# THE RISE OF SILAS LAPHAM

### AN AUTHORITATIVE TEXT
### COMPOSITION AND BACKGROUNDS
### CONTEMPORARY RESPONSES
### CRITICISM

>>> A NORTON CRITICAL EDITION <<<

*WILLIAM DEAN HOWELLS*

# THE RISE OF SILAS LAPHAM

## AN AUTHORITATIVE TEXT
## COMPOSITION AND BACKGROUNDS
## CONTEMPORARY RESPONSES
## CRITICISM

>>> <<<

*Edited by*

### DON L. COOK
INDIANA UNIVERSITY

W • W • NORTON & COMPANY
*New York*                    *London*

CENTER FOR EDITIONS OF
AMERICAN AUTHORS

*AN APPROVED TEXT*

MODERN LANGUAGE
ASSOCIATION OF AMERICA

®

Since this page cannot legibly accommodate all the copyright notices, the page
that follows constitutes an extension of the copyright page.

Library of Congress Cataloging in Publication Data
Howells, William Dean, 1837–1920.
  The Rise of Silas Lapham.
  (A Norton critical edition)
  Bibliography: p.
1. Howells, William Dean, 1837–1920. The rise
of Silas Lapham.  I. Cook, Don Lewis, 1928–  II.
Title.
PZ3.H84Ri  1980  [PS2025]  813'.4  80–12149

4  5  6  7  8  9  0

ISBN 0-393-04433-5
ISBN 0-393-09165-1 {PBK.}

ACKNOWLEDGMENTS

Ellen B. Ballou: "Gentlemen Publishers," from *The Building of the House: Houghton Mifflin's Formative Years.* Copyright © 1970 by Houghton Mifflin Company. Reprinted by permission of the publisher.

George N. Bennett: *William Dean Howells: The Development of a Novelist.* Copyright 1959 by the University of Oklahoma Press. Used by permission.

Edwin H. Cady: "The Chief American Realist: 1881–1885," in *The Road to Realism.* Copyright 1956 by Syracuse University Press. Used by permission.

Charles L. Campbell: "Realism and the Romance of Real Life: Multiple Fictional Worlds in Howells' Novels," *Modern Fiction Studies,* Vol.16, No.3, © 1970 by Purdue Research Foundation, West Lafayette, Indiana. Used by permission.

Everett Carter: *Howells and the Age of Realism.* Copyright 1954 by Everett Carter. Reprinted by permission of J. B. Lippincott Company.

Robert P. Falk: "W. D. Howells: Maturity in Fiction," from *The Victorian Mode in American Fiction, 1865–1885.* Copyright 1965 by The Michigan State University Press. Used by permission.

Robert M. Figg III: "Naturalism as a Literary Form." Copyright © 1964 by the University of Georgia. Reprinted by permission of *The Georgia Review.*

John E. Hart: "The Commonplace as Heroic in *The Rise of Silas Lapham,*" *Modern Fiction Studies,* Vol. 8, No. 4, © 1962 by Purdue Research Foundation, West Lafayette, Indiana. Used by permission.

C. Hugh Holman: "Notes on How to Read American Realism." Copyright © 1964 by the University of Georgia. Reprinted by permission of *The Georgia Review.*

William Dean Howells: Act II of "The Rise of Silas Lapham, a Play" reprinted by permission of New York University Press from *The Complete Plays of W. D. Howells,* edited by Walter Meserve. "The Rise of Silas Needham" reprinted by permission of W. W. Howells, Literary Executor. "Savings Bank" notebook selection reprinted by permission of W. W. Howells, Literary Executor, and the Harvard College Library. Selection from *Their Wedding Journey* by W. D. Howells, edited by John K. Reeves, copyright © 1968 by Indiana University Press and the Howells Edition Editorial Board, reprinted by permission of Indiana University Press. Letter from W. D. Howells to Clarence E. Buel, 11 May 1885, reprinted by permission of W. W. Howells, Literary Executor, and the Miami University Library; no other publication may be made without this permission. Letter to Samuel Clemens, 10 August 1884, reprinted by permission of W. W. Howells, Literary Executor, and The Mark Twain Papers at The Bancroft Library, University of California, Berkeley. Letter to Richard Watson Gilder, 31 July 1884, reprinted by permission of W. W. Howells, Literary Executor, and Rosamund Gilder. Letters to William Cooper Howells, 10 August 1884, and Henry James, 22 August 1884, reprinted by permission of W. W. Howells, Literary Executor, and the Harvard College Library. Letter to Cyrus L. Sulzberger, 17 July 1885, reprinted by permission of W. W. Howells, Literary Executor. Letters to W. D. Howells from various correspondents reprinted by permission of the Harvard College Library.

Harold Kolb: *The Illusion of Life: American Realism as a Literary Form.* The University Press of Virginia, 1969. Reprinted by permission.

Robie Macauley: "Let Me Tell You About the Rich," *Kenyon Review,* 27 (Autumn 1965). Copyright © 1965 by Robie Macauley. Reprinted by permission of International Creative Management.

William R. Manierre II: "*The Rise of Silas Lapham*: Retrospective Discussion as Dramatic Technique," *College English,* February 1962. Copyright © 1962 by the National Council of Teachers of English. Reprinted by permission of the publisher and the author.

Donald Pizer: "The Ethical Unity of *The Rise of Silas Lapham,*" *American Literature,* 32 (1960). Copyright 1960 by Duke University Press. Reprinted by permission of the publisher.

G. Thomas Tanselle: "The Architecture of *The Rise of Silas Lapham,*" *American Literature,* 37 (1966). Copyright 1966 by Duke University Press. Reprinted by permission of the publisher.

Larzer Ziff: *The American 1890's: Life and Times of a Lost Generation.* Copyright © 1966 by Larzer Ziff. Reprinted by permission of Viking Penguin, Inc.

*For Becky*

# Contents

# Preface

The reputation of William Dean Howells (1837–1920) has varied enormously over the years and is still far from settled. After a childhood of poverty and hard work in his father's Ohio printing office he became a newspaper reporter. Though he had little formal schooling, he taught himself foreign languages and literatures, and began publishing poems, first in local newspapers and finally in the prestigious *Atlantic* magazine. A campaign biography of Abraham Lincoln, written for the election of 1860, earned Howells an appointment as American consul in Venice, and it was there that he completed his literary apprenticeship, writing poems, travel letters, and translations and criticisms of Italian literature which he sent back to the United States for publication. Shortly after his return to America in 1865 he became assistant editor of the *Atlantic*, and settled in Boston. He succeeded to the chief-editorship in 1871 and, during the next ten years, established himself as a major essayist, novelist, and literary critic as well as a sponsor of foreign and domestic authors as yet unfamiliar to the American reading public. He was the early advocate and friend of Henry James and Mark Twain, and later defended and explained the works of Ibsen, Tolstoy, Zola, Turgenev, and many others to an often hostile public. By the end of the century Howells was recognized as the semi-official "dean of American letters," had received honorary degrees from Yale, Columbia, Princeton, and Oxford universities (he had long before refused a professorship at Harvard), and was elected first president of the American Academy of Arts and Letters. But during the next two decades changing public tastes and the self-assertive rejection of Howells' quiet realism by a new generation of writers diminished his readership and fastened on him the damning labels of "tea-cup realist" and "pious Victorian." It was not until after World War II that a revival of interest in Howells began. Even now, though a handful of his novels are recognized as American classics, the unavailability of most of his books and the resulting unawareness of the scope and quality of his works, even among generally well-informed readers, keep his reputation well below that of many of his contemporaries.

One aim of this volume is to make available to the largest possible reading public a reliable text of Howells' most popular novel, along with a record of the major variants that he chose, or was forced, to introduce into its subsequent editions. The text printed here is that of *A Selected Edition of W. D. Howells,* published by the Indiana University Press in 1971. That text was established by Walter J. Meserve and David J. Nordloh, who selected as their copy-text the novel as it was serialized in *The Century Illustrated Monthly Magazine* in ten installments between 8 October 1884 and 11 July 1885. Then, after careful examination of the seven other English and American editions and impressions over which Howells may have had some control, they introduced into the serial text those alterations that they felt represented Howells' intentions rather than the editorial stylings and inadvertent corruptions that occured in the printing plants. They were at all times reluctant to alter the serial text since it was the text closest to Howells' manuscript (no longer extant) and involved the least opportunity for departures from what Howells had written. The decisions to emend this text were based on research in the correspondence between Howells and his publishers, friends, and readers (some of that correspondence is reproduced in this volume), and on records of the publishing houses and the copyright depositories. The fascinating details of this scholarly detective work can be found in the Textual Apparatus section of the Indiana University Press volume, a feature of all the volumes that bear the seal of textual reliability awarded, after scrupulous inspection, by the Modern Language Association's Center for Editions of American Authors.

This Critical Edition provides the surviving sources of Howells' story and the author's comments (as well as some of the advice he received) on the composition of the book. Like most enduring works of popular fiction, *The Rise of Silas Lapham* embodies (often critically) some of the deep, even subconscious, public attitudes and values prevalent at the time the book was written. The second group of letters and articles focuses attention on some of these popular myths and on the way Howells uses them to comment on American society. The initial responses to the book, both from his literary friends and from the often hostile book reviewers, are provided in order to help the reader see the book in its historical context. There follows a series of critical articles written from the perspective of years, articles chosen not only because they say sound and stimulating things about Howells' book, but because they illustrate the diversity of critical viewpoints from which *The Rise of Silas Lapham* has been fruitfully examined. And, finally, a group of articles considers the book and its author as literary-historical phenomena, as products and agents of an intellectual and literary movement away from an ideal, romantic conception of the individual and society and toward a realistic, pragmatic acceptance of the limited choices and virtues with which people have to get by in the world in which they find themselves.

I wish to thank the scholars whose work is reprinted in this volume as well as the many others who continue to contribute to the dialogue that helps each of us better to understand what an author has written and what we can sensibly read out of it. I am particularly indebted to Edwin H. Cady and David J. Nordloh for their generous contributions to my understanding of Howells and his age, and to Jerry Herron for assistance in research.

DON L. COOK

The Text of
# The Rise of Silas Lapham

# I

When Bartley Hubbard went to interview Silas Lapham for the "Solid Men of Boston" series, which he undertook to finish up in "The Events," after he replaced their original projector on that newspaper, Lapham received him in his private office by previous appointment.[1]

"Walk right in!" he called out to the journalist, whom he caught sight of through the door of the counting-room.

He did not rise from the desk at which he was writing, but he gave Bartley his left hand for welcome, and he rolled his large head in the direction of a vacant chair. "Sit down! I'll be with you in just half a minute."

"Take your time," said Bartley, with the ease he instantly felt. "I'm in no hurry." He took a note-book from his pocket, laid it on his knee, and began to sharpen a pencil.

"There!" Lapham pounded with his great hairy fist on the envelope he had been addressing. "William!" he called out, and he handed the letter to a boy who came to get it. "I want that to go right away. Well, sir," he continued, wheeling round in his leather-cushioned swivel-chair, and facing Bartley, seated so near that their knees almost touched, "so you want my life, death, and Christian sufferings, do you, young man?"

"That's what I'm after," said Bartley. "Your money or your life."

"I guess you wouldn't want my life without the money," said Lapham, as if he were willing to prolong these moments of preparation.

"Take 'em both," Bartley suggested. "Don't want your money without your life, if you come to that. But you're just one million times more interesting to the public than if you hadn't a dollar; and you know that as well as I do, Mr. Lapham. There's no use beating about the bush."

"No," said Lapham, somewhat absently. He put out his huge foot and pushed the ground-glass door shut between his little den and the book-keepers, in their larger den outside.

"In personal appearance," wrote Bartley in the sketch for which he now studied his subject, while he waited patiently for

1. Bartley Hubbard and his wife Marcia Gaylord Hubbard are the central characters in Howells' novel *A Modern Instance*, where they are divorced after Bartley's journalistic career, and his personality, degenerate.

him to continue, "Silas Lapham is a fine type of the successful American. He has a square, bold chin, only partially concealed by the short, reddish-gray beard, growing to the edges of his firmly closing lips. His nose is short and straight; his forehead good, but broad rather than high; his eyes blue, and with a light in them that is kindly or sharp according to his mood. He is of medium height, and fills an average arm-chair with a solid bulk, which, on the day of our interview, was unpretentiously clad in a business suit of blue serge. His head droops somewhat from a short neck, which does not trouble itself to rise far from a pair of massive shoulders."

"I don't know as I know just where you want me to begin," said Lapham.

"Might begin with your birth; that's where most of us begin," replied Bartley.

A gleam of humorous appreciation shot into Lapham's blue eyes.

"I didn't know whether you wanted me to go quite so far back as that," he said. "But there's no disgrace in having been born, and I was born in the State of Vermont, pretty well up under the Canada line—so well up, in fact, that I came very near being an adoptive citizen; for I was bound to be an American of *some* sort, from the word Go! That was about—well, let me see!— pretty near sixty years ago: this is '75, and that was '20. Well, say I'm fifty-five years old; and I've *lived* 'em, too; not an hour of waste time about *me*, anywheres! I was born on a farm, and ____"

"Worked in the fields summers and went to school winters: regulation thing?" Bartley cut in.

"Regulation thing," said Lapham, accepting this irreverent version of his history somewhat dryly.

"Parents poor, of course," suggested the journalist. "Any barefoot business? Early deprivations of any kind, that would encourage the youthful reader to go and do likewise? Orphan myself, you know," said Bartley, with a smile of cynical good comradery.

Lapham looked at him silently, and then said with quiet self-respect, "I guess if you see these things as a joke, my·life wont inter*est* you."

"Oh, yes, it will," returned Bartley, unabashed. "You'll see;

it'll come out all right." And in fact it did so, in the interview which Bartley printed.

"Mr. Lapham," he wrote, "passed rapidly over the story of his early life, its poverty and its hardships, sweetened, however, by the recollections of a devoted mother, and a father who, if somewhat her inferior in education, was no less ambitious for the advancement of his children. They were quiet, unpretentious people, religious, after the fashion of that time, and of sterling morality, and they taught their children the simple virtues of the Old Testament and Poor Richard's Almanac."[2]

Bartley could not deny himself this gibe; but he trusted to Lapham's unliterary habit of mind for his security in making it, and most other people would consider it sincere reporter's rhetoric.

"You know," he explained to Lapham, "that we have to look at all these facts as material, and we get the habit of classifying them. Sometimes a leading question will draw out a whole line of facts that a man himself would never think of." He went on to put several queries, and it was from Lapham's answers that he generalized the history of his childhood. "Mr. Lapham, although he did not dwell on his boyish trials and struggles, spoke of them with deep feeling and an abiding sense of their reality." This was what he added in the interview, and by the time he had got Lapham past the period where risen Americans are all pathetically alike in their narrow circumstances, their sufferings, and their aspirations, he had beguiled him into forgetfulness of the check he had received, and had him talking again in perfect enjoyment of his autobiography.

"Yes, sir," said Lapham, in a strain which Bartley was careful not to interrupt again, "a man never sees all that his mother has been to him till it's too late to let her know that he sees it. Why, *my* mother—" he stopped. "It gives me a lump in the throat," he said apologetically, with an attempt at a laugh. Then he went on: "She was a little, frail thing, not bigger than a good-sized intermediate school-girl; but she did the whole work of a family of boys, and boarded the hired men besides. She cooked, swept, washed, ironed, made and mended from daylight till dark—

2. *Poor Richard's Almanac* was published by Benjamin Franklin and contained such good advice as "A penny saved is a penny earned," and "Early to bed and early to rise make a man healthy wealthy and wise."

and from dark till daylight, I was going to say; for I don't know how she got any time for sleep. But I suppose she did. She got time to go to church, and to teach us to read the Bible, and to misunderstand it in the old way. She was *good*. But it aint her on her knees in church that comes back to me so much like the sight of an angel, as her on her knees before me at night, washing my poor, dirty little feet, that I'd run bare in all day, and making me decent for bed. There were six of us boys; it seems to me we were all of a size; and she was just so careful with all of us. I can feel her hands on my feet yet!" Bartley looked at Lapham's No. 10 boots and softly whistled through his teeth. "We were patched all over; but we wa'n't ragged. *I* don't know how she got through it. She didn't seem to think it was anything; and I guess it was no more than my father expected of her. *He* worked like a horse in doors and out—up at daylight, feeding the stock, and groaning round all day with his rheumatism, but not stopping."

Bartley hid a yawn over his note-book, and probably, if he could have spoken his mind, he would have suggested to Lapham that he was not there for the purpose of interviewing his ancestry. But Bartley had learned to practice a patience with his victims which he did not always feel, and to feign an interest in their digressions till he could bring them up with a round turn.

"I tell you," said Lapham, jabbing the point of his penknife into the writing-pad on the desk before him, "when I hear women complaining nowadays that their lives are stunted and empty, I want to tell 'em about my *mother's* life. *I* could paint it out for 'em."

Bartley saw his opportunity at the word paint, and cut in. "And you say, Mr. Lapham, that you discovered this mineral paint on the old farm yourself?"

Lapham acquiesced in the return to business. "*I* didn't discover it," he said, scrupulously. "My father found it one day, in a hole made by a tree blowing down. There it was, laying loose in the pit, and sticking to the roots that had pulled up a big cake of dirt with 'em. *I* don't know what give him the idea that there was money in it, but he did think so from the start. I guess, if they'd had the word in those days, they'd considered him pretty much of a crank about it. He was trying as long as he lived to get that paint introduced; but he couldn't make it go. The country was so poor they couldn't paint their houses with anything; and father hadn't any facilities. It got to be a kind of joke with us; and I guess that paint-mine did as much as any one thing to make us boys clear out as soon as we got old enough.[3] All my brothers went West and took up land; but I hung on to New England, and I hung on to the old farm, not because the paint-mine was on it, but because the old house was—and the graves. Well," said Lapham, as if unwilling to give himself too much credit, "there wouldn't been any market for it, anyway. You can go through that part of the State and buy more farms than you can shake a stick at for less money than it cost to build the barns on 'em. Of course, it's turned out a good thing. I keep the old house up in good shape, and we spend a month or so there every summer. M' wife kind of likes it, and the girls. Pretty place; sightly all round it. I've got a force of men at work there the whole time, and I've got a man and his wife in the house. Had a family meeting there last year; the whole connection from out West. There!" Lapham rose from his seat and took down a large warped, unframed photograph from the top of his desk, passing his hand over it, and then blowing vigorously upon it, to clear it of the dust. "There we are, *all* of us."

"I don't need to look twice at *you*," said Bartley, putting his finger on one of the heads.

"Well, that's Bill," said Lapham, with a gratified laugh. "He's about as brainy as any of us, I guess. He's one of their leading lawyers, out Dubuque way; been judge of the Common Pleas once or twice. That's his son—just graduated at Yale—alongside of my youngest girl. Good-looking chap, aint he?"

"*She's* a good-looking chap," said Bartley, with prompt irreverence. He hastened to add, at the frown which gathered between Lapham's eyes, "What a beautiful creature she is! What a lovely, refined, sensitive face! And she looks *good*, too."

"She *is* good," said the father, relenting.

"And, after all, that's about the best thing in a woman," said the potential reprobate. "If my wife wasn't good enough to keep both of us straight, I don't know what would become of me."

"My other daughter," said Lapham, indicating a girl with eyes that showed large, and a face of singular gravity. "Mis' Lapham," he continued, touching his wife's effigy with his little

---

3. The paint mine consists of a deposit of an iron compound which when burned, pulverized, and mixed with linseed oil produces a high-quality paint.

finger. "My brother Willard and his family—farm at Kankakee. Hazard Lapham and his wife—Baptist preacher in Kansas. Jim and his three girls—milling business at Minneapolis. Ben and his family—practicing medicine in Fort Wayne."

The figures were clustered in an irregular group in front of an old farm-house, whose original ugliness had been smartened up with a coat of Lapham's own paint and heightened with an incongruous piazza. The photographer had not been able to conceal the fact that they were all decent, honest-looking, sensible people, with a very fair share of beauty among the young girls; some of these were extremely pretty, in fact. He had put them into awkward and constrained attitudes, of course; and they all looked as if they had the instrument of torture which photographers call a head-rest under their occiputs. Here and there an elderly lady's face was a mere blur; and some of the younger children had twitched themselves into wavering shadows, and might have passed for spirit-photographs of their own little ghosts. It was the standard family-group photograph, in which most Americans have figured at some time or other; and Lapham exhibited a just satisfaction in it. "I presume," he mused aloud, as he put it back on top of his desk, "that we sha'n't soon get together again, all of us."

"And you say," suggested Bartley, "that you staid right along on the old place, when the rest cleared out West?"

"No-o-o-o," said Lapham, with a long, loud drawl; "I cleared out West too, first off. Went to Texas. Texas was all the cry in those days. But I got enough of the Lone Star in about three months, and I come back with the idea that Vermont was good enough for me."

"Fatted calf business?" queried Bartley, with his pencil poised above his note-book.

"I presume they were glad to see me," said Lapham, with dignity. "Mother," he added gently, "died that winter, and I staid on with father. I buried him in the spring; and then I came down to a little place called Lumberville, and picked up what jobs I could get. I worked round at the saw-mills, and I was ostler awhile at the hotel—I always *did* like a good horse. Well, I *wa'n't* exactly a college graduate, and I went to school odd times. I got to driving the stage after while, and by and by I *bought* the stage and run the business myself. Then I hired the tavern-stand, and—well, to make a long story short, then I got married. Yes," said Lapham, with pride, "I married the school-teacher. We did pretty well with the hotel, and my wife she was always at me to paint up. Well, I put it off, and *put* it off, as a man will, till one day I give in, and says I, 'Well, *let's* paint up. Why, Pert,'—m'wife's name's Persis,[4]—'I've got a whole paint-mine out on the farm. Let's go out and look at it.' So we drove out. I'd let the place for seventy-five dollars a year to a shif'less kind of a Kanuck that had come down that way;[5] and I'd hated to see the house with him in it; but we drove out one Saturday afternoon, and we brought back about a bushel of the stuff in the buggy-seat, and I tried it crude, and I tried it burnt; and I liked it. M'wife she liked it, too. There wa'n't any painter by trade in the village, and I mixed it myself. Well, sir, that tavern's got that coat of paint on it yet, and it haint ever had any other, and I don't know's it ever will. Well, you know, I felt as if it was a kind of a harumscarum experiment, all the while; and I presume I shouldn't have tried it, but I kind of liked to do it because father'd always set so much store by his paint-mine. And when I'd got the first coat on,"—Lapham called it *cut,*—"I presume I must have set as much as half an hour, looking at it and thinking how he would have enjoyed it. I've had my share of luck in this world, and I aint a-going to complain on my *own* account, but I've noticed that most things get along too late for most people. It made me feel bad, and it took all the pride out my success with the paint, thinking of father. Seemed to me I might 'a' taken more interest in it when he was by to see; but we've got to live and learn. Well, I called my wife out,—I'd tried it on the back of the house, you know,—and she left her dishes,—I can re-member she came out with her sleeves rolled up and set down alongside of me on the trestle,—and says I, 'What do you think, Persis?' And says she, 'Well, you haint got a paint-mine, Silas Lapham; you've got a *gold*-mine.' She always was just so enthu-siastic about things. Well, it was just after two or three boats had burnt up out West, and a lot of lives lost, and there was a great cry about non-inflammable paint, and I guess that was what was

<hr>

4. The name "Persis" comes from the New Testament, Romans 16:12, which says: "Salute the beloved Persis, which labored much in the Lord." The name suggests that Persis should be able to provide moral guidance for her husband and family.

5. "Kanuck" is a derogatory slang term for Canadians, especially Canadian immigrants to New England.

in her mind. 'Well, I guess it aint any gold-mine, Persis,' says I; 'but I guess it *is* a paint-mine. I'm going to have it analyzed, and if it turns out what I think it is, I'm going to work it. And if father hadn't had such a long name, I should call it the Nehemiah Lapham Mineral Paint. But, any rate, every barrel of it, and every keg, and every bottle, and every package, big or little, has got to have the initials and figures N. L. f. 1835, S. L. t. 1855, on it. Father found it in 1835, and I tried it in 1855.' "

" 'S. T.—1860—X.' business," said Bartley.[6]

"Yes," said Lapham, "but I hadn't heard of Plantation Bitters then, and I hadn't seen any of the fellow's labels. I set to work and I got a man down from Boston; and I carried him out to the farm, and he analyzed it—made a regular job of it. Well, sir, we built a kiln, and we kept a lot of that paint-ore red-hot for forty-eight hours; kept the Kanuck and his family up, firing. The presence of iron in the ore showed with the magnet from the start; and when he came to test it, he found out that it contained about seventy-five per cent. of the peroxide of iron."

Lapham pronounced the scientific phrases with a sort of reverent satisfaction, as if awed through his pride by a little lingering uncertainty as to what peroxide was. He accented it as if it were purr-ox-*eyed*; and Bartley had to get him to spell it.

"Well, and what then?" he asked, when he had made a note of the percentage.

"What then?" echoed Lapham. "Well, then, the fellow set down and told me, 'You've got a paint here,' says he, 'that's going to drive every other mineral paint out of the market. Why,' says he, 'it'll drive 'em right into the Back Bay!'[7] Of course, *I* didn't know what the Back Bay was then; but I begun to open my eyes; thought I'd had 'em open before, but I guess I hadn't. Says he, 'That paint has got hydraulic cement in it, and it can stand fire and water and acids'; he named over a lot of things. Says he, 'It'll mix easily with linseed oil, whether you want to use it boiled or raw; and it aint a-going to crack nor fade any; and it aint a-going to scale. When you've got your arrangements for burning it properly, you're going to have a paint that will

6. The label of Plantation Bitters, a popular dyspepsia remedy, bore the date of the "discovery" of the formula. Bartley apparently assumes that Silas has merely copied the idea for the label of his own product.
7. Back Bay is a portion of Boston west of the Common, built on filled swampland, and very fashionable in the late nineteenth century. It is here, on Beacon Street, that Silas builds his house. In 1884 Howells bought and redecorated a house on the "water side" of Beacon Street— that is, overlooking the Charles River.

stand like the everlasting hills, in every climate under the sun.'
Then he went into a lot of particulars, and I begun to think he was
drawing a long bow, and meant to make his bill accordingly. So
I kept pretty cool; but the fellow's bill didn't amount to anything
hardly—said I might pay him after I got going; young chap, and
pretty easy; but every word he said was gospel. Well, I aint
a-going to brag up my paint; I don't suppose you came here to
hear me blow——"

"Oh, yes, I did," said Bartley. "That's what I want. Tell all
there is to tell, and I can boil it down afterward. A man can't
make a greater mistake with a reporter than to hold back anything out of modesty. It may be the very thing we want to know.
What we want is the whole truth, and more; we've got so much
modesty of our own that we can temper almost any statement."

Lapham looked as if he did not quite like this tone, and he
resumed a little more quietly. "Oh, there isn't really very much
more to say about the paint itself. But you can use it for almost
anything where a paint is wanted, inside or out. It'll prevent
decay, and it'll stop it, after it's begun, in tin or iron. You can
paint the inside of a cistern or a bath-tub with it, and water wont
hurt it; and you can paint a steam-boiler with it, and heat wont.
You can cover a brick wall with it, or a railroad car, or the deck
of a steam-boat, and you can't do a better thing for either."

"Never tried it on the human conscience, I suppose," suggested Bartley.

"No, sir," replied Lapham, gravely. "I guess you want to keep
that as free from paint as you can, if you want much use of it. I
never cared to try any of it on mine." Lapham suddenly lifted
his bulk up out of his swivel-chair, and led the way out into the
wareroom beyond the office partitions, where rows and ranks of
casks, barrels, and kegs stretched dimly back to the rear of the
building, and diffused an honest, clean, wholesome smell of oil
and paint. They were labeled and branded as containing each
so many pounds of Lapham's Mineral Paint, and each bore the
mystic devices, *N. L. f. 1835—S. L. t. 1855.* "There!" said Lapham, kicking one of the largest casks with the toe of his boot,
"that's about our biggest package; and here," he added, laying
his hand affectionately on the head of a very small keg, as if it
were the head of a child, which it resembled in size, "this is the
smallest. We used to put the paint on the market dry, but now

we grind every ounce of it in oil—very best quality of linseed oil—and warrant it. We find it gives more satisfaction. Now, come back to the office, and I'll show you our fancy brands."

It was very cool and pleasant in that dim wareroom, with the rafters showing overhead in a cloudy perspective, and darkening away into the perpetual twilight at the rear of the building; and Bartley had found an agreeable seat on the head of a half-barrel of the paint, which he was reluctant to leave. But he rose and followed the vigorous lead of Lapham back to the office, where the sun of a long summer afternoon was just beginning to glare in at the window. On shelves opposite Lapham's desk were tin cans of various sizes, arranged in tapering cylinders, and showing, in a pattern diminishing toward the top, the same label borne by the casks and barrels in the wareroom. Lapham merely waved his hand toward these; but when Bartley, after a comprehensive glance at them, gave his whole attention to a row of clean, smooth jars, where different tints of the paint showed through flawless glass, Lapham smiled and waited in pleased expectation.

"Hello!" said Bartley. "That's pretty!"

"Yes," assented Lapham, "it is rather nice. It's our latest thing, and we find it takes with customers first-rate. Look here!" he said, taking down one of the jars, and pointing to the first line of the label.

Bartley read, "THE PERSIS BRAND," and then he looked at Lapham and smiled.

"After *her*, of course," said Lapham. "Got it up and put the first of it on the market her last birthday. She was pleased."

"I should think she might have been," said Bartley, while he made a note of the appearance of the jars.

"I don't know about your mentioning it in your interview," said Lapham, dubiously.

"That's going into the interview, Mr. Lapham, if nothing else does. Got a wife myself, and I know just how you feel." It was in the dawn of Bartley's prosperity on the "Boston Events," before his troubles with Marcia had seriously begun.

"Is that so?" said Lapham, recognizing with a smile another of the vast majority of married Americans; a few underrate their wives, but the rest think them supernal in intelligence and capability. "Well," he added, "we must see about that. Where'd you say you lived?"

"We don't live; we board. Mrs. Nash, 13 Canary Place."

"Well, we've all got to commence that way," suggested Lapham, consolingly.

"Yes; but we've about got to the end of our string. I expect to be under a roof of my own on Clover street before long. I suppose," said Bartley, returning to business, "that you didn't let the grass grow under your feet much after you found out what was in your paint-mine?"

"No, sir," answered Lapham, withdrawing his eyes from a long stare at Bartley, in which he had been seeing himself a young man again, in the first days of his married life. "I went right back to Lumberville and sold out everything, and put all I could rake and scrape together into paint. And Mis' Lapham was with me every time. No hang back about *her*. I tell you she was a *woman!*"

Bartley laughed. "That's the sort most of us marry."

"No, we don't," said Lapham. "Most of us marry silly little girls grown up to *look* like women."

"Well, I guess that's about so," assented Bartley, as if upon second thought.

"If it hadn't been for her," resumed Lapham, "the paint wouldn't have come to anything. I used to tell her it wa'n't the seventy-five per cent. of purr-ox-eyed of iron in the *ore* that made that paint go; it was the seventy-five per cent. of purr-ox-eyed of iron in *her*."

"Good!" cried Bartley. "I'll tell Marcia that."

"In less'n six months there wa'n't a board-fence, nor a bridge-girder, nor a dead wall, nor a barn, nor a face of rock in that whole region that didn't have 'Lapham's Mineral Paint— Specimen' on it in the three colors we begun by making." Bartley had taken his seat on the window-sill, and Lapham, standing before him, now put up his huge foot close to Bartley's thigh; neither of them minded that.

"I've heard a good deal of talk about that S. T.—1860—X. man, and the stove-blacking man, and the kidney-cure man, because they advertised in that way; and I've read articles about it in the papers; but I don't see where the joke comes in, exactly. So long as the people that own the barns and fences don't object, I don't see what the public has got to do with it. And I never saw anything so very sacred about a big rock, along a river or in a pasture that it wouldn't do to put mineral paint on it in three colors. I wish some of the people that talk about the landscape, and *write* about it, had to bu'st one of them rocks *out* of the landscape with powder, or dig a hole to bury it in, as we used to have to do up on the farm; I guess they'd sing a little different tune about the profanation of scenery.[8] There aint any man enjoys a sightly bit of nature—a smooth piece of interval, with half a dozen good-sized wine-glass elms in it—more than *I* do. But I aint a-going to stand up for every big ugly rock I come across, as if we were all a set of dumn Druids. I say the landscape was made for man, and not man for the landscape."[9]

"Yes," said Bartley, carelessly; "it was made for the stove-polish man and the kidney-cure man."

"It was made for any man that knows how to use it," Lapham returned, insensible to Bartley's irony. "Let 'em go and live with nature in the *winter*, up there along the Canada line, and I guess they'll get enough of her for one while. Well—where was I?"

"Decorating the landscape," said Bartley.

"Yes, sir; I started right there at Lumberville, and it give the place a start, too. You wont find it on the map now; and you wont find it in the gazetteer. I give a pretty good lump of money to build a town-hall, about five years back, and the first meeting they held in it they voted to change the name,—Lumberville *wa'n't* a name,—and it's Lapham now."

"Isn't it somewhere up in that region that they get the old Brandon red?" asked Bartley.

"We're about ninety miles from Brandon. The Brandon's a good paint," said Lapham, conscientiously. "Like to show you round up at our place some odd time, if you get off."

"Thanks. I should like it first-rate. Works there?"

"Yes; Works there. Well, sir, just about the time I got started, the war broke out; and it knocked my paint higher than a kite. The thing dropped perfectly dead. I presume that if I'd had any sort of influence, I might have got it into government hands, for gun-carriages and army-wagons, and may be on board govern-

8. Well into the twentieth century, farmers leased the sides and roofs of their barns as advertising space, especially for tobacco and patent medicine signs. Any large surface such as a wall, a cliff, or a large boulder (or city building) might be similarly used. Silas is voicing the classic views of the public-be-damned school of nineteenth-century industrialism. But by the 1880s, some Americans were objecting to the desecration of the environment for private profit.
9. Silas' use of "dumn" rather than "damn" reflects his Yankee compromise with the Puritan prohibition against profanity.

ment vessels. But I hadn't, and we had to face the music. I was about broken-hearted, but m'wife she looked at it another way. '*I* guess it's a providence,' says she. 'Silas, I guess you've got a country that's worth fighting for. Any rate, you better go out and give it a chance.' Well, sir, I went. I knew she meant business. It might kill her to have me go, but it would kill her sure if I staid. She was one of that kind. I went. Her last words was, 'I'll look after the paint, Si.' We hadn't but just one little girl then,—boy'd died,—and Mis' Lapham's mother was livin' with us; and I knew if times *did* anyways come up again, m'wife'd know just what to do. So I went. I got through; and you can call me Colonel, if you want to. Feel there!" Lapham took Bartley's thumb and forefinger and put them on a bunch in his leg, just above the knee. "Anything hard?"

"Ball?"

Lapham nodded. "Gettysburg. That's my thermometer. If it wa'n't for that, I shouldn't know enough to come in when it rains."

Bartley laughed at a joke which betrayed some evidences of wear. "And when you came back, you took hold of the paint and rushed it."

"I took hold of the paint and rushed it—all I could," said Lapham, with less satisfaction than he had hitherto shown in his autobiography. "But I found that I had got back to another world. The day of small things was past, and I don't suppose it will ever come again in this country. My wife was at me all the time to take a partner—somebody with capital; but I couldn't seem to bear the idea. That paint was like my own blood to me. To have anybody else concerned in it was like—well, I don't know what. I saw it was the thing to do; but I tried to fight it off, and I tried to joke it off. I used to say, 'Why didn't you take a partner yourself, Persis, while I was away?' And she'd say, 'Well, if you hadn't come back, I should, Si.' Always *did* like a joke about as well as any woman *I* ever saw. Well, I had to come to it. I took a partner." Lapham dropped the bold blue eyes with which he had been till now staring into Bartley's face, and the reporter knew that here was a place for asterisks in his interview, if interviews were faithful. "He had money enough," continued Lapham, with a suppressed sigh; "but he didn't know anything about paint. We hung on together for a year or two. And then we quit."

"And he had the experience," suggested Bartley, with companionable ease.

"I had some of the experience too," said Lapham, with a scowl; and Bartley divined, through the freemasonry of all who have sore places in their memories, that this was a point which he must not touch again.

"And since that, I suppose, you've played it alone."

"I've played it alone."

"You must ship some of this paint of yours to foreign countries, Colonel?" suggested Bartley, putting on a professional air.

"We ship it to all parts of the world. It goes to South America, lots of it. It goes to Australia, and it goes to India, and it goes to China, and it goes to the Cape of Good Hope. It'll stand any climate. Of course, we don't export these fancy brands much. They're for home use. But we're introducing them elsewhere. Here." Lapham pulled open a drawer, and showed Bartley a lot of labels in different languages—Spanish, French, German, and Italian. "We expect to do a good business in all those countries. We've got our agencies in Cadiz now, and in Paris, and in Hamburg, and in Leghorn. It's a thing that's bound to make its way. Yes, sir. Wherever a man has got a ship, or a bridge, or a dock, or a house, or a car, or a fence, or a pig-pen, anywhere in God's universe, to paint, that's the paint for him, and he's bound to find it out sooner or later. You pass a ton of that paint dry through a blast-furnace, and you'll get a quarter of a ton of pig-iron. I believe in my paint. I believe it's a blessing to the world. When folks come in, and kind of smell round, and ask me what I mix it with, I always say, 'Well, in the first place, I mix it with *Faith*, and after that I grind it up with the best quality of boiled linseed oil that money will buy.'"

Lapham took out his watch and looked at it, and Bartley perceived that his audience was drawing to a close. " 'F you ever want to run down and take a look at our Works, pass you over the road,"—he called it *rud*,—"and it sha'n't cost you a cent."

"Well, may be I shall, sometime," said Bartley. "Good afternoon, Colonel."

"Good afternoon. Or—hold on! My horse down there yet, William?" he called to the young man in the counting-room, who had taken his letter at the beginning of the interview. "Oh! All right!" he added, in response to something the young man said. "Can't I set you down somewhere, Mr. Hubbard? I've got my horse at the door, and I can drop you on my way home. I'm going to take Mis' Lapham to look at a house I'm driving piles for, down on the New Land."

"Don't care if I do," said Bartley.

Lapham put on a straw hat, gathered up some papers lying on his desk, pulled down its rolling cover, turned the key in it, and gave the papers to an extremely handsome young woman at one of the desks in the outer office. She was stylishly dressed, as Bartley saw, and her smooth, yellow hair was sculpturesquely waved over a low, white forehead. "Here," said Lapham, with the same prompt, gruff kindness that he had used in addressing the young man, "I want you should put these in shape, and give me a type-writer copy to-morrow."

"What an uncommonly pretty girl!" said Bartley, as they descended the rough stairway and found their way out to the street, past the dangling rope of a block and tackle wandering up into the cavernous darkness overhead.

"She does her work," said Lapham, shortly.

Bartley mounted to the left side of the open buggy standing at the curb-stone, and Lapham, gathering up the hitching-weight, slid it under the buggy-seat and mounted beside him.

"No chance to speed a horse here, of course," said Lapham, while the horse with a spirited gentleness picked her way, with a high, long action, over the pavement of the street. The streets were all narrow, and most of them crooked, in that quarter of the town; but at the end of one the spars of a vessel penciled themselves delicately against the cool blue of the afternoon sky. The air was full of a smell pleasantly compounded of oakum, of leather, and of oil. It was not the busy season, and they met only two or three trucks heavily straggling toward the wharf with their long string teams; but the cobble-stones of the pavement were worn with the dint of ponderous wheels, and discolored with iron-rust from them; here and there, in wandering streaks over its surface, was the gray stain of the salt water with which the street had been sprinkled.

After an interval of some minutes, which both men spent in looking round the dashboard from opposite sides to watch the stride of the horse, Bartley said, with a light sigh, "I had a colt once down in Maine that stepped just like that mare."

"Well!" said Lapham, sympathetically recognizing the bond that this fact created between them. "Well, now, I tell you what you do. You let me come for you 'most any afternoon, now, and take you out over the Milldam, and speed this mare a little. I'd like to show you what this mare can do. Yes, I would."

"All right," answered Bartley; "I'll let you know my first day off."

"Good," cried Lapham.

"Kentucky?" queried Bartley.

"No, sir. I don't ride behind anything but Vermont; never did. Touch of Morgan,[1] of course; but you can't have much Morgan in a horse if you want speed. Hambletonian mostly. Where'd you say you wanted to get out?"

"I guess you may put me down at the 'Events' office, just round the corner here. I've got to write up this interview while it's fresh."

"All right," said Lapham, impersonally assenting to Bartley's use of him as material.

He had not much to complain of in Bartley's treatment, unless it was the strain of extravagant compliment which it involved. But the flattery was mainly for the paint, whose virtues Lapham did not believe could be overstated, and himself and his history had been treated with as much respect as Bartley was capable of showing any one. He made a very picturesque thing of the discovery of the paint-mine. "Deep in the heart of the virgin forests of Vermont, far up toward the line of the Canadian snows, on a desolate mountain-side, where an autumnal storm had done its wild work, and the great trees, strewn hither and thither, bore witness to its violence, Nehemiah Lapham discovered, just forty years ago, the mineral which the alchemy of his son's enterprise and energy has transmuted into solid ingots of the most precious of metals. The colossal fortune of Colonel Silas Lapham lay at the bottom of a hole which an uprooted tree had dug for him, and which for many years remained a paint-mine of no more appreciable value than a soap-mine."

Here Bartley had not been able to forego another grin; but he compensated for it by the high reverence with which he spoke

1. Justin Morgan (1791–1821), a horse named after his original owner, was sire of a breed of Vermont trotting horses renowned for their endurance and beauty. The Hambletonian breed later replaced the Morgan in popularity and gave its name to America's most famous trotting-race event.

of Colonel Lapham's record during the war of the rebellion, and of the motives which impelled him to turn aside from an enterprise in which his whole heart was engaged and take part in the struggle. "The Colonel bears imbedded in the muscle of his right leg a little memento of the period in the shape of a minie-ball, which he jocularly referred to as his thermometer, and which relieves him from the necessity of reading 'The Probabilities' in his morning paper. This saves him just so much time; and for a man who, as he said, has not a moment of waste time on him anywhere, five minutes a day are something in the course of a year. Simple, clear, bold, and straightforward in mind and action, Colonel Silas Lapham, with a prompt comprehensiveness and a never-failing business sagacity, is, in the best sense of that much-abused term, one of nature's noblemen, to the last inch of his five eleven and a half. His life affords an example of single-minded application and unwavering perseverance which our young business men would do well to emulate. There is nothing showy or meretricious about the man. He believes in mineral paint, and he puts his heart and soul into it. He makes it a religion; though we would not imply that it *is* his religion. Colonel Lapham is a regular attendant at the Rev. Dr. Langworthy's church. He subscribes liberally to the Associated Charities, and no good object or worthy public enterprise fails to receive his support. He is not now actively in politics, and his paint is not partisan; but it is an open secret that he is, and always has been, a stanch Republican. Without violating the sanctities of private life, we cannot speak fully of various details which came out in the free and unembarrassed interview which Colonel Lapham accorded our representative. But we may say that the success of which he is justly proud he is also proud to attribute in great measure to the sympathy and energy of his wife—one of those women who, in whatever walk of life, seem born to honor the name of American Woman, and to redeem it from the national reproach of Daisy Millerism.[2] Of Colonel Lapham's family, we will simply add that it consists of two young lady daughters.

2. Henry James' novella *Daisy Miller* (1878) tells of a beautiful and headstrong young American girl who is ostracized by the American colony in Rome because of her independent behavior. The book provoked widespread public discussion. Some readers felt that it was a harsh portrait of a crude, insensitive, and perhaps immoral type of American girl, while more penetrating readers saw it as a tribute to the innocence and vulnerability of the young girl faced with the hypocrisy of corrupt, Europeanized Americans. The reference suggests that Bartley Hubbard is taking the conventional, moralistic side, against "Daisy Millerism."

"The subject of this very inadequate sketch is building a house on the water side of Beacon street, after designs by one of our leading architectural firms, which, when complete, will be one of the finest ornaments of that exclusive avenue. It will, we believe, be ready for the occupancy of the family sometime in the spring."

When Bartley had finished his article, which he did with a good deal of inward derision, he went home to Marcia, still smiling over the thought of Lapham, whose burly simplicity had peculiarly amused him.

"He regularly turned himself inside out to me," he said, as he sat describing his interview to Marcia.

"Then I know you could make something nice out of it," said his wife; "and that will please Mr. Witherby."

"Oh, yes, I've done pretty well; but I couldn't let myself loose on him the way I wanted to. Confound the limitations of decency, anyway! I should like to have told just what Colonel Lapham thought of landscape advertising in Colonel Lapham's own words. I'll tell you one thing, Marsh: he had a girl there at one of the desks that you wouldn't let *me* have within gunshot of *my* office. Pretty? It aint any name for it!" Marcia's eyes began to blaze, and Bartley broke out into a laugh, in which he arrested himself at sight of a formidable parcel in the corner of the room.

"Hello! What's that?"

"Why, I don't know what it is," replied Marcia, tremulously. "A man brought it just before you came in, and I didn't like to open it."

"Think it was some kind of infernal machine?" asked Bartley, getting down on his knees to examine the package. "*Mrs. B. Hubbard*, heigh?" He cut the heavy hemp string with his pen-knife. "We must look into this thing. I should like to know who's sending packages to Mrs. Hubbard in my absence." He unfolded the wrappings of paper, growing softer and finer inward, and presently pulled out a handsome square glass jar, through which a crimson mass showed richly. "The Persis Brand!" he yelled. "I knew it!"

"Oh, what is it, Bartley?" quavered Marcia. Then, courageously drawing a little nearer: "Is it some kind of jam?" she implored.

"Jam? No!" roared Bartley. "It's *paint* ! It's mineral paint—Lapham's paint!"

"Paint?" echoed Marcia, as she stood over him while he stripped their wrappings from the jars which showed the dark blue, dark green, light brown, dark brown, and black, with the dark crimson, forming the gamut of color of the Lapham paint. "Don't *tell* me it's paint that *I* can use, Bartley!"

"Well, I shouldn't advise you to use much of it—all at once," replied her husband. "But it's paint that you can use in moderation."

Marcia cast her arms round his neck and kissed him. "O Bartley, I think I'm the happiest girl in the world! I was just wondering what I should do. There are places in that Clover street house that need touching up so dreadfully. I shall be very careful. You needn't be afraid I shall overdo. But this just saves my life. Did you *buy* it, Bartley? You know we couldn't afford it, and you oughtn't to have done it! And what does the Persis Brand mean?"

"Buy it?" cried Bartley. "No! The old fool's sent it to you as a present. You'd better wait for the facts before you pitch into me for extravagance, Marcia. Persis is the name of his wife; and he named it after her because it's his finest brand. You'll see it in my interview. Put it on the market her last birthday for a surprise to her."

"What old fool?" faltered Marcia.

"Why, Lapham—the mineral paint man."

"Oh, what a good man!" sighed Marcia from the bottom of her soul. "Bartley! you *wont* make fun of him, as you do of some of those people? *Will* you?"

"Nothing that *he*'ll ever find out," said Bartley, getting up and brushing off the carpet-lint from his knees.

## II

After dropping Bartley Hubbard at the "Events" building, Lapham drove on down Washington street to Nankeen Square at the South End, where he had lived ever since the mistaken movement of society in that direction ceased. He had not built, but had bought very cheap of a terrified gentleman of good extraction who discovered too late that the South End was not the thing, and who in the eagerness of his flight to the Back Bay threw in his carpets and shades for almost nothing. Mrs. Lapham was even better satisfied with their bargain than the Colonel himself, and they had lived in Nankeen Square for twelve years. They had seen the saplings planted in the pretty oval round which the houses were built flourish up into sturdy young trees, and their two little girls in the same period had grown into young ladies; the Colonel's tough frame had expanded into the bulk which Bartley's interview indicated; and Mrs. Lapham, while keeping a more youthful outline, showed the sharp print of the crow's-foot at the corners of her motherly eyes, and certain slight creases in her wholesome cheeks. The fact that they lived in an unfashionable neighborhood was something that they had never been made to feel to their personal disadvantage, and they had hardly known it till the summer before this story opens, when Mrs. Lapham and her daughter Irene had met some other Bostonians far from Boston, who made it memorable. They were people whom chance had brought for the time under a singular obligation to the Lapham ladies, and they were gratefully recognizant of it. They had ventured—a mother and two daughters— as far as a rather wild little Canadian watering-place on the St. Lawrence, below Quebec, and had arrived some days before their son and brother was expected to join them. Two of their trunks had gone astray, and on the night of their arrival the mother was taken violently ill. Mrs. Lapham came to their help, with her skill as nurse, and with the abundance of her own and her daughter's wardrobe, and a profuse, single-hearted kindness. When a doctor could be got at, he said that but for Mrs. Lapham's timely care, the lady would hardly have lived. He was a very effusive little Frenchman, and fancied he was saying something very pleasant to everybody.

A certain intimacy inevitably followed, and when the son came he was even more grateful than the others. Mrs. Lapham could not quite understand why he should be as attentive to her as to Irene; but she compared him with other young men about the place, and thought him nicer than any of them. She had not the means of a wider comparison; for in Boston, with all her husband's prosperity, they had not had a social life. Their first years there were given to careful getting on Lapham's part, and careful saving on his wife's. Suddenly the money began to come so abundantly that she need not save; and then they did not know what to do with it. A certain amount could be spent on horses, and Lapham spent it; his wife spent on rich and rather ugly clothes and a luxury of household appointments. Lapham had not yet reached the picture-buying stage of the rich man's development, but they decorated their house with the costliest and most abominable frescoes; they went upon journeys, and lavished upon cars and hotels; they gave with both hands to their church and to all the charities it brought them acquainted with; but they did not know how to spend on society. Up to a certain period Mrs. Lapham had the ladies of her neighborhood in to tea, as her mother had done in the country in her younger days. Lapham's idea of hospitality was still to bring a heavy-buying customer home to pot-luck; neither of them imagined dinners.

Their two girls had gone to the public schools, where they had not got on as fast as some of the other girls; so that they were a year behind in graduating from the grammar-school, where Lapham thought that they had got education enough. His wife was of a different mind; she would have liked them to go to some private school for their finishing. But Irene did not care for study; she preferred housekeeping, and both the sisters were afraid of being snubbed by the other girls, who were of a different sort from the girls of the grammar-school; these were mostly from the parks and squares, like themselves. It ended in their going part of a year. But the elder had an odd taste of her own for reading, and she took some private lessons, and read books out of the circulating library; the whole family were amazed at the number she read, and rather proud of it.

They were not girls who embroidered or abandoned themselves to needle-work. Irene spent her abundant leisure in shopping for herself and her mother, of whom both daughters made a kind of idol, buying her caps and laces out of their pin-money, and getting her dresses far beyond her capacity to wear. Irene dressed herself very stylishly, and spent hours on her toilet every day. Her sister had a simpler taste, and, if she had done altogether as she liked, might even have slighted dress. They all three took long naps every day, and sat hours together minutely discussing what they saw out of the window. In her self-guided search for self-improvement, the elder sister went to many church lectures on a vast variety of secular subjects, and usually came home with a comic account of them, and that made more matter of talk for the whole family. She could make fun of nearly everything; Irene complained that she scared away the young men whom they got acquainted with at the dancing-school sociables. They were, perhaps, not the wisest young men.

The girls had learned to dance at Papanti's; but they had not belonged to the private classes. They did not even know of them, and a great gulf divided them from those who did. Their father did not like company, except such as came informally in their way; and their mother had remained too rustic to know how to attract it in the sophisticated city fashion. None of them had grasped the idea of European travel; but they had gone about to mountain and sea-side resorts, the mother and the two girls, where they witnessed the spectacle which such resorts present throughout New England, of multitudes of girls, lovely, accomplished, exquisitely dressed, humbly glad of the presence of any sort of young man; but the Laphams had no skill or courage to make themselves noticed, far less courted by the solitary invalid, or clergyman, or artist. They lurked helplessly about in the hotel parlors, looking on and not knowing how to put themselves forward. Perhaps they did not care a great deal to do so. They had not a conceit of themselves, but a sort of content in their own ways that one may notice in certain families. The very strength of their mutual affection was a barrier to worldly knowledge; they dressed for one another; they equipped their house for their own satisfaction; they lived richly to themselves, not because they were selfish, but because they did not know how to do otherwise. The elder daughter did not care for society, apparently. The younger, who was but three years younger, was not yet quite old enough to be ambitious of it. With all her wonderful beauty, she had an innocence almost vegetable. When her beauty, which in its immaturity was crude and harsh, suddenly ripened, she bloomed and glowed with the unconsciousness of a flower; she not merely did not feel herself admired, but hardly knew herself discovered. If she dressed well, perhaps too well, it was because she had the instinct of dress; but till she met this young man who was so nice to her at Baie St. Joan, she had scarcely lived a detached, individual life, so wholly had she depended on her mother and her sister for her opinions, almost her sensations. She took account of everything he did and said, pondering it, and trying to make out exactly what he meant, to the inflection of a syllable, the slightest movement or gesture. In this way she began for the first time to form ideas which she had not derived from her family, and they were none the less her own because they were often mistaken.

Some of the things that he partly said, partly looked, she reported to her mother, and they talked them over, as they did everything relating to these new acquaintances, and wrought them into the novel point of view which they were acquiring. When Mrs. Lapham returned home, she submitted all the accumulated facts of the case, and all her own conjectures, to her husband, and canvassed them anew.

At first he was disposed to regard the whole affair as of small importance, and she had to insist a little beyond her own convictions in order to counteract his indifference.

"Well, I can tell you," she said, "that if you think they were not the nicest people *you* ever saw, you're mightily mistaken. They had about the best manners; and they had been everywhere, and knew everything. I declare it made me feel as if we had always lived in the backwoods. I don't know but the mother and the daughters would have *let* you feel so a little, if they'd showed out all they thought; but they never did; and the son— well, I can't express it, Silas! But that young man had about perfect ways."

"Seem struck up on Irene?" asked the Colonel.

"How can *I* tell? He seemed just about as much struck up on me. Anyway, he paid me as much attention as he did her. Perhaps it's more the way, now, to notice the mother than it used to be."

Lapham ventured no conjecture, but asked, as he had asked already, who the people were.

Mrs. Lapham repeated their name. Lapham nodded his head. "Do you know them? What business is he in?"

"I guess he aint in anything," said Lapham.

"They were very nice," said Mrs. Lapham, impartially.

"Well, they'd ought to be," returned the Colonel. "Never done anything else."

"They didn't seem stuck up," urged his wife.

"They'd no need to—with you. I could buy him and sell him, twice over."

This answer satisfied Mrs. Lapham rather with the fact than with her husband. "Well, I guess I wouldn't brag, Silas," she said.

In the winter the ladies of this family, who returned to town very late, came to call on Mrs. Lapham. They were again very polite. But the mother let drop, in apology for their calling almost at nightfall, that the coachman had not known the way exactly.

"Nearly all our friends are on the New Land or on the Hill."[3]

There was a barb in this that rankled after the ladies had gone; and on comparing notes with her daughter, Mrs. Lapham found that a barb had been left to rankle in her mind also.

"They said they had never been in this part of the town before."

Upon a strict search of her memory, Irene could not report that the fact had been stated with anything like insinuation, but it was that which gave it a more penetrating effect.

"Oh, well, of course," said Lapham, to whom these facts were referred. "Those sort of people haven't got much business up our way, and they don't come. It's a fair thing all round. We don't trouble the Hill or the New Land much."

"We know where they are," suggested his wife, thoughtfully.

"Yes," assented the Colonel. "*I* know where they are. I've got a lot of land over on the Back Bay."

"You have?" eagerly demanded his wife.

"Want me to build on it?" he asked in reply, with a quizzical smile.

"I guess we can get along here for a while."

This was at night. In the morning Mrs. Lapham said:

"I suppose we ought to do the best we can for the children, in every way."

"I supposed we always had," replied her husband.

"Yes, we have, according to our light."

"Have you got some new light?"

"I don't know as it's light. But if the girls are going to keep on living in Boston and marry here, I presume we ought to try to get them into society, some way; or ought to do something."

"Well, who's ever done more for their children than we have?" demanded Lapham, with a pang at the thought that he could possibly have been outdone. "Don't they have everything they want? Don't they dress just as you say? Don't you go everywhere

3. The two most fashionable residential areas in Boston of this era were on Beacon Hill or on the new land created by filling the tidal flats in Back Bay. The implication is that the Corey family would know only people of high social standing.

with 'em? Is there ever anything going on that's worth while that they don't see it or hear it? *I* don't know what you mean. Why don't you get them into society? There's money enough!"

"There's got to be something besides money, I guess," said Mrs. Lapham, with a hopeless sigh. "I presume we didn't go to work just the right way about their schooling. We ought to have got them into some school where they'd have got acquainted with city girls—girls who could help them along. Nearly everybody at Miss Smillie's was from somewhere else."

"Well, it's pretty late to think about that now," grumbled Lapham.

"And we've always gone our own way, and not looked out for the future. We ought to have gone out more, and had people come to the house. Nobody comes."

"Well, is that my fault? I guess nobody ever makes people welcomer."

"We ought to have invited company more."

"Why don't you do it now? If it's for the girls, I don't care if you have the house full all the while."

Mrs. Lapham was forced to a confession full of humiliation. "I don't know who to ask."

"Well, you can't expect me to tell you."

"No; we're both country people, and we've kept our country ways, and we don't, either of us, know what to do. You've had to work so hard, and your luck was so long coming, and then it came with such a rush, that we haven't had any chance to learn what to do with it. It's just the same with Irene's looks; I didn't expect she was ever going to have any, she *was* such a plain child, and, all at once, she's blazed out this way. As long as it was Pen that didn't seem to care for society, I didn't give much mind to it. But I can see it's going to be different with Irene. I don't believe but what we're in the wrong neighborhood."

"Well," said the Colonel, "there aint a prettier lot on the Back Bay than mine. It's on the water side of Beacon, and it's twenty-eight feet wide and a hundred and fifty deep. Let's build on it."

Mrs. Lapham was silent awhile. "No," she said finally; "we've always got along well enough here, and I guess we better stay."

At breakfast she said, casually: "Girls, how would you like to have your father build on the New Land?"

The girls said they did not know. It was more convenient to the horse-cars where they were.

Mrs. Lapham stole a look of relief at her husband, and nothing more was said of the matter.

The mother of the family who had called upon Mrs. Lapham brought her husband's cards, and when Mrs. Lapham returned the visit she was in some trouble about the proper form of acknowledging the civility. The Colonel had no card but a business card, which advertised the principal depot and the several agencies of the mineral paint; and Mrs. Lapham doubted, till she wished to goodness that she had never seen nor heard of those people, whether to ignore her husband in the transaction altogether, or to write his name on her own card. She decided finally upon this measure, and she had the relief of not finding the family at home. As far as she could judge, Irene seemed to suffer a little disappointment from the fact.

For several months there was no communication between the families. Then there came to Nankeen Square a lithographed circular from the people on the Hill, signed in ink by the mother, and affording Mrs. Lapham an opportunity to subscribe for a charity of undeniable merit and acceptability. She submitted it to her husband, who promptly drew a check for five hundred dollars.

She tore it in two. "I will take a check for a hundred, Silas," she said.

"Why?" he asked, looking up guiltily at her.

"Because a hundred is enough; and I don't want to show off before them."

"Oh, I thought may be you did. Well, Pert," he added, having satisfied human nature by the preliminary thrust, "I guess you're about right. When do you want I should begin to build on Beacon street?" He handed her the new check, where she stood over him, and then leaned back in his chair and looked up at her.

"I don't want you should begin at all. What do you mean, Silas?" She rested against the side of his desk.

"Well, I don't know as I mean anything. But shouldn't you like to build? Everybody builds, at least once in a life-time."

"Where is your lot? They say it's unhealthy over there."

Up to a certain point in their prosperity Mrs. Lapham had kept strict account of all her husband's affairs; but as they expanded, and ceased to be of the retail nature with which women successfully grapple, the intimate knowledge of them made her nervous. There was a period in which she felt that they were being ruined, but the crash had not come; and, since his great success, she had abandoned herself to a blind confidence in her husband's judgment, which she had hitherto felt needed her revision. He came and went, day by day, unquestioned. He bought and sold and got gain. She knew that he would tell her if ever things went wrong, and he knew that she would ask him whenever she was anxious.

"It ain't unhealthy where I've bought," said Lapham, rather enjoying her insinuation. "I looked after that when I was trading; and I guess it's about as healthy on the Back Bay as it is here, anyway. I got that lot for *you*, Pert; I thought you'd want to build on the Back Bay some day."

"Pshaw!" said Mrs. Lapham, deeply pleased inwardly, but not going to show it, as she would have said. "I guess you want to build there yourself." She insensibly got a little nearer to her husband. They liked to talk to each other in that blunt way; it is the New England way of expressing perfect confidence and tenderness.

"Well, I guess I do," said Lapham, not insisting upon the unselfish view of the matter. "I always did like the water side of Beacon. There aint a sightlier place in the world for a house. And some day there's bound to be a drive-way all along behind them houses, between them and the water, and then a lot there is going to be worth the gold that will cover it—*coin*. I've had offers for that lot, Pert, twice over what I give for it. Yes, I *have*. Don't you want to ride over there some afternoon with me and see it?"

"I'm satisfied where we be, Si," said Mrs. Lapham, recurring to the parlance of her youth in her pathos at her husband's kindness. She sighed anxiously, for she felt the trouble a woman knows in view of any great change. They had often talked of altering over the house in which they lived, but they had never come to it; and they had often talked of building, but it had always been a house in the country that they had thought of. "I wish you had sold that lot."

"I haint," said the Colonel, briefly.

"I don't know as I feel much like changing our way of living."

"Guess we could live there pretty much as we live here. There's all kinds of people on Beacon street; you mustn't think they're all big-bugs. I know one party that lives in a house he built to sell, and his wife don't keep any girl. You can have just as much style there as you want, or just as little. I guess we live as well as most of 'em now, and set as good a table. And if you come to style, I don't know as anybody has got more of a right to put it on than what we have."

"Well, I don't want to build on Beacon street, Si," said Mrs. Lapham, gently.

"Just as you please, Persis. I aint in any hurry to leave."

Mrs. Lapham stood flapping the check which she held in her right hand against the edge of her left.

The Colonel still sat looking up at her face, and watching the effect of the poison of ambition which he had artfully instilled into her mind.

She sighed again—a yielding sigh. "What are you going to do this afternoon?"

"I'm going to take a turn on the Brighton road," said the Colonel.

"I don't believe but what I should like to go along," said his wife.

"All right. You haint ever rode behind that mare yet, Pert, and I want you should see me let her out once. They say the snow's all packed down already, and the going is A 1."

At four o'clock in the afternoon, with a cold, red winter sunset before them, the Colonel and his wife were driving slowly down Beacon street in the light, high-seated cutter, where, as he said, they were a pretty tight fit.[4] He was holding the mare in till the time came to speed her, and the mare was springily jolting over the snow, looking intelligently from side to side, and cocking this ear and that, while from her nostrils, her head tossing easily, she blew quick, irregular whiffs of steam.

"Gay, aint she?" proudly suggested the Colonel.

"She *is* gay," assented his wife.

They met swiftly dashing sleighs, and let them pass on either

---

4. "high-seated cutter": a lightweight "coupe" sled, a sort of sports model.

hand, down the beautiful avenue narrowing with an admirably even skyline in the perspective. They were not in a hurry. The mare jounced easily along, and they talked of the different houses on either side of the way. They had a crude taste in architecture, and they admired the worst. There were women's faces at many of the handsome windows, and once in a while a young man on the pavement caught his hat suddenly from his head, and bowed in response to some salutation from within.

"I don't think our girls would look very bad behind one of those big panes," said the Colonel.

"No," said his wife, dreamily.

"Where's the *young* man? Did he come with them?"

"No; he was to spend the winter with a friend of his that has a ranch in Texas. I guess he's got to do something."

"Yes; gentlemaning as a profession has got to play out in a generation or two."

Neither of them spoke of the lot, though Lapham knew perfectly well what his wife had come with him for, and she was aware that he knew it. The time came when he brought the mare down to a walk, and then slowed up almost to a stop, while they both turned their heads to the right and looked at the vacant lot, through which showed the frozen stretch of the Back Bay, a section of the Long Bridge, and the roofs and smoke-stacks of Charlestown.[5]

"Yes, it's sightly," said Mrs. Lapham, lifting her hand from the reins, on which she had unconsciously laid it.

Lapham said nothing, but he let the mare out a little.

The sleighs and cutters were thickening round them. On the Milldam it became difficult to restrict the mare to the long, slow trot into which he let her break. The beautiful landscape widened to right and left of them, with the sunset redder and redder, over the low, irregular hills before them. They crossed the Milldam into Longwood,[6] and here, from the crest of the first upland, stretched two endless lines, in which thousands of cutters went and came. Some of the drivers were already speeding their horses,

5. The Laphams are looking northeast from Beacon Street, across the building lot Silas has bought, across Charleston, which lies on a peninsula just north of Boston on the opposite side of the Charles River, and beyond to the long bridge that connects Charleston to the town of Chelsea.
6. The Laphams continue northwest on Beacon Street, at that time still called Milldam, to the suburb of Longwood, in the present Fenway area. Beacon Street was built atop a dam that enclosed a tidal basin south of the Charles River. The power of the ebbing and flowing tides had been used to drive machinery before the area was filled in to form the fashionable Back Bay residential section.

and these shot to and fro on inner lines, between the slowly moving vehicles on either side of the road. Here and there a burly mounted policeman, bulging over the pommel of his McClellan saddle, jolted by, silently gesturing and directing the course, and keeping it all under the eye of the law. It was what Bartley Hubbard called "a carnival of fashion and gayety on the Brighton road," in his account of it. But most of the people in those elegant sleighs and cutters had so little the air of the great world that one knowing it at all must have wondered where they and their money came from; and the gayety of the men, at least, was expressed, like that of Colonel Lapham, in a grim, almost fierce, alertness; the women wore an air of courageous apprehension. At a certain point the Colonel said, "I'm going to let her out, Pert," and he lifted and then dropped the reins lightly on the mare's back.

She understood the signal, and, as an admirer said, "she laid down to her work." Nothing in the immutable iron of Lapham's face betrayed his sense of triumph, as the mare left everything behind her on the road. Mrs. Lapham, if she felt fear, was too busy holding her flying wraps about her, and shielding her face from the scud of ice flung from the mare's heels, to betray it; except for the rush of her feet, the mare was as silent as the people behind her; the muscles of her back and thighs worked more and more swiftly, like some mechanism responding to an alien force, and she shot to the end of the course, grazing a hundred encountered and rival sledges in her passage, but unmolested by the policemen, who probably saw that the mare and the Colonel knew what they were about, and, at any rate, were not the sort of men to interfere with trotting like that. At the end of the heat Lapham drew her in, and turned off on a side street into Brookline.

"Tell you what, Pert," he said, as if they had been quietly jogging along, with time for uninterrupted thought since he last spoke, "I've about made up my mind to build on that lot."

"All right, Silas," said Mrs. Lapham; "I suppose you know what you're about. Don't build on it for me, that's all."

When she stood in the hall at home, taking off her things, she said to the girls, who were helping her, "Some day your father will get killed with that mare."

"Did he speed her?" asked Penelope, the elder. She was named after her grandmother, who had in her turn inherited from another ancestress the name of the Homeric matron whose peculiar merits won her a place even among the Puritan Faiths, Hopes, Temperances, and Prudences.[7] Penelope was the girl whose odd, serious face had struck Bartley Hubbard in the photograph of the family group Lapham showed him on the day of the interview. Her large eyes, like her hair, were brown; they had the peculiar look of near-sighted eyes which is called mooning; her complexion was of a dark pallor.

Her mother did not reply to a question which might be considered already answered. "He says he's going to build on that lot of his," she next remarked, unwinding the long veil which she had tied round her neck to hold her bonnet on. She put her hat and cloak on the hall table, to be carried upstairs later, and they all went in to tea: creamed oysters, birds, hot biscuit, two kinds of cake, and dishes of stewed and canned fruit and honey. The women dined alone at one, and the Colonel at the same hour down-town. But he liked a good hot meal when he got home in the evening. The house flared with gas, and the Colonel, before he sat down, went about shutting the registers, through which a welding heat came voluming up from the furnace.

"I'll be the death of that darkey *yet*," he said, "if he don't stop making on such a fire. The only way to get any comfort out of your furnace is to take care of it yourself."

"Well," answered his wife from behind the tea-pot, as he sat down at table with this threat, "there's nothing to prevent you, Si. And you can shovel the snow, too, if you want to—till you get over to Beacon street, anyway."

"I guess I can keep my own sidewalk on Beacon street clean, if I take the notion."

"I should like to see you at it," retorted his wife.

"Well, you keep a sharp lookout, and may be you will."

Their taunts were really expressions of affectionate pride in each other. They liked to have it, give and take, that way, as they would have said, right along.

"A man can be a man on Beacon street as well as anywhere, I guess."

"Well, I'll do the wash, as I used to in Lumberville," said Mrs. Lapham. "I presume you'll let me have set tubs, Si. You know

---

7. Penelope, the wife of Odysseus in the *Odyssey*, was noted for the peculiar merits of patience and faithfulness. She waited twenty years for the return of her warrior-husband.

I aint so young, any more." She passed Irene a cup of Oolong tea,—none of them had a sufficiently cultivated palate for Souchong,—and the girl handed it to her father.[8]

"Papa," she asked, "you don't really mean that you are going to build over there?"

"Don't I? You wait and see," said the Colonel, stirring his tea.

"I don't believe you do," pursued the girl.

"Is that so? I presume you'd hate to have me. Your mother does." He said *doos*, of course.

Penelope took the word. "I go in for it. I don't see any use in not enjoying money, if you've got it *to* enjoy. That's what it's for, I suppose; though you mightn't always think so." She had a slow, quaint way of talking, that seemed a pleasant personal modification of some ancestral Yankee drawl, and her voice was low and cozy, and so far from being nasal that it was a little hoarse.

"I guess the ayes has it, Pen," said her father. "How would it do to let Irene and your mother stick in the old place here, and us go into the new house?" At times the Colonel's grammar failed him.

The matter dropped, and the Laphams lived on as before, with joking recurrences to the house on the water side of Beacon. The Colonel seemed less in earnest than any of them about it; but that was his way, his girls said; you never could tell when he really meant a thing.

## III

TOWARD the end of the winter there came a newspaper addressed to Miss Irene Lapham; it proved to be a Texas newspaper, with a complimentary account of the ranch of the Hon. Loring G. Stanton, which the representative of the journal had visited.

"It must be his friend," said Mrs. Lapham, to whom her daughter brought the paper; "the one he's staying with."

The girl did not say anything, but she carried the paper to her room, where she scanned every line of it for another name. She did not find it, but she cut the notice out and stuck it into

---

8. Souchong was a more fashionable tea than Oolong because of its supposedly more subtle    flavor. The Laphams retain the simple tastes of country people.

the side of her mirror, where she could read it every morning when she brushed her hair, and the last thing at night when she looked at herself in the glass just before turning off the gas. Her sister often read it aloud, standing behind her and rendering it with elocutionary effects.

"The first time I ever heard of a love-letter in the form of a puff to a cattle-ranch. But perhaps that's the style on the Hill."

Mrs. Lapham told her husband of the arrival of the paper, treating the fact with an importance that he refused to see in it.

"How do you know the fellow sent it, anyway?" he demanded.

"Oh, I know he did."

"I don't see why he couldn't write to 'Rene, if he really meant anything."

"Well, I guess that wouldn't be their way," said Mrs. Lapham; she did not at all know what their way would be.

When the spring opened Colonel Lapham showed that he had been in earnest about building on the New Land. His idea of a house was a brown-stone front, four stories high, and a French roof with an air-chamber above. Inside, there was to be a reception-room on the street and a dining-room back. The parlors were to be on the second floor, and finished in black walnut or parti-colored paint. The chambers were to be on the three floors above, front and rear, with side rooms over the front door. Black walnut was to be used everywhere except in the attic, which was to be painted and grained to look like black walnut. The whole was to be very high-studded, and there were to be handsome cornices and elaborate center-pieces throughout, except, again, in the attic.[9]

These ideas he had formed from the inspection of many new buildings which he had seen going up, and which he had a passion for looking into. He was confirmed in his ideas by a master-builder who had put up a great many houses on the Back Bay as a speculation, and who told him that if he wanted to have a house in the style, that was the way to have it.

The beginnings of the process by which Lapham escaped from the master-builder and ended in the hands of an architect are so obscure that it would be almost impossible to trace them. But it all happened, and Lapham promptly developed his ideas of

---

9. The height of the ceilings depends upon the height of the studs that bear the second floor.

The Lapham house is intended to have very high ceilings, an expensive way to build.

black-walnut finish, high-studding, and cornices. The architect was able to conceal the shudder which they must have sent through him. He was skillful, as nearly all architects are, in playing upon that simple instrument Man. He began to touch Colonel Lapham's stops.

"Oh, certainly, have the parlors high-studded. But you've seen some of those pretty, old-fashioned country-houses, haven't you, where the entrance-story is very low-studded?"

"Yes," Lapham assented.

"Well, don't you think something of that kind would have a very nice effect? Have the entrance-story low-studded, and your parlors on the next floor as high as you please. Put your little reception-room here beside the door, and get the whole width of your house frontage for a square hall, and an easy low-tread staircase running up three sides of it. I'm sure Mrs. Lapham would find it much pleasanter." The architect caught toward him a scrap of paper lying on the table at which they were sitting and sketched his idea. "Then have your dining-room behind the hall, looking on the water."

He glanced at Mrs. Lapham, who said, "Of course," and the architect went on:

"That gets you rid of one of those long, straight, ugly staircases,"—until that moment Lapham had thought a long, straight staircase the chief ornament of a house,—"and gives you an effect of amplitude and space."

"That's so!" said Mrs. Lapham. Her husband merely made a noise in his throat.

"Then, were you thinking of having your parlors together, connected by folding doors?" asked the architect deferentially.

"Yes, of course," said Lapham. "They're always so, aint they?"

"Well, nearly," said the architect. "I was wondering how would it do to make one large square room at the front, taking the whole breadth of the house, and, with this hall-space between, have a music-room back for the young ladies?"

Lapham looked helplessly at his wife, whose quicker apprehension had followed the architect's pencil with instant sympathy. "First-rate!" she cried.

The Colonel gave way. "I guess that would do. It'll be kind of odd, wont it?"

"Well, I don't know," said the architect. "Not so odd, I hope, as the other thing will be a few years from now." He went on to plan the rest of the house, and he showed himself such a master in regard to all the practical details that Mrs. Lapham began to feel a motherly affection for the young man, and her husband could not deny in his heart that the fellow seemed to understand his business. He stopped walking about the room, as he had begun to do when the architect and Mrs. Lapham entered into the particulars of closets, drainage, kitchen arrangements, and all that, and came back to the table. "I presume," he said, "you'll have the drawing-room finished in black walnut?"

"Well, yes," replied the architect, "if you like. But some less expensive wood can be made just as effective with paint. Of course you can paint black walnut, too."

"Paint it?" gasped the Colonel.

"Yes," said the architect quietly. "White, or a little off white."

Lapham dropped the plan he had picked up from the table. His wife made a little move toward him of consolation or support.

"Of course," resumed the architect, "I know there has been a great craze for black walnut. But it's an ugly wood; and for a drawing-room there is really nothing like white paint. We should want to introduce a little gold here and there. Perhaps we might run a painted frieze round under the cornice—garlands of roses on a gold ground; it would tell wonderfully in a white room."

The Colonel returned less courageously to the charge. "I presume you'll want Eastlake mantel-shelves and tiles?" He meant this for a sarcastic thrust at a prevailing foible of the profession.[1]

"Well, no," gently answered the architect. "I was thinking perhaps a white marble chimney-piece, treated in the refined Empire style, would be the thing for that room."[2]

"White marble!" exclaimed the Colonel. "I thought that had gone out long ago."

"Really beautiful things can't go out. They may disappear for a little while, but they must come back. It's only the ugly things that stay out after they've had their day."

1. Under the influence of English critic-designers Charles Locke Eastlake and John Ruskin many fashionable post–Civil War homes in America were decorated in dark colors, heavy draperies, textured wallpapers, and tiles. The style was expensive and oppressive.

2. The architect recommends a simple, open, light Empire style that takes its name from its identification with the reign of Napoleon in France.

Lapham could only venture very modestly, "Hard-wood floors?"

"In the music-room, of course," consented the architect.

"And in the drawing-room?"

"Carpet. Some sort of moquette, I should say. But I should prefer to consult Mrs. Lapham's taste in that matter."[3]

"And in the other rooms?"

"Oh, carpets, of course."

"And what about the stairs?"

"Carpet. And I should have the rail and banisters white— banisters turned or twisted."

The Colonel said under his breath, "Well, I'm dumned!" but he gave no utterance to his astonishment in the architect's presence. When he went at last,—the session did not end till eleven o'clock,—Lapham said, "Well, Pert, I guess that fellow's fifty years behind, or ten years ahead. I wonder what the Ongpeer style is?"

"I don't know. I hated to ask. But he seemed to understand what he was talking about. I declare, he knows what a woman wants in a house better than she does herself."

"And a man's simply nowhere in comparison," said Lapham. But he respected a fellow who could beat him at every point, and have a reason ready, as this architect had; and when he recovered from the daze into which the complete upheaval of all his preconceived notions had left him, he was in a fit state to swear by the architect. It seemed to him that he had discovered the fellow (as he always called him) and owned him now, and the fellow did nothing to disturb this impression. He entered into that brief but intense intimacy with the Laphams which the sympathetic architect holds with his clients. He was privy to all their differences of opinion and all their disputes about the house. He knew just where to insist upon his own ideas, and where to yield. He was really building several other houses, but he gave the Laphams the impression that he was doing none but theirs.

The work was not begun till the frost was thoroughly out of the ground, which that year was not before the end of April. Even then it did not proceed very rapidly. Lapham said they might as well take their time to it; if they got the walls up and the thing closed in before the snow flew, they could be working at it

3. Moquette was a sort of velvety woolen carpeting.

all winter. It was found necessary to dig for the kitchen; at that point the original salt marsh lay near the surface, and before they began to put in the piles for the foundation they had to pump. The neighborhood smelt like the hold of a ship after a three years' voyage. People who had cast their fortunes with the New Land went by professing not to notice it; people who still "hung on to the Hill" put their handkerchiefs to their noses, and told each other the old terrible stories of the material used in filling up the Back Bay.

Nothing gave Lapham so much satisfaction in the whole construction of his house as the pile-driving. When this began, early in the summer, he took Mrs. Lapham every day in his buggy and drove round to look at it; stopping the mare in front of the lot, and watching the operation with even keener interest than the little loafing Irish boys who superintended it in force. It pleased him to hear the portable engine chuckle out a hundred thin whiffs of steam, in carrying the big iron weight to the top of the framework above the pile, then seem to hesitate, and cough once or twice in pressing the weight against the detaching apparatus. There was a moment in which the weight had the effect of poising before it fell; then it dropped with a mighty whack on the iron-bound head of the pile and drove it a foot into the earth.

"By gracious!" he would say, "there aint anything like that in *this* world for *business*, Persis!"

Mrs. Lapham suffered him to enjoy the sight twenty or thirty times before she said, "Well, now drive on, Si."

By the time the foundation was in and the brick walls had begun to go up, there were so few people left in the neighborhood that she might indulge with impunity her husband's passion for having her clamber over the floor-timbers and the skeleton staircases with him. Many of the householders had boarded up their front doors before the buds had begun to swell and the assessor to appear in early May; others had followed soon; and Mrs. Lapham was as safe from remark as if she had been in the depth of the country. Ordinarily she and her girls left town early in July, going to one of the hotels at Nantasket,[4] where it was convenient for the Colonel to get to and from his business by the

4. The beach hotels along the Nantasket penin-   Bay, were more convenient than fashionable.
sula, at the extreme southeast end of the Boston

boat. But this summer they were all lingering a few weeks later, under the novel fascination of the new house, as they called it, as if there were no other in the world.

Lapham drove there with his wife after he had set Bartley Hubbard down at the "Events" office, but on this day something happened that interfered with the solid pleasure they usually took in going over the house. As the Colonel turned from casting anchor at the mare's head with the hitching-weight, after helping his wife to alight, he encountered a man to whom he could not help speaking, though the man seemed to share his hesitation if not his reluctance at the necessity. He was a tallish, thin man, with a dust-colored face, and a dead, clerical air, which somehow suggested at once feebleness and tenacity.

Mrs. Lapham held out her hand to him.

"Why, Mr. Rogers!" she exclaimed, and then, turning toward her husband, seemed to refer the two men to each other. They shook hands, but Lapham did not speak. "I didn't know you were in Boston," pursued Mrs. Lapham. "Is Mrs. Rogers with you?"

"No," said Mr. Rogers, with a voice which had the flat, succinct sound of two pieces of wood clapped together. "Mrs. Rogers is still in Chicago."

A little silence followed, and then Mrs. Lapham said:

"I presume you are quite settled out there."

"No; we have left Chicago. Mrs. Rogers has merely remained to finish up a little packing."

"Oh, indeed! Are you coming back to Boston?"

"I cannot say as yet. We some think of so doing."

Lapham turned away and looked up at the building. His wife pulled a little at her glove, as if embarrassed or even pained. She tried to make a diversion.

"We are building a house," she said, with a meaningless laugh.

"Oh, indeed," said Mr. Rogers, looking up at it.

Then no one spoke again, and she said, helplessly:

"If you come to Boston, I hope I shall see Mrs. Rogers."

"She will be happy to have you call," said Mr. Rogers.

He touched his hat-brim, and made a bow forward rather than in Mrs. Lapham's direction.

She mounted the planking that led into the shelter of the bare brick walls, and her husband slowly followed. When she turned her face toward him her cheeks were burning, and tears that looked hot stood in her eyes.

"You left it all to me!" she cried. "Why couldn't you speak a word?"

"I hadn't anything to say to him," replied Lapham sullenly.

They stood awhile, without looking at the work which they had come to enjoy, and without speaking to each other.

"I suppose we might as well go on," said Mrs. Lapham at last, as they returned to the buggy. The Colonel drove recklessly toward the Milldam. His wife kept her veil down and her face turned from him. After a time she put her handkerchief up under her veil and wiped her eyes, and he set his teeth and squared his jaw.

"I don't see how he always manages to appear just at the moment when he seems to have gone fairly out of our lives, and blight everything," she whimpered.

"I supposed he was dead," said Lapham.

"Oh, don't *say* such a thing! It sounds as if you wished it."

"Why do you mind it? What do you let him blight everything for?"

"I can't help it, and I don't believe I ever shall. I don't know as his being dead would help it any. I can't ever see him without feeling just as I did at first."

"I tell you," said Lapham, "it was a perfectly square thing. And I wish, once for all, you would quit bothering about it. My conscience is easy as far as he's concerned, and it always was."

"And I can't look at him without feeling as if you'd ruined him, Silas."

"Don't look at him, then," said her husband with a scowl. "I want you should recollect in the first place, Persis, that I never wanted a partner."

"If he hadn't put his money in when he did, you'd 'a' broken down."

"Well, he got his money out again, and more too," said the Colonel with a sulky weariness.

"He didn't want to take it out."

"I gave him his choice: buy out or go out."

"You know he couldn't buy out then. It was no choice at all."

"It was a business chance."

"No; you had better face the truth, Silas. It was no chance at all. You crowded him out. A man that had saved you! No, you had got greedy, Silas. You had made your paint your god, and you couldn't bear to let anybody else share in its blessings."

"I tell you he was a drag and a brake on me from the word go. You say he saved me. Well, if I hadn't got him out he'd 'a' ruined me sooner or later. So it's an even thing, as far forth as that goes."

"No, it aint an even thing, and you know it, Silas. Oh, if I could only get you once to acknowledge that you did wrong about it, then I should have some hope. I don't say you meant wrong exactly, but you took an advantage. Yes, you took an advantage! You had him where he couldn't help himself, and then you wouldn't show him any mercy."

"I'm sick of this," said Lapham. "If you'll 'tend to the house, I'll manage my business without your help."

"You were very glad of my help once."

"Well, I'm tired of it now. Don't meddle."

"I *will* meddle. When I see you hardening yourself in a wrong thing, it's time for me to meddle, as you call it, and I will. I can't ever get you to own up the least bit about Rogers, and I feel as if it was hurting you all the while."

"What do you want I should own up about a thing for when I don't feel wrong? I tell you Rogers haint got anything to complain of, and that's what I told you from the start. It's a thing that's done every day. I was loaded up with a partner that didn't know anything, and couldn't do anything, and I unloaded; that's all."

"You unloaded just at the time when you knew that your paint was going to be worth about twice what it ever had been; and you wanted all the advantage for yourself."

"I had a right to it. I made the success."

"Yes, you made it with Rogers's money; and when you'd made it you took his share of it. I guess you thought of that when you saw him, and that's why you couldn't look him in the face."

At these words Lapham lost his temper.

"I guess you don't want to ride with me any more to-day," he said, turning the mare abruptly round.

"I'm as ready to go back as what you are," replied his wife. "And don't you ask me to go to that house with you any more. You can sell it, for all me. I sha'n't live in it. There's blood on it."

# IV

THE silken texture of the marriage tie bears a daily strain of
wrong and insult to which no other human relation can be subjected without lesion; and sometimes the strength that knits
society together might appear to the eye of faltering faith the
curse of those immediately bound by it. Two people by no means
reckless of each other's rights and feelings, but even tender of
them for the most part, may tear at each other's heart-strings in
this sacred bond with perfect impunity; though if they were any
other two they would not speak or look at each other again after
the outrages they exchange. It is certainly a curious spectacle,
and doubtless it ought to convince an observer of the divinity of
the institution. If the husband and wife are blunt, outspoken
people like the Laphams, they do not weigh their words; if they
are more refined, they weigh them very carefully, and know
accurately just how far they will carry, and in what most sensitive spot they may be planted with most effect.

Lapham was proud of his wife, and when he married her it
had been a rise in life for him. For a while he stood in awe of his
good fortune, but this could not last, and he simply remained
supremely satisfied with it. The girl who had taught school with
a clear head and a strong hand was not afraid of work; she
encouraged and helped him from the first, and bore her full
share of the common burden. She had health, and she did not
worry his life out with peevish complaints and vagaries; she had
sense and principle, and in their simple lot she did what was
wise and right. Their marriage was hallowed by an early sorrow:
they lost their boy, and it was years before they could look each
other in the face and speak of him. No one gave up more than
they when they gave up each other, and Lapham went to the
war. When he came back and began to work, her zeal and courage formed the spring of his enterprise. In that affair of the
partnership she had tried to be his conscience, but perhaps she
would have defended him if he had accused himself; it was one
of those things in this life which seem destined to await justice,
or at least judgment, in the next. As he said, Lapham had dealt
fairly by his partner in money; he had let Rogers take more
money out of the business than he put into it; he had, as he said,
simply forced out of it a timid and inefficient participant in

advantages which he had created. But Lapham had not created them all. He had been dependent at one time on his partner's capital. It was a moment of terrible trial. Happy is the man forever after who can choose the ideal, the unselfish part in such an exigency! Lapham could not rise to it. He did what he could maintain to be perfectly fair. The wrong, if any, seemed to be condoned to him, except when from time to time his wife brought it up. Then all the question stung and burned anew, and had to be reasoned out and put away once more. It seemed to have an inextinguishable vitality. It slept, but it did not die.

His course did not shake Mrs. Lapham's faith in him. It astonished her at first, and it always grieved her that he could not see that he was acting solely in his own interest. But she found excuses for him, which at times she made reproaches. She vaguely perceived that his paint was something more than business to him; it was a sentiment, almost a passion. He could not share its management and its profit with another without a measure of self-sacrifice far beyond that which he must make with something less personal to him. It was the poetry of that nature, otherwise so intensely prosaic; and she understood this, and for the most part forbore. She knew him good and true and blameless in all his life, except for this wrong, if it were a wrong; and it was only when her nerves tingled intolerably with some chance renewal of the pain she had suffered that she shared her anguish with him in true wifely fashion.

With those two there was never anything like an explicit reconciliation. They simply ignored a quarrel; and Mrs. Lapham had only to say a few days after at breakfast, "I guess the girls would like to go round with you this afternoon, and look at the new house," in order to make her husband grumble out as he looked down into his coffee-cup, "I guess we better all go, hadn't we?"

"Well, I'll see," she said.

There was not really a great deal to look at when Lapham arrived on the ground in his four-seated beach-wagon. But the walls were up, and the studding had already given skeleton shape to the interior. The floors were roughly boarded over, and the stairways were in place, with provisional treads rudely laid. They had not begun to lath and plaster yet, but the clean, fresh smell of the mortar in the walls mingling with the pungent fragrance of the pine shavings neutralized the Venetian odor that drew in over the water. It was pleasantly shady there, though for the matter of that the heat of the morning had all been washed out of the atmosphere by a tide of east wind setting in at noon, and the thrilling, delicious cool of a Boston summer afternoon bathed every nerve.

The foreman went about with Mrs. Lapham, showing her where the doors were to be; but Lapham soon tired of this, and having found a pine stick of perfect grain, he abandoned himself to the pleasure of whittling it in what was to be the reception-room, where he sat looking out on the street from what was to be the bay-window. Here he was presently joined by his girls, who, after locating their own room on the water side above the music-room, had no more wish to enter into details than their father.

"Come and take a seat in the bay-window, ladies," he called out to them, as they looked in at him through the ribs of the wall. He jocosely made room for them on the trestle on which he sat.

They came gingerly and vaguely forward, as young ladies do when they wish not to seem to be going to do a thing they have made up their minds to do. When they had taken their places on their trestle, they could not help laughing with scorn, open and acceptable to their father; and Irene curled her chin up, in a little way she had, and said, "How ridiculous!" to her sister.

"Well, I can tell you what," said the Colonel, in fond enjoyment of their young-ladyishness, "your mother wasn't ashamed to sit with me on a trestle when I called her out to look at the first coat of my paint that I ever tried on a house."

"Yes; we've heard that story," said Penelope, with easy security of her father's liking what she said. "We were brought up on that story."

"Well, it's a good story," said her father.

At that moment a young man came suddenly in range, who began to look up at the signs of building as he approached. He dropped his eyes in coming abreast of the bay-window, where Lapham sat with his girls, and then his face lightened, and he took off his hat and bowed to Irene. She rose mechanically from the trestle, and her face lightened too. She was a very pretty figure of a girl, after our fashion of girls, round and slim and flexible, and her face was admirably regular. But her great beauty—and it was very great—was in her coloring. This was of an effect for which there is no word but delicious, as we use it of fruit or flowers. She had red hair, like her father in his earlier days, and the tints of her cheeks and temples were such as suggested May-flowers and apple-blossoms and peaches. Instead of the gray that often dulls this complexion, her eyes were of a blue at once intense and tender, and they seemed to burn on what they looked at with a soft, lambent flame. It was well understood by her sister and mother that her eyes always expressed a great deal more than Irene ever thought or felt; but this is not saying that she was not a very sensible girl and very honest.

The young man faltered perceptibly, and Irene came a little forward, and then there gushed from them both a smiling exchange of greeting, of which the sum was that he supposed she was out of town, and that she had not known that he had got back. A pause ensued, and flushing again in her uncertainty as to whether she ought or ought not to do it, she said, "My father, Mr. Corey; and my sister."

The young man took off his hat again, showing his shapely head, with a line of wholesome sunburn ceasing where the recently and closely clipped hair began. He was dressed in a fine summer check, with a blue white-dotted neckerchief, and he had a white hat, in which he looked very well when he put it back on his head. His whole dress seemed very fresh and new, and, in fact, he had cast aside his Texan habiliments only the day before.

"How do you do, sir?" said the Colonel, stepping to the window, and reaching out of it the hand which the young man advanced to take. "Wont you come in? We're at home here. House I'm building."

"Oh, indeed?" returned the young man; and he came promptly up the steps, and through its ribs into the reception-room.

"Have a trestle?" asked the Colonel, while the girls exchanged little shocks of terror and amusement at the eyes.

"Thank you," said the young man, simply, and sat down.

"Mrs. Lapham is upstairs interviewing the carpenter, but she'll be down in a minute."

"I hope she's quite well," said Corey. "I supposed—I was afraid she might be out of town."

"Well, we are off to Nantasket next week. The house kept us in town pretty late."

"It must be very exciting, building a house," said Corey to the elder sister.

"Yes, it is," she assented, loyally refusing in Irene's interest the opportunity of saying anything more.

Corey turned to the latter. "I suppose you've all helped to plan it?"

"Oh, no; the architect and mamma did that."

"But they allowed the rest of us to agree, when we were good," said Penelope.

Corey looked at her, and saw that she was shorter than her sister, and had a dark complexion.

"It's very exciting," said Irene.

"Come up," said the Colonel, rising, "and look round if you'd like to."

"I should like to, very much," said the young man.

He helped the young ladies over crevasses of carpentry and along narrow paths of planking, on which they had made their way unassisted before. The elder sister left the younger to profit solely by these offices as much as possible. She walked between them and her father, who went before, lecturing on each apartment and taking the credit of the whole affair more and more as he talked on.

"There!" he said, "we're going to throw out a bay-window here, so as get the water all the way up and down. This is my girls' room," he added, looking proudly at them both.

It seemed terribly intimate. Irene blushed deeply and turned her head away.

But the young man took it all, apparently, as simply as their father. "What a lovely lookout," he said. The Back Bay spread its glassy sheet before them, empty but for a few smaller boats and a large schooner, with her sails close-furled and dripping like snow from her spars, which a tug was rapidly towing toward Cambridge. The carpentry of that city, embanked and embowered in foliage, shared the picturesqueness of Charlestown in the distance.

"Yes," said Lapham, "I go in for using the best rooms in your house yourself. If people come to stay with you, they can put up with the second best. Though we don't intend to have any second best. There aint going to be an unpleasant room in the whole house, from top to bottom."

"Oh, I wish papa wouldn't brag so!" breathed Irene to her sister, where they stood a little apart looking away together.

The Colonel went on. "No, sir," he swelled out, "I have gone in for making a regular job of it. I've got the best architect in Boston, and I'm building a house to suit myself. And if money can do it, I guess I'm going to be suited."

"It seems very delightful," said Corey, "and very original."

"Yes, sir. That fellow hadn't talked five minutes before I saw that he knew what he was about every time."

"I wish mamma would come!" breathed Irene again. "I shall certainly go through the floor if papa says anything more."

"They are making a great many very pretty houses nowadays," said the young man. "It's very different from the old-fashioned building."

"Well," said the Colonel, with a large toleration of tone and a deep breath that expanded his ample chest, "we spend more on our houses nowadays. I started out to build a forty-thousand-dollar house. Well, sir! that fellow has got me in for more than sixty thousand already, and I doubt if I get out of it much under a hundred. You can't have a nice house for nothing. It's just like ordering a picture of a painter. You pay him enough, and he can afford to paint you a first-class picture; and if you don't, he can't. That's all there is of it. Why, they tell me that A. T. Stewart gave one of those French fellows sixty thousand dollars for a little seven-by-nine picture the other day. Yes, sir, give an architect money enough and he'll give you a nice house, every time."

"I've heard that they're sharp at getting money to realize their ideas," assented the young man, with a laugh.

"Well, I should say so!" exclaimed the Colonel. "They come to you with an improvement that you can't resist. It has good looks and common sense and everything in its favor, and it's like throwing money away to refuse. And they always manage to get you when your wife is around, and then you're helpless."

The Colonel himself set the example of laughing at this joke, and the young man joined him less obstreperously. The girls turned, and he said: "I don't think I ever saw this view to better advantage. It's surprising how well the Memorial Hall and the Cambridge spires work up, over there. And the sunsets must be magnificent."

Lapham did not wait for them to reply.

"Yes, sir, it's about the sightliest view I know of. I always did like the water side of Beacon. Long before I owned property here, or ever expected to, m'wife and I used to ride down this way, and stop the buggy to get this view over the water. When people talk to me about the Hill, I can understand 'em. It's snug, and it's old-fashioned, and it's where they've always lived. But when they talk about Commonwealth Avenue,[5] I don't know what they mean. It don't hold a candle to the water side of Beacon. You've got just as much wind over there, and you've got just as much dust, and all the view you've got is the view across the street. No, sir! When you come to the Back Bay at all, give me the water side of Beacon."

"Oh, I think you're quite right," said the young man. "The view here is everything."

Irene looked "I wonder what papa is going to say next!" at her sister, when their mother's voice was heard overhead, approaching the opening in the floor where the stairs were to be; and she presently appeared, with one substantial foot a long way ahead. She was followed by the carpenter, with his rule sticking out of his overalls pocket, and she was still talking to him about some measurements they had been taking, when they reached the bottom, so that Irene had to say, "Mamma, Mr. Corey," before Mrs. Lapham was aware of him.

He came forward with as much grace and speed as the uncertain footing would allow, and Mrs. Lapham gave him a stout squeeze of her comfortable hand.

"Why, Mr. Corey! When did you get back?"

"Yesterday. It hardly seems as if I *had* got back. I didn't expect to find you in a new house."

"Well, you are our first caller. I presume you won't expect I should make excuses for the state you find it in. Has the Colonel been doing the honors?"

"Oh, yes. And I've seen more of your house than I ever shall again, I suppose."

"Well, I hope not," said Lapham. "There'll be several chances to see us in the old one yet, before we leave."

He probably thought this a neat, off-hand way of making the

invitation, for he looked at his womankind as if he might expect their admiration.

"Oh, yes, indeed!" said his wife. "We shall be very glad to see Mr. Corey, any time."

"Thank you; I shall be glad to come."

He and the Colonel went before, and helped the ladies down the difficult descent. Irene seemed less sure-footed than the others; she clung to the young man's hand an imperceptible moment longer than need be, or else he detained her. He found opportunity of saying, "It's so pleasant seeing you again," adding, "All of you."

"Thank you," said the girl. "They must all be glad to have you at home again."

Corey laughed.

"Well, I suppose they would be, if they were at home to have me. But the fact is, there's nobody in the house but my father and myself, and I'm only on my way to Bar Harbor."[6]

"Oh! Are they there?"

"Yes; it seems to be the only place where my mother can get just the combination of sea and mountain air that she wants."

"We go to Nantasket—it's convenient for papa; and I don't believe we shall go anywhere else this summer, mamma's so taken up with building. We do nothing but talk house; and Pen says we eat and sleep house. She says it would be a sort of relief to go and live in tents for a while."

"She seems to have a good deal of humor," the young man ventured, upon the slender evidence.

The others had gone to the back of the house a moment, to look at some suggested change. Irene and Corey were left standing in the doorway. A lovely light of happiness played over her face and etherealized its delicious beauty. She had some ado to keep herself from smiling outright, and the effort deepened the dimples in her cheeks; she trembled a little, and the pendants shook in the tips of her pretty ears.

The others came back directly, and they all descended the front steps together. The Colonel was about to renew his invitation, but he caught his wife's eye, and, without being able to

6. Bar Harbor is a very fashionable vacation retreat on the coast of northern Maine. Its dis- tance and social tone contrast with Nantasket, a closer, more middle-class resort.

interpret its warning exactly, was able to arrest himself, and went about gathering up the hitching-weight, while the young man handed the ladies into the beach-wagon. Then he lifted his hat, and the ladies all bowed, and the Laphams drove off, Irene's blue ribbons fluttering backward from her hat, as if they were her clinging thoughts.

"So that's young Corey, is it?" said the Colonel, letting the stately stepping, tall coupé horse make his way homeward at will with the beach-wagon. "Well, he aint a bad-looking fellow, and he's got a good, fair and square, honest eye. But I don't see how a fellow like that, that's had every advantage in this world, can hang round home and let his father support him. Seems to me, if I had his health and his education, I should want to strike out and do something for myself."

The girls on the back seat had hold of each other's hands, and they exchanged electrical pressures at the different points their father made.

"I presume," said Mrs. Lapham, "that he was down in Texas looking after something."

"He's come back without finding it, I guess."

"Well, if his father has the money to support him, and don't complain of the burden, I don't see why *we* should."

"Oh, I know it's none of my business; but I don't like the principle. I like to see a man *act* like a man. I don't like to see him taken care of like a young lady. Now, I suppose that fellow belongs to two or three clubs, and hangs around 'em all day, lookin' out the window,—I've seen 'em,—instead of tryin' to hunt up something to do for an honest livin'."

"If I was a young man," Penelope struck in, "I would belong to twenty clubs, if I could find them, and I would hang around them all, and look out the window till I dropped."

"Oh, you would, would you?" demanded her father, delighted with her defiance, and twisting his fat head around over his shoulder to look at her. "Well, you wouldn't do it on *my* money, if you were a son of *mine*, young lady."

"Oh, you wait and see," retorted the girl.

This made them all laugh. But the Colonel recurred seriously to the subject that night, as he was winding up his watch preparatory to putting it under his pillow.

"I could make a man of that fellow, if I had him in the business with me. There's stuff in him. But I spoke up the way I did because I didn't choose Irene should think I would stand any kind of a loafer 'round—I don't care who he is, or how well educated or brought up. And I guess, from the way Pen spoke up, that 'Rene saw what I was driving at."

The girl, apparently, was less anxious about her father's ideas and principles than about the impression which he had made upon the young man. She talked it over and over with her sister before they went to bed, and she asked in despair, as she stood looking at Penelope brushing out her hair before the glass,

"Do you suppose he'll think papa always talks in that bragging way?"

"He'll be right if he does," answered her sister. "It's the way father always does talk. You never noticed it so much, that's all. And I guess if he can't make allowance for father's bragging, he'll be a little too good. *I* enjoyed hearing the Colonel go on."

"I know you did," returned Irene in distress. Then she sighed. "Didn't you think he looked very nice?"

"Who? The Colonel?" Penelope had caught up the habit of calling her father so from her mother, and she used his title in all her jocose and perverse moods.

"You know very well I don't mean papa," pouted Irene.

"Oh! Mr. Corey! Why didn't you say Mr. Corey if you meant Mr. Corey? If I meant Mr. Corey, I should say Mr. Corey. It isn't swearing! Corey, Corey, Co——"

Her sister clapped her hand over her mouth. "Will you *hush*, you wretched thing?" she whimpered. "The whole house can hear you."

"Oh, yes, they can hear me all over the square. Well, I think he looked well enough for a plain youth, who hadn't taken his hair out of curl-papers for some time."

"It *was* clipped pretty close," Irene admitted; and they both laughed at the drab effect of Mr. Corey's skull, as they remembered it. "Did you like his nose?" asked Irene, timorously.

"Ah, now you're *coming* to something," said Penelope. "I don't know whether, if I had so much of a nose, I should want it all Roman."

"I don't see how you can expect to have a nose part one kind and part another," argued Irene.

"Oh, *I* do. Look at mine!" She turned aside her face, so as to get a three-quarters view of her nose in the glass, and crossing her hands, with the brush in one of them, before her, regarded it judicially. "Now, my nose started Grecian, but changed its mind before it got over the bridge, and concluded to be snub the rest of the way."

"You've got a very pretty nose, Pen," said Irene, joining in the contemplation of its reflex in the glass.

"Don't say that in hopes of getting me to compliment *his*, Mrs."—she stopped, and then added deliberately—"C.!"

Irene also had her hair-brush in her hand, and now she sprang at her sister and beat her very softly on the shoulder with the flat of it. "You mean thing!" she cried, between her shut teeth, blushing hotly.

"Well, *D.*, then," said Penelope. "You've nothing to say against D.? Though I think C. is just as nice an initial."

"Oh!" cried the younger, for all expression of unspeakable things.

"I think he has very good eyes," admitted Penelope.

"Oh, he *has* ! And didn't you like the way his sack-coat set? So close to him, and yet free—kind of peeling away at the lapels?"

"Yes, I should say he was a young man of great judgment. He knows how to choose his tailor."

Irene sat down on the edge of a chair. "It was so nice of you, Pen, to come in, that way, about clubs."

"Oh, I didn't mean anything by it except opposition," said Penelope. "I couldn't have father swelling on so, without saying something."

"How he *did* swell!" sighed Irene. "Wasn't it a relief to have mamma come down, even if she did seem to be all stocking at first?"

The girls broke into a wild giggle and hid their faces in each other's necks. "I thought I *should* die," said Irene.

" 'It's just like ordering a painting,' " said Penelope, recalling her father's talk, with an effect of dreamy absent-mindedness. " 'You give the painter money enough, and he can afford to paint you a first-class picture. Give an architect money enough, and he'll give you a first-class house, every time.' "

"Oh, wasn't it awful!" moaned her sister. "No one would ever have supposed that he had fought the very idea of an architect for weeks, before he gave in."

Penelope went on. " 'I always did like the water side of Beacon —long before I owned property there. When you come to the Back Bay at all, give me the water side of Beacon.' "

"Ow-w-w-w!" shrieked Irene. "*Do* stop!"

The door of their mother's chamber opened below, and the voice of the real Colonel called, "What are you doing up there, girls? Why don't you go to bed?"

This extorted nervous shrieks from both of them. The Colonel heard a sound of scurrying feet, whisking drapery, and slamming doors. Then he heard one of the doors opened again, and Penelope said, "I was only repeating something you said when you talked to Mr. Corey."

"Very well, now," answered the Colonel. "You postpone the rest of it till to-morrow at breakfast, and see that you're up in time to let *me* hear it."

# V

AT THE same moment young Corey let himself in at his own door with his latch-key, and went to the library, where he found his father turning the last leaves of a story in the "Revue des Deux Mondes."[7] He was a white-mustached old gentleman, who had never been able to abandon his *pince-nez* for the superior comfort of spectacles, even in the privacy of his own library. He knocked the glasses off as his son came in, and looked up at him with lazy fondness, rubbing the two red marks that they always leave on the side of the nose.

"Tom," he said, "where did you get such good clothes?"

"I stopped over a day in New York," replied the son, finding himself a chair. "I'm glad you like them."

"Yes, I always do like your clothes, Tom," returned the father thoughtfully, swinging his glasses. "But I don't see how you can afford 'em. *I* can't."

"Well, sir," said the son, who dropped the sir into his speech with his father, now and then, in an old-fashioned way that was rather charming, "you see I have an indulgent parent."

"Smoke?" suggested the father, pushing toward his son a box of cigarettes, from which he had taken one.

---

7. The *Revue des Deux Mondes* was an international periodical published in Paris noted for its sophistication.

"No, thank you," said the son. "I've dropped that."

"Ah, is that so?" The father began to feel about on the table for matches, in the purblind fashion of elderly men. His son rose, lighted one, and handed it to him. "Well,—oh, thank you, Tom! —I believe some statisticians prove that if you will give up smoking you can dress very well on the money your tobacco costs, even if you haven't got an indulgent parent. But I'm too old to try. Though, I confess, I should rather like the clothes. Whom did you find at the club?"

"There were a lot of fellows there," said young Corey, watching the accomplished fumigation of his father in an absent way.

"It's astonishing what a hardy breed the young club-men are," observed his father. "All summer through, in weather that sends the sturdiest female flying to the sea-shore, you find the clubs filled with young men, who don't seem to mind the heat in the least."

"Boston isn't a bad place, at the worst, in summer," said the son, declining to take up the matter in its ironical shape.

"I dare say it isn't, compared with Texas," returned the father, smoking tranquilly on. "But I don't suppose you find many of your friends in town outside of the club."

"No; you're requested to ring at the rear door, all the way down Beacon street and up Commonwealth Avenue. It's rather a blank reception for the returning prodigal."

"Ah, the prodigal must take his chance if he comes back out of season. But I'm glad to have you back, Tom, even as it is, and I hope you're not going to hurry away. You must give your energies a rest."

"I'm sure you never had to reproach me with abnormal activy," suggested the son, taking his father's jokes in good part.

"No, I don't know that I have," admitted the elder. "You've always shown a fair degree of moderation, after all. What do you think of taking up next? I mean after you have embraced your mother and sisters at Mount Desert.[8] Real estate? It seems to me that it is about time for you to open out as a real-estate broker. Or did you ever think of matrimony?"

"Well, not just in that way, sir," said the young man. "I shouldn't quite like to regard it as a career, you know."

8. Bar Harbor is located on Mount Desert Island.

"No, no. I understand that. And I quite agree with you. But you know I've always contended that the affections could be made to combine pleasure and profit. I wouldn't have a man marry for money,—that would be rather bad,—but I don't see why, when it comes to falling in love, a man shouldn't fall in love with a rich girl as easily as a poor one. Some of the rich girls are very nice, and I should say that the chances of a quiet life with them were rather greater. They've always had everything, and they wouldn't be so ambitious and uneasy. Don't you think so?"

"It would depend," said the son, "upon whether a girl's people had been rich long enough to have given her position before she married. If they hadn't, I don't see how she would be any better than a poor girl in that respect."

"Yes, there's sense in that. But the suddenly rich are on a level with any of us nowadays. Money buys position at once. I don't say that it isn't all right. The world generally knows what it's about, and knows how to drive a bargain. I dare say it makes the new rich pay too much. But there's no doubt but money is to the fore now. It is the romance, the poetry of our age. It's the thing that chiefly strikes the imagination. The Englishmen who come here are more curious about the great new millionaires than about any one else, and they respect them more. It's all very well. I don't complain of it."

"And you would like a rich daughter-in-law, quite regardless, then?"

"Oh, not quite so bad as that, Tom," said his father. "A little youth, a little beauty, a little good sense and pretty behavior— one mustn't object to those things; and they go just as often with money as without it. And I suppose I should like her people to be rather grammatical."

"It seems to me that you're exacting, sir," said the son. "How can you expect people who have been strictly devoted to business to be grammatical? Isn't that rather too much?"

"Perhaps it is. Perhaps you're right. But I understood your mother to say that those benefactors of hers, whom you met last summer, were very passably grammatical."

"The father isn't."

The elder, who had been smoking with his profile toward his son, now turned his face full upon him. "I didn't know you had seen him?"

"I hadn't until to-day," said young Corey, with a little heightening of his color. "But I was walking down street this afternoon, and happened to look round at a new house some one was putting up, and I saw the whole family in the window. It appears that Mr. Lapham is building the house."

The elder Corey knocked the ash of his cigarette into the holder at his elbow. "I am more and more convinced, the longer I know you, Tom, that we are descended from Giles Corey? The gift of holding one's tongue seems to have skipped me, but you have it in full force. I can't say just how you would behave under *peine forte et dure,*[1] but under ordinary pressure you are certainly able to keep your own counsel. Why didn't you mention this encounter at dinner? You weren't asked to plead to an accusation of witchcraft."

"No, not exactly," said the young man. "But I didn't quite see my way to speaking of it. We had a good many other things before us."

"Yes, that's true. I suppose you wouldn't have mentioned it now if I hadn't led up to it, would you?"

"I don't know, sir. It was rather on my mind to do so. Perhaps it was I who led up to it."

His father laughed. "Perhaps you did, Tom; perhaps you did. Your mother would have known you were leading up to something, but I'll confess that I didn't. What is it?"

"Nothing very definite. But do you know that in spite of his syntax I rather liked him?"

The father looked keenly at the son; but unless the boy's full confidence was offered, Corey was not the man to ask it. "Well?" was all that he said.

"I suppose that in a new country one gets to looking at people a little out of our tradition; and I dare say that if I hadn't passed a winter in Texas I might have found Colonel Lapham rather too much."

"You mean that there are worse things in Texas?"

"Not that exactly. I mean that I saw it wouldn't be quite fair to test him by our standards."

"This comes of the error which I have often deprecated," said

9. Giles Corey is the fictitious, but representative, founder of this fictitious family of Boston aristocrats.

1. *peine forte et dure:* (*French*), "strong and hard pain," in other words, torture.

the elder Corey. "In fact I am always saying that the Bostonian ought never to leave Boston. Then he knows—and then only— that there can *be* no standard but ours. But we are constantly going away, and coming back with our convictions shaken to their foundations. One man goes to England, and returns with the conception of a grander social life; another comes home from Germany with the notion of a more searching intellectual activity; a fellow just back from Paris has the absurdest ideas of art and literature; and you revert to us from the cowboys of Texas, and tell us to our faces that we ought to try Papa Lapham by a jury of his peers. It ought to be stopped—it ought, really. The Bostonian who leaves Boston ought to be condemned to perpetual exile."

The son suffered the father to reach his climax with smiling patience. When he asked finally, "What are the characteristics of Papa Lapham that place him beyond our jurisdiction?" the younger Corey crossed his long legs, and leaned forward to take one of his knees between his hands.

"Well, sir, he bragged, rather."

"Oh, I don't know that bragging should exempt him from the ordinary processes. I've heard other people brag in Boston."

"Ah, not just in that personal way—not about money."

"No, that was certainly different."

"I don't mean," said the young fellow, with the scrupulosity which people could not help observing and liking in him, "that it was more than an indirect expression of satisfaction in the ability to spend."

"No. I should be glad to express something of the kind myself, if the facts would justify me."

The son smiled tolerantly again. "But if he was enjoying his money in that way, I didn't see why he shouldn't show his pleasure in it. It might have been vulgar, but it wasn't sordid. And I don't know that it was vulgar. Perhaps his successful strokes of business were the romance of his life——"

The father interrupted with a laugh. "The girl must be uncommonly pretty. What did she seem to think of her father's brag?"

"There were two of them," answered the son evasively.

"Oh, two! And is the sister pretty, too?"

"Not pretty, but rather interesting. She is like her mother."

"Then the pretty one isn't the father's pet?"

"I can't say, sir. I don't believe," added the young fellow, "that I can make you see Colonel Lapham just as I did. He struck me as very simple-hearted and rather wholesome. Of course he could be tiresome; we all can; and I suppose his range of ideas is limited. But he is a force, and not a bad one. If he hasn't got over being surprised at the effect of rubbing his lamp——"

"Oh, one could make out a case. I suppose you know what you are about, Tom. But remember that we are Essex County people,[2] and that in savor we are just a little beyond the salt of the earth. I will tell you plainly that I don't like the notion of a man who has rivaled the hues of nature in her wildest haunts with the tints of his mineral paint; but I don't say there are not worse men. He isn't to my taste, though he might be ever so much to my conscience."

"I suppose," said the son, "that there is nothing really to be ashamed of in mineral paint. People go into all sorts of things."

His father took his cigarette from his mouth and once more looked his son full in the face. "Oh, is *that* it?"

"It has crossed my mind," admitted the son. "I must do something. I've wasted time and money enough. I've seen much younger men all through the West and Southwest taking care of themselves. I don't think I was particularly fit for anything out there, but I am ashamed to come back and live upon you, sir."

His father shook his head with an ironical sigh. "Ah, we shall never have a real aristocracy while this plebeian reluctance to live upon a parent or a wife continues the animating spirit of our youth. It strikes at the root of the whole feudal system. I really think you owe me an apology, Tom. I supposed you wished to marry the girl's money, and here you are, basely seeking to go into business with her father."

Young Corey laughed again like a son who perceives that his father is a little antiquated, but keeps a filial faith in his wit. "I don't know that it's quite so bad as that; but the thing had certainly crossed my mind. I don't know how it's to be approached, and I don't know that it's at all possible. But I confess that I 'took to' Colonel Lapham from the moment I saw him. He looked as if he 'meant business,' and I mean business too."

2. Essex County, just north of Boston, centers at Salem and is one of the oldest and most venerable districts of New England.

The father smoked thoughtfully. "Of course people do go into all sorts of things, as you say, and I don't know that one thing is more ignoble than another, if it's decent, and large enough. In my time you would have gone into the China trade or the India trade—though *I* didn't; and a little later cotton would have been your manifest destiny—though it wasn't mine; but now a man may do almost anything. The real-estate business *is* pretty full. Yes, if you have a deep inward vocation for it, I don't see why mineral paint shouldn't do. I fancy it's easy enough approaching the matter. We will invite Papa Lapham to dinner, and talk it over with him."

"Oh, I don't think that would be exactly the way, sir," said the son, smiling at his father's patrician unworldliness.

"No? Why not?"

"I'm afraid it would be a bad start. I don't think it would strike him as business-like."

"I don't see why he should be punctilious, if we're not."

"Ah, we might say that if he were making the advances."

"Well, perhaps you are right, Tom. What is your idea?"

"I haven't a very clear one. It seems to me I ought to get some business friend of ours, whose judgment he would respect, to speak a good word for me."

"Give you a character?"

"Yes. And of course I must go to Colonel Lapham. My notion would be to inquire pretty thoroughly about him, and then, if I liked the look of things, to go right down to Republic street and let him see what he could do with me, if anything."

"That sounds tremendously practical to me, Tom, though it may be just the wrong way. When are you going down to Mount Desert?"

"To-morrow, I think, sir," said the young man. "I shall turn it over in my mind while I'm off."

The father rose, showing something more than his son's height, with a very slight stoop, which the son's figure had not. "Well," he said, whimsically, "I admire your spirit, and I don't deny that it is justified by necessity. It's a consolation to think that while I've been spending and enjoying, I have been preparing the noblest future for you—a future of industry and self-reliance. You never could draw, but this scheme of going into the mineral-paint business shows that you have inherited something of my feeling for color."

The son laughed once more, and waiting till his father was well on his way upstairs, turned out the gas and then hurried after him and preceded him into his chamber. He glanced over it, to see that everything was there, to his father's hand. Then he said, "Good-night, sir," and the elder responded, "Good-night, my son," and the son went to his own room.

Over the mantel in the elder Corey's room hung a portrait which he had painted of his own father, and now he stood a moment and looked at this as if struck by something novel in it. The resemblance between his son and the old India merchant, who had followed the trade from Salem to Boston when the larger city drew it away from the smaller, must have been what struck him. Grandfather and grandson had both the Roman nose which appears to have flourished chiefly at the formative period of the republic, and which occurs more rarely in the descendants of the conscript fathers, though it still characterizes the profiles of a good many Boston ladies. Bromfield Corey had not inherited it, and he had made his straight nose his defense when the old merchant accused him of a want of energy. He said, "What could a man do whose unnatural father had left his own nose away from him?" This amused but did not satisfy the merchant. "You must do something," he said; "and it's for you to choose. If you don't like the India trade, go into something else. Or, take up law or medicine. No Corey yet ever proposed to do nothing." "Ah, then, it's quite time one of us made a beginning," urged the man who was then young, and who was now old, looking into the somewhat fierce eyes of his father's portrait. He had inherited as little of the fierceness as of the nose, and there was nothing predatory in his son either, though the aquiline beak had come down to him in such force. Bromfield Corey liked his son Tom for the gentleness which tempered his energy.

"Well, let us compromise," he seemed to be saying to his father's portrait. "I will travel." "Travel? How long?" the keen eyes demanded. "Oh, indefinitely. I wont be hard with you, father." He could see the eyes soften, and the smile of yielding come over his father's face; the merchant could not resist a son who was so much like his dead mother. There was some vague understanding between them that Bromfield Corey was to come back and go into business after a time, but he never did so. He traveled about over Europe, and traveled handsomely, frequenting good society everywhere, and getting himself presented at several courts, at a period when it was a distinction to do so. He had always sketched, and with his father's leave he fixed himself at Rome, where he remained studying art and rounding the being inherited from his Yankee progenitors, till there was very little left of the ancestral angularities. After ten years he came home and painted that portrait of his father. It was very good, if a little amateurish, and he might have made himself a name as a painter of portraits if he had not had so much money. But he had plenty of money, though by this time he was married and beginning to have a family. It was absurd for him to paint portraits for pay, and ridiculous to paint them for nothing; so he did not paint them at all. He continued a dilettante, never quite abandoning his art, but working at it fitfully, and talking more about it than working at it. He had his theory of Titian's method; and now and then a Bostonian insisted upon buying a picture of him. After a while he hung it more and more inconspicuously, and said apologetically, "Oh, yes! that's one of Bromfield Corey's things. It has nice qualities, but it's amateurish." [3]

In process of time the money seemed less abundant. There were shrinkages of one kind and another, and living had grown much more expensive and luxurious. For many years he talked about going back to Rome, but he never went, and his children grew up in the usual way. Before he knew it his son had him out to his class-day spread at Harvard, and then he had his son on his hands. The son made various unsuccessful provisions for himself, and still continued upon his father's hands, to their common dissatisfaction, though it was chiefly the younger who repined. He had the Roman nose and the energy without the opportunity, and at one of the reversions his father said to him, "You ought not to have that nose, Tom; then you would do very well. You would go and travel, as I did."

Lapham and his wife continued talking after he had quelled the disturbance in his daughters' room overhead; and their talk was not altogether of the new house.

"I tell you," he said, "if I had that fellow in the business with me I would make a man of him."

"Well, Silas Lapham," returned his wife, "I do believe you've got mineral paint on the brain. Do you suppose a fellow like

---

3. The Venetian painter Tiziano Vecellio (1490–1576), usually called Titian, is especially admired for his mastery of color.

young Corey, brought up the way he's been, would touch mineral paint with a ten-foot pole?"

"Why not?" haughtily asked the Colonel.

"Well, if you don't know already, there's no use trying to tell you."

# VI

THE COREYS had always had a house at Nahant,[4] but after letting it for a season or two they found they could get on without it, and sold it at the son's instance, who foresaw that if things went on as they were going, the family would be straitened to the point of changing their mode of life altogether. They began to be of the people of whom it was said that they staid in town very late; and when the ladies did go away, it was for a brief summering in this place and that. The father remained at home altogether; and the son joined them in the intervals of his enterprises, which occurred only too often.

At Bar Harbor, where he now went to find them, after his winter in Texas, he confessed to his mother that there seemed no very good opening there for him. He might do as well as Loring Stanton, but he doubted if Stanton was doing very well. Then he mentioned the new project which he had been thinking over. She did not deny that there was something in it, but she could not think of any young man who had gone into such a business as that, and it appeared to her that he might as well go into a patent medicine or a stove-polish.

"There was one of his hideous advertisements," she said, "painted on a reef that we saw as we came down."

Corey smiled. "Well, I suppose, if it was in a good state of preservation, that is proof positive of the efficacy of the paint on the hulls of vessels."

"It's very distasteful to me, Tom," said his mother; and if there was something else in her mind, she did not speak more plainly of it than to add: "It's not only the kind of business, but the kind of people you would be mixed up with."

"I thought you didn't find them so very bad," suggested Corey.

"I hadn't seen them in Nankeen Square then."

4. Nahant is a resort town on a peninsula extending into Massachusetts Bay northeast of Boston.

"You can see them on the water side of Beacon street when you go back."

Then he told of his encounter with the Lapham family in their new house. At the end his mother merely said, "It is getting very common down there," and she did not try to oppose anything further to his scheme.

The young man went to see Colonel Lapham shortly after his return to Boston. He paid his visit at Lapham's office, and if he had studied simplicity in his summer dress he could not have presented himself in a figure more to the mind of a practical man. His hands and neck still kept the brown of the Texan suns and winds, and he looked as business-like as Lapham himself.

He spoke up promptly and briskly in the outer office, and caused the pretty girl to look away from her copying at him. "Is Mr. Lapham in?" he asked; and after that moment for reflection which an array of book-keepers so addressed likes to give the inquirer, a head was lifted from a ledger and nodded toward the inner office.

Lapham had recognized the voice, and he was standing, in considerable perplexity of mind, to receive Corey, when the young man opened his painted glass door. It was a hot afternoon, and Lapham was in his shirt-sleeves. Scarcely a trace of the boastful hospitality with which he had welcomed Corey to his house a few days before lingered in his present address. He looked at the young man's face, as if he expected him to dispatch whatever unimaginable affair he had come upon.

"Wont you sit down? How are you? You'll excuse me," he added, in brief allusion to the shirt-sleeves. "I'm about roasted."

Corey laughed. "I wish you'd let me take off *my* coat."

"Why, *take* it off!" cried the Colonel, with instant pleasure. There is something in human nature which causes the man in his shirt-sleeves to wish all other men to appear in the same dishabille.

"I will, if you ask me after I've talked with you two minutes," said the young fellow, companionably pulling up the chair offered him toward the desk where Lapham had again seated himself. "But perhaps you haven't got two minutes to give me?"

"Oh, yes, I have," said the Colonel. "I was just going to knock off. I can give you twenty, and then I shall have fifteen minutes to catch the boat."

"All right," said Corey. "I want you to take me into the mineral paint business."

The Colonel sat dumb. He twisted his thick neck, and looked round at the door to see if it was shut. He would not have liked to have any of those fellows outside hear him, but there is no saying what sum of money he would not have given if his wife had been there to hear what Corey had just said.

"I suppose," continued the young man, "I could have got several people whose names you know to back my industry and sobriety, and say a word for my business capacity. But I thought I wouldn't trouble anybody for certificates till I found whether there was a chance, or the ghost of one, of your wanting me. So I came straight to you."

Lapham gathered himself together as well as he could. He had not yet forgiven Corey for Mrs. Lapham's insinuation that he would feel himself too good for the mineral paint business; and though he was dispersed by that astounding shot at first, he was not going to let any one even hypothetically despise his paint with impunity. "How do you think I am going to take you on?" They took on hands at the works; and Lapham put it as if Corey were a hand coming to him for employment. Whether he satisfied himself by this or not, he reddened a little after he had said it.

Corey answered, ignorant of the offense: "I haven't a very clear idea, I'm afraid; but I've been looking a little into the matter from the outside——"

"I hope you haint been paying any attention to that fellow's stuff in the 'Events'?" Lapham interrupted. Since Bartley's interview had appeared, Lapham had regarded it with very mixed feelings. At first it gave him a glow of secret pleasure, blended with doubt as to how his wife would like the use Bartley had made of her in it. But she had not seemed to notice it much, and Lapham had experienced the gratitude of the man who escapes. Then his girls had begun to make fun of it; and though he did not mind Penelope's jokes much, he did not like to see that Irene's gentility was wounded. Business friends met him with the kind of knowing smile about it that implied their sense of the fraudulent character of its praise—the smile of men who had been there and who knew how it was themselves. Lapham had his misgivings as to how his clerks and underlings looked at it; he treated them with stately severity for a while after it came out, and he ended by feeling rather sore about it. He took it for granted that everybody had read it.

"I don't know what you mean," replied Corey. "I don't see the 'Events' regularly."

"Oh, it was nothing. They sent a fellow down here to interview me, and he got everything about as twisted as he could."

"I believe they always do," said Corey. "I hadn't seen it. Perhaps it came out before I got home."

"Perhaps it did."

"My notion of making myself useful to you was based on a hint I got from one of your own circulars."

Lapham was proud of those circulars; he thought they read very well. "What was that?"

"I could put a little capital into the business," said Corey, with the tentative accent of a man who chances a thing. "I've got a little money, but I didn't imagine you cared for anything of that kind."

"No, sir, I don't," returned the Colonel bluntly. "I've had one partner, and one's enough."

"Yes," assented the young man, who doubtless had his own ideas as to eventualities—or perhaps rather had the vague hopes of youth. "I didn't come to propose a partnership. But I see that you are introducing your paint into the foreign markets, and there I really thought I might be of use to you, and to myself, too."

"How?" asked the Colonel scantly.

"Well, I know two or three languages pretty well. I know French, and I know German, and I've got a pretty fair sprinkling of Spanish."

"You mean that you can talk them?" asked the Colonel, with the mingled awe and slight that such a man feels for such accomplishments.

"Yes; and I can write an intelligible letter in either of them."

Lapham rubbed his nose. "It's easy enough to get all the letters we want translated."

"Well," pursued Corey, not showing his discouragement if he felt any, "I know the countries where you want to introduce this paint of yours. I've been there. I've been in Germany and France, and I've been in South America and Mexico; I've been in Italy, of course. I believe I could go to any of those countries and place it to advantage."

Lapham had listened with a trace of persuasion in his face, but now he shook his head.

"It's placing itself as fast as there's any call for it. It wouldn't pay us to send anybody out to look after it. Your salary and expenses would eat up about all we should make on it."

"Yes," returned the young man intrepidly, "if you had to pay me any salary and expenses."

"You don't propose to work for nothing?"

"I propose to work for a commission." The Colonel was beginning to shake his head again, but Corey hurried on. "I haven't come to you without making some inquiries about the paint, and I know how it stands with those who know best. I believe in it."

Lapham lifted his head and looked at the young man, deeply moved.

"It's the best paint in God's universe," he said, with the solemnity of prayer.

"It's the best in the market," said Corey; and he repeated, "I believe in it."

"You believe in it," began the Colonel, and then he stopped. If there had really been any purchasing power in money, a year's income would have bought Mrs. Lapham's instant presence. He warmed and softened to the young man in every way, not only because he must do so to any one who believed in his paint, but because he had done this innocent person the wrong of listening to a defamation of his instinct and good sense, and had been willing to see him suffer for a purely supposititious offense.

Corey rose.

"You mustn't let me outstay my twenty minutes," he said, taking out his watch. "I don't expect you to give a decided answer on the spot. All that I ask is that you'll consider my proposition."

"Don't hurry," said Lapham. "Sit still! I want to tell you about this paint," he added, in a voice husky with the feeling that his hearer could not divine. "I want to tell you *all* about it."

"I could walk with you to the boat," suggested the young man.

"Never mind the boat! I can take the next one. Look here!" The Colonel pulled open a drawer, as Corey sat down again, and took out a photograph of the locality of the mine. "Here's where we get it. This photograph don't half do the place justice," he said, as if the imperfect art had slighted the features of a beloved face. "It's one of the sightliest places in the country, and here's the very spot"—he covered it with his huge forefinger—"where my father found that paint, more than forty—years—ago. Yes, sir!"

He went on, and told the story in unsparing detail, while his chance for the boat passed unheeded, and the clerks in the outer office hung up their linen office coats and put on their seersucker or flannel street coats. The young lady went, too, and nobody was left but the porter, who made from time to time a noisy demonstration of fastening a distant blind, or putting something in place. At last the Colonel roused himself from the autobiographical delight of the history of his paint. "Well, sir, that's the story."

"It's an interesting story," said Corey, with a long breath, as they rose together, and Lapham put on his coat.

"That's what it is," said the Colonel. "Well!" he added, "I don't see but what we've got to have another talk about this thing. It's a surprise to me, and I don't see exactly how you're going to make it pay."

"I'm willing to take the chances," answered Corey. "As I said, I believe in it. I should try South America first. I should try Chili."

"Look here!" said Lapham, with his watch in his hand. "I like to get things over. We've just got time for the six o'clock boat. Why don't you come down with me to Nantasket? I can give you a bed as well as not. And then we can finish up."

The impatience of youth in Corey responded to the impatience of temperament in his elder.

"Why, I don't see why I shouldn't," he allowed himself to say. "I confess I should like to have it finished up myself, if it could be finished up in the right way."

"Well, we'll see. Dennis!" Lapham called to the remote porter, and the man came. "Want to send any word home?" he asked Corey.

"No; my father and I go and come as we like, without keeping account of each other. If I don't come home, he knows that I'm not there. That's all."

"Well, that's convenient. You'll find you can't do that when you're married. Never mind, Dennis," said the Colonel.

He had time to buy two newspapers on the wharf before he jumped on board the steam-boat with Corey. "Just made it," he said; "and that's what I like to do. I can't stand it to be aboard much more than a minute before she shoves out." He gave one of the newspapers to Corey as he spoke, and set him the example of catching up a camp-stool on their way to that point on the boat which his experience had taught him was the best. He opened his paper at once and began to run over its news, while the young man watched the spectacular recession of the city, and was vaguely conscious of the people about him, and of the gay life of the water round the boat. The air freshened; the craft thinned in number; they met larger sail, lagging slowly inward in the afternoon light; the islands of the bay waxed and waned as the steamer approached and left them behind.

"I hate to see them stirring up those Southern fellows again," said the Colonel, speaking into the paper on his lap. "Seems to me it's time to let those old issues go."

"Yes," said the young man. "What are they doing now?"

"Oh, stirring up the Confederate brigadiers in Congress.[5] I don't like it. Seems to me, if our party haint got any other stock-in-trade, we better shut up shop altogether." Lapham went on, as he scanned his newspaper, to give his ideas of public questions, in a fragmentary way, while Corey listened patiently, and waited for him to come back to business. He folded up his paper at last, and stuffed it into his coat pocket. "There's one thing I always make it a rule to do," he said, "and that is to give my mind a complete rest from business while I'm going down on the boat. I like to get the fresh air all through me, soul and body. I believe a man can give his mind a rest, just the same as he can give his legs a rest, or his back. All he's got to do is to use his will-power. Why, I suppose, if I hadn't adopted some such rule, with the strain I've had on me for the last ten years, I should 'a' been a dead man long ago. That's the reason I like a horse. You've got to give your mind to the horse; you can't help it, unless you want to break your neck; but a boat's different, and there you got to use your will-power. You got to take your mind right up and put it where you want it. I make it a rule to read the paper on the boat— Hold on!" he interrupted himself to prevent Corey

5. "Confederate brigadeers in Congress" refers to Democratic congressmen, usually southerners and often former officers in the army of the Confederacy. For several decades after the Civil War, the Grand Old Party (Republican) found it useful to "wave the bloody shirt," that is, to raise the issue of treason, whenever the predominantly southern Democratic party seemed to be gaining strength.

from paying his fare to the man who had come round for it. "I've got tickets. And when I get through the paper, I try to get somebody to talk to, or I watch the people. It's an astonishing thing to me where they all come from. I've been riding up and down on these boats for six or seven years, and I don't know but very few of the faces I see on board. Seems to be a perfectly fresh lot every time. Well, of course! Town's full of strangers in the summer season, anyway, and folks keep coming down from the country. They think it's a great thing to get down to the beach, and they've all heard of the electric light on the water, and they want to see it. But you take faces now! The astonishing thing to me is not what a face tells, but what it don't tell. When you think of what a man is, or a woman is, and what most of 'em have been through before they get to be thirty, it seems as if their experience would burn right through. But it don't. I like to watch the couples, and try to make out which are engaged, or going to be, and which are married, or better be. But half the time I can't make any sort of guess. Of course, where they're young and kittenish, you can tell; but where they're anyways on, you can't. Heigh?"

"Yes, I think you're right," said Corey, not perfectly reconciled to philosophy in the place of business, but accepting it as he must.

"Well," said the Colonel, "I don't suppose it was meant we should know what was in each other's minds. It would take a man out of his own hands. As long as he's in his own hands, there's some hopes of his doing something with himself; but if a fellow has been found out—even if he hasn't been found out to be so very bad—it's pretty much all up with him. No, sir. I don't want to know people through and through."

The greater part of the crowd on board—and, of course, the boat was crowded—looked as if they might not only be easily but safely known. There was little style and no distinction among them; they were people who were going down to the beach for the fun or the relief of it, and were able to afford it. In face they were commonplace, with nothing but the American poetry of vivid purpose to light them up, where they did not wholly lack fire. But they were nearly all shrewd and friendly-looking, with an apparent readiness for the humorous intimacy native to us all. The women were dandified in dress, according to their means and taste, and the men differed from each other in degrees of indifference to it. To a straw-hatted population, such as ours is in summer, no sort of personal dignity is possible. We have not even the power over observers which comes from the fantasticality of an Englishman when he discards the conventional dress. In our straw hats and our serge or flannel sacks we are no more imposing than a crowd of boys.

"Some day," said Lapham, rising as the boat drew near the wharf of the final landing, "there's going to be an awful accident on these boats. Just look at that jam."

He meant the people thickly packed on the pier, and under strong restraint of locks and gates, to prevent them from rushing on board the boat and possessing her for the return trip before she had landed her Nantasket passengers.

"Overload 'em every time," he continued, with a sort of dry, impersonal concern at the impending calamity, as if it could not possibly include him. "They take about twice as many as they ought to carry, and about ten times as many as they could save if anything happened. Yes, sir, it's bound to come. Hello! There's my girl!" He took out his folded newspaper and waved it toward a group of phaetons and barouches drawn up on the pier a little apart from the pack of people, and a lady in one of them answered with a flourish of her parasol.[6]

When he had made his way with his guest through the crowd, she began to speak to her father before she noticed Corey. "Well, Colonel, you've improved your last chance. We've been coming to every boat since four o'clock,—or Jerry has,—and I told mother that I would come myself once, and see if *I* couldn't fetch you; and if I failed, you could walk next time. You're getting perfectly spoiled."

The Colonel enjoyed letting her scold him to the end before he said, with a twinkle of pride in his guest and satisfaction in her probably being able to hold her own against any discomfiture, "I've brought Mr. Corey down for the night with me, and I was showing him things all the way, and it took time."

The young fellow was at the side of the open beach-wagon, making a quick, gentlemanly bow, and Penelope Lapham was cozily drawling, "Oh, how do you do, Mr. Corey?" before the Colonel had finished his explanation.

6. Phaetons and barouches were two- and four-seat, horse-drawn carriages.

"Get right in there, alongside of Miss Lapham, Mr. Corey," he said, pulling himself up into the place beside the driver. "No, no," he had added quickly, at some signs of polite protest in the young man, "I don't give up the best place to anybody. Jerry, suppose you let me have hold of the leathers a minute."

This was his way of taking the reins from the driver; and in half the time he specified, he had skillfully turned the vehicle on the pier, among the crooked lines and groups of foot-passengers, and was spinning up the road toward the stretch of verandaed hotels and restaurants in the sand along the shore. "Pretty gay down here," he said, indicating all this with a turn of his whip, as he left it behind him. "But I've got about sick of hotels; and this summer I made up my mind that I'd take a cottage. Well, Pen, how are the folks?" He looked half-way round for her answer, and with the eye thus brought to bear upon her he was able to give her a wink of supreme content. The Colonel, with no sort of ulterior design, and nothing but his triumph over Mrs. Lapham definitely in his mind, was feeling, as he would have said, about right.

The girl smiled a daughter's amusement at her father's boyishness. "I don't think there's much change since morning. Did Irene have a headache when you left?"

"No," said the Colonel.

"Well, then, there's that to report."

"Pshaw!" said the Colonel, with vexation in his tone.

"I'm sorry Miss Irene isn't well," said Corey politely.

"I think she must have got it from walking too long on the beach. The air is so cool here that you forget how hot the sun is."

"Yes, that's true," assented Corey.

"A good night's rest will make it all right," suggested the Colonel, without looking round. "But you girls have got to look out."

"If you're fond of walking," said Corey, "I suppose you find the beach a temptation."

"Oh, it isn't so much that," returned the girl. "You keep walking on and on because it's so smooth and straight before you. We've been here so often that we know it all by heart—just how it looks at high tide, and how it looks at low tide, and how it looks after a storm. We're as well acquainted with the crabs and stranded jelly-fish as we are with the children digging in the sand

and the people sitting under umbrellas. I think they're always the same, all of them."

The Colonel left the talk to the young people. When he spoke next it was to say, "Well, here we are!" and he turned from the highway and drove up in front of a brown cottage with a vermilion roof, and a group of geraniums clutching the rock that cropped up in the loop formed by the road. It was treeless and bare all round, and the ocean, unnecessarily vast, weltered away a little more than a stone's cast from the cottage. A hospitable smell of supper filled the air, and Mrs. Lapham was on the veranda, with that demand in her eyes for her belated husband's excuses, which she was obliged to check on her tongue at sight of Corey.

## VII

THE exultant Colonel swung himself lightly down from his seat. "I've brought Mr. Corey with me," he nonchalantly explained.

Mrs. Lapham made their guest welcome, and the Colonel showed him to his room, briefly assuring himself that there was nothing wanting there. Then he went to wash his own hands, carelessly ignoring the eagerness with which his wife pursued him to their chamber.

"What gave Irene a headache?" he asked, making himself a fine lather for his hairy paws.

"Never you mind Irene," promptly retorted his wife. "How came he to come? Did you press him? If you *did*, I'll never forgive you, Silas!"

The Colonel laughed, and his wife shook him by the shoulder to make him laugh lower. "'Sh!" she whispered. "Do you want him to hear *every* thing? *Did* you urge him?"

The Colonel laughed the more. He was going to get all the good out of this. "No, I didn't urge him. Seemed to want to come."

"I don't believe it. Where did you meet him?"

"At the office."

"What office?"

"Mine."

"Nonsense! What was he doing there?"

"Oh, nothing much."

"What did he come for?"

"Come for? Oh! He *said* he wanted to go into the mineral paint business."

Mrs. Lapham dropped into a chair, and watched his bulk shaken with smothered laughter. "Silas Lapham," she gasped, "if you try to get off any more of those things on me——"

The Colonel applied himself to the towel. "Had a notion he could work it in South America. *I* don't know what he's up to."

"Never mind!" cried his wife. "I'll get even with you *yet*."

"So I told him he had better come down and talk it over," continued the Colonel, in well-affected simplicity. "I knew he wouldn't touch it with a ten-foot pole."

"Go on!" threatened Mrs. Lapham.

"Right thing to do, wa'n't it?"

A tap was heard at the door, and Mrs. Lapham answered it. A maid announced supper. "Very well," she said, "come to tea now. But I'll make you pay for this, Silas."

Penelope had gone to her sister's room as soon as she entered the house.

"Is your head any better, 'Rene?" she asked.

"Yes, a little," came a voice from the pillows. "But I shall not come to tea. I don't want anything. If I keep still, I shall be all right by morning."

"Well, I'm sorry," said the elder sister. "He's come down with father."

"He hasn't! Who?" cried Irene, starting up in simultaneous denial and demand.

"Oh, well, if you say he hasn't, what's the use of my telling you who?"

"Oh, how can you treat me so!" moaned the sufferer. "What do you mean, Pen?"

"I guess I'd better not tell you," said Penelope, watching her like a cat playing with a mouse. "If you're not coming to tea, it would just excite you for nothing."

The mouse moaned and writhed upon the bed.

"Oh, I wouldn't treat *you* so!"

The cat seated herself across the room and asked quietly:

"Well, what could you do if it *was* Mr. Corey? You couldn't come to tea, you say. But *he*'ll excuse you. *I*'ve told him you had a headache. Why, of course you can't come! It would be too

barefaced. But you needn't be troubled, Irene; I'll do my best
to make the time pass pleasantly for him." Here the cat gave a
low titter, and the mouse girded itself up with a momentary
courage and self-respect.

"I should think you would be ashamed to come here and tease
me so."

"I don't see why you shouldn't believe me," argued Penelope.
"Why shouldn't he come down with father, if father asked him?
and he'd be sure to if he thought of it. I don't see any p'ints about
that frog that's any better than any other frog."

The sense of her sister's helplessness was too much for the tease;
she broke down in a fit of smothered laughter, which convinced
her victim that it was nothing but an ill-timed joke.

"Well, Pen, I wouldn't use you so," she whimpered.

Penelope threw herself on the bed beside her.

"Oh, poor Irene! He *is* here. It's a solemn fact." And she
caressed and soothed her sister, while she choked with laughter.
"You must get up and come out. I don't know what brought him
here, but here he *is*."

"It's too late now," said Irene, desolately. Then she added,
with a wilder despair: "What a fool I was to take that walk!"

"Well," coaxed her sister, "come out and get some tea. The
tea will do you good."

"No, no; I can't come. But send me a cup here."

"Yes, and then perhaps you can see him later in the evening."

"I shall not see him at all."

An hour after Penelope came back to her sister's room and
found her before her glass. "You might as well have kept still,
and been well by morning, 'Rene," she said. "As soon as we were
done father said, 'Well, Mr. Corey and I have got to talk over a
a little matter of business, and we'll excuse you, ladies.' He looked
at mother in a way that I guess was pretty hard to bear. 'Rene,
you ought to have heard the Colonel swelling at supper. It would
have made you feel that all he said the other day was nothing."

Mrs. Lapham suddenly opened the door.

"Now, see here, Pen," she said, as she closed it behind her,
"I've had just as much as I can stand from your father, and if
you don't tell me this instant what it all means——"

She left the consequences to imagination, and Penelope replied, with her mock soberness:

"Well, the Colonel does seem to be on his high horse, ma'am. But you mustn't ask me what his business with Mr. Corey is, for I don't know. All that I know is that I met them at the landing, and that they conversed all the way down—on literary topics."

"Nonsense! What do you think it is?"

"Well, if you want my candid opinion, I think this talk about business is nothing but a blind. It seems a pity Irene shouldn't have been up to receive him," she added.

Irene cast a mute look of imploring at her mother, who was too much preoccupied to afford her the protection it asked.

"Your father said he wanted to go into the business with him."

Irene's look changed to a stare of astonishment and mystification, but Penelope preserved her imperturbability.

"Well, it's a lucrative business, I believe."

"Well, I don't believe a word of it!" cried Mrs. Lapham. "And so I told your father."

"Did it seem to convince him?" inquired Penelope.

Her mother did not reply. "I know one thing," she said. "He's got to tell me every word, or there'll be no sleep for him *this* night."

"Well, ma'am," said Penelope, breaking down in one of her queer laughs, "I shouldn't be a bit surprised if you were right."

"Go on and dress, Irene," ordered her mother, "and then you and Pen come out into the parlor. They can have just two hours for business, and then we must all be there to receive him. You haven't got headache enough to hurt you."

"Oh, it's all gone now," said the girl.

At the end of the limit she had given the Colonel, Mrs. Lapham looked into the dining-room, which she found blue with his smoke.

"I think you gentlemen will find the parlor pleasanter now, and we can give it up to you."

"Oh, no, you needn't," said her husband. "We've got about through." Corey was already standing, and Lapham rose too. "I guess we can join the ladies now. We can leave that little point till to-morrow."

Both of the young ladies were in the parlor when Corey entered with their father, and both were frankly indifferent to the few books and the many newspapers scattered about on the table where the large lamp was placed. But after Corey had greeted Irene he glanced at the novel under his eye, and said, in the dearth that sometimes befalls people at such times: "I see you're reading "Middlemarch.' Do you like George Eliot?"[7]

"Who?" asked the girl.

Penelope interposed. "I don't believe Irene's read it yet. I've just got it out of the library; I heard so much talk about it. I wish she would let you find out a little about the people for yourself," she added. But here her father struck in:

"I can't get the time for books. It's as much as I can do to keep up with the newspapers; and when night comes, I'm tired, and I'd rather go out to the theater, or a lecture, if they've got a good stereopticon to give you views of the places[8] But I guess we all like a play better than 'most anything else. I want something that'll make me laugh. I don't believe in tragedy. I think there's enough of that in real life without putting it on the stage. Seen 'Joshua Whitcomb'?"[9]

The whole family joined in the discussion, and it appeared that they all had their opinions of the plays and actors. Mrs. Lapham brought the talk back to literature. "I guess Penelope does most of our reading."

"Now, mother, you're not going to put it all on me!" said the girl, in comic protest.

Her mother laughed, and then added, with a sigh: "I used to like to get hold of a good book when I was a girl; but we weren't allowed to read many novels in those days. My mother called them all *lies*. And I guess she wasn't so very far wrong about some of them."

"They're certainly fictions," said Corey, smiling.

"Well, we do buy a good many books, first and last," said the Colonel, who probably had in mind the costly volumes which they presented to one another on birthdays and holidays. "But I get about all the reading I want in the newspapers. And when the girls want a novel, I tell 'em to get it out of the library. That's what the library's for. Phew!" he panted, blowing away the whole unprofitable subject. "How close you women-folks like to

7. George Eliot's novel *Middlemarch* was first published in England in 1871–72 and would have been immediately available in this country. Earlier mention of *Daisy Miller* (1878) and later of the Park Street Theater (opened in 1879) suggests that the action is taking place in the early 1880s. The point is that unlike the Coreys, who read the *Revue des Deux Mondes*, Penelope, the only "literary Lapham," lags behind in her tastes.

8. A stereopticon was a device using two or three projectors to throw a slide image on a screen.

9. Joshua Whitcomb was the title character in a popular comedy. The American actor Denman Thompson (1833–1911) based the broadly drawn character on rustic New England farmers he had known. Silas' taste for broad comedy is intended to contrast with Tom's more cultivated taste.

keep a room! You go down to the sea-side or up to the mountains for a change of air, and then you cork yourselves into a room so tight you don't have any air at all. Here! You girls get on your bonnets and go and show Mr. Corey the view of the hotels from the rocks."

Corey said that he should be delighted. The girls exchanged looks with each other, and then with their mother. Irene curved her pretty chin in comment upon her father's incorrigibility, and Penelope made a droll mouth, but the Colonel remained serenely content with his finesse. "I got 'em out of the way," he said, as soon as they were gone, and before his wife had time to fall upon him, "because I've got through my talk with him, and now I want to talk with *you*. It's just as I said, Persis; he wants to go into the business with me."

"It's lucky for you," said his wife, meaning that now he would not be made to suffer for attempting to hoax her. But she was too intensely interested to pursue that matter further. "What in the world do you suppose he means by it?"

"Well, I should judge by his talk that he had been trying a good many different things since he left college, and he haint found just the thing he likes—or the thing that likes him. It aint so easy. And now he's got an idea that he can take hold of the paint and push it in other countries—push it in Mexico and push it in South America. He's a splendid Spanish scholar,"—this was Lapham's version of Corey's modest claim to a smattering of the language,—"and he's been among the natives enough to know their ways. And he believes in the paint," added the Colonel.

"I guess he believes in something else besides the paint," said Mrs. Lapham.

"What do you mean?"

"Well, Silas Lapham, if you can't see *now* that he's after Irene, I don't know what ever *can* open your eyes. That's all."

The Colonel pretended to give the idea silent consideration, as if it had not occurred to him before. "Well, then, all I've got to say is, that he's going a good way round. I don't say you're wrong, but if it's Irene, I don't see why he should want to go off to South America to get her. And that's what he proposes to do. I guess there's some paint about it too, Persis. He says he believes in it,"—the Colonel devoutly lowered his voice,—"and he's willing to take the agency on his own account down there, and run it for a commission on what he can sell."

"Of course! He isn't going to take hold of it any way so as to feel beholden to you. He's got too much pride for that."

"He aint going to take hold of it at all, if he don't mean paint in the first place and Irene afterward. I don't object to him, as I know, either way, but the two things wont mix; and I don't propose he shall pull the wool over my eyes—or anybody else. But, as far as heard from, up to date, he means paint first, last, and all the time. At any rate, I'm going to take him on that basis. He's got some pretty good ideas about it, and he's been stirred up by this talk, just now, about getting our manufactures into the foreign markets. There's an overstock in everything, and we've got to get rid of it, or we've got to shut down till the home demand begins again. We've had two or three such flurries before now, and they didn't amount to much. They say we can't extend our commerce under the high tariff system we've got now, because there aint any sort of reciprocity on our side,—we want to have the other fellows show all the reciprocity,—and the English have got the advantage of us every time. I don't know whether it's so or not; but I don't see why it should apply to my paint. Anyway, he wants to try it, and I've about made up my mind to let him. Of course I aint going to let him take all the risk. I believe in the paint *too*, and I shall pay his expenses anyway."

"So you want another partner after all?" Mrs. Lapham could not forbear saying.

"Yes, if that's your idea of a partner. It isn't mine," returned her husband dryly.

"Well, if you've made up your mind, Si, I suppose you're ready for advice," said Mrs. Lapham.

The Colonel enjoyed this. "Yes, I *am*. What have you got to say against it?"

"I don't know as I've got anything. I'm satisfied if you are."

"Well?"

"When is he going to start for South America?"

"I shall take him into the office awhile. He'll get off some time in the winter. But he's got to know the business first."

"Oh, indeed! Are you going to take him to board in the family?"

"What are you after, Persis?"

"Oh, nothing! I presume he will feel free to visit in the family, even if he don't board with us."

"I presume he will."

"And if he don't use his privileges, do you think he'll be a fit person to manage your paint in South America?"

The Colonel reddened consciously. "I'm not taking him on that basis."

"Oh, yes, you are! You may pretend you aint to yourself, but you mustn't pretend so to me. Because I know you."

The Colonel laughed. "Pshaw!" he said.

Mrs. Lapham continued: "I don't see any harm in hoping that he'll take a fancy to her. But if you really think it wont do to mix the two things, I advise you not to take Mr. Corey into the business. It will do all very well if he *does* take a fancy to her; but if he don't, you know how you'll feel about it. And I know you well enough, Silas, to know that you can't do him justice if that happens. And I don't think it's right you should take this step unless you're pretty sure. I can see that you've set your heart on this thing——"

"I haven't set my heart on it at all," protested Lapham.

"And if you can't bring it about, you're going to feel unhappy over it," pursued his wife, regardless of his protest.

"Oh, very well," he said. "If you know more about what's in my mind than I do, there's no use arguing, as I can see."

He got up, to carry off his consciousness, and sauntered out of the door on to his piazza. He could see the young people down on the rocks, and his heart swelled in his breast. He had always said that he did not care what a man's family was, but the presence of young Corey as an applicant to him for employment, as his guest, as the possible suitor of his daughter, was one of the sweetest flavors that he had yet tasted in his success. He knew who the Coreys were very well, and, in his simple, brutal way, he had long hated their name as a symbol of splendor which, unless he should live to see at least three generations of his descendants gilded with mineral paint, he could not hope to realize in his own. He was acquainted in a business way with the tradition of old Phillips Corey, and he had heard a great many things about the Corey who had spent his youth abroad and his father's money everywhere, and done nothing but say smart things. Lapham could not see the smartness of some of them which had been repeated to him. Once he had encountered the fellow, and it seemed to Lapham that the tall, slim, white-mustached man, with the slight stoop, was everything that was offensively aristocratic. He had bristled up aggressively at the name when his wife told how she had made the acquaintance of the fellow's family the summer before, and he had treated the notion of young Corey's caring for Irene with the contempt which such a ridiculous superstition deserved. He had made up his mind about young Corey beforehand; yet when he met him he felt an instant liking for him, which he frankly acknowledged, and he had begun to assume the burden of his wife's superstition, of which she seemed now ready to accuse him of being the inventor.

Nothing had moved his thick imagination like this day's events since the girl who taught him spelling and grammar in the school at Lumberville had said she would have him for her husband.

The dark figures, stationary on the rocks, began to move, and he could see that they were coming toward the house. He went indoors so as not to appear to have been watching them.

# VIII

A WEEK after she had parted with her son at Bar Harbor, Mrs. Corey suddenly walked in upon her husband in their house in Boston. He was at breakfast, and he gave her the patronizing welcome with which the husband who has been staying in town all summer receives his wife when she drops down upon him from the mountains or the sea-side. For a little moment she feels herself strange in the house, and suffers herself to be treated like a guest, before envy of his comfort vexes her back into possession and authority. Mrs. Corey was a lady, and she did not let her envy take the form of open reproach.

"Well, Anna, you find me here in the luxury you left me to. How did you leave the girls?"

"The girls were well," said Mrs. Corey, looking absently at her husband's brown velvet coat, in which he was so handsome. No man had ever grown gray more beautifully. His hair, while not remaining dark enough to form a theatrical contrast with his mustache, was yet some shades darker, and, in becoming a little thinner, it had become a little more gracefully wavy. His skin had the pearly tint which that of elderly men sometimes assumes, and the lines which time had traced upon it were too delicate for the name of wrinkles. He had never had any personal vanity, and there was no consciousness in his good looks now.

"I am glad of that. The boy I have with me," he returned; "that is, when he *is* with me."

"Why, where is he?" demanded the mother.

"Probably carousing with the boon Lapham somewhere. He left me yesterday afternoon to go and offer his allegiance to the Mineral Paint King, and I haven't seen him since."

"Bromfield!" cried Mrs. Corey. "Why didn't you stop him?"

"Well, my dear, I'm not sure that it isn't a very good thing."

"A good thing? It's horrid!"

"No, I don't think so. It's decent. Tom had found out—without consulting the landscape, which I believe proclaims it everywhere——"

"Hideous!"

"That it's really a good thing; and he thinks that he has some ideas in regard to its dissemination in the parts beyond seas."

"Why shouldn't he go into something else?" lamented the mother.

"I believe he has gone into nearly everything else, and come out of it. So there is a chance of his coming out of this. But as I had nothing to suggest in place of it, I thought it best not to interfere. In fact, what good would my telling him that mineral paint was nasty have done? I dare say *you* told him it was nasty."

"Yes! I did."

"And you see with what effect, though he values your opinion three times as much as he values mine. Perhaps you came up to tell him again that it was nasty?"

"I feel very unhappy about it. He is throwing himself away. Yes, I should like to prevent it if I could!"

The father shook his head.

"If Lapham hasn't prevented it, I fancy it's too late. But there may be some hopes of Lapham. As for Tom's throwing himself away, I don't know. There's no question but he is one of the best fellows under the sun. He's tremendously energetic, and he has plenty of the kind of sense which we call horse; but he isn't brilliant. No, Tom is not brilliant. I don't think he would get on in a profession, and he's instinctively kept out of everything of the kind. But he has got to do something. What shall he do? He says mineral paint, and really I don't see why he shouldn't. If money is fairly and honestly earned, why should we pretend to care what it comes out of, when we don't really care? That superstition is exploded everywhere."

"Oh, it isn't the paint alone," said Mrs. Corey; and then she perceptibly arrested herself, and made a diversion in continuing: "I wish he had married some one."

"With money?" suggested her husband. "From time to time I have attempted Tom's corruption from that side, but I suspect Tom has a conscience against it, and I rather like him for it. I married for love myself," said Corey, looking across the table at his wife.

She returned his look tolerantly, though she felt it right to say, "What nonsense!"

"Besides," continued her husband, "if you come to money, there is the paint princess. She will have plenty."

"Ah, that's the worst of it," sighed the mother. "I suppose I could get on with the paint——"

"But not with the princess? I thought you said she was a very pretty, well-behaved girl?"

"She is very pretty, and she is well-behaved; but there is nothing of her. She is insipid; she is very insipid."

"But Tom seemed to like her flavor, such as it was?"

"How can I tell? We were under a terrible obligation to them, and I naturally wished him to be polite to them. In fact, I asked him to be so."

"And he was too polite?"

"I can't say that he was. But there is no doubt that the child is extremely pretty."

"Tom says there are two of them. Perhaps they will neutralize each other."

"Yes, there is another daughter," assented Mrs. Corey. "I don't see how you can joke about such things, Bromfield," she added.

"Well, I don't either, my dear, to tell you the truth. My hardihood surprises me. Here is a son of mine whom I see reduced to making his living by a shrinkage in values. It's very odd," interjected Corey, "that some values should have this peculiarity of shrinking. You never hear of values in a picture shrinking; but rents, stocks, real estate—all those values shrink abominably. Perhaps it might be argued that one should put all his values into pictures; I've got a good many of mine there."

"Tom needn't earn his living," said Mrs. Corey, refusing her husband's jest. "There's still enough for all of us."

"That is what I have sometimes urged upon Tom. I have proved to him that with economy, and strict attention to business, he need do nothing as long as he lives. Of course he would be somewhat restricted, and it would cramp the rest of us; but it is a world of sacrifices and compromises. He couldn't agree with me, and he was not in the least moved by the example of persons of quality in Europe, which I alleged in support of the life of idleness. It appears that he wishes to do something—to do something for himself. I am afraid that Tom is selfish."

Mrs. Corey smiled wanly. Thirty years before, she had married the rich young painter in Rome, who said so much better things than he painted—charming things, just the things to please the fancy of a girl who was disposed to take life a little too seriously and practically. She saw him in a different light when she got him home to Boston; but he had kept on saying the charming things, and he had not done much else. In fact, he had fulfilled the promise of his youth. It was a good trait in him that he was not actively but only passively extravagant. He was not adventurous with his money; his tastes were as simple as an Italian's; he had no expensive habits. In the process of time he had grown to lead a more and more secluded life. It was hard to get him out anywhere, even to dinner. His patience with their narrowing circumstances had a pathos which she felt the more the more she came into charge of their joint life. At times it seemed too bad that the children and their education and pleasures should cost so much. She knew, besides, that if it had not been for them she would have gone back to Rome with him, and lived princely there for less than it took to live respectably in Boston.

"Tom hasn't consulted me," continued his father, "but he has consulted other people. And he has arrived at the conclusion that mineral paint is a good thing to go into. He has found out all about it, and about its founder or inventor. It's quite impressive to hear him talk. And if he must do something for himself, I don't see why his egotism shouldn't as well take that form as another. Combined with the paint princess, it isn't so agreeable; but that's only a remote possibility, for which your principal ground is your motherly solicitude. But even if it were probable and imminent, what could you do? The chief consolation that we American parents have in these matters is that we can do nothing. If we were Europeans, even English, we should take some cognizance of our children's love affairs, and in some measure teach their young affections how to shoot. But it is our custom to ignore them until they have shot, and then they ignore us. We are altogether too delicate to arrange the marriages of our children; and when they have arranged them we don't like to say anything, for fear we should only make bad worse. The right way is for us to school ourselves to indifference. That is what the young people have to do elsewhere, and that is the only logical result of our position here. It is absurd for us to have any feeling about what we don't interfere with."

"Oh, people do interfere with their children's marriages very often," said Mrs. Corey.

"Yes, but only in a half-hearted way, so as not to make it disagreeable for themselves if the marriages go on in spite of them, as they're pretty apt to do. Now, my idea is that I ought to cut Tom off with a shilling. That would be very simple, and it would be economical. But you would never consent, and Tom wouldn't mind it."

"I think our whole conduct in regard to such things is wrong," said Mrs. Corey.

"Oh, very likely. But our whole civilization is based upon it. And who is going to make a beginning? To which father in our acquaintance shall I go and propose an alliance for Tom with his daughter? I should feel like an ass. And will you go to some mother, and ask her sons in marriage for our daughters? You would feel like a goose. No; the only motto for us is, Hands off altogether."

"I shall certainly speak to Tom when the time comes," said Mrs. Corey.

"And I shall ask leave to be absent from your discomfiture, my dear," answered her husband.

The son returned that afternoon, and confessed his surprise at finding his mother in Boston. He was so frank that she had not quite the courage to confess in turn why she had come, but trumped up an excuse.

"Well, mother," he said promptly, "I have made an engagement with Mr. Lapham."

"Have you, Tom?" she asked faintly.

"Yes. For the present I am going to have charge of his foreign correspondence, and if I see my way to the advantage I expect to find in it, I am going out to manage that side of his business in South America and Mexico. He's behaved very handsomely about it. He says that if it appears for our common interest, he shall pay me a salary as well as a commission. I've talked with Uncle Jim, and he thinks it's a good opening."

"Your Uncle Jim does?" queried Mrs. Corey in amaze.

"Yes; I consulted him the whole way through, and I've acted on his advice."

This seemed an incomprehensible treachery on her brother's part.

"Yes; I thought you would like to have me. And besides, I couldn't possibly have gone to any one so well fitted to advise me."

His mother said nothing. In fact, the mineral paint business, however painful its interest, was, for the moment, superseded by a more poignant anxiety. She began to feel her way cautiously toward this.

"Have you been talking about your business with Mr. Lapham all night?"

"Well, pretty much," said her son, with a guiltless laugh. "I went to see him yesterday afternoon, after I had gone over the whole ground with Uncle Jim, and Mr. Lapham asked me to go down with him and finish up."

"Down?" repeated Mrs. Corey.

"Yes, to Nantasket. He has a cottage down there."

"At Nantasket?" Mrs. Corey knitted her brows a little. "What in the world can a cottage at Nantasket be like?"

"Oh, very much like a 'cottage' anywhere. It has the usual allowance of red roof and veranda. There are the regulation rocks by the sea; and the big hotels on the beach about a mile off, flaring away with electric lights and roman-candles at night. We didn't have them at Nahant."

"No," said his mother. "Is Mrs. Lapham well? And her daughter?"

"Yes, I think so," said the young man. "The young ladies walked me down to the rocks in the usual way after dinner, and then I came back and talked paint with Mr. Lapham till midnight. We didn't settle anything till this morning coming up on the boat."

"What sort of people do they seem to be at home?"

"What sort? Well, I don't know that I noticed." Mrs. Corey permitted herself the first part of a sigh of relief; and her son laughed, but apparently not at her. "They're just reading 'Middlemarch.' They say there's so much talk about it. Oh, I suppose they're very good people. They seemed to be on very good terms with each other."

"I suppose it's the plain sister who's reading 'Middlemarch.' "

"Plain? Is she plain?" asked the young man, as if searching his consciousness. "Yes, it's the older one who does the reading, apparently. But I don't believe that even she overdoes it. They like to talk better. They reminded me of Southern people in that." The young man smiled, as if amused by some of his impressions of the Lapham family. "The living, as the country people call it, is tremendously good. The Colonel—he's a colonel—talked of the coffee as his wife's coffee, as if she had personally made it in the kitchen, though I believe it was merely inspired by her. And there was everything in the house that money could buy. But money has its limitations."

This was a fact which Mrs. Corey was beginning to realize more and more unpleasantly in her own life; but it seemed to bring her a certain comfort in its application to the Laphams. "Yes, there is a point where taste has to begin," she said.

"They seemed to want to apologize to me for not having more books," said Corey. "I don't know why they should. The Colonel said they bought a good many books, first and last; but apparently they don't take them to the sea-side."

"I dare say they *never* buy a *new* book. I've met some of these moneyed people lately, and they lavish on every conceivable luxury, and then borrow books, and get them in the cheap paper editions."

"I fancy that's the way with the Lapham family," said the young man, smilingly. "But they are very good people. The other daughter is humorous."

"Humorous?" Mrs. Corey knitted her brows in some perplexity. "Do you mean like Mrs. Sayre?" she asked, naming the lady whose name must come into every Boston mind when humor is mentioned.

"Oh, no; nothing like that. She never says anything that you can remember; nothing in flashes or ripples; nothing the least literary. But it's a sort of droll way of looking at things; or a droll medium through which things present themselves. I don't know. She tells what she's seen, and mimics a little."

"Oh," said Mrs. Corey, coldly. After a moment she asked: "And is Miss Irene as pretty as ever?"

"She's a wonderful complexion," said the son, unsatisfactorily. "I shall want to be by when father and Colonel Lapham meet," he added, with a smile.

"Ah, yes, your father!" said the mother, in that way in which a wife at once compassionates and censures her husband to their children.

"Do you think it's really going to be a trial to him?" asked the young man, quickly.

"No, no, I can't say it is. But I confess I wish it was some other business, Tom."

"Well, mother, I don't see why. The principal thing looked at now is the amount of money; and while I would rather starve than touch a dollar that was dirty with any sort of dishonesty ____"

"Of course you would, my son!" interposed his mother, proudly.

"I shouldn't at all mind its having a little mineral paint on it. I'll use my influence with Colonel Lapham—if I ever have any— to have his paint scraped off the landscape."

"I suppose you wont begin till the autumn."

"Oh, yes, I shall," said the son, laughing at his mother's simple ignorance of business. "I shall begin to-morrow morning."

"To-morrow morning!"

"Yes. I've had my desk appointed already, and I shall be down there at nine in the morning to take possession."

"Tom!" cried his mother, "why do you think Mr. Lapham has taken you into business so readily? I've always heard that it was so hard for young men to get in."

"And do you think I found it easy with him? We had about twelve hours' solid talk."

"And you don't suppose it was any sort of—personal consideration?"

"Why, I don't know exactly what you mean, mother. I suppose he likes me."

Mrs. Corey could not say just what she meant. She answered, ineffectually enough:

"Yes. You wouldn't like it to be a favor, would you?"

"I think he's a man who may be trusted to look after his own interest. But I don't mind his beginning by liking me. It'll be my own fault if I don't make myself essential to him."

"Yes," said Mrs. Corey.

"Well," demanded her husband, at their first meeting after her interview with their son, "what did you say to Tom?"

"Very little, if anything. I found him with his mind made up, and it would only have distressed him if I had tried to change it."

"That is precisely what I said, my dear."

"Besides, he had talked the matter over fully with James, and seems to have been advised by him. I can't understand James."

"Oh! it's in regard to the paint, and not the princess, that he's made up his mind. Well, I think you were wise to let him alone, Anna. We represent a faded tradition. We don't really care what business a man is in, so it is large enough, and he doesn't advertise offensively; but we think it fine to affect reluctance."

"Do you really feel so, Bromfield?" asked his wife, seriously.

"Certainly I do. There was a long time in my misguided youth when I supposed myself some sort of porcelain; but it's a relief to be of the common clay, after all, and to know it. If I get broken, I can be easily replaced."

"If Tom must go into such a business," said Mrs. Corey, "I'm glad James approves of it."

"I'm afraid it wouldn't matter to Tom if he didn't; and I don't know that I should care," said Corey, betraying the fact that he had perhaps had a good deal of his brother-in-law's judgment in the course of his life. "You had better consult him in regard to Tom's marrying the princess."

"There is no necessity at present for that," said Mrs. Corey, with dignity. After a moment, she asked, "Should you feel quite so easy if it were a question of that, Bromfield?"

"It would be a little more personal."

"You feel about it as I do. Of course, we have both lived too long, and seen too much of the world, to suppose we can control such things. The child is good, I haven't the least doubt, and all those things can be managed so that they wouldn't disgrace us. But she has had a certain sort of bringing up. I should prefer Tom to marry a girl with another sort, and this business venture of his increases the chances that he wont. That's all."

" "'Tis not so deep as a well, nor so wide as a church door, but 'twill serve.' "[1]

"I shouldn't like it."

"Well, it hasn't happened yet."

"Ah, you never can realize anything beforehand."

"Perhaps that has saved me some suffering. But you have at least the consolation of two anxieties at once. I always find that a great advantage. You can play one off against the other."

Mrs. Corey drew a long breath as if she did not experience the suggested consolation; and she arranged to quit, the following afternoon, the scene of her defeat, which she had not had the courage to make a battle-field. Her son went down to see her off on the boat, after spending his first day at his desk in Lapham's office. He was in a gay humor, and she departed in a reflected gleam of his good spirits. He told her all about it, as he sat talking with her at the stern of the boat, lingering till the last moment, and then stepping ashore, with as little waste of time as Lapham himself, on the gang-plank which the deck-hands had laid hold of. He touched his hat to her from the wharf to reassure her of his escape from being carried away with her, and the next moment his smiling face hid itself in the crowd.

He walked on smiling up the long wharf, encumbered with trucks and hacks and piles of freight, and, taking his way through the deserted business streets beyond this bustle, made a point of passing the door of Lapham's warehouse, on the jambs of which his name and paint were lettered in black on a square ground of white. The door was still open, and Corey loitered a moment before it, tempted to go upstairs and fetch away some foreign letters which he had left on his desk, and which he thought he might finish up at home. He was in love with his work, and he felt the enthusiasm for it which nothing but the work we can do well inspires in us. He believed that he had found his place in the world, after a good deal of looking, and he had the relief, the repose, of fitting into it. Every little incident of the momentous, uneventful day was a pleasure in his mind, from his sitting down at his desk, to which Lapham's boy brought him the foreign letters, till his rising from it an hour ago. Lapham had been in view within his own office, but he had given Corey no formal

---

1. " 'Tis not so deep as a well . . ." is a misquotation of the words with which Mercutio, in *Romeo* *and Juliet* (iii.i.100–101) refers jokingly to the sword wound from which he will soon die.

reception, and had, in fact, not spoken to him till toward the end of the forenoon, when he suddenly came out of his den with some more letters in his hand, and after a brief "How d'ye do?" had spoken a few words about them, and left them with him. He was in his shirt-sleeves again, and his sanguine person seemed to radiate the heat with which he suffered. He did not go out to lunch, but had it brought to him in his office, where Corey saw him eating it before he left his own desk to go out and perch on a swinging seat before the long counter of a down-town restaurant. He observed that all the others lunched at twelve, and he resolved to anticipate his usual hour. When he returned, the pretty girl who had been clicking away at a type-writer all the morning was neatly putting out of sight the evidences of pie from the table where her machine stood, and was preparing to go on with her copying. In his office Lapham lay asleep in his arm-chair, with a newspaper over his face.

Now, while Corey lingered at the entrance to the stairway, these two came down the stairs together, and he heard Lapham saying, "Well, then, you better get a divorce."

He looked red and excited, and the girl's face, which she veiled at sight of Corey, showed traces of tears. She slipped round him into the street.

But Lapham stopped, and said, with the show of no feeling but surprise: "Hello, Corey! Did you want to go up?"

"Yes; there were some letters I hadn't quite got through with."

"You'll find Dennis up there. But I guess you better let them go till to-morrow. I always make it a rule to stop work when I'm done."

"Perhaps you're right," said Corey, yielding.

"Come along down as far as the boat with me. There's a little matter I want to talk over with you."

It was a business matter, and related to Corey's proposed connection with the house.

The next day the head book-keeper, who lunched at the long counter of the same restaurant with Corey, began to talk with him about Lapham. Walker had not apparently got his place by seniority; though, with his bald head, and round, smooth face, one might have taken him for a plump elder, if he had not looked equally like a robust infant. The thick, drabbish-yellow mustache was what arrested decision in either direction, and the prompt vigor of all his movements was that of a young man of thirty, which was really Walker's age. He knew, of course, who Corey was, and he had waited for a man who might look down on him socially to make the overtures toward something more than business acquaintance; but, these made, he was readily responsive, and drew freely on his philosophy of Lapham and his affairs.

"I think about the only difference between people in this world is that some know what they want, and some don't. Well, now," said Walker, beating the bottom of his salt-box to make the salt come out, "the old man knows what he wants every time. And generally he gets it. Yes, sir, he generally gets it. He knows what he's about, but I'll be blessed if the rest of us do half the time. Anyway, we don't till he's ready to let us. You take my position in most business houses. It's confidential. The head book-keeper knows right along pretty much everything the house has got in hand. I'll give you my word *I* don't. He may open up to you a little more in your department, but, as far as the rest of us go, he don't open up any more than an oyster on a hot brick. They say he had a partner once; I guess he's dead. *I* wouldn't like to be the old man's partner. Well, you see, this paint of his is like his heart's blood. Better not try to joke him about it. I've seen people come in occasionally and try it. They didn't get much fun out of it."

While he talked, Walker was plucking up morsels from his plate, tearing off pieces of French bread from the long loaf, and feeding them into his mouth in an impersonal way, as if he were firing up an engine.

"I suppose he thinks," suggested Corey, "that if he doesn't tell, nobody else will."

Walker took a draught of beer from his glass, and wiped the foam from his mustache.

"Oh, but he carries it too far! It's a weakness with him. He's just so about everything. Look at the way he keeps it up about that type-writer girl of his. You'd think she was some princess traveling incognito. There isn't one of us knows who she is, or where she came from, or who she belongs to. He brought her and her machine into the office one morning, and set 'em down at a table, and that's all there is about it, as far as we're concerned. It's pretty hard on the girl, for I guess she'd like to talk; and to any one that didn't know the old man—" Walker broke off and drained his glass of what was left in it.

Corey thought of the words he had overheard from Lapham to the girl. But he said, "She seems to be kept pretty busy."

"Oh, yes," said Walker; "there aint much loafing round the place, in any of the departments, from the old man's down. That's just what I say. He's got to work just twice as hard, if he wants to keep everything in his own mind. But he aint afraid of work. That's one good thing about him. And Miss Dewey has to keep step with the rest of us. But she don't look like one that would take to it naturally. Such a pretty girl as that generally thinks she does enough when she looks her prettiest."

"She's a pretty girl," said Corey, non-committally. "But I suppose a great many pretty girls have to earn their living."

"Don't any of 'em like to do it," returned the book-keeper. "They think it's a hardship, and I don't blame 'em. They have got a right to get married, and they ought to have the chance. And Miss Dewey's smart, too. She's as bright as a biscuit. I guess she's had trouble. I shouldn't be much more than half surprised if Miss Dewey wasn't Miss Dewey, or hadn't always been. Yes, sir," continued the book-keeper, who prolonged the talk as they walked back to Lapham's warehouse together, "I don't know exactly what it is,—it isn't any one thing in particular,—but I should say that girl had been married. I wouldn't speak so freely to any of the rest, Mr. Corey,—I want you to understand that,— and it isn't any of my business, anyway; but that's my opinion."

Corey made no reply, as he walked beside the book-keeper, who continued:

"It's curious what a difference marriage makes in people. Now, I know that I don't look any more like a bachelor of my age than I do like the man in the moon, and yet I couldn't say where the difference came in, to save me. And it's just so with a woman. The minute you catch sight of her face, there's something in it that tells you whether she's married or not. What do you suppose it is?"

"I'm sure I don't know," said Corey, willing to laugh away the topic. "And from what I read occasionally of some people who go about repeating their happiness, I shouldn't say that the intangible evidences were always unmistakable."

"Oh, of course," admitted Walker, easily surrendering his position. "All signs fail in dry weather. Hello! What's that?" He caught Corey by the arm, and they both stopped.

At a corner, half a block ahead of them, the summer noon

solitude of the place was broken by a bit of drama. A man and woman issued from the intersecting street, and at the moment of coming into sight the man, who looked like a sailor, caught the woman by the arm, as if to detain her. A brief struggle ensued, the woman trying to free herself, and the man half coaxing, half scolding. The spectators could now see that he was drunk; but before they could decide whether it was a case for their interference or not, the woman suddenly set both hands against the man's breast and gave him a quick push. He lost his footing and tumbled into a heap in the gutter. The woman faltered an instant, as if to see whether he was seriously hurt, and then turned and ran.

When Corey and the book-keeper reëntered the office, Miss Dewey had finished her lunch, and was putting a sheet of paper into her type-writer. She looked up at them with her eyes of turquoise blue, under her low white forehead, with the hair neatly rippled over it, and then began to beat the keys of her machine.

## IX

LAPHAM had the pride which comes of self-making, and he would not openly lower his crest to the young fellow he had taken into his business. He was going to be obviously master in his own place to every one; and during the hours of business he did nothing to distinguish Corey from the half-dozen other clerks and book-keepers in the outer office, but he was not silent about the fact that Bromfield Corey's son had taken a fancy to come to him. "Did you notice that fellow at the desk facing my type-writer girl? Well, sir, that's the son of Bromfield Corey—old Phillips Corey's grandson. And I'll say this for him, that there isn't a man in the office that looks after his work better. There isn't anything he's too good for. He's right here at nine every morning, before the clock gets in the word. I guess it's his grandfather coming out in him. He's got charge of the foreign correspondence. We're pushing the paint everywhere." He flattered himself that he did not lug the matter in. He had been warned against that by his wife, but he had the right to do Corey justice, and his brag took the form of illustration. "Talk about training for business—I tell you it's all in the man himself! I used to believe in what old

Horace Greeley said about college graduates being the poorest
kind of horned cattle;[2] but I've changed my mind a little. You
take that fellow Corey. He's been through Harvard, and he's
had about every advantage that a fellow could have. Been everywhere, and talks half a dozen languages like English. I suppose
he's got money enough to live without lifting a hand, any more
than his father does; son of Bromfield Corey, you know. But the
thing was in him. He's a natural-born business man; and I've
had many a fellow with me that had come up out of the street,
and worked hard all his life, without ever losing his original
opposition to the thing. But Corey likes it. I believe the fellow
would like to stick at that desk of his night and day. I don't know
where he got it. I guess it must be his grandfather, old Phillips
Corey; it often skips a generation, you know. But what I say is,
a thing has got to be born in a man; and if it ain't born in him,
all the privations in the world won't put it there, and if it is, all
the college training won't take it out."

Sometimes Lapham advanced these ideas at his own table,
to a guest whom he had brought to Nantasket for the night. Then
he suffered exposure and ridicule at the hands of his wife, when
opportunity offered. She would not let him bring Corey down
to Nantasket at all.

"No, indeed!" she said. "I am not going to have them think
we're running after him. If he wants to see Irene, he can find
out ways of doing it for himself."

"Who wants him to see Irene?" retorted the Colonel angrily.

"I do," said Mrs. Lapham. "And I want him to see her without
any of your connivance, Silas. I'm not going to have it said that
I put my girls *at* anybody. Why don't you invite some of your
other clerks?"

"He ain't just like the other clerks. He's going to take charge
of a part of the business. It's quite another thing."

"Oh, indeed!" said Mrs. Lapham vexatiously. "Then you
*are* going to take a partner."

"I shall ask him down if I choose!" returned the Colonel,
disdaining her insinuation.

His wife laughed with the fearlessness of a woman who knows
her husband.

2. Horace Greeley (1811–72) was an American
newspaper editor, reformer, and candidate for
president in 1872. Noted for his homespun wisdom, he was credited with originating the advice
"Go West, young man."

"But you won't choose when you've thought it over, Si." Then she applied an emollient to his chafed surface. "Don't you suppose I feel as you do about it? I know just how proud you are, and I'm not going to have you do anything that will make you feel meeching afterward.[3] You just let things take their course. If he wants Irene, he's going to find out some way of seeing her; and if he don't, all the plotting and planning in the world isn't going to make him."

"Who's plotting?" again retorted the Colonel, shuddering at the utterance of hopes and ambitions which a man hides with shame, but a woman talks over as freely and coolly as if they were items of a milliner's bill.

"Oh, not *you!*" exulted his wife. "I understand what *you* want. You want to get this fellow, who is neither partner nor clerk, down here to talk business with him. Well, now, you just talk business with him at the office."

The only social attention which Lapham succeeded in offering Corey was to take him in his buggy, now and then, for a spin out over the Milldam. He kept the mare in town, and on a pleasant afternoon he liked to knock off early, as he phrased it, and let the mare out a little. Corey understood something about horses, though in a passionless way, and he would have preferred to talk business when obliged to talk horse. But he deferred to his business superior with the sense of discipline which is innate in the apparently insubordinate American nature. If Corey could hardly have helped feeling the social difference between Lapham and himself, in his presence he silenced his traditions, and showed him all the respect that he could have exacted from any of his clerks. He talked horse with him, and when the Colonel wished he talked house. Besides himself and his paint Lapham had not many other topics; and if he had a choice between the mare and the edifice on the water side of Beacon street, it was just now the latter. Sometimes, in driving in or out, he stopped at the house, and made Corey his guest there, if he might not at Nantasket; and one day it happened that the young man met Irene there again. She had come up with her mother alone, and they were in the house, interviewing the carpenter as before, when the Colonel jumped out of his buggy and cast anchor at the pavement. More exactly, Mrs. Lapham was interviewing the car-

3. "meeching": cringing, sneaky.

penter, and Irene was sitting in the bow-window on a trestle, and looking out at the driving. She saw him come up with her father, and bowed and blushed. Her father went on upstairs to find her mother, and Corey pulled up another trestle which he found in the back part of the room. The first floorings had been laid throughout the house, and the partitions had been lathed so that one could realize the shape of the interior.

"I suppose you will sit at this window a good deal," said the young man.

"Yes, I think it will be very nice. There's so much more going on than there is in the Square."

"It must be very interesting to you to see the house grow."

"It is. Only it doesn't seem to grow so fast as I expected."

"Why, I'm amazed at the progress your carpenter has made every time I come."

The girl looked down, and then lifting her eyes she said, with a sort of timorous appeal:

"I've been reading that book since you were down at Nantasket."

"Book?" repeated Corey, while she reddened with disappointment. "Oh, yes. 'Middlemarch.' Did you like it?"

"I haven't got through with it yet. Pen has finished it."

"What does she think of it?"

"Oh, I think she likes it very well. I haven't heard her talk about it much. Do you like it?"

"Yes; I liked it immensely. But it's several years since I read it."

"I didn't know it was so old. It's just got into the Seaside Library," she urged, with a little sense of injury in her tone.

"Oh, it hasn't been out such a very great while," said Corey, politely. "It came a little before 'Daniel Deronda.' "[4]

The girl was again silent. She followed the curl of a shaving on the floor with the point of her parasol.

"Do you like that Rosamond Vincy?" she asked, without looking up.[5]

Corey smiled in his kind way.

"I didn't suppose she was expected to have any friends. I can't

---

4. George Eliot's novel *Daniel Deronda* was published in installments from 1874–76, about two years after *Middlemarch*.
5. Rosamond Vincy, in *Middlemarch*, is a beautiful, blond, spoiled girl, not unlike Irene, who fancies herself too fine for village life. She finally forces her husband, a potentially brilliant doctor, into a trivial but lucrative practice among hypochondriacs at a health spa.

say I liked her. But I don't think I disliked her so much as the author does. She's pretty hard on her good-looking"—he was going to say girls, but as if that might have been rather personal, he said—"people."

"Yes, that's what Pen says. She says she doesn't give her any chance to be good. She says she should have been just as bad as Rosamond if she had been in her place."

The young man laughed. "Your sister is very satirical, isn't she?"

"I don't know," said Irene, still intent upon the convolutions of the shaving. "She keeps us laughing. Papa thinks there's nobody that can talk like her." She gave the shaving a little toss from her, and took the parasol up across her lap. The unworldliness of the Lapham girls did not extend to their dress; Irene's costume was very stylish, and she governed her head and shoulders stylishly. "We are going to have the back room upstairs for a music-room and library," she said abruptly.

"Yes?" returned Corey. "I should think that would be charming."

"We expected to have book-cases, but the architect wants to build the shelves in."

The fact seemed to be referred to Corey for his comment.

"It seems to me that would be the best way. They'll look like part of the room then. You can make them low, and hang your pictures above them."

"Yes, that's what he said." The girl looked out of the window in adding, "I presume with nice bindings it will look very well."

"Oh, nothing furnishes a room like books."

"No. There will have to be a good many of them."

"That depends upon the size of your room and the number of your shelves."

"Oh, of course! I presume," said Irene, thoughtfully, "we shall have to have Gibbon."

"If you want to read him," said Corey, with a laugh of sympathy for an imaginable joke.

"We had a great deal about him at school. I believe we had one of his books. Mine's lost, but Pen will remember."

The young man looked at her, and then said, seriously, "You'll want Greene, of course, and Motley, and Parkman."

"Yes. What kind of writers are they?"

"They're historians, too."

"Oh, yes; I remember now. That's what Gibbon was. Is it Gibbon or Gibbons?" [6]

The young man decided the point with apparently superfluous delicacy. "Gibbon, I think."

"There used to be so many of them," said Irene, gayly. "I used to get them mixed up with each other, and I couldn't tell them from the poets. Should you want to have poetry?"

"Yes; I suppose some edition of the English poets."

"We don't any of us like poetry. Do you like it?"

"I'm afraid I don't very much," Corey owned. "But, of course, there was a time when Tennyson was a great deal more to me than he is now."

"We had something about him at school, too. I think I remember the name. I think we ought to have *all* the American poets."

"Well, not all. Five or six of the best: you want Longfellow and Bryant and Whittier and Holmes and Emerson and Lowell." [7]

The girl listened attentively, as if making mental note of the names.

"And Shakspere," she added. "Don't you like Shakspere's plays?"

"Oh, yes, very much."

"I used to be perfectly crazy about his plays. Don't you think 'Hamlet' is splendid? We had ever so much about Shakspere. Weren't you perfectly astonished when you found out how many other plays of his there were? I always thought there was nothing but 'Hamlet' and 'Romeo and Juliet' and 'Macbeth' and

---

6. Edward Gibbon (1737–94), English historian, was author of *The History of the Decline and Fall of the Roman Empire*; George Washington Greene (1811–83), American historian, wrote *Historical View of the American Revolution*; John Lathrop Motley (1814–77), American historian, was author of *The Rise of the Dutch Republic*; Francis Parkman (1823–93), American historian, wrote *The California and Oregon Trail* and many other volumes on the American frontier. Tom Corey's implication is that any gentleman's library would doubtless be furnished with the works of these historians. He proceeds to mention "five or six of the best" American poets. Irene suggests the English novelist Scott. Novels were often considered much less serious reading than either poetry or history.

7. Henry Wadsworth Longfellow (1807–82) is best known for his long narrative poems such as *Evangeline* and *The Song of Hiawatha*; William

Cullen Bryant (1794–1878) wrote "Thanatopsis," "To a Waterfowl," and much nature poetry; John Greenleaf Whittier (1807–92) was an American Quaker poet and reformer, author of *Snow-bound* and such ballads as "Barbara Frietchie"; Oliver Wendell Holmes (1809–94) was both author and physician, and among his most popular poems are "Old Ironsides" and "The Deacon's Masterpiece" ("the wonderful one-horse shay"); Ralph Waldo Emerson (1803–82) was a poet, essayist, and lecturer, whose best known poems include "Brahma," "The Rhodora," and "The Concord Hymn"; James Russell Lowell (1819–91), poet and critic, was author of romantic poetry as well as the satirical Yankee dialect *Biglow Papers*. While he was editor of the *Atlantic Monthly* magazine (1871–81) Howells knew and published work by all of these "fireside poets."

'Richard III.' and 'King Lear,' and that one that Robeson and Crane have—oh, yes! 'Comedy of Errors.' "[8]

"Those are the ones they usually play," said Corey.

"I presume we shall have to have Scott's works," said Irene, returning to the question of books.

"Oh, yes."

"One of the girls used to think he was *great*. She was always talking about Scott." Irene made a pretty little, amiably contemptuous mouth. "He isn't American, though?" she suggested.

"No," said Corey; "he's Scotch, I believe."

Irene passed her glove over her forehead. "I always get him mixed up with Cooper.[9] Well, papa has got to get them. If we have a library, we have got to have books in it. Pen says it's perfectly ridiculous having one. But papa thinks whatever the architect says is right. He fought him hard enough at first. I don't see how any one can keep the poets and the historians and novelists separate in their mind. Of course papa will buy them if we say so. But I don't see how I'm ever going to tell him which ones." The joyous light faded out of her face and left it pensive.

"Why, if you like," said the young man, taking out his pencil, "I'll put down the names we've been talking about."

He clapped himself on his breast pockets to detect some lurking scrap of paper.

"Will you?" she cried delightedly. "Here! take one of my cards," and she pulled out her card-case. "The carpenter writes on a three-cornered block and puts it into his pocket, and it's so uncomfortable he can't help remembering it. Pen says she's going to adopt the three-cornered-block plan with papa."[1]

"Thank you," said Corey. "I believe I'll use your card." He crossed over to her, and after a moment sat down on the trestle beside her. She looked over the card as he wrote. "Those are the ones we mentioned, but perhaps I'd better add a few others."

"Oh, thank you," she said, when he had written the card full on both sides. "He has got to get them in the nicest binding, too.

8. Stuart Robson (1836–1903) and Henry Crane (1845–1928) were American actors who collaborated with great success from 1877 until 1889. They had particular success in playing the double twins in Shakespeare's *Comedy of Errors*.
9. Sir Walter Scott (1771–1832) and James Fenimore Cooper (1789–1851) were two of the leading authors of romantic adventure novels. Howells particularly objected to the distorted pictures of life and human nature these heroic melodramas provided, and in having Irene recall them he is suggesting her own unrealistic and simple-minded attitudes.
1. A carpenter may write a memo on a scrap of wood and stuff it in his pocket, knowing that the discomfort will act as a reminder. A three-cornered block is more uncomfortable yet and therefore a better reminder. It is typical of Penelope's droll wit to appreciate this down-to-earth system and threaten to adopt it.

79111

I shall tell him about their helping to furnish the room, and then he can't object." She remained with the card, looking at it rather wistfully.

Perhaps Corey divined her trouble of mind.

"If he will take that to any book-seller, and tell him what bindings he wants, he will fill the order for him."

"Oh, thank you very much," she said, and put the card back into her card-case with great apparent relief. Then she turned her lovely face toward the young man, beaming with the triumph a woman feels in any bit of successful manœuvring, and began to talk with recovered gayety of other things, as if, having got rid of a matter annoying out of all proportion to its importance, she was now going to indemnify herself.

Corey did not return to his own trestle. She found another shaving within reach of her parasol, and began poking that with it, and trying to follow it through its folds. Corey watched her awhile.

"You seem to have a great passion for playing with shavings," he said. "Is it a new one?"

"New what?"

"Passion."

"I don't know," she said, dropping her eyelids, and keeping on with her effort. She looked shyly aslant at him. "Perhaps you don't approve of playing with shavings?"

"Oh, yes, I do. I admire it very much. But it seems rather difficult. I've a great ambition to put my foot on the shaving's tail and hold it for you."

"Well," said the girl.

"Thank you," said the young man. He did so, and now she ran her parasol point easily through it. They looked at each other and laughed. "That was wonderful. Would you like to try another?" he asked.

"No, I thank you," she replied. "I think one will do."

They both laughed again, for whatever reason or no reason, and then the young girl became sober. To a girl everything a young man does is of significance; and if he holds a shaving down with his foot while she pokes through it with her parasol, she must ask herself what he means by it.

"They seem to be having rather a long interview with the carpenter to-day," said Irene, looking vaguely toward the ceil-

ing. She turned with polite ceremony to Corey. "I'm afraid
you're letting them keep you. You mustn't."

"Oh, no. You're letting me stay," he returned.

She bridled, and bit her lip for pleasure. "I presume they
will be down before a great while. Don't you like the smell of
the wood and the mortar? It's so fresh."

"Yes, it's delicious." He bent forward and picked up from the
floor the shaving with which they had been playing, and put it
to his nose. "It's like a flower. May I offer it to you?" he asked,
as if it had been one.

"Oh, thank you, thank you!" She took it from him and put
it into her belt, and then they both laughed once more.

Steps were heard descending. When the elder people reached
the floor where they were sitting, Corey rose and presently took
his leave.

"What makes you so solemn, 'Rene?" asked Mrs. Lapham.

"Solemn?" echoed the girl. "I'm not a *bit* solemn. What *can*
you mean?"

Corey dined at home that evening, and as he sat looking
across the table at his father, he said, "I wonder what the average
literature of non-cultivated people is."

"Ah," said the elder, "I suspect the average is pretty low even
with cultivated people. You don't read a great many books
yourself, Tom."

"No, I don't," the young man confessed. "I read more books
when I was with Stanton, last winter, than I had since I was a
boy. But I read them because I must—there was nothing else to
do. It wasn't because I was fond of reading. Still, I think I read
with some sense of literature and the difference between authors.
I don't suppose that people generally do that; I have met people
who had read books without troubling themselves to find out even
the author's name, much less trying to decide upon his quality.
I suppose that's the way the vast majority of people read."

"Yes. If authors were not almost necessarily recluses, and
ignorant of the ignorance about them, I don't see how they could
endure it. Of course they are fated to be overwhelmed by oblivion
at last, poor fellows; but to see it weltering all round them while
they are in the very act of achieving immortality must be
tremendously discouraging. I don't suppose that we who have

the habit of reading, and at least a nodding acquaintance with literature, can imagine the bestial darkness of the great mass of people—even people whose houses are rich, and whose linen is purple and fine. But occasionally we get glimpses of it. I suppose you found the latest publications lying all about in Lapham cottage when you were down there?"

Young Corey laughed. "It wasn't exactly cumbered with them."

"No?"

"To tell the truth, I don't suppose they ever buy books. The young ladies get novels that they hear talked of out of the circulating library."

"Had they knowledge enough to be ashamed of their ignorance?"

"Yes, in certain ways—to a certain degree."

"It's a curious thing, this thing we call civilization," said the elder, musingly. "We think it is an affair of epochs and of nations. It's really an affair of individuals. One brother will be civilized and the other a barbarian. I've occasionally met young girls who were so brutally, insolently, willfully indifferent to the arts which make civilization that they ought to have been clothed in the skins of wild beasts and gone about barefoot with clubs over their shoulders. Yet they were of polite origin, and their parents were at least respectful of the things that these young animals despised."

"I don't think that is exactly the case with the Lapham family," said the son, smiling. "The father and mother rather apologized about not getting time to read, and the young ladies by no means scorned it."

"They are quite advanced!"

"They are going to have a library in their Beacon street house."

"Oh, poor things! How are they ever going to get the books together?"

"Well, sir," said the son, coloring a little, "*I* have been indirectly applied to for help."

"You, Tom!" His father dropped back in his chair and laughed.

"I recommended the standard authors," said the son.

"Oh, I never supposed your *prudence* would be at fault, Tom!"

"But seriously," said the young man, generously smiling in

sympathy with his father's enjoyment, "they're not unintelligent people. They are very quick, and they are shrewd and sensible."

"I have no doubt that some of the Sioux are so. But that is not saying that they are civilized. All civilization comes through literature now, especially in our country. A Greek got his civilization by talking and looking, and in some measure a Parisian may still do it. But we, who live remote from history and monuments, we must read or we must barbarize. Once we were softened, if not polished, by religion; but I suspect that the pulpit counts for much less now in civilizing."

"They're enormous devourers of newspapers, and theatergoers; and they go a great deal to lectures. The Colonel prefers them with the stereopticon."

"They might get a something in that way," said the elder, thoughtfully. "Yes, I suppose one must take those things into account—especially the newspapers and the lectures. I doubt if the theater is a factor in civilization among us. I dare say it doesn't deprave a great deal, but from what I've seen of it I should say that it was intellectually degrading. Perhaps they might get some sort of lift from it; I don't know. Tom!" he added, after a moment's reflection. "I really think I ought to see this patron of yours. Don't you think it would be rather decent in me to make his acquaintance?"

"Well, if you have the fancy, sir," said the young man. "But there's no sort of obligation. Colonel Lapham would be the last man in the world to want to give our relation any sort of social character. The meeting will come about in the natural course of things."

"Ah, I didn't intend to propose anything immediate," said the father. "One can't do anything in the summer, and I should prefer your mother's superintendence. Still, I can't rid myself of the idea of a dinner. It appears to me that there ought to be a dinner."

"Oh, pray don't feel that there's any necessity."

"Well," said the elder, with easy resignation, "there's at least no hurry."

"There is one thing I don't like," said Lapham, in the course of one of those talks which came up between his wife and himself concerning Corey, "or at least I don't understand it; and that's the way his father behaves. I don't want to force myself on any man; but it seems to me pretty queer the way he holds off. I should think he would take enough interest in his son to want to know something about his. business. What is he afraid of?" demanded Lapham angrily. "Does he think I'm going to jump at a chance to get in with him, if he gives me one? He's mightily mistaken if he does. *I* don't want to know him."

"Silas," said his wife, making a wife's free version of her husband's words, and replying to their spirit rather than their letter, "I hope you never said a word to Mr. Corey to let him know the way you feel."

"I never mentioned his father to him!" roared the Colonel. "That's the way I feel about it!"

"Because it would spoil everything. I wouldn't have them think we cared the least thing in the world for their acquaintance. We shouldn't be a bit better off. We don't know the same people they do, and we don't care for the same kind of things."

Lapham was breathless with resentment of his wife's implication. "Don't I tell you," he gasped, "that I don't want to know them? Who began it? They're friends of yours if they're anybody's."

"They're distant acquaintances of mine," returned Mrs. Lapham quietly; "and this young Corey is a clerk of yours. And I want we should hold ourselves so that when they get ready to make the advances we can meet them half-way or not, just as we choose."

"That's what grinds me," cried her husband. "Why should we wait for them to make the advances? Why shouldn't we make 'em? Are they any better than we are? My note of hand would be worth ten times what Bromfield Corey's is on the street to-day. And I made *my* money. I haven't loafed my life away."

"Oh, it isn't what you've got, and it isn't what you've done exactly. It's what you are."

"Well, then, what's the difference?"

"None that really amounts to anything, or that need give you any trouble, if you don't think of it. But he's been all his life in society, and he knows just what to say and what to do, and he can talk about the things that society people like to talk about, and you—can't."

Lapham gave a furious snort. "And does that make him any better?"

"No. But it puts him where he can make the advances without

demeaning himself, and it puts you where you can't. Now, look here, Silas Lapham! You understand this thing as well as I do. You know that I appreciate you, and that I'd sooner die than have you humble yourself to a living soul. But I'm not going to have you coming to me, and pretending that you can meet Bromfield Corey as an equal on his own ground. You can't. He's got a better education than you, and if he hasn't got more brains than you, he's got different. And he and his wife, and their fathers and grandfathers before 'em, have always had a high position, and you can't help it. If you want to know them, you've got to let them make the advances. If you don't, all well and good."

"I guess," said the chafed and vanquished Colonel, after a moment for swallowing the pill, "that they'd have been in a pretty fix if you'd waited to let them make the advances last summer."

"That was a different thing altogether. I didn't know who they were, or may be I should have waited. But all I say now is that if you've got young Corey into business with you, in hopes of our getting into society with his father, you better ship him at once. For I ain't going to have it on that basis."

"Who wants to have it on that basis?" retorted her husband.

"Nobody, if you don't," said Mrs. Lapham tranquilly.

Irene had come home with the shaving in her belt, unnoticed by her father, and unquestioned by her mother. But her sister saw it at once, and asked her what she was doing with it.

"Oh, nothing," said Irene, with a joyful smile of self-betrayal, taking the shaving carefully out, and laying it among the laces and ribbons in her drawer.

"Hadn't you better put it in water, 'Rene? It'll be all wilted by morning," said Pen.

"You mean thing!" cried the happy girl. "It isn't a flower!"

"Oh, I thought it was a whole bouquet. Who gave it to you?"

"I sha'n't tell you," said Irene saucily.

"Oh, well, never mind. Did you know Mr. Corey had been down here this afternoon, walking on the beach with me?"

"He wasn't—he wasn't at all! He was at the house with *me*. There! I've caught you fairly."

"Is that so?" drawled Penelope. "Then I never could guess who gave you that precious shaving."

"No, you couldn't!" said Irene, flushing beautifully. "And you may guess, and you may guess, and you may guess!" With her lovely eyes she coaxed her sister to keep on teasing her, and Penelope continued the comedy with the patience that women have for such things.

"Well, I'm not going to try, if it's no use. But I didn't know it had got to be the fashion to give shavings instead of flowers. But there's some sense in it. They can be used for kindlings when they get old, and you can't do anything with old flowers. Perhaps he'll get to sending 'em by the barrel."

Irene laughed for pleasure in this tormenting. "Oh, Pen, I want to tell you how it all happened."

"Oh, he *did* give it to you, then? Well, I guess I don't care to hear."

"You shall, and you've got to!" Irene ran and caught her sister, who feigned to be going out of the room, and pushed her into a chair. "There, now!" She pulled up another chair, and hemmed her in with it. "He came over, and sat down on the trestle alongside of me ——"

"What? As close as you are to me now?"

"You wretch! I will *give* it to you! No, at a proper distance. And here was this shaving on the floor, that I'd been poking with my parasol ——"

"To hide your embarrassment."

"Pshaw! I wasn't a bit embarrassed. I was just as much at my ease! And then he asked me to let him hold the shaving down with his foot, while I went on with my poking. And I said yes he might ——"

"What a bold girl! You said he might hold a shaving down for you?"

"And then—and then—"continued Irene, lifting her eyes absently, and losing herself in the beatific recollection, "and then— Oh, yes! Then I asked him if he didn't like the smell of pine shavings. And then he picked it up, and said it smelt like a flower. And then he asked if he might offer it to me—just for a joke, you know. And I took it, and stuck it in my belt. And we had such a laugh! We got into a regular gale. And oh, Pen, what do you suppose he meant by it?" She suddenly caught herself to her sister's breast, and hid her burning face on her shoulder.

"Well, there used to be a book about the language of flowers.

But I never knew much about the language of shavings, and I can't say exactly ——"

"Oh, don't—*don't*, Pen!" and here Irene gave over laughing, and began to sob in her sister's arms.

"Why, 'Rene!" cried the elder girl.

"You *know* he didn't mean anything. He doesn't care a bit about me. He hates me! He despises me! Oh, what shall I do?"

A trouble passed over the face of the sister as she silently comforted the child in her arms; then the drolling light came back into her eyes. "Well, 'Rene, *you* haven't got to do *any*thing. That's one advantage girls have got—if it *is* an advantage. I'm not always sure."

Irene's tears turned to laughing again. When she lifted her head it was to look into the mirror confronting them, where her beauty showed all the more brilliant for the shower that had passed over it. She seemed to gather courage from the sight.

"It must be awful to have to *do*," she said, smiling into her own face. "I don't see how they ever can."

"Some of 'em can't—especially when there's such a tearing beauty around."

"Oh, pshaw, Pen! You know that isn't so. You've got a real pretty mouth, Pen," she added thoughtfully, surveying the feature in the glass, and then pouting her own lips for the sake of that effect on them.

"It's a useful mouth," Penelope admitted; "I don't believe I could get along without it now, I've had it so long."

"It's got such a funny expression—just the mate of the look in your eyes; as if you were just going to say something ridiculous. He said, the very first time he saw you, that he knew you were humorous."

"Is it possible? It must be so, if the Grand Mogul said it. Why didn't you tell me so before, and not let me keep on going round just like a common person?"

Irene laughed as if she liked to have her sister take his praises in that way rather than another. "I've got such a stiff, prim kind of mouth," she said, drawing it down, and then looking anxiously at it.

"I hope you didn't put on that expression when he offered you the shaving. If you did, I don't believe he'll ever give you another splinter."

The severe mouth broke into a lovely laugh, and then pressed itself in a kiss against Penelope's cheek.

"There! Be done, you silly thing! I'm not going to have you accepting *me* before I've offered myself, *anyway*." She freed herself from her sister's embrace, and ran from her round the room.

Irene pursued her, in the need of hiding her face against her shoulder again. "Oh, Pen! Oh, Pen!" she cried.

The next day, at the first moment of finding herself alone with her eldest daughter, Mrs. Lapham asked, as if knowing that Penelope must have already made it subject of inquiry: "What was Irene doing with that shaving in her belt yesterday?"

"Oh, just some nonsense of hers with Mr. Corey. He gave it to her at the new house." Penelope did not choose to look up and meet her mother's grave glance.

"What do you think he meant by it?"

Penelope repeated Irene's account of the affair, and her mother listened without seeming to derive much encouragement from it.

"He doesn't seem like one to flirt with her," she said at last. Then, after a thoughtful pause: "Irene is as good a girl as ever breathed, and she's a perfect beauty. But I should hate the day when a daughter of mine was married for her beauty."

"You're safe as far as I'm concerned, mother."

Mrs. Lapham smiled ruefully. "She isn't really equal to him, Pen. I misdoubted that from the first, and it's been borne in upon me more and more ever since. She hasn't mind enough."

"I didn't know that a man fell in love with a girl's intellect," said Penelope quietly.

"Oh, no. He hasn't fallen in love with Irene at all. If he had, it wouldn't matter about the intellect."

Penelope let the self-contradiction pass.

"Perhaps he has, after all."

"No," said Mrs. Lapham. "She pleases him when he sees her. But he doesn't try to see her."

"He has no chance. You won't let father bring him here."

"He would find excuses to come without being brought, if he wished to come," said the mother. "But she isn't in his mind enough to make him. He goes away and doesn't think anything more about her. She's a child. She's a good child, and I shall always say it; but she's nothing but a child. No, she's got to forget him."

"Perhaps that won't be so easy."

"No, I presume not. And now your father has got the notion in his head, and he will move heaven and earth to bring it to pass. I can see that he's always thinking about it."

"The Colonel has a will of his own," observed the girl, rocking to and fro where she sat looking at her mother.

"I wish we had never met them!" cried Mrs. Lapham. "I wish we had never thought of building! I wish he had kept away from your father's business!"

"Well, it's too late now, mother," said the girl. "Perhaps it isn't so bad as you think."

"Well, we must stand it, anyway," said Mrs. Lapham, with the grim antique Yankee submission.

"Oh, yes, we've got to stand it," said Penelope, with the quaint modern American fatalism.

# X

It was late June, almost July, when Corey took up his life in Boston again, where the summer slips away so easily. If you go out of town early, it seems a very long summer when you come back in October; but if you stay, it passes swiftly, and, seen foreshortened in its flight, seems scarcely a month's length. It has its days of heat, when it is very hot, but for the most part it is cool, with baths of the east wind that seem to saturate the soul with delicious freshness. Then there are stretches of gray, westerly weather, when the air is full of the sentiment of early autumn, and the frying of the grasshopper in the blossomed weed of the vacant lots on the Back Bay is intershot with the carol of crickets; and the yellowing leaf on the long slope of Mt. Vernon street smites the sauntering observer with tender melancholy. The caterpillar, gorged with the spoil of the lindens on Chestnut, and weaving his own shroud about him in his lodgment on the brickwork, records the passing of summer by mid-July; and if after that comes August, its breath is thick and short, and September is upon the sojourner before he has fairly had time to philosophize the character of the town out of season.[2]

2. Mt. Vernon and Chestnut are two streets in the fashionable Beacon Hill section of Boston.

But it must have appeared that its most characteristic feature was the absence of everybody he knew. This was one of the things that commended Boston to Bromfield Corey during the summer; and if his son had any qualms about the life he had entered upon with such vigor, it must have been a relief to him that there was scarcely a soul left to wonder or pity. By the time people got back to town the fact of his connection with the mineral paint man would be an old story, heard afar off with different degrees of surprise, and considered with different degrees of indifference. A man has not reached the age of twenty-six in any community where he was born and reared without having had his capacity pretty well ascertained; and in Boston the analysis is conducted with an unsparing thoroughness which may fitly impress the un-Bostonian mind, darkened by the popular superstition that the Bostonians blindly admire one another. A man's qualities are sifted as closely in Boston as they doubtless were in Florence or Athens; and, if final mercy was shown in those cities because a man was, with all his limitations, an Athenian or Florentine, some abatement might as justly be made in Boston for like reason. Corey's powers had been gauged in college, and he had not given his world reason to think very differently of him since he came out of college. He was rated as an energetic fellow, a little indefinite in aim, with the smallest amount of inspiration that can save a man from being commonplace. If he was not commonplace, it was through nothing remarkable in his mind, which was simply clear and practical, but through some combination of qualities of the heart that made men trust him, and women call him sweet —a word of theirs which conveys otherwise indefinable excellences. Some of the more nervous and excitable said that Tom Corey was as sweet as he could live; but this perhaps meant no more than the word alone. No man ever had a son less like him than Bromfield Corey. If Tom Corey had ever said a witty thing, no one could remember it; and yet the father had never said a witty thing to a more sympathetic listener than his own son. The clear mind which produced nothing but practical results reflected everything with charming lucidity; and it must have been this which endeared Tom Corey to every one who spoke ten words with him. In a city where people have good reason for liking to shine, a man who did not care to shine must be little short of universally acceptable without any other effort for popularity;

and those who admired and enjoyed Bromfield Corey loved his
son. Yet, when it came to accounting for Tom Corey, as it often
did in a community where every one's generation is known to
the remotest degrees of cousinship, they could not trace his sweetness to his mother, for neither Anna Bellingham nor any of her
family, though they were so many blocks of Wenham ice ³ for
purity and rectangularity, had ever had any such savor; and, in
fact, it was to his father, whose habit of talk wronged it in himself,
that they had to turn for this quality of the son's. They traced to
the mother the traits of practicality and common sense in which
he bordered upon the commonplace, and which, when they had
dwelt upon them, made him seem hardly worth the close inquiry
they had given him.

While the summer wore away he came and went methodically
about his business, as if it had been the business of his life, sharing
his father's bachelor liberty and solitude, and expecting with
equal patience the return of his mother and sisters in the autumn.
Once or twice he found time to run down to Mt. Desert and see
them; and then he heard how the Philadelphia and New York
people were getting in everywhere, and was given reason to regret
the house at Nahant which he had urged to be sold. He came
back and applied himself to his desk with a devotion that was
exemplary rather than necessary; for Lapham made no difficulty
about the brief absences which he asked, and set no term to the
apprenticeship that Corey was serving in the office before setting
off upon that mission to South America in the early winter, for
which no date had yet been fixed.

The summer was a dull season for the paint as well as for everything else. Till things should brisk up, as Lapham said, in the fall,
he was letting the new house take a great deal of his time.
Æsthetic ideas had never been intelligibly presented to him
before, and he found a delight in apprehending them that was
very grateful to his imaginative architect. At the beginning, the
architect had foreboded a series of mortifying defeats and disastrous victories in his encounters with his client; but he had never
had a client who could be more reasonably led on from one
outlay to another. It appeared that Lapham required but to
understand or feel the beautiful effect intended, and he was ready

---

3. Wenham ice: a particularly pure ice was cut
each winter from a small lake near Wenham, a
town about five miles north of Salem in Essex
County, Mass.

to pay for it. His bull-headed pride was concerned in a thing which the architect made him see, and then he believed that he had seen it himself, perhaps conceived it. In some measure the architect seemed to share his delusion, and freely said that Lapham was very suggestive. Together they blocked out windows here, and bricked them up there; they changed doors and passages; pulled down cornices and replaced them with others of different design; experimented with costly devices of decoration, and went to extravagant lengths in novelties of finish. Mrs. Lapham, beginning with a woman's adventurousness in the unknown region, took fright at the reckless outlay at last, and refused to let her husband pass a certain limit. He tried to make her believe that a far-seeing economy dictated the expense; and that if he put the money into the house, he could get it out any time by selling it. She would not be persuaded.

"I don't want you should sell it. And you've put more money into it now than you'll ever get out again, unless you can find as big a goose to buy it, and that isn't likely. No, sir! You just stop at a hundred thousand, and don't you let him get you a cent beyond. Why, you're perfectly bewitched with that fellow! You've lost your head, Silas Lapham, and if you don't look out you'll lose your money too."

The Colonel laughed; he liked her to talk that way, and promised he would hold up awhile.

"But there's no call to feel anxious, Pert. It's only a question what to do with the money. I can reinvest it; but I never had so much of it to spend before."

"Spend it, then," said his wife; "don't throw it away! And how came you to have so much more money than you know what to do with, Silas Lapham?" she added.

"Oh, I've made a very good thing in stocks lately."

"In stocks? When did you take up gambling for a living?"

"Gambling? Stuff! What gambling? Who said it was gambling?"

"You have; many a time."

"Oh, yes, buying and selling on a margin. But this was a *bona fide* transaction. I bought at forty-three for an investment, and I sold at a hundred and seven; and the money passed both times."

"Well, you better let stocks alone," said his wife, with the conservatism of her sex. "Next time you'll buy at a hundred and seven and sell at forty-three. Then where'll you be?"

"Left," admitted the Colonel.

"You better stick to paint awhile yet."

The Colonel enjoyed this, too, and laughed again with the ease of a man who knows what he is about. A few days after that he came down to Nantasket with the radiant air which he wore when he had done a good thing in business and wanted his wife's sympathy. He did not say anything of what had happened till he was alone with her in their own room; but he was very gay the whole evening, and made several jokes which Penelope said nothing but very great prosperity could excuse: they all understood these moods of his.

"Well, what is it, Silas?" asked his wife when the time came. "Any more big-bugs wanting to go into the mineral paint business with you?"

"Something better than that."

"I could think of a good many better things," said his wife, with a sigh of latent bitterness. "What's this one?"

"I've had a visitor."

"Who?"

"Can't you guess?"

"I don't want to try. Who was it?"

"Rogers."

Mrs. Lapham sat down with her hands in her lap, and stared at the smile on her husband's face, where he sat facing her.

"I guess you wouldn't want to joke on that subject, Si," she said, a little hoarsely, "and you wouldn't grin about it unless you had some good news. I don't know what the miracle is, but if you could tell quick——"

She stopped like one who can say no more.

"I will, Persis," said her husband, and with that awed tone in which he rarely spoke of anything but the virtues of his paint. "He came to borrow money of me, and I lent him it. That's the short of it. The long——"

"Go on," said his wife, with gentle patience.

"Well, Pert, I was never so much astonished in my life as I was to see that man come into my office. You might have knocked me down with—I don't know what."

"I don't wonder. Go on!"

"And he was as much embarrassed as I was. There we stood,

gaping at each other, and I hadn't hardly sense enough to ask him to take a chair. I don't know just how we got at it. And I don't remember just how it was that he said he came to come to me. But he had got hold of a patent right that he wanted to go into on a large scale, and there he was wanting me to supply him the funds."

"Go on!" said Mrs. Lapham, with her voice further in her throat.

"I never felt the way you did about Rogers, but I know how you always did feel, and I guess I surprised him with my answer. He had brought along a lot of stock as security——"

"You didn't take it, Silas!" his wife flashed out.

"Yes, I did, though," said Lapham. "You wait. We settled our business, and then we went into the old thing, from the very start. And we talked it all over. And when we got through we shook hands. Well, I don't know when it's done me so much good to shake hands with anybody."

"And you told him—you owned up to him that you were in the wrong, Silas?"

"No, I didn't," returned the Colonel, promptly; "for I wasn't. And before we got through, I guess he saw it the same as I did."

"Oh, no matter! so you had the chance to show how you felt."

"But I never felt that way," persisted the Colonel. "I've lent him the money, and I've kept his stocks. And he got what he wanted out of me."

"Give him back his stocks!"

"No, I sha'n't. Rogers came to borrow. He didn't come to beg. You needn't be troubled about his stocks. They're going to come up in time; but just now they're so low down that no bank would take them as security, and I've got to hold them till they do rise. I hope you're satisfied now, Persis," said her husband; and he looked at her with the willingness to receive the reward of a good action which we all feel when we have performed one. "I lent him the money you kept me from spending on the house."

"Truly, Si? Well, I'm satisfied," said Mrs. Lapham, with a deep, tremulous breath. "The Lord has been good to you, Silas," she continued, solemnly. "You may laugh if you choose, and I don't know as *I* believe in his interfering a great deal; but I believe he's interfered this time; and I tell you, Silas, it ain't always he gives people a chance to make it up to others in this life. I've been afraid you'd die, Silas, before you got the chance; but he's let you live to make it up to Rogers."

"I'm glad to be let live," said Lapham, stubbornly; "but I hadn't anything to make up to Milton K. Rogers. And if God has let me live for that——"

"Oh, say what you please, Si! Say what you please, now you've done it! I sha'n't stop you. You've taken the one spot—the one *speck*—off you that was ever there, and I'm satisfied."

"There wa'n't ever any speck there," Lapham held out, lapsing more and more into his vernacular; "and what I done, I done for you, Persis."

"And I thank you for your own soul's sake, Silas."

"I guess my soul's all right," said Lapham.

"And I want you should promise me one thing more."

"Thought you said you were satisfied?"

"I am. But I want you should promise me this: that you won't let anything tempt you—anything!—to ever trouble Rogers for that money you lent him. No matter what happens—no matter if you lose it all. Do you promise?"

"Why, I don't ever *expect* to press him for it. That's what I said to myself when I lent it. And of course I'm glad to have that old trouble healed up. I don't *think* I ever did Rogers any wrong, and I never did think so; but if I *did* do it—*if* I did—I'm willing to call it square, if I never see a cent of my money back again."

"Well, that's all," said his wife.

They did not celebrate his reconciliation with his old enemy—for such they had always felt him to be since he ceased to be an ally—by any show of joy or affection. It was not in their tradition, as stoical for the woman as for the man, that they should kiss or embrace each other at such a moment. She was content to have told him that he had done his duty, and he was content with her saying that. But before she slept she found words to add that she always feared the selfish part he had acted toward Rogers had weakened him, and left him less able to overcome any temptation that might beset him; and that was one reason why she could never be easy about it. Now she should never fear for him again.

This time he did not explicitly deny her forgiving impeachment.

"Well, it's all past and gone now, anyway; and I don't want you should think anything more about it."

He was man enough to take advantage of the high favor in

which he stood when he went up to town, and to abuse it by
bringing Corey down to supper. His wife could not help con-
doning the sin of disobedience in him at such a time. Penelope
said that between the admiration she felt for the Colonel's boldness and her mother's forbearance, she was hardly in a state to
entertain company that evening; but she did what she could.

Irene liked being talked to better than talking, and when her
sister was by she was always, tacitly or explicitly, referring to her
for confirmation of what she said. She was content to sit and look
pretty as she looked at the young man and listened to her sister's
drolling. She laughed, and kept glancing at Corey to make sure
that he was understanding her. When they went out on the
veranda to see the moon on the water, Penelope led the way and
Irene followed.

They did not look at the moonlight long. The young man
perched on the rail of the veranda, and Irene took one of the
red-painted rocking-chairs where she could conveniently look at
him and at her sister, who sat leaning forward lazily and running
on, as the phrase is. That low, crooning note of hers was delicious;
her face, glimpsed now and then in the moonlight as she turned
it or lifted it a little, had a fascination which kept his eye. Her
talk was very unliterary, and its effect seemed hardly conscious.
She was far from epigram in her funning. She told of this trifle
and that; she sketched the characters and looks of people who
had interested her, and nothing seemed to have escaped her
notice; she mimicked a little, but not much; she suggested, and
then the affair represented itself as if without her agency. She
did not laugh; when Corey stopped, she made a soft cluck in her
throat, as if she liked his being amused, and went on again.

The Colonel, left alone with his wife for the first time since he
had come from town, made haste to take the word. "Well, Pert,
I've arranged the whole thing with Rogers, and I hope you'll
be satisfied to know that he owes me twenty thousand dollars,
and that I've got security from him to the amount of a fourth of
that, if I was to force his stocks to a sale."

"How came he to come down with you?" asked Mrs. Lapham.

"Who? Rogers?"

"Mr. Corey."

"Corey? Oh!" said Lapham, affecting not to have thought
she could mean Corey. "He proposed it."

"Likely!" jeered his wife, but with perfect amiability.

"It's so," protested the Colonel. "We got talking about a matter just before I left, and he walked down to the boat with me; and then he said if I didn't mind he guessed he'd come along down and go back on the return boat. Of course I couldn't let him do that."

"It's well for you you couldn't."

"And I couldn't do less than bring him here to tea."

"Oh, certainly not."

"But he ain't going to stay the night—unless," faltered Lapham, "you want him to."

"Oh, of course, *I* want him to! I guess he'll stay, probably."

"Well, you know how crowded that last boat always is, and he can't get any other now."

Mrs. Lapham laughed at the simple wile. "I hope you'll be just as well satisfied, Si, if it turns out he doesn't want Irene after all."

"Pshaw, Persis! What are you always bringing that up for?" pleaded the Colonel. Then he fell silent, and presently his rude, strong face was clouded with an unconscious frown.

"There!" cried his wife, startling him from his abstraction. "I see how you'd feel; and I hope that you'll remember who you've got to blame."

"I'll risk it," said Lapham, with the confidence of a man used to success.

From the veranda the sound of Penelope's lazy tone came through the closed windows, with joyous laughter from Irene and peals from Corey.

"Listen to that!" said her father within, swelling up with inexpressible satisfaction. "That girl can talk for twenty, right straight along. She's better than a circus any day. I wonder what she's up to now."

"Oh, she's probably getting off some of those yarns of hers, or telling about some people. She can't step out of the house without coming back with more things to talk about than most folks would bring back from Japan. There ain't a ridiculous person she's ever seen but what she's got something from them to make you laugh at; and I don't believe we've ever had anybody in the house since the girl could talk that she hain't got some saying from, or some trick that'll pint 'em out so 't you can see 'em and hear 'em. Sometimes I want to stop her; but when she gets into

one of her gales there ain't any standing up against her. I guess
it's lucky for Irene that she's got Pen there to help entertain her
company. I can't ever feel down where Pen is."

"That's so," said the Colonel. "And I guess she's got about
as much culture as any of them. Don't you?"

"She reads a great deal," admitted her mother. "She seems
to be at it the whole while. I don't want she should injure her
health, and sometimes I feel like snatchin' the books away from
her. I don't know as it's good for a girl to read so much, anyway,
especially novels. I don't want she should get notions."

"Oh, I guess Pen'll know how to take care of herself," said
Lapham.

"She's got sense enough. But she ain't so practical as Irene.
She's more up in the clouds—more of what you may call a
dreamer. Irene's wide-awake every minute; and I declare, any
one to see these two together when there's anything to be done,
or any lead to be taken, would say Irene was the oldest, nine
times out of ten. It's only when they get to talking that you can
see Pen's got twice as much brains."

"Well," said Lapham, tacitly granting this point, and leaning
back in his chair in supreme content. "Did you ever see much
nicer girls anywhere?"

His wife laughed at his pride. "I presume they're as much
swans as anybody's geese."

"No; but honestly, now!"

"Oh, they'll do; but don't you be silly, if you can help it, Si."

The young people came in, and Corey said it was time for his
boat. Mrs. Lapham pressed him to stay, but he persisted, and he
would not let the Colonel send him to the boat; he said he would
rather walk. Outside, he pushed along toward the boat, which
presently he could see lying at her landing in the bay, across the
sandy tract to the left of the hotels. From time to time he almost
stopped in his rapid walk, as a man does whose mind is in a
pleasant tumult; and then he went forward at a swifter pace.

"She's charming!" he said, and he thought he had spoken
aloud. He found himself floundering about in the deep sand,
wide of the path; he got back to it, and reached the boat just
before she started. The clerk came to take his fare, and Corey
looked radiantly up at him in his lantern-light, with a smile that
he must have been wearing a long time; his cheek was stiff with

it. Once some people who stood near him edged suddenly and fearfully away, and then he suspected himself of having laughed outright.

# XI

COREY put off his set smile with the help of a frown, of which he first became aware after reaching home, when his father asked:

"Anything gone wrong with your department of the fine arts to-day, Tom?"

"Oh, no—no, sir," said the son, instantly relieving his brows from the strain upon them, and beaming again. "But I was thinking whether you were not perhaps right in your impression that it might be well for you to make Colonel Lapham's acquaintance before a great while."

"Has he been suggesting it in any way?" asked Bromfield Corey, laying aside his book and taking his lean knee between his clasped hands.

"Oh, not at all!" the young man hastened to reply. "I was merely thinking whether it might not begin to seem intentional, your not doing it."

"Well, Tom, you know I have been leaving it altogether to you——"

"Oh, I understand, of course, and I didn't mean to urge anything of the kind——"

"You are so very much more of a Bostonian than I am, you know, that I've been waiting your motion in entire confidence that you would know just what to do, and when to do it. If I had been left quite to my own lawless impulses, I think I should have called upon your *padrone* at once. It seems to me that *my* father would have found some way of showing that he expected as much as that from people placed in the relation to him that we hold to Colonel Lapham."

"Do you think so?" asked the young man.

"Yes. But you know I don't pretend to be an authority in such matters. As far as they go, I am always in the hands of your mother and you children."

"I'm very sorry, sir. I had no idea I was overruling your judgment. I only wanted to spare you a formality that didn't seem quite a necessity yet. I'm very sorry," he said again, and this time with more comprehensive regret. "I shouldn't like to have seemed remiss with a man who has been so considerate of me. They are all very good-natured."

"I dare say," said Bromfield Corey, with the satisfaction which no elder can help feeling in disabling the judgment of a younger man, "that it won't be too late if I go down to your office with you to-morrow."

"No, no. I didn't imagine your doing it at once, sir."

"Ah, but nothing can prevent me from doing a thing when once I take the bit in my teeth," said the father, with the pleasure which men of weak will sometimes take in recognizing their weakness. "How does their new house get on?"

"I believe they expect to be in it before New Year's."

"Will they be a great addition to society?" asked Bromfield Corey, with unimpeachable seriousness.

"I don't quite know what you mean," returned the son, a little uneasily.

"Ah, I see that you do, Tom."

"No one can help feeling that they are all people of good sense and—right ideas."

"Oh, that won't do. If society took in all the people of right ideas and good sense, it would expand beyond the calling capacity of its most active members. Even your mother's social conscientiousness could not compass it. Society is a very different sort of thing from good sense and right ideas. It is based upon them, of course, but the airy, graceful, winning superstructure which we all know demands different qualities. Have your friends got these qualities,—which may be felt, but not defined?"

The son laughed. "To tell you the truth, sir, I don't think they have the most elemental ideas of society, as we understand it. I don't believe Mrs. Lapham ever gave a dinner."

"And with all that money!" sighed the father.

"I don't believe they have the habit of wine at table. I suspect that when they don't drink tea and coffee with their dinner, they drink ice-water."

"Horrible!" said Bromfield Corey.

"It appears to me that this defines them."

"Oh, yes. There are people who give dinners, and who are

not cognoscible. But people who have never yet given a dinner, how is society to assimilate them?"[4]

"It digests a great many people," suggested the young man.

"Yes; but they have always brought some sort of sauce piquante with them. Now, as I understand you, these friends of yours have no such sauce."

"Oh, I don't know about that!" cried the son.

"Oh, rude, native flavors, I dare say. But that isn't what I mean. Well, then, they must spend. There is no other way for them to win their way to general regard. We must have the Colonel elected to the Ten O'clock Club,[5] and he must put himself down in the list of those willing to entertain. Any one can manage a large supper. Yes, I see a gleam of hope for him in that direction."

In the morning Bromfield Corey asked his son whether he should find Lapham at his place as early as eleven.

"I think you might find him even earlier. I've never been there before him. I doubt if the porter is there much sooner."

"Well, suppose I go with you, then?"

"Why, if you like, sir," said the son, with some deprecation.

"Oh, the question is, will *he* like?"

"I think he will, sir"; and the father could see that his son was very much pleased.

Lapham was rending an impatient course through the morning's news when they appeared at the door of his inner room. He looked up from the newspaper spread on the desk before him, and then he stood up, making an indifferent feint of not knowing that he knew Bromfield Corey by sight.

"Good-morning, Colonel Lapham," said the son, and Lapham waited for him to say further, "I wish to introduce my father."

Then he answered "Good-morning," and added rather sternly for the elder Corey, "How do you do, sir? Will you take a chair?" and he pushed him one.

---

4. "cognoscible": literally, capable of being known. Bromfield Corey is suggesting that the Laphams are neither in the category of people who have the manners and customs that make them at ease in society nor in the category of people one does not invite to dinner—one's washerwoman or chimney-sweep, for instance. The Laphams *are* "knowable," but their lack of social abilities will make relations difficult for everyone.

5. A joking reference to the various dining clubs to which business, professional, and literary men of Boston belonged. The contrast between Ten O'Clock (with its suggestion of a hasty daily coffee break) and the prestigious Saturday Club, to which such Boston notables as Emerson, Longfellow, and Howells belonged, may indicate Bromfield Corey's estimate of the kind of club appropriate for Lapham.

They shook hands and sat down, and Lapham said to his subordinate, "Have a seat"; but young Corey remained standing, watching them in their observance of each other with an amusement which was a little uneasy. Lapham made his visitor speak first by waiting for him to do so.

"I'm glad to make your acquaintance, Colonel Lapham, and I ought to have come sooner to do so. My father in your place would have expected it of a man in my place at once, I believe. But I can't feel myself altogether a stranger as it is. I hope Mrs. Lapham is well? And your daughter?"

"Thank you," said Lapham, "they're quite well."

"They were very kind to my wife——"

"Oh, that was nothing!" cried Lapham. "There's nothing Mrs. Lapham likes better than a chance of that sort. Mrs. Corey and the young ladies well?"

"Very well, when I heard from them. They're out of town."

"Yes, so I understood," said Lapham, with a nod toward the son. "I believe Mr. Corey, here, told Mrs. Lapham." He leaned back in his chair, stiffly resolute to show that he was not incommoded by the exchange of these civilities.

"Yes," said Bromfield Corey. "Tom has had the pleasure which I hope for of seeing you all. I hope you're able to make him useful to you here?" Corey looked round Lapham's room vaguely, and then out at the clerks in their railed inclosure, where his eye finally rested on an extremely pretty girl, who was operating a type-writer.

"Well, sir," replied Lapham, softening for the first time with this approach to business, "I guess it will be our own fault if we don't. By the way, Corey," he added, to the younger man, as he gathered up some letters from his desk, "here's something in your line. Spanish or French, I guess."

"I'll run them over," said Corey, taking them to his desk.

His father made an offer to rise.

"Don't go," said Lapham, gesturing him down again. "I just wanted to get him away a minute. I don't care to say it to his face,—I don't like the principle,—but since you ask me about it, I'd just as lief say that I've never had any young man take hold here equal to your son. I don't know as you care——"

"You make me very happy," said Bromfield Corey. "Very happy indeed. I've always had the idea that there was something in my son, if he could only find the way to work it out. And he seems to have gone into your business for the love of it."

"He went to work in the right way, sir! He told me about it. He looked into it. And that paint is a thing that will bear looking into."

"Oh, yes. You might think he had invented it, if you heard him celebrating it."

"Is that so?" demanded Lapham, pleased through and through. "Well, there ain't any other way. You've got to believe in a thing before you can put any heart in it. Why, I had a partner in this thing once, along back just after the war, and he used to be always wanting to tinker with something else. 'Why,' says I, 'you've got the best thing in God's universe now. Why ain't you satisfied?' I had to get rid of him at last. I stuck to my paint, and that fellow's drifted round pretty much all over the whole country, whittling his capital down all the while, till here the other day I had to lend him some money to start him new. No, sir, you've got to believe in a thing. And I believe in your son. And I don't mind telling you that, so far as he's gone, he's a success."

"That's very kind of you."

"No kindness about it. As I was saying the other day to a friend of mine, I've had many a fellow right out of the street that had to work hard all his life, and didn't begin to take hold like this son of yours."

Lapham expanded with profound self-satisfaction. As he probably conceived it, he had succeeded in praising, in a perfectly casual way, the supreme excellence of his paint, and his own sagacity and benevolence; and here he was sitting face to face with Bromfield Corey, praising his son to him, and receiving his grateful acknowledgments as if he were the father of some office-boy whom Lapham had given a place half out of charity.

"Yes, sir, when your son proposed to take hold here, I didn't have much faith in his ideas, that's the truth. But I had faith in him, and I saw that he meant business from the start. I could see it was born in him. Any one could."

"I'm afraid he didn't inherit it directly from me," said Bromfield Corey; "but it's in the blood, on both sides."

"Well, sir, we can't help those things," said Lapham, compassionately. "Some of us have got it, and some of us haven't. The idea is to make the most of what we *have* got."

"Oh, yes; that is the idea. By all means."

"And you can't ever tell what's in you till you try. Why, when I started this thing, I didn't more than half understand my own strength. I wouldn't have said, looking back, that I could have stood the wear and tear of what I've been through. But I developed as I went along. It's just like exercising your muscles in a gymnasium. You can lift twice or three times as much after you've been in training a month as you could before. And I can see that it's going to be just so with your son. His going through college won't hurt him,—he'll soon slough all that off,—and his bringing up won't; don't be anxious about it. I noticed in the army that some of the fellows that had the most go-ahead were fellows that hadn't ever had much more to do than girls before the war broke out. Your son will get along."

"Thank you," said Bromfield Corey, and smiled—whether because his spirit was safe in the humility he sometimes boasted, or because it was triply armed in pride against anything the Colonel's kindness could do.

"He'll get along. He's a good business man and he's a fine fellow. *Must* you go?" asked Lapham, as Bromfield Corey now rose more resolutely. "Well, glad to see you. It was natural you should want to come and see what he was about, and I'm glad you did. I should have felt just so about it. Here is some of our stuff," he said, pointing out the various packages in his office, including the Persis Brand.

"Ah, that's very nice, very nice indeed," said his visitor. "That color through the jar—very rich—delicious. Is Persis Brand a name?"

Lapham blushed.

"Well, Persis is. I don't know as you saw an interview that fellow published in the 'Events' awhile back?"

"What is the 'Events'?" [6]

6. The *Events* is a fictitious newspaper, but the kind of article Bartley Hubbard is writing for it suggests that it is a tabloid devoted largely to local personalities, sensational stories, and advertising. In Howells' earlier novel, *A Modern Instance*, Bartley Hubbard is employed by the editor of the *Events* who tells Bartley, "I hold that the first duty of a public journal is to make money for the owner; all the rest follows naturally." By contrast *The Daily Advertiser* was a highly respectable paper that had begun publication in the printing office where Benjamin Franklin learned his trade. Howells misses no opportunity to contrast the naive commercialism of Silas Lapham with the conservative respectability of Bromfield Corey.

"Well, it's that new paper Witherby's started."

"No," said Bromfield Corey, "I haven't seen it. I read 'The Daily,'" he explained; by which he meant "The Daily Advertiser," the only daily there is in the old-fashioned Bostonian sense.

"He put a lot of stuff in my mouth that I never said," resumed Lapham; "but that's neither here nor there, so long as you haven't seen it. Here's the department your son's in," and he showed him the foreign labels. Then he took him out into the warehouse to see the large packages. At the head of the stairs, where his guest stopped to nod to his son and say "Good-bye, Tom," Lapham insisted upon going down to the lower door with him. "Well, call again," he said in hospitable dismissal. "I shall always be glad to see you. There ain't a great deal doing at this season." Bromfield Corey thanked him, and let his hand remain perforce in Lapham's lingering grasp. "If you ever like to ride after a good horse——" the Colonel began.

"Oh, no, no, no; thank you! The better the horse, the more I should be scared. Tom has told me of your driving!"

"Ha, ha, ha!" laughed the Colonel. "Well! every one to his taste. Well, good-morning, sir!" and he suffered him to go.

"Who is the old man blowing to this morning?" asked Walker, the book-keeper, making an errand to Corey's desk.

"My father."

"Oh! That your father? I thought he must be one of your Italian correspondents that you'd been showing round, or Spanish."

In fact, as Bromfield Corey found his way at his leisurely pace up through the streets on which the prosperity of his native city was founded, hardly any figure could have looked more alien to its life. He glanced up and down the façades and through the crooked vistas like a stranger, and the swarthy fruiterer of whom he bought an apple, apparently for the pleasure of holding it in his hand, was not surprised that the purchase should be transacted in his own tongue.

Lapham walked back through the outer office to his own room without looking at Corey, and during the day he spoke to him only of business matters. That must have been his way of letting Corey see that he was not overcome by the honor of his father's visit. But he presented himself at Nantasket with the event so perceptibly on his mind that his wife asked: "Well, Silas, has Rogers been borrowing any more money of you? I don't want you should let that thing go too far. You've done enough."

"You needn't be afraid. I've seen the last of Rogers for one while." He hesitated, to give the fact an effect of no importance. "Corey's father called this morning."

"Did he?" said Mrs. Lapham, willing to humor his feint of indifference. "Did *he* want to borrow some money too?"

"Not as I understood." Lapham was smoking at great ease, and his wife had some crocheting on the other side of the lamp from him.

The girls were on the piazza looking at the moon on the water again. "There's no man in it to-night," Penelope said, and Irene laughed forlornly.

"What *did* he want, then?" asked Mrs. Lapham.

"Oh, I don't know. Seemed to be just a friendly call. Said he ought to have come before."

Mrs. Lapham was silent awhile. Then she said: "Well, I hope you're satisfied now."

Lapham rejected the sympathy too openly offered. "I don't know about being satisfied. I wa'n't in any hurry to see him."

His wife permitted him this pretense also. "What sort of a person is he, anyway?"

"Well, not much like his son. There's no sort of business about him. I don't know just how you'd describe him. He's tall; and he's got white hair and a mustache; and his fingers are very long and limber. I couldn't help noticing them as he sat there with his hands on the top of his cane. Didn't seem to be dressed very much, and acted just like anybody. Didn't talk much. Guess I did most of the talking. Said he was glad I seemed to be getting along so well with his son. He asked after you and Irene; and he said he couldn't feel just like a stranger. Said you had been very kind to his wife. Of course I turned it off. Yes," said Lapham thoughtfully, with his hands resting on his knees, and his cigar between the fingers of his left hand, "I guess he meant to do the right thing, every way. Don't know as I ever saw a much pleasanter man. Dunno but what he's about the pleasantest man I ever did see." He was not letting his wife see in his averted face the struggle that revealed itself there—

the struggle of stalwart achievement not to feel flattered at the notice of sterile elegance, not to be sneakingly glad of its amiability, but to stand up and look at it with eyes on the same level. God, who made us so much like himself, but out of the dust, alone knows when that struggle will end. The time had been when Lapham could not have imagined any worldly splendor which his dollars could not buy if he chose to spend them for it; but his wife's half discoveries, taking form again in his ignorance of the world, filled him with helpless misgiving. A cloudy vision of something unpurchasable, where he had supposed there was nothing, had cowed him in spite of the burly resistance of his pride.

"I don't see why he shouldn't be pleasant," said Mrs. Lapham. "He's never done anything else."

Lapham looked up consciously, with an uneasy laugh. "Pshaw, Persis! you never forget anything!"

"Oh, I've got more than that to remember. I suppose you asked h 1 to ride after the mare?"

"Well," said Lapham, reddening guiltily, "he said he was afraid of a good horse."

"Then, of course, you hadn't asked him." Mrs. Lapham crocheted in silence, and her husband leaned back in his chair and smoked.

At last he said, "I'm going to push that house forward. They're loafing on it. There's no reason why we shouldn't be in it by Thanksgiving. I don't believe in moving in the dead of winter."

"We can wait till spring. We're very comfortable in the old place," answered his wife. Then she broke out on him: "What are you in such a hurry to get into that house for? Do you want to invite the Coreys to a house-warming?"

Lapham looked at her without speaking.

"Don't you suppose I can see through you? I declare, Silas Lapham, if I didn't know different, I should say you *were* about the biggest fool! Don't you know *anything*? Don't you know that it wouldn't do to ask those people to our house before they've asked us to theirs? They'd laugh in our faces!"

"I don't believe they'd laugh in our faces. What's the difference between our asking them and their asking us?" demanded the Colonel, sulkily.

"Oh, well! If you don't see!"

"Well, I *don't* see. But *I* don't want to ask them to the house. I suppose, if I want to, I can invite him down to a fish dinner at Taft's."[7]

Mrs. Lapham fell back in her chair, and let her work drop in her lap with that "Tckk!" in which her sex knows how to express utter contempt and despair.

"What's the matter?"

"Well, if you *do* such a thing, Silas, I'll never speak to you again! It's no *use*! It's *no* use! I did think, after you'd behaved so well about Rogers, I might trust you a little. But I see I can't. I presume as long as you live you'll have to be nosed about like a perfect—*I* don't know what!"

"What are you making such a fuss about?" demanded Lapham, terribly crest-fallen, but trying to pluck up a spirit. "I haven't done anything yet. I can't ask your advice about anything any more without having you fly out. Confound it! I shall do as I please after this."

But as if he could not endure that contemptuous atmosphere, he got up, and his wife heard him in the dining-room pouring himself out a glass of ice-water, and then heard him mount the stairs to their room, and slam its door after him.

"Do you know what your father's wanting to do now?" Mrs. Lapham asked her eldest daughter, who lounged into the parlor a moment with her wrap stringing from her arm, while the younger went straight to bed. "He wants to invite Mr. Corey's father to a fish dinner at Taft's!"

Penelope was yawning with her hand on her mouth; she stopped, and, with a laugh of amused expectance, sank into a chair, her shoulders shrugged forward.

"Why! what in the world has put the Colonel up to that?"

"Put him up to it! There's that fellow, who ought have come to see him long ago, drops into his office this morning, and talks five minutes with him, and your father is flattered out of his five senses. He's crazy to get in with those people, and I shall have a perfect battle to keep him within bounds."

---

7. Taft's was probably a fictitious restaurant, since Howells is unlikely to have wished to offend a respectable establishment by suggesting that it was a place where a vulgarian like Lapham would be likely to entertain at lunch.

"Well, Persis, ma'am, you can't say but what you began it," said Penelope.

"Oh, yes, I began it," confessed Mrs. Lapham. "Pen," she broke out, "what do you suppose he means by it?"

"Who? Mr. Corey's father? What does the Colonel think?"

"Oh, the Colonel!" cried Mrs. Lapham. She added tremulously: "Perhaps he *is* right. He *did* seem to take a fancy to her last summer, and now if he's called in that way—" She left her daughter to distribute the pronouns aright, and resumed: "Of course, I should have said once that there wasn't any question about it. I should have said so last year; and I don't know what it is keeps me from saying so now. I suppose I know a little more about things than I did; and your father's being so bent on it sets me all in a twitter. He thinks his money can do everything. Well, I don't say but what it can, a good many. And 'Rene is as good a child as ever there was; and I don't see but what she's pretty-appearing enough to suit any one. She's pretty-behaved, too; and she *is* the most capable girl. I presume young men don't care very much for such things nowadays; but there ain't a great many girls can go right into the kitchen, and make such a custard as she did yesterday. And look at the way she does, through the whole house! She can't seem to go into a room without the things fly right into their places. And if she had to do it to-morrow, she could make all her own dresses a great deal better than them we pay to do it. I don't say but what he's about as nice a fellow as ever stepped. But there! I'm ashamed of going on so."

"Well, mother," said the girl after a pause, in which she looked as if a little weary of the subject, "why do you worry about it? If it's to be it'll be, and if it isn't——"

"Yes, that's what I tell your father. But when it comes to myself, I see how hard it is for him to rest quiet. I'm afraid we shall all do something we'll repent of afterwards."

"Well, ma'am," said Penelope, "*I* don't intend to do anything wrong; but if I do, I promise not to be sorry for it. I'll go that far. And I think I wouldn't be sorry for it beforehand, if I were in your place, mother. Let the Colonel go on! He likes to manœuvre, and he isn't going to hurt any one. The Corey family can take care of themselves, I guess."

She laughed in her throat, drawing down the corners of her

mouth, and enjoying the resolution with which her mother tried to fling off the burden of her anxieties. "Pen! I believe you're, right. You always do see things in such a light! There! I don't care if he brings him down every day."

"Well, ma'am," said Pen, "I don't believe 'Rene would, either. She's just so indifferent!"

The Colonel slept badly that night, and in the morning Mrs. Lapham came to breakfast without him.

"Your father ain't well," she reported. "He's had one of his turns."

"*I* should have thought he had two or three of them," said Penelope, "by the stamping round I heard. Isn't he coming to breakfast?"

"Not just yet," said her mother. "He's asleep, and he'll be all right if he gets his nap out. I don't want you girls should make any great noise."

"Oh, we'll be quiet enough," returned Penelope. "Well, I'm glad the Colonel isn't sojering. At first I thought he might be sojering." She broke into a laugh, and, struggling indolently with it, looked at her sister. "You don't think it'll be necessary for anybody to come down from the office and take orders from him while he's laid up, do you, mother?" she inquired.

"Pen!" cried Irene.

"He'll be well enough to go up on the ten o'clock boat," said the mother, sharply.

"I think papa works too hard all through the summer. Why don't you make him take a rest, mamma?" asked Irene.

"Oh, take a rest! The man slaves harder every year. It used to be so that he'd take a little time off now and then; but I declare, he hardly ever seems to breathe now away from his office. And this year he says he doesn't intend to go down to Lapham, except to see after the works for a few days. *I* don't know what to do with the man any more! Seems as if the more money he got, the more he wanted to get. It scares me to think what would happen to him if he lost it. I know one thing," concluded Mrs. Lapham. "He shall not go back to the office to-day."

"Then he won't go up on the ten o'clock boat," Pen reminded her.

"No, he won't. You can just drive over to the hotel as soon

as you're through, girls, and telegraph that he's not well, and won't be at the office till to-morrow. I'm not going to have them send anybody down here to bother him."

"That's a blow," said Pen. "I didn't know but they might send——" she looked demurely at her sister— "Dennis!"

"Mamma!" cried Irene.

"Well, I declare, there's no living with this family any more," said Penelope.

"There, Pen, be done!" commanded her mother. But perhaps she did not intend to forbid her teasing. It gave a pleasant sort of reality to the affair that was in her mind, and made what she wished appear not only possible but probable.

Lapham got up and lounged about, fretting and rebelling as each boat departed without him, through the day; before night he became very cross, in spite of the efforts of the family to soothe him, and grumbled that he had been kept from going up to town. "I might as well have gone as not," he repeated, till his wife lost her patience.

"Well, you shall go to-morrow, Silas, if you have to be carried to the boat."

"I declare," said Penelope, "the Colonel don't pet worth a cent."[8]

The six o'clock boat brought Corey. The girls were sitting on the piazza, and Irene saw him first.

"Oh, Pen!" she whispered, with her heart in her face; and Penelope had no time for mockery before he was at the steps.

"I hope Colonel Lapham isn't ill," he said, and they could hear their mother engaged in a moral contest with their father indoors.

"Go and put on your coat! I say you shall! It don't matter *how* he sees you at the office, shirt-sleeves or not. You're in a gentleman's house now—or you ought to be—and you sha'n't see company in your dressing-gown."

Penelope hurried in to subdue her mother's anger.

"Oh, he's very much better, thank you!" said Irene, speaking up loudly to drown the noise of the controversy.

"I'm glad of that," said Corey, and when she led him indoors the vanquished Colonel met his visitor in a double-

8. Howells uses Penelope's affectionate and colloquial familiarity with her father to contrast with the witty formality of Tom Corey's conversations with his father. Penelope means that her father does not know how to submit gracefully to being pampered by his family.

breasted frock-coat, which he was still buttoning up. He could not persuade himself at once that Corey had not come upon some urgent business matter, and when he was clear that he had come out of civility, surprise mingled with his gratification that he should be the object of solicitude to the young man. In Lapham's circle of acquaintance they complained when they were sick, but they made no womanish inquiries after one another's health, and certainly paid no visits of sympathy till matters were serious. He would have enlarged upon the particulars of his indisposition if he had been allowed to do so; and after tea, which Corey took with them, he would have remained to entertain him if his wife had not sent him to bed. She followed him to see that he took some medicine she had prescribed for him, but she went first to Penelope's room, where she found the girl with a book in her hand, which she was not reading.

"You better go down," said the mother. "I've got to go to your father, and Irene is all alone with Mr. Corey; and I know she'll be on pins and needles without you're there to help make it go off."

"She'd better try to get along without me, mother," said Penelope soberly. "I can't always be with them."

"Well," replied Mrs. Lapham, "then *I* must. There'll be a perfect Quaker meeting down there."[9]

"Oh, I guess 'Rene will find something to say if you leave her to herself. Or if she don't, *he* must. It'll be all right for you to go down when you get ready; but I sha'n't go till toward the last. If he's coming here to see Irene—and I don't believe he's come on father's account—he wants to see her and not me. If she can't interest him alone, perhaps he'd as well find it out now as any time. At any rate, I guess you'd better make the experiment. You'll know whether it's a success if he comes again."

"Well," said the mother, "may be you're right. I'll go down directly. It does seem as if he did mean something, after all."

Mrs. Lapham did not hasten to return to her guest. In her own girlhood it was supposed that if a young man seemed to be coming to see a girl, it was only common sense to suppose that he wished to see her alone; and her life in town had left Mrs. Lap-

9. The religious meetings of the Quakers begin with a period of silent meditation that continues until someone feels moved to speak to the group.

ham's simple traditions in this respect unchanged. She did with her daughter as her mother would have done with her.

Where Penelope sat with her book, she heard the continuous murmur of voices below, and after a long interval she heard her mother descend. She did not read the open book that lay in her lap, though she kept her eyes fast on the print. Once she rose and almost shut the door, so that she could scarcely hear; then she opened it wide again with a self-disdainful air, and resolutely went back to her book, which again she did not read. But she remained in her room till it was nearly time for Corey to return to his boat.

When they were alone again, Irene made a feint of scolding her for leaving her to entertain Mr. Corey.

"Why! didn't you have a pleasant call?" asked Penelope.

Irene threw her arms round her. "Oh, it was a *splendid* call! I didn't suppose I could make it go off so well. We talked nearly the whole time about you!"

"I don't think *that* was a very interesting subject."

"He kept asking about you. He asked everything. You don't know how much he thinks of you, Pen. Oh, Pen! what do you think made him come? Do you think he really did come to see how papa was?" Irene buried her face in her sister's neck.

Penelope stood with her arms at her side, submitting. "Well," she said, "I don't think he did, altogether."

Irene, all glowing, released her. "Don't you—don't you *really?* Oh! Pen, don't you think he *is* nice? Don't you think he's handsome? Don't you think I behaved horridly when we first met him this evening, not thanking him for coming? I know he thinks I've no manners. But it seemed as if it would be thanking him for coming to see me. Ought I to have asked him to come again, when he said good-night? I didn't; I couldn't. Do you believe he'll think I don't want him to? You don't believe he would keep coming if he didn't—want to——"

"He hasn't kept coming a great deal, yet," suggested Penelope.

"No; I know he hasn't. But if he—if he should?"

"Then I should think he wanted to."

"Oh, would you—*would* you? Oh, how good you always are, Pen! And you always say what you think. I wish there was some one coming to see you too. That's all that I don't like about it. Perhaps—— He was telling about his friend there in Texas——"

"Well," said Penelope, "his friend couldn't call often from Texas. You needn't ask Mr. Corey to trouble about me, 'Rene. I think I can manage to worry along, if you're satisfied."

"Oh, I *am*, Pen. When do you suppose he'll come again?" Irene pushed some of Penelope's things aside on the dressing-case, to rest her elbow and talk at ease. Penelope came up and put them back.

"Well, not to-night," she said; "and if that's what you're sitting up for——"

Irene caught her round the neck again, and ran out of the room.

The Colonel was packed off on the eight o'clock boat the next morning; but his recovery did not prevent Corey from repeating his visit in a week. This time Irene came radiantly up to Penelope's room, where she had again withdrawn herself. "You must come down, Pen," she said. "He's asked if you're not well, and mamma says you've got to come."

After that Penelope helped Irene through with her calls, and talked them over with her far into the night after Corey was gone. But when the impatient curiosity of her mother pressed her for some opinion of the affair, she said, "You know as much as I do, mother."

"Don't he ever say anything to you about her—praise her up, any?"

"He's never mentioned Irene to me."

"He hasn't to me, either," said Mrs. Lapham, with a sigh of trouble. "Then what makes him keep coming?"

"I can't tell you. One thing, he says there isn't a house open in Boston where he's acquainted. Wait till some of his friends get back, and then if he keeps coming, it'll be time to inquire."

"Well!" said the mother; but as the weeks passed she was less and less able to attribute Corey's visits to his loneliness in town, and turned to her husband for comfort.

"Silas, I don't know as we ought to let young Corey keep coming so. I don't quite like it, with all his family away."

"He's of age," said the Colonel. "He can go where he pleases. It don't matter whether his family's here or not."

"Yes, but if they don't want he should come? Should you feel just right about letting him?"

"How're you going to stop him? I swear, Persis, I don't know what's got over you! What is it? You didn't use to be so. But to hear you talk, you'd think those Coreys were too good for this world, and we wa'n't fit for 'em to walk on."

"I'm not going to have 'em say we took an advantage of their being away and tolled him on." [1]

"I should like to *hear* 'em say it!" cried Lapham. "Or anybody!"

"Well," said his wife, relinquishing this point of anxiety, "I can't make out whether he cares anything for her or not. And Pen can't tell either; or else she won't."

"Oh, I guess he cares for her, fast enough," said the Colonel.

"I can't make out that he's said or done the first thing to show it."

"Well, I was better than a year getting *my* courage up."

"Oh, that was different," said Mrs. Lapham, in contemptuous dismissal of the comparison, and yet with a certain fondness. "I guess, if he cared for her, a fellow in his position wouldn't be long getting up his courage to speak to Irene."

Lapham brought his fist down on the table between them.

"Look here, Persis! Once for all, now, don't you ever let me hear you say anything like that again! I'm worth nigh on to a million, and I've made it every cent myself; and my girls are the equals of anybody, I don't care who it is. He ain't the fellow to take on any airs; but if he ever tries it with me, I'll send him to the right about mighty quick. I'll have a talk with him, if——"

"No, no; don't do that!" implored his wife. "I didn't mean anything. I don't know as I meant *anything*. He's just as unassuming as he can be, and I think Irene's a match for anybody. You just let things go on. It'll be all right. You never can tell how it is with young people. Perhaps *she's* offish. Now you ain't—you ain't going to say anything?"

Lapham suffered himself to be persuaded, the more easily, no doubt, because after his explosion he must have perceived that his pride itself stood in the way of what his pride had threatened. He contented himself with his wife's promise that she would never again present that offensive view of the case, and she did not remain without a certain support in his sturdy self-assertion.

1. "tolled him on": *tole* is an old-fashioned term meaning "to allure or lead on." The Laphams have a good many such old-fashioned or country terms in their conversation.

Mrs. Corey returned with her daughters in the early days of October, having passed three or four weeks at Intervale after leaving Bar Harbor.² They were somewhat browner than they were when they left town in June, but they were not otherwise changed. Lily, the elder of the girls, had brought back a number of studies of kelp and toadstools, with accessory rocks and rotten logs, which she would never finish up and never show any one, knowing the slightness of their merit. Nanny, the younger, had read a great many novels with a keen sense of their inaccuracy as representations of life, and had seen a great deal of life with a sad regret for its difference from fiction. They were both nice girls, accomplished, well dressed of course, and well-enough looking; but they had met no one at the seaside or the mountains whom their taste would allow to influence their fate, and they had come home to the occupations they had left, with no hopes and no fears to distract them.

In the absence of these they were fitted to take the more vivid interest in their brother's affairs, which they could see weighed upon their mother's mind after the first hours of greeting.

"Oh, it seems to have been going on, and your father has never written a word about it," she said, shaking her head.

"What good would it have done?" asked Nanny, who was little and fair, with rings of light hair that filled a bonnet-front very prettily; she looked best in a bonnet. "It would only have worried you. He could not have stopped Tom; you couldn't, when you came home to do it."

"I dare say papa didn't know much about it," suggested Lily. She was a tall, lean, dark girl, who looked as if she were not quite warm enough, and whom you always associated with wraps of different æsthetic effect after you had once seen her.

It is a serious matter always to the women of his family when a young man gives them cause to suspect that he is interested in some other woman. A son-in-law or brother-in-law does not enter the family; he need not be caressed or made anything of; but the

---

2. Intervale, New Hampshire, was a rural summer resort in the White Mountains that Howells visited occasionally. Such summer retreats provided simple, healthful vacations for society ladies whose nerves were traditionally in bad repair after a strenuous winter season of elegant entertaining. In *A Traveller from Altruria* and several of his novels Howells explores, and criticizes, this phenomenon.

son's or brother's wife has a claim upon his mother and sisters which they cannot deny. Some convention of their sex obliges them to show her affection, to like or to seem to like her, to take her to their intimacy, however odious she may be to them. With the Coreys it was something more than an affair of sentiment. They were by no means poor, and they were not dependent money-wise upon Tom Corey; but the mother had come, without knowing it, to rely upon his sense, his advice in everything, and the sisters, seeing him hitherto so indifferent to girls, had insensibly grown to regard him as altogether their own till he should be released, not by his marriage, but by theirs, an event which had not approached with the lapse of time. Some kinds of girls—they believed that they could readily have chosen a kind —might have taken him without taking him from them; but this generosity could not be hoped for in such a girl as Miss Lapham.

"Perhaps," urged their mother, "it would not be so bad. She seemed an affectionate little thing with her mother, without a great deal of character, though she was so capable about some things."

"Oh, she'll be an affectionate little thing with Tom too, you may be sure," said Nanny. "And that characterless capability becomes the most intense narrow-mindedness. She'll think we were against her from the beginning."

"She has no cause for that," Lily interposed, "and we shall not give her any."

"Yes, we shall," retorted Nanny. "We can't help it; and if we can't, her own ignorance would be cause enough."

"I can't feel that she's altogether ignorant," said Mrs. Corey, justly.

"Of course she can read and write," admitted Nanny.

"I can't imagine what he finds to talk about with her," said Lily.

"Oh, *that's* very simple," returned her sister. "They talk about themselves, with occasional references to each other. I have heard people 'going on' on the hotel piazzas. She's embroidering, or knitting, or tatting, or something of that kind; and he says she seems quite devoted to needle-work; and she says, yes, she has a perfect passion for it, and everybody laughs at her for it; but she can't help it, she always was so from a child, and supposes she always shall be,—with remote and minute particulars. And she ends by saying that perhaps he does not like people to tat, or knit, or embroider, or whatever. And he says, oh, yes, he does; what could make her think such a thing? but for his part he likes boating rather better, or if you're in the woods camping. Then she lets him take up one corner of her work, and perhaps touch her fingers; and that encourages him to say that he supposes nothing could induce her to drop her work long enough to go down on the rocks, or out among the huckleberry bushes; and she puts her head on one side, and says she doesn't know really. And then they go, and he lies at her feet on the rocks, or picks huckleberries and drops them in her lap, and they go on talking about themselves, and comparing notes to see how they differ from each other. And——"

"That will do, Nanny," said her mother.

Lily smiled autumnally. "Oh, disgusting!"

"Disgusting? Not at all!" protested her sister. "It's very amusing when you see it, and when you do it——"

"It's always a mystery what people see in each other," observed Mrs. Corey, severely.

"Yes," Nanny admitted, "but I don't know that there is much comfort for us in the application."

"No, there isn't," said her mother.

"The most that we can do is to hope for the best till we know the worst. Of course we shall make the best of the worst when it comes."

"Yes, and perhaps it would not be so very bad. I was saying to your father when I was here in July that those things can always be managed. You must face them as if they were nothing out of the way, and try not to give any cause for bitterness among ourselves."

"That's true. But I don't believe in too much resignation beforehand. It amounts to concession," said Nanny.

"Of course we should oppose it in all proper ways," returned her mother.

Lily had ceased to discuss the matter. In virtue of her artistic temperament, she was expected not to be very practical. It was her mother and her sister who managed, submitting to the advice and consent of Corey what they intended to do.

"Your father wrote me that he had called on Colonel Lapham at his place of business," said Mrs. Corey, seizing her first chance of approaching the subject with her son.

"Yes," said Corey. "A dinner was father's idea, but he came down to a call, at my suggestion."

"Oh," said Mrs. Corey, in a tone of relief, as if the statement threw a new light on the fact that Corey had suggested the visit. "He said so little about it in his letter that I didn't know just how it came about."

"I thought it was right they should meet," explained the son, "and so did father. I was glad that I suggested it, afterward; it was extremely gratifying to Colonel Lapham."

"Oh, it was quite right in every way. I suppose you have seen something of the family during the summer."

"Yes, a good deal. I've been down at Nantasket rather often."

Mrs. Corey let her eyes droop. Then she asked: "Are they well?"

"Yes, except Lapham himself, now and then. I went down once or twice to see him. He hasn't given himself any vacation this summer; he has such a passion for his business that I fancy he finds it hard being away from it at any time, and he's made his new house an excuse for staying——"

"Oh, yes, his house! Is it to be something fine?"

"Yes; it's a beautiful house. Seymour is doing it."

"Then, of course, it will be very handsome. I suppose the young ladies are very much taken up with it; and Mrs. Lapham."

"Mrs. Lapham, yes. I don't think the young ladies care so much about it."

"It must be for them. Aren't they ambitious?" asked Mrs. Corey, delicately feeling her way.

Her son thought awhile. Then he answered with a smile:

"No, I don't really think they are. They are unambitious, I should say." Mrs. Corey permitted herself a long breath. But her son added, "It's the parents who are ambitious for them," and her respiration became shorter again.

"Yes," she said.

"They're very simple, nice girls," pursued Corey. "I think you'll like the elder, when you come to know her."

When you come to know her. The words implied an expectation that the two families were to be better acquainted.

"Then she is more intellectual than her sister?" Mrs. Corey ventured.

"Intellectual?" repeated her son. "No; that isn't the word, quite. Though she certainly has more mind."

"The younger seemed very sensible."

"Oh, sensible, yes. And as practical as she's pretty. She can do all sorts of things, and likes to be doing them. Don't you think she's an extraordinary beauty?"

"Yes—yes, she is," said Mrs. Corey, at some cost.

"She's good, too," said Corey, "and perfectly innocent and transparent. I think you will like her the better the more you know her."

"I thought her very nice from the beginning," said the mother, heroically; and then nature asserted itself in her. "But I should be afraid that she might perhaps be a little bit tiresome at last; her range of ideas seemed so extremely limited."

"Yes, that's what I was afraid of. But, as a matter of fact, she isn't. She interests you by her very limitations. You can see the working of her mind, like that of a child. She isn't at all conscious even of her beauty."

"I don't believe young men can tell whether girls are conscious or not," said Mrs. Corey. "But I am not saying the Miss Laphams are not—" Her son sat musing, with an inattentive smile on his face. "What is it?"

"Oh, nothing. I was thinking of Miss Lapham and something she was saying. She's very droll, you know."

"The elder sister? Yes, you told me that. Can you see the workings of her mind too?"

"No; she's everything that's unexpected." Corey fell into another revery, and smiled again; but he did not offer to explain what amused him, and his mother would not ask.

"I don't know what to make of his admiring the girl so frankly," she said afterward to her husband. "That couldn't come naturally till after he had spoken to her, and I feel sure that he hasn't yet."

"You women haven't risen yet—it's an evidence of the backwardness of your sex—to a conception of the Bismarck idea in diplomacy. If a man praises one woman, you still think he's in love with another. Do you mean that because Tom didn't praise the elder sister so much, he *has* spoken to *her?*"[3]

3. Otto Von Bismarck (1815–98), known as the "Iron Chancellor" of Germany, was alleged to have revolutionized European diplomacy by telling his opponents exactly what he was going to do, and then actually doing it.

Mrs. Corey refused the consequence, saying that it did not follow. "Besides, he did praise her."

"You ought to be glad that matters are in such good shape, then. At any rate, you can do absolutely nothing."

"Oh! I know it," sighed Mrs. Corey. "I wish Tom would be a little opener with me."

"He's as open as it's in the nature of an American-born son to be with his parents. I dare say if you'd ask him plumply what he meant in regard to the young lady, he would have told you— if he knew."

"Why, don't you think he does know, Bromfield?"

"I'm not at all sure he does. You women think that because a young man dangles after a girl, or girls, he's attached to them. It doesn't at all follow. He dangles because he must, and doesn't know what to do with his time, and because they seem to like it. I dare say that Tom has dangled a good deal in this instance because there was nobody else in town."

"Do you really think so?"

"I throw out the suggestion. And it strikes me that a young lady couldn't do better than stay in or near Boston during the summer. Most of the young men are here, kept by business through the week, with evenings available only on the spot, or a few miles off. What was the proportion of the sexes at the sea-shore and the mountains?"

"Oh, twenty girls at least for even an excuse of a man. It's shameful."

"You see, I am right in one part of my theory. Why shouldn't I be right in the rest?"

"I wish you were. And yet I can't say that I do. Those things are very serious with girls. I shouldn't like Tom to have been going to see those people if he meant nothing by it."

"And you wouldn't like it if he did. You are difficult, my dear." Her husband pulled an open newspaper toward him from the table.

"I feel that it wouldn't be at all like him to do so," said Mrs. Corey, going on to entangle herself in her words, as women often do when their ideas are perfectly clear. "Don't go to reading, please, Bromfield! I am really worried about this matter. I must know how much it means. I can't let it go on so. I don't see how you can rest easy without knowing."

"I don't in the least know what's going to become of me when I die; and yet I sleep well," replied Bromfield Corey, putting his newspaper aside.

"Ah, but this is a very different thing."

"So much more serious? Well, what can you do? We had this out when you were here in the summer, and you agreed with me then that we could do nothing. The situation hasn't changed at all."

"Yes, it has; it has continued the same," said Mrs. Corey, again expressing the fact by a contradiction in terms. "I think I must ask Tom outright."

"You know you can't do that, my dear."

"Then why doesn't he tell us?"

"Ah, that's what *he* can't do, if he's making love to Miss Irene —that's her name, I believe—on the American plan. He will tell us after he has told *her*. That was the way I did. Don't ignore our own youth, Anna. It was a long while ago, I'll admit."

"It was very different," said Mrs. Corey, a little shaken.

"I don't see how. I dare say Mamma Lapham knows whether Tom is in love with her daughter or not; and no doubt Papa Lapham knows it at second hand. But we shall not know it until the girl herself does. Depend upon that. Your mother knew, and she told your father; but my poor father knew nothing about it till we were engaged; and I had been hanging about—dangling, as you call it——"

"No, no; *you* called it that."

"Was it I?—for a year or more."

The wife could not refuse to be a little consoled by the image of her young love which the words conjured up, however little she liked its relation to her son's interest in Irene Lapham. She smiled pensively. "Then you think it hasn't come to an understanding with them yet?"

"An understanding? Oh, probably."

"An explanation, then?"

"The only logical inference from what we've been saying is that it hasn't. But I don't ask you to accept it on that account. May I read now, my dear?"

"Yes, you may read now," said Mrs. Corey, with one of those

sighs which perhaps express a feminine sense of the unsatisfactoriness of husbands in general, rather than a personal discontent with her own.

"Thank you, my dear; then I think I'll smoke too," said Bromfield Corey, lighting a cigar.

She left him in peace, and she made no further attempt upon her son's confidence. But she was not inactive for that reason. She did not, of course, admit to herself, and far less to others, the motive with which she went to pay an early visit to the Laphams, who had now come up from Nantasket to Nankeen Square. She said to her daughters that she had always been a little ashamed of using her acquaintance with them to get money for her charity, and then seeming to drop it. Besides, it seemed to her that she ought somehow to recognize the business relation that Tom had formed with the father; they must not think that his family disapproved of what he had done.

"Yes, business is business," said Nanny, with a laugh. "Do you wish us to go with you again?"

"No; I will go alone this time," replied the mother with dignity.

Her coupé now found its way to Nankeen Square without difficulty, and she sent up a card, which Mrs. Lapham received in the presence of her daughter Penelope. [4]

"I presume I've got to see her," she gasped.

"Well, don't look so guilty, mother," joked the girl; "you haven't been doing anything so *very* wrong."

"It seems as if I *had*. I don't know what's come over me. I wasn't afraid of the woman before, but now I don't seem to feel as if I could look her in the face. He's been coming here of his own accord, and I fought against his coming long enough, goodness knows. I didn't want him to come. And as far forth as that goes, we're as respectable as they are; and your father's got twice their money, any day. We've no need to go begging for their favor. I guess they were glad enough to get him in with your father."

"Yes, those are all good points, mother," said the girl; "and if you keep saying them over, and count a hundred every time before you speak, I guess you'll worry through."

---

4. A coupé was a stylish four-wheel enclosed   carriage for two passengers with  the  driver's seat outside.

Mrs. Lapham had been fussing distractedly with her hair and ribbons, in preparation for her encounter with Mrs. Corey. She now drew in a long quivering breath, stared at her daughter without seeing her, and hurried downstairs. It was true that when she met Mrs. Corey before she had not been awed by her; but since then she had learned at least her own ignorance of the world, and she had talked over the things she had misconceived and the things she had shrewdly guessed so much that she could not meet her on the former footing of equality. In spite of as brave a spirit and as good a conscience as woman need have, Mrs. Lapham cringed inwardly, and tremulously wondered what her visitor had come for. She turned from pale to red, and was hardly coherent in her greetings; she did not know how they got to where Mrs. Corey was saying exactly the right things about her son's interest and satisfaction in his new business, and keeping her eyes fixed on Mrs. Lapham's, reading her uneasiness there, and making her feel, in spite of her indignant innocence, that she had taken a base advantage of her in her absence to get her son away from her and marry him to Irene. Then, presently, while this was painfully revolving itself in Mrs. Lapham's mind, she was aware of Mrs. Corey's asking if she was not to have the pleasure of seeing Miss Irene.

"No; she's out, just now," said Mrs. Lapham. "I don't know just when she'll be in. She went to get a book." And here she turned red again, knowing that Irene had gone to get the book because it was one that Corey had spoken of.

"Oh! I'm sorry," said Mrs. Corey. "I had hoped to see her. And your other daughter, whom I never met?"

"Penelope?" asked Mrs. Lapham, eased a little. "She is at home. I will go and call her." The Laphams had not yet thought of spending their superfluity on servants who could be rung for; they kept two girls and a man to look after the furnace, as they had for the last ten years. If Mrs. Lapham had rung in the parlor, her second girl would have gone to the street door to see who was there. She went upstairs for Penelope herself, and the girl, after some rebellious derision, returned with her.

Mrs. Corey took account of her, as Penelope withdrew to the other side of the room after their introduction, and sat down, indolently submissive on the surface to the tests to be applied, and following Mrs. Corey's lead of the conversation in her odd drawl.

"You young ladies will be glad to be getting into your new house," she said, politely.

"I don't know," said Penelope. "We're so used to this one."

Mrs. Corey looked a little baffled, but she said sympathetically, "Of course, you will be sorry to leave your old home."

Mrs. Lapham could not help putting in on behalf of her daughters: "I guess if it was left to the girls to say, we shouldn't leave it at all."

"Oh, indeed!" said Mrs. Corey; "are they so much attached? But I can quite understand it. My children would be heartbroken too if we were to leave the old place." She turned to Penelope. "But you must think of the lovely new house, and the beautiful position."

"Yes, I suppose we shall get used to them too," said Penelope, in response to this didactic consolation.

"Oh, I could even imagine your getting very fond of them," pursued Mrs. Corey, patronizingly. "My son has told me of the lovely outlook you're to have over the water. He thinks you have such a beautiful house. I believe he had the pleasure of meeting you all there when he first came home."

"Yes, I think he was our first visitor."

"He is a great admirer of your house," said Mrs. Corey, keeping her eyes very sharply, however politely, on Penelope's face, as if to surprise there the secret of any other great admiration of her son's that might helplessly show itself.

"Yes," said the girl, "he's been there several times with father; and he wouldn't be allowed to overlook any of its good points."

Her mother took a little more courage from her daughter's tranquillity.

"The girls make such fun of their father's excitement about his building, and the way he talks it into everybody."

"Oh, indeed!" said Mrs. Corey, with civil misunderstanding and inquiry.

Penelope flushed, and her mother went on: "I tell him he's more of a child about it than any of them."

"Young people are very philosophical nowadays," remarked Mrs. Corey.

"Yes, indeed," said Mrs. Lapham. "I tell them they've always had everything, so that nothing's a surprise to them. It was different with us in our young days."

"Yes," said Mrs. Corey, without assenting.

"I mean the Colonel and myself," explained Mrs. Lapham.

"Oh, yes—*yes!*" said Mrs. Corey.

"I'm sure," the former went on, rather helplessly, "*we* had to work hard enough for everything we got. And so we appreciated it."

"So many things were not done for young people then," said Mrs. Corey, not recognizing the early-hardships stand-point of Mrs. Lapham. "But I don't know that they are always the better for it now," she added, vaguely, but with the satisfaction we all feel in uttering a just commonplace.

"It's rather hard living up to blessings that you've always had," said Penelope.

"Yes," replied Mrs. Corey, distractedly, and coming back to her slowly from the virtuous distance to which she had absented herself. She looked at the girl searchingly again, as if to determine whether this were a touch of the drolling her son had spoken of. But she only added: "You will enjoy the sunsets on the Back Bay so much."

"Well, not unless they're new ones," said Penelope. "I don't believe I could promise to enjoy any sunsets that I was used to, a great deal."

Mrs. Corey looked at her with misgiving, hardening into dislike. "No," she breathed, vaguely. "My son spoke of the fine effect of the lights about the hotel from your cottage at Nantasket," she said to Mrs. Lapham.

"Yes, they're splendid!" exclaimed that lady. "I guess the girls went down every night with him to see them from the rocks."

"Yes," said Mrs. Corey, a little dryly; and she permitted herself to add: "He spoke of those rocks. I suppose both you young ladies spend a great deal of your time on them when you're there. At Nahant my children were constantly on them."

"Irene likes the rocks," said Penelope. "I don't care much about them,—especially at night."

"Oh, indeed! I suppose you find it quite as well looking at the lights comfortably from the veranda."

"No; you can't see them from the house."

"Oh," said Mrs. Corey. After a perceptible pause, she turned to Mrs. Lapham. "I don't know what my son would have done for a breath of sea air this summer, if you had not allowed him to come to Nantasket. He wasn't willing to leave his business long enough to go anywhere else."

"Yes, he's a born business man," responded Mrs. Lapham enthusiastically. "If it's born in you, it's bound to come out. That's what the Colonel is always saying about Mr. Corey. He says it's born in him to be a business man, and he can't help it." She recurred to Corey gladly because she felt that she had not said enough of him when his mother first spoke of his connection with the business. "I don't believe," she went on excitedly, "that Colonel Lapham has ever had anybody with him that he thought more of."

"You have *all* been very kind to my son," said Mrs. Corey in acknowledgment, and stiffly bowing a little, "and we feel greatly indebted to you. Very much so."

At these grateful expressions Mrs. Lapham reddened once more, and murmured that it had been very pleasant to them, she was sure. She glanced at her daughter for support, but Penelope was looking at Mrs. Corey, who doubtless saw her from the corner of her eyes, though she went on speaking to her mother.

"I was sorry to hear from him that Mr.—Colonel?—Lapham had not been quite well this summer. I hope he's better now?"

"Oh, yes, indeed," replied Mrs. Lapham; "he's all right now. He's hardly ever been sick, and he don't know how to take care of himself. That's all. We don't any of us; we're all so well."

"Health is a great blessing," sighed Mrs. Corey.

"Yes, so it is. How is your oldest daughter?" inquired Mrs. Lapham. "Is she as delicate as ever?"

"She seems to be rather better since we returned." And now Mrs. Corey, as if forced to the point, said bunglingly that the young ladies had wished to come with her, but had been detained. She based her statement upon Nanny's sarcastic demand; and, perhaps seeing it topple a little, she rose hastily, to get away from its fall. "But we shall hope for some—some other occasion," she said vaguely, and she put on a parting smile, and shook hands with Mrs. Lapham and Penelope, and then, after some lingering commonplaces, got herself out of the house.

Penelope and her mother were still looking at each other, and trying to grapple with the effect or purport of the visit, when Irene burst in upon them from the outside.

"Oh, mamma! wasn't that Mrs. Corey's carriage just drove away?"

Penelope answered with her laugh. "Yes! You've just missed the most delightful call, 'Rene. So easy and pleasant every way. Not a bit stiff! Mrs. Corey was so friendly! She didn't make *me* feel at all as if she'd bought me, and thought she'd given too much; and mother held up her head as if she were all wool and a yard wide, and she would just like to have anybody deny it."

In a few touches of mimicry she dashed off a sketch of the scene: her mother's trepidation, and Mrs. Corey's well-bred repose and polite scrutiny of them both. She ended by showing how she herself had sat huddled up in a dark corner, mute with fear.

"If she came to make us say and do the wrong thing, she must have gone away happy; and it's a pity you weren't here to help, Irene. I don't know that I aimed to make a bad impression, but I guess I succeeded—even beyond my deserts." She laughed; then suddenly she flashed out in fierce earnest. "If I missed doing anything that could make me as hateful to her as she made her-self to me——" She checked herself, and began to laugh. Her laugh broke, and the tears started into her eyes; she ran out of the room, and up the stairs.

"What—what does it mean?" asked Irene, in a daze.

Mrs. Lapham was still in the chilly torpor to which Mrs. Corey's call had reduced her. Penelope's vehemence did not rouse her. She only shook her head absently, and said, "I don't know."

"Why should Pen care what impression she made? I didn't suppose it would make any difference to her whether Mrs. Corey liked her or not."

"I didn't, either. But I could see that she was just as nervous as she could be, every minute of the time. I guess she didn't like Mrs. Corey any too well from the start, and she couldn't seem to act like herself."

"Tell me about it, mamma," said Irene, dropping into a chair.

Mrs. Corey described the interview to her husband on her return home. "Well, and what are your inferences?" he asked.

"They were extremely embarrassed and excited—that is, the

mother. I don't wish to do her injustice, but she certainly behaved consciously."

"You made her feel so, I dare say, Anna. I can imagine how terrible you must have been, in the character of an accusing spirit, too lady-like to say anything. What did you hint?"

"I hinted nothing," said Mrs. Corey, descending to the weakness of defending herself. "But I saw quite enough to convince me that the girl is in love with Tom, and the mother knows it."

"That was very unsatisfactory. I supposed you went to find out whether Tom was in love with the girl. Was she as pretty as ever?"

"I didn't see her; she was not at home; I saw her sister."

"I don't know that I follow you quite, Anna. But no matter. What was the sister like?"

"A thoroughly disagreeable young woman."

"What did she do?"

"Nothing. She's far too sly for that. But that was the impression."

"Then you didn't find her so amusing as Tom does?"

"I found her pert. There's no other word for it. She says things to puzzle you and put you out."

"Ah, that was worse than pert, Anna; that was criminal. Well, let us thank heaven the younger one is so pretty."

Mrs. Corey did not reply directly. "Bromfield," she said, after a moment of troubled silence, "I have been thinking over your plan, and I don't see why it isn't the right thing."

"What is my plan?" inquired Bromfield Corey.

"A dinner."

Her husband began to laugh. "Ah, you overdid the accusing-spirit business, and this is reparation." But Mrs. Corey hurried on, with combined dignity and anxiety:

"We can't ignore Tom's intimacy with them—it amounts to that; it will probably continue even if it's merely a fancy, and we must seem to know it; whatever comes of it, we can't disown it. They are very simple, unfashionable people, and unworldly; but I can't say that they are offensive, unless—unless," she added, in propitiation of her husband's smile, "unless the father—how *did* you find the father?" she implored.

"He will be very entertaining," said Corey, "if you start him on his paint. What was the disagreeable daughter like? Shall you have her?"

"She's little and dark. We must have them all," Mrs. Corey sighed. "Then you don't think a dinner would do?"

"Oh, yes, I do. As you say, we can't disown Tom's relation to them, whatever it is. We had much better recognize it, and make the best of the inevitable. I think a Lapham dinner would be delightful." He looked at her with delicate irony in his voice and smile, and she fetched another sigh, so deep and sore now that he laughed outright. "Perhaps," he suggested, "it would be the best way of curing Tom of his fancy, if he has one. He has been seeing her with the dangerous advantages which a mother knows how to give her daughter in the family circle, and with no means of comparing her with other girls. You must invite several other very pretty girls."

"Do you really think so, Bromfield?" asked Mrs. Corey, taking courage a little. "That might do." But her spirits visibly sank again. "I don't know any other girl half so pretty."

"Well, then, better bred."

"She is very lady-like, very modest, and pleasing."

"Well, more cultivated."

"Tom doesn't get on with such people."

"Oh, you *wish* him to marry her, I see."

"No, no——"

"Then you'd better give the dinner to bring them together, to promote the affair."

"You know I don't want to do that, Bromfield. But I feel that we must do something. If we don't, it has a clandestine appearance. It isn't just to them. A dinner won't leave us in any worse position, and may leave us in a better. Yes," said Mrs. Corey, after another thoughtful interval, "we must have them—have them all. It could be very simple."

"Ah, you can't give a dinner under a bushel, if I take your meaning, my dear. If we do this at all, we mustn't do it as if we were ashamed of it. We must ask people to meet them."

"Yes," sighed Mrs. Corey. "There are not many people in town yet," she added, with relief that caused her husband another smile. "There really seems a sort of fatality about it," she concluded, religiously.

"Then you had better not struggle against it. Go and reconcile Lily and Nanny to it as soon as possible."

Mrs. Corey blanched a little. "But don't you think it will be the best thing, Bromfield?"

"I do indeed, my dear. The only thing that shakes my faith in the scheme is the fact that I first suggested it. But if you have adopted it, it must be all right, Anna. I can't say that I expected it."

"No," said his wife, "it wouldn't do."

# XIII

HAVING distinctly given up the project of asking the Laphams to dinner, Mrs. Corey was able to carry it out with the courage of sinners who have sacrificed to virtue by frankly acknowledging its superiority to their intended transgression. She did not question but the Laphams would come; and she only doubted as to the people whom she should invite to meet them. She opened the matter with some trepidation to her daughters, but neither of them opposed her; they rather looked at the scheme from her own point of view, and agreed with her that nothing had really yet been done to wipe out the obligation to the Laphams helplessly contracted the summer before, and strengthened by that ill-advised application to Mrs. Lapham for charity. Not only the principal of their debt of gratitude remained, but the accruing interest. They said, What harm could giving the dinner possibly do them? They might ask any or all of their acquaintance without disadvantage to themselves; but it would be perfectly easy to give the dinner just the character they chose, and still flatter the ignorance of the Laphams. The trouble would be with Tom, if he were really interested in the girl; but he could not say anything if they made it a family dinner; he could not feel anything. They had each turned in her own mind, as it appeared from a comparison of ideas, to one of the most comprehensive of those cousinships which form the admiration and terror of the adventurer in Boston society. He finds himself hemmed in and left out at every turn by ramifications that forbid him all hope of safe personality in his comments on people; he is never less secure than when he hears some given Bostonian denouncing or ridiculing another. If he will be advised, he will guard himself from concurring in these criticisms, however just they appear, for the probability is that their object is a cousin of not more than one remove from the censor. When the alien hears a group of Boston ladies calling one another, and speaking of all their gentlemen friends, by the familiar abbreviations of their Christian names, he must feel keenly the exile to which he was born; but he is then, at least, in comparatively little danger; while these latent and tacit cousinships open pitfalls at every step around him, in a society where Middlesexes have married Essexes and produced Suffolks for two hundred and fifty years.[5]

These conditions, however, so perilous to the foreigner, are a source of strength and security to those native to them. An uncertain acquaintance may be so effectually involved in the meshes of such a cousinship, as never to be heard of outside of it; and tremendous stories are told of people who have spent a whole winter in Boston, in a whirl of gayety, and who, the original guests of the Suffolks, discover upon reflection that they have met no one but Essexes and Middlesexes.

Mrs. Corey's brother James came first into her mind, and she thought with uncommon toleration of the easy-going, uncritical good-nature of his wife. James Bellingham had been the adviser of her son throughout, and might be said to have actively promoted his connection with Lapham. She thought next of the widow of her cousin, Henry Bellingham, who had let her daughter marry that Western steamboat man, and was fond of her son-in-law; she might be expected at least to endure the paint-king and his family. The daughters insisted so strongly upon Mrs. Bellingham's son, Charles, that Mrs. Corey put him down—if he were in town; he might be in Central America; he got on with all sorts of people. It seemed to her that she might stop at this: four Laphams, five Coreys, and four Bellinghams were enough.

"That makes thirteen," said Nanny. "You can have Mr. and Mrs. Sewell."

"Yes, that is a good idea," assented Mrs. Corey. "He is our minister, and it is very proper."

"I don't see why you don't have Robert Chase. It is a pity he shouldn't see her—for the color."

"I don't quite like the idea of that," said Mrs. Corey; "but we can have him too, if it won't make too many." The painter had married into a poorer branch of the Coreys, and his wife was dead. "Is there any one else?"

5. Suffolk is the county in which Boston is located. Middlesex County, with its seat at Concord, and Essex County, with its seat at Salem, connect with Suffolk County on the north and west, and the three were inhabited by some of the oldest and therefore most prestigious families of New England.

"There is Miss Kingsbury."

"We have had her so much. She will begin to think we are using her."

"She won't mind; she's so good-natured."

"Well, then," the mother summed up, "there are four Laphams, five Coreys, four Bellinghams, one Chase, and one Kingsbury—fifteen. Oh! and two Sewells. Seventeen. Ten ladies and seven gentlemen. It doesn't balance very well, and it's too large."

"Perhaps some of the ladies won't come," suggested Lily.

"Oh, the ladies always come," said Nanny.

Their mother reflected. "Well, I will ask them. The ladies will refuse in time to let us pick up some gentlemen somewhere; some more artists. Why! we must have Mr. Seymour, the architect; he's a bachelor, and he's building their house, Tom says."

Her voice fell a little when she mentioned her son's name, and she told him of her plan, when he came home in the evening, with evident misgiving.

"What are you doing it for, mother?" he asked, looking at her with his honest eyes.

She dropped her own in a little confusion. "I won't do it at all, my dear," she said, "if you don't approve. But I thought——
You know we have never made any proper acknowledgment of their kindness to us at Baie St. Joan. Then in the winter, I'm ashamed to say, I got money from her for a charity I was interested in; and I hate the idea of merely *using* people in that way. And now your having been at their house this summer—we can't seem to disapprove of that; and your business relations to him——"

"Yes, I see," said Corey. "Do you think it amounts to a dinner?"

"Why, I don't know," returned his mother. "We shall have hardly any one out of our family connection."

"Well," Corey assented, "it might do. I suppose what you wish is to give them a pleasure."

"Why, certainly. Don't you think they'd like to come?"

"Oh, they'd like to come; but whether it would be a pleasure after they were here is another thing. I should have said that if you wanted to have them, they would enjoy better being simply asked to meet our own immediate family."

"That's what I thought of in the first place, but your father seemed to think it implied a social distrust of them; and we couldn't afford to have that appearance, even to ourselves."

"Perhaps he was right."

"And besides, it might seem a little significant."

Corey seemed inattentive to this consideration. "Whom did you think of asking?" His mother repeated the names. "Yes, that would do," he said, with a vague dissatisfaction.

"I won't have it at all, if you don't wish, Tom."

"Oh, yes, have it; perhaps you ought. Yes, I dare say it's right. What did you mean by a family dinner seeming significant?"

His mother hesitated. When it came to that, she did not like to recognize in his presence the anxieties that had troubled her. But "I don't know," she said, since she must. "I shouldn't want to give that young girl, or her mother, the idea that we wished to make more of the acquaintance than—than you did, Tom."

He looked at her absent-mindedly, as if he did not take her meaning. But he said, "Oh, yes, of course," and Mrs. Corey, in the uncertainty in which she seemed destined to remain concerning this affair, went off and wrote her invitation to Mrs. Lapham. Later in the evening, when they again found themselves alone, her son said, "I don't think I understood you, mother, in regard to the Laphams. I think I do now. I certainly don't wish you to make more of the acquaintance than I have done. It wouldn't be right; it might be very unfortunate. Don't give the dinner!"

"It's too late now, my son," said Mrs. Corey. "I sent my note to Mrs. Lapham an hour ago." Her courage rose at the trouble which showed in Corey's face. "But don't be annoyed by it, Tom. It isn't a family dinner, you know, and everything can be managed without embarrassment. If we take up the affair at this point, you will seem to have been merely acting for us; and they can't possibly understand anything more."

"Well, well! Let it go! I dare say it's all right. At any rate, it can't be helped now."

"I don't wish to help it, Tom," said Mrs. Corey, with a cheerfulness which the thought of the Laphams had never brought her before. "I am sure it is quite fit and proper, and we can make them have a very pleasant time. They are good, inoffensive people, and we owe it to ourselves not to be afraid to show that we have felt their kindness to us, and his appreciation of you."

"Well," consented Corey. The trouble that his mother had suddenly cast off was in his tone; but she was not sorry. It was quite time that he should think seriously of his attitude toward these people if he had not thought of it before, but, according to his father's theory, had been merely dangling.

It was a view of her son's character that could hardly have pleased her in different circumstances; yet it was now unquestionably a consolation if not wholly a pleasure. If she considered the Laphams at all, it was with the resignation which we feel at the evils of others, even when they have not brought them on themselves.

Mrs. Lapham, for her part, had spent the hours between Mrs. Corey's visit and her husband's coming home from business in reaching the same conclusion with regard to Corey; and her spirits were at the lowest when they sat down to supper. Irene was downcast with her; Penelope was purposely gay; and the Colonel was beginning, after his first plate of the boiled ham,— which, bristling with cloves, rounded its bulk on a wide platter before him,—to take note of the surrounding mood, when the door-bell jingled peremptorily, and the girl left waiting on the table to go and answer it. She returned at once with a note for Mrs. Lapham, which she read, and then, after a helpless survey of her family, read again.

"Why, what *is* it, mamma?" asked Irene; while the Colonel, who had taken up his carving-knife for another attack on the ham, held it drawn half across it.

"Why, *I* don't know what it *does* mean," answered Mrs. Lapham tremulously, and she let the girl take the note from her.

Irene ran it over, and then turned to the name at the end with a joyful cry and a flush that burned to the top of her forehead. Then she began to read it once more.

The Colonel dropped his knife and frowned impatiently, and Mrs. Lapham said, "You read it out loud, if you know what to make of it, Irene." But Irene, with a nervous scream of protest, handed it to her father, who performed the office.

"DEAR MRS. LAPHAM:

"Will you and General Lapham——"

"I didn't know I was a general," grumbled Lapham. "I

guess I shall have to be looking up my back pay. Who is it writes this, anyway?" he asked, turning the letter over for the signature.

"Oh, never mind. Read it through!" cried his wife, with a kindling glance of triumph at Penelope, and he resumed:
"—and your daughters give us the pleasure of your company at dinner on Thursday, the 28th, at half-past six.

"Yours sincerely,

"Anna B. Corey."

The brief invitation had been spread over two pages, and the Colonel had difficulties with the signature which he did not instantly surmount. When he had made out the name and pronounced it, he looked across at his wife for an explanation.

"*I* don't know what it all means," she said, shaking her head and speaking with a pleased flutter. "She was here this afternoon, and I should have said she had come to see how bad she *could* make us feel. I declare, I never felt so put down in my life by anybody."

"Why, what did she do? What did she say?" Lapham was ready, in his dense pride, to resent any affront to his blood, but doubtful, with the evidence of this invitation to the contrary, if any affront had been offered. Mrs. Lapham tried to tell him, but there was really nothing tangible; and when she came to put it into words, she could not make out a case. Her husband listened to her excited attempt, and then he said, with judicial superiority, "*I* guess nobody's been trying to make you feel bad, Persis. What would she go right home and invite you to dinner for, if she'd acted the way you say?"

In this view it did seem improbable, and Mrs. Lapham was shaken. She could only say, "Penelope felt just the way I did about it."

Lapham looked at the girl, who said, "Oh, *I* can't prove it! I begin to think it never happened. I guess it didn't."

"Humph!" said her father, and he sat frowning thoughtfully awhile—ignoring her mocking irony, or choosing to take her seriously. "You can't really put your finger on anything," he said to his wife, "and it ain't likely there *is* anything. Anyway, she's done the proper thing by you now."

Mrs. Lapham faltered between her lingering resentment and the appeals of her flattered vanity. She looked from Penelope's impassive face to the eager eyes of Irene. "Well—just as you *say*,

Silas. I don't know as she *was* so very bad. I guess may be she was embarrassed some——"

"That's what I told you, mamma, from the start," interrupted Irene. "Didn't I tell you she didn't mean anything by it? It's just the way she acted at Baie St. Joan, when she got well enough to realize what you'd done for her!"

Penelope broke into a laugh. "Is *that* her way of showing her gratitude? I'm sorry I didn't understand that before."

Irene made no effort to reply. She merely looked from her mother to her father with a grieved face for their protection, and Lapham said, "When we've done supper, you answer her, Persis. Say we'll come."

"With one exception," said Penelope.

"What do you mean?" demanded her father, with a mouth full of ham.

"Oh, nothing of importance. Merely that I'm not going."

Lapham gave himself time to swallow his morsel, and his rising wrath went down with it. "I guess you'll change your mind when the time comes," he said. "Anyway, Persis, you say we'll all come, and then, if Penelope don't want to go, you can excuse her after we get there. That's the best way."

None of them, apparently, saw any reason why the affair should not be left in this way, or had a sense of the awful and binding nature of a dinner-engagement. If she believed that Penelope would not finally change her mind and go, no doubt Mrs. Lapham thought that Mrs. Corey would easily excuse her absence. She did not find it so simple a matter to accept the invitation. Mrs. Corey had said "Dear Mrs. Lapham," but Mrs. Lapham had her doubts whether it would not be a servile imitation to say "Dear Mrs. Corey" in return; and she was tormented as to the proper phrasing throughout and the precise temperature which she should impart to her politeness. She wrote an unpracticed, uncharacteristic round hand, the same in which she used to set the children's copies at school, and she subscribed herself, after some hesitation between her husband's given name and her own, "Yours truly, Mrs. S. Lapham."

Penelope had gone to her room, without waiting to be asked to advise or criticise; but Irene had decided upon the paper, and, on the whole, Mrs. Lapham's note made a very decent appearance on the page.

When the furnace-man came, the Colonel sent him out to post it in the box at the corner of the square. He had determined not to say anything more about the matter before the girls, not choosing to let them see that he was elated; he tried to give the effect of its being an every-day sort of thing, abruptly closing the discussion with his order to Mrs. Lapham to accept; but he had remained swelling behind his newspaper during her prolonged struggle with her note, and he could no longer hide his elation when Irene followed her sister upstairs.

"Well, Pers," he demanded, "what do you say now?"

Mrs. Lapham had been sobered into something of her former misgiving by her difficulties with her note. "Well, I don't know what *to* say. I declare, I'm all mixed up about it, and I don't know as we've begun as we can carry out in promising to go. I presume," she sighed, "that we can *all* send some excuse at the last moment, if we don't want to go."

"I guess we can carry out, and I guess we sha'n't want to send any excuse," bragged the Colonel. "If we're ever going to be anybody at all, we've got to go and see how it's done. I presume we've got to give some sort of party when we get into the new house, and this gives the chance to ask 'em back again. You can't complain now but what they've made the advances, Persis?"

"No," said Mrs. Lapham, lifelessly; "I wonder why they wanted to do it. Oh, I suppose it's all right," she added in deprecation of the anger with her humility which she saw rising in her husband's face; "but if it's all going to be as much trouble as that letter, I'd rather be whipped. *I* don't know what I'm going to wear; or the girls, either. I do wonder—I've heard that people go to dinner in low-necks. Do you suppose it's the custom?"

"How should *I* know?" demanded the Colonel. "I guess you've got clothes enough. Any rate, you needn't fret about it. You just go round to White's, or Jordan & Marsh's, and ask for a dinner dress. I guess that'll settle it; they'll know. Get some of them imported dresses. I see 'em in the window every time I pass; lots of 'em." [6]

"Oh, it ain't the dress!" said Mrs. Lapham. "I don't suppose but what we could get along with that; and I want to do the best we can for the children; but *I* don't know what we're going to

6. Ralph H. White & Co. was a dry goods store on Winter Street in Boston. Jordan and Marsh & Co. began as "dressmakers" in the 1870s, but later became a leading department store.

talk about to those people when we get there. We haven't got anything in common with them. Oh, I don't say they're any better," she again made haste to say in arrest of her husband's resentment. "I don't believe they are; and I don't see why they should be. And there ain't anybody has got a better right to hold up their head than you have, Silas. You've got plenty of money, and you've made every cent of it."

"I guess I shouldn't amounted to much without you, Persis," interposed Lapham, moved to this justice by her praise.

"Oh, don't talk about *me !*" protested the wife. "Now that you've made it all right about Rogers, there ain't a thing in this world against you. But still, for all that, I can see—and I can feel it when I can't see it—that we're different from those people. They're well-meaning enough, and they'd excuse it, I presume, but we're too old to learn to be like them."

"The children ain't," said Lapham, shrewdly.

"No, the children ain't," admitted his wife, "and that's the only thing that reconciles me to it."

"You see how pleased Irene looked when I read it?"

"Yes, she was pleased."

"And I guess Penelope'll think better of it before the time comes."

"Oh, yes, we do it for them. But whether we're doing the best thing for 'em, goodness knows. I'm not saying anything against *him*. Irene'll be a lucky girl to get him, if she wants him. But there! I'd ten times rather she was going to marry such a fellow as *you* were, Si, that had to make every inch of his own way, and she had to help him. It's *in* her!"

Lapham laughed aloud for pleasure in his wife's fondness; but neither of them wished that he should respond directly to it. "I guess, if it wa'n't for me, he wouldn't have a much easier time. But don't you fret! It's all coming out right. That dinner ain't a thing for you to be uneasy about. It'll pass off perfectly easy and natural."

Lapham did not keep his courageous mind quite to the end of the week that followed. It was his theory not to let Corey see that he was set up about the invitation, and when the young man said politely that his mother was glad they were able to come, Lapham was very short with him. He said yes, he believed that Mrs. Lapham and the girls were going. Afterward he was afraid

Corey might not understand that he was coming too; but he did not know how to approach the subject again, and Corey did not, so he let it pass. It worried him to see all the preparation that his wife and Irene were making, and he tried to laugh at them for it; and it worried him to find that Penelope was making no preparation at all for herself, but only helping the others. He asked her what should she do if she changed her mind at the last moment and concluded to go, and she said she guessed she should not change her mind, but if she did, she would go to White's with him and get him to choose her an imported dress, he seemed to like them so much. He was too proud to mention the subject again to her.

Finally, all that dress-making in the house began to scare him with vague apprehensions in regard to his own dress. As soon as he had determined to go, an ideal of the figure in which he should go presented itself to his mind. He should not wear any dress-coat, because, for one thing, he considered that a man looked like a fool in a dress-coat, and, for another thing, he had none—had none on principle. He would go in a frock-coat and black pantaloons, and perhaps a white waistcoat, but a black cravat, anyway. But as soon as he developed this ideal to his family, which he did in pompous disdain of their anxieties about their own dress, they said he should not go so. Irene reminded him that he was the only person without a dress-coat at a corps-reunion dinner which he had taken her to some years before, and she remembered feeling awfully about it at the time. Mrs. Lapham, who would perhaps have agreed of herself, shook her head with misgiving. "I don't see but what you'll have to get you one, Si," she said. "I don't believe they *ever* go without 'em to a private house."

He held out openly, but on his way home the next day, in a sudden panic, he cast anchor before his tailor's door and got measured for a dress-coat. After that he began to be afflicted about his waistcoat, concerning which he had hitherto been airily indifferent. He tried to get opinion out of his family, but they were not so clear about it as they were about the frock. It ended in their buying a book of etiquette, which settled the question adversely to a white waistcoat. The author, however, after being very explicit in telling them not to eat with their knives, and above all not to pick their teeth with their forks,—a thing which he said no lady or gentleman ever did,—was still far from decided as to the kind of cravat Colonel Lapham ought to wear: shaken on other points, Lapham had begun to waver also concerning the black cravat. As to the question of gloves for the Colonel, which suddenly flashed upon him one evening, it appeared never to have entered the thoughts of the etiquette man, as Lapham called him. Other authors on the same subject were equally silent, and Irene could only remember having heard, in some vague sort of way, that gentlemen did not wear gloves so much any more.

Drops of perspiration gathered on Lapham's forehead in the anxiety of the debate; he groaned, and he swore a little in the compromise profanity which he used.

"I declare," said Penelope, where she sat purblindly sewing on a bit of dress for Irene, "the Colonel's clothes are as much trouble as anybody's. Why don't you go to Jordan & Marsh's and order one of the imported dresses for yourself, father?" That gave them all the relief of a laugh over it, the Colonel joining in piteously.

He had an awful longing to find out from Corey how he ought to go. He formulated and repeated over to himself an apparently careless question, such as, "Oh, by the way, Corey, where do you get your gloves?" This would naturally lead to some talk on the subject, which would, if properly managed, clear up the whole trouble. But Lapham found that he would rather die than ask this question, or any question that would bring up the dinner again. Corey did not recur to it, and Lapham avoided the matter with positive fierceness. He shunned talking with Corey at all, and suffered in grim silence.

One night, before they fell asleep, his wife said to him, "I was reading in one of those books to-day, and I don't believe but what we've made a mistake if Pen holds out that she won't go."

"Why?" demanded Lapham, in the dismay which beset him at every fresh recurrence to the subject.

"The book says that it's very impolite not to answer a dinner invitation promptly. Well, we've done that all right,—at first I didn't know but what we had been a little too quick, may be,—but then it says if you're not going, that it's the height of rudeness not to let them know at once, so that they can fill your place at the table."

The Colonel was silent for a while. "Well, I'm dumned," he

said finally, "if there seems to be any end to this thing. If it was to do over again, I'd say no for all of us."

"I've wished a hundred times they hadn't asked us; but it's too late to think about that *now*. The question is, what are we going to do about Penelope?"

"Oh, I guess she'll go, at the last moment."

"She says she won't. She took a prejudice against Mrs. Corey that day, and she can't seem to get over it."

"Well, then, hadn't you better write in the morning, as soon as you're up, that she ain't coming?"

Mrs. Lapham sighed helplessly. "I shouldn't know how to get it in. It's so late now; I don't see how I could have the face."

"Well, then, she's got to go, that's all."

"She's set she won't."

"And I'm set she shall," said Lapham, with the loud obstinacy of a man whose women always have their way.

Mrs. Lapham was not supported by the sturdiness of his proclamation.

But she did not know how to do what she knew she ought to do about Penelope, and she let matters drift. After all, the child had a right to stay at home if she did not wish to go. That was what Mrs. Lapham felt, and what she said to her husband next morning, bidding him let Penelope alone, unless she chose herself to go. She said it was too late now to do anything, and she must make the best excuse she could when she saw Mrs. Corey. She began to wish that Irene and her father would go and excuse her too. She could not help saying this, and then she and Lapham had some unpleasant words.

"Look here!" he cried. "Who wanted to go in for these people in the first place? Didn't you come home full of 'em last year, and want me to sell out here and move somewheres else because it didn't seem to suit 'em? And now you want to put it all on me! I ain't going to stand it."

"Hush!" said his wife. "Do you want to raise the house? I *didn't* put it on you, as you say. You took it on yourself. Ever since that fellow happened to come into the new house that day, you've been perfectly crazy to get in with them. And now you're so afraid you shall do something wrong before 'em, you don't hardly dare to say your life's your own. I declare, if you pester me any more about those gloves, Silas Lapham, I won't go."

"Do you suppose I want to go on my own account?" he demanded furiously.

"No," she admitted. "Of course I don't. I know very well that you're doing it for Irene; but, for goodness gracious sake, don't worry our lives out, and make yourself a perfect laughing-stock before the children."

With this modified concession from her, the quarrel closed in sullen silence on Lapham's part. The night before the dinner came, and the question of his gloves was still unsettled, and in a fair way to remain so. He had bought a pair, so as to be on the safe side, perspiring in company with the young lady who sold them, and who helped him try them on at the shop; his nails were still full of the powder which she had plentifully peppered into them in order to overcome the resistance of his blunt fingers. But he was uncertain whether he should wear them. They had found a book at last that said the ladies removed their gloves on sitting down at table, but it said nothing about gentlemen's gloves. He left his wife where she stood half hook-and-eyed at her glass in her new dress, and went down to his own den beyond the parlor. Before he shut his door he caught a glimpse of Irene trailing up and down before the long mirror in *her* new dress, followed by the seamstress on her knees; the woman had her mouth full of pins, and from time to time she made Irene stop till she could put one of the pins into her train; Penelope sat in a corner criticising and counseling. It made Lapham sick, and he despised himself and all his brood for the trouble they were taking. But another glance gave him a sight of the young girl's face in the mirror, beautiful and radiant with happiness; and his heart melted again with paternal tenderness and pride. It was going to be a great pleasure to Irene, and Lapham felt that she was bound to cut out anything there. He was vexed with Penelope that she was not going, too; he would have liked to have those people hear her talk. He held his door a little open, and listened to the things she was "getting off" there to Irene. He showed that he felt really hurt and disappointed about Penelope, and the girl's mother made her console him the next evening before they all drove away without her. "You try to look on the bright side of it, father. I guess you'll see that it's best I didn't go when you get there. Irene needn't open her lips, and they can all see how pretty she is; but they wouldn't know how smart I was unless I talked, and may be then they wouldn't."

This thrust at her father's simple vanity in her made him laugh; and then they drove away, and Penelope shut the door, and went upstairs with her lips firmly shutting in a sob.

# XIV

THE COREYS were one of the few old families who lingered in Bellingham Place, the handsome, quiet old street which the sympathetic observer must grieve to see abandoned to boarding-houses. The dwellings are stately and tall, and the whole place wears an air of aristocratic seclusion, which Mrs. Corey's father might well have thought assured when he left her his house there at his death. It is one of two evidently designed by the same architect who built some houses in a characteristic taste on Beacon street opposite the Common. It has a wooden portico, with slender fluted columns, which have always been painted white, and which, with the delicate moldings of the cornice, form the sole and sufficient decoration of the street front; nothing could be simpler, and nothing could be better. Within, the architect has again indulged his preference for the classic; the roof of the vestibule, wide and low, rests on marble columns, slim and fluted like the wooden columns without, and an ample staircase climbs in a graceful, easy curve from the tessellated pavement. Some carved Venetian *scrigni* stretched along the wall; a rug lay at the foot of the stairs; but otherwise the simple adequacy of the architectural intention had been respected, and the place looked bare to the eyes of the Laphams when they entered.[7] The Coreys had once kept a man, but when young Corey began his retrenchments the man had yielded to the neat maid who showed the Colonel into the reception-room and asked the ladies to walk up two flights.

He had his charges from Irene not to enter the drawing-room without her mother, and he spent five minutes in getting on his gloves, for he had desperately resolved to wear them at last. When he had them on, and let his large fists hang down on either

---

7. Venetian *scrigni*: (*Italian*), a chest or cabinet frequently used to safeguard jewels or other valuable objects.

side, they looked, in the saffron tint which the shop-girl said his gloves should be of, like canvased hams. He perspired with doubt as he climbed the stairs, and while he waited on the landing for Mrs. Lapham and Irene to come down from above, before going into the drawing-room, he stood staring at his hands, now open and now shut, and breathing hard. He heard quiet talking beyond the *portière* [8] within, and presently Tom Corey came out.

"Ah, Colonel Lapham! Very glad to see you."

Lapham shook hands with him and gasped, "Waiting for Mis' Lapham," to account for his presence. He had not been able to button his right glove, and he now began, with as much indifference as he could assume, to pull them both off, for he saw that Corey wore none. By the time he had stuffed them into the pocket of his coat-skirt his wife and daughter descended.

Corey welcomed them very cordially too, but looked a little mystified. Mrs. Lapham knew that he was silently inquiring for Penelope, and she did not know whether she ought to excuse her to him first or not. She said nothing, and after a glance toward the regions where Penelope might conjecturably be lingering, he held aside the *portière* for the Laphams to pass, and entered the room with them.

Mrs. Lapham had decided against low-necks on her own responsibility, and had intrenched herself in the safety of a black silk, in which she looked very handsome. Irene wore a dress of one of those shades which only a woman or an artist can decide to be green or blue, and which to other eyes looks both or neither, according to their degrees of ignorance. If it was more like a ball dress than a dinner dress, that might be excused to the exquisite effect. She trailed, a delicate splendor, across the carpet in her mother's somber wake, and the consciousness of success brought a vivid smile to her face. Lapham, pallid with anxiety lest he should somehow disgrace himself, giving thanks to God that he should have been spared the shame of wearing gloves where no one else did, but at the same time despairing that Corey should have seen him in them, had an unwonted aspect of almost pathetic refinement.

Mrs. Corey exchanged a quick glance of surprise and relief with her husband as she started across the room to meet her guests, and in her gratitude to them for being so irreproachable,

8. *portière*: (French) a door curtain.

she threw into her manner a warmth that people did not always find there. "General Lapham?" she said, shaking hands in quick succession with Mrs. Lapham and Irene, and now addressing herself to him.

"No, ma'am, only Colonel," said the honest man, but the lady did not hear him. She was introducing her husband to Lapham's wife and daughter, and Bromfield Corey was already shaking his hand and saying he was very glad to see him again, while he kept his artistic eye on Irene, and apparently could not take it off. Lily Corey gave the Lapham ladies a greeting which was physically rather than socially cold, and Nanny stood holding Irene's hand in both of hers a moment, and taking in her beauty and her style with a generous admiration which she could afford, for she was herself faultlessly dressed in the quiet taste of her city, and looking very pretty. The interval was long enough to let every man present confide his sense of Irene's beauty to every other; and then, as the party was small, Mrs. Corey made everybody acquainted. When Lapham had not quite understood, he held the person's hand, and, leaning urbanely forward, inquired, "What name?" He did that because a great man to whom he had been presented on the platform at a public meeting had done so to him, and he knew it must be right.

A little lull ensued upon the introductions, and Mrs. Corey said quietly to Mrs. Lapham, "Can I send any one to be of use to Miss Lapham?" as if Penelope must be in the dressing-room.

Mrs. Lapham turned fire-red, and the graceful forms in which she had been intending to excuse her daughter's absence went out of her head. "She isn't upstairs," she said, at her bluntest, as country people are when embarrassed. "She didn't feel just like coming to-night. I don't know as she's feeling very well."

Mrs. Corey emitted a very small "O!"—very small, very cold, —which began to grow larger and hotter and to burn into Mrs. Lapham's soul before Mrs. Corey could add, "I'm very sorry. It's nothing serious, I hope?"

Robert Chase, the painter, had not come, and Mrs. James Bellingham was not there, so that the table really balanced better without Penelope; but Mrs. Lapham could not know this, and did not deserve to know it. Mrs. Corey glanced round the room, as if to take account of her guests, and said to her husband, "I think we are all here, then," and he came forward and gave his arm to Mrs. Lapham. She perceived then that in their determination not to be the first to come, they had been the last, and must have kept the others waiting for them.

Lapham had never seen people go down to dinner arm-in-arm before, but he knew that his wife was distinguished in being taken out by the host, and he waited in jealous impatience to see if Tom Corey would offer his arm to Irene. He gave it to that big girl they called Miss Kingsbury, and the handsome old fellow whom Mrs. Corey had introduced as her cousin took Irene out. Lapham was startled from the misgiving in which this left him by Mrs. Corey's passing her hand through his arm, and he made a sudden movement forward, but felt himself gently restrained. They went out the last of all; he did not know why, but he submitted, and when they sat down he saw that Irene, although she had come in with that Mr. Bellingham, was seated beside young Corey, after all.

He fetched a long sigh of relief when he sank into his chair and felt himself safe from error if he kept a sharp lookout and did only what the others did. Bellingham had certain habits which he permitted himself, and one of these was tucking the corner of his napkin into his collar; he confessed himself an uncertain shot with a spoon, and defended his practice on the ground of neatness and common sense. Lapham put his napkin into his collar too, and then, seeing that no one but Bellingham did it, became alarmed and took it out again slyly. He never had wine on his table at home, and on principle he was a prohibitionist; but now he did not know just what to do about the glasses at the right of his plate. He had a notion to turn them all down, as he had read of a well-known politician's doing at a public dinner, to show that he did not take wine; but, after twiddling with one of them a moment, he let them be, for it seemed to him that would be a little too conspicuous, and he felt that every one was looking. He let the servant fill them all, and he drank out of each, not to appear odd. Later, he observed that the young ladies were not taking wine, and he was glad to see that Irene had refused it, and that Mrs. Lapham was letting it stand untasted. He did not know but he ought to decline some of the dishes, or at least leave most of some on his plate, but he was not able to decide; he took everything and ate everything.

He noticed that Mrs. Corey seemed to take no more trouble about the dinner than anybody, and Mr. Corey rather less; he was talking busily to Mrs. Lapham, and Lapham caught a word here and there that convinced him she was holding her own. He was getting on famously himself with Mrs. Corey, who had begun with him about his new house; he was telling her all about it, and giving her his ideas. Their conversation naturally included his architect across the table; Lapham had been delighted and secretly surprised to find the fellow there; and at something Seymour said the talk spread suddenly, and the pretty house he was building for Colonel Lapham became the general theme. Young Corey testified to its loveliness, and the architect said laughingly that if he had been able to make a nice thing of it, he owed it to the practical sympathy of his client.

"Practical sympathy is good," said Bromfield Corey; and, slanting his head confidentially to Mrs. Lapham, he added, "Does he bleed your husband, Mrs. Lapham? He's a terrible fellow for appropriations!"

Mrs. Lapham laughed, reddening consciously, and said she guessed the Colonel knew how to take care of himself. This struck Lapham, then draining his glass of sauterne, as wonderfully discreet in his wife.

Bromfield Corey leaned back in his chair a moment. "Well, after all, you can't say, with all your modern fuss about it, that you do much better now than the old fellows who built such houses as this."

"Ah," said the architect, "nobody can do better than well. Your house is in perfect taste; you know I've always admired it; and I don't think it's at all the worse for being old-fashioned. What we've done is largely to go back of the hideous style that raged after they forgot how to make this sort of house. But I think we may claim a better feeling for structure. We use better material, and more wisely; and by and by we shall work out something more characteristic and original."

"With your chocolates and olives, and your clutter of bric-à-brac?"

"All that's bad, of course, but I don't mean that. I don't wish to make you envious of Colonel Lapham, and modesty prevents my saying that his house is prettier,—though I may have my convictions,—but it's better built. All the new houses are better built. Now, your house——"

"Mrs. Corey's house," interrupted the host, with a burlesque haste in disclaiming responsibility for it that made them all laugh. "*My* ancestral halls are in Salem, and I'm told you couldn't drive a nail into their timbers; in fact, I don't know that you would want to do it."

"I should consider it a species of sacrilege," answered Seymour, "and I shall be far from pressing the point I was going to make against a house of Mrs. Corey's."

This won Seymour the easy laugh, and Lapham silently wondered that the fellow never got off any of those things to him.

"Well," said Corey, "you architects and the musicians are the true and only artistic creators. All the rest of us, sculptors, painters, novelists, and tailors, deal with forms that we have before us; we try to imitate, we try to represent. But you two sorts of artists create form. If you represent, you fail. Somehow or other you do evolve the camel out of your inner consciousness."[9]

"I will not deny the soft impeachment," said the architect, with a modest air.

"I dare say. And you'll own that it's very handsome of me to say this, after your unjustifiable attack on Mrs. Corey's property."

Bromfield Corey addressed himself again to Mrs. Lapham, and the talk subdivided itself as before. It lapsed so entirely away from the subject just in hand, that Lapham was left with rather a good idea, as he thought it, to perish in his mind, for want of a chance to express it. The only thing like a recurrence to what they had been saying was Bromfield Corey's warning Mrs. Lapham, in some connection that Lapham lost, against Miss Kingsbury. "She's worse," he was saying, "when it comes to appropriations than Seymour himself. Depend upon it, Mrs. Lapham, she will give you no peace of your mind, now she's met you, from this out. Her tender mercies are cruel; and I leave you to supply the context from your own scriptural knowledge. Beware of her, and all her works. She calls them works of charity; but heaven knows whether they are. It don't stand to reason that she gives the poor *all* the money she gets out of people. I have my own belief"—he gave it in a whisper for the whole table to hear— "that she spends it for champagne and cigars."

9. Bromfield Corey is wittily suggesting that the camel is such an astonishing looking animal that, like music, it must have been a mental invention; it certainly was not a shape already existing in nature that one could copy.

Lapham did not know about that kind of talking; but Miss Kingsbury seemed to enjoy the fun as much as anybody, and he laughed with the rest.

"You shall be asked to the very next debauch of the committee, Mr. Corey; then you won't dare expose us," said Miss Kingsbury.

"I wonder you haven't been down upon Corey to go to the Chardon street home and talk with your indigent Italians in their native tongue," said Charles Bellingham.[1] "I saw in the 'Transcript' the other night that you wanted some one for the work."[2]

"We did think of Mr. Corey," replied Miss Kingsbury; "but we reflected that he probably wouldn't talk with them at all; he would make them keep still to be sketched, and forget all about their wants."

Upon the theory that this was a fair return for Corey's pleasantry, the others laughed again.

"There is one charity," said Corey, pretending superiority to Miss Kingsbury's point, "that is so difficult I wonder it hasn't occurred to a lady of your courageous invention."

"Yes?" said Miss Kingsbury. "What is that?"

"The occupation, by deserving poor of neat habits, of all the beautiful, airy, wholesome houses that stand empty the whole summer long, while their owners are away in their lowly cots beside the sea."

"Yes, that is terrible," replied Miss Kingsbury, with quick earnestness, while her eyes grew moist. "I have often thought of our great, cool houses standing useless here, and the thousands of poor creatures stifling in their holes and dens, and the little children dying for wholesome shelter. How cruelly selfish we are!"

"That is a very comfortable sentiment, Miss Kingsbury," said Corey, "and must make you feel almost as if you had thrown open No. 931 to the whole North End. But I am serious about this matter. I spend my summers in town, and I occupy my own house, so that I can speak impartially and intelligently; and I tell you that in some of my walks on the Hill and down on the Back Bay, nothing but the surveillance of the local policeman

1. Chardon Street lay below Beacon Hill, to the north a few blocks, at the edge of an area that was to become the Italian enclave of North End. Evidently Miss Kingsbury is conducting some philanthropic work in the area.

2. *The Boston Evening Transcript,* founded in 1830, was a newspaper of such stifling respectability that in 1915 Thomas Stearns Eliot used the newspaper as a symbol of stuffiness in his satiric poem "The Boston Evening Transcript."

prevents me from applying dynamite to those long rows of close-shuttered, handsome, brutally insensible houses. If I were a poor man, with a sick child pining in some garret or cellar at the North End, I should break into one of them, and camp out on the grand piano.''

''Surely, Bromfield,'' said his wife, ''you don't consider what havoc such people would make with the furniture of a nice house!''

''That is true,'' answered Corey, with meek conviction. ''I never thought of that.''

''And if you were a poor man with a sick child, I doubt if you'd have so much heart for burglary as you have now,'' said James Bellingham.

''It's wonderful how patient they are,'' said the minister. ''The spectacle of the hopeless comfort the hard-working poor man sees must be hard to bear.''

Lapham wanted to speak up and say that he had been there himself, and knew how such a man felt. He wanted to tell them that generally a poor man was satisfied if he could make both ends meet; that he didn't envy any one his good luck, if he had earned it, so long as he wasn't running under himself. But before he could get the courage to address the whole table, Sewell added, ''I suppose he don't always think of it.''

''But some day he *will* think about it,'' said Corey. ''In fact, we rather invite him to think about it, in this country.''

''My brother-in-law,'' said Charles Bellingham, with the pride a man feels in a mentionably remarkable brother-in-law, ''has no end of fellows at work under him out there at Omaha, and he says it's the fellows from countries where they've been kept from thinking about it that are discontented. The Americans never make any trouble. They seem to understand that so long as we give unlimited opportunity, nobody has a right to complain.''

''What do you hear from Leslie?'' asked Mrs. Corey, turning from these profitless abstractions to Mrs. Bellingham.

''You know,'' said that lady in a lower tone, ''that there is another baby?''

''No! I hadn't heard of it!''

''Yes; a boy. They have named him after his uncle.''

''Yes,'' said Charles Bellingham, joining in. ''He is said to be a noble boy and to resemble me.''

"All boys of that tender age are noble," said Corey, "and look like anybody you wish them to resemble. Is Leslie still homesick for the bean-pots of her native Boston?"

"She is getting over it, I fancy," replied Mrs. Bellingham. "She's very much taken up with Mr. Blake's enterprises, and leads a very exciting life. She says she's like people who have been home from Europe three years; she's past the most poignant stage of regret, and hasn't reached the second, when they feel that they *must* go again."

Lapham leaned a little toward Mrs. Corey, and said of a picture which he saw on the wall opposite, "Picture of your daughter, I presume?"

"No; my daughter's grandmother. It's a Stuart Newton; he painted a great many Salem beauties. She was a Miss Polly Burroughs. My daughter *is* like her, don't you think?" They both looked at Nanny Corey and then at the portrait.[3] "Those pretty old-fashioned dresses are coming in again. I'm not surprised you took it for her. The others"—she referred to the other portraits more or less darkling on the walls—"are my people; mostly Copleys."[4]

These names, unknown to Lapham, went to his head like the wine he was drinking; they seemed to carry light for the moment, but a film of deeper darkness followed. He heard Charles Bellingham telling funny stories to Irene and trying to amuse the girl; she was laughing and seemed very happy. From time to time Bellingham took part in the general talk between the host and James Bellingham and Miss Kingsbury and that minister, Mr. Sewell. They talked of people mostly; it astonished Lapham to hear with what freedom they talked. They discussed these persons unsparingly; James Bellingham spoke of a man known to Lapham for his business success and great wealth as not a gentleman; his cousin Charles said he was surprised that the fellow had kept from being governor so long.

3. The painter Gilbert Stuart Newton (1794–1835) was born in Halifax, Nova Scotia, and studied in Boston under his uncle Gilbert Stuart, famous for his numerous portraits of George Washington. Newton is generally thought of as an English painter and remembered for his portraits of Thomas More and Sir Walter Scott. Miss Polly Burroughs is a fictitious grandmother, but the name Burroughs appears often in Massachusetts history. For instance, the Reverend George Burroughs, who graduated from Harvard in 1670, was the only clergyman executed as a witch during the Salem witch trials in 1692. Perhaps Howells intended some connection between this distinguished forebear and Mrs. Corey's character.

4. John S. Copley (1738–1815), a Boston portrait painter, fled to England at the start of the Revolution, which indicates that the portraits of Mrs. Corey's ancestors were painted before 1774.

When the latter turned from Irene to make one of these excursions into the general talk, young Corey talked to her; and Lapham caught some words from which it seemed that they were speaking of Penelope. It vexed him to think she had not come; she could have talked as well as any of them; she was just as bright; and Lapham was aware that Irene was not as bright, though when he looked at her face, triumphant in its young beauty and fondness, he said to himself that it did not make any difference. He felt that he was not holding up his end of the line, however. When some one spoke to him he could only summon a few words of reply, that seemed to lead to nothing; things often came into his mind appropriate to what they were saying, but before he could get them out they were off on something else; they jumped about so, he could not keep up; but he felt, all the same, that he was not doing himself justice.

At one time the talk ran off upon a subject that Lapham had never heard talked of before; but again he was vexed that Penelope was not there, to have her say; he believed that her say would have been worth hearing.

Miss Kingsbury leaned forward and asked Charles Bellingham if he had read "Tears, Idle Tears,"[5] the novel that was making such a sensation; and when he said no, she said she wondered at him. "It's perfectly heart-breaking, as you'll imagine from the name; but there's such a dear old-fashioned hero and heroine in it, who keep dying for each other all the way through and making the most wildly satisfactory and unnecessary sacrifices for each other. You feel as if you'd done them yourself."

"Ah, that's the secret of its success," said Bromfield Corey. "It flatters the reader by painting the characters colossal, but with his limp and stoop, so that he feels himself of their supernatural proportions. You've read it, Nanny?"

"Yes," said his daughter. "It ought to have been called 'Slop, Silly Slop.'"

"Oh, not quite *slop*, Nanny," pleaded Miss Kingsbury.

"It's astonishing," said Charles Bellingham, "how we do like the books that go for our heart-strings. And I really suppose that

---

5. "Tears, Idle Tears" is also the title of a sentimental poem by Alfred, Lord Tennyson (1809–92). The poem begins: "Tears, idle tears, I know not what they mean;/Tears from the depth of some divine despair/Rise in the heart, and gather to the eyes,/In looking on the happy autumn-fields/And thinking of the days that are no more" and continues to celebrate and cause sweet sadness.

you can't put a more popular thing than self-sacrifice into a novel. We do like to see people suffering sublimely."

"There was talk some years ago," said James Bellingham, "about novels going out."

"They're just coming in!" cried Miss Kingsbury.

"Yes," said Mr. Sewell, the minister. "And I don't think there ever was a time when they formed the whole intellectual experience of more people. They do greater mischief than ever."

"Don't be envious, parson," said the host.

"No," answered Sewell. "I should be glad of their help. But those novels with old-fashioned heroes and heroines in them— excuse me, Miss Kingsbury—are ruinous!"

"Don't you feel like a moral wreck, Miss Kingsbury?" asked the host.

But Sewell went on: "The novelists might be the greatest possible help to us if they painted life as it is, and human feelings in their true proportion and relation, but for the most part they have been and are altogether noxious."

This seemed sense to Lapham; but Bromfield Corey asked: "But what if life as it is isn't amusing? Aren't we to be amused?"

"Not to our hurt," sturdily answered the minister. "And the self-sacrifice painted in most novels like this——"

"Slop, Silly Slop?" suggested the proud father of the inventor of the phrase.

"Yes—is nothing but psychical suicide, and is as wholly immoral as the spectacle of a man falling upon his sword."

"Well, I don't know but you're right, parson," said the host; and the minister, who had apparently got upon a battle-horse of his, careered onward in spite of some tacit attempts of his wife to seize the bridle.

"Right? To be sure I am right. The whole business of love, and love-making and marrying, is painted by the novelists in a monstrous disproportion to the other relations of life. Love is very sweet, very pretty——"

"Oh, *thank* you, Mr. Sewell," said Nanny Corey in a way that set them all laughing.

"But it's the affair, commonly, of very young people, who have not yet character and experience enough to make them interesting. In novels it's treated, not only as if it were the chief interest of life, but the sole interest of the lives of two ridiculous young persons; and it is taught that love is perpetual, that the glow of a true passion lasts forever; and that it is sacrilege to think or act otherwise."

"Well, but isn't that true, Mr. Sewell?" pleaded Miss Kingsbury.

"I have known some most estimable people who had married a second time," said the minister, and then he had the applause with him. Lapham wanted to make some open recognition of his good sense, but could not.

"I suppose the passion itself has been a good deal changed," said Bromfield Corey, "since the poets began to idealize it in the days of chivalry."

"Yes; and it ought to be changed again," said Mr. Sewell.

"What! Back?"

"I don't say that. But it ought to be recognized as something natural and mortal, and divine honors, which belong to righteousness alone, ought not to be paid it."

"Oh, you ask too much, parson," laughed his host, and the talk wandered away to something else.

It was not an elaborate dinner; but Lapham was used to having everything on the table at once, and this succession of dishes bewildered him; he was afraid perhaps he was eating too much. He now no longer made any pretense of not drinking his wine, for he was thirsty, and there was no more water, and he hated to ask for any. The ice-cream came, and then the fruit. Suddenly Mrs. Corey rose and said across the table to her husband, "I suppose you will want your coffee here." And he replied, "Yes; we'll join you at tea."

The ladies all rose, and the gentlemen got up with them. Lapham started to follow Mrs. Corey, but the other men merely stood in their places, except young Corey, who ran and opened the door for his mother. Lapham thought with shame that it was he who ought to have done that; but no one seemed to notice, and he sat down again gladly, after kicking out one of his legs which had gone to sleep.

They brought in cigars with coffee, and Bromfield Corey advised Lapham to take one that he chose for him. Lapham confessed that he liked a good cigar about as well as anybody, and Corey said: "These are new. I had an Englishman here the other day who was smoking old cigars in the superstition that tobacco improved with age, like wine."

"Ah," said Lapham, "anybody who had ever lived off a tobacco country could tell him better than that." With the fuming cigar between his lips he felt more at home than he had before. He turned sidewise in his chair and, resting one arm on the back, intertwined the fingers of both hands, and smoked at large ease.

James Bellingham came and sat down by him. "Colonel Lapham, weren't you with the 96th Vermont when they charged across the river in front of Pickensburg, and the rebel battery opened fire on them in the water?" [6]

Lapham slowly shut his eyes and slowly dropped his head for assent, letting out a white volume of smoke from the corner of his mouth.

"I thought so," said Bellingham. "I was with the 85th Massachusetts, and I sha'n't forget that slaughter. We were all new to it still. Perhaps that's why it made such an impression."

"I don't know," suggested Charles Bellingham. "Was there anything much more impressive afterward? I read of it out in Missouri, where I was stationed at the time, and I recollect the talk of some old army men about it. They said that death-rate couldn't be beaten. I don't know that it ever was."

"About one in five of us got out safe," said Lapham, breaking his cigar-ash off on the edge of a plate. James Bellingham reached him a bottle of Apollinaris. He drank a glass, and then went on smoking. [7]

They all waited, as if expecting him to speak, and then Corey said: "How incredible those things seem already! You gentlemen *know* that they happened; but are you still able to believe it?"

"Ah, nobody *feels* that anything happened," said Charles Bellingham. "The past of one's experience doesn't differ a great deal from the past of one's knowledge. It isn't much more probable; it's really a great deal less vivid than some scenes in a novel that one read when a boy."

"I'm not sure of that," said James Bellingham.

"Well, James, neither am I," consented his cousin, helping himself from Lapham's Apollinaris bottle. "There would be very little talking at dinner if one only said the things that one was sure of."

6. The 96th Vermont is a fictional Civil War regiment. The Pickensburg charge is also fictional.

7. Apollinaris was an imported, bottled mineral water.

The others laughed, and Bromfield Corey remarked thought-fully, "What astonishes the craven civilian in all these things is the abundance—the superabundance—of heroism. The cowards were the exception; the men that were ready to die, the rule."

"The woods were full of them," said Lapham, without taking his cigar from his mouth.

"That's a nice little touch in 'School,' " interposed Charles Bellingham, "where the girl says to the fellow who was at Inker-man, 'I should think you would be so proud of it,' and he reflects awhile, and says, 'Well, the fact is, you know, there were so many of us.' " [8]

"Yes, I remember that," said James Bellingham, smiling for pleasure in it. "But I don't see why you claim the credit of being a craven civilian, Bromfield," he added, with a friendly glance at his brother-in-law, and with the willingness Boston men often show to turn one another's good points to the light in company; bred so intimately together at school and college and in society, they all know these points. "A man who was out with Garibaldi in '48," continued James Bellingham. [9]

"Oh, a little amateur red-shirting," Corey interrupted in deprecation. "But even if you choose to dispute my claim, what has become of all the heroism? Tom, how many club men do you know who would think it sweet and fitting to die for their country?"

"I can't think of a great many at the moment, sir," replied the son, with the modesty of his generation.

"And I couldn't in '61," said his uncle. "Nevertheless they were there."

"Then your theory is that it's the occasion that is wanting," said Bromfield Corey. "But why shouldn't civil-service reform, and the resumption of specie payment, and a tariff for revenue only, inspire heroes? They are all good causes."

"It's the occasion that's wanting," said James Bellingham, ignoring the *persiflage.* "And I'm very glad of it."

"So am I," said Lapham, with a depth of feeling that expressed itself in spite of the haze in which his brain seemed to float. There

8. *School* (1869) is a play by the English actor and dramatist Thomas William Robertson (1829–71). Inkerman was a suburb of Sevastopol where in 1854 the British and French defeated the Russians in the Crimean War.

9. Giuseppe Garibaldi (1807–82), Italian patriot and soldier, attempted in 1848 to drive the occupying Austrian army out of Italy. The volunteer soldiers who served with Garibaldi were called the Red Shirts.

was a great deal of the talk that he could not follow; it was too quick for him; but here was something he was clear of. "I don't want to see any more men killed in my time." Something serious, something somber must lurk behind these words, and they waited for Lapham to say more; but the haze closed round him again, and he remained silent, drinking Apollinaris.

"We non-combatants were notoriously reluctant to give up fighting," said Mr. Sewell, the minister; "but I incline to think Colonel Lapham and Mr. Bellingham may be right. I dare say we shall have the heroism again if we have the occasion. Till it comes, we must content ourselves with the every-day generosities and sacrifices. They make up in quantity what they lack in quality, perhaps."

"They're not so picturesque," said Bromfield Corey. "You can paint a man dying for his country, but you can't express on canvas a man fulfilling the duties of a good citizen."

"Perhaps the novelists will get at him by and by," suggested Charles Bellingham. "If I were one of these fellows, I shouldn't propose to myself anything short of that."

"What: the commonplace?" asked his cousin.

"Commonplace? The commonplace is just that light, impalpable, aërial essence which they've never got into their confounded books yet. The novelist who could interpret the common feelings of commonplace people would have the answer to 'the riddle of the painful earth' on his tongue."[1]

"Oh, not so bad as that, I hope," said the host; and Lapham looked from one to the other, trying to make out what they were at. He had never been so up a tree before.

"I suppose it isn't well for us to see human nature at white heat habitually," continued Bromfield Corey, after a while. "It would make us vain of our species. Many a poor fellow in that war and in many another has gone into battle simply and purely for his country's sake, not knowing whether, if he laid down his life, he should ever find it again, or whether, if he took it up hereafter, he should take it up in heaven or hell. Come, parson!" he said, turning to the minister, "what has ever been conceived of omnipotence, of omniscience, so sublime, so divine as that?"

"Nothing," answered the minister, quietly. "God has never

---

1. "The riddle of the painful earth" occurs in Tennyson's "The Palace of Art" (1. 213), a poem in which he affirms the need for even the artistic soul to pay heed to ordinary human nature.

been imagined at all. But if you suppose such a man as that was Authorized, I think it will help you to imagine what God must be."

"There's sense in that," said Lapham. He took his cigar out of his mouth, and pulled his chair a little toward the table, on which he placed his ponderous fore-arms. "I want to tell you about a fellow I had in my own company when we first went out. We were all privates to begin with; after a while they elected me captain—I'd had the tavern stand, and most of 'em knew me. But Jim Millon never got to be anything more than corporal; corporal when he was killed." The others arrested themselves in various attitudes of attention, and remained listening to Lapham with an interest that profoundly flattered him. Now, at last, he felt that he was holding up his end of the rope. "I can't say he went into the thing from the highest motives, altogether; our motives are always pretty badly mixed, and when there's such a hurrah-boys as there was then, you can't tell which is which. I suppose Jim Millon's wife was enough to account for his going, herself. She was a pretty bad assortment," said Lapham, lowering his voice and glancing round at the door to make sure that it was shut, "and she used to lead Jim *one* kind of life. Well, sir," continued Lapham, synthetizing his auditors in that form of address, "that fellow used to save every cent of his pay and send it to that woman. Used to get me to do it for him. I tried to stop him. 'Why, Jim,' said I, 'you know what she'll do with it.' 'That's so, Cap,' says he, 'but I don't know what she'll do without it.' And it did keep her straight—straight as a string—as long as Jim lasted. Seemed as if there was something mysterious about it. They had a little girl,—about as old as my oldest girl,—and Jim used to talk to me about her. Guess he done it as much for her as for the mother; and he said to me before the last action we went into, 'I should like to turn tail and run, Cap. I ain't comin' out o' this one. But I don't suppose it would do.' 'Well, not for you, Jim,' said I. 'I want to live,' he says; and he bust out crying right there in my tent. 'I want to live for poor Molly and Zerrilla'— that's what they called the little one; I dunno where they got the name. 'I ain't ever had half a chance; and now she's doing better, and I believe we should get along after this.' He set there cryin' like a baby. But he wa'n't no baby when he went into action. I hated to look at him after it was over, not so much because he'd got a ball that was meant for me by a sharp-shooter—he saw the devil takin' aim, and he jumped to warn me—as because he didn't look like Jim; he looked like—fun; all desperate and savage. I guess he died hard."

The story made its impression, and Lapham saw it. "Now I say," he resumed, as if he felt that he was going to do himself justice, and say something to heighten the effect his story had produced. At the same time, he was aware of a certain want of clearness. He had the idea, but it floated vague, elusive, in his brain. He looked about as if for something to precipitate it in tangible shape.

"Apollinaris?" asked Charles Bellingham, handing the bottle from the other side. He had drawn his chair closer than the rest to Lapham's, and was listening with great interest. When Mrs. Corey asked him to meet Lapham he accepted gladly. "You know I go in for that sort of thing, Anna. Since Leslie's affair we're rather bound to do it. And I think we meet these practical fellows too little. There's always something original about them." He might naturally have believed that the reward of his faith was coming. [2]

"Thanks, I will take some of this wine," said Lapham, pouring himself a glass of Madeira from a black and dusty bottle caressed by a label bearing the date of the vintage.[3] He tossed off the wine, unconscious of its preciousness, and waited for the result. That cloudiness in his brain disappeared before it, but a mere blank remained. He not only could not remember what he was going to say, but he could not recall what they had been talking about. They waited, looking at him, and he stared at them in return. After a while he heard the host saying, "Shall we join the ladies?"

Lapham went, trying to think what had happened. It seemed to him a long time since he had drunk that wine.

Miss Corey gave him a cup of tea, where he stood aloof from his wife, who was talking with Miss Kingsbury and Mrs. Sewell; Irene was with Miss Nanny Corey. He could not hear what they were talking about; but if Penelope had come he knew that she would have done them all credit. He meant to let her know how he felt about her behavior when he got home. It was a shame for

---

2. Charles Bellingham is referring to the marriage of his sister to a "Western steamboat man," mentioned in Chapter XIII.

3. Madiera is a fortified wine which resembles sherry.

her to miss such a chance. Irene was looking beautiful, as pretty as all the rest of them put together, but she was not talking, and Lapham perceived that at a dinner party you ought to talk. He was himself conscious of having talked very well. He now wore an air of great dignity, and, in conversing with the other gentlemen, he used a grave and weighty deliberation. Some of them wanted him to go into the library. There he gave his ideas of books. He said he had not much time for anything but the papers; but he was going to have a complete library in his new place. He made an elaborate acknowledgment to Bromfield Corey of his son's kindness in suggesting books for his library; he said that he had ordered them all, and that he meant to have pictures. He asked Mr. Corey who was about the best American painter going now. "I don't set up to be a judge of pictures, but I know what I like," he said. He lost the reserve which he had maintained earlier, and began to boast. He himself introduced the subject of his paint, in a natural transition from pictures; he said Mr. Corey must take a run up to Lapham with him some day, and see the Works; they would interest him, and he would drive him round the country; he kept most of his horses up there, and he could show Mr. Corey some of the finest Jersey grades in the country.[4] He told about his brother William, the judge at Dubuque; and a farm he had out there that paid for itself every year in wheat. As he cast off all fear, his voice rose, and he hammered his arm-chair with the thick of his hand for emphasis. Mr. Corey seemed impressed; he sat perfectly quiet, listening, and Lapham saw the other gentlemen stop in their talk every now and then to listen. After this proof of his ability to interest them, he would have liked to have Mrs. Lapham suggest again that he was unequal to their society, or to the society of anybody else. He surprised himself by his ease among men whose names had hitherto overawed him. He got to calling Bromfield Corey by his surname alone. He did not understand why young Corey seemed so preoccupied, and he took occasion to tell the company how he had said to his wife the first time he saw that fellow that he could make a man of him if he had him in the business; and he guessed he was not mistaken. He began to tell stories of the different

---

4. "Jersey grades": in cattle breeding "grades" are produced by cross-breeding native stock with pedigreed pure breeds. Silas seems to imply that he is a gentleman farmer who keeps stock not so much for profit as to improve American stock through scientific experiment.

young men he had had in his employ. At last he had the talk altogether to himself; no one else talked, and he talked unceasingly. It was a great time; it was a triumph.

He was in this successful mood when word came to him that Mrs. Lapham was going; Tom Corey seemed to have brought it, but he was not sure. Anyway, he was not going to hurry. He made cordial invitations to each of the gentlemen to drop in and see him at his office, and would not be satisfied till he had exacted a promise from each. He told Charles Bellingham that he liked him, and assured James Bellingham that it had always been his ambition to know him, and that if any one had said when he first came to Boston that in less than ten years he should be hobnobbing with Jim Bellingham, he should have told that person he lied. He would have told anybody he lied that had told him ten years ago that a son of Bromfield Corey would have come and asked him to take him into the business. Ten years ago he, Silas Lapham, had come to Boston, a little worse off than nothing at all, for he was in debt for half the money that he had bought out his partner with, and here he was now worth a million, and meeting you gentlemen like one of you. And every cent of that was honest money,—no speculation,—every copper of it for value received. And here, only the other day, his old partner, who had been going to the dogs ever since he went out of the business, came and borrowed twenty thousand dollars of him! Lapham lent it because his wife wanted him to: she had always felt bad about the fellow's having to go out of the business.

He took leave of Mr. Sewell with patronizing affection, and bade him come to him if he ever got into a tight place with his parish work; he would let him have all the money he wanted; he had more money than he knew what to do with. "Why, when your wife sent to mine last fall," he said, turning to Mr. Corey, "I drew my check for five hundred dollars, but my wife wouldn't take more than one hundred; said she wasn't going to show off before Mrs. Corey. I call that a pretty good joke on Mrs. Corey. I must tell her how Mrs. Lapham done her out of a cool four hundred dollars."

He started toward the door of the drawing-room to take leave of the ladies; but Tom Corey was at his elbow, saying, "I think Mrs. Lapham is waiting for you below, sir," and in obeying the direction Corey gave him toward another door he forgot all about his purpose, and came away without saying good-night to his hostess.

Mrs. Lapham had not known how soon she ought to go, and had no idea that in her quality of chief guest she was keepihg the others. She staid till eleven o'clock, and was a little frightened when she found what time it was; but Mrs. Corey, without pressing her to stay longer, had said it was not at all late. She and Irene had had a perfect time. Everybody had been very polite; on the way home they celebrated the amiability of both the Miss Coreys and of Miss Kingsbury. Mrs. Lapham thought that Mrs. Bellingham was about the pleasantest person she ever saw; she had told her all about her married daughter who had married an inventor and gone to live in Omaha—a Mrs. Blake.

"If it's that car-wheel Blake," said Lapham, proudly, "I know all about him. I've sold him tons of the paint."

"Pooh, papa! How you do smell of smoking!" cried Irene.

"Pretty strong, eh?" laughed Lapham, letting down a window of the carriage. His heart was throbbing wildly in the close air, and he was glad of the rush of cold that came in, though it stopped his tongue, and he listened more and more drowsily to the rejoicings that his wife and daughter exchanged. He meant to have them wake Penelope up and tell her what she had lost; but when he reached home he was too sleepy to suggest it. He fell asleep as soon as his head touched the pillow, full of supreme triumph.

But in the morning his skull was sore with the unconscious, night-long ache; and he rose cross and taciturn. They had a silent breakfast. In the cold gray light of the morning the glories of the night before showed poorer. Here and there a painful doubt obtruded itself and marred them with its awkward shadow. Penelope sent down word that she was not well, and was not coming to breakfast, and Lapham was glad to go to his office without seeing her.

He was severe and silent all day with his clerks, and peremptory with customers. Of Corey he was slyly observant, and as the day wore away he grew more restively conscious. He sent out word by his office-boy that he would like to see Mr. Corey for a few minutes after closing. The type-writer girl had lingered too, as if she wished to speak with him, and Corey stood in abeyance as she went toward Lapham's door.

"Can't see you to-night, Zerrilla," he said bluffly, but not unkindly. "Perhaps I'll call at the house, if it's important."

"It is," said the girl, with a spoiled air of insistence.

"Well," said Lapham; and, nodding to Corey to enter, he closed the door upon her. Then he turned to the young man and demanded: "Was I drunk last night?"

## XV

LAPHAM's strenuous face was broken up with the emotions that had forced him to this question: shame, fear of the things that must have been thought of him, mixed with a faint hope that he might be mistaken, which died out at the shocked and pitying look in Corey's eyes.

"Was I drunk?" he repeated. "I ask you, because I was never touched by drink in my life before, and I don't know." He stood with his huge hands trembling on the back of his chair, and his dry lips apart, as he stared at Corey.

"That is what every one understood, Colonel Lapham," said the young man. "Every one saw how it was. Don't——"

"Did they talk it over after I left?" asked Lapham, vulgarly.

"Excuse me," said Corey, blushing, "my father doesn't talk his guests over with one another." He added, with youthful superfluity, "You were among gentlemen."

"I was the only one that wasn't a gentleman there!" lamented Lapham. "I disgraced you! I disgraced my family! I mortified your father before his friends!" His head dropped. "I showed that I wasn't fit to go with you. I'm not fit for any decent place. What did I say? What did I do?" he asked, suddenly lifting his head and confronting Corey. "Out with it! If you could bear to see it and hear it, I had ought to bear to know it!"

"There was nothing—really nothing," said Corey. "Beyond the fact that you were not quite yourself, there was nothing whatever. My father *did* speak of it to me," he confessed, "when we were alone. He said that he was afraid we had not been thoughtful of you, if you were in the habit of taking only water; I told him I had not seen wine at your table. The others said nothing about you."

"Ah, but what did they think!"

"Probably what we did: that it was purely a misfortune—an accident."

"I wasn't fit to be there," persisted Lapham. "Do you want to leave?" he asked, with savage abruptness.

"Leave?" faltered the young man.

"Yes; quit the business? Cut the whole connection?"

"I haven't the remotest idea of it!" cried Corey in amazement. "Why in the world should I?"

"Because you're a gentleman, and I'm not, and it ain't right I should be over you. If you want to go, I know some parties that would be glad to get you. I will give you up if you want to go before anything worse happens, and I sha'n't blame you. I can help you to something better than I can offer you here, and I will."

"There's no question of my going, unless you wish it," said Corey. "If you do——"

"Will you tell your father," interrupted Lapham, "that I had a notion all the time that I was acting the drunken blackguard, and that I've suffered for it all day? Will you tell him I don't want him to notice me if we ever meet, and that I know I'm not fit to associate with gentlemen in anything but a business way, if I am that?"

"Certainly, I shall do nothing of the kind," retorted Corey. "I can't listen to you any longer. What you say is shocking to me—shocking in a way you can't think."

"Why, man!" exclaimed Lapham, with astonishment; "if *I* can stand it, *you* can!"

"No," said Corey, with a sick look, "that doesn't follow. You may denounce yourself, if you will; but I have my reasons for refusing to hear you—my reasons why I *can't* hear you. If you say another word I must go away."

"*I* don't understand you," faltered Lapham, in bewilderment, which absorbed even his shame.

"You exaggerate the effect of what has happened," said the young man. "It's enough, more than enough, for you to have mentioned the matter to me, and I think it's unbecoming in me to hear you."

He made a movement toward the door, but Lapham stopped him with the tragic humility of his appeal. "Don't go yet! I can't let you. I've disgusted you,—I see that; but I didn't mean to. I—I take it back."

"Oh, there's nothing to take back," said Corey, with a repressed shudder for the abasement which he had seen. "But let us say no more about it—think no more. There wasn't one of the gentlemen present last night who didn't understand the matter precisely as my father and I did, and that fact must end it between us two."

He went out into the larger office beyond, leaving Lapham helpless to prevent his going. It had become a vital necessity with him to think the best of Lapham, but his mind was in a whirl of whatever thoughts were most injurious. He thought of him the night before in the company of those ladies and gentlemen, and he quivered in resentment of his vulgar, braggart, uncouth nature. He recognized his own allegiance to the exclusiveness to which he was born and bred, as a man perceives his duty to his country when her rights are invaded. His eye fell on the porter going about in his shirt-sleeves to make the place fast for the night, and he said to himself that Dennis was not more plebeian than his master; that the gross appetites, the blunt sense, the purblind ambition, the stupid arrogance were the same in both, and the difference was in a brute will that probably left the porter the gentler man of the two. The very innocence of Lapham's life in the direction in which he had erred wrought against him in the young man's mood: it contained the insult of clownish inexperience. Amidst the stings and flashes of his wounded pride, all the social traditions, all the habits of feeling, which he had silenced more and more by force of will during the past months, asserted their natural sway, and he rioted in his contempt of the offensive boor, who was even more offensive in his shame than in his trespass. He said to himself that he was a Corey, as if that were somewhat; yet he knew that at the bottom of his heart all the time was that which must control him at last, and which seemed sweetly to be suffering his rebellion, secure of his submission in the end. It was almost with the girl's voice that it seemed to plead with him, to undo in him, effect by effect, the work of his indignant resentment, to set all things in another and fairer light, to give him hopes, to suggest palliations, to protest against injustices. It *was* in Lapham's favor that he was so guiltless in the past, and now Corey asked himself if it were the first time he could have wished a guest at his father's table to have taken less wine; whether Lapham was not rather to be honored for not knowing how to contain his folly where a veteran transgressor might have held his tongue. He asked himself, with a thrill of sudden remorse, whether, when Lapham humbled himself in the dust so shockingly, he had shown him the sympathy to which such *abandon* had the right; and he had to own that he had met him on the gentlemanly ground, sparing himself and asserting the superiority of his sort, and not recognizing that Lapham's humiliation came from the sense of wrong, which he had helped to accumulate upon him by superfinely standing aloof and refusing to touch him.

He shut his desk and hurried out into the early night, not to go anywhere, but to walk up and down, to try to find his way out of the chaos, which now seemed ruin, and now the materials out of which fine actions and a happy life might be shaped. Three hours later he stood at Lapham's door.

At times what he now wished to do had seemed forever impossible, and again it had seemed as if he could not wait a moment longer. He had not been careless, but very mindful of what he knew must be the feelings of his own family in regard to the Laphams, and he had not concealed from himself that his family had great reason and justice on their side in not wishing him to alienate himself from their common life and associations. The most that he could urge to himself was that they had not all the reason and justice; but he had hesitated and delayed because they had so much. Often he could not make it appear right that he should merely please himself in what chiefly concerned himself. He perceived how far apart in all their experiences and ideals the Lapham girls and his sisters were; how different Mrs. Lapham was from his mother; how grotesquely unlike were his father and Lapham; and the disparity had not always amused him.

He had often taken it very seriously, and sometimes he said that he must forego the hope on which his heart was set. There had been many times in the past months when he had said that he must go no farther, and as often as he had taken this stand he had yielded it, upon this or that excuse, which he was aware of trumping up. It was part of the complication that he should be unconscious of the injury he might be doing to some one besides his family and himself; this was the defect of his diffidence; and it had come to him in a pang for the first time when his mother said that she would not have the Laphams think she wished to make more of the acquaintance than he did; and then it had come too late. Since that he had suffered quite as much from the fear that it might not be as that it might be so; and now, in the mood, romantic and exalted, in which he found himself concerning Lapham, he was as far as might be from vain confidence. He ended the question in his own mind by affirming to himself that he was there, first of all, to see Lapham and give him an ultimate proof of his own perfect faith and unabated respect, and to offer him what reparation this involved for that want of sympathy—of humanity—which he had shown.

# XVI

The Nova Scotia second-girl who answered Corey's ring said that Lapham had not come home yet.

"Oh," said the young man, hesitating on the outer step.

"I guess you better come in," said the girl. "I'll go and see when they're expecting him."

Corey was in the mood to be swayed by any chance. He obeyed the suggestion of the second-girl's patronizing friendliness, and let her shut him into the drawing-room, while she went upstairs to announce him to Penelope.

"Did you tell him father wasn't at home?"

"Yes. He seemed so kind of disappointed, I told him to come in, and I'd see when he *would* be in," said the girl, with the human interest which sometimes replaces in the American domestic the servile deference of other countries.

A gleam of amusement passed over Penelope's face, as she glanced at herself in the glass. "Well," she cried, finally, dropping from her shoulders the light shawl in which she had been huddled over a book when Corey rang, "I will go down."

"All right," said the girl, and Penelope began hastily to amend the disarray of her hair, which she tumbled into a mass on the top of her little head, setting off the pale dark of her complexion with a flash of crimson ribbon at her throat. She moved across the carpet once or twice with the quaint grace that belonged to her small figure, made a dissatisfied grimace at it in the glass, caught a handkerchief out of a drawer and slid it into her pocket, and then descended to Corey.

The Lapham drawing-room in Nankeen Square was in the

parti-colored paint which the Colonel had hoped to repeat in his new house: the trim of the doors and windows was in light green and the panels in salmon; the walls were a plain tint of French gray paper, divided by gilt moldings into broad panels with a wide stripe of red velvet paper running up the corners; the chandelier was of massive imitation bronze; the mirror over the mantel rested on a fringed mantel-cover of green reps, and heavy curtains of that stuff hung from gilt lambrequin frames at the window;[5] the carpet was of a small pattern in crude green, which, at the time Mrs. Lapham bought it, covered half the new floors in Boston. In the paneled spaces on the walls were some stone-colored landscapes, representing the mountains and cañons of the West, which the Colonel and his wife had visited on one of the early official railroad excursions. In front of the long windows looking into the square were statues, kneeling figures which turned their backs upon the company within doors, and represented allegories of Faith and Prayer to people without. A white marble group of several figures, expressing an Italian conception of Lincoln Freeing the Slaves,—a Latin negro and his wife,— with our Eagle flapping his wings in approval, at Lincoln's feet, occupied one corner, and balanced the what-not of an earlier period in another.[6] These phantasms added their chill to that imparted by the tone of the walls, the landscapes, and the carpets, and contributed to the violence of the contrast when the chandelier was lighted up full glare, and the heat of the whole furnace welled up from the registers into the quivering atmosphere on one of the rare occasions when the Laphams invited company.

Corey had not been in this room before; the family had always received him in what they called the sitting-room. Penelope looked into this first, and then she looked into the parlor, with a smile that broke into a laugh as she discovered him standing under the single burner, which the second-girl had lighted for him in the chandelier.

"I don't understand how you came to be put in there," she said, as she led the way to the cozier place, "unless it was because Alice thought you were only here on probation, anyway. Father hasn't got home yet, but I'm expecting him every moment; I

---

5. "Lambrequin" probably refers to a valance or molding at the top of the window, carved to resemble draperies and then gilded. All the details of the room reveal the Laphams' lack of taste.
6. A what-not is a small shelf or cabinet on which decorative knickknacks are displayed.

don't know what's keeping him. Did the girl tell you that mother and Irene were out?"

"No, she didn't say. It's very good of you to see me." She had not seen the exaltation which he had been feeling, he perceived with half a sigh; it must all be upon this lower level; perhaps it was best so. "There was something I wished to say to your father——I hope," he broke off, "you're better to-night."

"Oh, yes, thank you," said Penelope, remembering that she had not been well enough to go to dinner the night before.

"We all missed you very much."

"Oh, thank you! I'm afraid you wouldn't have missed me if I had been there."

"Oh, yes, we should," said Corey, "I assure you."

They looked at each other.

"I really think I believed I was saying something," said the girl.

"And so did I," replied the young man. They laughed rather wildly, and then they both became rather grave.

He took the chair she gave him, and looked across at her, where she sat on the other side of the hearth, in a chair lower than his, with her hands dropped in her lap, and the back of her head on her shoulders as she looked up at him. The soft-coal fire in the grate purred and flickered; the drop-light cast a mellow radiance on her face. She let her eyes fall, and then lifted them for an irrelevant glance at the clock on the mantel.

"Mother and Irene have gone to the Spanish Students' concert."

"Oh, have they?" asked Corey; and he put his hat, which he had been holding in his hand, on the floor beside his chair.

She looked down at it for no reason, and then looked up at his face for no other, and turned a little red. Corey turned a little red himself. She who had always been so easy with him now became a little constrained.

"Do you know how warm it is out-of-doors?" he asked.

"No; is it warm? I haven't been out all day."

"It's like a summer night."

She turned her face towards the fire, and then started abruptly. "Perhaps it's too warm for you here?"

"Oh, no, it's very comfortable."

"I suppose it's the cold of the last few days that's still in the house. I was reading with a shawl on when you came."

"I interrupted you."

"Oh, no. I had finished the book. I was just looking over it again."

"Do you like to read books over?"

"Yes; books that I like at all."

"What was it?" asked Corey.

The girl hesitated. "It has rather a sentimental name. Did you ever read it?—'Tears, Idle Tears.'"

"Oh, yes; they were talking of that last night; it's a famous book with ladies. They break their hearts over it. Did it make you cry?"

"Oh, it's pretty easy to cry over a book," said Penelope, laughing; "and that one *is* very natural till you come to the main point. Then the naturalness of all the rest makes that seem natural too; but I guess it's rather forced."

"Her giving him up to the other one?"

"Yes; simply because she happened to know that the other one had cared for him first. Why should she have done it? What right had she?"

"I don't know. I suppose that the self-sacrifice——"

"But it *wasn't* self-sacrifice—or not self-sacrifice alone. She was sacrificing him, too; and for some one who couldn't appreciate him half as much as she could. I'm provoked with myself when I think how I cried over that book—for I did cry. It's silly—it's wicked for any one to do what that girl did. Why can't they let people have a chance to behave reasonably in stories?"

"Perhaps they couldn't make it so attractive," suggested Corey, with a smile.

"It would be novel, at any rate," said the girl. "But so it would in real life, I suppose," she added.

"I don't know. Why shouldn't people in love behave sensibly?"

"That's a very serious question," said Penelope, gravely. "*I* couldn't answer it," and she left him the embarrassment of supporting an inquiry which she had certainly instigated herself. She seemed to have finally recovered her own ease in doing this. "Do you admire our autumnal display, Mr. Corey?"

"Your display?"

"The trees in the square. *We* think it's quite equal to an opening at Jordan & Marsh's."

"Ah, I'm afraid you wouldn't let me be serious even about your maples."

"Oh, yes, I should—if you like to be serious."

"Don't you?"

"Well, not about serious matters. That's the reason that book made me cry."

"You make fun of everything. Miss Irene was telling me last night about you."

"Then it's no use for me to deny it so soon. I must give Irene a talking to."

"I hope you won't forbid her to talk about you!"

She had taken up a fan from the table, and held it, now between her face and the fire, and now between her face and him. Her little visage, with that arch, lazy look in it, topped by its mass of dusky hair, and dwindling from the full cheeks to the small chin, had a Japanese effect in the subdued light, and it had the charm which comes to any woman with happiness. It would be hard to say how much of this she perceived that he felt. They talked about other things awhile, and then she came back to what he had said. She glanced at him obliquely round her fan, and stopped moving it. "Does Irene talk about me?" she asked.

"I think so—yes. Perhaps it's only I who talk about you. You must blame me if it's wrong," he returned.

"Oh, I didn't say it was wrong," she replied. "But I hope if you said anything very bad of me, you'll let me know what it was, so that I can reform——"

"No, don't change, please!" cried the young man.

Penelope caught her breath, but went on resolutely, "Or rebuke you for speaking evil of dignities." She looked down at the fan, now flat in her lap, and tried to govern her head, but it trembled, and she remained looking down. Again they let the talk stray, and then it was he who brought it back to themselves, as if it had not left them.

"I have to talk *of* you," said Corey, "because I get to talk *to* you so seldom."

"You mean that I do all the talking, when we're—together?" She glanced sidewise at him; but she reddened after speaking the last word.

"We're so seldom together," he pursued.

"I don't know what you mean——"

"Sometimes I've thought—I've been afraid—that you avoided me."

"Avoided you?"

"Yes! Tried not to be alone with me."

She might have told him that there was no reason why she should be alone with him, and that it was very strange he should make this complaint of her. But she did not. She kept looking down at the fan, and then she lifted her burning face and looked at the clock again. "Mother and Irene will be sorry to miss you," she gasped.

He instantly rose and came towards her. She rose too, and mechanically put out her hand. He took it as if to say good-night. "I didn't mean to send you away," she besought him.

"Oh, I'm not going," he answered, simply. "I wanted to say —to say that it's I who make her talk about you. To say I— There is something I want to say to you; I've said it so often to myself that I feel as if you must know it." She stood quite still, letting him keep her hand, and questioning his face with a bewildered gaze. "You *must* know—she must have told you—she must have guessed——" Penelope turned white, but outwardly quelled the panic that sent the blood to her heart. "I—I didn't expect—I hoped to have seen your father—but I must speak now, whatever —— I love you!"

She freed her hand from both of those he had closed upon it, and went back from him across the room with a sinuous spring. "*Me!*" Whatever potential complicity had lurked in her heart, his words brought her only immeasurable dismay.

He came towards her again. "Yes, *you*. Who else?"

She fended him off with an imploring gesture. "I thought—I —it was——"

She shut her lips tight, and stood looking at him where he remained in silent amaze. Then her words came again, shudderingly. "Oh, what have you done?"

"Upon my soul," he said, with a vague smile, "I don't know. I hope no harm?"

"Oh, don't laugh!" she cried, laughing hysterically herself. "Unless you want me to think you the greatest wretch in the world!"

"I?" he responded. "For heaven's sake tell me what you mean!"

"You know I can't tell you. Can you say—can you put your hand on your heart and say that—you—say you never meant—that you meant me—all along?"

"Yes!— Yes! Who else? I came here to see your father, and to tell him that I wished to tell you this—to ask him—— But what does it matter? You must have known it—you must have seen—and it's for you to answer me. I've been abrupt, I know, and I've startled you; but if you love me, you can forgive that to my loving you so long before I spoke."

She gazed at him with parted lips.

"Oh, mercy! What shall I do? If it's true—what you say—you must go!" she said. "And you must never come any more. Do you promise that?"

"Certainly not," said the young man. "Why should I promise such a thing—so abominably wrong? I could obey if you didn't love me——"

"Oh, I don't! Indeed I don't! Now will you obey?"

"No. I don't believe you."

"Oh!"

He possessed himself of her hand again.

"My love—my dearest! What is this trouble, that you can't tell it? It can't be anything about yourself. If it is anything about any one else, it wouldn't make the least difference in the world, no matter what it was. I would be only too glad to show by any act or deed I could that nothing could change me towards you."

"Oh, you don't understand!"

"No, I don't. You must tell me."

"I will never do that."

"Then I will stay here till your mother comes, and ask her what it is."

"Ask *her*?"

"Yes! Do you think I will give you up till I know why I must?"

"You force me to it! Will you go if I tell you, and never let any human creature know what you have said to me?"

"Not unless you give me leave."

"That will be never. Well, then——" She stopped, and made two or three ineffectual efforts to begin again. "No, no! I can't.

You must go!"

"I will not go!"

"You said you—loved me. If you do, you will go."

He dropped the hands he had stretched towards her, and she hid her face in her own.

"There!" she said, turning it suddenly upon him. "Sit down there. And will you promise me—on your honor—not to speak —not to try to persuade me—not to—touch me? You won't touch me?"

"I will obey you, Penelope."

"As if you were never to see me again? As if I were dying?"

"I will do what you say. But I shall see you again; and don't talk of dying. This is the beginning of life——"

"No. It's the end," said the girl, resuming at last something of the hoarse drawl which the tumult of her feeling had broken into those half-articulate appeals. She sat down too, and lifted her face towards him. "It's the end of life for me, because I know now that I must have been playing false from the beginning. You don't know what I mean, and I can never tell you. It isn't my secret—it's some one else's. You—you must never come here again. I can't tell you why, and you must never try to know. Do you promise?"

"You can forbid me. I must do what you say."

"I do forbid you, then. And you shall not think I am cruel——"

"How could I think that?"

"Oh, how hard you make it!"

Corey laughed for very despair. "Can I make it easier by disobeying you?"

"I know I am talking crazily. But I'm not crazy."

"No, no," he said, with some wild notion of comforting her; "but try to tell me this trouble! There is nothing under heaven— no calamity, no sorrow—that I wouldn't gladly share with you, or take all upon myself if I could!"

"I know! But this you can't. Oh, my——"

"Dearest! Wait! Think! Let me ask your mother—your father——"

She gave a cry.

"No! If you do that, you will make me hate you! Will you——"

The rattling of a latch-key was heard in the outer door.

"Promise!" cried Penelope.

"Oh, I promise!"

"Good-bye!" She suddenly flung her arms round his neck, and, pressing her cheek tight against his, flashed out of the room by one door as her father entered it by another.

Corey turned to him in a daze. "I—I called to speak with you—about a matter—— But it's so late now. I'll—I'll see you to-morrow."

"No time like the present," said Lapham, with a fierceness that did not seem referable to Corey. He had his hat still on, and he glared at the young man out of his blue eyes with a fire that something else must have kindled there.

"I really can't, now," said Corey, weakly. "It will do quite as well to-morrow. Good-night, sir."

"Good-night," answered Lapham abruptly, following him to the door, and shutting it after him. "I think the devil must have got into pretty much everybody to-night," he muttered, coming back to the room, where he put down his hat. Then he went to the kitchen-stairs and called down, "Hello, Alice! I want something to eat!"

## XVII

"WHAT's the reason the girls never get down to breakfast any more?" asked Lapham when he met his wife at the table in the morning. He had been up an hour and a half, and he spoke with the severity of a hungry man. "It seems to me they don't amount to *any*thing. Here I am, at my time of life, up the first one in the house. I ring the bell for the cook at quarter-past six every morning, and the breakfast is on the table at half-past seven right along, like clock-work, but I never see anybody but you till I go to the office."

"Oh, yes, you do, Si," said his wife, soothingly. "The girls are nearly always down. But they're young, and it tires them more than it does us to get up early."

"They can rest afterwards. They don't do anything after they *are* up," grumbled Lapham.

"Well, that's your fault, ain't it? You oughtn't to have made so much money, and then they'd have had to work." She laughed at Lapham's Spartan mood, and went on to excuse the young people. "Irene's been up two nights hand running, and Penelope says she ain't well. What makes you so cross about the girls? Been doing something you're ashamed of?"

"I'll tell you when I've been doing anything to be ashamed of," growled Lapham.

"Oh, no, you won't!" said his wife, jollily. "You'll only be hard on the rest of us. Come, now, Si; what is it?"

Lapham frowned into his coffee with sulky dignity, and said, without looking up, "I wonder what that fellow wanted here last night?"

"What fellow?"

"Corey. I found him here when I came home, and he said he wanted to see me; but he wouldn't stop."

"Where was he?"

"In the sitting-room."

"Was Pen there?"

"*I* didn't see her."

Mrs. Lapham paused, with her hand on the cream-jug. "Why, what in the land *did* he want? Did he say he wanted you?"

"That's what he said."

"And then he wouldn't stay?"

"No."

"Well, then, I'll tell you just what it is, Silas Lapham. He came here"—she looked about the room and lowered her voice—"to see you about Irene, and then he hadn't the courage."

"I guess he's got courage enough to do pretty much what he wants to," said Lapham, glumly. "All I know is, he was here. You better ask Pen about it, if she ever gets down."

"I guess I sha'n't wait for her," said Mrs. Lapham; and, as her husband closed the front door after him, she opened that of her daughter's room and entered abruptly.

The girl sat at the window, fully dressed, and as if she had been sitting there a long time. Without rising, she turned her face towards her mother. It merely showed black against the light, and revealed nothing till her mother came close to her with successive questions. "Why, how long have you been up, Pen? Why don't you come to your breakfast? Did you see Mr. Corey when he called last night? Why, what's the matter with you? What have you been crying about?"

"Have I been crying?"

"Yes! Your cheeks are all wet!"

"I thought they were on fire. Well, I'll tell you what's happened." She rose and then fell back in her chair. "Lock the door!" she ordered, and her mother mechanically obeyed. "I don't want Irene in here. There's nothing the matter. Only, Mr. Corey offered himself to me last night."

Her mother remained looking at her, helpless, not so much with amaze, perhaps, as dismay.

"Oh, I'm not a ghost! I wish I was! You had better sit down, mother. You have got to know all about it."

Mrs. Lapham dropped nervelessly into the chair at the other window, and while the girl went slowly but briefly on, touching only the vital points of the story, and breaking at times into a bitter drollery, she sat as if without the power to speak or stir.

"Well, that's all, mother. I should say I had dreamt it, if I had slept any last night; but I guess it really happened."

The mother glanced round at the bed, and said, glad to occupy herself delayingly with the minor care: "Why, you have been sitting up all night! You will kill yourself."

"I don't know about killing myself, but I've been sitting up all night," answered the girl. Then, seeing that her mother remained blankly silent again, she demanded, "Why don't you blame me, mother? Why don't you say that I led him on, and tried to get him away from her? Don't you believe I did?"

Her mother made her no answer, as if these ravings of self-accusal needed none. "Do you think," she asked, simply, "that he got the idea you cared for him?"

"He knew it! How could I keep it from him? I said I didn't —at first!"

"It was no use," sighed the mother. "You might as well said you did. It couldn't help Irene any, if you didn't."

"I always tried to help her with him, even when I——"

"Yes, I know. But she never was equal to him. I saw that from the start; but I tried to blind myself to it. And when he kept coming——"

"You never thought of me!" cried the girl, with a bitterness that reached her mother's heart. "I was nobody! I couldn't feel! No one could care for me!" The turmoil of despair, of triumph, of remorse and resentment, which filled her soul, tried to express itself in the words.

"No," said the mother humbly. "I didn't think of you. Or I

didn't think of you enough. It did come across me sometimes that maybe—— But it didn't seem as if—— And your going on so for Irene——"

"You let me go on. You made me always go and talk with him for her, and you didn't think I would talk to him for myself. Well, I didn't!"

"I'm punished for it. When did you—begin to care for him?"

"How do I know? What difference does it make? It's all over now, no matter when it began. He won't come here any more, unless I let him." She could not help betraying her pride in this authority of hers, but she went on anxiously enough: "What will you say to Irene? She's safe as far as I'm concerned; but if he don't care for her, what will you do?"

"I don't know what to do," said Mrs. Lapham. She sat in an apathy from which she apparently could not rouse herself. "I don't see as anything can be done."

Penelope laughed in a pitying derision.

"Well, let things go on then. But they won't *go* on."

"No, they won't go on," echoed her mother. "She's pretty enough, and she's capable; and your father's got the money— I don't know what I'm saying! She ain't equal to him, and she never was. I kept feeling it all the time, and yet I kept blinding myself."

"If he had ever cared for her," said Penelope, "it wouldn't have mattered whether she was equal to him or not. *I'm* not equal to him either."

Her mother went on: "I might have thought it was you; but I had got set—— Well! I can see it all clear enough, now it's too late. *I* don't know what to do."

"And what do you expect *me* to do?" demanded the girl. "Do you want *me* to go to Irene and tell her that I've got him away from her?"

"Oh, good Lord!" cried Mrs. Lapham. "What shall I do? What do you want I should do, Pen?"

"Nothing for me," said Penelope. "I've had it out with myself. Now do the best you can for Irene."

"I couldn't say you had done wrong, if you was to marry him to-day."

"Mother!"

"No, I couldn't. I couldn't say but what you had been good and faithful all through, and you had a perfect right to do it. There ain't any one to blame. He's behaved like a gentleman, and I can see now that he never thought of her, and that it was you all the while. Well, marry him, then! He's got the right, and so have you."

"What about Irene? I don't want you to talk about me. I can take care of myself."

"She's nothing but a child. It's only a fancy with her. She'll get over it. She hain't really got her heart set on him."

"She's got her heart set on him, mother. She's got her whole life set on him. You know that."

"Yes, that's so," said the mother, as promptly as if she had been arguing to that rather than the contrary effect.

"If I could give him to her, I would. But he isn't mine to give." She added in a burst of despair, "He isn't mine to keep!"

"Well," said Mrs. Lapham, "she has got to bear it. I don't know what's to come of it all. But she's got to bear her share of it." She rose and went toward the door.

Penelope ran after her in a sort of terror. "You're not going to tell Irene?" she gasped, seizing her mother by either shoulder.

"Yes, I am," said Mrs. Lapham. "If she's a woman grown, she can bear a woman's burden."

"I can't let you tell Irene," said the girl, letting fall her face on her mother's neck. "Not Irene," she moaned. "I'm afraid to let you. How can I ever look at her again?"

"Why, you haven't done anything, Pen," said her mother, soothingly.

"I wanted to! Yes, I must have done something. How could I help it? I did care for him from the first, and I must have tried to make him like me. Do you think I did? No, no! You mustn't tell Irene! Not—not—yet! Mother! Yes! I did try to get him from her!" she cried, lifting her head, and suddenly looking her mother in the face with those large dim eyes of hers. "What do you think? Even last night! It was the first time I ever had him all to myself, for myself, and I know now that I tried to make him think that I was pretty and—funny. And I didn't try to make him think of her. I knew that I pleased him, and I tried to please him more. Perhaps I could have kept him from saying that he cared for me; but when I saw he did—I must have seen it—I couldn't. I had never had him to myself, and for myself, before. I needn't have seen him at all, but I wanted to see him; and when I was sitting there alone with him, how do I know what I did to let him feel that I cared for him? Now, will you tell Irene? I never thought he did care for me, and never expected him to. But I liked him. Yes—I did like him! Tell her that! Or else *I* will."

"If it was to tell her he was dead," began Mrs. Lapham, absently.

"How easy it would be!" cried the girl in self-mockery. "But he's worse than dead to her; and so am I. I've turned it over a million ways, mother; I've looked at it in every light you can put it in, and I can't make anything but misery out of it. You can see the misery at the first glance, and you can't see more or less if you spend your life looking at it." She laughed again, as if the hopelessness of the thing amused her. Then she flew to the extreme of self-assertion. "Well, I *have* a right to him, and he has a right to me. If he's never done anything to make her think he cared for her,—and I know he hasn't; it's all been our doing,—then he's free and I'm free. We can't make her happy, whatever we do; and why shouldn't I—— No, that won't do! I reached that point before!" She broke again into her desperate laugh. "*You* may try now, mother!"

"I'd best speak to your father first——"

Penelope smiled a little more forlornly than she had laughed.

"Well, yes; the Colonel will have to know. It isn't a trouble that I can keep to myself exactly. It seems to belong to too many other people."

Her mother took a crazy encouragement from her return to her old way of saying things. "Perhaps he can think of something."

"Oh, I don't doubt but the Colonel will know just what to do!"

"You mustn't be too down-hearted about it. It—it'll all come right——"

"You tell Irene that, mother."

Mrs. Lapham had put her hand on the door-key; she dropped it, and looked at the girl with a sort of beseeching appeal for the comfort she could not imagine herself. "Don't look at me, mother," said Penelope, shaking her head. "You know that if Irene were to die without knowing it, it wouldn't come right for me."

"Pen!"

"I've read of cases where a girl gives up the man that loves her so as to make some other girl happy that the man doesn't love. That might be done."

"Your father would think you were a fool," said Mrs. Lapham, finding a sort of refuge in her strong disgust for the pseudo-heroism. "No! If there's to be any giving up, let it be by the one that sha'n't make anybody but herself suffer. There's trouble and sorrow enough in the world, without *making* it on purpose!"

She unlocked the door, but Penelope slipped round and set herself against it. "Irene shall not give up!"

"I will see your father about it," said the mother. "Let me out now——"

"Don't let Irene come here!"

"No. I will tell her that you haven't slept. Go to bed now, and try to get some rest. She isn't up herself yet. You must have some breakfast."

"No; let me sleep if I can. I can get something when I wake up. I'll come down if I can't sleep. Life has got to go on. It does when there's a death in the house, and this is only a little worse."

"Don't you talk nonsense!" cried Mrs. Lapham, with angry authority.

"Well, a little better, then," said Penelope, with meek concession.

Mrs. Lapham attempted to say something, and could not. She went out and opened Irene's door. The girl lifted her head drowsily from her pillow. "Don't disturb your sister when you get up, Irene. She hasn't slept well——"

"*Please* don't talk! I'm almost *dead* with sleep!" returned Irene. "Do go, mamma! I sha'n't disturb her." She turned her face down in the pillow, and pulled the covering up over her ears.

The mother slowly closed the door and went down-stairs, feeling bewildered and baffled almost beyond the power to move. The time had been when she would have tried to find out why this judgment had been sent upon her. But now she could not feel that the innocent suffering of others was inflicted for her fault; she shrank instinctively from that cruel and egotistic misinterpretation of the mystery of pain and loss. She saw her two children, equally if differently dear to her, destined to trouble that nothing could avert, and she could not blame either of them; she could not blame the means of this misery to them; he was as innocent as they, and though her heart was sore against him in this first moment, she could still be just to him in it. She was a woman who had been used to seek the light by striving; she had hitherto literally worked to it. But it is the curse of prosperity that it takes work away from us, and shuts that door to hope and health of spirit. In this house, where everything had come to be done for her, she had no tasks to interpose between her and her despair. She sat down in her own room and let her hands fall in her lap,—the hands that had once been so helpful and busy,—and tried to think it all out. She had never heard of the fate that was once supposed to appoint the sorrows of men irrespective of their blamelessness or blame, before the time when it came to be believed that sorrows were penalties; but in her simple way she recognized something like that mythic power when she rose from her struggle with the problem, and said aloud to herself, "Well, the witch is in it." Turn which way she would, she saw no escape from the misery to come—the misery which had come already to Penelope and herself, and that must come to Irene and her father. She started when she definitely thought of her husband, and thought with what violence it would work in every fiber of his rude strength. She feared that, and she feared something worse—the effect which his pride and ambition might seek to give it; and it was with terror of this, as well as the natural trust with which a woman must turn to her husband in any anxiety at last, that she felt she could not wait for evening to take counsel with him. When she considered how wrongly he might take it all, it seemed as if it were already known to him, and she was impatient to prevent his error.

She sent out for a messenger, whom she dispatched with a note to his place of business: "Silas, I should like to ride with you this afternoon. Can't you come home early? Persis." And she was at dinner with Irene, evading her questions about Penelope, when answer came that he would be at the house with the buggy at half-past two. It is easy to put off a girl who has but one thing in her head; but, though Mrs. Lapham could escape without telling anything of Penelope, she could not escape seeing how wholly Irene was engrossed with hopes now turned so vain and impossible. She was still talking of that dinner, of nothing but that dinner, and begging for flattery of herself and praise of him, which her mother had till now been so ready to give.

"Seems to me you don't take very much interest, mamma!" she said, laughing and blushing, at one point.

"Yes,—yes, I do," protested Mrs. Lapham, and then the girl prattled on.

"I guess I shall get one of those pins that Nanny Corey had in her hair. I think it would become me, don't you?"

"Yes; but, Irene—I don't like to have you go on so, till— unless he's said something to show— You oughtn't to give yourself up to thinking——" But at this the girl turned so white, and looked such reproach at her, that she added, frantically: "Yes, get the pin. It is just the thing for you! But don't disturb Penelope. Let her alone till I get back. I'm going out to ride with your father. He'll be here in half an hour. Are you through? Ring, then. Get yourself that fan you saw the other day. Your father won't say anything; he likes to have you look well. I could see his eyes on you half the time the other night."

"I should have liked to have Pen go with me," said Irene, restored to her normal state of innocent selfishness by these flatteries. "Don't you suppose she'll be up in time? What's the matter with her that she didn't sleep?"

"I don't know. Better let her alone."

"Well," submitted Irene.

# XVIII

Mrs. Lapham went away to put on her bonnet and cloak, and she was waiting at the window when her husband drove up. She opened the door and ran down the steps. "Don't get out; I can help myself in," and she clambered to his side, while he kept the fidgeting mare still with voice and touch.

"Where do you want I should go?" he asked, turning the buggy.

"Oh, I don't care. Out Brookline way, I guess. I wish you hadn't brought this fool of a horse," she gave way, petulantly. "I wanted to have a talk."[7]

"When I can't drive this mare and talk too, I'll sell out altogether," said Lapham. "She'll be quiet enough when she's had her spin."

"Well," said his wife; and while they were making their way

7. Brookline is a suburb west of Boston.

across the city to the Milldam she answered certain questions he asked about some points in the new house.

"I should have liked to have you stop there," he began; but she answered so quickly, "Not to-day," that he gave it up and turned his horse's head westward, when they struck Beacon street.

He let the mare out, and he did not pull her in till he left the Brighton road and struck off under the low boughs that met above one of the quiet streets of Brookline, where the stone cottages, with here and there a patch of determined ivy on their northern walls, did what they could to look English amid the glare of the autumnal foliage. The smooth earthen track under the mare's hoofs was scattered with flakes of the red and yellow gold that made the air luminous around them, and the perspective was gay with innumerable tints and tones.

"Pretty sightly," said Lapham, with a long sigh, letting the reins lie loose in his vigilant hand, to which he seemed to relegate the whole charge of the mare. "I want to talk with you about Rogers, Persis. He's been getting in deeper and deeper with me; and last night he pestered me half to death to go in with him in one of his schemes. I ain't going to blame anybody, but I hain't got very much confidence in Rogers. And I told him so last night."

"Oh, don't talk to me about Rogers!" his wife broke in. "There's something a good deal more important than Rogers in the world, and more important than your business. It seems as if you couldn't think of anything else—that and the new house. Did you suppose I wanted to ride so as to talk Rogers with you?" she demanded, yielding to the necessity a wife feels of making her husband pay for her suffering, even if he has not inflicted it. "I declare——"

"Well, hold on, now!" said Lapham. "What *do* you want to talk about? I'm listening."

His wife began, "Why, it's just this, Silas Lapham!" and then she broke off to say, "Well, you may wait, now—starting me wrong, when it's hard enough anyway."

Lapham silently turned his whip over and over in his hand and waited.

"Did you suppose," she asked at last, "that that young Corey had been coming to see Irene?"

"I don't know what I supposed," replied Lapham sullenly.

"You always said so." He looked sharply at her under his lowering brows.

"Well, he hasn't," said Mrs. Lapham; and she replied to the frown that blackened on her husband's face, "And I can tell you what, if you take it in that way I sha'n't speak another word."

"Who's takin' it what way?" retorted Lapham savagely. "What are you drivin' at?"

"I want you should promise that you'll hear me out quietly."

"I'll hear you out if you'll give me a chance. I haven't said a word yet."

"Well, I'm not going to have you flying into forty furies, and looking like a perfect thunder-cloud at the very start. I've had to bear it, and you've got to bear it too."

"Well, let me have a chance at it, then."

"It's nothing to blame anybody about, as I can see, and the only question is, what's the best thing to do about it. There's only one thing we can do; for if he don't care for the child, nobody wants to make him. If he hasn't been coming to see her, he hasn't, and that's all there is to it."

"No, it ain't!" exclaimed Lapham.

"There!" protested his wife.

"If he hasn't been coming to see her, what *has* he been coming for?"

"He's been coming to see Pen!" cried the wife. "*Now* are you satisfied?" Her tone implied that he had brought it all upon them; but at the sight of the swift passions working in his face to a perfect comprehension of the whole trouble, she fell to trembling, and her broken voice lost all the spurious indignation she had put into it. "Oh, Silas! what are we going to do about it? I'm afraid it'll kill Irene."

Lapham pulled off the loose driving-glove from his right hand with the fingers of his left, in which the reins lay. He passed it over his forehead, and then flicked from it the moisture it had gathered there. He caught his breath once or twice, like a man who meditates a struggle with superior force and then remains passive in its grasp.

His wife felt the need of comforting him, as she had felt the need of afflicting him. "I don't say but what it can be made to come out all right in the end. All I say is, I don't see my way clear yet."

"What makes you think he likes Pen?" he asked, quietly.

"He told her so last night, and she told me this morning. Was he at the office to-day?"

"Yes, he was there. I haven't been there much myself. He didn't say anything to me. Does Irene know?"

"No; I left her getting ready to go out shopping. She wants to get a pin like the one Nanny Corey had on."

"Oh, my Lord!" groaned Lapham.

"It's been Pen from the start, I guess, or almost from the start. I don't say but what he was attracted some by Irene at the *very* first; but I guess it's been Pen ever since he saw her; and we've taken up with a notion, and blinded ourselves with it. Time and again I've had my doubts whether he cared for Irene any; but I declare to goodness, when he kept coming, I never hardly thought of Pen, and I couldn't help believing at last he *did* care for Irene. Did it ever strike you he might be after Pen?"

"No. I took what you said. I supposed you knew."

"Do you blame me, Silas?" she asked timidly.

"No. What's the use of blaming? We don't either of us want anything but the children's good. What's it all of it for, if it ain't for that? That's what we've both slaved for all our lives."

"Yes, I know. Plenty of people *lose* their children," she suggested.

"Yes, but that don't comfort me any. I never was one to feel good because another man felt bad. How would you have liked it if some one had taken comfort because his boy lived when ours died? No, I can't do it. And this is worse than death, someways. That comes and it goes; but this looks as if it was one of those things that had come to stay. The way I look at it, there ain't any hope for anybody. Suppose we don't want Pen to have him; will that help Irene any, if he don't want her? Suppose we don't want to let him have either; does that help either?"

"You talk," exclaimed Mrs. Lapham, "as if our say was going to settle it. Do you suppose that Penelope Lapham is a girl to take up with a fellow that her sister is in love with, and that she always thought was in love with her sister, and go off and be happy with him? Don't you believe but what it would come back to her, as long as she breathed the breath of life, how she'd teased her about him, as I've heard Pen tease Irene, and helped to make her think he was in love with her, by showing that she thought so herself? It's ridiculous!"

Lapham seemed quite beaten down by this argument. His huge head hung forward over his breast; the reins lay loose in his moveless hand; the mare took her own way. At last he lifted his face and shut his heavy jaws.

"Well?" quavered his wife.

"Well," he answered, "if he wants her, and she wants him, I don't see what that's got to do with it." He looked straight forward, and not at his wife.

She laid her hands on the reins. "Now, you stop right here, Silas Lapham! If I thought that—if I really believed you could be willing to break that poor child's heart, and let Pen disgrace herself by marrying a man that had as good as killed her sister, just because you wanted Bromfield Corey's son for a son-in-law——"

Lapham turned his face now, and gave her a look. "You had better *not* believe that, Persis! Get up!" he called to the mare, without glancing at her, and she sprang forward. "I see you've got past being any use to yourself on this subject."

"Hello!" shouted a voice in front of him. "Where the devil you goin' to?"

"Do you want to *kill* somebody?" shrieked his wife.

There was a light crash, and the mare recoiled her length, and separated their wheels from those of the open buggy in front which Lapham had driven into. He made his excuses to the occupant; and the accident relieved the tension of their feelings and left them far from the point of mutual injury which they had reached in their common trouble and their unselfish will for their children's good.

It was Lapham who resumed the talk. "I'm afraid we can't either of us see this thing in the right light. We're too near to it. I wish to the Lord there was somebody to talk to about it."

"Yes," said his wife; "but there ain't anybody."

"Well, I dunno," suggested Lapham, after a moment; "why not talk to the minister of your church? May be he could see some way out of it."

Mrs. Lapham shook her head hopelessly. "It wouldn't do. I've never taken up my connection with the church, and I don't feel as if I'd got any claim on him."

"If he's anything of a man, or anything of a preacher, you *have* got a claim on him," urged Lapham; and he spoiled his argument by adding, "I've contributed enough *money* to his church."

"Oh, that's nothing," said Mrs. Lapham. "I ain't well enough acquainted with Dr. Langworthy, or else I'm *too* well. No; if I was to ask any one, I should want to ask a total stranger. But what's the use, Si? Nobody could make us see it any different from what it is, and I don't know as I should want they should."

It blotted out the tender beauty of the day and weighed down their hearts ever more heavily within them. They ceased to talk of it a hundred times, and still came back to it. They drove on and on. It began to be late. "I guess we better go back, Si," said his wife; and as he turned without speaking, she pulled her veil down and began to cry softly behind it, with low little broken sobs.

Lapham started the mare up and drove swiftly homeward. At last his wife stopped crying and began trying to find her pocket. "Here, take mine, Persis," he said kindly, offering her his handkerchief, and she took it and dried her eyes with it. "There was one of those fellows there the other night," he spoke again, when his wife leaned back against the cushions in peaceful despair, "that I liked the looks of about as well as any man I ever saw. I guess he was a pretty good man. It was that Mr. Sewell." He looked at his wife, but she did not say anything. "Persis," he resumed, "I can't bear to go back with nothing settled in our minds. I can't bear to let you."

"We must, Si," returned his wife, with gentle gratitude. Lapham groaned. "Where does he live?" she asked.

"On Bolingbroke street. He gave me his number."

"Well, it wouldn't do any good. What could he say to us?"

"Oh, I don't know as he could say anything," said Lapham hopelessly; and neither of them said anything more till they crossed the Milldam and found themselves between the rows of city houses.

"Don't drive past the new house, Si," pleaded his wife. "I couldn't bear to see it. Drive—drive up Bolingbroke street. We might as well see where he *does* live."

"Well," said Lapham. He drove along slowly. "That's the place," he said finally, stopping the mare and pointing with his whip.

"It wouldn't do any good," said his wife, in a tone which he understood as well as he understood her words. He turned the mare up to the curbstone.

"You take the reins a minute," he said, handing them to his wife.

He got down and rang the bell, and waited till the door opened; then he came back and lifted his wife out. "He's in," he said.

He got the hitching-weight from under the buggy-seat and made it fast to the mare's bit.

"Do you think she'll stand with that?" asked Mrs. Lapham.

"I guess so. If she don't, no matter."

"Ain't you afraid she'll take cold," she persisted, trying to make delay.

"Let her!" said Lapham. He took his wife's trembling hand under his arm, and drew her to the door.

"He'll think we're crazy," she murmured, in her broken pride.

"Well, we *are*," said Lapham. "Tell him we'd like to see him alone awhile," he said to the girl who was holding the door ajar for him, and she showed him into the reception-room, which had been the Protestant confessional for many burdened souls before their time, coming, as they did, with the belief that they were bowed down with the only misery like theirs in the universe; for each one of us must suffer long to himself before he can learn that he is but one in a great community of wretchedness which has been pitilessly repeating itself from the foundation of the world.

They were as loath to touch their trouble when the minister came in as if it were their disgrace; but Lapham did so at last, and, with a simple dignity which he had wanted in his bungling and apologetic approaches, he laid the affair clearly before the minister's compassionate and reverent eye. He spared Corey's name, but he did not pretend that it was not himself and his wife and their daughters who were concerned.

"I don't know as I've got any right to trouble you with this thing," he said, in the moment while Sewell sat pondering the case, "and I don't know as I've got any warrant for doing it. But, as I told my wife here, there was something about you—I don't know whether it was anything you *said* exactly—that made me feel as if you could help us. I guess I didn't say so much as that to her; but that's the way I felt. And here we are. And if it ain't all right——"

"Surely," said Sewell, "it's all right. I thank you for coming —for trusting your trouble to me. A time comes to every one of us when we can't help ourselves, and then we must get others to help us. If people turn to me at such a time, I feel sure that I was put into the world for something—if nothing more than to give my pity, my sympathy."

The brotherly words, so plain, so sincere, had a welcome in them that these poor outcasts of sorrow could not doubt.

"Yes," said Lapham huskily, and his wife began to wipe the tears again under her veil.

Sewell remained silent, and they waited till he should speak. "We can be of use to one another here, because we can always be wiser for some one else than we can for ourselves. We can see another's sins and errors in a more merciful light—and that is always a fairer light—than we can our own; and we can look more sanely at others' afflictions." He had addressed these words to Lapham; now he turned to his wife. "If some one had come to you, Mrs. Lapham, in just this perplexity, what would you have thought?"

"I don't know as I understand you," faltered Mrs. Lapham.

Sewell repeated his words, and added, "I mean, what do you think some one else ought to do in your place?"

"Was there ever any poor creatures in such a strait before?" she asked, with pathetic incredulity.

"There's no new trouble under the sun," said the minister.

"Oh, if it was any one else, I should say—I should say— Why, of course! I should say that their duty was to let——" She paused.

"One suffer instead of three, if none is to blame?" suggested Sewell. "That's sense, and that's justice. It's the economy of pain which naturally suggests itself, and which would insist upon itself, if we were not all perverted by traditions which are the figment of the shallowest sentimentality. Tell me, Mrs. Lapham, didn't this come into your mind when you first learned how matters stood?"

"Why, yes, it flashed across me. But I didn't think it could be right."

"And how was it with you, Mr. Lapham?"

"Why, that's what *I* thought, of course. But I didn't see my way——"

"No," cried the minister, "we are all blinded, we are all weakened by a false ideal of self-sacrifice. It wraps us round with its meshes, and we can't fight our way out of it. Mrs. Lapham, what made you feel that it might be better for three to suffer than one?"

"Why, she did herself. I know she would die sooner than take him away from her."

"I supposed so!" cried the minister bitterly. "And yet she is a sensible girl, your daughter?"

"She has more common sense——"

"Of course! But in such a case we somehow think it must be wrong to use our common sense. I don't know where this false ideal comes from, unless it comes from the novels that befool and debauch almost every intelligence in some degree. It certainly doesn't come from Christianity, which instantly repudiates it when confronted with it. Your daughter believes, in spite of her common sense, that she ought to make herself and the man who loves her unhappy, in order to assure the lifelong wretchedness of her sister, whom he doesn't love, simply because her sister saw him and fancied him first! And I'm sorry to say that ninety-nine young people out of a hundred—oh, nine hundred and ninety-nine out of a thousand!—would consider that noble and beautiful and heroic; whereas you know at the bottom of your hearts that it would be foolish and cruel and revolting. You know what marriage is! And what it must be without love on both sides."

The minister had grown quite heated and red in the face.

"I lose all patience!" he went on vehemently. "This poor child of yours has somehow been brought to believe that it will kill her sister if her sister does not have what does not belong to her, and what it is not in the power of all the world, or any soul in the world, to give her. Her sister will suffer—yes, keenly!—in heart and in pride; but she will not die. You will suffer, too, in your tenderness for her; but you must do your duty. You must help her to give up. You would be guilty if you did less. Keep clearly in mind that you are doing right, and the only possible good. And God be with you!"

# XIX

"He talked sense, Persis," said Lapham gently, as he mounted to his wife's side in the buggy and drove slowly homeward through the dusk.

"Yes, he talked sense," she admitted. But she added, bitterly, "I guess, if he had it to *do* ! Oh, he's right, and it's got to be done. There ain't any other way for it. It's sense; and, yes, it's justice." They walked to their door after they left the horse at the livery stable around the corner, where Lapham kept it. "I want you should send Irene up to our room as soon as we get in, Silas."

"Why, ain't you going to have any supper first?" faltered Lapham, with his latch-key in the lock.

"No. I can't lose a minute. If I do, I sha'n't do it at all."

"Look here, Persis," said her husband tenderly, "let *me* do this thing."

"Oh, *you* !" said his wife, with a woman's compassionate scorn for a man's helplessness in such a case. "Send her right up. And I shall feel—" She stopped, to spare him.

Then she opened the door, and ran up to her room, without waiting to speak to Irene, who had come into the hall at the sound of her father's key in the door.

"I guess your mother wants to see you upstairs," said Lapham, looking away.

Her mother turned round and faced the girl's wondering look as Irene entered the chamber, so close upon her that she had not yet had time to lay off her bonnet; she stood with her wraps still on her arm.

"Irene!" she said harshly, "there is something you have got to bear. It's a mistake we've all made. He don't care anything for you. He never did. He told Pen so last night. He cares for her."

The sentences had fallen like blows. But the girl had taken them without flinching. She stood up immovable, but the delicate rose-light of her complexion went out and left her snow-white. She did not offer to speak.

"Why don't you say something?" cried her mother. "Do you want to kill me, Irene?"

"Why should I want to hurt *you*, mamma?" the girl replied steadily, but in an alien voice. "There's nothing to say. I want to see Pen a minute."

She turned and left the room. As she mounted the stairs that led to her own and her sister's rooms on the floor above, her mother helplessly followed. Irene went first to her own room at the front of the house, and then came out, leaving the door open and the gas flaring behind her. The mother could see that she had tumbled many things out of the drawers of her bureau upon the marble top.

She passed her mother, where she stood in the entry. "You can come too, if you want to, mamma," she said.

She opened Penelope's door without knocking, and went in. Penelope sat at the window, as in the morning. Irene did not go to her; but she went and laid a gold hair-pin on her bureau, and said, without looking at her, "There's a pin that I got to-day, because it was like his sister's. It won't become a dark person so well, but you can have it."

She stuck a scrap of paper in the side of Penelope's mirror. "There's that account of Mr. Stanton's ranch. You'll want to read it, I presume."

She laid a withered *boutonnière* on the bureau beside the pin. "There's his button-hole bouquet. He left it by his plate, and I stole it."

She had a pine-shaving, fantastically tied up with a knot of ribbon, in her hand. She held it a moment; then, looking deliberately at Penelope, she went up to her, and dropped it in her lap without a word. She turned, and, advancing a few steps, tottered and seemed about to fall.

Her mother sprang forward with an imploring cry, "Oh, 'Rene, 'Rene, 'Rene!"

Irene recovered herself before her mother could reach her. "Don't touch me," she said icily. "Mamma, I'm going to put on my things. I want papa to walk with me. I'm choking here."

"I—I can't let you go out, Irene, child," began her mother.

"You've got to," replied the girl. "Tell papa to hurry his supper."

"Oh, poor soul! He doesn't want any supper. *He* knows it too."

"I don't want to talk about that. Tell him to get ready."

She left them once more.

Mrs. Lapham turned a hapless glance upon Penelope.

"Go and tell him, mother," said the girl. "I would, if I could. If she can walk, let her. It's the only thing for her." She sat still;

she did not even brush to the floor the fantastic thing that lay in her lap, and that sent up faintly the odor of the sachet powder with which Irene liked to perfume her boxes.

Lapham went out with the unhappy child, and began to talk with her, crazily, incoherently enough.

She mercifully stopped him. "Don't talk, papa. I don't want any one should talk with me."

He obeyed, and they walked silently on and on. In their aimless course they reached the new house on the water side of Beacon, and she made him stop, and stood looking up at it. The scaffolding which had so long defaced the front was gone, and in the light of the gas-lamp before it all the architectural beauty of the façade was suggested, and much of the finely felt detail was revealed. Seymour had pretty nearly satisfied himself in that rich façade; certainly Lapham had not stinted him of the means.

"Well," said the girl, "I shall never live in it," and she began to walk on.

Lapham's sore heart went down, as he lumbered heavily after her. "Oh, yes, you will, Irene. You'll have lots of good times there yet."

"No," she answered, and said nothing more about it. They had not talked of their trouble at all, and they did not speak of it now. Lapham understood that she was trying to walk herself weary, and he was glad to hold his peace and let her have her way. She halted him once more before the red and yellow lights of an apothecary's window.

"Isn't there something they give you to make you sleep?" she asked vaguely. "I've got to sleep to-night!"

Lapham trembled. "I guess you don't want anything, Irene."

"Yes, I do! Get me something!" she retorted willfully. "If you don't, I shall die. I *must* sleep."

They went in, and Lapham asked for something to make a nervous person sleep. Irene stood poring over the show-case full of brushes and trinkets, while the apothecary put up the bromide, which he guessed would be about the best thing. She did not show any emotion; her face was like a stone, while her father's expressed the anguish of his sympathy. He looked as if he had not slept for a week; his fat eyelids drooped over his glassy eyes, and his cheeks and throat hung flaccid. He started as the apothecary's cat stole smoothly up and rubbed itself against his leg;

and it was to him that the man said, "You want to take a table-spoonful of that as long as you're awake. I guess it won't take a great many to fetch you."

"All right," said Lapham, and paid and went out. "I don't know but I *shall* want some of it," he said, with a joyless laugh.

Irene came closer up to him and took his arm. He laid his heavy paw on her gloved fingers. After a while she said, "I want you should let me go up to Lapham to-morrow."

"To Lapham? Why, to-morrow's Sunday, Irene! You can't go to-morrow."

"Well, Monday, then. I can live through one day here."

"Well," said the father passively. He made no pretense of asking her why she wished to go, nor any attempt to dissuade her.

"Give me that bottle," she said, when he opened the door at home for her, and she ran up to her own room.

The next morning Irene came to breakfast with her mother; the Colonel and Penelope did not appear, and Mrs. Lapham looked sleep-broken and careworn.

The girl glanced at her. "Don't you fret about me, mamma," she said. "I shall get along." She seemed herself as steady and strong as rock.

"I don't like to see you keeping up so, Irene," replied her mother. "It'll be all the worse for you when you do break. Better give way a little at the start."

"I sha'n't break, and I've given way all I'm going to. I'm going to Lapham to-morrow,—I want you should go with me, mamma,—and I guess I can keep up one day here. All about it is, I don't want you should say anything, or *look* anything. And, whatever I do, I don't want you should try to stop me. And, the first thing, I'm going to take her breakfast up to her. Don't!" she cried, intercepting the protest on her mother's lips. "I shall not let it hurt Pen, if I can help it. She's never done a thing nor thought a thing to wrong me. I had to fly out at her last night; but that's all over now, and I know just what I've got to bear."

She had her way unmolested. She carried Penelope's breakfast to her, and omitted no care or attention that could make the sacrifice complete, with an heroic pretense that she was performing no unusual service. They did not speak, beyond her saying, in a clear, dry note, "Here's your breakfast, Pen," and her sister's answering, hoarsely and tremulously, "Oh, thank you, Irene." And, though two or three times they turned their faces toward each other while Irene remained in the room, mechanically putting its confusion to rights, their eyes did not meet. Then Irene descended upon the other rooms, which she set in order, and some of which she fiercely swept and dusted. She made the beds; and she sent the two servants away to church as soon as they had eaten their breakfast, telling them that she would wash their dishes. Throughout the morning her father and mother heard her about the work of getting dinner, with certain silences which represented the moments when she stopped and stood stock-still, and then, readjusting her burden, forced herself forward under it again.

They sat alone in the family-room, out of which their two girls seemed to have died. Lapham could not read his Sunday papers, and she had no heart to go to church, as she would have done earlier in life when in trouble. Just then she was obscurely feeling that the church was somehow to blame for that counsel of Mr. Sewell's on which they had acted.

"I should like to know," she said, having brought the matter up, "whether he would have thought it was such a light matter if it had been his own children. Do you suppose he'd have been so ready to act on his own advice if it *had* been?"

"He told us the right thing to do, Persis,—the only thing. We couldn't let it go on," urged her husband gently.

"Well, it makes me despise Pen! Irene's showing twice the character that she is, this very minute."

The mother said this so that the father might defend her daughter to her. He did not fail. "Irene's got the easiest part, the way I look at it. And you'll see that Pen'll know how to behave when the time comes."

"What do you want she should do?"

"I haven't got so far as that yet. What are we going to do about Irene?"

"What do you want Pen should do," repeated Mrs. Lapham, "when it comes to it?"

"Well, I don't want she should take him, for *one* thing," said Lapham.

This seemed to satisfy Mrs. Lapham as to her husband, and she said, in defense of Corey, "Why, I don't see what *he's* done. It's all been our doing."

"Never mind that now. What about Irene?"

"She says she's going to Lapham to-morrow. She feels that she's got to get away somewhere. It's natural she should."

"Yes. And I presume it will be about the best thing *for* her. Shall you go with her?"

"Yes."

"Well." He comfortlessly took up a newspaper again, and she rose with a sigh, and went to her room to pack some things for the morrow's journey.

After dinner, when Irene had cleared away the last trace of it in kitchen and dining-room with unsparing punctilio, she came downstairs, dressed to go out, and bade her father come to walk with her again. It was a repetition of the aimlessness of the last night's wanderings. They came back, and she got tea for them, and after that they heard her stirring about in her own room, as if she were busy about many things; but they did not dare to look in upon her, even after all the noises had ceased, and they knew she had gone to bed.

"Yes; it's a thing she's got to fight out by herself," said Mrs. Lapham.

"I guess she'll get along," said Lapham. "But I don't want you should misjudge Pen either. She's all right too. She ain't to blame."

"Yes, I know. But I can't work round to it all at once. I sha'n't misjudge her, but you can't expect me to get over it right away."

"Mamma," said Irene, when she was hurrying their departure the next morning, "what did she tell him when he asked her?"

"Tell him?" echoed the mother; and after a while she added, "She didn't tell him anything."

"Did she say anything about me?"

"She said he mustn't come here any more."

Irene turned and went into her sister's room. "Good-bye, Pen," she said, kissing her with an effect of not seeing or touching her. "I want you should tell him all about it. If he's half a man, he won't give up till he knows why you won't have him; and he has a right to know."

"It wouldn't make any difference. I couldn't have him after ——"

"That's for you to say. But if you don't tell him about me, *I* will."

"'Rene!"

"Yes! You needn't say I cared for him. But you can say that you all thought he—cared for—me."

"Oh, Irene——"

"Don't!" Irene escaped from the arms that tried to cast themselves about her. "You are all right, Pen. You haven't done anything. You've helped me all you could. But I can't—yet."

She went out of the room and summoned Mrs. Lapham with a sharp "Now, mamma!" and went on putting the last things into her trunks.

The Colonel went to the station with them, and put them on the train. He got them a little compartment to themselves in the Pullman car; and as he stood leaning with his lifted hands against the sides of the doorway, he tried to say something consoling and hopeful: "I guess you'll have an easy ride, Irene. I don't believe it'll be dusty, any, after the rain last night."

"Don't you stay till the train starts, papa," returned the girl, in rigid rejection of his futilities. "Get off now."

"Well, if you want I should," he said, glad to be able to please her in anything. He remained on the platform till the cars started. He saw Irene bustling about in the compartment, making her mother comfortable for the journey; but Mrs. Lapham did not lift her head. The train moved off, and he went heavily back to his business.

From time to time during the day, when he caught a glimpse of him, Corey tried to make out from his face whether he knew what had taken place between him and Penelope. When Rogers came in about time of closing, and shut himself up with Lapham in his room, the young man remained till the two came out together and parted in their salutationless fashion.

Lapham showed no surprise at seeing Corey still there, and merely answered, "Well!" when the young man said that he wished to speak with him, and led the way back to his room.

Corey shut the door behind them. "I only wish to speak to you in case you know of the matter already; for otherwise I'm bound by a promise."

"I guess I know what you mean. It's about Penelope."

"Yes, it's about Miss Lapham. I am greatly attached to her—you'll excuse my saying it; I couldn't excuse myself if I were not."

"Perfectly excusable," said Lapham. "It's all right."

"Oh, I'm *glad* to hear you say that!" cried the young fellow joyfully. "I want you to believe that this isn't a new thing or an unconsidered thing with me—though it seemed so unexpected to her."

Lapham fetched a deep sigh. "It's all right as far as I'm concerned—or her mother. We've both liked you first-rate."

"Yes?"

"But there seems to be something in Penelope's mind—I don't know——" The Colonel consciously dropped his eyes.

"She referred to something—I couldn't make out what—but I hoped—I hoped—that with your leave I might overcome it—the barrier—whatever it was. Miss Lapham—Penelope—gave me the hope—that I was—wasn't—indifferent to her——"

"Yes, I guess that's so," said Lapham. He suddenly lifted his head, and confronted the young fellow's honest face with his own face, so different in its honesty. "Sure you never made up to any one else at the same time?"

"*Never!* Who could imagine such a thing? If that's all, I can easily——"

"I don't say that's all, nor that that's it. I don't want you should go upon that idea. I just thought, may be—you hadn't thought of it."

"No, I certainly hadn't thought of it! Such a thing would have been so impossible to me that I *couldn't* have thought of it; and it's so shocking to me now that I don't know what to say to it."

"Well, don't take it too much to heart," said Lapham, alarmed at the feeling he had excited; "I don't say she thought so. I was trying to guess—trying to——"

"If there is *any*thing I can say or do to convince you——"

"Oh, it ain't necessary to say anything. I'm all right."

"But Miss Lapham! I may see her again? I may try to convince her that——"

He stopped in distress, and Lapham afterwards told his wife that he kept seeing the face of Irene as it looked when he parted with her in the car; and whenever he was going to say yes, he could not open his lips. At the same time he could not help feeling that Penelope had a right to what was her own, and Sewell's words came back to him. Besides, they had already put Irene to the worst suffering. Lapham compromised, as he imagined.

"You can come round to-night and see *me*, if you want to," he said; and he bore grimly the gratitude that the young man poured out upon him.

Penelope came down to supper and took her mother's place at the head of the table.

Lapham sat silent in her presence as long as he could bear it. Then he asked, "How do you feel to-night, Pen?"

"Oh, like a thief," said the girl. "A thief that hasn't been arrested yet."

Lapham waited awhile before he said, "Well, now, your mother and I want you should hold up on that awhile."

"It isn't for you to say. It's something I *can't* hold up on."

"Yes, I guess you can. If I know what's happened, then what's happened is a thing that nobody is to blame for. And we want you should make the best of it, and not the worst. Heigh? It ain't going to help Irene any for you to hurt yourself—or anybody else; and I don't want you should take up with any such crazy notion. As far as heard from, you haven't stolen anything, and whatever you've got belongs to you."

"Has he been speaking to you, father?"

"Your mother's been speaking to me."

"Has *he* been speaking to you?"

"That's neither here nor there."

"Then he's broken his word, and I will never speak to him again!"

"If he was any such fool as to promise that he wouldn't talk to me on a subject"—Lapham drew a deep breath, and then made the plunge—"that I brought up——"

"Did you bring it up?"

"The same as brought up—the quicker he broke his word the better; and I want you should act upon that idea. Recollect that it's my business, and your mother's business, as well as yours, and we're going to have our say. He hain't done anything wrong, Pen, nor anything that he's going to be punished for. Understand that. He's got to have a reason, if you're not going to have him. I don't say you've got to have him; I want you should feel perfectly free about that; but I *do* say you've got to give him a reason."

"Is he coming here?"

"I don't know as you'd call it *coming*——"

"Yes, you do, father!" said the girl, in forlorn amusement at his shuffling.

"He's coming here to see *me*——"

"When's he coming?"

"I don't know but he's coming to-night."

"And you want I should see him?"

"I don't know but you'd better."

"All right. I'll see him."

Lapham drew a long, deep breath of suspicion inspired by this acquiescence. "What you going to do?" he asked presently.

"I don't know yet," answered the girl sadly. "It depends a good deal upon what *he* does."

"Well," said Lapham, with the hungriness of unsatisfied anxiety in his tone. When Corey's card was brought into the family-room where he and Penelope were sitting, he went into the parlor to find him. "I guess Penelope wants to see you," he said; and, indicating the family-room, he added, "She's in there," and did not go back himself.

Corey made his way to the girl's presence with open trepidation, which was not allayed by her silence and languor. She sat in the chair where she had sat the other night, but she was not playing with a fan now.

He came toward her, and then stood faltering. A faint smile quivered over her face at the spectacle of his subjection. "Sit down, Mr. Corey," she said. "There's no reason why we shouldn't talk it over quietly; for I know you will think I'm right."

"I'm sure of that," he answered hopefully. "When I saw that your father knew of it to-day, I asked him to let me see you again. I'm afraid that I broke my promise to you—technically——"

"It had to be broken."

He took more courage at her words. "But I've only come to do whatever you say, and not to be an—annoyance to you——"

"Yes, you have to know; but I couldn't tell you before. Now they all think I should."

A tremor of anxiety passed over the young man's face, on which she kept her eyes steadily fixed.

"We supposed it—it was—Irene——"

He remained blank a moment, and then he said with a smile

of relief, of deprecation, of protest, of amazement, of compassion:

"*Oh !* Never! Never for an instant! How could you think such a thing? It was impossible! I never thought of her. But I see—I see! I can explain—no, there's nothing to explain! I have never knowingly done or said a thing from first to last to make you think that. I see how terrible it is!" he said; but he still smiled, as if he could not take it seriously. "I admired her beauty—who could help doing that?—and I thought her very good and sensible. Why, last winter in Texas, I told Stanton about our meeting in Canada, and we agreed—I only tell you to show you how far I always was from what you thought—that he must come North and try to see her, and—and—of course, it all sounds very silly! —and he sent her a newspaper with an account of his ranch in it——"

"She thought it came from you."

"Oh, good heavens! He didn't tell me till after he'd done it. But he did it for a part of our foolish joke. And when I met your sister again, I only admired her as before. I can see, now, how I must have seemed to be seeking her out; but it was to talk of you with her—I never talked of anything else if I could help it, except when I changed the subject because I was ashamed to be always talking of you. I see how distressing it is for all of you. But tell me that you believe me!"

"Yes, I must. It's all been our mistake——"

"It has indeed! But there's no mistake about my loving *you*, Penelope," he said; and the old-fashioned name, at which she had often mocked, was sweet to her from his lips.

"That only makes it worse!" she answered.

"Oh, no!" he gently protested. "It makes it better. It makes it right. How is it worse? How is it wrong?"

"Can't you see? You must understand all now! Don't you see that if she believed so too, and if she——" She could not go on.

"Did she—did your sister—think that too?" gasped Corey.

"She used to talk with me about you; and when you say you care for me now, it makes me feel like the vilest hypocrite in the world. That day you gave her the list of books, and she came down to Nantasket, and went on about you, I helped her to flatter herself—oh! I don't see how she can forgive me. But she knows I

can never forgive myself! That's the reason she can do it. I can
see now," she went on, "how I must have been trying to get you
from her. I can't endure it! The only way is for me never to see
you or speak to you again!" She laughed forlornly. "That would
be pretty hard on you, if you cared."

"I do care—all the world!"

"Well, then, it would if you were going to keep on caring. You
won't long, if you stop coming now."

"Is this all, then? Is it the end?"

"It's—whatever it is. I can't get over the thought of her. Once
I thought I could, but now I see that I can't. It seems to grow
worse. Sometimes I feel as if it would drive me crazy."

He sat looking at her with lack-luster eyes. The light suddenly
came back into them. "Do you think I could love you if you had
been false to her? I know you have been true to her, and truer
still to yourself. I never tried to see her, except with the hope of
seeing you too. I supposed she must know that I was in love with
you. From the first time I saw you there that afternoon, you filled
my fancy. Do you think I was flirting with the child, or—no, you
*don't* think that! We have not done wrong. We have not harmed
any one knowingly. We have a right to each other——"

"No! no! you must never speak to me of this again. If you do,
I shall know that you despise me."

"But how will that help her? I don't love *her.*"

"Don't say that to me! I have said that to myself too much."

"If you forbid me to love you, it won't make me love her," he
persisted.

She was about to speak, but she caught her breath without
doing so, and merely stared at him.

"I must do what you say," he continued. "But what good will
it do her? You can't make her happy by making yourself unhappy."

"Do you ask me to profit by a wrong?"

"Not for the world. But there *is* no wrong!"

"There is something—I don't know what. There's a wall between us. I shall dash myself against it as long as I live; but that
won't break it."

"Oh!" he groaned. "We have done no wrong. Why should
we suffer from another's mistake as if it were our sin?"

"I don't know. But we must suffer."

"Well, then, I *will* not, for my part, and I will not let you. If you care for me——"

"You had no right to know it."

"You make it my privilege to keep you from doing wrong for the right's sake. I'm sorry, with all my heart and soul, for this error; but I can't blame myself, and I won't deny myself the happiness I haven't done anything to forfeit. I will never give you up. I will wait as long as you please for the time when you shall feel free from this mistake; but you shall be mine at last. Remember that. I might go away for months—a year, even; but that seems a cowardly and guilty thing, and I'm not afraid, and I'm not guilty, and I'm going to stay here and try to see you."

She shook her head. "It won't change anything. Don't you see that there's no hope for us?"

"When is she coming back?" he asked.

"I don't know. Mother wants father to come and take her out West for a while."

"She's up there in the country with your mother yet?"

"Yes."

He was silent; then he said, desperately:

"Penelope, she is very young; and perhaps—perhaps she might meet——"

"It would make no difference. It wouldn't change it for me."

"You are cruel—cruel to yourself, if you love me, and cruel to me. Don't you remember that night—before I spoke—you were talking of that book; and you said it was foolish and wicked to do as that girl did. Why is it different with you, except that you give me nothing, and can never give me anything when you take yourself away? If it were anybody else, I am sure you would say——"

"But it isn't anybody else, and that makes it impossible. Sometimes I think it might be if I would only say so to myself, and then all that I said to her about you comes up——"

"I will wait. It can't always come up. I won't urge you any longer now. But you will see it differently—more clearly. Good-bye—no! Good-night! I shall come again to-morrow. It will surely come right, and, whatever happens, you have done no wrong. Try to keep that in mind. I am so happy, in spite of all!"

He tried to take her hand, but she put it behind her. "No, no! I can't let you—yet!"

# XX

AFTER a week Mrs. Lapham returned, leaving Irene alone at the old homestead in Vermont. "She's comfortable there—as comfortable as she can be anywheres, I guess," she said to her husband, as they drove together from the station, where he had met her in obedience to her telegraphic summons. "She keeps herself busy helping about the house; and she goes round amongst the hands in their houses. There's sickness, and you know how helpful she is where there's sickness. She don't complain any. I don't know as I've heard a word out of her mouth since we left home; but I'm afraid it'll wear on her, Silas."

"You don't look over and above well yourself, Persis," said her husband kindly.

"Oh, don't talk about me. What I want to know is whether you can't get the time to run off with her somewhere? I wrote to you about Dubuque. She'll work herself down, I'm afraid; and *then* I don't know as she'll be over it. But if she could go off, and be amused—see new people——"

"I could *make* the time," said Lapham, "if I had to. But, as it happens, I've got to go out West on business,—I'll tell you about it,—and I'll take Irene along."

"Good!" said his wife. "That's about the best thing I've heard yet. Where you going?"

"Out Dubuque way."

"Anything the matter with Bill's folks?"

"No. It's business."

"How's Pen?"

"I guess she ain't much better than Irene."

"He been about any?"

"Yes. But I can't see as it helps matters much."

"Tchk!" Mrs. Lapham fell back against the carriage cushions. "I declare, to see her willing to take the man that we all thought wanted her sister! I can't make it seem right."

"It's right," said Lapham stoutly; "but I guess she ain't willing; I wish she was. But there don't seem to be any way out of the thing, anywhere. It's a perfect snarl. But I don't want you should be anyways ha'sh with Pen."

Mrs. Lapham answered nothing; but when she met Penelope she gave the girl's wan face a sharp look, and began to whimper on her neck.

Penelope's tears were all spent. "Well, mother," she said, "you come back almost as cheerful as you went away. I needn't ask if 'Rene's in good spirits. We all seem to be overflowing with them. I suppose this is one way of congratulating me. Mrs. Corey hasn't been round to do it yet."

"Are you—are you engaged to him, Pen?" gasped her mother.

"Judging by my feelings, I should say not. I feel as if it was a last will and testament. But you'd better ask him when he comes."

"I can't bear to look at him."

"I guess he's used to that. He don't seem to expect to be looked at. Well! we're all just where we started. I wonder how long it will keep up?"

Mrs. Lapham reported to her husband when he came home at night—he had left his business to go and meet her, and then, after a desolate dinner at the house, had returned to the office again—that Penelope was fully as bad as Irene. "And she don't know how to work it off. Irene keeps doing; but Pen just sits in her room and mopes. She don't even read. I went up this afternoon to scold her about the state the house was in—you can see that Irene's away by the perfect mess; but when I saw her through the crack of the door I hadn't the heart. She sat there with her hands in her lap, just staring. And, my goodness! she *jumped* so when she saw me; and then she fell back, and began to laugh, and said she, 'I thought it was my ghost, mother!' I felt as if I should give way."

Lapham listened jadedly, and answered far from the point. "I guess I've got to start out there pretty soon, Persis."

"How soon?"

"Well, to-morrow morning."

Mrs. Lapham sat silent. Then, "All right," she said. "I'll get you ready."

"I shall run up to Lapham for Irene, and then I'll push on through Canada. I can get there about as quick."

"Is it anything you can tell me about, Silas?"

"Yes," said Lapham. "But it's a long story, and I guess you've got your hands pretty full as it is. I've been throwing good money after bad,—the usual way,—and now I've got to see if I can save the pieces."

After a moment Mrs. Lapham asked, "Is it—Rogers?"

"It's Rogers."

"I didn't want you should get in any deeper with him."

"No. You didn't want I should press him either; and I had to do one or the other. And so I got in deeper."

"Silas," said his wife, "I'm afraid I made you!"

"It's all right, Persis, as far forth as that goes. I was glad to make it up with him—I jumped at the chance. I guess Rogers saw that he had a soft thing in me, and he's worked it for all it was worth. But it'll all come out right in the end."

Lapham said this as if he did not care to talk any more about it. He added, casually, "Pretty near everybody but the fellows that owe *me* seem to expect me to do a cash business, all of a sudden."

"Do you mean that you've got payments to make, and that people are not paying *you* ?"

Lapham winced a little. "Something like that," he said, and he lighted a cigar. "But when I tell you it's all right, I mean it, Persis. I ain't going to let the grass grow under my feet, though, —especially while Rogers digs the ground away from the roots."

"What are you going to do?"

"If it has to come to that, I'm going to squeeze him." Lapham's countenance lighted up with greater joy than had yet visited it since the day they had driven out to Brookline. "Milton K. Rogers is a rascal, if you want to know; or else all the signs fail. But I guess he'll find he's got his come-uppance." Lapham shut his lips so that the short, reddish-gray beard stuck straight out on them.

"What's he done?"

"What's he done? Well, now, I'll tell you what he's done, Persis, since you think Rogers is such a saint, and that I used him so badly in getting him out of the business. He's been dabbling in every sort of fool thing you can lay your tongue to,— wild-cat stocks, patent-rights, land speculations, oil claims,— till he's run through about everything. But he did have a big milling property out on the line of the P. Y. & X.,—saw-mills and grist-mills and lands,—and for the last eight years he's been doing a land-office business with 'em—business that would have made anybody else rich. But you can't make Milton K. Rogers rich, any more than you can fat a hide-bound colt. It ain't *in* him. He'd run through Vanderbilt, Jay Gould, and Tom Scott rolled into one,[8] in less than six months, give him a chance, and come out and want to borrow money of you. Well, he won't borrow any more money of *me*; and if he thinks I don't know as much about that milling property as he does, he's mistaken. I've taken his mills, but I guess I've got the inside track; Bill's kept me posted; and now I'm going out there to see how I can unload; and I sha'n't mind a great deal if Rogers is under the load when it's off, once."

"I don't understand you, Silas."

"Why, it's just this. The Great Lacustrine & Polar Railroad has leased the P. Y. & X. for ninety-nine years,—*bought* it, practically,—and it's going to build car-works right by those mills, and it may want them. And Milton K. Rogers knew it when he turned 'em in on me."[9]

"Well, if the road wants them, don't that make the mills valuable? You can get what you ask for them!"

"Can I? The P. Y. & X. is the only road that runs within fifty miles of the mills, and you can't get a foot of lumber nor a pound of flour to market any other way. As long as he had a little local road like the P. Y. & X. to deal with, Rogers could manage; but when it come to a big through line like the G. L. & P., he couldn't stand any chance at all. If such a road as that took a fancy to his mills, do you think it would pay what he asked? *No*, sir! He would take what the road offered, or else the road would tell him to carry his flour and lumber to market himself."

"And do you suppose he knew the G. L. & P. wanted the mills when he turned them in on you?" asked Mrs. Lapham, aghast, and falling helplessly into his alphabetical parlance.

The Colonel laughed scoffingly. "Well, when Milton K. Rogers don't know which side his bread's buttered on! I don't understand," he added thoughtfully, "how he's always letting it fall on the buttered side. But such a man as that is sure to have a screw loose in him somewhere."

Mrs. Lapham sat discomfited. All that she could say was, "Well, I want you should ask yourself whether Rogers would

8. Cornelius Vanderbilt (1794–1877), Jay Gould (1836–92), and Thomas Alexander Scott (1823–81) were American businessmen who made themselves wealthy and powerful through railroad speculation and management.
9. The names and initials of the railroads are fictitious, though they suggest the splendid titles often given to fly-by-night business enterprises.

ever have gone wrong, or got into these ways of his, if it hadn't been for your forcing him out of the business when you did. I want you should think whether you're not responsible for everything he's done since."

"You go and get that bag of mine ready," said Lapham sullenly. "I guess I can take care of myself. And Milton K. Rogers too," he added.

That evening Corey spent the time after dinner in his own room, with restless excursions to the library, where his mother sat with his father and sisters, and showed no signs of leaving them. At last, in coming down, he encountered her on the stairs, going up. They both stopped consciously.

"I would like to speak with you, mother. I have been waiting to see you alone."

"Come to my room," she said.

"I have a feeling that you know what I want to say," he began there.

She looked up at him where he stood by the chimney-piece, and tried to put a cheerful note into her questioning "Yes?"

"Yes; and I have a feeling that you won't like it—that you won't approve of it. I wish you did—I wish you could!"

"I'm used to liking and approving everything you do, Tom. If I don't like this at once, I shall try to like it—you know that —for your sake, whatever it is."

"I'd better be short," he said, with a quick sigh. "It's about Miss Lapham." He hastened to add, "I hope it *isn't* surprising to you. I'd have told you before, if I could."

"No, it isn't surprising. I was afraid—I suspected something of the kind."

They were both silent in a painful silence.

"Well, mother?" he asked at last.

"If it's something you've quite made up your mind to——"

"It is!"

"And if you've already spoken to her——"

"I had to do that first, of course."

"There would be no use of my saying anything, even if I disliked it."

"You do dislike it!"

"No—no! I can't say that. Of course, I should have preferred it if you had chosen some nice girl among those that you had been brought up with—some friend or associate of your sisters, whose people we had known——"

"Yes, I understand that, and I can assure you that I haven't been indifferent to your feelings. I have tried to consider them from the first, and it kept me hesitating in a way that I'm ashamed to think of; for it wasn't quite right towards—others. But your feelings and my sisters' have been in my mind, and if I couldn't yield to what I supposed they must be, entirely——"

Even so good a son and brother as this, when it came to his love affair, appeared to think that he had yielded much in considering the feelings of his family at all.

His mother hastened to comfort him. "I know—I know. I've seen for some time that this might happen, Tom, and I have prepared myself for it. I have talked it over with your father, and we both agreed from the beginning that you were not to be hampered by our feeling. Still—it is a surprise. It must be."

"I know it. I can understand your feeling. But I'm sure that it's one that will last only while you don't know her well."

"Oh, I'm sure of that, Tom. I'm sure that we shall all be fond of her,—for your sake at first, even,—and I hope she'll like us."

"I am quite certain of that," said Corey, with that confidence which experience does not always confirm in such cases. "And your taking it as you do lifts a tremendous load off me."

But he sighed so heavily, and looked so troubled, that his mother said, "Well, now, you mustn't think of that any more. We wish what is for your happiness, my son, and we will gladly reconcile ourselves to anything that might have been disagreeable. I suppose we needn't speak of the family. We must both think alike about them. They have their—drawbacks, but they are thoroughly good people, and I satisfied myself the other night that they were not to be dreaded." She rose, and put her arm round his neck. "And I wish you joy, Tom! If she's half as good as you are, you will both be very happy." She was going to kiss him, but something in his looks stopped her—an absence, a trouble, which broke out in his words.

"I must tell you, mother! There's been a complication—a mistake—that's a blight on me yet, and that it sometimes seems as if we couldn't escape from. I wonder if you can help us! They all thought I meant—the other sister."

"Oh, Tom! But how *could* they?"

"I don't know. It seemed so glaringly plain—I was ashamed of making it so outright from the beginning. But they did. Even she did, herself!"

"But where could they have thought your eyes were—your taste? It wouldn't be surprising if any one were taken with that wonderful beauty; and I'm sure she's good too. But I'm astonished at them! To think you could prefer that little, black, odd creature, with her joking and——"

"*Mother!*" cried the young man, turning a ghastly face of warning upon her.

"What do you mean, Tom?"

"Did you—did—did *you* think so, too,—that it was *Irene* I meant?"

"Why, of course!"

He stared at her hopelessly.

"Oh, my son!" she said, for all comment on the situation.

"Don't reproach me, mother! I couldn't stand it."

"No. I didn't mean to do that. But how—*how* could it happen?"

"I don't know. When she first told me that they had understood it so, I laughed—almost—it was so far from me. But now, when you seem to have had the same idea— Did you all think so?"

"Yes."

They remained looking at each other. Then Mrs. Corey began: "It did pass through my mind once—that day I went to call upon them—that it might not be as we thought; but I knew so little of—of——"

"Penelope," Corey mechanically supplied.

"Is that her name?—I forgot—that I only thought of you in relation to her long enough to reject the idea; and it was natural, after our seeing something of the other one last year, that I might suppose you had formed some—attachment——"

"Yes; that's what they thought too. But I never thought of her as anything but a pretty child. I was civil to her because you wished it; and when I met her here again, I only tried to see her so that I could talk with her about her sister."

"You needn't defend yourself to *me*, Tom," said his mother, proud to say it to him in his trouble. "It's a terrible business for them, poor things," she added. "I don't know how they could get over it. But, of course, sensible people must see——"

"They haven't got over it. At least *she* hasn't. Since it's happened, there's been nothing that hasn't made me prouder and fonder of her! At first I *was* charmed with her—my fancy was taken; she delighted me—I don't know how; but she was simply the most fascinating person I ever saw. Now I never think of that. I only think how good she is—how patient she is with me, and how unsparing she is of herself. If she were concerned alone—if I were not concerned too—it would soon end. She's never had a thought for anything but her sister's feeling and mine from the beginning. I go there,—I know that I oughtn't, but I can't help it,—and she suffers it, and tries not to let me see that she is suffering it. There never was any one like her—so brave, so true, so noble. I won't give her up—I can't. But it breaks my heart when she accuses herself of what was all *my* doing. We spend our time trying to reason out of it, but we always come back to it at last, and I have to hear her morbidly blaming herself. Oh!"

Doubtless Mrs. Corey imagined some reliefs to this suffering, some qualifications of this sublimity in a girl she had disliked so distinctly; but she saw none in her son's behavior, and she gave him her further sympathy. She tried to praise Penelope, and said that it was not to be expected that she could reconcile herself at once to everything. "I shouldn't have liked it in her if she had. But time will bring it all right. And if she really cares for you——"

"I extorted that from her."

"Well, then, you must look at it in the best light you can. There is no blame anywhere, and the mortification and pain is something that must be lived down. That's all. And don't let what I said grieve you, Tom. You know I scarcely knew her, and I—I shall be sure to like any one you like, after all."

"Yes, I know," said the young man drearily. "Will you tell father?"

"If you wish."

"He must know. And I couldn't stand any more of this, just yet—any more mistake."

"I will tell him," said Mrs. Corey; and it was naturally the next thing for a woman who dwelt so much on decencies to propose: "We must go to call on her—your sisters and I. They have never seen her even; and she mustn't be allowed to think we're indifferent to her, especially under the circumstances."

"Oh, no! Don't go—not yet," cried Corey, with an instinctive perception that nothing could be worse for him. "We must wait —we must be patient. I'm afraid it would be painful to her now."

He turned away without speaking further; and his mother's eyes followed him wistfully to the door. There were some questions that she would have liked to ask him; but she had to content herself with trying to answer them when her husband put them to her.

There was this comfort for her always in Bromfield Corey, that he never was much surprised at anything, however shocking or painful. His standpoint in regard to most matters was that of the sympathetic humorist who would be glad to have the victim of circumstance laugh with him, but was not too much vexed when the victim could not. He laughed now when his wife, with careful preparation, got the facts of his son's predicament fully under his eye.

"Really, Bromfield," she said, "I don't see how you *can* laugh. Do you see any way out of it?"

"It seems to me that the way has been found already. Tom has told his love to the right one, and the wrong one knows it. Time will do the rest."

"If I had so low an opinion of them all as that, it would make me very unhappy. It's shocking to think of it."

"It is, upon the theory of ladies and all young people," said her husband, with a shrug, feeling his way to the matches on the mantel, and then dropping them with a sigh, as if recollecting that he must not smoke there. "I've no doubt Tom feels himself an awful sinner. But apparently he's resigned to his sin; he isn't going to give her up."

"I'm glad to say, for the sake of human nature, that *she* isn't resigned—little as I like her," cried Mrs. Corey.

Her husband shrugged again. "Oh, there mustn't be any indecent haste. She will instinctively observe the proprieties. But come, now, Anna! you mustn't pretend to me here, in the sanctuary of home, that practically the human affections don't reconcile themselves to any situation that the human sentiments condemn. Suppose the wrong sister had died: would the right one have had any scruple in marrying Tom, after they had both 'waited a proper time,' as the phrase is?"

"Bromfield, you're shocking!"

"Not more shocking than reality. You may regard this as a second marriage." He looked at her with twinkling eyes, full of the triumph the spectator of his species feels in signal exhibitions of human nature. "Depend upon it, the right sister will be reconciled; the wrong one will be consoled; and all will go merry as a marriage bell—a second marriage bell. Why, it's quite like a romance!" Here he laughed outright again.

"Well," sighed the wife, "I could almost wish the right one, as you call her, would reject Tom. I dislike her so much."

"Ah, now you're talking business, Anna," said her husband, with his hands spread behind the back he turned comfortably to the fire. "The whole Lapham tribe is distasteful to *me*. As I don't happen to have seen our daughter-in-law elect, I have still the hope—which you're disposed to forbid me—that she may not be quite so unacceptable as the others."

"Do you really feel so, Bromfield?" anxiously inquired his wife.

"Yes—I think I do"; and he sat down, and stretched out his long legs toward the fire.

"But it's very inconsistent of you to oppose the matter now, when you've shown so much indifference up to this time. You've told me, all along, that it was of no use to oppose it."

"So I have. I was convinced of that at the beginning, or my reason was. You know very well that I am equal to any trial, any sacrifice, day after to-morrow; but when it comes to-day it's another thing. As long as this crisis decently kept its distance, I could look at it with an impartial eye; but now that it seems at hand, I find that, while my reason is still acquiescent, my nerves are disposed to—excuse the phrase—kick. I ask myself, what have I done nothing for, all my life, and lived as a gentleman should, upon the earnings of somebody else, in the possession of every polite taste and feeling that adorns leisure, if I'm to come to this at last? And I find no satisfactory answer. I say to myself that I might as well have yielded to the pressure all round me, and gone to work, as Tom has."

Mrs. Corey looked at him forlornly, divining the core of real repugnance that existed in his self-satire.

"I assure you, my dear," he continued, "that the recollection of what I suffered from the Laphams at that dinner of yours is an anguish still. It wasn't their behavior,—they behaved well enough—or ill enough; but their conversation was terrible. Mrs. Lapham's range was strictly domestic; and when the Colonel got me in the library, he poured mineral paint all over me, till I could have been safely warranted not to crack or scale in any climate. I suppose we shall have to see a good deal of them. They will probably come here every Sunday night to tea. It's a perspective without a vanishing-point."

"It may not be so bad, after all," said his wife; and she suggested for his consolation that he knew very little about the Laphams yet.

He assented to the fact. "I know very little about them, and about my other fellow-beings. I dare say that I should like the Laphams better if I knew them better. But in any case, I resign myself. And we must keep in view the fact that this is mainly Tom's affair, and if his affections have regulated it to his satisfaction, we must be content."

"Oh, yes," sighed Mrs. Corey. "And perhaps it won't turn out so badly. It's a great comfort to know that you feel just as I do about it."

"I do," said her husband, "and more too."

It was she and her daughters who would be chiefly annoyed by the Lapham connection; she knew that. But she had to begin to bear the burden by helping her husband to bear his light share of it. To see him so depressed dismayed her, and she might well have reproached him more sharply than she did for showing so much indifference, when she was so anxious, at first. But that would not have served any good end now. She even answered him patiently when he asked her, "What did you say to Tom when he told you it was the other one?"

"What could I say? I could do nothing, but try to take back what I had said against her."

"Yes, you had quite enough to do, I suppose. It's an awkward business. If it had been the pretty one, her beauty would have been our excuse. But the plain one—what do you suppose attracted him in her?"

Mrs. Corey sighed at the futility of the question. "Perhaps I did her injustice. I only saw her a few moments. Perhaps I got a false impression. I don't think she's lacking in sense, and that's a great thing. She'll be quick to see that we don't mean unkindness, and can't, by anything we say or do, when she's Tom's wife." She pronounced the distasteful word with courage, and went on: "The pretty one might not have been able to see that. She might have got it into her head that we were looking down on her; and those insipid people are terribly stubborn. We can come to some understanding with *this* one; I'm sure of that." She ended by declaring that it was now their duty to help Tom out of his terrible predicament.

"Oh, even the Lapham cloud has a silver lining," said Corey. "In fact, it seems really to have all turned out for the best, Anna; though it's rather curious to find you the champion of the Lapham side, at last. Confess, now, that the right girl has secretly been your choice all along, and that while you sympathize with the wrong one, you rejoice in the tenacity with which the right one is clinging to her own!" He added with final seriousness, "It's just that she should, and, so far as I understand the case, I respect her for it."

"Oh, yes," sighed Mrs. Corey. "It's natural, and it's right." But she added, "I suppose they're glad of him on any terms."

"That is what I have been taught to believe," said her husband. "When shall we see our daughter-in-law elect? I find myself rather impatient to have that part of it over."

Mrs. Corey hesitated. "Tom thinks we had better not call, just yet."

"She has told him of your terrible behavior when you called before?"

"No, Bromfield! She couldn't be so vulgar as *that?*"

"But anything short of it?"

## XXI

LAPHAM was gone a fortnight. He was in a sullen humor when he came back, and kept himself shut close within his own den at the office the first day. He entered it in the morning without a word to his clerks as he passed through the outer room, and he made no sign throughout the forenoon, except to strike savagely on his desk-bell from time to time, and send out to Walker for some book of accounts or a letter-file. His boy confidentially reported to Walker that the old man seemed to have got a lot of papers round; and at lunch the book-keeper said to Corey, at the

little table which they had taken in a corner together, in default
of seats at the counter, "Well, sir, I guess there's a cold wave
coming."

Corey looked up innocently, and said, "I haven't read the
weather report."

"Yes, sir," Walker continued, "it's coming. Areas of rain
along the whole coast, and increased pressure in the region of
the private office. Storm-signals up at the old man's door now."

Corey perceived that he was speaking figuratively, and that
his meteorology was entirely personal to Lapham. "What do you
mean?" he asked, without vivid interest in the allegory, his mind
being full of his own tragi-comedy.

"Why, just this: I guess the old man's takin' in sail. And I
guess he's got to. As I told you the first time we talked about him,
there don't any one know one-quarter as much about the old
man's business as the old man does himself; and I ain't betraying
any confidence when I say that I guess that old partner of his has
got pretty deep into his books. I guess he's over head and ears in
'em, and the old man's gone in after him, and he's got a drownin'
man's grip round his neck. There seems to be a kind of a lull—
kind of a dead calm, *I* call it—in the paint market just now; and
then again a ten-hundred-thousand-dollar man don't build a
hundred-thousand-dollar house without feeling the drain, unless
there's a regular boom. And just now there ain't any boom at all.
Oh, I don't say but what the old man's got anchors to windward;
guess he *has*; but if he's *goin'* to leave me his money, I wish he'd
left it six weeks ago. Yes, sir, I guess there's a cold wave comin';
but you can't generally 'most always tell, as a usual thing, where
the old man's concerned, and it's *only* a guess." Walker began to
feed in his breaded chop with the same nervous excitement with
which he abandoned himself to the slangy and figurative excesses
of his talks. Corey had listened with a miserable curiosity and
compassion up to a certain moment, when a broad light of hope
flashed upon him. It came from Lapham's potential ruin; and
the way out of the labyrinth that had hitherto seemed so hopeless
was clear enough, if another's disaster would befriend him, and
give him the opportunity to prove the unselfishness of his con-
stancy. He thought of the sum of money that was his own, and
that he might offer to lend, or practically give, if the time came;
and with his crude hopes and purposes formlessly exulting in his

heart, he kept on listening with an unchanged countenance.

Walker could not rest till he had developed the whole situation, so far as he knew it. "Look at the stock we've got on hand. There's going to be an awful shrinkage on that, now! And when everybody is shutting down, or running half time, the works up at Lapham are going full chip, just the same as ever. Well, it's his pride. I don't say but what it's a good sort of pride, but he likes to make his brags that the fire's never been out in the works since they started, and that no man's work or wages has ever been cut down yet at Lapham, it don't matter *what* the times are. Of course," explained Walker, "I shouldn't talk so to everybody; don't know as I should talk so to *any*body but you, Mr. Corey."

"Of course," assented Corey.

"Little off your feed to-day," said Walker, glancing at Corey's plate.

"I got up with a headache."

"Well, sir, if you're like me you'll carry it round all day, then. I don't know a much meaner thing than a headache—unless it's earache, or toothache, or some other kind of ache. I'm pretty hard to suit, when it comes to diseases. Notice how yellow the old man looked when he came in this morning? I don't like to see a man of his build look yellow—much."

About the middle of the afternoon the dust-colored face of Rogers, now familiar to Lapham's clerks, showed itself among them. "Has Colonel Lapham returned yet?" he asked, in his dry, wooden tones, of Lapham's boy.

"Yes, he's in his office," said the boy; and as Rogers advanced, he rose and added, "I don't know as you can see him to-day. His orders are not to let anybody in."

"Oh, indeed!" said Rogers; "I think he will see *me* !" and he pressed forward.

"Well, I'll have to ask," returned the boy; and hastily preceding Rogers, he put his head in at Lapham's door, and then withdrew it. "Please to sit down," he said; "he'll see you pretty soon;" and, with an air of some surprise, Rogers obeyed. His sere, dull-brown whiskers and the mustache closing over both lips were incongruously and illogically clerical in effect, and the effect was heightened for no reason by the parchment texture of his skin; the baldness extending to the crown of his head was like a baldness made up for the stage. What his face expressed chiefly was a bland and beneficent caution. Here, you must have said to yourself, is a man of just, sober, and prudent views, fixed purposes, and the good citizenship that avoids debt and hazard of every kind.

"What do you want?" asked Lapham, wheeling round in his swivel-chair as Rogers entered his room, and pushing the door shut with his foot, without rising.

Rogers took the chair that was not offered him, and sat with his hat-brim on his knees, and its crown pointed towards Lapham. "I want to know what you are going to do," he answered, with sufficient self-possession.

"I'll tell you, first, what I've *done*," said Lapham. "I've been to Dubuque, and I've found out all about that milling property you turned in on me. Did you know that the G. L. & P. had leased the P. Y. & X.?"

"I some suspected that it might."

"Did you know it when you turned the property in on me? Did you know that the G. L. & P. wanted to buy the mills?"

"I presumed the road would give a fair price for them," said Rogers, winking his eyes in outward expression of inwardly blinking the point.

"You lie," said Lapham, as quietly as if correcting him in a slight error; and Rogers took the word with equal *sang froid.* "You knew the road wouldn't give a fair price for the mills! You knew it would give what it chose, and that I couldn't help myself, when you let me take them. You're a thief, Milton K. Rogers, and you stole money I lent you." Rogers sat listening, as if respectfully considering the statements. "You knew how I felt about that old matter—or my wife did; and that I wanted to make it up to you, if you felt anyway badly used. And you took advantage of it. You've got money out of me, in the first place, on securities that wa'n't worth thirty-five cents on the dollar, and you've let me in for this thing, and that thing, and you've bled me every time. And all I've got to show for it is a milling property on a line of road that can squeeze me, whenever it wants to, as dry as it pleases. And you want to know what I'm going to do? I'm going to squeeze *you*. I'm going to sell these collaterals of yours,"—he touched a bundle of papers among others that littered his desk,

---

1. *"sang froid"*: (*French*), cold blood; coolness; indifference.

—"and I'm going to let the mills go for what they'll fetch. *I* ain't going to fight the G. L. & P."

Lapham wheeled about in his chair and turned his burly back on his visitor, who sat wholly unmoved.

"There are some parties," he began, with a dry tranquillity ignoring Lapham's words, as if they had been an outburst against some third person, who probably merited them, but in whom he was so little interested that he had been obliged to use patience in listening to his condemnation,—"there are some English parties who have been making inquiries in regard to those mills."

"I guess you're lying, Rogers," said Lapham, without looking round.

"Well, all that I have to ask is that you will not act hastily."

"I see you don't think I'm in earnest!" cried Lapham, facing fiercely about. "You think I'm fooling, do you?" He struck his bell, and "William," he ordered the boy who answered it, and who stood waiting while he dashed off a note to the brokers and inclosed it with the bundle of securities in a large envelope, "take these down to Gallop & Paddock's, in State street, right away. Now go!" he said to Rogers, when the boy had closed the door after him; and he turned once more to his desk.

Rogers rose from his chair, and stood with his hat in his hand. He was not merely dispassionate in his attitude and expression, he was impartial. He wore the air of a man who was ready to return to business whenever the wayward mood of his interlocutor permitted. "Then I understand," he said, "that you will take no action in regard to the mills till I have seen the parties I speak of."

Lapham faced about once more, and sat looking up into the visage of Rogers in silence. "I wonder what you're up to," he said at last; "I *should* like to know." But as Rogers made no sign of gratifying his curiosity, and treated this last remark of Lapham's as of the irrelevance of all the rest, he said, frowning, "You bring me a party that will give me enough for those mills to clear me of you, and I'll talk to you. But don't you come here with any man of straw. And I'll give you just twenty-four hours to prove yourself a swindler again."

Once more Lapham turned his back, and Rogers, after looking thoughtfully into his hat a moment, cleared his throat, and quietly withdrew, maintaining to the last his unprejudiced demeanor.

Lapham was not again heard from, as Walker phrased it, during the afternoon, except when the last mail was taken in to him; then the sound of rending envelopes, mixed with that of what seemed suppressed swearing, penetrated to the outer office. Somewhat earlier than the usual hour for closing, he appeared there with his hat on and his overcoat buttoned about him. He said briefly to his boy, "William, I sha'n't be back again this afternoon," and then went to Miss Dewey and left a number of letters on her table to be copied, and went out. Nothing had been said, but a sense of trouble subtly diffused itself through those who saw him go out.

That evening, as he sat down with his wife alone at tea, he asked, "Ain't Pen coming to supper?"

"No, she ain't," said his wife. "I don't know as I like the way she's going on, any too well. I'm afraid, if she keeps on, she'll be down sick. She's got deeper feelings than Irene."

Lapham said nothing, but, having helped himself to the abundance of his table in his usual fashion, he sat and looked at his plate with an indifference that did not escape the notice of his wife. "What's the matter with *you*?" she asked.

"Nothing. I haven't got any appetite."

"What's the matter?" she persisted.

"Trouble's the matter; bad luck and lots of it's the matter," said Lapham. "I haven't ever hid anything from you, Persis, when you asked me, and it's too late to begin now. I'm in a fix. I'll tell you what kind of a fix, if you think it'll do you any good; but I guess you'll be satisfied to know that it's a fix."

"How much of a one?" she asked, with a look of grave, steady courage in her eyes.

"Well, I don't know as I can tell, just yet," said Lapham, avoiding this look. "Things have been dull all the fall, but I thought they'd brisk up, come winter. They haven't. There have been a lot of failures, and some of 'em owed me, and some of 'em had me on their paper; and——" Lapham stopped.

"And what?" prompted his wife.

He hesitated before he added, "And then—Rogers."

"I'm to blame for that," said Mrs. Lapham. "I forced you to it."

"No; I was as willing to go into it as what you were," answered Lapham. "I don't want to blame anybody."

Mrs. Lapham had a woman's passion for fixing responsibility; she could not help saying, as soon as acquitted, "I warned you against him, Silas. I told you not to let him get in any deeper with you."

"Oh, yes. I had to help him to try to get my money back. I might as well poured water into a sieve. And now——" Lapham stopped.

"Don't be afraid to speak out to me, Silas Lapham. If it comes to the worst, I want to know it—I've got to know it. What did I ever care for the money? I've had a happy home with you ever since we were married, and I guess I shall have as long as you live, whether we go on to the Back Bay, or go back to the old house at Lapham. I know who's to blame, and I blame myself. It was my forcing Rogers on to you." She came back to this, with her helpless longing, inbred in all Puritan souls, to have some one specifically suffer for the evil in the world, even if it must be herself.

"It hasn't come to the worst yet, Persis," said her husband. "But I shall have to hold up on the new house a little while, till I can see where I am."

"I shouldn't care if we had to sell it," cried his wife, in passionate self-condemnation. "I should be *glad* if we had to, as far as I'm concerned."

"I shouldn't," said Lapham.

"I know!" said his wife; and she remembered ruefully how his heart was set on it.

He sat musing. "Well, I guess it's going to come out all right in the end. Or, if it ain't," he sighed, "we can't help it. May be Pen needn't worry so much about Corey, after all," he continued, with a bitter irony new to him. "It's an ill wind that blows nobody good. And there's a chance," he ended, with a still bitterer laugh, "that Rogers will come to time, after all."

"I don't believe it!" exclaimed Mrs. Lapham, with a gleam of hope in her eyes. "What chance?"

"One in ten million," said Lapham; and her face fell again. "He says there are some English parties after him to buy these mills."

"Well?"

"Well, I gave him twenty-four hours to prove himself a liar."

"You don't believe there are any such parties?"

"Not in *this* world."

"But if there were?"

"Well, if there were, Persis—— But pshaw!"

"No, no!" she pleaded eagerly. "It don't seem as if he *could* be such a villain. What would be the use of his pretending? If he brought the parties to you——"

"Well," said Lapham scornfully, "I'd let them have the mills at the price Rogers turned 'em in on me at. *I* don't want to make anything on 'em. But guess I shall hear from the G. L. & P. first. And when they make their offer, I guess I'll have to accept it, whatever it is. I don't think they'll have a great many competitors."

Mrs. Lapham could not give up her hope. "If you could get your price from those English parties before they knew that the G. L. & P. wanted to buy the mills, would it let you out with Rogers?"

"Just about," said Lapham.

"Then I know he'll move heaven and earth to bring it about. I *know* you won't be allowed to suffer for doing him a kindness, Silas. He *can't* be so ungrateful! Why, why *should* he pretend to have any such parties in view when he hasn't? Don't you be down-hearted, Si. You'll see that he'll be round with them to-morrow."

Lapham laughed, but she urged so many reasons for her belief in Rogers that Lapham began to rekindle his own faith a little. He ended by asking for a hot cup of tea; and Mrs. Lapham sent the pot out and had a fresh one steeped for him. After that he made a hearty supper in the revulsion from his entire despair; and they fell asleep that night talking hopefully of his affairs, which he laid before her fully, as he used to do when he first started in business. That brought the old times back, and he said: "If this had happened then, I shouldn't have cared much. I was young then, and I wasn't afraid of anything. But I noticed that after I passed fifty I began to get scared easier. I don't believe I could pick up, now, from a regular knockdown."

"Pshaw! *You* scared, Silas Lapham?" cried his wife, proudly. "I should like to see the thing that ever scared you; or the knockdown that *you* couldn't pick up from!"

"Is that so, Persis?" he asked, with the joy her courage gave him.

In the middle of the night she called to him, in a voice which the darkness rendered still more deeply troubled: "Are you awake, Silas?"

"Yes; I'm awake."

"I've been thinking about those English parties, Si——"

"So've I."

"And I can't make it out but what you'd be just as bad as Rogers, every bit and grain, if you were to let them have the mills——"

"And not tell 'em what the chances were with the G. L. & P.? I thought of that, and you needn't be afraid."

She began to bewail herself, and to sob convulsively: "Oh, Silas! Oh, Silas!" Heaven knows in what measure the passion of her soul was mixed with pride in her husband's honesty, relief from an apprehended struggle, and pity for him.

"Hush, hush, Persis!" he besought her. "You'll wake Pen if you keep on that way. Don't cry any more! You mustn't."

"Oh, let me cry, Silas! It'll help me. I shall be all right in a minute. Don't you mind." She sobbed herself quiet. "It does seem too hard," she said, when she could speak again, "that you have to give up this chance when Providence had fairly raised it up for you."

"I guess it wa'n't *Providence* raised it up," said Lapham. "Any rate, it's got to go. Most likely Rogers was lyin', and there ain't any such parties; but if there were, they couldn't have the mills from me without the whole story. Don't you be troubled, Persis. I'm going to pull through all right."

"Oh, I ain't afraid. I don't suppose but what there's plenty would help you, if they knew you needed it, Si."

"They would if they knew I *didn't* need it," said Lapham sardonically.

"Did you tell Bill how you stood?"

"No, I couldn't bear to. I've been the rich one so long, that I couldn't bring myself to own up that I was in danger."

"Yes."

"Besides, it didn't look so ugly till to-day. But I guess we sha'n't let ugly looks scare us."

"No."

# XXII

THE morning postman brought Mrs. Lapham a letter from Irene, which was chiefly significant because it made no reference whatever to the writer or her state of mind. It gave the news of her uncle's family; it told of their kindness to her; her cousin Will was going to take her and his sisters ice-boating on the river, when it froze.

By the time this letter came, Lapham had gone to his business, and the mother carried it to Penelope to talk over. "What do you make out of it?" she asked; and without waiting to be answered, she said, "I don't know as I believe in cousins marrying, a great deal; but if Irene and Will were to fix it up between 'em—" She looked vaguely at Penelope.

"It wouldn't make any difference as far as I was concerned," replied the girl, listlessly.

Mrs. Lapham lost her patience.

"Well, then, I'll tell you what, Penelope!" she exclaimed. "Perhaps it'll make a difference to you if you know that your father's in *real* trouble. He's harassed to death, and he was awake half the night, talking about it. That abominable old Rogers has got a lot of money away from him; and he's lost by others that he's helped,"—Mrs. Lapham put it in this way because she had no time to be explicit,—"and I want you should come out of your room now, and try to be of some help and comfort to him when he comes home to-night. I guess Irene wouldn't mope round much, if she was here," she could not help adding.

The girl lifted herself on her elbow. "What's that you say about father?" she demanded, eagerly. "Is he in trouble? Is he going to lose his money? Shall we have to stay in this house?"

"We may be very *glad* to stay in this house," said Mrs. Lapham, half angry with herself for having given cause for the girl's conjectures, and half with the habit of prosperity in her child, which could conceive no better of what adversity was. "And I want you should get up and show that you've got some feeling for somebody in the world besides yourself."

"Oh, I'll get *up!*" said the girl, promptly, almost cheerfully.

"I don't say it's as bad now as it looked a little while ago," said her mother, conscientiously hedging a little from the statement which she had based rather upon her feelings than her facts. "Your father thinks he'll pull through all right, and I don't know but what he will. But I want you should see if you can't do something to cheer him up and keep him from getting so perfectly down-hearted as he seems to get, under the load he's got to carry. And stop thinking about yourself awhile, and behave yourself like a sensible girl."

"Yes, yes," said the girl; "I will. You needn't be troubled about me any more."

Before she left her room she wrote a note, and when she came down she was dressed to go out-of-doors and post it herself. The note was to Corey:

"Do not come to see me any more till you hear from me. I have a reason which I cannot give you now; and you must not ask what it is."

All day she went about in a buoyant desperation, and she came down to meet her father at supper.

"Well, Persis," he said scornfully, as he sat down, "we might as well saved our good resolutions till they were wanted. I guess those English parties have gone back on Rogers."

"Do you mean he didn't come?"

"He hadn't come up to half-past five," said Lapham.

"Tchk!" uttered his wife.

"But I guess I shall pull through without Mr. Rogers," continued Lapham. "A firm that I didn't think *could* weather it is still afloat, and so far forth as the danger goes of being dragged under with it, I'm all right." Penelope came in. "Hello, Pen!" cried her father. "It ain't often I meet *you* nowadays." He put up his hand as she passed his chair, and pulled her down and kissed her.

"No," she said; "but I thought I'd come down to-night and cheer you up a little. I shall not talk; the sight of me will be enough."

Her father laughed out. "Mother been telling you? Well, I *was* pretty blue last night; but I guess I was more scared than hurt. How'd you like to go to the theater to-night? Sellers at the Park. Heigh?"[2]

2. Sellers is probably a reference to Samuel Clemens' (Mark Twain's) character Colonel Mulberry Sellers who first appeared in *The Gilded Age* (1873). The actor John T. Raymond (1836–87) brought Clemens' character to the stage the following year in the play, *Colonel Sellers*.

"Well, I don't know. Don't you think they could get along without me there?"

"No; couldn't work it at all," cried the Colonel. "Let's all go. Unless," he added, inquiringly, "there's somebody coming here?"

"There's nobody coming," said Penelope.

"Good! Then we'll go. Mother, don't you be late now."

"Oh, *I* sha'n't keep you waiting," said Mrs. Lapham. She had thought of telling what a cheerful letter she had got from Irene; but upon the whole it seemed better not to speak of Irene at all just then. After they returned from the theater, where the Colonel roared through the comedy, with continual reference of his pleasure to Penelope, to make sure that she was enjoying it too, his wife said, as if the whole affair had been for the girl's distraction rather than his, "I don't believe but what it's going to come out all right about the children;" and then she told him of the letter, and the hopes she had founded upon it.

"Well, perhaps you're right, Persis," he consented.

"I haven't seen Pen so much like herself since it happened. I declare, when I see the way she came out to-night, just to please you, I don't know as I want you should get over all your troubles right away."

"I guess there'll be enough to keep Pen going for a while yet," said the Colonel, winding up his watch.

But for a time there was a relief, which Walker noted, in the atmosphere at the office, and then came another cold wave, slighter than the first, but distinctly felt there, and succeeded by another relief. It was like the winter which was wearing on to the end of the year, with alternations of freezing weather, and mild days stretching to weeks, in which the snow and ice wholly disappeared. It was none the less winter, and none the less harassing for these fluctuations, and Lapham showed in his face and temper the effect of like fluctuations in his affairs. He grew thin and old, and both at home and at his office he was irascible to the point of offense. In these days Penelope shared with her mother the burden of their troubled home, and united with her in supporting the silence or the petulance of the gloomy, secret man who replaced the presence of jolly prosperity there. Lapham had now ceased to talk of his troubles, and savagely resented his wife's interference. "You mind your own business, Persis," he said one day, "if you've got any;" and after that she left him mainly to Penelope, who did not think of asking him questions.

"It's pretty hard on you, Pen," she said.

"That makes it easier for me," returned the girl, who did not otherwise refer to her own trouble. In her heart she had wondered a little at the absolute obedience of Corey, who had made no sign since receiving her note. She would have liked to ask her father if Corey was sick; she would have liked him to ask her why Corey did not come any more. Her mother went on:

"I don't believe your father knows *where* he stands. He works away at those papers he brings home here at night, as if he didn't half know what he was about. He always did have that close streak in him, and I don't suppose but what he's been going into things he don't want anybody else to know about, and he's kept these accounts of his own."

Sometimes he gave Penelope figures to work at, which he would not submit to his wife's nimbler arithmetic. Then she went to bed and left them sitting up till midnight, struggling with problems in which they were both weak. But she could see that the girl was a comfort to her father, and that his troubles were a defense and shelter to her. Some nights she could hear them going out together, and then she lay awake for their return from their long walk. When the hour or day of respite came again, the home felt it first. Lapham wanted to know what the news from Irene was; he joined his wife in all her cheerful speculations, and tried to make her amends for his sullen reticence and irritability. Irene was staying on at Dubuque. There came a letter from her, saying that her uncle's people wanted her to spend the winter there. "Well, let her," said Lapham. "It'll be the best thing for her." Lapham himself had letters from his brother at frequent intervals. His brother was watching the G. L. & P., which as yet had made no offer for the mills. Once, when one of these letters came, he submitted to his wife whether, in the absence of any positive information that the road wanted the property, he might not, with a good conscience, dispose of it to the best advantage to anybody who came along.

She looked wistfully at him; it was on the rise from a season of deep depression with him. "No, Si," she said; "I don't see how you could do that."

He did not assent and submit, as he had done at first, but began to rail at the unpracticality of women; and then he shut some papers he had been looking over into his desk, and flung out of the room.

One of the papers had slipped through the crevice of the lid, and lay upon the floor. Mrs. Lapham kept on at her sewing, but after a while she picked the paper up to lay it on the desk. Then she glanced at it, and saw that it was a long column of dates and figures, recording successive sums, never large ones, paid regularly to "Wm. M." The dates covered a year, and the sum amounted at least to several hundreds.

Mrs. Lapham laid the paper down on the desk, and then she took it up again and put it into her work-basket, meaning to give it to him. When he came in she saw him looking absent-mindedly about for something, and then going to work upon his papers, apparently without it. She thought she would wait till he missed it definitely, and then give him the scrap she had picked up. It lay in her basket, and after some days it found its way under the work in it, and she forgot it.

## XXIII

Since New Year's there had scarcely been a mild day, and the streets were full of snow, growing foul under the city feet and hoofs, and renewing its purity from the skies with repeated falls, which in turn lost their whiteness, beaten down, and beaten black and hard into a solid bed like iron. The sleighing was incomparable, and the air was full of the din of bells; but Lapham's turnout was not of those that thronged the Brighton road every afternoon; the man at the livery-stable sent him word that the mare's legs were swelling.

He and Corey had little to do with each other. He did not know how Penelope had arranged it with Corey; his wife said she knew no more than he did, and he did not like to ask the girl herself, especially as Corey no longer came to the house. He saw that she was cheerfuller than she had been, and helpfuller with him and her mother. Now and then Lapham opened his troubled soul to her a little, letting his thought break into speech without preamble or conclusion. Once he said:

"Pen, I presume you know I'm in trouble."

"We all seem to be there," said the girl.

"Yes, but there's a difference between being there by your own fault and being there by somebody else's."

"I don't call it his fault," she said.

"I call it mine," said the Colonel.

The girl laughed. Her thought was of her own care, and her father's wholly of his. She must come to his ground. "What have you been doing wrong?"

"I don't know as you'd call it wrong. It's what people do all the time. But I wish I'd let stocks alone. It's what I always promised your mother I would do. But there's no use cryin' over spilt milk; or watered stock, either."

"I don't think there's much use crying about anything. If it could have been cried straight, it would have been all right from the start," said the girl, going back to her own affair; and if Lapham had not been so deeply engrossed in his, he might have seen how little she cared for all that money could do or undo. He did not observe her enough to see how variable her moods were in those days, and how often she sank from some wild gayety into abject melancholy; how at times she was fiercely defiant of nothing at all, and at others inexplicably humble and patient. But no doubt none of these signs had passed unnoticed by his wife, to whom Lapham said one day, when he came home, "Persis, what's the reason Pen don't marry Corey?"

"You know as well as I do, Silas," said Mrs. Lapham, with an inquiring look at him for what lay behind his words.

"Well, I think it's all tomfoolery, the way she's going on. There ain't any rhyme nor reason to it." He stopped, and his wife waited. "If she said the word, I could have some help from them." He hung his head, and would not meet his wife's eye.

"I guess you're in a pretty bad way, Si," she said pityingly, "or you wouldn't have come to that."

"I'm in a hole," said Lapham, "and I don't know where to turn. You won't let me do anything about those mills——"

"Yes, I'll let you," said his wife sadly.

He gave a miserable cry. "You know I can't do anything, if you do. Oh, my Lord!"

She had not seen him so low as that before. She did not know what to say. She was frightened, and could only ask, "Has it come to the worst?"

"The new house has got to go," he answered evasively.

She did not say anything. She knew that the work on the house had been stopped since the beginning of the year. Lapham had told the architect that he preferred to leave it unfinished till the spring, as there was no prospect of their being able to get into it that winter; and the architect had agreed with him that it would not hurt it to stand. Her heart was heavy for him, though she could not say so. They sat together at the table, where she had come to be with him at his belated meal. She saw that he did not eat, and she waited for him to speak again, without urging him to take anything. They were past that.

"And I've sent orders to shut down at the Works," he added.

"Shut down at the Works!" she echoed with dismay. She could not take it in. The fire at the Works had never been out before since it was first kindled. She knew how he had prided himself upon that; how he had bragged of it to every listener, and had always lugged the fact in as the last expression of his sense of success. "Oh, Silas!"

"What's the use?" he retorted. "I saw it was coming a month ago. There are some fellows out in West Virginia that have been running the paint as hard as they could. They couldn't do much; they used to put it on the market raw. But lately they got to baking it, and now they've struck a vein of natural gas right by their works, and they pay ten cents for fuel where I pay a dollar, and they make as good a paint. Anybody can see where it's going to end. Besides, the market's overstocked. It's glutted. There wa'n't anything to do but to shut *down*, and I've *shut down*."

"I don't know what's going to become of the hands in the middle of the winter, this way," said Mrs. Lapham, laying hold of one definite thought which she could grasp in the turmoil of ruin that whirled before her eyes.

"I don't care what becomes of the hands," cried Lapham. "They've shared my luck; now let 'em share the other thing. And if you're so very sorry for the hands, I wish you'd keep a little of your pity for *me*. Don't you know what shutting down the Works means?"

"Yes, indeed I do, Silas," said his wife tenderly.

"Well, then!" He rose, leaving his supper untasted, and went into the sitting-room, where she presently found him, with that everlasting confusion of papers before him on the desk. That made her think of the paper in her work-basket, and she decided not to make the careworn, distracted man ask her for it, after all. She brought it to him.

He glanced blankly at it and then caught it from her, turning red and looking foolish. "Where'd you get that?"

"You dropped it on the floor the other night, and I picked it up. Who is 'Wm. M.'?"

" 'Wm. M.'?" he repeated, looking confusedly at her, and then at the paper. "Oh,—it's nothing." He tore the paper into small pieces, and went and dropped them into the fire. When Mrs. Lapham came into the room in the morning, before he was down, she found a scrap of the paper, which must have fluttered to the hearth; and glancing at it she saw that the words were "Mrs. M." She wondered what dealings with a woman her husband could have, and she remembered the confusion he had shown about the paper, and which she had thought was because she had surprised one of his business secrets. She was still thinking of it when he came down to breakfast, heavy-eyed, tremulous, with deep seams and wrinkles in his face.

After a silence which he did not seem inclined to break, "Silas," she asked, "who is 'Mrs. M.'?"

He stared at her. "I don't know what you're talking about."

"Don't you?" she returned mockingly. "When you do, you tell me. Do you want any more coffee?"

"No."

"Well, then, you can ring for Alice when you've finished. I've got some things to attend to." She rose abruptly, and left the room. Lapham looked after her in a dull way, and then went on with his breakfast. While he still sat at his coffee, she flung into the room again, and dashed some papers down beside his plate. "Here are some more things of yours, and I'll thank you to lock them up in your desk and not litter my room with them, if you please." Now he saw that she was angry, and it must be with him. It enraged him that in such a time of trouble she should fly out at him in that way. He left the house without trying to speak to her.

That day Corey came just before closing, and, knocking at Lapham's door, asked if he could speak with him a few moments.

"Yes," said Lapham, wheeling round in his swivel-chair and kicking another towards Corey. "Sit down. I want to talk to you. I'd ought to tell you you're wasting your time here. I spoke the other day about your placin' yourself better, and I can help you to do it, yet. There ain't going to be the outcome for the paint in the foreign markets that we expected, and I guess you better give it up."

"I don't wish to give it up," said the young fellow, setting his lips. "I've as much faith in it as ever; and I want to propose now what I hinted at in the first place. I want to put some money into the business."

"Some money!" Lapham leaned towards him, and frowned as if he had not quite understood, while he clutched the arms of his chair.

"I've got about thirty thousand dollars that I could put in, and if you don't want to consider me a partner—I remember that you objected to a partner—you can let me regard it as an investment. But I think I see the way to doing something at once in Mexico, and I should like to feel that I had something more than a drummer's interest in the venture."[3]

The men sat looking into each other's eyes. Then Lapham leaned back in his chair, and rubbed his hand hard and slowly over his face. His features were still twisted with some strong emotion when he took it away. "Your family know about this?"

"My uncle James knows."

"He thinks it would be a good plan for you?"

"He thought that by this time I ought to be able to trust my own judgment."

"Do you suppose I could see your uncle at his office?"

"I imagine he's there."

"Well, I want to have a talk with him, one of these days." He sat pondering awhile, and then rose, and went with Corey to his door. "I guess I sha'n't change my mind about taking you into the business in that way," he said coldly. "If there was any reason why I shouldn't at first, there's more now."

"Very well, sir," answered the young man, and went to close his desk. The outer office was empty; but while Corey was putting his papers in order it was suddenly invaded by two women, who pushed by the protesting porter on the stairs and made their way towards Lapham's room. One of them was Miss Dewey, the type-writer girl, and the other was a woman

---

3. A drummer is a travelling salesman.

whom she would resemble in face and figure twenty years hence, if she led a life of hard work varied by paroxysms of hard drinking.

"That his room, Z'rilla?" asked this woman, pointing towards Lapham's door with a hand that had not freed itself from the fringe of dirty shawl under which it had hung. She went forward without waiting for the answer, but before she could reach it the door opened, and Lapham stood filling its space.

"Look here, Colonel Lapham!" began the woman, in a high key of challenge. "I want to know if this is the way you're goin' back on me and Z'rilla?"

"What do you want?" asked Lapham.

"What do I want? What do you s'pose I want? I want the money to pay my month's rent; there ain't a bite to eat in the house; and I want some money to market."

Lapham bent a frown on the woman, under which she shrank back a step. "You've taken the wrong way to get it. Clear out!"

"I *won't* clear out!" said the woman, beginning to whimper.

"Corey!" said Lapham, in the peremptory voice of a master, —he had seemed so indifferent to Corey's presence that the young man thought he must have forgotten he was there,—"is Dennis anywhere round?"

"Yissor," said Dennis, answering for himself from the head of the stairs, and appearing in the wareroom.

Lapham spoke to the woman again. "Do you want I should call a hack, or do you want I should call an officer?"

The woman began to cry into an end of her shawl. "*I* don't know what we're goin' to do."

"You're going to clear out," said Lapham. "Call a hack, Dennis. If you ever come here again, I'll have you arrested. Mind that! Zerrilla, I shall want you early to-morrow morning."

"Yes, sir," said the girl meekly; she and her mother shrank out after the porter.

Lapham shut his door without a word.

At lunch the next day Walker made himself amends for Corey's reticence by talking a great deal. He talked about Lapham, who seemed to have, more than ever since his apparent difficulties began, the fascination of an enigma for his bookkeeper, and he ended by asking, "Did you see that little circus last night?"

"What little circus?" asked Corey in his turn.

"Those two women and the old man. Dennis told me about it. I told him if he liked his place he'd better keep his mouth shut."

"That was very good advice," said Corey.

"Oh, all right, if you don't want to talk. Don't know as I should in your place," returned Walker, in the easy security he had long felt that Corey had no intention of putting on airs with him. "But I'll tell you what: the old man can't expect it of everybody. If he keeps this thing up much longer, it's going to be talked about. You can't have a woman walking into your place of business, and trying to bulldoze you before your porter, without setting your porter to thinking. And the last thing you want a porter to do is to think; for when a porter thinks, he thinks wrong."

"I don't see why even a porter couldn't think right about that affair," replied Corey. "I don't know who the woman was, though I believe she was Miss Dewey's mother; but I couldn't see that Colonel Lapham showed anything but a natural resentment of her coming to him in that way. I should have said she was some rather worthless person whom he'd been befriending, and that she had presumed upon his kindness."

"Is that so? What do you think of his never letting Miss Dewey's name go on the books?"

"That it's another proof it's a sort of charity of his. That's the only way to look at it."

"Oh, *I'm* all right." Walker lighted a cigar and began to smoke, with his eyes closed to a fine straight line. "It won't do for a book-keeper to think wrong, any more than a porter, I suppose. But I guess you and I don't think very different about this thing."

"Not if you think as I do," replied Corey steadily; "and I know you would do that if you had seen the 'circus' yourself. A man doesn't treat people who have a disgraceful hold upon him as he treated them."

"It depends upon who he is," said Walker, taking his cigar from his mouth. "I never said the old man was afraid of anything."

"And character," continued Corey, disdaining to touch the

matter further, except in generalities, "must go for something. If it's to be the prey of mere accident and appearance, then it goes for nothing."

"Accidents will happen in the best-regulated families," said Walker, with vulgar, good-humored obtuseness that filled Corey with indignation. Nothing, perhaps, removed his matter-of-fact nature farther from the common-place than a certain generosity of instinct, which I should not be ready to say was always infallible.

That evening it was Miss Dewey's turn to wait for speech with Lapham after the others were gone. He opened his door at her knock, and stood looking at her with a worried air. "Well, what do you want, Zerrilla?" he asked, with a sort of rough kindness.

"I want to know what I'm going to do about Hen. He's back again; and he and mother have made it up, and they both got to drinking last night after I went home, and carried on so that the neighbors came in."

Lapham passed his hand over his red and heated face. "I don't know what I'm going to do. You're twice the trouble that my own family is, now. But I know what I'd do, mighty quick, if it wasn't for you, Zerrilla," he went on relentingly. "I'd shut your mother up somewheres, and if I could get that fellow off for a three years' voyage——"

"I declare," said Miss Dewey, beginning to whimper, "it seems as if he came back just so often to spite me. He's never gone more than a year at the furthest, and you can't make it out habitual drunkenness, either, when it's just sprees. I'm at my wit's end."

"Oh, well, you mustn't cry around here," said Lapham soothingly.

"I know it," said Miss Dewey. "If I could get rid of Hen, I could manage well enough with mother. Mr. Wemmel would marry me if I could get the divorce. He's said so over and over again."

"I don't know as I like that very well," said Lapham, frowning. "I don't know as I want you should get married in any hurry again. I don't know as I like your going with anybody else just yet."

"Oh, you needn't be afraid but what it'll be all right. It'll be the best thing all round, if I can marry him."

"Well!" said Lapham impatiently; "I can't think about it now. I suppose they've cleaned everything out again?"

"Yes, they have," said Zerrilla; "there isn't a cent left."

"You're a pretty expensive lot," said Lapham. "Well, here!" He took out his pocket-book and gave her a note. "I'll be round to-night and see what can be done."

He shut himself into his room again, and Zerrilla dried her tears, put the note into her bosom, and went her way.

Lapham kept the porter nearly an hour later. It was then six o'clock, the hour at which the Laphams usually had tea; but all custom had been broken up with him during the past months, and he did not go home now. He determined, perhaps in the extremity in which a man finds relief in combating one care with another, to keep his promise to Miss Dewey, and at the moment when he might otherwise have been sitting down at his own table he was climbing the stairs to her lodging in the old-fashioned dwelling which had been portioned off into flats. It was in a region of depots, and of the cheap hotels, and "ladies' and gents' " dining-rooms, and restaurants with bars, which abound near depots; and Lapham followed to Miss Dewey's door a waiter from one of these, who bore on a salver before him a supper covered with a napkin. Zerrilla had admitted them, and at her greeting a young fellow in the shabby shore-suit of a sailor, buttoning imperfectly over the nautical blue flannel of his shirt, got up from where he had been sitting, on one side of the stove, and stood infirmly on his feet, in token of receiving the visitor. The woman who sat on the other side did not rise, but began a shrill, defiant apology.

"Well, I don't suppose but what you'll think we're livin' on the fat o' the land, right straight along, all the while. But it's just like this. When that child came in from her work, she didn't seem to have the spirit to go to cookin' anything, and I had such a bad night last night I was feelin' all broke up, and s'd I, what's the use, anyway? By the time the butcher's heaved in a lot o' bone, and made you pay for the suet he cuts away, it comes to the same thing, and why not *git* it from the rest'rant first off, and save the cost o' your fire? s'd I."

"What have you got there under your apron? A bottle?" demanded Lapham, who stood with his hat on and his hands in his pockets, indifferent alike to the ineffective reception of the sailor and the chair Zerrilla had set him.

"Well, yes, it's a bottle," said the woman, with an assumption of virtuous frankness. "It's whisky; I got to have *some*thing to rub my rheumatism with."

"Humph!" grumbled Lapham. "You've been rubbing *his* rheumatism too, I see."

He twisted his head in the direction of the sailor, now softly and rhythmically waving to and fro on his feet.

"He hain't had a drop to-day in *this* house!" cried the woman.

"What are you doing around here?" said Lapham, turning fiercely upon him. "You've got no business ashore. Where's your ship? Do you think I'm going to let you come here and eat your wife out of house and home, and then give money to keep the concern going?"

"Just the very words I said when he first showed his face here, yist'day. Didn't I, Z'rilla?" said the woman, eagerly joining in the rebuke of her late boon companion. "You got no business here, Hen, s'd I. You can't come here to live on me and Z'rilla, s'd I. You want to go back to your ship, s'd I. That's what I said."

The sailor mumbled, with a smile of tipsy amiability for Lapham, something about the crew being discharged.

"Yes," the woman broke in, "that's always the way with these coasters. Why don't you go off on some them long v'y'ges? s'd I. It's pretty hard, when Mr. Wemmel stands ready to marry Z'rilla and provide a comfortable home for us both,—I hain't got a great many years more to live, and I *should* like to get some satisfaction out of 'em and not be beholden and dependent all my days,—to have Hen, here, blockin' the way. I tell him there'd be more money for him in the end; but he can't seem to make up his mind to it."

"Well, now, look here," said Lapham. "I don't care anything about all that. It's your own business, and I'm not going to meddle with it. But it's my business who lives off me; and so I tell you all three, I'm willing to take care of Zerrilla, and I'm willing to take care of her mother——"

"I guess if it hadn't been for that child's father," the mother interpolated, "you wouldn't been here to tell the tale, Colonel Lapham."

"I know all about that," said Lapham. "But I'll tell you what, Mr. Dewey, I'm not going to support *you*."

"I don't see what Hen's done," said the old woman, impartially.

"He hasn't done anything, and I'm going to stop it. He's got to get a ship, and he's got to get out of this. And Zerrilla needn't come back to work till he does. I'm done with you all."

"Well, I vow," said the mother, "if I ever heard anything like it! Didn't that child's father lay down his life for you? Hain't you said it yourself a hundred times? And don't she work for her money, and slave for it mornin', noon, and night? You talk as if we was beholden to you for the very bread in our mouths. I guess if it hadn't been for Jim, you wouldn't been here crowin' over us."

"You mind what I say. I mean business this time," said Lapham, turning to the door.

The woman rose and followed him, with her bottle in her hand. "Say, Colonel! what should you advise Z'rilla to do about Mr. Wemmel? I tell her there ain't any use goin' to the trouble to git a divorce without she's sure about him. Don't you think we'd ought to git him to sign a paper, or something, that he'll marry her if she gits it? I don't like to have things going at loose ends the way they are. It ain't sense. It ain't right."

Lapham made no answer to the mother anxious for her child's future, and concerned for the moral questions involved. He went out and down the stairs, and on the pavement at the lower door he almost struck against Rogers, who had a bag in his hand, and seemed to be hurrying towards one of the depots. He halted a little, as if to speak to Lapham; but Lapham turned his back abruptly upon him, and took the other direction.

The days were going by in a monotony of adversity to him, from which he could no longer escape, even at home. He attempted once or twice to talk of his troubles to his wife, but she repulsed him sharply; she seemed to despise and hate him; but he set himself doggedly to make a confession to her, and he stopped her one night, as she came into the room where he sat— hastily upon some errand that was to take her directly away again.

"Persis, there's something I've got to tell you."

She stood still, as if fixed against her will, to listen.

"I guess you know something about it already, and I guess it's set you against me."

"Oh, I guess not, Colonel Lapham. You go your way, and I go mine. That's all."

She waited for him to speak, listening with a cold, hard smile on her face.

"I don't say it to make favor with you, because I don't want you to spare me, and I don't ask you; but I got into it through Milton K. Rogers."

"Oh!" said Mrs. Lapham contemptuously.

"I always felt the way I said about it—that it wa'n't any better than gambling, and I say so now. It's like betting on the turn of a card; and I give you my word of honor, Persis, that I never was in it at all till that scoundrel began to load me up with those wild-cat securities of his. Then it seemed to me as if I ought to try to do something to get somewhere even. I know it's no excuse; but watching the market to see what the infernal things were worth from day to day, and seeing it go up, and seeing it go down, was too much for me; and, to make a long story short, I began to buy and sell on a margin—just what I told you I never would do. I seemed to make something—I did make something; and I'd have stopped, I do believe, if I could have reached the figure I'd set in my own mind to start with; but I couldn't fetch it. I began to lose, and then I began to throw good money after bad, just as I always did with everything that Rogers ever came within a mile of. Well, what's the use? I lost the money that would have carried me out of this, and I shouldn't have had to shut down the Works, or sell the house, or——"

Lapham stopped. His wife, who at first had listened with mystification, and then dawning incredulity, changing into a look of relief that was almost triumph, lapsed again into severity. "Silas Lapham, if you was to die the next minute, is this what you started to tell me?"

"Why, of course it is. What did you suppose I started to tell you?"

"And—look me in the eyes!—you haven't got anything else on your mind now?"

"No! There's trouble enough, the Lord knows; but there's nothing else to tell you. I suppose Pen gave you a hint about it.

I dropped something to her. I've been feeling bad about it, Persis, a good while, but I hain't had the heart to speak of it. I can't expect you to say you like it. I've been a fool, I'll allow, and I've been something worse, if you choose to say so; but that's all. I haven't hurt anybody but myself—and you and the children."

Mrs. Lapham rose and said, with her face from him, as she turned towards the door, "It's all right, Silas. I sha'n't ever bring it up against you."

She fled out of the room, but all that evening she was very sweet with him, and seemed to wish in all tacit ways to atone for her past unkindness.

She made him talk of his business, and he told her of Corey's offer, and what he had done about it. She did not seem to care for his part in it, however; at which Lapham was silently disappointed a little, for he would have liked her to praise him.

"He did it on account of Pen!"

"Well, he didn't insist upon it, anyway," said Lapham, who must have obscurely expected that Corey would recognize his own magnanimity by repeating his offer. If the doubt that follows a self-devoted action—the question whether it was not after all a needless folly—is mixed, as it was in Lapham's case, with the vague belief that we might have done ourselves a good turn without great risk of hurting any one else by being a little less unselfish, it becomes a regret that is hard to bear. Since Corey spoke to him, some things had happened that gave Lapham hope again.

"I'm going to tell her about it," said his wife, and she showed herself impatient to make up for the time she had lost. "Why didn't you tell me before, Silas?"

"I didn't know we were on speaking terms before," said Lapham sadly.

"Yes, that's true," she admitted, with a conscious flush. "I hope he won't think Pen's known about it all this while."

## XXIV

THAT evening James Bellingham came to see Corey after dinner, and went to find him in his own room.

"I've come at the instance of Colonel Lapham," said the uncle. "He was at my office to-day, and I had a long talk with him. Did you know that he was in difficulties?"

"I fancied that he was in some sort of trouble. And I had the book-keeper's conjectures—he doesn't really know much about it."

"Well, he thinks it time—on all accounts—that you should know how he stands, and why he declined that proposition of yours. I must say he has behaved very well—like a gentleman."

"I'm not surprised."

"I am. It's hard to behave like a gentleman where your interest is vitally concerned. And Lapham doesn't strike me as a man who's in the habit of acting from the best in him always."

"Do any of us?" asked Corey.

"Not all of us, at any rate," said Bellingham. "It must have cost him something to say no to you, for he's just in that state when he believes that this or that chance, however small, would save him."

Corey was silent. "Is he really in such a bad way?"

"It's hard to tell just where he stands. I suspect that a hopeful temperament and fondness for round numbers have always caused him to set his figures beyond his actual worth. I don't say that he's been dishonest about it, but he's had a loose way of estimating his assets; he's reckoned his wealth on the basis of his capital, and some of his capital is borrowed. He's lost heavily by some of the recent failures, and there's been a terrible shrinkage in his values. I don't mean merely in the stock of paint on hand, but in a kind of competition which has become very threatening. You know about that West Virginia paint?"

Corey nodded.

"Well, he tells me that they've struck a vein of natural gas out there which will enable them to make as good a paint as his own at a cost of manufacturing so low that they can undersell him everywhere. If this proves to be the case, it will not only drive his paint out of the market, but will reduce the value of his Works —the whole plant—at Lapham to a merely nominal figure."

"I see," said Corey dejectedly. "I've understood that he had put a great deal of money into his Works."

"Yes, and he estimated his mine there at a high figure. Of course it will be worth little or nothing if the West Virginia paint drives his out. Then, besides, Lapham has been into several things outside of his own business, and, like a good many other men who try outside things, he's kept account of them himself;

and he's all mixed up about them. He's asked me to look into his affairs with him, and I've promised to do so. Whether he can be tided over his difficulties remains to be seen. I'm afraid it will take a good deal of money to do it—a great deal more than he thinks, at least. He believes comparatively little would do it. I think differently. I think that anything less than a great deal would be thrown away on him. If it were merely a question of a certain sum—even a large sum—to keep him going, it might be managed; but it's much more complicated. And, as I say, it must have been a trial to him to refuse your offer."

This did not seem to be the way in which Bellingham had meant to conclude. But he said no more; and Corey made him no response.

He remained pondering the case, now hopefully, now doubtfully, and wondering, whatever his mood was, whether Penelope knew anything of the fact with which her mother went nearly at the same moment to acquaint her.

"Of course, he's done it on your account," Mrs. Lapham could not help saying.

"Then he was very silly. Does he think I would have let him give father money? And if father lost it for him, does he suppose it would make it any easier for me? I think father acted twice as well. It was very silly."

In repeating the censure, her look was not so severe as her tone; she even smiled a little, and her mother reported to her father that she acted more like herself than she had yet since Corey's offer.

"I think, if he was to repeat his offer, she would have him now," said Mrs. Lapham.

"Well, I'll let her know if he does," said the Colonel.

"I guess he won't do it to you!" she cried.

"Who else will he do it to?" he demanded.

They perceived that they had each been talking of a different offer.

After Lapham went to his business in the morning the postman brought another letter from Irene, which was full of pleasant things that were happening to her; there was a great deal about her cousin Will, as she called him. At the end she had written, "Tell Pen I don't want she should be foolish."

"There!" said Mrs. Lapham. "I guess it's going to come out

right, all round;" and it seemed as if even the Colonel's difficulties were past. "When your father gets through this, Pen," she asked impulsively, "what shall you do?"

"What have you been telling Irene about me?"

"Nothing much. What should you do?"

"It would be a good deal easier to say what I should do if father didn't," said the girl.

"I know you think it was nice in him to make your father that offer," urged the mother.

"It was nice, yes; but it was silly," said the girl. "Most nice things are silly, I suppose," she added.

She went to her room and wrote a letter. It was very long, and very carefully written; and when she read it over, she tore it into small pieces. She wrote another one, short and hurried, and tore that up too. Then she went back to her mother, in the family room, and asked to see Irene's letter, and read it over to herself. "Yes, she seems to be having a good time," she sighed. "Mother, do you think I ought to let Mr. Corey know that I know about it?"

"Well, I should think it would be a pleasure to him," said Mrs. Lapham judicially.

"I'm not so sure of that—the way I should have to tell him. I should begin by giving him a scolding. Of course, he meant well by it, but can't you see that it wasn't very flattering? How did he expect it would change me?"

"I don't believe he ever thought of that."

"Don't you? Why?"

"Because you can see that he isn't one of that kind. He might want to please you without wanting to change you by what he did."

"Yes. He must have known that nothing would change me,—at least, nothing that he could do. I thought of that. I shouldn't like him to feel that I couldn't appreciate it, even if I did think it was silly. Should you write to him?"

"I don't see why not."

"It would be too pointed. No, I shall just let it go. I wish he hadn't done it."

"Well, he has done it."

"And I've tried to write to him about it—two letters: one so humble and grateful that it couldn't stand up on its edge, and the other so pert and flippant. Mother, I wish you could have seen those two letters! I wish I had kept them to look at if I ever got to thinking I had any sense again. They would take the conceit out of me."

"What's the reason he don't come here any more?"

"Doesn't he come?" asked Penelope in turn, as if it were something she had not noticed particularly.

"You'd ought to know."

"Yes." She sat silent awhile. "If he doesn't come, I suppose it's because he's offended at something I did."

"What did you do?"

"Nothing. I—wrote to him—a little while ago. I suppose it was very blunt, but I didn't believe he would be angry at it. But this—this that he's done shows he was angry, and that he wasn't just seizing the first chance to get out of it."

"What have you done, Pen?" demanded her mother sharply.

"Oh, I don't know. All the mischief in the world, I suppose. I'll tell you. When you first told me that father was in trouble with his business, I wrote to him not to come any more till I let him. I said I couldn't tell him why, and he hasn't been here since. I'm sure *I* don't know what it means."

Her mother looked at her with angry severity. "Well, Penelope Lapham! For a sensible child, you *are* the greatest goose I ever saw. Did you think he would come here and *see* if you wouldn't let him come?"

"He might have written," urged the girl.

Her mother made that despairing "Tchk!" with her tongue, and fell back in her chair. "I should have *despised* him if he had written. He's acted just exactly right, and you—you've acted— I don't know *how* you've acted. I'm ashamed of you. A girl that could be so sensible for her sister, and always say and do just the right thing, and then when it comes to herself to be such a *disgusting* simpleton!"

"I thought I ought to break with him at once, and not let him suppose that there was any hope for him or me if father was poor. It was my one chance, in this whole business, to do anything heroic, and I jumped at it. You mustn't think, because I can laugh at it now, that I wasn't in earnest, mother! I *was*—dead! But the Colonel has gone to ruin so gradually, that he's spoilt everything. I expected that he would be bankrupt the next day, and that then *he* would understand what I meant. But to have it drag along for a fortnight seems to take all the heroism out of it, and leave it as flat!" She looked at her mother with a smile that shone through her tears, and a pathos that quivered round her jesting lips. "It's easy enough to be sensible for other people. But when it comes to myself, there I am! Especially, when I want to do what I oughtn't so much that it seems as if doing what I didn't want to do *must* be doing what I ought! But it's been a great success one way, mother. It's helped me to keep up before the Colonel. If it hadn't been for Mr. Corey's staying away, and my feeling so indignant with him for having been badly treated by me, I shouldn't have been worth anything at all."

The tears started down her cheeks, but her mother said, "Well, now, go along, and write to him. It don't matter what you say, much; and don't be so very particular."

Her third attempt at a letter pleased her scarcely better than the rest, but she sent it, though it seemed so blunt and awkward. She wrote:

> DEAR FRIEND:
> I expected when I sent you that note, that you would understand, almost the next day, why I could not see you any more. You must know now, and you must not think that if anything happened to my father, I should wish you to help him. But that is no reason why I should not thank you, and I do thank you, for offering. It was like you, I will say that.
> Yours sincerely, PENELOPE LAPHAM.

She posted her letter, and he sent his reply in the evening, by hand:

> DEAREST:
> What I did was nothing, till you praised it. Everything I have and am is yours. Won't you send a line by the bearer, to say that I may come to see you? I know how you feel; but I am sure that I can make you think differently. You must consider that I loved you without a thought of your father's circumstances, and always shall.
> T. C.

The generous words were blurred to her eyes by the tears that sprang into them. But she could only write in answer:

> "Please do not come; I have made up my mind. As long as

this trouble is hanging over us, I cannot see you. And if father is unfortunate, all is over between us."

She brought his letter to her mother, and told her what she had written in reply. Her mother was thoughtful awhile before she said, with a sigh, "Well, I hope you've begun as you can carry out, Pen."

"Oh, I shall not have to carry out at all. I shall not have to do anything. That's one comfort—the only comfort." She went away to her own room, and when Mrs. Lapham told her husband of the affair, he was silent at first, as she had been. Then he said, "I don't know as I should have wanted her to done differently; I don't know as she could. If I ever come right again, she won't have anything to feel meeching about; and if I don't, I don't want she should be beholden to anybody. And I guess that's the way she feels."

The Coreys in their turn sat in judgment on the fact which their son felt bound to bring to their knowledge.

"She has behaved very well," said Mrs. Corey, to whom her son had spoken.

"My dear," said her husband, with his laugh, "she has behaved *too* well. If she had studied the whole situation with the most artful eye to its mastery, she could not possibly have behaved better."

The process of Lapham's financial disintegration was like the course of some chronic disorder, which has fastened itself upon the constitution, but advances with continual reliefs, with apparent amelioration, and at times seems not to advance at all, when it gives hope of final recovery not only to the sufferer, but to the eye of science itself. There were moments when James Bellingham, seeing Lapham pass this crisis and that, began to fancy that he might pull through altogether; and at these moments, when his adviser could not oppose anything but experience and probability to the evidence of the fact, Lapham was buoyant with courage, and imparted his hopefulness to his household. Our theory of disaster, of sorrow, of affliction, borrowed from the poets and novelists, is that it is incessant; but every passage in our own lives and in the lives of others, so far as we have witnessed them, teaches us that this is false. The house of mourning is decorously darkened to the world, but within itself it is also the house of laughing. Bursts of gayety, as heartfelt as its grief, relieve the gloom, and the stricken survivors have their jests together, in which the thought of the dead is tenderly involved, and a fond sense, not crazier than many others, of sympathy and enjoyment beyond the silence, justifies the sunnier mood before sorrow rushes back, deploring and despairing, and making it all up again with the conventional fitness of things. Lapham's adversity had this quality in common with bereavement. It was not always like the adversity we figure in allegory; it had its moments of being like prosperity, and if upon the whole it was continual, it was not incessant. Sometimes there was a week of repeated reverses, when he had to keep his teeth set and to hold on hard to all his hopefulness; and then days came of negative result or slight success, when he was full of his jokes at the tea-table, and wanted to go to the theater, or to do something to cheer Penelope up. In some miraculous way, by some enormous stroke of success which should eclipse the brightest of his past prosperity, he expected to do what would reconcile all difficulties, not only in his own affairs, but in hers too. "You'll see," he said to his wife; "it's going to come out all right. Irene'll fix it up with Bill's boy, and then she'll be off Pen's mind; and if things go on as they've been going for the last two days, I'm going to be in a position to do the favors myself, and Pen can feel that *she's* makin' a sacrifice, and then I guess may be she'll do it. If things turn out as I expect now, and times ever *do* get any better generally, I can show Corey that I appreciate his offer. I can offer him the partnership myself then."

Even in the other moods, which came when everything had been going wrong, and there seemed no way out of the net, there were points of consolation to Lapham and his wife. They rejoiced that Irene was safe beyond the range of their anxieties, and they had a proud satisfaction that there had been no engagement between Corey and Penelope, and that it was she who had forbidden it. In the closeness of interest and sympathy in which their troubles had reunited them, they confessed to each other that nothing would have been more galling to their pride than the idea that Lapham should not have been able to do everything for his daughter that the Coreys might have expected. Whatever happened now, the Coreys could not have it to say that the Laphams had tried to bring any such thing about.

Bellingham had lately suggested an assignment to Lapham, as the best way out of his difficulties.[4] It was evident that he had not the money to meet his liabilities at present, and that he could not raise it without ruinous sacrifices, that might still end in ruin after all. If he made the assignment, Bellingham argued, he could gain time and make terms; the state of things generally would probably improve, since it could not be worse, and the market, which he had glutted with his paint, might recover and he could start again. Lapham had not agreed with him. When his reverses first began, it had seemed easy for him to give up everything, to let the people he owed take all, so only they would let him go out with clean hands; and he had dramatized this feeling in his talk with his wife, when they spoke together of the mills on the G. L. & P. But ever since then it had been growing harder, and he could not consent even to seem to do it now in the proposed assignment. He had not found other men so very liberal or faithful with him; a good many of them appeared to have combined to hunt him down; a sense of enmity towards all his creditors asserted itself in him; he asked himself why they should not suffer a little too. Above all, he shrank from the publicity of the assignment. It was open confession that he had been a fool in some way; he could not bear to have his family—his brother the judge, especially, to whom he had always appeared the soul of business wisdom—think him imprudent or stupid. He would make any sacrifice before it came to that. He determined in parting with Bellingham to make the sacrifice which he had oftenest in his mind, because it was the hardest, and to sell his new house. That would cause the least comment. Most people would simply think that he had got a splendid offer, and with his usual luck had made a very good thing of it; others who knew a little more about him would say that he was hauling in his horns, but they could not blame him; a great many other men were doing the same in those hard times—the shrewdest and safest men; it might even have a good effect.

He went straight from Bellingham's office to the real-estate broker in whose hands he meant to put his house, for he was not the sort of man to shilly-shally when he had once made up his

4. Assignment refers to the legal transfer of the control of his company to other managers who would settle the company's debts. This would have protected Lapham's personal property even though his company failed.

mind. But he found it hard to get his voice up out of his throat, when he said he guessed he would get the broker to sell that new house of his on the water side of Beacon. The broker answered cheerfully, yes; he supposed Colonel Lapham knew it was a pretty dull time in real estate? and Lapham said yes, he knew that, but he should not sell at a sacrifice, and he did not care to have the broker name him or describe the house definitely unless parties meant business. Again the broker said yes; and he added, as a joke Lapham would appreciate, that he had half a dozen houses on the water side of Beacon on the same terms; that no-body wanted to be named or to have his property described.

It did, in fact, comfort Lapham a little to find himself in the same boat with so many others; he smiled grimly, and said in his turn, yes, he guessed that was about the size of it with a good many people. But he had not the heart to tell his wife what he had done, and he sat taciturn that whole evening, without even going over his accounts, and went early to bed, where he lay tossing half the night before he fell asleep. He slept at last only upon the promise he made himself that he would withdraw the house from the broker's hands; but he went heavily to his own business in the morning without doing so. There was no such rush, anyhow, he reflected bitterly; there would be time to do that a month later, probably.

It struck him with a sort of dismay when a boy came with a note from the broker, saying that a party who had been over the house in the fall had come to him to know whether it could be bought, and was willing to pay the cost of the house up to the time he had seen it. Lapham took refuge in trying to think who the party could be; he concluded that it must have been some-body who had gone over it with the architect, and he did not like that; but he was aware that this was not an answer to the broker, and he wrote that he would give him an answer in the morning.

Now that it had come to the point, it did not seem to him that he could part with the house. So much of his hope for himself and his children had gone into it that the thought of selling it made him tremulous and sick. He could not keep about his work stead-ily, and with his nerves shaken by want of sleep, and the shock of this sudden and unexpected question, he left his office early, and went over to look at the house and try to bring himself to some conclusion there. The long procession of lamps on the beautiful street was flaring in the clear red of the sunset towards which it marched, and Lapham, with a lump in his throat, stopped in front of his house and looked at their multitude. They were not merely a part of the landscape; they were a part of his pride and glory, his success, his triumphant life's work which was fading into failure in his helpless hands. He ground his teeth to keep down that lump, but the moisture in his eyes blurred the lamps, and the keen, pale crimson against which it made them flicker. He turned and looked up, as he had so often done, at the window-spaces, neatly glazed for the winter with white linen, and recalled the night when he had stopped with Irene before the house, and she had said that she should never live there, and he had tried to coax her into courage about it. There was no such façade as that on the whole street, to his thinking. Through his long talks with the architect, he had come to feel almost as intimately and fondly as the architect himself the satisfying simplicity of the whole design and the delicacy of its detail. It appealed to him as an exquisite bit of harmony appeals to the unlearned ear, and he recognized the difference between this fine work and the obstreperous pretentiousness of the many overloaded house-fronts which Seymour had made him notice for his instruction elsewhere on the Back Bay. Now, in the depths of his gloom, he tried to think what Italian city it was where Seymour said he had first got the notion of treating brickwork in that way.

He unlocked the temporary door with the key he always carried, so that he could let himself in and out whenever he liked, and entered the house, dim and very cold with the accumulated frigidity of the whole winter in it, and looking as if the arrest of work upon it had taken place a thousand years before. It smelt of the unpainted woods and the clean, hard surfaces of the plaster, where the experiments in decoration had left it untouched; and mingled with these odors was that of some rank pigments and metallic compositions which Seymour had used in trying to realize a certain daring novelty of finish, which had not proved successful. Above all, Lapham detected the peculiar odor of his own paint, with which the architect had been greatly interested one day, when Lapham showed it to him at the office. He had asked Lapham to let him try the Persis Brand in realizing a little idea he had for the finish of Mrs. Lapham's room. If it succeeded, they could tell her what it was, for a surprise.

Lapham glanced at the bay-window in the reception-room, where he sat with his girls on the trestles when Corey first came by; and then he explored the whole house to the attic, in the light faintly admitted through the linen sashes. The floors were strewn with shavings and chips which the carpenters had left, and in the music-room these had been blown into long irregular windrows by the draughts through a wide rent in the linen sash. Lapham tried to pin it up, but failed, and stood looking out of it over the water. The ice had left the river, and the low tide lay smooth and red in the light of the sunset. The Cambridge flats showed the sad, sodden yellow of meadows stripped bare after a long sleep under snow; the hills, the naked trees, the spires and roofs had a black outline, as if they were objects in a landscape of the French school.

The whim seized Lapham to test the chimney in the music-room; it had been tried in the dining-room below, and in his girls' fire-places above, but here the hearth was still clean. He gathered some shavings and blocks together, and kindled them, and as the flame mounted gayly from them, he pulled up a nail-keg which he found there and sat down to watch it. Nothing could have been better; the chimney was a perfect success; and as Lapham glanced out of the torn linen sash he said to himself that that party, whoever he was, who had offered to buy his house might go to the devil; he would never sell it as long as he had a dollar. He said that he should pull through yet; and it suddenly came into his mind that, if he could raise the money to buy out those West Virginia fellows, he should be all right, and would have the whole game in his own hand. He slapped himself on the thigh, and wondered that he had never thought of that before; and then, lighting a cigar with a splinter from the fire, he sat down again to work the scheme out in his own mind.

He did not hear the feet heavily stamping up the stairs, and coming towards the room where he sat; and the policeman to whom the feet belonged had to call out to him, smoking at his chimney-corner, with his back turned to the door, "Hello! what are you doing here?"

"What's that to you?" retorted Lapham, wheeling half round on his nail-keg.

"I'll show you," said the officer, advancing upon him, and then stopping short as he recognized him. "Why, Colonel Lapham! I thought it was some tramp got in here!"

"Have a cigar?" said Lapham hospitably. "Sorry there ain't another nail-keg."

The officer took the cigar. "I'll smoke it outside. I've just come on, and I can't stop. Tryin' your chimney?"

"Yes, I thought I'd see how it would draw, in here. It seems to go first-rate."

The policeman looked about him with an eye of inspection. "You want to get that linen window, there, mended up."

"Yes, I'll speak to the builder about that. It can go for one night."

The policeman went to the window and failed to pin the linen together where Lapham had failed before. "*I* can't fix it." He looked round once more, and saying, "Well, good-night," went out and down the stairs.

Lapham remained by the fire till he had smoked his cigar; then he rose and stamped upon the embers that still burned with his heavy boots, and went home. He was very cheerful at supper. He told his wife that he guessed he had a sure thing of it now, and in another twenty-four hours he should tell her just how. He made Penelope go to the theater with him, and when they came out, after the play, the night was so fine that he said they must walk round by the new house and take a look at it in the starlight. He said he had been there before he came home, and tried Seymour's chimney in the music-room, and it worked like a charm.

As they drew near Beacon street they were aware of unwonted stir and tumult, and presently the still air transmitted a turmoil of sound, through which a powerful and incessant throbbing made itself felt. The sky had reddened above them, and turning the corner at the Public Garden, they saw a black mass of people obstructing the perspective of the brightly-lighted street, and out of this mass a half dozen engines, whose strong heart-beats had already reached them, sent up volumes of fire-tinged smoke and steam from their funnels. Ladders were planted against the façade of a building, from the roof of which a mass of flame burnt smoothly upward, except where here and there it seemed to pull contemptuously away from the heavy streams of water which the firemen, clinging like great beetles to their ladders, poured in upon it.

Lapham had no need to walk down through the crowd, gazing and gossiping, with shouts and cries and hysterical laughter, before the burning house, to make sure that it was his.

"I guess I done it, Pen," was all he said.

Among the people who were looking at it were a party who seemed to have run out from dinner in some neighboring house; the ladies were fantastically wrapped up, as if they had flung on the first things they could seize.

"Isn't it perfectly magnificent!" cried a pretty girl. "I wouldn't have missed it on any account. Thank you *so* much, Mr. Symington, for bringing us out!"

"Ah, I thought you'd like it," said this Mr. Symington, who must have been the host; "and you can enjoy it without the least compunction, Miss Delano, for I happen to know that the house belongs to a man who could afford to burn one up for you once a year."

"Oh, do you think he would, if I came again?"

"I haven't the least doubt of it. We don't do things by halves in Boston."

"He ought to have had a coat of his non-combustible paint on it," said another gentleman of the party.

Penelope pulled her father away toward the first carriage she could reach of a number that had driven up. "Here, father! get into this."

"No, no; I couldn't ride," he answered heavily, and he walked home in silence. He greeted his wife with, "Well, Persis, our house is gone! And I guess I set it on fire myself;" and while he rummaged among the papers in his desk, still with his coat and hat on, his wife got the facts as she could from Penelope. She did not reproach him. Here was a case in which his self-reproach must be sufficiently sharp without any edge from her. Besides, her mind was full of a terrible thought.

"Oh, Silas," she faltered, "they'll think you set it on fire to get the insurance!"

Lapham was staring at a paper which he held in his hand. "I had a builder's risk on it, but it expired last week. It's a dead loss."

"Oh, thank the merciful Lord!" cried his wife.

"Merciful!" said Lapham. "Well, it's a queer way of showing it."

He went to bed, and fell into the deep sleep which sometimes follows a great moral shock. It was perhaps rather a torpor than a sleep.

# XXV

LAPHAM awoke confused, and in a kind of remoteness from the loss of the night before, through which it loomed mistily. But before he lifted his head from the pillow, it gathered substance and weight against which it needed all his will to bear up and live. In that moment he wished that he had not wakened, that he might never have wakened; but he rose, and faced the day and its cares.

The morning papers brought the report of the fire, and the conjectured loss. The reporters somehow had found out the fact that the loss fell entirely upon Lapham; they lighted up the hackneyed character of their statements with the picturesque interest of the coincidence that the policy had expired only the week before; heaven knows how they knew it. They said that nothing remained of the building but the walls; and Lapham, on his way to business, walked up past the smoke-stained shell. The windows looked like the eye-sockets of a skull down upon the blackened and trampled snow of the street; the pavement was a sheet of ice, and the water from the engines had frozen, like streams of tears, down the face of the house, and hung in icy tags from the window-sills and copings.

He gathered himself up as well as he could, and went on to his office. The chance of retrieval that had flashed upon him, as he sat smoking by that ruined hearth the evening before, stood him in such stead now as a sole hope may; and he said to himself that, having resolved not to sell his house, he was no more crippled by its loss than he would have been by letting his money lie idle in it; what he might have raised by mortgage on it could be made up in some other way; and if they would sell, he could still buy out the whole business of that West Virginia company, mines, plant, stock on hand, good-will, and everything, and unite it with his own. He went early in the afternoon to see Bellingham, whose expressions of condolence for his loss he cut short with as much politeness as he knew how to throw into his impatience. Bellingham seemed at first a little dazzled with the splendid courage of his scheme; it was certainly fine in its way; but then he began to have his misgivings.

"I happen to know that they haven't got much money behind them," urged Lapham. "They'll jump at an offer."

Bellingham shook his head. "If they can show profit on the old manufacture, and prove they can make their paint still cheaper and better hereafter, they can have all the money they want. And it will be very difficult for you to raise it if you're threatened by them. With that competition, you know what your plant at Lapham would be worth, and what the shrinkage on your manufactured stock would be. Better sell out to them," he concluded, "if they will buy."

"There ain't money enough in this country to buy out my paint," said Lapham, buttoning up his coat in a quiver of resentment. "Good-afternoon, sir." Men are but grown-up boys, after all. Bellingham watched this perversely proud and obstinate child fling petulantly out of his door, and felt a sympathy for him which was as truly kind as it was helpless.

But Lapham was beginning to see through Bellingham, as he believed. Bellingham was, in his way, part of that conspiracy by which Lapham's creditors were trying to drive him to the wall. More than ever now he was glad that he had nothing to do with that cold-hearted, self-conceited race, and that the favors so far were all from his side. He was more than ever determined to show them, every one of them, high and low, that he and his children could get along without them, and prosper and triumph without them. He said to himself that if Penelope were engaged to Corey that very minute, he would make her break with him.

He knew what he should do now, and he was going to do it without loss of time. He was going on to New York to see those West Virginia people; they had their principal office there, and he intended to get at their ideas, and then he intended to make them an offer. He managed this business better than could possibly have been expected of a man in his impassioned mood. But when it came really to business, his practical instincts, alert and wary, came to his aid against the passions that lay in wait to betray after they ceased to dominate him. He found the West Virginians full of zeal and hope, but in ten minutes he knew that they had not yet tested their strength in the money market, and had not ascertained how much or how little capital they could command. Lapham himself, if he had had so much, would not have hesitated to put a million dollars into their business. He saw, as they did not see, that they had the game in their own hands, and that if they could raise the money to extend their business, they could ruin him. It was only a question of time, and he was on the ground first. He frankly proposed a union of their interests. He admitted that they had a good thing, and that he should have to fight them hard; but he meant to fight them to the death unless they could come to some sort of terms. Now, the question was whether they had better go on and make a heavy loss for both sides by competition, or whether they had better form a partnership to run both paints and command the whole market. Lapham made them three propositions, each of which was fair and open: to sell out to them altogether; to buy them out altogether; to join facilities and forces with them, and go on in an invulnerable alliance. Let them name a figure at which they would buy, a figure at which they would sell, a figure at which they would combine,— or, in other words, the amount of capital they needed.

They talked all day, going out to lunch together at the Astor House, and sitting with their knees against the counter on a row of stools before it for fifteen minutes of reflection and de-glutition,[5] with their hats on, and then returning to the basement from which they emerged. The West Virginia company's name was lettered in gilt on the wide low window, and its paint, in the form of ore, burnt, and mixed, formed a display on the window shelf. Lapham examined it and praised it; from time to time they all recurred to it together; they sent out for some of Lapham's paint and compared it, the West Virginians admitting its former superiority. They were young fellows, and country persons, like Lapham, by origin, and they looked out with the same amused, undaunted, provincial eyes at the myriad metropolitan legs passing on the pavement above the level of their window. He got on well with them. At last, they said what they would do. They said it was nonsense to talk of buying Lapham out, for they had not the money; and as for selling out, they would not do it, for they knew they had a big thing. But they would as soon use his capital to develop it as anybody else's, and if he could put in a certain sum for this purpose, they would go in with him. He should run the works at Lapham and manage the business in Boston, and they would run the works at Kanawha Falls and manage the business in New York. The two brothers with whom Lapham talked named their

5. "deglutition": swallowing.

figure, subject to the approval of another brother at Kanawha
Falls, to whom they would write, and who would telegraph his
answer, so that Lapham could have it inside of three days. But
they felt perfectly sure that he would approve; and Lapham
started back on the eleven o'clock train with an elation that
gradually left him as he drew near Boston, where the difficulties
of raising this sum were to be overcome. It seemed to him, then,
that those fellows had put it up on him pretty steep, but he
owned to himself that they had a sure thing, and that they
were right in believing they could raise the same sum elsewhere;
it would take all of it, he admitted, to make their paint pay on
the scale they had the right to expect. At their age, he would
not have done differently; but when he emerged, old, sore, and
sleep-broken, from the sleeping-car in the Albany depot at
Boston, he wished with a pathetic self-pity that they knew how
a man felt at his age. A year ago, six months ago, he would have
laughed at the notion that it would be hard to raise the money.
But he thought ruefully of that immense stock of paint on hand,
which was now a drug in the market, of his losses by Rogers
and by the failures of other men, of the fire that had licked up
so many thousands in a few hours; he thought with bitterness
of the tens of thousands that he had gambled away in stocks,
and of the commissions that the brokers had pocketed whether
he won or lost; and he could not think of any securities on which
he could borrow, except his house in Nankeen Square, or the
mine and works at Lapham. He set his teeth in helpless rage
when he thought of that property out on the G. L. & P., that
ought to be worth so much, and was worth so little if the road
chose to say so.

He did not go home, but spent most of the day shinning
round, as he would have expressed it, and trying to see if he
could raise the money. But he found that people of whom he
hoped to get it were in the conspiracy which had been formed
to drive him to the wall. Somehow, there seemed a sense of his
embarrassments abroad. Nobody wanted to lend money on the
plant at Lapham without taking time to look into the state of
the business; but Lapham had no time to give, and he knew
that the state of the business would not bear looking into. He
could raise fifteen thousand on his Nankeen Square house, and
another fifteen on his Beacon street lot, and this was all that a

man who was worth a million by rights could do! He said a million, and he said it in defiance of Bellingham, who had subjected his figures to an analysis which wounded Lapham more than he chose to show at the time, for it proved that he was not so rich and not so wise as he had seemed. His hurt vanity forbade him to go to Bellingham now for help or advice; and if he could have brought himself to ask his brothers for money, it would have been useless; they were simply well-to-do Western people, but not capitalists on the scale he required.

Lapham stood in the isolation to which adversity so often seems to bring men. When its test was applied, practically or theoretically, to all those who had seemed his friends, there was none who bore it; and he thought with bitter self-contempt of the people whom he had befriended in their time of need. He said to himself that he had been a fool for that; and he scorned himself for certain acts of scrupulosity by which he had lost money in the past. Seeing the moral forces all arrayed against him, Lapham said that he would like to have the chance offered him to get even with them again; he thought he should know how to look out for himself. As he understood it, he had several days to turn about in, and he did not let one day's failure dishearten him. The morning after his return he had, in fact, a gleam of luck that gave him the greatest encouragement for the moment. A man came in to inquire about one of Rogers's wild-cat patents,[6] as Lapham called them, and ended by buying it. He got it, of course, for less than Lapham took it for, but Lapham was glad to be rid of it for something, when he had thought it worth nothing; and when the transaction was closed, he asked the purchaser rather eagerly if he knew where Rogers was; it was Lapham's secret belief that Rogers had found there was money in the thing, and had sent the man to buy it. But it appeared that this was a mistake; the man had not come from Rogers, but had heard of the patent in another way; and Lapham was astonished in the afternoon, when his boy came to tell him that Rogers was in the outer office, and wished to speak with him.

"All right," said Lapham, and he could not command at once the severity for the reception of Rogers which he would have

6. Wild-cat patents are those on unlikely inventions that are bought chiefly for purposes of speculation.

liked to use. He found himself, in fact, so much relaxed towards him by the morning's touch of prosperity that he asked him to sit down, gruffly, of course, but distinctly; and when Rogers said in his lifeless way, and with the effect of keeping his appointment of a month before, "Those English parties are in town, and would like to talk with you in reference to the mills," Lapham did not turn him out-of-doors.

He sat looking at him, and trying to make out what Rogers was after; for he did not believe that the English parties, if they existed, had any notion of buying his mills.

"What if they are not for sale?" he asked. "You know that I've been expecting an offer from the G. L. & P."

"I've kept watch of that. They haven't made you any offer," said Rogers quietly.

"And did you think," demanded Lapham, firing up, "that I would turn them in on somebody else as you turned them in on me, when the chances are that they won't be worth ten cents on the dollar six months from now?"

"I didn't know what you would do," said Rogers, non-committally. "I've come here to tell you that these parties stand ready to take the mills off your hands at a fair valuation—at the value I put upon them when I turned them in."

"I don't believe you!" cried Lapham brutally, but a wild, predatory hope made his heart leap so that it seemed to turn over in his breast. "I don't believe there are any such parties to begin with; and in the next place, I don't believe they would buy at any such figure; unless—unless you've lied to them, as you've lied to me. Did you tell them about the G. L. & P.?"

Rogers looked compassionately at him, but he answered, with unvaried dryness, "I did not think that necessary."

Lapham had expected this answer, and he had expected or intended to break out in furious denunciation of Rogers when he got it; but he only found himself saying, in a sort of baffled gasp, "I wonder what your game is!"

Rogers did not reply categorically, but he answered, with his impartial calm, and as if Lapham had said nothing to indicate that he differed at all with him as to disposing of the property in the way he had suggested: "If we should succeed in selling, I should be able to repay you your loans, and should have a little capital for a scheme that I think of going into."

"And do you think that I am going to steal these men's money to help you plunder somebody in a new scheme?" answered Lapham. The sneer was on behalf of virtue, but it was still a sneer.

"I suppose the money would be useful to you too, just now."

"Why?"

"Because I know that you have been trying to borrow."

At this proof of wicked omniscience in Rogers, the question whether he had better not regard the affair as a fatality, and yield to his destiny, flashed upon Lapham; but he answered, "I shall want money a great deal worse than I've ever wanted it yet, before I go into such rascally business with you. Don't you know that we might as well knock these parties down on the street, and take the money out of their pockets?"

"They have come on," answered Rogers, "from Portland to see you. I expected them some weeks ago, but they disappointed me. They arrived on the *Circassian* last night; they expected to have got in five days ago, but the passage was very stormy."

"Where are they?" asked Lapham, with helpless irrelevance, and feeling himself somehow drifted from his moorings by Rogers's shipping intelligence.

"They are at Young's. I told them we would call upon them after dinner this evening; they dine late."

"Oh, you did, did you?" asked Lapham, trying to drop another anchor for a fresh clutch on his underlying principles. "Well, now, you go and tell them that I said I wouldn't come."

"Their stay is limited," remarked Rogers. "I mentioned this evening because they were not certain they could remain over another night. But if to-morrow would suit you better——"

"Tell 'em I sha'n't come at all," roared Lapham, as much in terror as defiance, for he felt his anchor dragging. "Tell 'em I sha'n't come at all! Do you understand that?"

"I don't see why you should stickle as to the matter of going to them," said Rogers; "but if you think it will be better to have them approach you, I suppose I can bring them to you."

"No, you can't! I sha'n't let you! I sha'n't see them! I sha'n't have anything to do with them. *Now* do you understand?"

"I inferred from our last interview," persisted Rogers, unmoved by all this violent demonstration of Lapham's, "that you wished to meet these parties. You told me that you would give me time to produce them; and I have promised them that you would meet them; I have committed myself."

It was true that Lapham had defied Rogers to bring on his

men, and had implied his willingness to negotiate with them. That was before he had talked the matter over with his wife, and perceived his moral responsibility in it; even she had not seen this at once. He could not enter into this explanation with Rogers; he could only say, "I said I'd give you twenty-four hours to prove yourself a liar, and you did it. I didn't say twenty-four days."

"I don't see the difference," returned Rogers. "The parties are here now, and that proves that I was acting in good faith at the time. There has been no change in the posture of affairs. You don't know now any more than you knew then that the G. L. & P. is going to want the property. If there's any difference, it's in favor of the Road's having changed its mind."

There was some sense in this, and Lapham felt it—felt it only too eagerly, as he recognized the next instant.

Rogers went on quietly: "You're not obliged to sell to these parties when you meet them; but you've allowed me to commit myself to them by the promise that you would talk with them."

"'Twa'n't a promise," said Lapham.

"It was the same thing; they have come out from England on my guaranty that there was such and such an opening for their capital; and now what am I to say to them? It places me in a ridiculous position." Rogers urged his grievance calmly, almost impersonally, making his appeal to Lapham's sense of justice. "I *can't* go back to those parties and tell them you won't see them. It's no answer to make. They've got a right to know *why* you won't see them."

"Very well, then!" cried Lapham; "I'll come and *tell* them why. Who shall I ask for? When shall I be there?"

"At eight o'clock, please," said Rogers, rising, without apparent alarm at his threat, if it was a threat. "And ask for me; I've taken a room at the hotel for the present."

"I won't keep you five minutes when I get there," said Lapham; but he did not come away till ten o'clock.

It appeared to him as if the very devil was in it. The Englishmen treated his downright refusal to sell as a piece of bluff, and talked on as though it were merely the opening of the negotiation. When he became plain with them in his anger, and told them why he would not sell, they seemed to have been prepared for this as a stroke of business, and were ready to meet it.

"Has this fellow," he demanded, twisting his head in the direction of Rogers, but disdaining to notice him otherwise, "been telling you that it's part of my game to say this? Well, sir, I can tell you, on my side, that there isn't a slipperier rascal unhung in America than Milton K. Rogers!"

The Englishmen treated this as a piece of genuine American humor, and returned to the charge with unabated courage. They owned now, that a person interested with them had been out to look at the property, and that they were satisfied with the appearance of things. They developed further the fact that they were not acting solely, or even principally, in their own behalf, but were the agents of people in England who had projected the colonization of a sort of community on the spot, somewhat after the plan of other English dreamers, and that they were satisfied, from a careful inspection, that the resources and facilities were those best calculated to develop the energy and enterprise of the proposed community. They were prepared to meet Mr. Lapham —Colonel, they begged his pardon, at the instance of Rogers— at any reasonable figure, and were quite willing to assume the risks he had pointed out. Something in the eyes of these men, something that lurked at an infinite depth below their speech, and was not really in their eyes when Lapham looked again, had flashed through him a sense of treachery in them. He had thought them the dupes of Rogers; but in that brief instant he had seen them—or thought he had seen them—his accomplices, ready to betray the interests of which they went on to speak with a certain comfortable jocosity, and a certain incredulous slight of his show of integrity. It was a deeper game than Lapham was used to, and he sat looking with a sort of admiration from one Englishman to the other, and then to Rogers, who maintained an exterior of modest neutrality, and whose air said, "I have brought you gentlemen together as the friend of all parties, and I now leave you to settle it among yourselves. I ask nothing, and expect nothing, except the small sum which shall accrue to me after the discharge of my obligations to Colonel Lapham."

While Rogers's presence expressed this, one of the Englishmen was saying, "And if you have any scruple in allowin' us to assume this risk, Colonel Lapham, perhaps you can console yourself with the fact that the loss, if there is to be any, will fall upon people who are able to bear it—upon an association of rich and charitable people. But we're quite satisfied there will be no loss," he added savingly. "All you have to do is to name your price, and we will do our best to meet it."

There was nothing in the Englishman's sophistry very shocking to Lapham. It addressed itself in him to that easy-going, not evilly intentioned, potential immorality which regards common property as common prey, and gives us the most corrupt municipal governments under the sun—which makes the poorest voter, when he has tricked into place, as unscrupulous in regard to others' money as an hereditary prince. Lapham met the Englishman's eye, and with difficulty kept himself from winking. Then he looked away, and tried to find out where he stood, or what he wanted to do. He could hardly tell. He had expected to come into that room and unmask Rogers, and have it over. But he had unmasked Rogers without any effect whatever, and the play had only begun. He had a whimsical and sarcastic sense of its being very different from the plays at the theater. He could not get up and go away in silent contempt; he could not tell the Englishmen that he believed them a pair of scoundrels and should have nothing to do with them; he could no longer treat them as innocent dupes. He remained baffled and perplexed, and the one who had not spoken hitherto remarked:

"Of course we sha'n't 'aggle about a few pound, more or less. If Colonel Lapham's figure should be a little larger than ours, I've no doubt 'e'll not be too 'ard upon us in the end."

Lapham appreciated all the intent of this subtle suggestion, and understood as plainly as if it had been said in so many words, that if they paid him a larger price, it was to be expected that a certain portion of the purchase money was to return to their own hands. Still he could not move; and it seemed to him that he could not speak.

"Ring that bell, Mr. Rogers," said the Englishman who had last spoken, glancing at the annunciator button in the wall near Rogers's head, "and 'ave up something 'ot, can't you? I should like to wet me w'istle, as you say 'ere, and Colonel Lapham seems to find it rather dry work."

Lapham jumped to his feet, and buttoned his overcoat about him. He remembered with terror the dinner at Corey's where he had disgraced and betrayed himself, and if he went into this thing at all, he was going into it sober. "I can't stop," he said, "I must be going."

"But you haven't given us an answer yet, Mr. Lapham," said the first Englishman with a successful show of dignified surprise.

"The only answer I can give you now is, *No*," said Lapham. "If you want another, you must let me have time to think it over."

"But 'ow much time?" said the other Englishman. "We're pressed for time ourselves, and we hoped for an answer—'oped for a hanswer," he corrected himself, "at once. That was our understandin' with Mr. Rogers."

"I can't let you know till morning, anyway," said Lapham, and he went out, as his custom often was, without any parting salutation. He thought Rogers might try to detain him; but Rogers had remained seated when the others got to their feet, and paid no attention to his departure.

He walked out into the night air, every pulse throbbing with the strong temptation. He knew very well those men would wait, and gladly wait, till the morning, and that the whole affair was in his hands. It made him groan in spirit to think that it was. If he had hoped that some chance might take the decision from him, there was no such chance, in the present or future, that he could see. It was for him alone to commit this rascality—if it was a rascality—or not.

He walked all the way home, letting one car after another pass him on the street, now so empty of other passing, and it was almost eleven o'clock when he reached home. A carriage stood before his house, and when he let himself in with his key, he heard talking in the family-room. It came into his head that Irene had got back unexpectedly, and that the sight of her was some-how going to make it harder for him; then he thought it might be Corey, come upon some desperate pretext to see Penelope; but when he opened the door he saw, with a certain absence of surprise, that it was Rogers. He was standing with his back to the fire-place, talking to Mrs. Lapham, and he had been shed-ding tears; dry tears they seemed, and they had left a sort of sandy, glistening trace on his cheeks. Apparently he was not ashamed of them, for the expression with which he met Lapham was that of a man making a desperate appeal in his own cause, which was identical with that of humanity, if not that of justice.

"I some expected," began Rogers, "to find you here——"

"No, you didn't," interrupted Lapham; "you wanted to come here and make a poor mouth to Mrs. Lapham before I got home."

"I knew that Mrs. Lapham would know what was going on," said Rogers, more candidly, but not more virtuously, for that he could not, "and I wished her to understand a point that I hadn't put to you at the hotel, and that I want you should consider. And I want you should consider me a little in this business, too; you're not the only one that's concerned, I tell you, and I've been telling Mrs. Lapham that it's my one chance; that if you don't meet me on it, my wife and children will be reduced to beggary."

"So will mine," said Lapham, "or the next thing to it."

"Well, then, I want you to give me this chance to get on my feet again. You've no right to deprive me of it; it's unchristian. In our dealings with each other we should be guided by the Golden Rule, as I was saying to Mrs. Lapham before you came in. I told her that if I knew myself, I should in your place consider the circumstances of a man in mine, who had honorably endeavored to discharge his obligations to me, and had patiently borne my undeserved suspicions. I should consider that man's family, I told Mrs. Lapham."

"Did you tell her that if I went in with you and those fellows, I should be robbing the people who trusted them?"

"I don't see what you've got to do with the people that sent them here. They are rich people, and could bear it if it came to the worst. But there's no likelihood, now, that it will come to the worst; you can see yourself that the Road has changed its mind about buying. And here am I without a cent in the world; and my wife is an invalid. She needs comforts, she needs little luxuries, and she hasn't even the necessaries; and you want to sacrifice her to a mere idea! You don't know in the first place that the Road will ever want to buy; and if it does, the probability is that with a colony like that planted on its line, it would make very different terms from what it would with you or me. These agents are not afraid, and their principals are rich people; and if there was any loss, it would be divided up amongst them so that they wouldn't any of them feel it."

Lapham stole a troubled glance at his wife, and saw that there was no help in her. Whether she was daunted and confused in her own conscience by the outcome, so evil and disastrous, of the reparation to Rogers which she had forced her husband to make, or whether her perceptions had been blunted and darkened by the appeals which Rogers had now used, it would be difficult to say. Probably there was a mixture of both causes in the effect which her husband felt in her, and from which he turned, girding himself anew, to Rogers.

"I have no wish to recur to the past," continued Rogers, with growing superiority. "You have shown a proper spirit in regard to that, and you have done what you could to wipe it out."

"I should think I had," said Lapham. "I've used up about a hundred and fifty thousand dollars trying."

"Some of my enterprises," Rogers admitted, "have been unfortunate, seemingly; but I have hopes that they will yet turn out well—in time. I can't understand why you should be so mindful of others now, when you showed so little regard for me then. I had come to your aid at a time when you needed help, and when you got on your feet you kicked me out of the business. I don't complain, but that is the fact; and I had to begin again, after I had supposed myself settled in life, and establish myself elsewhere."

Lapham glanced again at his wife; her head had fallen; he could see that she was so rooted in her old remorse for that questionable act of his, amply and more than fully atoned for since, that she was helpless, now in the crucial moment, when he had the utmost need of her insight. He had counted upon her; he perceived now that when he had thought it was for him alone to decide, he had counted upon her just spirit to stay his own in its struggle to be just. He had not forgotten how she held out against him only a little while ago, when he asked her whether he might not rightfully sell in some such contingency as this; and it was not now that she said or even looked anything in favor of Rogers, but that she was silent against him, which dismayed Lapham. He swallowed the lump that rose in his throat, the self-pity, the pity for her, the despair, and said gently, "I guess you better go to bed, Persis. It's pretty late."

She turned towards the door, when Rogers said, with the obvious intention of detaining her through her curiosity:

"But I let that pass. And I don't ask now that you should sell to these men."

Mrs. Lapham paused, irresolute.

"What are you making this bother for, then?" demanded Lapham. "What *do* you want?"

"What I've been telling your wife here. I want you should sell to *me*. I don't say what I'm going to do with the property, and you will not have an iota of responsibility, whatever happens."

Lapham was staggered, and he saw his wife's face light up with eager question.

"I want that property," continued Rogers, "and I've got the money to buy it. What will you take for it? If it's the price you're standing out for——"

"Persis," said Lapham, "go to bed," and he gave her a look that meant obedience for her. She went out of the door, and left him with his tempter.

"If you think I'm going to help you whip the devil round the stump, you're mistaken in your man, Milton Rogers," said Lapham, lighting a cigar. "As soon as I sold to you, you would sell to that other pair of rascals. *I* smelt 'em out in half a minute."

"They are Christian gentlemen," said Rogers. "But I don't purpose defending them; and I don't purpose telling you what I shall or shall not do with the property when it is in my hands again. The question is, Will you sell, and, if so, what is your figure? You have got nothing whatever to do with it after you've sold."

It was perfectly true. Any lawyer would have told him the same. He could not help admiring Rogers for his ingenuity, and every selfish interest of his nature joined with many obvious duties to urge him to consent. He did not see why he should refuse. There was no longer a reason. He was standing out alone for nothing, any one else would say. He smoked on as if Rogers were not there, and Rogers remained before the fire as patient as the clock ticking behind his head on the mantel, and showing the gleam of its pendulum beyond his face on either side. But at last he said, "Well?"

"Well," answered Lapham, "you can't expect me to give you an answer to-night, any more than before. You know that what you've said now hasn't changed the thing a bit. I wish it had. The Lord knows, I want to be rid of the property fast enough."

"Then why don't you sell to me? Can't you see that you will not be responsible for what happens after you have sold?"

"No, I *can't* see that; but if I can by morning, I'll sell."

"Why do you expect to know any better by morning? You're

wasting time for nothing!" cried Rogers, in his disappointment. "Why are you so particular? When you drove me out of the business you were not so very particular."

Lapham winced. It was certainly ridiculous for a man who had once so selfishly consulted his own interests to be stickling now about the rights of others.

"I guess nothing's going to happen over-night," he answered sullenly. "Anyway, I sha'n't say what I shall do till morning."

"What time can I see you in the morning?"

"Half-past nine."

Rogers buttoned his coat, and went out of the room without another word. Lapham followed him to close the street-door after him.

His wife called down to him from above as he approached the room again, "Well?"

"I've told him I'd let him know in the morning."

"Want I should come down and talk with you?"

"No," answered Lapham, in the proud bitterness which his isolation brought, "you couldn't do any good." He went in and shut the door, and by and by his wife heard him begin walking up and down; and then the rest of the night she lay awake and listened to him walking up and down. But when the first light whitened the window, the words of the Scripture came into her mind: "And there wrestled a man with him until the breaking of the day. . . . And he said, Let me go, for the day breaketh. And he said, I will not let thee go, except thou bless me."[7]

She could not ask him anything when they met, but he raised his dull eyes after the first silence and said, "*I* don't know what I'm going to say to Rogers."

She could not speak; she did not know what to say, and she saw her husband, when she followed him with her eyes from the window, drag heavily down toward the corner, where he was to take the horse-car.

He arrived rather later than usual at his office, and he found his letters already on his table. There was one, long and official-looking, with a printed letter-heading on the outside, and Lapham had no need to open it in order to know that it was the offer

---

7. "And there wrestled. . . ." The quotation comes from Genesis 32:24. Jacob wrestles with an angel and, by overcoming him, gains his blessing. Jacob reflects," I have seen God face to face and my life is preserved." Howells no doubt intends us to notice the ironic inappropriateness of Persis' pious Biblical citation.

of the Great Lacustrine & Polar Railroad for his mills. But he went mechanically through the verification of his prophetic fear, which was also his sole hope, and then sat looking blankly at it.

Rogers came promptly at the appointed time, and Lapham handed him the letter. He must have taken it all in at a glance, and seen the impossibility of negotiating any further now, even with victims so pliant and willing as those Englishmen.

"You've ruined me!" Rogers broke out. "I haven't a cent left in the world! God help my poor wife!"

He went out, and Lapham remained staring at the door which closed upon him. This was his reward for standing firm for right and justice to his own destruction: to feel like a thief and a murderer.

## XXVI

LATER in the forenoon came the dispatch from the West Virginians in New York, saying their brother assented to their agreement; and it now remained for Lapham to fulfill his part of it. He was ludicrously far from able to do this; and unless he could get some extension of time from them, he must lose this chance, his only chance, to retrieve himself. He spent the time in a desperate endeavor to raise the money, but he had not raised the half of it when the banks closed. With shame in his heart he went to Bellingham, from whom he had parted so haughtily, and laid his plan before him. He could not bring himself to ask Bellingham's help, but he told him what he proposed to do. Bellingham pointed out that the whole thing was an experiment, and that the price asked was enormous, unless a great success were morally certain. He advised delay, he advised prudence; he insisted that Lapham ought at least to go out to Kanawha Falls, and see the mines and works, before he put any such sum into the development of the enterprise.

"That's all well enough," cried Lapham; "but if I don't clinch this offer within twenty-four hours, they'll withdraw it, and go into the market; and then where am I?"

"Go on and see them again," said Bellingham. "They can't be so peremptory as that with you. They must give you time to look at what they want to sell. If it turns out what you hope, then—I'll see what can be done. But look into it thoroughly."

"Well!" cried Lapham, helplessly submitting. He took out his watch, and saw that he had forty minutes to catch the four o'clock train. He hurried back to his office, put together some papers preparatory to going, and dispatched a note by his boy to Mrs. Lapham saying that he was starting for New York, and did not know just when he should get back.

The early spring day was raw and cold. As he went out through the office he saw the clerks at work with their street coats and hats on; Miss Dewey had her jacket dragged up on her shoulders and looked particularly comfortless as she operated her machine with her red fingers. "What's up?" asked Lapham, stopping a moment.

"Seems to be something the matter with the steam," she answered, with the air of unmerited wrong habitual with so many pretty women who have to work for a living.

"Well, take your writer into my room; there's a fire in the stove there," said Lapham, passing out.

Half an hour later his wife came into the outer office. She had passed the day in a passion of self-reproach, gradually mounting from the mental numbness in which he had left her, and now she could wait no longer to tell him that she saw how she had forsaken him in his hour of trial and left him to bear it alone. She wondered at herself in shame and dismay; she wondered that she could have been so confused as to the real point by that old wretch of a Rogers, that she could have let him hoodwink her so, even for a moment. It astounded her that such a thing should have happened, for if there was any virtue upon which this good woman prided herself, in which she thought herself superior to her husband, it was her instant and steadfast perception of right and wrong, and the ability to choose the right to her own hurt. But she had now to confess, as each of us has had likewise to confess in his own case, that the very virtue on which she had prided herself was the thing that had played her false; that she had kept her mind so long upon that old wrong which she believed her husband had done this man that she could not detach it, but clung to the thought of reparation for it when she ought to have seen that he was proposing a piece of roguery as the means. The suffering which Lapham must inflict on him if he decided against him had been more to her apprehension than the harm he might do if he decided for him. But now she owned her limitations to herself, and above everything in the world she wished the man whom her conscience had roused and driven on whither her intelligence had not followed, to do right, to do what he felt to be right, and nothing else. She admired and revered him for going beyond her, and she wished to tell him that she did not know what he had determined to do about Rogers, but that she knew it was right, and would gladly abide the consequences with him, whatever they were.

She had not been near his place of business for nearly a year, and her heart smote her tenderly as she looked about her there, and thought of the early days when she knew as much about the paint as he did; she wished that those days were back again. She saw Corey at his desk, and she could not bear to speak to him; she dropped her veil that she need not recognize him, and pushed on to Lapham's room, and, opening the door without knocking, shut it behind her.

Then she became aware with intolerable disappointment that her husband was not there. Instead, a very pretty girl sat at his desk, operating a type-writer. She seemed quite at home, and she paid Mrs. Lapham the scant attention which such young women often bestow upon people not personally interesting to them. It vexed the wife that any one else should seem to be helping her husband about business that she had once been so intimate with; and she did not at all like the girl's indifference to her presence. Her hat and sack hung on a nail in one corner, and Lapham's office coat, looking intensely like him to his wife's familiar eye, hung on a nail in the other corner; and Mrs. Lapham liked even less than the girl's good looks this domestication of her garments in her husband's office. She began to ask herself exitedly why he should be away from his office when she happened to come; and she had not the strength at the moment to reason herself out of her unreasonableness.

"When will Colonel Lapham be in, do you suppose?" she sharply asked of the girl.

"I couldn't say exactly," replied the girl, without looking round.

"Has he been out long?"

"I don't know as I noticed," said the girl, looking up at the clock, without looking at Mrs. Lapham. She went on working her machine.

"Well, I can't wait any longer," said the wife abruptly. "When Colonel Lapham comes in, you please tell him Mrs. Lapham wants to see him."

The girl started to her feet and turned toward Mrs. Lapham with a red and startled face, which she did not lift to confront her. "Yes—yes—I will," she faltered.

The wife went home with a sense of defeat mixed with an irritation about this girl which she could not quell or account for. She found her husband's message, and it seemed intolerable that he should have gone to New York without seeing her; she asked herself in vain what the mysterious business could be that took him away so suddenly. She said to herself that he was neglecting her; he was leaving her out a little too much; and in demanding of herself why he had never mentioned that girl there in his office, she forgot how much she had left herself out of his business life. That was another curse of their prosperity. Well, she was glad the prosperity was going; it had never been happiness. After this she was going to know everything as she used.

She tried to dismiss the whole matter till Lapham returned; and if there had been anything for her to do in that miserable house, as she called it in her thought, she might have succeeded. But again the curse was on her; there was nothing to do; and the looks of that girl kept coming back to her vacancy, her disoccupation. She tried to make herself something to do, but that beauty, which she had not liked, followed her amid the work of overhauling the summer clothing, which Irene had seen to putting away in the fall. Who was the thing, anyway? It was very strange, her being there; why did she jump up in that frightened way when Mrs. Lapham had named herself?

After dark that evening, when the question had worn away its poignancy from mere iteration, a note for Mrs. Lapham was left at the door by a messenger who said there was no answer. "A note for me?" she said, staring at the unknown, and somehow artificial-looking, handwriting of the superscription. Then she opened it and read: "Ask your husband about his lady copying-clerk. A Friend and Well-wisher," who signed the note, gave no other name.

Mrs. Lapham sat helpless with it in her hand. Her brain

reeled; she tried to fight the madness off; but before Lapham came back the second morning, it had become, with lessening intervals of sanity and release, a demoniacal possession. She passed the night without sleep, without rest, in the frenzy of the cruelest of the passions, which covers with shame the unhappy soul it possesses, and murderously lusts for the misery of its object. If she had known where to find her husband in New York, she would have followed him; she waited his return in an ecstasy of impatience. In the morning he came back, looking spent and haggard. She saw him drive up to the door, and she ran to let him in herself.

"Who is that girl you've got in your office, Silas Lapham?" she demanded, when her husband entered.

"Girl in my office?"

"Yes! Who is she? What is she doing there?"

"Why, what have you heard about her?"

"Never you mind what I've heard. Who is she? *Is it Mrs. M. that you gave that money to?* I want to know who she is! I want to know what a respectable man, with grown-up girls of his own, is doing with such a looking thing as that in his office! I want to know how long she's been there! I want to know what she's there at all for!"

He had mechanically pushed her before him into the long, darkened parlor, and he shut himself in there with her now, to keep the household from hearing her lifted voice. For a while he stood bewildered, and could not have answered if he would; and then he would not. He merely asked, "Have I ever accused you of anything wrong, Persis?"

"You no need to!" she answered furiously, placing herself against the closed door.

"Did you ever know me to do anything out of the way?"

"That isn't what I asked you."

"Well, I guess you may find out about that girl yourself. Get away from the door."

"I won't get away from the door."

She felt herself set lightly aside, and her husband opened the door and went out. "I *will* find out about her," she screamed after him. "I'll find out, and I'll disgrace you—I'll teach you how to treat me!"

The air blackened round her; she reeled to the sofa; and

then she found herself waking from a faint. She did not know how long she had lain there; she did not care. In a moment her madness came whirling back upon her. She rushed up to his room; it was empty; the closet-doors stood ajar and the drawers were open; he must have packed a bag hastily and fled. She went out, and wandered crazily up and down till she found a hack. She gave the driver her husband's business address, and told him to drive there as fast as he could; and three times she lowered the window to put her head out and ask him if he could not hurry. A thousand things thronged into her mind to support her in her evil will. She remembered how glad and proud that man had been to marry her, and how everybody said she was marrying beneath her when she took him. She remembered how good she had always been to him, how perfectly devoted, slaving early and late to advance him, and looking out for his interests in all things, and sparing herself in nothing. If it had not been for her, he might have been driving stage yet; and since their troubles had begun, the troubles which his own folly and imprudence had brought on them, her conduct had been that of a true and faithful wife. Was *he* the sort of man to be allowed to play her false with impunity? She set her teeth and drew her breath sharply through them, when she thought how willingly she had let him befool her and delude her about that memorandum of payments to Mrs. M., because she loved him so much, and pitied him for his cares and anxieties. She recalled his confusion, his guilty looks.

She plunged out of the carriage so hastily when she reached the office that she did not think of paying the driver; and he had to call after her when she had got half-way up the stairs. Then she went straight to Lapham's room, with outrage in her heart. There was again no one there but that type-writer girl; she jumped to her feet in a fright, as Mrs. Lapham dashed the door to behind her and flung up her veil.

The two women confronted each other.

"Why, the good land!" cried Mrs. Lapham, "ain't you Zerrilla Millon?"

"I—I'm married," faltered the girl. "My name's Dewey now."

"You're Jim Millon's daughter, anyway. How long have you been here?"

"I haven't been here regularly; I've been here off and on ever since last May."

"Where's your mother?"

"She's here—in Boston."

Mrs. Lapham kept her eyes on the girl, but she dropped, trembling, into her husband's chair, and a sort of amaze and curiosity were in her voice instead of the fury she had meant to put there.

"The Colonel," continued Zerrilla, "he's been helping us, and he's got me a type-writer, so that I can help myself a little. Mother's doing pretty well now; and when Hen isn't around we can get along."

"That your husband?"

"I never wanted to marry him; but he promised to try to get something to do on shore; and mother was all for it, because he had a little property then, and I thought maybe I'd better. But it's turned out just as I said, and if he don't stay away long enough this time to let me get the divorce,—he's agreed to it, time and again,—I don't know what we're going to do." Zerrilla's voice fell, and the trouble which she could keep out of her face usually, when she was comfortably warmed and fed and prettily dressed, clouded it in the presence of a sympathetic listener. "I saw it was you when you came in the other day," she went on; "but you didn't seem to know me. I suppose the Colonel's told you that there's a gentleman going to marry me— Mr. Wemmel's his name—as soon as I get the divorce; but sometimes I'm completely discouraged; it don't seem as if I ever *could* get it."

Mrs. Lapham would not let her know that she was ignorant of the fact attributed to her knowledge. She remained listening to Zerrilla, and piecing out the whole history of her presence there from the facts of the past, and the traits of her husband's character. One of the things she had always had to fight him about was that idea of his that he was bound to take care of Jim Millon's worthless wife and her child because Millon had got the bullet that was meant for him. It was a perfect superstition of his; she could not beat it out of him; but she had made him promise the last time he had done anything for that woman that it should *be* the last time. He had then got her a little house in one of the fishing ports, where she could take the sailors to board and wash for, and earn an honest living if she would keep straight. That was five or six years ago, and Mrs. Lapham had heard nothing of Mrs. Millon since; she had heard quite enough of her before, and had known her idle and baddish ever since she was the worst little girl at school in Lumberville, and all through her shameful girlhood, and the married days which she had made so miserable to the poor fellow who had given her his decent name and a chance to behave herself. Mrs. Lapham had no mercy on Moll Millon, and she had quarreled often enough with her husband for befriending her. As for the child, if the mother would put Zerrilla out with some respectable family, that would be *one* thing; but as long as she kept Zerrilla with her, she was against letting her husband do anything for either of them. He had done ten times as much for them now as he had any need to, and she had made him give her his solemn word that he would do no more. She saw now that she was wrong to make him give it, and that he must have broken it again and again for the reason that he had given when she once scolded him for throwing away his money on that hussy:

"When I think of Jim Millon, I've *got* to; that's all."

She recalled now that whenever she had brought up the subject of Mrs. Millon and her daughter, he had seemed shy of it, and had dropped it with some guess that they were getting along now. She wondered that she had not thought at once of Mrs. Millon when she saw that memorandum about Mrs. M.; but the woman had passed so entirely out of her life, that she had never dreamt of her in connection with it. Her husband had deceived her, yet her heart was no longer hot against him, but rather tenderly grateful that his deceit was in this sort, and not in that other. All cruel and shameful doubt of him went out of it. She looked at this beautiful girl, who had blossomed out of her knowledge since she saw her last, and she knew that she was only a blossomed weed, of the same worthless root as her mother, and saved, if saved, from the same evil destiny by the good of her father in her; but so far as the girl and her mother were concerned, Mrs. Lapham knew that her husband was to blame for nothing but his willful, wrong-headed kind-heartedness, which her own exactions had turned into deceit. She remained awhile, questioning the girl quietly about herself and her mother, and then, with a better mind towards Zerrilla, at least, than she had ever had before, she rose up and went out. There must have been some outer hint of the exhaustion in which the subsidence of her excitement had left her within, for before she had reached the head of the stairs, Corey came towards her.

"Can I be of any use to you, Mrs. Lapham? The Colonel was here just before you came in, on his way to the train."

"Yes,—yes. I didn't know—I thought perhaps I could catch him here. But it don't matter. I wish you would let some one go with me to get a carriage," she begged feebly.

"I'll go with you myself," said the young fellow, ignoring the strangeness in her manner. He offered her his arm in the twilight of the staircase, and she was glad to put her trembling hand through it, and keep it there till he helped her into a hack which he found for her. He gave the driver her direction, and stood looking a little anxiously at her.

"I thank you; I am all right now," she said, and he bade the man drive on.

When she reached home she went to bed, spent with the tumult of her emotions and sick with shame and self-reproach. She understood now, as clearly as if he had told her in so many words, that if he had befriended these worthless jades—the Millons characterized themselves so, even to Mrs. Lapham's remorse—secretly and in defiance of her, it was because he dreaded her blame, which was so sharp and bitter, for what he could not help doing. It consoled her that he had defied her; deceived her; when he came back she should tell him that; and then it flashed upon her that she did not know where he was gone, or whether he would ever come again. If he never came, it would be no more than she deserved; but she sent for Penelope, and tried to give herself hopes of escape from this just penalty.

Lapham had not told his daughter where he was going; she had heard him packing his bag, and had offered to help him; but he had said he could do it best, and had gone off, as he usually did, without taking leave of any one.

"What were you talking about so loud, down in the parlor," she asked her mother, "just before he came up? Is there any new trouble?"

"No; it was nothing."

"I couldn't tell. Once I thought you were laughing." She went about, closing the curtains on account of her mother's headache, and doing awkwardly and imperfectly the things that Irene would have done so skillfully for her comfort.

The day wore away to nightfall, and then Mrs. Lapham said she *must* know. Penelope said there was no one to ask; the clerks would all be gone home; and her mother said yes, there was Mr. Corey; they could send and ask him; he would know.

The girl hesitated. "Very well," she said then, scarcely above a whisper, and she presently laughed huskily. "Mr. Corey seems fated to come in somewhere. I guess it's a Providence, mother."

She sent off a note, inquiring whether he could tell her just where her father had expected to be that night; and the answer came quickly back that Corey did not know, but would look up the book-keeper and inquire. This office brought him in person, an hour later, to tell Penelope that the Colonel was to be at Lapham that night and next day.

"He came in from New York in a great hurry, and rushed off as soon as he could pack his bag," Penelope explained, "and we hadn't a chance to ask him where he was to be to-night. And mother wasn't very well, and——"

"I thought she wasn't looking well when she was at the office to-day; and so I thought I would come rather than send," Corey explained, in his turn.

"Oh, thank you!"

"If there is anything I can do—telegraph Colonel Lapham, or anything?"

"Oh, no, thank you; mother's better now. She merely wanted to be sure where he was."

He did not offer to go upon this conclusion of his business, but hoped he was not keeping her from her mother. She thanked him once again, and said no, that her mother was much better since she had had a cup of tea; and then they looked at each other, and without any apparent exchange of intelligence he remained, and at eleven o'clock he was still there. He was honest in saying he did not know it was so late; but he made no pretense of being sorry, and she took the blame to herself.

"I oughtn't to have let you stay," she said. "But with father gone, and all that trouble hanging over us——"

She was allowing him to hold her hand a moment at the door, to which she had followed him.

"I'm so glad you could let me!" he said; "and I want

to ask you now when I may come again. But if you need me, you'll——"

A sharp pull at the door-bell outside made them start asunder, and at a sign from Penelope, who knew that the maids were abed by this time, he opened it.

"Why, Irene!" shrieked the girl.

Irene entered, with the hackman, who had driven her un-heard to the door, following with her small bags, and kissed her sister with resolute composure. "That's all," she said to the hackman. "I gave my checks to the expressman," she explained to Penelope.

Corey stood helpless. Irene turned upon him, and gave him her hand. "How do you do, Mr. Corey?" she said, with a courage that sent a thrill of admiring gratitude through him. "Where's mamma, Pen? Papa gone to bed?"

Penelope faltered out some reply embodying the facts, and Irene ran up the stairs to her mother's room. Mrs. Lapham started up in bed at her apparition.

"Irene Lapham!"

"Uncle William thought he ought to tell me the trouble papa was in; and did you think I was going to stay off there junketing, while you were going through all this at home, and Pen acting so silly too? You ought to have been ashamed to let me stay so long! I started just as soon as I could pack. Did you get my dispatch? I telegraphed from Springfield. But it don't matter now. Here I am. And I don't think I need have hurried on Pen's account," she added, with an accent prophetic of the sort of old maid she would become if she happened never to marry.

"Did you see him?" asked her mother. "It's the first time he's been here since she told him he mustn't come."

"I guess it isn't the last time, by the looks," said Irene; and before she took off her bonnet she began to undo some of Penel-ope's mistaken arrangements of the room.

At breakfast, where Corey and his mother met the next morning before his father and sisters came down, he told her, with embarrassment which told much more, that he wished now that she would go and call upon the Laphams.

Mrs. Corey turned a little pale, but shut her lips tight and mourned in silence whatever hopes she had lately permitted herself. She answered with Roman fortitude: "Of course, if there's ʼanything between you and Miss Lapham, your family ought to recognize it."

"Yes," said Corey.

"You were reluctant to have me call at first, but now if the affair is going on——"

"It is! I hope—yes, it is!"

"Then I ought to go and see her, with your sisters; and she ought to come here and—we ought all to see her and make the matter public. We can't do so too soon. It will seem as if we were ashamed if we don't."

"Yes, you are quite right, mother," said the young man gratefully, "and I feel how kind and good you are. I have tried to consider you in this matter, though I don't seem to have done so; I know what your rights are, and I wish with all my heart that I were meeting even your tastes perfectly. But I know you will like her when you come to know her. It's been very hard for her every way,—about her sister,—and she's made a great sacrifice for me. She's acted nobly."

Mrs. Corey, whose thoughts cannot always be reported, said she was sure of it, and that all she desired was her son's happiness.

"She's been very unwilling to consider it an engagement on that account, and on account of Colonel Lapham's difficulties. I should like to have you go, now, for that very reason. I don't know just how serious the trouble is; but it isn't a time when we can seem indifferent."

The logic of this was not perhaps so apparent to the glasses of fifty as to the eyes of twenty-six; but Mrs. Corey, however she viewed it, could not allow herself to blench before the son whom she had taught that to want magnanimity was to be less than gentlemanly. She answered, with what composure she could, "I will take your sisters," and then she made some natural inquiries about Lapham's affairs.

"Oh, I hope it will come out all right," Corey said, with a lover's vague smile, and left her. When his father came down, rubbing his long hands together, and looking aloof from all the cares of the practical world, in an artistic withdrawal, from which his eye ranged over the breakfast-table before he sat down, Mrs. Corey told him what she and their son had been saying.

He laughed, with a delicate impersonal appreciation of the predicament. "Well, Anna, you can't say but if you ever were guilty of supposing yourself porcelain, this is a just punishment of your arrogance. Here you are bound by the very quality on which you've prided yourself to behave well to a bit of earthenware who is apparently in danger of losing the gilding that rendered her tolerable."

"We never cared for the money," said Mrs. Corey. "You know that."

"No; and now we can't seem to care for the loss of it. That would be still worse. Either horn of the dilemma gores us. Well, we still have the comfort we had in the beginning; we can't help ourselves, and we should only make bad worse by trying. Unless we can look to Tom's inamorata herself for help."

Mrs. Corey shook her head so gloomily that her husband broke off with another laugh. But at the continued trouble of her face he said, sympathetically: "My dear, I know it's a very disagreeable affair; and I don't think either of us has failed to see that it was so from the beginning. I have had my way of expressing my sense of it, and you yours, but we have always been of the same mind about it. We would both have preferred to have Tom marry in his own set; the Laphams are about the last set we could have wished him to marry into. They *are* uncultivated people, and, so far as I have seen them, I'm not able to believe that poverty will improve them. Still, it may. Let us hope for the best, and let us behave as well as we know how. I'm sure *you* will behave well, and I shall try. I'm going with you to call on Miss Lapham. This is a thing that can't be done by halves!"

He cut his orange in the Neapolitan manner, and ate it in quarters.

# XXVII

Irene did not leave her mother in any illusion concerning her cousin Will and herself. She said they had all been as nice to her as they could be, and when Mrs. Lapham hinted at what had been in her thoughts,—or her hopes, rather,—Irene severely snubbed the notion. She said that he was as good as engaged to a girl out there, and that he had never dreamt of her. Her mother wondered at her severity; in these few months the girl had toughened and hardened; she had lost all her babyish dependence and pliability; she was like iron; and here and there she was sharpened to a cutting edge. It had been a life and death struggle with her; she had conquered, but she had also necessarily lost much. Perhaps what she had lost was not worth keeping; but at any rate she had lost it.

She required from her mother a strict and accurate account of her father's affairs, so far as Mrs. Lapham knew them; and she showed a business-like quickness in comprehending them that Penelope had never pretended to. With her sister she ignored the past as completely as it was possible to do; and she treated both Corey and Penelope with the justice which their innocence of voluntary offense deserved. It was a difficult part, and she kept away from them as much as she could. She had been easily excused, on a plea of fatigue from her journey, when Mr. and Mrs. Corey had called the day after her arrival, and, Mrs. Lapham being still unwell, Penelope received them alone.

The girl had instinctively judged best that they should know the worst at once, and she let them have the full brunt of the drawing-room, while she was screwing her courage up to come down and see them. She was afterwards—months afterwards—able to report to Corey that when she entered the room his father was sitting with his hat on his knees, a little tilted away from the Emancipation group, as if he expected the Lincoln to hit him with that lifted hand of benediction; and that Mrs. Corey looked as if she were not sure but the Eagle pecked. But for the time being Penelope was as nearly crazed as might be by the complications of her position, and received her visitors with a piteous distraction which could not fail of touching Bromfield Corey's Italianized sympatheticism. He was very polite and tender with her at first, and ended by making a joke with her, to which Penelope responded in her sort. He said he hoped they parted friends, if not quite acquaintances; and she said she hoped they would be able to recognize each other if they ever met again.

"That is what I meant by her pertness," said Mrs. Corey, when they were driving away.

"Was it very pert?" he queried. "The child had to answer something."

"I would much rather she had answered nothing, under the circumstances," said Mrs. Corey. "However!" she added hopelessly.

"Oh, she's a merry little grig,[8] you can see that, and there's no harm in her. I can understand a little why a formal fellow like Tom should be taken with her. She hasn't the least reverence, I suppose, and joked with the young man from the beginning. You must remember, Anna, that there was a time when you liked my joking."

"It was a very different thing!"

"But that drawing-room!" pursued Corey; "really, I don't see how Tom stands that. Anna, a terrible thought occurs to me! Fancy Tom being married in front of that group, with a floral horse-shoe in tuberoses coming down on either side of it!"

"Bromfield!" cried his wife, "you are unmerciful."

"No, no, my dear," he argued; "merely imaginative. And I can even imagine that little thing finding Tom just the least bit slow at times, if it were not for his goodness. Tom is so kind that I'm convinced he sometimes feels your joke in his heart when his head isn't quite clear about it. Well, we will not despond, my dear."

"Your father seemed actually to like her," Mrs. Corey reported to her daughters, very much shaken in her own prejudices by the fact. If the girl were not so offensive to his fastidiousness, there might be some hope that she was not so offensive as Mrs. Corey had thought. "I wonder how she will strike *you*," she concluded, looking from one daughter to another, as if trying to decide which of them would like Penelope least.

Irene's return and the visit of the Coreys formed a distraction for the Laphams in which their impending troubles seemed to hang farther aloof; but it was only one of those reliefs which mark the course of adversity, and it was not one of the cheerful reliefs. At any other time, either incident would have been an anxiety and care for Mrs. Lapham which she would have found hard to bear; but now she almost welcomed them. At the end of three days Lapham returned, and his wife met him as if nothing unusual had marked their parting; she reserved her atonement for a fitter time; he would know now from the way she acted that she felt all right towards him. He took very little note of her manner, but met his family with an austere quiet that puzzled her, and a sort of pensive dignity that refined his rudeness to an

8. A "grig" is an extravagantly lively person, one full of jests. It makes a nice contrast with Pene-  lope's image of herself.

effect that sometimes comes to such natures after long sickness, when the animal strength has been taxed and lowered. He sat silent with her at the table after their girls had left them alone; and seeing that he did not mean to speak, she began to explain why Irene had come home, and to praise her.

"Yes, she done right," said Lapham. "It was time for her to come," he added gently.

Then he was silent again, and his wife told him of Corey's having been there, and of his father's and mother's calling. "I guess Pen's concluded to make it up," she said.

"Well, we'll see about that," said Lapham; and now she could no longer forbear to ask him about his affairs.

"I don't know as I've got any right to know anything about it," she said humbly, with remote allusion to her treatment of him. "But I can't help wanting to know. How *are* things going, Si?"

"Bad," he said, pushing his plate from him, and tilting himself back in his chair. "Or they ain't going at all. They've stopped."

"What do you mean, Si?" she persisted tenderly.

"I've got to the end of my string. To-morrow I shall call a meeting of my creditors, and put myself in their hands. If there's enough left to satisfy them, I'm satisfied." His voice dropped in his throat; he swallowed once or twice, and then did not speak.

"Do you mean that it's all over with you?" she asked fearfully.

He bowed his big head, wrinkled and grizzled; and after a while he said, "It's hard to realize it; but I guess there ain't any doubt about it." He drew a long breath, and then he explained to her about the West Virginia people, and how he had got an extension of the first time they had given him, and had got a man to go up to Lapham with him and look at the works,—a man that had turned up in New York, and wanted to put money in the business. His money would have enabled Lapham to close with the West Virginians. "The devil was in it, right straight along," said Lapham. "All I had to do was to keep quiet about that other company. It was Rogers and his property right over again. He liked the look of things, and he wanted to go into the business, and he had the money—plenty; it would have saved me with those West Virginia folks. But I had to tell him how I stood. I had to tell him all about it, and what I wanted to do. He began to back water in a minute, and the next morning I saw that it was up with him. He's gone back to New York. I've lost my last chance. Now all I've got to do is to save the pieces."

"Will—will—everything go?" she asked.

"I can't tell yet. But they shall have a chance at everything— every dollar, every cent. I'm sorry for you, Persis—and the girls."

"Oh, don't talk of *us* !" She was trying to realize that the simple, rude soul to which her heart clove in her youth, but which she had put to such cruel proof with her unsparing conscience and her unsparing tongue, had been equal to its ordeals, and had come out unscathed and unstained. He was able in his talk to make so little of them; he hardly seemed to see what they were; he was apparently not proud of them, and certainly not glad; if they were victories of any sort, he bore them with the patience of defeat. His wife wished to praise him, but she did not know how; so she offered him a little reproach, in which alone she touched the cause of her behavior at parting. "Silas," she asked after a long gaze at him, "why didn't you tell me you had Jim Millon's girl there?"

"I didn't suppose you'd like it, Persis," he answered. "I did intend to tell you at first, but then I put it off. I thought you'd come round some day, and find it out for yourself."

"I'm punished," said his wife, "for not taking enough interest in your business to even come near it. If we're brought back to the day of small things, I guess it's a lesson for me, Silas."

"Oh, I don't know about the lesson," he said wearily.

That night she showed him the anonymous scrawl which had kindled her fury against him. He turned it listlessly over in his hand. "I guess I know who it's from," he said, giving it back to her, "and I guess you do too, Persis."

"But how—how could he——"

"Mebbe he believed it," said Lapham, with patience that cut her more keenly than any reproach. "*You* did."

Perhaps because the process of his ruin had been so gradual, perhaps because the excitement of preceding events had exhausted their capacity for emotion, the actual consummation of his bankruptcy brought a relief, a repose to Lapham and his family, rather than a fresh sensation of calamity. In the shadow of his disaster they returned to something like their old, united life; they were at least all together again; and it will be intelligible to those whom life has blessed with vicissitude, that Lapham should come home the evening after he had given up everything to his creditors, and should sit down to his supper so cheerful that Penelope could joke him in the old way, and tell him that she thought from his looks they had concluded to pay him a hundred cents on every dollar he owed them.

As James Bellingham had taken so much interest in his troubles from the first, Lapham thought he ought to tell him, before taking the final step, just how things stood with him, and what he meant to do. Bellingham made some futile inquiries about his negotiations with the West Virginians, and Lapham told him they had come to nothing. He spoke of the New York man, and the chance that he might have sold out half his business to him. "But, of course, I had to let him know how it was about those fellows."

"Of course," said Bellingham, not seeing till afterwards the full significance of Lapham's action.

Lapham said nothing about Rogers and the Englishmen. He believed that he had acted right in that matter, and he was satisfied; but he did not care to have Bellingham, or anybody, perhaps think he had been a fool.

All those who were concerned in his affairs said he behaved well, and even more than well, when it came to the worst. The prudence, the good sense, which he had shown in the first years of his success, and of which his great prosperity seemed to have bereft him, came back; and these qualities, used in his own behalf, commended him as much to his creditors as the anxiety he showed that no one should suffer by him; this even made some of them doubtful of his sincerity. They gave him time, and there would have been no trouble in his resuming on the old basis, if the ground had not been cut from under him by the competition of the West Virginia company. He saw himself that it was useless to try to go on in the old way, and he preferred to go back and begin the world anew where he had first begun it, in the hills at Lapham. He put the house at Nankeen Square, with everything else he had, into the payment of his debts, and Mrs. Lapham found it easier to leave it for the old farmstead in Vermont than it would have been to go from that home of many years to the new house on the water side of Beacon. This thing and that is embittered to us, so that we may be willing to relinquish it; the world, life itself, is embittered to most of us, so that we are glad to have done with them at last; and this home was haunted with such memories to each of those who abandoned it that to go was less exile than escape. Mrs. Lapham could not look into Irene's room without seeing the girl there before her glass, tearing the poor little keepsakes of her hapless fancy from their hiding-places to take them and fling them in passionate renunciation upon her sister; she could not come into the sitting-room, where her little ones had grown up, without starting at the thought of her husband sitting so many weary nights at his desk there, trying to fight his way back to hope out of the ruin into which he was slipping. When she remembered that night when Rogers came, she hated the place. Irene accepted her release from the house eagerly, and was glad to go before and prepare for the family at Lapham. Penelope was always ashamed of her engagement there; it must seem better somewhere else, and she was glad to go too. No one but Lapham, in fact, felt the pang of parting in all its keenness. Whatever regret the others had was softened to them by the likeness of their flitting to many of those removals for the summer which they made in the late spring when they left Nankeen Square; they were going directly into the country instead of to the sea-side first; but Lapham, who usually remained in town long after they had gone, knew all the difference. For his nerves there was no mechanical sense of coming back; this was as much the end of his proud, prosperous life as death itself could have been. He was returning to begin life anew, but he knew, as well as he knew that he should not find his vanished youth in his native hills, that it could never again be the triumph that it had been. That was impossible, not only in his stiffened and weakened forces, but in the very nature of things. He was going back, by grace of the man whom he owed money, to make what he could out of the one chance which his successful rivals had left him.

In one phase his paint had held its own against bad times and ruinous competition, and it was with the hope of doing still more with the Persis Brand that he now set himself to work. The West Virginia people confessed that they could not produce those fine grades, and they willingly left the field to him. A strange, not ignoble friendliness existed between Lapham and the three brothers; they had used him fairly; it was their facilities that had conquered him, not their ill-will; and he recognized in them without enmity the necessity to which he had yielded. If he succeeded in his efforts to develop his paint in this direction, it must be for a long time on a small scale compared with his former business, which it could never equal, and he brought to them the flagging energies of an elderly man. He was more broken than he knew by his failure; it did not kill, as it often does, but it weakened the spring once so strong and elastic. He lapsed more and more into acquiescence with his changed condition, and that bragging note of his was rarely sounded. He worked faithfully enough in his enterprise, but sometimes he failed to seize occasions that in his younger days he would have turned to golden account. His wife saw in him a daunted look that made her heart ache for him.

One result of his friendly relations with the West Virginia people was that Corey went in with them, and the fact that he did so solely upon Lapham's advice, and by means of his recommendation, was perhaps the Colonel's proudest consolation. Corey knew the business thoroughly, and after half a year at Kanawha Falls and in the office at New York, he went out to Mexico and Central America, to see what could be done for them upon the ground which he had theoretically studied with Lapham.

Before he went he came up to Vermont, and urged Penelope to go with him. He was to be first in the city of Mexico, and if his mission was successful he was to be kept there and in South America several years, watching the new railroad enterprises and the development of mechanical agriculture and whatever other undertakings offered an opening for the introduction of the paint. They were all young men together, and Corey, who had put his money into the company, had a proprietary interest in the success which they were eager to achieve.

"There's no more reason now and no less than ever there was," mused Penelope, in counsel with her mother, "why I should say Yes, or why I should say No. Everything else changes, but this is just where it was a year ago. It don't go backward, and it don't go forward. Mother, I believe I shall take the bit in my teeth—if anybody will put it there!"

"It isn't the same as it was," suggested her mother. "You can see that Irene's all over it."

"That's no credit to me," said Penelope. "I ought to be just as much ashamed as ever."

"You no need ever to be ashamed."

"That's true, too," said the girl. "And I can sneak off to Mexico with a good conscience if I could make up my mind to it." She laughed. "Well, if I could be *sentenced* to be married, or somebody would up and forbid the banns! *I* don't know what to do about it."

Her mother left her to carry her hesitation back to Corey, and she said now they had better go all over it and try to reason it out. "And I hope that whatever I do, it won't be for my own sake, but for—others!"

Corey said he was sure of that, and looked at her with eyes of patient tenderness.

"I don't say it is wrong," she proceeded, rather aimlessly, "but I can't make it seem right. I don't know whether I can make you understand, but the idea of being happy, when everybody else is so miserable, is more than I can endure. It makes me wretched."

"Then perhaps that's your share of the common suffering," suggested Corey, smiling.

"Oh, you know it isn't! You know it's nothing. Oh! One of the reasons is what I told you once before, that as long as father is in trouble I can't let you think of me. Now that he's lost everything——" She bent her eyes inquiringly upon him, as if for the effect of this argument.

"I don't think that's a very good reason," he answered seriously, but smiling still. "Do you believe me when I tell you that I love you?"

"Why, I suppose I must," she said, dropping her eyes.

"Then why shouldn't I think all the more of you on account of your father's loss? You didn't suppose I cared for you because he was prosperous?" There was a shade of reproach, ever so delicate and gentle, in his smiling question, which she felt.

"No, I couldn't think such a thing of you. I—I don't know what I meant. I meant that——" She could not go on and say that she had felt herself more worthy of him because of her father's money; it would not have been true; yet there was no other explanation. She stopped and cast a helpless glance at him.

He came to her aid. "I understand why you shouldn't wish me to suffer by your father's misfortunes."

"Yes, that was it; and there is too great a difference every way. We ought to look at that again. You mustn't pretend that you don't know it, for that wouldn't be true. Your mother will never like me, and perhaps—perhaps I shall not like her."

"Well," said Corey, a little daunted, "you won't have to marry my family."

"Ah, that isn't the point!"

"I know it," he admitted. "I won't pretend that I don't see what you mean; but I'm sure that all the differences would disappear when you came to know my family better. I'm not afraid but you and my mother will like each other—she can't help it!" he exclaimed, less judicially than he had hitherto spoken, and he went on to urge some points of doubtful tenability. "We have our ways, and you have yours; and while I don't say but what you and my mother and sisters would be a little strange together at first, it would soon wear off on both sides. There can't be anything hopelessly different in you all, and if there were it wouldn't be any difference to me."

"Do you think it would be pleasant to have you on my side against your mother?"

"There won't be any sides. Tell me just what it is you're afraid of."

"Afraid?"

"Thinking of, then."

"I don't know. It isn't anything they say or do," she explained, with her eyes intent on his. "It's what they are. I couldn't be natural with them, and if I can't be natural with people, I'm disagreeable."

"Can you be natural with me?"

"Oh, I'm not afraid of you. I never was. That was the trouble from the beginning."

"Well, then, that's all that's necessary. And it never was the least trouble to me!"

"It made me untrue to Irene."

"You mustn't say that! You were always true to her."

"She cared for you first."

"Well, but I never cared for her at all!" he besought her.

"She thought you did."

"That was nobody's fault, and I can't let you make it yours. My dear——"

"Wait. We must understand each other," said Penelope,

rising from her seat to prevent an advance he was making from his; "I want you to realize the whole affair. Should you want a girl who hadn't a cent in the world, and felt different in your mother's company, and had cheated and betrayed her own sister?"

"I want you!"

"Very well, then, you can't have me. I should always despise myself. I ought to give you up for all these reasons. Yes, I must." She looked at him intently, and there was a tentative quality in her affirmations.

"Is this your answer?" he said. "I must submit. If I asked too much of you, I was wrong. And—good-bye."

He held out his hand, and she put hers in it. "You think I'm capricious and fickle!" she said. "I can't help it—I don't know myself. I can't keep to one thing for half a day at a time. But it's right for us to part—yes, it must be. It must be," she repeated; "and I shall try to remember that. Good-bye! I will try to keep that in my mind, and you will too—you won't care, very soon! I didn't mean *that*—no; I know how true you are; but you will soon look at me differently, and see that even if there hadn't been this about Irene, I was not the one for you. You do think so, don't you?" she pleaded, clinging to his hand. "I am not at all what they would like—your family; I felt that. I am little, and black, and homely, and they don't understand my way of talking, and now that we've lost everything—— No, I'm not fit. Good-bye. You're quite right not to have patience with me any longer. I've tried you enough. I ought to be willing to marry you against their wishes if you want me to, but I can't make the sacrifice—I'm too selfish for that." All at once she flung herself on his breast. "I can't even give you up! I shall never dare look any one in the face again. Go, go! But take me with you! I tried to do without you! I gave it a fair trial, and it was a dead failure. Oh, poor Irene! How could *she* give you up?"

Corey went back to Boston immediately, and left Penelope, as he must, to tell her sister that they were to be married. She was spared from the first advance toward this by an accident or a misunderstanding. Irene came straight to her after Corey was gone, and demanded, "Penelope Lapham, have you been such a ninny as to send that man away on my account?"

Penelope recoiled from this terrible courage; she did not

answer directly, and Irene went on, "Because if you did, I'll thank you to bring him back again. I'm not going to have him thinking that I'm dying for a man that never cared for me. It's insulting, and I'm not going to stand it. Now, you just send for him!"

"Oh, I will, 'Rene," gasped Penelope. And then she added, shamed out of her prevarication by Irene's haughty magnanimity, "I have. That is—he's coming back——"

Irene looked at her a moment, and then, whatever thought was in her mind, said fiercely, "Well!" and left her to her dismay—her dismay and her relief, for they both knew that this was the last time they should ever speak of that again.

The marriage came after so much sorrow and trouble, and the fact was received with so much misgiving for the past and future, that it brought Lapham none of the triumph in which he had once exulted at the thought of an alliance with the Coreys. Adversity had so far been his friend that it had taken from him all hope of the social success for which people crawl and truckle, and restored him, through failure and doubt and heartache, the manhood which his prosperity had so nearly stolen from him. Neither he nor his wife thought now that their daughter was marrying a Corey; they thought only that she was giving herself to the man who loved her, and their acquiescence was sobered still further by the presence of Irene. Their hearts were far more with her.

Again and again Mrs. Lapham said she did not see how she could go through it. "I can't make it seem right," she said.

"It *is* right," steadily answered the Colonel.

"Yes, I know. But it don't *seem* so."

It would be easy to point out traits in Penelope's character which finally reconciled all her husband's family and endeared her to them. These things continually happen in novels; and the Coreys, as they had always promised themselves to do, made the best, and not the worst, of Tom's marriage.

They were people who could value Lapham's behavior as Tom reported it to them. They were proud of him, and Bromfield Corey, who found a delicate, æsthetic pleasure in the heroism with which Lapham had withstood Rogers and his temptations,—something finely dramatic and unconsciously effective,—wrote him a letter which would once have flattered the rough soul almost to ecstasy, though now he affected to slight it in showing it. "It's all right if it makes it more comfortable for Pen," he said to his wife.

But the differences remained uneffaced, if not uneffaceable, between the Coreys and Tom Corey's wife. "If he had only married the Colonel!" subtly suggested Nanny Corey.

There was a brief season of civility and forbearance on both sides, when he brought her home before starting for Mexico, and her father-in-law made a sympathetic feint of liking Penelope's way of talking, but it is questionable if even he found it so delightful as her husband did. Lily Corey made a little, ineffectual sketch of her, which she put by with other studies to finish up some time, and found her rather picturesque in some ways. Nanny got on with her better than the rest, and saw possibilities for her in the country to which she was going. "As she's quite unformed socially," she explained to her mother, "there is a chance that she will form herself on the Spanish manner, if she stays there long enough, and that when she comes back she will have the charm of not olives, perhaps, but *tortillas*, whatever they are: something strange and foreign, even if it's borrowed. I'm glad she's going to Mexico. At that distance we can—correspond."

Her mother sighed, and said bravely that she was sure they all got on very pleasantly as it was, and that she was perfectly satisfied if Tom was.

There was, in fact, much truth in what she said of their harmony with Penelope. Having resolved, from the beginning, to make the best of the worst, it might almost be said that they were supported and consoled in their good intentions by a higher power. This marriage had not, thanks to an overruling Providence, brought the succession of Lapham teas upon Bromfield Corey which he had dreaded; the Laphams were far off in their native fastnesses, and neither Lily nor Nanny Corey was obliged to sacrifice herself to the conversation of Irene; they were not even called upon to make a social demonstration for Penelope at a time when, most people being still out of town, it would have been so easy; she and Tom had both begged that there might be nothing of that kind; and though none of the

Coreys learned to know her very well in the week she spent with them, they did not find it hard to get on with her. There were even moments when Nanny Corey, like her father, had glimpses of what Tom had called her humor, but it was perhaps too unlike their own to be easily recognizable.

Whether Penelope, on her side, found it more difficult to harmonize, I cannot say. She had much more of the harmonizing to do, since they were four to one; but then she had gone through so much greater trials before. When the door of their carriage closed and it drove off with her and her husband to the station, she fetched a long sigh.

"What is it?" asked Corey, who ought to have known better.

"Oh, nothing. I don't think I shall feel strange amongst the Mexicans now."

He looked at her with a puzzled smile, which grew a little graver, and then he put his arm round her and drew her closer to him. This made her cry on his shoulder. "I only meant that I should have you all to myself." There is no proof that she meant more, but it is certain that our manners and customs go for more in life than our qualities. The price that we pay for civilization is the fine yet impassable differentiation of these. Perhaps we pay too much; but it will not be possible to persuade those who have the difference in their favor that this is so. They may be right; and at any rate the blank misgiving, the recurring sense of disappointment to which the young people's departure left the Coreys is to be considered. That was the end of their son and brother for them; they felt that; and they were not mean or unamiable people.

He remained three years away. Some changes took place in that time. One of these was the purchase by the Kanawha Falls Company of the mines and works at Lapham. The transfer relieved Lapham of the load of debt which he was still laboring under, and gave him an interest in the vaster enterprise of the younger men, which he had once vainly hoped to grasp all in his own hand. He began to tell of this coincidence as something very striking; and pushing on more actively the special branch of the business left to him, he bragged, quite in his old way, of its enormous extension. His son-in-law, he said, was pushing it in Mexico and Central America: an idea that they had originally had in common. Well, young blood was what was wanted in a thing of that kind. Now, those fellows out in West Virginia: all young, and a perfect team!

For himself, he owned that he had made mistakes; he could see just where the mistakes were—put his finger right on them. But one thing he could say: he had been no man's enemy but his own; every dollar, every cent had gone to pay his debts; he had come out with clean hands. He said all this, and much more, to Mr. Sewell the summer after he sold out, when the minister and his wife stopped at Lapham on their way across from the White Mountains to Lake Champlain; Lapham had found them on the cars, and pressed them to stop off.

There were times when Mrs. Lapham had as great pride in the clean-handedness with which Lapham had come out as he had himself, but her satisfaction was not so constant. At those times, knowing the temptations he had resisted, she thought him the noblest and grandest of men; but no woman could endure to live in the same house with a perfect hero, and there were other times when she reminded him that if he had kept his word to her about speculating in stocks, and had looked after the insurance of his property half as carefully as he had looked after a couple of worthless women who had no earthly claim on him, they would not be where they were now. He humbly admitted it all, and left her to think of Rogers herself. She did not fail to do so, and the thought did not fail to restore him to her tenderness again.

I do not know how it is that clergymen and physicians keep from telling their wives the secrets confided to them; perhaps they can trust their wives to find them out for themselves whenever they wish. Sewell had laid before his wife the case of the Laphams after they came to consult with him about Corey's proposal to Penelope, for he wished to be confirmed in his belief that he had advised them soundly; but he had not given her their names, and he had not known Corey's himself. Now he had no compunctions in talking the affair over with her without the veil of ignorance which she had hitherto assumed, for she declared that as soon as she heard of Corey's engagement to Penelope, the whole thing had flashed upon her. "And that night at dinner, I could have told the child that he was in love with her sister by the way he talked about her; I heard him; and if she had not been so blindly in love with him herself, she would have known it too. I must say, I can't help feeling a sort of contempt for her sister."

"Oh, but you must not!" cried Sewell. "That is wrong, cruelly wrong. I'm sure that's out of your novel-reading, my dear, and not out of your heart. Come! it grieves me to hear you say such a thing as that."

"Oh, I dare say this pretty thing has got over it—how much character she has got!—and I suppose she'll see somebody else."

Sewell had to content himself with this partial concession. As a matter of fact, unless it was the young West Virginian who had come on to arrange the purchase of the Works, Irene had not yet seen any one, and whether there was ever anything between them is a fact that would need a separate inquiry. It is certain that at the end of five years after the disappointment which she met so bravely, she was still unmarried. But she was even then still very young, and her life at Lapham had been varied by visits to the West. It had also been varied by an invitation, made with the politest resolution by Mrs. Corey, to visit in Boston, which the girl was equal to refusing in the same spirit.

Sewell was intensely interested in the moral spectacle which Lapham presented under his changed conditions. The Colonel, who was more the Colonel in those hills than he could ever have been on the Back Bay, kept him and Mrs. Sewell over night at his house; and he showed the minister minutely round the Works and drove him all over his farm. For this expedition he employed a lively colt which had not yet come of age, and an open buggy long past its prime, and was no more ashamed of his turnout than of the finest he had ever driven on the Milldam. He was rather shabby and slovenly in dress, and he had fallen unkempt, after the country fashion, as to his hair and beard and boots. The house was plain, and was furnished with the simpler movables out of the house in Nankeen Square. There were certainly all the necessaries, but no luxuries, unless the statues of Prayer and Faith might be so considered. The Laphams now burned kerosene, of course, and they had no furnace in the winter; these were the only hardships the Colonel complained of; but he said that as soon as the company got to

paying dividends again,—he was evidently proud of the out-
lays that for the present prevented this,—he should put in
steam-heat and naphtha-gas. He spoke freely of his failure, and
with a confidence that seemed inspired by his former trust in
Sewell, whom, indeed, he treated like an intimate friend, rather
than an acquaintance of two or three meetings. He went back
to his first connection with Rogers, and he put before Sewell
hypothetically his own conclusions in regard to the matter.

"Sometimes," he said, "I get to thinking it all over, and it
seems to me I done wrong about Rogers in the first place; that
the whole trouble came from that. It was just like starting a row
of bricks. I tried to catch up, and stop 'em from going, but they
all tumbled, one after another. It wa'n't in the nature of things
that they could be stopped till the last brick went. I don't talk
much with my wife any more about it; but I should like to know
how it strikes you."

"We can trace the operation of evil in the physical world,"
replied the minister, "but I'm more and more puzzled about it
in the moral world. There its course is often so very obscure;
and often it seems to involve, so far as we can see, no penalty
whatever. And in your own case, as I understand, you don't
admit—you don't feel sure—that you ever actually did wrong
this man."

"Well, no; I don't. That is to say——"

He did not continue, and after a while Sewell said, with that
subtle kindness of his, "I should be inclined to think—nothing
can be thrown quite away; and it can't be that our sins only
weaken us—that your fear of having possibly behaved selfishly
toward this man kept you on your guard, and strengthened you
when you were brought face to face with a greater"—he was
going to say temptation, but he saved Lapham's pride, and said
—"emergency."

"Do you think so?"

"I think that there may be truth in what I suggest."

"Well, I don't know what it was," said Lapham; "all I know
is that when it came to the point, although I could see that I'd
got to go under unless I did it, that I couldn't sell out to those
Englishmen, and I couldn't let that man put his money into my
business without I told him just how things stood."

As Sewell afterwards told his wife, he could see that the loss of his fortune had been a terrible trial to Lapham, just because his prosperity had been so gross and palpable; and he had now a burning desire to know exactly how, at the bottom of his heart, Lapham still felt. "And do you ever have any regrets?" he delicately inquired of him.

"About what I done? Well, it don't always seem as if I done it," replied Lapham. "Seems sometimes as if it was a hole opened for me, and I crept out of it. I don't know," he added thoughtfully, biting the corner of his stiff mustache—"I don't know as I should always say it paid; but if I done it, and the thing was to do over again, right in the same way, I guess I should have to do it."

**THE END**

# Textual Note: Hyphenation
## of Divided Words

List A records compounds or possible compounds hyphenated at the end of the line in the copy-text (or in other texts at points where readings have been adopted from them) and resolved as hyphenated or one word as listed below. If Howells' manuscripts of this period fairly consistently followed one practice respecting the particular compound or possible compound, the resolution was made on that basis. Otherwise his *Century* and other periodical texts of this period were used as guides. List B is a guide to transcription of compounds or possible compounds hyphenated at the end of the line in the present text: compounds recorded here should be transcribed as given; words divided at the end of the line and not listed should be transcribed as one word.

## LIST A

| | | | |
|---|---|---|---|
| | | 36.7 | old-fashioned |
| 3.19 | leather-cushioned | 36.14 | low-tread |
| 3.33 | ground-glass | 36.38 | First-rate |
| 4.23 | anywheres | 37.11 | drawing-room |
| 8.14 | head-rest | 38.24–25 | preconceived |
| 9.1 | tavern-stand | 39.31 | floor-timbers |
| 9.12 | buggy-seat | 40.12 | dust-colored |
| 10.14 | red-hot | 44.18 | self-sacrifice |
| 13.23 | seventy-five | 45.13 | music-room |
| 13.24 | seventy-five | 45.25 | young-ladyishness |
| 13.27 | board-fence | 54.19 | white-mustached |
| 17.60 | stairway | 54.24 | -in-law |
| 17.38 | dashboard | 61.13 | Grandfather |
| 19.5 | minie-ball | 64.16 | book-keepers |
| 19.13 | never-failing | 64.22 | shirt-sleeves |
| 20.5 | sometime | 64.32 | shirt-sleeves |
| 20.12 | interview | 69.34 | will-power |
| 27.35 | twenty-eight | 70.38 | friendly-looking |
| 31.2 | skyline | 76.26 | headache |
| 33.7 | near-sighted | 76.29 | dining-room |
| 35.19–20 | reception-room | 77.9 | newspapers |
| 36.1 | black-walnut | 81.15 | indoors |

| | | | |
|---|---|---|---|
| 89.27 | brother-in- | 219.6 | newspaper |
| 90.11 | afternoon | 219.11 | downstairs |
| 91.15 | arm-chair | 220.13 | doorway |
| 92.9 | salt-box | 223.14 | family-room |
| 92.15 | book-keeper | 226.37 | to-morrow |
| 93.14 | hardship | 229.34 | patent-rights |
| 98.2 | good-looking | 233.3 | outright |
| 107.17 | alongside | 237.13 | fellow-beings |
| 117.17 | red-painted | 239.12 | tragi-comedy |
| 121.27 | superstructure | 240.23 | dust-colored |
| 126.21 | good-morning | 245.24 | down-hearted |
| 130.36 | beforehand | 253.26 | overstocked |
| 137.12 | well-enough | 257.30 | book-keeper |
| 145.5 | misconceived | 258.5 | good-humored |
| 147.18 | sunsets | 258.7 | common-place |
| 150.5 | lady-like | 259.7 | pocket-book |
| 151.3 | disown | 264.30 | undersell |
| 152.17 | ill-advised | 273.24 | brickwork |
| 152.22 | disadvantage | 275.13 | good-night |
| 153.17 | good-nature | 275.30 | brightly-lighted |
| 161.20 | waistcoat | 276.17 | non-combustible |
| 163.31 | somewheres | 278.11 | grown-up |
| 164.18 | hook-and- | 278.19 | cold-hearted |
| 165.29 | reception-room | 280.14 | sleep-broken |
| 166.5 | drawing-room | 282.7 | -of-doors |
| 166.22 | low-necks | 291.7 | over-night |
| 167.30 | to-night | 292.33 | twenty-four |
| 169.27 | old-fashioned | 295.36 | artificial-looking |
| 172.15 | hard-working | 298.10 | type-writer |
| 173.2 | homesick | 299.37 | kind-heartedness |
| 173.17 | old-fashioned | 305.20 | drawing-room |
| 175.1 | self-sacrifice | 307.20 | To-morrow |
| 175.11 | old-fashioned | 310.7 | sitting-room |
| 191.34 | -of-doors | 310.21 | sea-side |
| 192.20 | self-sacrifice | 314.26 | Good-bye |
| 192.21 | self-sacrifice | 320.3 | naphtha-gas |
| 197.15 | Good-night | | |
| 208.2 | to-day | | |
| 211.20 | reception-room | | LIST B |
| 212.11 | outcasts | | |
| 214.21 | upstairs | 4.37 | self-respect |
| 215.20 | button-hole | 7.5 | paint-mine |
| 219.1 | to-morrow | 9.2 | school-teacher |

| | | | |
|---|---|---|---|
| 9.6 | paint-mine | 165.8 | boarding-houses |
| 13.27 | bridge-girder | 169.33 | -à-brac |
| 14.12 | stove-polish | 172.1 | close-shuttered |
| 17.21 | hitching-weight | 199.25 | self-accusal |
| 19.15 | single-minded | 209.13 | -in-law |
| 35.31 | master-builder | 213.24 | ninety-nine |
| 45.10 | reception-room | 214.32 | snow-white |
| 45.13 | music-room | 217.1 | table-spoonful |
| 46.30 | reception-room | 223.14 | family-room |
| 48.13 | old-fashioned | 226.36 | Good-bye |
| 48.17 | -thousand-dollar | 245.24 | to-morrow |
| 60.38 | self-reliance | 251.14 | absent-mindedly |
| 69.18 | stock-in- | 256.39 | book-keeper |
| 104.11 | theater-goers | 259.25 | shore-suit |
| 126.11 | Good-bye | 273.9 | window-spaces |
| 132.38 | double-breasted | 274.15 | music-room |
| 146.10 | heart-broken | 274.19 | nail-keg |
| 150.29 | accusing-spirit | 289.13 | self-pity |
| 153.22 | paint-king | 291.35 | official-looking |

# Composition and
# Backgrounds

# Composition

By 1884, when he began to write *The Rise of Silas Lapham,* William Dean Howells was a well-established author of international reputation. His publications included *Their Wedding Journey* (1872), *The Undiscovered Country* (1880), *A Modern Instance* (1882) and a dozen other volumes of fiction, poetry, and travel sketches. James R. Osgood was acting as his literary agent, placing his stories in magazines and arranging for the most profitable publication of his books. Howells normally sold his novels before they were written, providing a prospective publisher with a brief outline of the story, but refusing to expand it very much for fear that he would restrict the free operation of his imagination upon which the growth of the story depended. Howells was considered so professionally reliable and the sales of his books so dependable that publishers were willing to buy on the basis of a sketch alone and to begin serialization of a novel long before it was completed.

Howells usually had several literary projects going simultaneously, and his correspondence suggests that when Osgood sold Roswell Smith, the publisher of *Century* magazine, the right to serialize Howells' novel, Howells may have been intending to submit an international novel about an American's return to Italy after many years' absence, an idea he later developed in *Indian Sumer* (1886). But by the time he began to work on the novel that his contract with *Century* called for, he summarized instead "The Rise of Silas Needham." This synopsis cannot be dated precisely, but it evidently preceded the entries in Howells' "Savings Bank" notebook since the notebook entries use the name Lapham and develop details of the story more fully than does the synopsis. The notebook bears the dates 1883–1897, so we know that the outline of the story and, more important, the kind of rise that Lapham was to experience were clear in Howells' mind before he began the actual composition.

His letters show that while he was writing the novel, during the summer of 1884, Howells was drawing on his own experience and researching details about which he was unsure. In her essay in this section, Ellen B. Ballou suggests that for at least the professional side of his characters Howells drew on his acquaintances in the publishing business. Even while the novel was being serialized in the *Century* (November 1884–August 1885), Howells was making major revisions, first to quiet the fears of his publisher, Roswell Smith, and of Richard Watson Gilder, editor of the *Century,* that the story would incite violence and result in the seizure of the magazine. Later he found it necessary to remove his ironic treatment of the widespread ethnic prejudice against Jews, having overestimated the ability of some of his readers to grasp his irony.

The continuing public interest in the novel caused several theatrical producers to feel that *Silas Lapham* would be successful on the stage. In collaboration with Paul Kester, Howells undertook to dramatize his story, but the theatrical producer James A. Hearn demanded more changes in the play than Howells was willing to make and the project finally collapsed. The surviving dramatization is interesting, however, for the reordering and extreme compression of events demanded in a play as opposed to Howells' more congenial genre, the novel.

# W. D. HOWELLS

## The Rise of Silas Needham†

The story opens with an Interview of Needham by Bartley Hubhard, who includes him in his Solid Men series for the Boston Events. In this interview the outlines of Needham's career are traced from his hard, squalid childhood to the moment of his greatest prosperity as the proprietor and manufacturer of Needham's Mineral Paint (or Stove-Blacking, or Boys' Clothing, etc.) Then the story takes him, and touching the points indicated by the Interview vitalizes them by bringing all into the strongest and most intimate relief. The man's character is carefully studied; his love story is told; the dramatic incidents of his rise are portrayed; an injustice to a partner whom he has crowded out of the business is narrated, and the fact that a sense of his wrong-doing has never ceased to rest heavily on Needham's conscience is indicated.

His family and its social status in Boston is depicted in a series of incidents all bearing on this main story. The romance of his daughter's love-story, and her marriage against his liking is told.

Nothing is spared, good or bad, as to the truth of Needham's life and character; the vulgarity of his nature in some respects is shown; his family troubles are dealt with; and the man's essential goodness and patience and moral strength are only covertly indicated.

He abandons his old business after amassing a fortune in it, and goes into speculation. The moment comes when in some railroad adventure, the choice is presented to him of cruelly and oppressively squeezing another man, or getting squeezed himself. *He feels the weakening effect of the old wrong that he committed.* The circumstances of his temptation are carefully pointed, and all its incidents. At last, almost by force of "that, not ourselves, which works for righteousness"[1] he resists the temptation and suffers ruin.

His after life of adversity *from which he does not recover,* is sketched. The reader is made to feel that this adversity, consciously and deliberately chosen, is The Rise of Silas Needham.

---

†The manuscript of this synopsis, in Howells' hand, is in The Huntington Library, San Marino, California. It is printed here without the occasional cancellations and false starts that occur in the author's manuscript.

1. Howells appears to have been quoting loosely from Matthew Arnold's (1822–88) *Literature and Dogma:* " . . . the enduring power, not ourselves, which makes for righteousness." [*Editor.*]

# W. D. HOWELLS

## The "Savings Bank" Notebook[†]

Lapham vulgar but not sordid
Make more of the fact that the Laphams don't know what to do with
their money.
Corey must make P. own that she loves him. They must talk it out all
[indecipherable word] fully. He cannot understand her but submits.
So, she must not own it at first nor let him know why. Perhaps he
goes away—to Mexico—mystified. Lapham's difficulty must be pend-
ing while his wife's jealousy comes on, and it is harder for him to do
the right thing because of his fury at that. —Before this, when it comes
out that Corey prefers P. he would naturally insist in his combination
that Irene must give C., and not stand in her sister's way.
The young trees growing out of the fallen logs in the forest—the
new life out of the old. Apply to Lapham's fall.
Reconcile Corey's saying that he doesn't like to live upon his father
to his having some money of his own.

# W. D. HOWELLS

## Letter to Richard Watson Gilder[†]

Wolfeboro, N.H.
July 31, 1884.

My dear Gilder:[1]
I hardly know what advertising material to give you about the story.
It will involve more interests, I find, and be more of a love story than I
expected, but the main idea of a rude, common, unrefined nature,
holding out against a temptation which must beset many business men
and accepting ruin rather than inflict it, remains the same. (I wouldn't
give this idea away.) The story opens with an interview by Bartley
Hubbard,[2] in which the hero's history and character are outlined. The
scene is always in Boston, except at the close, when it will be somewhere in Northern New England. I can't think what else to say.

\* \* \*

Yours ever
W. D. HOWELLS.

†Unpublished notebook in the Harvard College
Library.
†Unpublished letter in the Manuscript Division,
New York Public Library.
1. Richard Watson Gilder (1844–1909), editor of
*Century* magazine from 1881 until his death, was a
prominent New York literary and social figure; among
other things, he wrote sixteen volumes of verse, the best
of which is *The New Day* (1875). [*Editor.*]
2. Bartley Hubbard had appeared in Howells' earlier
novel *A Modern Instance*. [*Editor.*]

# W. D. HOWELLS

## Letter to Mark Twain[†]

Aug. 10, 1884

Dear Clemens:[1]

If I had written half as good a book as Huck Finn, I shouldn't ask anything better than to read the proofs; even as it is I don't. So send them on; they will always find me somewhere. I'm here in town for the present; but I'm going to Kennebunkport where the family are on Tuesday, and then to Campobello, N. B. Back to Boston the last of the month.

\* \* \*

I'm looking up, for my new story, facts about the general lack of literature in people, and I asked the teacher of a first-class ladies' school here how little literature a girl could carry away from her school. "Some go barely knowing that Shakespeare was an Englishman. One who had read all the 'love-part' of your (my) novels, didn't know that you were an American or a contemporary. We have to fight in eight months against fifteen or twenty years' absolute ignorance of literature."

I've got a mighty pretty house here on the water side of Beacon st., and Mrs. Howells wants Mrs. Clemens and you to consider yourself engaged for a visit to us when my opera comes out in November.[2]

Yours ever
W. D. Howells

†Unpublished letter from The Mark Twain Papers, The Bancroft Library, University of California, Berkeley.

1. Samuel Langhorne Clemens (1835–1910), who used the pen name "Mark Twain", met Howells by chance in the editorial offices of the *Atlantic* in 1869, thereby initiating one of the warmest and longest-lasting personal and professional friendships in American literary history. [*Editor.*]

2. Howells wrote the libretto for an opera, *A Sea Change or Love's Stowaway*, to which Georg Henschel (1850–1934) contributed the score. The opera was published in 1888, but it was never produced in Howells' lifetime. [*Editor.*]

# W. D. HOWELLS

## Letter to Henry James[†]

Kennebunkport, Maine,
Aug. 22, 1884

My Dear James:[1]

It is very good of you to write me when I've so long owed you a letter, and to make my buying a house "on the water side of Beacon" the occasion of forgiving my neglect. The greatest pleasure the house has yet brought me is this; but it is a pretty house and an extremely fine situation, and I hope it is not the only joy I shall have from it. I have spent some desolate weeks in it already, putting my books on their shelves, while the family were away at mountain-side and sea-side, and I can speak confidently and authoritatively of the sunsets from the library-windows. The sun goes down over Cambridge with as much apparent interest as if he were a Harvard graduate: possibly he is; and he spreads a glory over the Back Bay that is not to be equaled by the blush of a Boston Independent for such of us Republicans as are going to vote for Blaine.[2] – – – – Sometimes I feel it an extra-ordinary thing that I should have been able to buy a house on Beacon str., but I built one on Concord Avenue of nearly the same cost when I had far less money to begin with. In those doubting days I used to go and look at the cellar they were digging, and ask myself, knowing that I had had barely money to pay for the lot, "*Can* blood be got out of a turnip?" Now I know that some divine power loves turnips, and that somehow the blood will be got out of the particular turnip which I represent. Drolly enough, I am writing a story in which the chief personage builds a house on the water side of Beacon, and I shall be able to use all my experience, down to the quick. Perhaps the novel to may pay for the house.

\* \* \*

Yours ever
W. D. HOWELLS.

†Unpublished letter from the Harvard College Library.

1. Henry James met Howells in 1864 or 1865 in Cambridge, at a time when both men were first embarking on their literary careers. They remained friends and correspondents over the years, with Howells using his position as a respected editor, novelist, and critic to sponsor the early work of James. [*Editor.*]

2. James Gillespie Blaine (1830–93), congressman and senator from Maine, received the 1884 presidential nomination of the Republican party. He lost narrowly in the general election to the Democratic candidate, Grover Cleveland. [*Editor.*]

# ELLEN B. BALLOU

## Gentlemen Publishers[†]

In 1871 when Howells was writing *Their Wedding Journey*, he asked his sister to return his Niagara Falls guidebook. He wanted to be certain his recollections of the area were accurate in detail. In 1884 when he was writing *The Rise of Silas Lapham*, he could not rely on a map to check his memory of the years the novel mirrors.

\* \* \*

It embodies his recollections of things past; it also renders concrete his experience of things present. "An author," he once said, "is merely one who has had the fortune to remember more . . . than other men. A good many wise critics will tell you that writing is inventing; but I know better than that; it is only remembering . . . the history of your own life." In selecting the details for the *Silas Lapham* plot and the characters out of whom the plot grows, he drew not only from his well of memory but also on "the intensities" and "implications" of his day to day perceptions. The novel pictures a businessman's rise, at the expense of material well-being, from arrogant affluence to moral solvency. As he completed the novel in March 1885, he later recalled, "the bottom dropped out of everything." Possibly the reason for this sense of desolation was that reality had betrayed his subtle sermon. The facts had contradicted his ethical vision.

The characters, the setting, the plot of *Silas Lapham* are the product of Howells' creative imagination working evocatively with materials of his experience. Anyone reading the novel is struck by the accuracy of particulars, by the skillful economy of selection through which Howells creates an image apprehended by all the senses. The setting and characters have both substantial reality and an aura of supersensible experience. Of all the pictures in the novel none is more vivid than Lapham's house in the course of building on the water side of Beacon Street. The skeleton staircases with their provisional treads, the floor roughly laid, the crevasses of carpentry; the narrow paths of planking over which Mrs. Lapham clambers, the trestle on which Silas sits to whittle, the smell of mortar, the fragrance of pine shavings, the carpenter with his rule sticking out of his overall pocket create the house.

Howells, at the time he was working on *Silas Lapham*, himself bought a house on the water side of Beacon Street. In reporting his purchase to Henry James, he spoke of his novel and its hero, saying he would be able to use all his experience "down to the quick." Lapham's Beacon Street house is, of course, a composite picture of Howells'

†From *The Building of the House: Houghton Mifflin's Formative Years* (Boston: Houghton Mifflin, 1970), pp. 271–76. (Footnotes by Ballou unless otherwise indicated.—*Editor*.)

various residences.[1] The one at 302 Beacon he did not build, but simply renovated. He had had however two earlier opportunities to become acquainted with cellar holes, brick and mortar, raw boards and paint, his first when he built in Cambridge on Concord Avenue, his second with Redtop on Fairchild's land in Belmont. The reality of the Lapham house results from the mingling of details from these experiences. Lapham's office, more briefly sketched, has a comparable actuality and is an equally composite picture, derived from the Ticknor & Fields offices at 124 Tremont Street, the Cathedral Building, and the Riverside Press, from which he edited the *Atlantic Monthly* for over three years. Composite as the picture may be, to anyone who knows the Press today the similarity is startling. There on the second floor is Lapham's small den of an office with its glass door, swivel chair, and roll-top desk. Beyond the glass door is the larger den where Lapham's knowing bookkeeper watched and worked and where the beautiful enigmatic Miss Dewey beat the keys of her typewriter.

Just as the setting for *Silas Lapham* is made from Howells' years of perceptive observation so with the characters. To seek similarities too closely would be a "biographic fallacy." After all, Howells was an artist not a photographer. He had the privilege of arranging his objects according to his purpose. None of us is singular. We share characteristics with many others. The universal emerges in the particular. The individual provokes a shock of recognition because he is not unique. However, some of the parallels between the fictional characters and Howells' contemporaries are as striking as those between Lapham's office and that once used by Henry Oscar Houghton at the Riverside Press.

George Harrison Mifflin and Tom Corey, the young man who through his love for Lapham's daughter Penelope links the main plot with the subplot, have much in common. Mifflin with his aristocratic Crowninshield[2] background reflects Corey in detail after detail. His father, like Tom's, was a dilettante. Mifflin, like Tom, was a young man of wealth with a Harvard degree, determined despite his privilege to strike out and do something for himself. Like Corey, he was persistent in securing his job from a reluctant employer. Both through their gentleness, energy, reticence, and self-discipline won the unreserved support of their superiors.

In May 1880 the *Publishers' Weekly* ran the following paragraph on Houghton's junior partner. It could serve as a pen portrait of Tom Corey.

Mr. Mifflin is an excellent specimen of a Boston boy who believes in work. Coming from an old family, he might easily have sunk into a

1. Elinor Howells, the author's wife, designed the house at 37 Concord Avenue, in Cambridge, where the family moved in the summer of 1873. Five years later they left this house for Red Top, which they built on Charles Fairchild's (1838–1910) estate in Belmont, a Cambridge suburb. Three and a half years later, Howells and his family returned to Boston, where in August 1884 he bought and renovated the house at 302 Beacon Street, on the stylish Back Bay. [*Editor*.]
2. The Crowninshield family of Boston was one of the wealthiest in the East. [*Editor*.]

fashionable dilettante, a gentlemanly frequenter of clubs and drawing rooms, a *nobody*. Instead of this, immediately after graduating at Harvard, he went to the Riverside Press, began at the beginning, made himself master of all the steps and processes of book-making, became a member of the firm of Hurd & Houghton, then of Houghton, Osgood & Co., and for sometime has managed the Riverside Press with ability and success. No small part of the tasteful appearance and good workmanship of the present products of the Press is due to his skill and conscientious fidelity to his work.

As striking as the similarities between Mifflin and young Corey are those between Henry Oscar Houghton and Silas Lapham. Houghton, like Lapham, came from a numerous family and had been born in northern Vermont along the Canada line. He also was a man of simple, homely loyalties, devoted to his parents, his brothers and sisters, his wife and children. He, like Silas, married a schoolteacher. Both were clear, bold, straightforward, singleminded, and persevering. Beyond the sphere of the family, business was their being. In politics they were Republican. Physically they were large men, although Houghton was free of the grossness in Lapham's bearing. In speech he quite probably retained his Vermont twang; however, he was a literate, persuasive speaker, an accomplishment Howells denies Lapham. Both had emerged from poverty to opulence. Houghton's favorite extravagance was horses and their equipages; Lapham too loved the horse in harness. Houghton, however, did not think it proper "for the senior partner to be mounted on a Brewster trotting wagon[3] with side pieces with a Kossuth hat[4] knocked in at the side, on his head and shooting by every man on the road." Such display he left to his juniors. In this he differed from Lapham. Nor did he build on Beacon Street. He was content with his ample Cambridge residence. To this, in the early eighties, he added a spacious library done in oak and rich damask.

In the novel Lapham's wife Persis is his conscience, attenuating his business common sense to the tune of about $150,000, the sum he loans his former partner Milton K. Rogers as salve to his wife-inflicted feeling of guilt for having forced the man out of the firm at the moment of promising prosperity. Although Rogers' partnership capital had made possible the development of their paint business, the man had proved himself financially incompetent. Money had run through his fingers as through a sieve. "Buy out or go out," Lapham had told him. A letter from Albert Houghton's widow to her brother-in-law duplicates the anxiety that Persis had shown. Her husband had died in 1880 and she was considering withdrawing her inheritance from the firm and putting it in Government bonds.

3. A "sport model" carriage built by the carriage manufacturer Brewster & Co., of New York. [*Editor*.]
4. A style popularized by the Hungarian patriot Lajos Kossuth (1802–94), who was lionized during his visit to the United States following the failure of the 1848 revolution in his own country. [*Editor*.]

I know that if Albert had lived to take care of his interest [she wrote] he would have wanted his money to remain there as you say. He was a *great balance wheel,* and had to *hold* back—he did not believe in going into such great expense for show & he did not believe in getting deeply in debt—and he always would live within his means. Now bro H. O. I confess I have felt a *little* uneasy for you. When I see the great change that has taken place since he went out of the business, but it may be you are doing an immensely larger business than when he was in the concern and you can afford it. You certainly live in the style of a Millionaire which of course is all right & no one's business if you are out of debt and "owe no man anything."[5]

Houghton was able to reassure his sister-in-law, and she left her funds, over $100,000, with his firm. Indeed, in contrast to Silas Lapham, Houghton was punctilious in money matters, precise to the fraction. Nor was he attracted by risk. Given an inside tip on "Canada Lands,"[6] he was tempted, but replied, "I have scrupulously abstained from doing anything of a speculative nature and perhaps had better continue to do so." Publishing was enough of a gamble for him. Lapham's character is an amalgam. His stock deals, his love of round figures, his perennial optimism, his loose way of overstating his resources appear in James R. Osgood.[7]

A third character embodied in Silas Lapham and one who may have supplied the crux of the novel's plot is Lawson Valentine. In the late 1860s, Valentine, Cambridge-born of well-to-do parents, having had a variety of partnerships in the paint and varnish business in Boston, established his plant in Brighton. By this time, after fifteen years of experiment, Valentine & Company was boasting that its varnish was the best in the world, largely supplanting the English product. In 1872, Valentine's Brighton factory was burned to the ground, and he transferred his business to New York, where it prospered. According to Lyman Abbott,[8] Lawson Valentine was "a genius," "a seer in business," "an electric dynamo," "a fascinating enigma," "quick to see and bold to use commercial opportunities." "Business was to him a form of energy, not a game for money." Although paint was his business, publishing held for him a fascination. After his transfer to New York, he acquired a number of publishing activities, the most important, large shares in Orange, Judd & Company and the Christian Union Company, the latter organized after the failure of J. B. Ford and Company, the original publishers of the *Christian Union.* Valentine played a key roll in the founding of Houghton, Mifflin & Company.

5. Mrs. Albert G. Houghton to H. O. Houghton, 12 September 1882. (Houghton Library, Harvard).
6. There were many oppourtunities to speculate in Canadian land, which—it was hoped—would rise rapidly in value because of mining, railroading, and other commercial expansion. [*Editor.*]
7. James R. Osgood (1826–92), a close personal friend of Howells, served him as both publisher and literary agent. His publishing firm went bankrupt more than once because of his optimistic overexpansion. [*Editor.*]
8. Lyman Abbott (1835–1922), clergyman, author, and literary critic. [*Editor.*]

The counting room at the Riverside Press in the 1880s (from Ellen B. Ballou, *The Building of the House: Houghton Mifflin's Formative Years* [Boston, 1970], p. 273). The figure wearing the hat bears a striking resemblance to W. D. Howells, and the office might be quite similar to that maintained by Silas Lapham except for the number of books in evidence.

# W.D. HOWELLS
## Letter to His Father[†]

Boston
Aug. 10, 1884

Dear father:

I came down here last Monday, to put the house in order—or rather my books—leaving the family at Kennebunkport, Me. (I seem to have written you all this before.) And here I have been hard at work, and lonesome of course. There is not only nobody else in the house, but nobody else that I know sleeps in town. Altogether the effect is queer. There are miles of empty houses all around me. And how unequally things are divided in this world. While these beautiful, airy, wholesome houses are uninhabited, thousands upon thousands of poor creatures are stifling in wretched barracks in the city there, whole families in one room. I wonder that men are as patient with society as they are.

\* \* \*

With love to all,
Your aff'te son
WILL.

# W. D. HOWELLS
## [Summer in New York][†]

\* \* \*

Their afternoon's experience was something that Basil and Isabel could, when it was past, look upon only as a kind of vision, magnificent at times, and at other times full of indignity and pain. They seemed to have dreamed of a long horse-car pilgrimage through that squalid street by the river-side, where presently they came to a market, opening upon the view hideous vistas of carnage, and then into a wide avenue, with processions of cars like their own coming and going up and down the centre of a foolish and useless breadth, which made even the tall buildings (rising gauntly up among the older houses of one or two stories) on either hand look low, and let in the sun to bake the dust that the hot breaths of wind caught up and sent swirling into the shabby shops. Here they dreamed of the eternal demolition and construction of the city, and further on of vacant lots full of granite boulders, clambered over by goats. In their dream they had fellow-passengers, whose sufferings made them odious and whom they were glad to leave behind when they alighted from the car, and running out of the blaze of the avenue, quenched themselves in the shade of the cross-street. A little strip of shadow lay along the row of brown-stone

†Unpublished letter in the Harvard College Library.
†From *Their Wedding Journey* (1872), ed. John K. Reeves (Bloomington & London: Indiana University Press, 1968), pp. 30–31.

fronts, but there were intervals where the vacant lots cast no shadow. With great bestowal of thought they studied hopelessly how to avoid these spaces as if they had been difficult torrents or vast expanses of desert sand; they crept slowly along till they came to such a place, and dashed swiftly across it, and then, fainter than before, moved on. They seemed now and then to stand at doors, and to be told that people were out, and again that they were in; and they had a sense of cool dark parlors, and the airy rustling of light-muslined ladies, of chat and of fans and ice-water, and then they came forth again; and evermore

> "The day increased from heat to heat."[1]

At last they were aware of an end of their visits, and of a purpose to go down town again, and of seeking the nearest car by endless blocks of brown-stone fronts, which with their eternal brown-stone flights of steps, and their handsome, intolerable uniformity, oppressed them like a procession of houses trying to pass a given point and never getting by. Upon these streets there was seldom a soul to be seen, so that when their ringing at a door had evoked answer, it had startled them with a vague, sad surprise. In the distance on either hand they could see cars and carts and wagons toiling up and down the avenues, and on the next intersecting pavement sometimes a laborer with his jacket slung across his shoulder, or a dog that had plainly made up his mind to go mad. Up to the time of their getting into one of those phantasmal cars for the return downtownwards they had kept up a show of talk in their wretched dream; they had spoken of other hot days that they had known elsewhere; and they had wondered that the tragical character of heat had been so little recognized. They said that the daily New York murder might even at that moment be somewhere taking place; and that no murder of the whole homicidal year could have such proper circumstance; they morbidly wondered what that day's murder would be, and in what swarming tenement-house, or den of the assassin streets by the river-sides,—if indeed it did not befall in some such high, close-shuttered, handsome dwelling as those they passed, in whose twilight it would be so easy to strike down the master and leave him undiscovered and unmourned by the family ignorantly absent at the mountains or the seaside. They conjectured of the horror of midsummer battles, and pictured the anguish of shipwrecked men upon a tropical coast, and the grimy misery of stevedores unloading shiny cargoes of anthracite coal at city docks. But now at last, as they took seats opposite one another in the crowded car, they seemed to have drifted infinite distances and long epochs asunder. They looked hopelessly across the intervening gulf and mutely questioned when it was and from what far city they or some

---

1. From "Mariana in the South" (line 39), by Alfred, Lord Tennyson. [*Editor.*]

remote ancestors of theirs had set forth upon a wedding journey. They bade each other a tacit farewell, and with patient, pathetic faces awaited the end of the world.

# RICHARD WATSON GILDER
## Letter to W. D. Howells[†]

The CENTURY MAGAZINE

UNION SQUARE . NEW YORK
Feb. 18. 1885,

My dear Mr. Howells,

The leap made this year in the Century's circulation—up to 210,000 & *still rising*—has thrown upon us, we cannot help feeling, a greater responsibility than ever, & we cannot help being on guard against any false step which may injure our prestige & influence. A week or two ago we cancelled 150,000 pages in an article by Mr. Bigelow[1] (with his consent) in which he quoted an enthusiastic endorsement of dynamite war-fare on the Parliament buildings & reigning houses generally. We had not objected to this while dynamiting was an insignificant matter; but with recent events before our eyes the paragraph had a new significance—it would doubtless have been copied by dynamite journals as an endorsement of their methods, & possibly might have led to the seizure of the magazine in England.

I hope you will not think us super-sensitive when we call your attention to page 867 of your April installment—where some words written months ago assume a new meaning in the light of new events. It is the very word, *dynamite,* that is now so dangerous for any of us to use, except in condemnation. None but a crank would misinterpret your allusion, but it is the crank who does the deed. The other day it was found that dynamite had been built into all the hearths in a new house!—there is no telling where this sort of thing is going to break out—it is an unknown & horribly inflammable quantity, & we don't want, if we can help it, to be associated with the subject—except as opposing it. I am confident that on reflection you will take this view, & if so can you telegraph (and also write) a line or two to take the place of the phrase which introduces the word "dynamite"? If you cannot make the matter clear (at our expense) by telegraph then please telegraph that you have written. I have asked Mr. Smith to drop you a line to show how the matter struck him. With many regrets at the necessity of troubling you—

I remain
Sincerely yours
R W GILDER.

†Unpublished letter in the Harvard College Library.
1. Probably John Bigelow (1817–1911), New York journalist and editor of the *Evening Post* (1848–61). [*Editor.*]

# ROSWELL SMITH
## Letter to W. D. Howells[†]

THE CENTURY CO.
33 East 17th Street
New York.
Feby 18.85

My Dear Howells.

Last night Mrs Roswell Smith read aloud to me, the April installment of Silas Lapham—which we enjoyed greatly—but about noon
today I recalled Bromfield Corys utterance on the subject of Dynamite & went back & re-read it—Then I showed it to Buel[1] & Gilder &
the result is, we have stopped the Press & taken off the form—We did
not feel in justice to you that we could go on with the printing until
your attention had been called to it—I know what your first impression will be likely to be—& that is simply to let it stand as it is—but when
you have thought about it, twenty four hours I am sure you will come
to our conclusion—It may be well enough to joke about taking possession of the houses of the rich, &c—but blowing open the shutters with
a charge of Dynamite—suggests nihilism, destructiveness—revenge—etc—which to be sure is not fairly suggested even by the
language—nothing worse than getting in is stated—the other is not
even fairly suggested—But, think of the recent events in London[2] &
elsewhere abroad & in New York—I am sure it won't do—Then I
fancy the Law might stop the Magazine or make the Publisher trouble
in England—ie that, that is among the possibilities— Last month we
had to cancel four pages in an article after the sheets had gone to
England—& after 150,000- had been printed—Fortunately only
25,000- of this form are printed—& sheets have not gone to England— Please telegraph us whether you decide to change—& send by
mail the matter—a single line—or a whole page if you wish that you
wish substituted— Gilder agreed two hours ago to write you about
it—it comes better from the Editor that [*sic*] the Publisher—but since I
have had the honor publicly to differ with you over M. Everts[3]—
perhaps you will pardon me for privately calling your attention to
what may be a mistake for you & for us—.

I am Always Faithfully yrs

ROSWELL SMITH

†Unpublished letter in the Harvard College
Library.
1. Clarence Clough Buel (1850–1933), American
essayist and editor of the *Century* (1881–90).
[*Editor*.]
2. Dynamite explosions had recently occurred in
London in connection with political and economic
unrest. [*Editor*.]
3. Probably and erroneous reference to William M.
Evarts (1818–1901), a lawyer much involved in public
issues who was elected U.S. senator from New York in
1885. [*Editor*.]

# W. D. HOWELLS
## Textual Variations: The Dynamite Passages

"There is one charity," said Corey, pretending superiority to Miss Kingsbury's point, "that is so difficult I wonder it hasn't occurred to a lady of your courageous invention."

"Yes?" said Miss Kingsbury. "What is that?"

"The occupation, by deserving poor of neat habits, of all the beautiful, airy, wholesome houses that stand empty the whole summer long, while their owners are away in their lowly cots beside the sea."

"Yes, that is terrible," replied Miss Kingsbury, with quick earnestness, while her eyes grew moist. "I have often thought of our great, cool houses standing useless here, and the thousands of poor creatures stifling in their holes and dens, and the little children dying for wholesome shelter. How cruelly selfish we are!"

"That is a very comfortable sentiment, Miss Kingsbury," said Corey, "and must make you feel almost as if you had thrown open No. 931 to the whole North End. But I am serious about this matter. I spend my summers in town, and I occupy my own house, so that I can speak impartially and intelligently; and I tell you that in some of my walks on the Hill and down on the Back Bay, nothing but the surveillance of the local policeman

prevents me from applying dynamite to[1]

prevents me from personally affronting[2]

prevents my offering personal violence to[3]

those long rows of close-shuttered, handsome, brutally insensible houses. If I were a poor man, with a sick child pining in some garret or cellar at the North End, I should break into one of them, and camp out on the grand piano."

"Surely, Bromfield," said his wife, "you don't consider what havoc such people would make with the furniture of a nice house!"

"That is true," answered Corey, with meek conviction. "I never thought of the furniture. Probably a poor man with a dying child would consider it, and would not break into the house, after all."

"It's wonderful. . . ."[4]

"That is true,"answered Corey with meek conviction. "I never thought of that."

1. These are three variants of pp. 171–72. This is the earliest version of the book set in type. It is preserved in a prepublication version set in England by the publisher David Douglas and deposited in the British Museum in order to secure the British copyright.

2. This is the serial version, published in *Century* magazine (November 1884–August 1885) and containing the changes demanded by Smith and Gilder.

3. This is the version that appeared in the American and English book editions published in 1885.

4. See note 1.

"And if you were a poor man with a sick child, I doubt if you'd have so much heart for burglary as you have now," said James Bellingham.

"It's wonderful how patient they are," said Mr. Sewell, "The spectacle of the hopeless luxury and comfort the hard-working poor man sees around him must be hard to bear at times."[5]

"It's wonderful how patient they are," said the minister. "The spectacle of the hopeless comfort the hard-working poor man sees must be hard to bear."[6]

# CYRUS L. SULZBERGER

## Letter to W. D. Howells[†]

*The American Hebrew*
498–500 Third Avenue.
New York 12 July 1885

Dear Sir:

As "The Rise of Silas Lapham: is about approaching completion and will, I presume, soon appear in book form, I beg to call to your notice a slur (in chap II) upon a number of your readers and admirers—a slur as unmerited by the Jewish people as it is unworthy of its author. It is not alone upon the ignorant and uncultured of the Jews that you reflect for neither "the Saviour himself," nor the twelve apostles, nor the prophets, nor even Adam, were—so far as the records show, of that class which depreciated the value of property when they "got in."

The introduction of the lines in question cannot even be excused on the ground that it serves a literary purpose for no such end is accomplished. The sentiment is violently dragged in for no other ascertainable reason than to pander to a prejudice against which all educated and cultured Jews must battle.

The literary leaders of a country have so great a power in fomenting or in repressing popular prejudices that I make bold to hope that in the permanent form in which "Silas Lapham" will no doubt soon appear, these objectionable lines will be omitted.

I have the honor to be, Sir,

Very Respectfully Yours.
Cyrus L. Sulzberger

W. D. Howells Esq.

5. See note 2.
6. See note 3.
†Unpublished letter in the Harvard College Library. Cyrus L. Sulzberger (1858–1932) was editor of the *American Hebrew*, a Jewish newspaper of wide circulation.

# W. D. HOWELLS

## Letter to Cyrus L. Sulzberger[††]

Old Orchard Me.,
July 17, 1885.

My Dear Sir:

I thank you for your frank and manly letter.

I supposed that I was writing in reprobation of the prejudice of which you justly complain, but my irony seems to have fallen short of the mark—so far short that you are not the first Hebrew to accuse me of "pandering" to the stupid and cruel feeling against your race and religion. I will not ask you to read again, in the light of this statement, the passage of my story which you object to, for I have already struck it out of my book, and it will not re-appear. In that passage I merely recognized to rebuke it, the existence of a feeling which civilized men should be ashamed of. But perhaps it is better not to recognize all the facts.

Perhaps also you owe me an apology for making an unjust accusation. I leave that to you.

Very truly yours,
W. D. HOWELLS.

# CYRUS L. SULZBERGER

## Letter to W. D. Howells[†]

*The American Hebrew*
498–500 Third Avenue, New York
19 July 1885.

My dear Sir

Certainly in view of your kind note of 17 inst I do owe you an apology. Still in justification of my own stupidity in missing the point of your irony I may say that Silas's admission that "they" do depreciate the value of property when they get in—a fact concerning the financial accuracy of which I have some doubts—seemed to me rather as an endorsement than a rebuke of what you truly call the "stupid and cruel feeling" against us.

I am glad indeed to have your assurance that the passage will not appear in the book and still more pleased to know that the author

---

[††]From "Silas Lapham and the Jews," *American Hebrew*, xxiv (Sept. 4, 1885), 50.

[†]Unpublished letter in the Harvard College Library.

whom I have so much admired is not to be numbered counted among the number—unfortunately too large—of Jewhaters in America.

Very truly Yours

Cyrus L. Sulzberger

Mr. W D Howells
Old Orchard

As this correspondence will interest the readers of *The American Hebrew*, I trust you will have no objection to my laying it before them. Should you object however, will you please telegraph me (at my expense of course) and it will not appear.

# W. D. HOWELLS
## Textual Variations: The Jews

\* \* \* The fact that they lived in an unfashionable neighborhood was something that they had never been made to feel to their personal disadvantage, and they had hardly known it till the summer before this story opens, when Mrs. Lapham and her daughter Irene had met some other Bostonians far from Boston, who made it memorable. . . . (p. 22)

A certain intimacy inevitably followed, and when the son came he was even more grateful than the others. . . . (p. 22)

Some of the things that he partly said, partly looked, she reported to her mother, and they talked them over, as they did everything relating to these new acquaintances, and wrought them into the novel point of view which they were acquiring.

It was something that Mrs. Lapham especially submitted to her husband when they got home; she asked him if it were true, and if it made any difference.

"It makes a difference in the price of the property," replied the Colonel, promptly. "But as long as we don't want to sell, it don't matter."

"Why, Silas Lapham," said his wife, "do you mean to tell me that this house is worth less than we gave for it?"

"It's worth a good deal less. You see, they *have* got in—and pretty thick, too— it's no use denying it. And when they get in, they send down the price of property. Of course, there ain't any sense in it; *I* think it's all dumn foolishness. It's cruel, and folks ought to be ashamed. But there it is. You tell folks that the Savior himself was one, and the twelve apostles, and all the prophets,—I don't know but what Adam was—guess he *was*,—and it don't make a bit of difference. They send down the price of real estate. Prices begin to shade when the first one gets in."

Mrs. Lapham thought the facts over a few moments. "Well, what do we care, so long as we're comfortable in our home? And they're just as nice and as good neighbors as can be."

"Oh, it's all right as far as I'm concerned," said Lapham. "Who did you say those people were that stirred you up about it?"

Mrs. Lapham repeated their name.[1]

Some of the things that he partly said, partly looked, she reported to her mother, and they talked them over, as they did everything relating to these new acquaintances, and wrought them into the novel point of view which they were acquiring. When Mrs. Lapham returned home, she submitted all the accumulated facts of the case, and all her own conjectures, to her husband, and canvassed them anew.

At first he was disposed to regard the whole affair as of small importance, and she had to insist a little beyond her own convictions in order to counteract his indifference.

"Well, I can tell you," she said, "that if you think they were not the nicest people *you* ever saw, you're mightily mistaken. They had about the best manners; and they had been everywhere, and knew everything. I declare it made me feel as if we had always lived in the backwoods. I don't know but the mother and the daughters would have *let* you feel so a little, if they'd showed out all they thought; but they never did; and the son—well, I can't express it, Silas! But that young man had about perfect ways."

"Seem struck up on Irene?" asked the Colonel.

"How can *I* tell? He seemed just about as much struck up on me. Anyway, he paid me as much attention as he did her. Perhaps it's more the way, now, to notice the mother than it used to be."

Lapham ventured no conjecture, but asked, as he had asked already, who the people were.

Mrs. Lapham repeated their name.[2]

"Well, I don't want to build on Beacon street, Si." said Mrs. Lapham, gently.

"Just as you please, Persis. I ain't in any hurry to leave."

Mrs. Lapham stood flapping the check which she held in her right hand against the edge of her left. "A Mr. Liliengarten has bought the Gordon house across the square." she said, thoughtfully.

"Well, I'm agreeable. I suppose he's got the money to pay for it."

"Oh, yes, they've all got money," sighed Mrs. Lapham.

She sighed again—a yielding sigh. . . .[3]

---

1. This passage and next are variants of p. 25. This is the serial version, published in *Century* magazine (29 [Nov. 1884] p. 22) and containing a passage considered offensive by Cyrus L. Sulzberger.
2. This is the version that appeared in the Ameri-

can and English book editions published in 1885.
3. This passage and next are variants of p. 30. This is the serial version, published in *Century* magazine (29 [Nov. 1884] p. 25) and containing a passage considered offensive by Cyrus L. Sulzberger.

"Well, I don't want to build on Beacon street, Si," said Mrs. Lapham, gently.

"Just as you please, Persis. I aint in any hurry to leave."

Mrs. Lapham stood flapping the check which she held in her right hand against the edge of her left.

The Colonel still sat looking up at her face, and watching the effect of the poison of ambition which he had artfully instilled into her mind.

She sighed again—a yielding sigh.[4]

# W. D. HOWELLS and PAUL KESTER

## *The Rise of Silas Lapham:*
## A Play[†]

### *Act II*

SCENE: *The Corey's House. The scene shows a drawing room from which a dining room is separated by heavy curtains; the scene is so set that both rooms are virtually one when the curtains are drawn aside. A part of the hall with entrance through double doors opens from the drawing room. Doors lead to other rooms.*

*Discovered:* MR. *and* MRS. COREY, *in evening dress.* MR. COREY *has evening paper.* MRS. COREY *has some flowers which she can arrange in vase or later take to the dining room.*

MRS. COREY: Bromfield, I confess I wish this dinner were well over. It is all very distasteful to me.

COREY: Well, my dear, if it is any consolation to you, I think it is going to be as much of a trial to your Laphams as it is to you.

MRS. COREY: My Laphams!

COREY: Well, Tom's Laphams then. Come Anna, I thought you did not find them so bad at Baie St. Paul.

MRS. COREY: I hadn't seen them in Nankeen Square then.

COREY: You will see them on the waterside of Beacon Street before the winter is over.

MRS. COREY: Beacon Street is getting very common, Bromfield. When Tom first suggested going into this mineral paint business, why didn't you stop him? Tom need not earn his living—there is enough for us all.

COREY: I did urge it upon Tom, that with economy, and by cramping us a little, he need do nothing as long as he lived. But it appears that he wished to do something. I am afraid that Tom is selfish.

4. This is the version that appeared in the American and English book editions published in 1885.
†From *The Complete Plays of W. D. Howells*, ed. Walter J. Meserve (New York: New York University Press, 1960), pp. 495–504. Paul Kester (1870–1933), a cousin of Howells, wrote his first play in 1892.

MRS. COREY: I feel very unhappy about it—it isn't the paint alone— (*Checks herself.*) I wish he had married someone.

COREY: With money? From time to time I have attempted Tom's corruption from that side, but he has a conscience against it, and I rather like him for it. I married for love myself.

MRS. COREY: What nonsense!

COREY: Besides, if you come to money, there's the Mineral Paint princess—she'll have plenty.

MRS. COREY: Oh, that's the worst of it! I suppose I could get on with the paint—

COREY: But not with the princess?

MRS. COREY: It troubles me, Bromfield. The child is very pretty.

COREY: Oh, you feel sure it's the pretty one, then? Tom says the plain one is very humorous; and there's a sense of humor as well as a sense of color in our family.

MRS. COREY: Nonsense! He couldn't think of that little black, pert thing. She was fairly saucy to me when I called on her mother.

COREY: You don't think you patronized them, Anna? I've seen the time when if I had been the subject of your condescension I should have sauced you myself. Well, let's hope it's neither of the princesses. You haven't sounded Tom on the subject?

MRS. COREY: No, I wish you could do so, Bromfield.

COREY: It's a delicate matter. You can't very well ask your son if he's in love, and which one besides!

MRS. COREY: It will have to be done sooner or later. I must go and give a glance at the table.

> *Exit through portieres to dining room. At the same moment enter* TOM *from left.*

COREY: Ah, Tom! Your mother and I were just talking of you. (*Goes up and puts hands on son's shoulders, and gazes admiringly at him.*) Who's your tailor? I don't see how you can afford such nice clothes?

TOM: Why, you see, I have an indulgent father.

COREY: Ah, I wish *I* had. And sometimes I wish I was in the mineral paint line, like you; I should be more prosperous. But I must be satisfied to dine the mineral paint king. The royal family is disposed to make us do ante-chamber, it seems.

TOM: It's only a few minutes past eight. We must give them the quarter hour's grace.

COREY: Oh, yes. As all of them are coming they ought to have half an hour's grace, perhaps.

TOM: I'm not sure it was best to have them at all.

COREY: Your mother and I felt that we ought to.

TOM: I don't know quite what you mean.

COREY: I see you do, Tom.

TOM: No one can help feeling that they are people of good sense and right ideas.

COREY: Oh, that won't do. If society took in all the people of right ideas and good sense, it would expand beyond the calling capacity of its active members. Society is a very different sort of thing from good sense and right ideas. It is based upon them, of course, but the airy, graceful, winning superstructure which we all know demands different qualities. Have your friends got these qualities, which may be felt, but not defined?

TOM: To tell the truth, sir, I don't think they have the most elemental ideas of society as we understand it. I don't believe Mrs. Lapham ever gave a dinner.

COREY: With all that money!

TOM: I don't believe they have the habit of wine at table. I suspect that when they don't drink tea and coffee with their dinner, they drink icewater.

COREY: Horrible!

TOM: I don't believe that I can make you see Colonel Lapham quite as I do. I don't know that we can judge him rightly by our standards.

COREY: Oh, one could make out a case. I suppose you know what you are about, Tom. I suspect this all comes of your winter in Texas. I am always saying that the Bostonian ought never to leave Boston. Then he knows—and then only—that there can be no standard but ours. One man goes to England and returns with the conception of a grander social life; another comes home from Germany with the notion of a more searching intellectual activity; a fellow just back from Paris has the absurdest ideas of art and literature; and you revert to us from the cowboys of Texas, and tell us to our faces that we ought to try Papa Lapham by a jury of his peers. It ought to be stopped, it ought, really. The Bostonian who leaves Boston ought to be condemned to perpetual exile.

MRS. COREY *enters.* TOM *goes to her.*

MRS. COREY: Tom—

TOM: Mother, do you really think this dinner is going to be a trial for the Laphams?

MRS. COREY: No. No. I can't say it is, but I confess I wish it were well over. It's all very distasteful to me, Tom.

TOM: I'm sorry, mother, but you know I never suggested this dinner. I'm sure it is the right thing. I—I've forgotten my handkerchief. *Exit.*

MRS. COREY: If the dinner only ended it!

COREY: We will not despond, my dear. If Tom is really in love with one of the Misses Lapham, or even both of them, we have the consolation of knowing that we couldn't help it.

*Enter* NANNY COREY.

NANNY: Poor Tom! I met him on the stairs. He's so troubled about his Laphams. Perhaps it won't be so bad.

MRS. COREY: She seemed an affectionate little thing with her mother, and really so pretty.

NANNY: Oh, she'll be an affectionate little thing with Tom, too, you may be sure. She'll make him think we were all against her from the beginning.

MRS. COREY: She has no cause for that, and we shall not give her any. I can't imagine what he finds to talk about with her.

NANNY: Oh, that's very simple; they talk about themselves, with occasional references to each other. I have heard people go on, on the hotel piazzas. She's embroidering, or knitting, and he says she seems quite devoted to needlework, and she says yes, she has a perfect passion for it, and everybody laughs at her for it; she always was so from a child, and supposes she always shall be—with remote and minute particulars. And she ends by saying that perhaps he does not like people to knit or embroider, or whatever. And he says, oh, yes, he does; what could make her think such a thing? But for his part he likes boating rather better. Then she lets him take up one corner of her work, and perhaps touch her fingers; and that encourages him to say that he supposes nothing could induce her to drop her work long enough to go down on the rocks, or out among the huckleberry bushes; and she puts her head on one side and says she doesn't know really. And then they go, and he lies at her feet on the rocks, or picks huckleberries and drops them in her lap, and they go on talking about themselves, and comparing notes to see how they differ from each other and—

MRS. COREY: That will do, Nanny. Disgusting!

NANNY: Disgusting? Not at all. It's very amusing when you see it, and when you do it!

MRS. COREY: It's always a mystery what people see in each other.

NANNY: The most that we can do is to hope for the best till we know the worst.

MRS. COREY: Of course, we shall make the best of the worst when it comes.

*Exeunt* MR. *and* MRS. COREY, *R. Enter* TOM, *L.*

NANNY: Tom, we've been talking about you!

TOM: That's what father told me before. What have you been saying?

NANNY: Very nice things. That she's very sweet and good, and that if you *must* be happy, we hope you may be *very* happy!

TOM: Oh, thank you, Nan. It's a little premature—

NANNY: I dare say. But it isn't the less certain on that account. I don't know that I should have chosen to go to Nankeen Square for a sister; but I don't think I could have found a more beautiful one, anywhere.

TOM: Beautiful? Well, I don't know. Charming, yes; and quaint; but beautiful—

NANNY: Why, where are your eyes? She's divine—if that's all you want.

TOM: Do you think so, Nan? That's very sweet of you—

NANNY: I do, indeed. And her name suits her beauty so exactly. It's royal; though they don't know how to pronounce it. You must teach them to say, I-re-ne.

TOM, *aghast*: I-re-ne!

NANNY, *amazed*: You don't mean to say it's—

TOM: Penelope? Of course, I do! How could you dream of anything else? I never thought of Irene for a moment. She's pretty, and she's good, as you say; but Penelope is—I was in love with her from the first moment. She fascinated me!

NANNY: Oh, Tom, Tom, Tom!

TOM: What?

NANNY: Do you think *they* know it?

TOM: Know it? Of course, they know it! What do you mean?

NANNY: I'm afraid they don't. I'm afraid they think it's Irene. Oh, Tom, how could you! We all thought it was Irene.

TOM: You thought it was Irene! Nanny—

NANNY: Hush! They're coming down stairs at last. Come! (*She seizes his hand and pulls him through door, R.*) They mustn't find us here!

*Enter* LAPHAM, *pulling off his gloves; and* MRS. LAPHAM *after him.*

MRS. LAPHAM: I declare, Silas Lapham, you're pulling off those gloves again! Can't you do one way or another? You'll drive me wild with your fussing. Why didn't you find out whether you have to wear 'em or not?

LAPHAM, *putting on gloves:* Haven't I tried? I read all the behavior books, and they didn't say a word about it; and I asked the girl in the store where I bought 'em, and *she* couldn't tell, either. Just kept on peppering in that powdered soap to make 'em slip on, and split up the front or back till I got this pair. (*Glances down at them.*) My Lord, I don't know what to do. *One* while, I thought I'd ask Tom Corey—

MRS. LAPHAM: If you had, Silas Lapham, I'd have *left* you. What's keeping her, I wonder. And you made me accept for Penelope, you said it wouldn't make any difference whether she came or not; and now I'm afraid it will, and I shan't know *what* to say. Oh, I wish we'd never *thought* of coming. And we're too old to learn to be like them.

LAPHAM: The children ain't. I wish Pen had come. She could talk for twenty.

MRS. LAPHAM: She was set against it from the first. She said they wanted to see Irene. They didn't want *her.*

LAPHAM: I guess they wanted her or they wouldn't have asked her. Of course, if young Corey's taken with Irene—

MRS. LAPHAM: Irene'll be a lucky girl to get him, if she wants him. But there! I'd ten times rather she was going to marry such a fellow as you were, Si, that had to make every inch of his own way, and she had to help him. (*Looking anxiously at* LAPHAM *and then starting back.*) Silas, you've got something more than your *gloves* and your cravat on your mind!

LAPHAM: Yes, I have, Persis.

MRS. LAPHAM, *tenderly:* Is it anything you can tell me about, Silas?

LAPHAM: I haven't ever hid anything from you, Persis, when you asked me, and it's too late to begin now. I'm in a kind of fix. Things have been dull all fall, but I thought they'd brisk up come winter. They haven't. There's been a lot of failures and some of them owed me, and some of them had me on their paper, and—

MRS. LAPHAM: And what?

LAPHAM: And then—Rogers.

MRS. LAPHAM: I didn't want you should get in any deeper with him.

LAPHAM: No. And you didn't want I should press him either, and I had to do one or the other. And so I got in deeper.

MRS. LAPHAM: Silas, I'm afraid I made you!

LAPHAM: It's all right, Persis, as far forth as that goes. It'll all come out right in the end. Only pretty near everybody but the fellows that owe me money seem to expect me to do a cash business all of a sudden.

MRS. LAPHAM: Do you mean you've got payments to make, and that people are not paying you?

LAPHAM: Something like that. I ain't going to let the grass grow under my feet, though, especially while Rogers digs the ground away from the roots.

MRS. LAPHAM: What are you going to do?

LAPHAM: If it has to come to that, I'm going to squeeze him. Milton K. Rogers is a rascal, if you want to know; or else all the signs fail. But I guess he'll find he's got his come-uppance.

MRS. LAPHAM: What's he done?

LAPHAM: What's he done? He's been dabbling in every sort of fool thing you can lay your tongue to; wild-cat stocks, patent-rights, land speculations, oil claims—till he's run through about everything. But he did have a big milling property out on the line of the P. Y. & X., saw-mills and grist mills and timber lands: and for the last years he's been doing a land office business with them—business that would have made anybody else rich. But you can't make Milton K. Rogers rich any more than you can fat a hide bound colt. It ain't in him. He'd run through Vanderbilt, Rockefeller and Astor rolled into one in less than six months, give him a chance, and come out and want to borrow money of you. Well, he won't borrow any more of *me*; and if he thinks I don't know as much about that milling property as he does he's mistaken. I've taken his mills for security, and I guess I've got the inside track. Bill's kept me posted; and now I'm going out there to see how I can unload; and I shan't mind a great deal if Rogers is under the load when it's off once.

MRS. LAPHAM: I don't understand you, Silas.

LAPHAM: Why, it's just this. The G. L. & P. has leased the P. Y. & X. for ninety-nine years—bought it practically—and it's going to build car works right by those mills, and it wants the mills. And Milton K. Rogers knew it when he turned 'em in on me.

MRS. LAPHAM: Well, if the road wants the mills you can get what you ask for them.

LAPHAM: Can I? The G. L. & P. is the only road that runs within fifty miles of the mills, and you can't get a foot of lumber or a pound of flour to market any other way. As long as he had a little local road like the P. Y. & X. to deal with, Rogers could manage; but when it comes to a big through line like the G. L. & P. he couldn't stand any chance at all. If such a road as that takes a fancy to his mills, do you think it will pay what he asked? No, sir! He must take what the road offers, or else the road will tell him to carry his flour and lumber to market himself.

MRS. LAPHAM: And do you suppose he knew the G. L. & P. wanted the mills when he turned them in on you?

LAPHAM: Well, when Milton K. Rogers don't know which side his bread's buttered on!

MRS. LAPHAM: Well, I want you should ask yourself whether Rogers would ever have gone wrong if it hadn't been for your forcing him out of the business when you did. I want you should think whether you're not responsible for everything he's done since.

LAPHAM: You go and fetch Irene. I guess I can take care of myself and Milton K. Rogers, too.
> *Pulling off his gloves.*

MRS. LAPHAM: Oh, *don't* take them off again. (*He puts them on. Enter* IRENE.) Oh, there you are at last. Your father's fairly driving me distracted about his gloves.

IRENE: I think papa looks splendid!

LAPHAM: Good for you, Irene! My Lord, but you're pretty in that dress. It'll go off all right about Pen, Persis; you'll see. And I tell you what. You two just go in there, and see whether the men have got gloves on, and then one of you pretend you've forgot something and come out and tell me.

IRENE: Well, that's a good idea, papa. Come along, mama!
> MRS. LAPHAM *with a gesture of despair goes out R. to library with* IRENE; *while* JAMES BELLINGHAM[1] *enters L.*

BELLINGHAM: Ah, Colonel. Waiting for the ladies? They always make us do that.

LAPHAM, *looking at tie, aside*: Black! (*Observing that he has no gloves, pulls his off and puts them into his coat tail pocket.*) Well, well—not exactly. They're in there, (*nodding R*) but I—I'm mighty glad to see you a moment alone, Mr. Bellingham. Your nephew, Tom Corey, has been talking to me about putting some money into the business and I've kind of fought off from him. I'll tell you why. Between you and me, I've got caught a little in stocks, and I've lent money to an old partner of mine. Well, it's all right. It ain't anything that I can't swing with one hand tied behind me. But when I let your nephew put in his money, I don't want him to take the least risk in the world—nor the shadow of it. Understand?

BELLINGHAM: It's what I should have expected of you, Colonel Lapham. (*Offering hand.*) Not that I think there's the least risk, but—

LAPHAM, *swelling*: Not the least in the world! I can raise $100,000—on my own house any day,—and—But you know how I feel?

BELLINGHAM: I'm proud to say I do, Colonel Lapham—
> MRS. LAPHAM *enter from R.*

MRS. LAPHAM: Well, Colonel Lapham, ain't you *ever* coming? (*Seeing* BELLINGHAM.) Oh, *excuse* me!

LAPHAM: Introduce you to Mrs. Lapham, Mr. Bellingham.
> *They bow and all go toward library R. whence issues* MRS. COREY *followed slowly by the others.* MR. COREY, MR. SEYMOUR, IRENE, TOM, MISS KINGSBURY *and* NANNY.

TOM, *advancing, shaking hands with* LAPHAM: Ah, Colonel Lapham, very glad to see you. Mother—
> *Introducing* MRS. COREY *to* LAPHAM.

1. At first Howells used both Charles and James Bellingham; then he combined the two into one character without making changes consistent throughout the typescript. [Meserve's note—Editor.]

MRS. COREY, *advancing and shaking hands*: General Lapham?

LAPHAM: No, ma'am, only Colonel.

COREY, *to* LAPHAM: I am very glad to see you again.

LAPHAM, *observing* COREY'S *white tie, beaming with satisfaction, aside*: White!

*NANNY holds* IRENE'S *hand a moment;* MRS. COREY *turns to* MRS. LAPHAM.

MRS. COREY: Can I send any one to be of use to Miss Lapham?

MRS. LAPHAM: She isn't upstairs. (*Bluntly.*) She didn't feel just like coming tonight. I don't know as she's feeling very well.

MRS. COREY: Oh! (*Very coldly; with offense.*) I'm very sorry. It's nothing serious, I hope. (*To* MR. COREY.) I think we are all here then.

MR. COREY *crosses and gives his arm to* MRS. LAPHAM, *the curtains are drawn back opening the dining room into the scene.* MRS. COREY *slips her hand through* LAPHAM'S *arm and detains him as he would start forward. They follow the others into the dining room and all sit at the table.* LAPHAM *on* MRS. COREY'S *right.* MRS. LAPHAM *beside* MR. COREY. IRENE *beside* TOM. *Seeing* JAMES BELLINGHAM *tuck his napkin in his collar* LAPHAM *does likewise, then as none of the others do it he takes it out again.*

BELLINGHAM, *to* MISS KINGSBURY: I'm such an uncertain shot with a spoon. I defend my practice on the ground of neatness and commonsense.

*The servants move about with the courses, filling the glasses.* LAPHAM *watches the others, and tastes his wine.*

TOM, *to* IRENE: I can't tell you how sorry I am that your sister could not come. She is not really very ill, I hope?

IRENE: No, only a bad headache.

TOM: I don't believe Miss Lapham cares much for society. Do you know I sometimes imagine that she even avoids me. She doesn't dislike me?

IRENE: Oh, no, no! How can you think such a thing? Why Pen is lovely.

TOM: I know that!

*They converse together silently.*

MRS. COREY, *to* LAPHAM: We have been so interested in watching your house grow, across the way. Mr. Seymour has done wonders.

SEYMOUR: If I have been able to make a nice thing of it, I owe it all to the practical sympathy of my client.

COREY: Practical sympathy is good. Does he bleed your husband, Mrs. Lapham? He's a terrible fellow for appropriations.

MRS. LAPHAM: I guess the Colonel knows how to take care of himself.

COREY, *leaning back in his chair*: Well, after all, you can't say, with all your modern fuss about it, that you do much better now than the old fellows who built such houses as this.

SEYMOUR: Ah, nobody can do better than well. Your house is in perfect taste; you know I've always admired it; and I don't think it's at all the worse for being old-fashioned. But I think we may claim a better feeling for structure. We use better material, and more wisely; and by and by we shall work out something more characteristic and original.

COREY: With your chocolate and your olive greens and your clutter of bric-a-brac?

SEYMOUR: All that's bad, of course. I don't wish to make you envious of Colonel Lapham, and modesty prevents my saying that his house is prettier—though I may have my convictions—but it's better built. All the new houses are better built. Now your house—

COREY: Mrs. Corey's house! My ancestral halls are in Salem, and I'm told you couldn't drive a nail into their timbers; in fact, I don't know that you would want to.

SEYMOUR: I should consider it a species of sacrilege; and I shall be far from pressing the point I was going to make against a house of Mrs. Corey's.

COREY, *as all laugh:* Well, you architects and musicians are the only true artistic creators; somehow or other you do evolve the camel out of your inner consciousness!

SEYMOUR: I will not deny the soft impeachment.

COREY: I dare say, and you'll own that it's very handsome of me to say this, after your unjustifiable attack on Mrs. Corey's property.

BELLINGHAM, *to* MRS. LAPHAM: You mustn't listen to Miss Kingsbury. She's worse, when it comes to appropriations than Seymour himself. Depend upon it, Mrs. Lapham, she will give you no peace of your mind, now she's met you, from this out.

COREY: Beware of her and all her works. She calls them works of charity; but Heaven knows whether they are. It don't stand to reason that she gives the poor *all* the money she gets out of people. I have my own belief—(*in an audible whisper*) that she spends it for champagne and cigars.

MISS KINGSBURY: You shall be asked to the very next debauch of the committee, Mr. Corey; then you won't dare expose us.

BELLINGHAM: I wonder you haven't been down upon Corey to go to the Chardon Street home and talk with your indigent Italians in their native tongue. I saw in the *Transcript* the other night that you wanted someone for the work.

MISS KINGSBURY: We did think of Mr. Corey, but we reflected that he probably wouldn't talk with them at all; he would make them keep still to be sketched, and forget all about their wants.

COREY, *as the others laugh:* There is one charity that is so difficult, I wonder it hasn't occurred to a lady of your courageous invention.

MISS KINGSBURY: Yes? What is that?

COREY: The occupation, by deserving poor of neat habits, of all the beautiful, airy, wholesome houses that stand empty the whole summer long while their owners are away in their lowly cots beside the sea.

MISS KINGSBURY: Yes. It's terrible. I have often thought of our great, cool houses standing useless, and the thousands of poor creatures stifling in their holes and dens, and the little children dying for wholesome shelter. How cruelly selfish we are!

COREY: That is a very comfortable sentiment, Miss Kingsbury, and must make you feel almost as if you had thrown open No. 31 to the whole North End.

MRS. COREY: Surely, Bromfield, you don't consider what havoc such people would make with the furniture of a nice house.

COREY: That's true! I never thought of that.

LAPHAM, *to* MRS. COREY: Picture of your daughter, I presume?

MRS. COREY: No, my daughter's grandmother. It's a Stewart Newton—he painted a great many Salem beauties; she was a Miss Polly Burroughs. My daughter *is* like her, don't you think? Those pretty old-fashioned dresses are coming in again—I'm not surprised you took it for her.

LAPHAM, *to* NANNY COREY: It's a good thing to have a grandmother handsome enough to be painted in your place, Miss Corey.

COREY: Why, that's true, Colonel Lapham, I hadn't thought of it before.

BELLINGHAM, *to* MRS. LAPHAM: Does your husband often make those pretty speeches to young ladies, Mrs. Lapham?

MRS. LAPHAM: I guess he don't often have such a good chance.

NANNY: Spare my grandmother's blushes! I'm sure if she could speak, she would say: you ought to have seen both of Miss Irene's grandmothers.

> *They all laugh.* MRS. COREY *rises.*

MRS. COREY: I suppose you will want your coffee here?

COREY: Yes, we'll join you at tea.

> *All the ladies rise,* LAPHAM *starts to follow* MRS. COREY, *then pauses seeing the gentlemen remain.* TOM *opens the door for his mother. The ladies exeunt. The gentlemen light their cigars and re-seat themselves.*

COREY, *as* SERVANT *offers cigars*: Try this one, Colonel Lapham. These are new. I had an Englishman here the other day who was smoking *old* cigars in the superstition that tobacco improved with age, like wine.

LAPHAM: Anybody who had ever lived off a tobacco country could tell him better than that. I guess I like a good cigar about as well as anybody.

BELLINGHAM, *coming to* LAPHAM's *side as he smokes, half turned in his seat*: Colonel Lapham, weren't you with the 96th Vermont when they charged across the river in front of Pickensburg, and the rebel battery opened fire on them in the water? (LAPHAM *slowly closing his eyes, and nodding his head in assent as he smokes.*) I thought so. I was with the 85th Massachusetts, and I sha'n't forget that slaughter. We were all new to it still. Perhaps that's why it made such an impression.

COREY: I don't know. Was there anything much more impressive afterward? I recollect the talk of some old army men at the time. They said that death-rate couldn't be beaten.

LAPHAM: About one in five of us got out safe.

> *He breaks the ashes from his cigar.* BELLINGHAM *fills his glass.*

COREY: What astonishes the craven civilian in all these things is the abundance—the superabundance—of heroism. The cowards were the exception; the men that were ready to die, the rule.

LAPHAM: The woods were full of them!

BELLINGHAM, *to* COREY: I don't see why you claim the credit of being a craven civilian, Bromfield. A man who was out with Garibaldi in '48!

COREY: Oh, a little amateur red-shirting. What has become of all the heroism? Tom, how many club men do you know who would think it sweet and fit to die for their country?

TOM: I can't think of a great many at the moment, sir!

BELLINGHAM: And I couldn't in '61. Nevertheless they were there. It's the occasion that's wanting, and I'm glad of it.

LAPHAM: So am I. I don't want to see any more men killed in my time.

COREY: We non-combatants were notoriously reluctant to give up fighting. But I incline to think Colonel Lapham and James may be right. I dare say we shall have the heroism again if we have the occasion.

LAPHAM: Heroism? I want to tell you about a fellow I had in my own company when we first went out. We were all privates to begin with: after a while they elected me captain—I'd had the tavern stand and most of 'em knew me. But Jim Millon never got to be anything more than corporal; corporal when he was killed. I can't say he went into the thing from the highest motives, altogether. I suppose Jim Millon's wife was enough to account for his going, herself. She was a pretty bad assortment. And she used to lead Jim *one* kind of life. Well, sir, that fellow used to save every cent of his pay and send it to that woman. Used to get me to do it for him. I tried to stop him. "Why Jim," said I, "you know what she'll do with it." "That's so, Cap," says he, "but I don't know what she'll do without it." And it did keep her straight, straight as a string—as long as Jim lasted. Seemed as if there was something mysterious about it. They had a little girl—about as old as my oldest girl—and Jim used to talk to me about her. Guess he done it as much for her as for the mother; and he said to me before the last action he went into, "I should like to turn tail and run, Cap. I ain't comin' out o' this one. But I don't suppose it would do." "Well, not for *you*, Jim," said I. "I want to live," says he, and he bust out crying right there in my tent. "I want to live for poor Molly and Zarilla"—that's what they called the little one—I dunno where they got the name. "I ain't ever had half a chance; and now Molly's doin' better, and I believe we should get along after this." He set there cryin' like a baby. But he wan't no baby when he went into action. I hated to look at him when it was over, not so much because he'd got a ball that was meant for me by a sharpshooter—he saw the devil takin' aim, and he jumped to warn me—as because he didn't look like Jim; he looked like—fun, all desperate and savage. I guess he died hard. Now I say—

*He pauses flushed with wine—staring ahead.*

BELLINGHAM: Apollinaris?

LAPHAM: Thanks. I will take some of this wine. (*Pouring himself a glass.*) What—what's I sayin'?

BELLINGHAM: You were speaking of one of your men—Jim Millon.

LAPHAM, *with tipsy suspicion*: What's—what's Jim Millon got to do with it?

BELLINGHAM: Oh, nothing, I believe. We were speaking of the—of heroism in the war, and you were illustrating—

LAPHAM, *with a returning gleam*: Oh, yes. Well, what I want to say about

Jim, is this— *(He stops again, and stares blankly around with a hiccough. He reaches for the wine again.* TOM COREY *pretends to take some for himself, and puts the bottle beyond his reach.* BROMFIELD COREY *comes nearer, in hopes of diverting him.* LAPHAM *regards him in surprise)* Wa'—wan't you over there just now?

COREY: Yes, but I came round to speak with you about my boy. I hope, Colonel Lapham, that you are able to make Tom useful to you?

LAPHAM, *steadying himself, and sobered a little by the chance of bragging*: Well, sir, I guess it will be our fault if we don't. I don't like to say it to his face—I don't like the principle—but since you ask me about it, I'd just as lief say that I've never had any young man take hold equal to your son. I don't know as you care—

COREY: You make me very happy. I've always had the idea that there was something in my son, if he could only find the way to work it out. And he seems to have gone into your business for the love of it.

LAPHAM: He went to work in the right way, sir. He told me about it. He looked into the paint, first. And that paint is a thing that will bear looking into.

COREY: You might think he had invented it if you heard him celebrating it.

LAPHAM: Is that so? Well, there ain't any other way. You've got to believe in a thing before you can put any heart in it. Why I had a partner in this thing once, along back just after the war, and he used to be always wanting to tinker with something else. "Why," says I, "you've got the best thing in God's universe now. Why ain't you satisfied?" I had to get rid of him at last. I stuck to my paint, and that fellow's drifted round pretty much all over the whole country, whittling his capital down all the while, till here a couple of months ago I had to lend him twenty thousand dollars to start new, and I've had to keep him going ever since. I was tellin' your brother—*(nods at* JAMES BELLINGHAM) just before we come in to dinner that Rogers has done his best to get me into a hole lately. I felt pretty blue, one while, but I'm all right now. No, sir, you've got to believe in a thing, and I believe in your son, and I don't mind telling you that so far as he's gone he's a success!

TOM: That's very kind of you.

LAPHAM, *to* COREY: Yes, sir, when your son proposed to take hold I didn't have much faith in his ideas, that's the truth. But I had faith in him, and I saw that he meant business from the start. I could see it was born in him; anyone could!

COREY: I'm afraid he didn't inherit it directly from me.

LAPHAM: Well, sir, we can't help those things. Some of us have got it and some of us haven't. The idea is to make the most of what we have got.

COREY: Oh yes, that's the idea.

LAPHAM: And you can't ever tell what's in you till you try. Why, when I started this thing I didn't more than half understand my own strength. I wouldn't have said, looking back, that I could have stood the wear and tear of what I've been through. But I developed as I went along. His going through college won't hurt him, he'll soon slough all that off—and his society bringing up, won't; don't you be anxious about it. Your son will get along.

COREY: Thank you.

LAPHAM: He'll get along. He's a good business man and a fine fellow. If you ever like to ride after a good horse—

COREY: Oh no, no, no; thank you! The better the horse the more I should be scared. Tom has told me of your driving.

LAPHAM: Ha! Ha! Ha! Well, everyone to his taste. But you must run up to Lapham with me some day, and see the works. (*Raising his voice and striking the arm of his chair with his hand as the wine goes more and more to his head.*) Those works are worth seeing! They're what brought me to Boston, and they're what have kept me here! They're what's building my house there across the street on the waterside of Beacon. They're what has built my fortune! And they're going to build it bigger and bigger. (*As* LAPHAM *gets tipsy, he reaches out for more wine in every direction.* TOM COREY *now tries to substitute a bottle of apollinaris for the madeira before him. Savagely.*) What's that?

TOM: I thought you wanted the apollinaris, Colonel.

LAPHAM, *with drunken dignity*: I guess I know what I want, young man. When I want apollinaris, I'll ask for it. Where was I? Oh, yes; up at Lapham. (*Raising his voice again and addressing* COREY.) Yes, sir, the fires that Mrs. Lapham lighted in the works when they first opened hain't been out once day or night in all these years, and they never shall go out in my time! I tell you, Corey, that paint brought me to Boston ten years ago a little worse off than nothing at all, for I was in debt for the money that I bought out my partner with. And here I am now worth my million, and meeting you gentlemen like one of you, and every cent of it is honest money—no speculation—every copper of it for value received. I've got more money than I know what to do with. Why, when your wife sent to mine for that charity, a while back, I wrote my cheque for five hundred dollars but my wife wouldn't take more than one hundred; said she wasn't going to show off before Mrs. Corey. I call that a pretty good joke on Mrs. Corey. I must tell her how Mrs. Lapham done her out of a cool four hundred dollars—(*He looks about, and discovers that the ladies are gone.*) Why—why—what's got all the women?

*He starts up*

TOM: The ladies are in the drawing room, sir. We are going to join them in a moment.

LAPHAM: I want to see Mis' Corey *now*. This joke won't keep. I keep forgettin' things so, tonight—

COREY: I'll remind you of it, Colonel. Do sit down again.

BELLINGHAM: I want some more coffee, Bromfield. Wouldn't you like another cup, Colonel?

LAPHAM, *dropping back in his chair*: That's about it. I've got such a buzzin'—and this coffee goes to the right spot. I must get Mis' Corey to tell my wife how she makes it. I guess Irene could do it. She's the greatest little cook! Now Pen, she's more for readin', but Irene—

BELLINGHAM, *listening*: Isn't that a fire near here? I thought I heard an engine.

LAPHAM, *not regarding*: Gentlemen, I *like* you! (*To* JAMES BELLINGHAM.) It always was my ambition to know *you*; yes, sir. If anyone had said when I first come to Boston that in less than ten years I would be hob-nobbing here with Jim Bellingham, I would have told that person he lied; I would have told anybody he lied that had told me ten years ago that a son of Bromfield Corey would have come and asked me to take him into business!

TOM, *going to window*: The engines are here in the street.

*A light is seen beyond the window, the engines are heard throbbing and pulsing in the street below. A sound of distant bells and voices. An engine crashes by.*

SEYMOUR: There comes another! (*To* COREY.) May I—

COREY: By all means!

*Exit* SEYMOUR *for ladies. All crowd to the window, save* LAPHAM *who remains seated.*

BELLINGHAM: It seems to be quite near.

*Enter* SEYMOUR *with* MRS. LAPHAM, MRS. COREY, MISS KINGSBURY, IRENE *and* NANNY. *All crowd to the window.*

NANNY: Oh, isn't it perfectly magnificent! If you lean out you can see the flames!

MISS KINGSBURY: I wouldn't have missed it on any account. Thank you, Mr. Seymour, for bringing us out!

SEYMOUR: Oh, it's Mr. Corey's fire.

COREY: Ah, I thought you'd like it. I wish I could afford to have one for you every time you dined here.

MISS KINGSBURY: Oh, do you think you would if I came again?

MRS. LAPHAM: Irene!

IRENE: Papa! Papa!

MRS. LAPHAM, *looks from window*: Silas Lapham! Look! It's our house!

IRENE: Papa!

LAPHAM, *starting to window*: My house! (*All draw back, he stands in the now open window looking out, the curtains moving in the wind about him. The pulsing of the engines and the shouts and sounds of crackling—breaking glass—and flames sound near.* LAPHAM *puts his hand up to his forehead and steps back.* MRS. LAPHAM *goes to him.*) Persis, our new house is gone!

*The crash of engines, the shouts and the sounds of fire continue.*

MRS. LAPHAM: Oh, Silas, it was insured?

LAPHAM: I had a buildin' risk on it, and it expired last week. It's a dead loss, and I guess I done it.

CURTAIN

# Backgrounds: The Myth of Success

Howells is usually spoken of as a literary realist, and of course much of the vividness and conviction of his writing comes from his keen observation and accurate transcription of the life he saw about him. But he was also fully aware of the values and assumptions that underlay the actions and attitudes of his fellow citizens. His ability to dramatize these almost unconscious attitudes enabled him to create characters and tell stories in which his readers recognized their own aspirations, tensions, and fears. Unlike the sentimental authors of his day, Howells frequently depicted popular attitudes ironically in order to reveal their hollowness. In *The Rise of Silas Lapham*, for instance, he tests the accepted image of the self-made man and captain of industry against the reality he had observed. Penelope and Irene Lapham make mockery of the tradition of the dark temptress and the golden-haired heroine, and of the romantic cliches of ennobling self-sacrifice and beautiful suffering. The almost sacred belief that behind every great man there stands a great woman, the keeper of conscience and morality, is also called into question in the relationship of Silas and Persis Lapham.

The American success myth, popularly embodied in Horatio Alger, was so strongly entrenched in American culture that Howells himself was appropriated for use in the Rags-to-Riches Hall of Fame, and Theodore Dreiser, in a faked interview, lifted Howells' written remarks out of context and constructed a "conversation" that made Howells appear to celebrate his own virtuous rise to fame and wealth. Even Howells' publisher, Roswell Smith, an astute business man and a close observer of literature, found it difficult to believe that Howells did not intend to use Lapham's failures of sophistication to preach a sermon on the dangers of drink and gambling or that Howells could resist the opportunity to reinforce public morality by punishing and degrading Silas. To an age as disenchanted (not to say cynical) as our own it is perhaps difficult to conceive how strong a hold on the American imagination was once exercised by the myths surrounding Horatio Alger: the inseparability of wealth and virtue; the coincidence of piety and morality.

## ROBERT FALK

## W. D. Howells: Maturity in Fiction[†]

\* \* \*

Without retracing well-marked paths of comment upon *Silas Lapham*, it will be \* \* \* rewarding to consider it in the light of later patterns of historical commentary on the tradition of the business-

[†]From *The Victorian Mode in American Fiction, 1865–1885* (East Lansing: Michigan State University Press, 1964), pp. 131–35.

man in America and its relation to "the protestant ethic." *Silas Lapham,* along with its immediate successor, *The Minister's Charge, or the Apprenticeship of Lemuel Barker,* has a significant position in the fiction of the businessman, a tradition which is as old as Franklin's *Poor Richard's Almanack* and as new as the man in the gray flannel suit. Howells's two novels furthermore reflect clearly the influence upon this long tradition of the Horatio Alger theme. *Silas Lapham,* while it ultimately reverses the emphasis of the Alger story by "rising" in a quite different way, nevertheless reveals the essential spirit of the nineteenth-century, middle-class, protestant definition of success through hard work and virtuous conduct. It is not accurate to regard it as a parody of the Alger story. Actually it is a more serious and mature examination of the tradition. *The Minister's Charge,* on the other hand, with its Algeresque subtitle, belongs more clearly to the familiar pattern. It contains many of the classic features. A country boy adrift in the city and confronted by the duplicities of city life, ultimately triumphs over obstacles by innocence, patience, and a stubborn insistence upon the old verities.

It remained for a later generation of economic historians to denigrate the protestant ethic and create the image of "The Gilded Age," and it is necessary to understand the historical reasons for this change before applying all of its assumptions to a judgment of the period in which Howells wrote. During the 1930's when American social critics sought historical causes for the economic dislocation of the depression years, they began to define the meaning of such terms as "Social Darwinism," "the gospel of wealth," and "the protestant ethic." With the assistance of European scholars like Max Weber[1] they identified the spirit of capitalism with the period of the 1870's and 1880's which they regarded as the golden age of American business and the "apotheosis of the protestant ethic." Weber had traced the beginnings of this process back to John Calvin and found a latter-day illustration of it in Benjamin Franklin's success philosophy, especially in *The Way to Wealth.*[2] American critics applied the thesis to the dream of success, the rags-to-riches pattern as seen in Franklin's *Autobiography* and *Poor Richard.* In 1934 Nathanael West wrote a scathing parody-novel entitled *A Cool Million; or the Dismantling of Lemuel Pitkin* which was a great deal more than a clever caricature of the Horatio Alger idea of "rising in the ranks," as parodied in the subtitle. West extended his satire to include the whole concept of American innocence and free enterprise. For him the protestant virtues of middle-class business and virtue, the combination portrayed by Howells in Silas Lapham, were

1. Max Weber (1864–1920), a German sociologist, was the author of *The Protestant Ethic and the Spirit of Capitalism* (1920, Eng. tr. 1930). [*Editor.*]
2. *The Way to Wealth* is the title assigned to reprints from Benjamin Franklin's 1758 almanac version of *Father Abraham's Speech,* a set of discourses delivered by a wise old man to the people attending an auction. [*Editor.*]

merely an invitation to disaster in the America of the 1930's. Lem and his friend Shagpoke Whipple, former president of the United States, became in West's novel the unconscious dupes of communist and fascist demagogues.

A comparison of Howells's character with West's suggests the way in which Howells remained close to the spirit of the Alger tradition. West's Lemuel Pitkin is gradually "dismantled" of his arms, legs, his sight, his teeth, and his scalp. He has come to the city to make his fortune "in the honorable tradition of his country," but his virtuous efforts to win success bring him the rewards of jail, poverty, violence and death. West's purpose, hilariously and cruelly revealed, turns the original Alger tradition inside out. Howells, on the other hand, preserved the tradition in all its essentials, altering only the surface heroics and popular gilding by which Alger sentimentalized it for his juvenile readers. Lemuel Barker comes to Boston from "Willoughby Pastures" seeking literary success. When he realizes that his verses are not publishable, Lem undergoes the classic Alger experience in the city. He is the victim of confidence tricksters and loses his money. Too proud to ask assistance, he is arrested while chasing the swindlers and is falsely accused of purse-snatching. Jailed for a night, he is judged innocent but is forced to spend a second night in a charity flophouse where Sewell finally rescues him and starts him on the path to success with a job as janitor for a wealthy friend, Miss Vane. Lem gradually learns the ways of the city and the injustices of the social system, but like the Alger hero he educates himself and "rises" to a position of respectability. His rural-bred innocence has played him false in various ways, but it serves him well in the end, and he returns to the farm determined to assist his family in their poverty.

There is no direct evidence that Howells was consciously following the Alger plot, or even that he knew the *Ragged Dick* and *Tattered Tom* stories,[3] but in a letter to James R. Osgood, while writing the novel, he seemed uncomfortably aware that his purpose was misunderstood by H. M. Alden, the editor to whom he had submitted the manuscript. Alden had suggested to Howells that he "make more of the hero and heroine." Howells explained:

> I never meant to make what he seemed to think I would—that is, something farcical or comical. In the first place, I don't believe in heroes and heroines, and willingly avoid the heroic; but I meant to make a simple, earnest, and often very pathetic figure of my

3. According to Edwin H. Cady (*The Road to Realism* [Syracuse, N.Y., 1956], pp. 48–49), Howells' earliest piece of fiction was in the Horatio Alger pattern, almost fifteen years before Alger himself wrote *Ragged Dick*. Howells' youthful fiction, "A Tale of Love and Politics, Adventures of a Printer Boy," was printed in the Ashtabula *Sentinel*, 1 September 1853. It was a tale of an orphan who saves a judge's daughter from drowning and becomes a successful newspaper man.

country boy, whose adventures and qualities should win him the reader's entire sympathy and respect.[4]

Alger had written in *Ragged Dick:* "I hope my young readers will like him as I do without being blind to his faults. Perhaps, although he was only a bootblack, they may find something in him to emulate." If we subtract the obtrusive sermonizing, the money *mystique,* and the banalities of style of the typical Alger "juvenile" there remains much in *The Minister's Charge* that parallels the Alger stories. Thrift, hard work, respect for elders, self-education, pride are among the virtues Lemuel Barker owns in common with Alger's heroes. Howells insisted that his hero was "anything but a trivial or a farcical figure" (as Alden had apparently interpreted the story) and told Osgood that his tendency was toward tragic, rather than comic, effects. Before publication of the novel, two years after this letter, Howells superimposed upon the account of Lemuel Barker the character of Reverend Sewell and his circle together with the final sermon on "Complicity" which states the central thesis in Tolstoryan[5] terms. *The Minister's Charge,* which began as a modified Alger success story ended as a plea for universal brotherhood and Christian charity.

Howells's social philosophy, first cautiously indicated in his review of *The Breadwinners,*[6] and made explicit in *The Minister's Charge,* was kept beneath the surface in *The Rise of Silas Lapham.* Class distinctions in this novel remain largely matters of taste and etiquette. Only in the brief glimpses into Zerilla Dewey's life, her drunken husband and poor living conditions in a tenement apartment, does Howells desert the generally middle-class setting of the story. If one were to summarize Howells's social views from evidence in *Silas Lapham* alone, they would well represent the Victorian concept of class responsibility, somewhat as follows:

> Poverty and inequality of the laboring classes are increasing problems of American society, but they can best be solved within the existing class divisions, provided enough ethical leadership and responsibility is demonstrated by the two classes which hold places of influence—that is, the traditionally educated Back Bay families like the Coreys and the newer, energetic businessmen like Lapham. The Coreys and the Bellinghams represent the older, established order and the settled social authority of Boston, but they had become, like Bromfield Corey, cynical and withdrawn. Lapham, despite his humble origins, had hold of the driving force of American society. If he could achieve a measure of ethical

4. *Life in Letters of William Dean Howells,* ed. Mildred Howells (New York, 1928), I, 361. [*Editor.*]
5. The ethical ideals of Count Leo Tolstoy (1828–1910) were based upon the Christian tenets of forgiveness, pacifism, and selfless love.

6. John Hay (1838–1905), American statesman and author, anonymously published *The Bread-Winners* (1884), a novel dealing with contemporary social problems. [*Editor.*]

responsibility, he might compensate for his social deficiencies. But what was needed was the right combination of the two types.

Howells seems to suggest in the marriage of Tom Corey and Penelope Lapham that a hope for the future lay in joining these two classes of citizens. Tom Corey is the mediating force. He possesses his family's superior taste and education, but is equally sympathetic with Lapham's useful and productive ideas of business. And he tactfully brings the two men together and helps break down their reserves of suspicion toward each other.

Thus Howells was concerned to exhibit with the greatest impartiality the faults and virtues of both these families. Bromfield Corey, despite his idleness and caustic sense of superiority, is engaging in his manner, likeable, and self-critical. He sees clearly and states conditions frankly and articulately. It is Corey, not Lapham, who expresses one of the central concerns of the novel: "Money," he says, "is the romance, the poetry of our age. It's the thing that chiefly strikes the imagination. The Englishmen who come here are more curious about the great new millionaires than about anyone else, and they respect them more." Lapham has the money, and he likewise has an acute feeling of his responsibility to less fortunate people, like Zerilla Dewey, his secretary, whose father had saved him in the Civil War at the cost of his own life. Lapham's one act of injustice toward his former partner, Rogers, seems fully compensated in his other acts of charity and fair-mindedness even before the final temptation scene. Howells, too, is careful to limit the satire to matters of taste—his table manners, his ignorance of social amenities, his bragging about his possessions and his money, his crude pleasure in painted signboards advertising the Lapham paint. It is clear from the opening chapter that Howells sees Lapham as a hopeful element for the future of American society, and in the broad picture he has presented of a representative, nineteenth-century individualistic entrepreneur of business, he struck a vein of social analysis which has been a focal point for fiction and social analysis ever since.

The novel echoes the Alger theme mainly in the opening chapter when Lapham describes his boyhood to Bartley Hubbard, a boyhood not unlike that of Howells himself who also had risen from a rural environment to become a Solid Man of Boston and had built a large and comfortable home on the water side of Beacon Street. Howells directs his sympathy toward Lapham in the exchange with Bartley Hubbard when the latter satirically questions him about his boyhood. "Worked in the fields summers and went to school winters," Bartley notes, "regulation thing? Any barefoot business? Early deprivations of any kind that would encourage the reader to go and do likewise?" Lapham replies to Hubbard's professional flippancy "with quiet self-respect;" "I guess," he says, "if you see these things as a joke my life won't interest you." After the opening chapter the novel becomes a more serious examination of a recognizable type of the American business tycoon, a theme which touched a basic chord in the American experience.

Lapham's character does not, however, demonstrate later doctrinaire definitions of the protestant ethic. Nor does it exemplify the "gospel of wealth" or the cluster of ideas suggested by the term "Social Darwinism."[7] As the story developed Howells placed less emphasis upon Silas's acquisitive qualities and his low motives. When Persis, his wife, charges him with making his paint business a religion and with forcing out his partner to gain larger profits for himself, he defends his action on the grounds of sentiment, as a dedication to the memory of his father who discovered the mine on the family property. Though he boasts about his money and the power it gives him, he nowhere suggests that it was a providential sign of God's favor, nor does he imply that his good fortune was the result of an evolutionary process of struggle and competition. Lapham remains a human being, never becoming a symbol or the illustration of a thesis. As such Howells's portrait remains one of the most satisfying in the history of the fiction of the businessman. With his mixture of good and bad traits, he is more convincing than either Dreiser's Frank Cowperwood or Lewis's Babbitt.[8] Without either Dreiser's powerful statement of the robber-baron thesis or Lewis's sharp-edged satire upon small-minded rotarianism, he nonetheless managed to describe a businessman who was neither a monster nor a damn fool. By the oblique use of a popular tradition, he managed to find a large reading public for his realistic examination of a type which had already become central in American life.

# CLARK W. BRYAN

## The Literature of the Household[†]

A SKETCH OF AMERICA'S LEADING WRITER OF FICTION, W. D. HOWELLS.

One of the most prominent instances and pertinent illustrations of America's greatness, in rapidity of growth, simplicity of conduct and eminent attainment in the field of literature, is fairly presented in the proud yet modestly held position of America's leading writer of

7. Social Darwinism involved the notion that evolutionary principles (especially the "survival of the fittest") govern social, as well as biological, existence and is frequently associated with the English sociologist and philosopher, Herbert Spencer (1820–1903) who popularized the ideas in his book *First Principles* (1862). [*Editor.*]
8. Frank Cowperwood, a giant of industry and fi-

nance, is a major character in *The Financier* (1912), *The Titan* (1914), and *The Stoic* (1947) by Theodore Dreiser (1871–1945); George F. Babbitt, a small-town real estate broker, civic booster, and conformist, is the protagonist of *Babbitt* (1922) by Sinclair Lewis (1885–1951). [*Editor.*]
†From *Good Housekeeping*, I (11 July 1885), 2–3.

fiction, to-day—William Dean Howells. It is not only noteworthy, but marvelous, as well, that such a position should have been acquired without outside aids of any kind, without wealth and with but limited opportunities for acquiring an education, in so short a time, and from such unpromising beginnings as has been the case with Mr. Howells. In no other country but that of America could there have been developed so rapid attainment of literary supremacy—with such a wealth of fruitage in so short a season of growth and maturity. The story of Mr. Howells' life, told in simple narrative, seems far more like fiction itself than a relation of stern facts—a fiction having more of the character of a page from the Arabian Nights than like a plain unvarnished tale of American life.

Mr. Howells was born at Martin's Ferry, Ohio, opposite Wheeling, West Virginia, March 1st, 1837, of Welsh parentage on the father's side. The Howells were Quakers, and people of substance in Wales—the great-grandfather of the novelist had introduced the manufacture of flannel in his town and founded three mills there, but the grandfather, who was attracted to America by his democratic sympathies, became a fervid Methodist. The father in turn became a Swedenborgian,[1] in which belief the novelist was reared. His people were all, so far as he knows them, in past generations, people of literary taste and cultivation. When the boy was three years old, his father removed to Hamilton, Ohio, and bought the Hamilton *Intelligencer*, a weekly journal in the office of which the embryo author learned to set type at a very early age—so early, in fact, and in such a matter-of-fact way that he does not know himself when he first heard the "click, click, click, of the type in the stick." But he does remember distinctly that he set type on President Taylor's inaugural message, when he was about twelve years of age. His father remained in Hamilton until after the inauguration of President Taylor, in 1849, when, having had conscientious scruples about supporting a slave-holding president, he sold the *Intelligencer* and the family removed to Dayton, Ohio, the elder Howells purchasing the Dayton *Transcript*, a semi-weekly paper, which he changed into a daily, the enterprise proving a disastrous failure. The occurrences of those years may well seem, as the subject of our sketch once said in referring to the details of his early life, like a dream. The elder Mr. Howells found it necessary to husband all his resources, and these resources were forcibly augmented by his sons, every one of whom, as rapidly as might be, was taught to be a producer rather than a consumer, by taking up the "art preservative"—in short by learning to set type. During the two years of struggle for existence, which the daily paper had, it often fell to the subject of this sketch to set type till

1. Swedenborgianism is a religious system based on the mystical doctrines of the Swedish theologian, Emanuel Swedenborg (1688–1772), who held that belief is founded on spiritual essences immediately present in the everyday world. [Editor.]

eleven o'clock at night and then to get up at four o'clock the next morning to carry a newspaper route. The fight against fate was kept up for two years and when the crisis came and the elder Howells announced the true condition of affairs—the failure of the *Transcript*—says Mr. W. D. Howells, in recalling the circumstance, "we all went down to the Miami river and *went in swimming*." This was American philosophy. We have spoken of American greatness and this kind of American philosophy serves as one of the handmaids in pointing the former on to much of the eminent success it has achieved.

From Dayton the family removed to Greene county, where it was purposed to give the elder Mr. Howells the superintendence of a projected paper mill, but the enterprise failed of a successful organization and after waiting a year the field was abandoned.

In 1851 the now eminent author secured a situation as compositor on the Ohio State *Journal* at a salary of *four dollars a week*, his father being clerk of the House at the same time. This was the first money Mr. W. D. Howells ever earned and received as his own. But it was all turned into the family exchequer and helped to keep the wolf from the door of his father's home. Here he formed the acquaintance of John J. Piatt, who was a compositor on the *Journal* at that time, and conjointly with whom he published his first volume of verse.

In 1852 the family removed to Ashtabula, Ohio, the elder Mr. Howells purchasing the Ashtabula *Sentinel* and the whole family of boys working on the mechanical department of the paper. The *Sentinel* was afterwards removed to Jefferson, Ohio, where its publication was continued under the same management as at Ashtabula. Almost from the time he could read it was a pastime of Mr. Howells' to write verses, put them in type, print them on slips for the amusement of himself and some of his companions. This was the first round on the ladder of authorship which has since become so prominent a way-mark in the arena of American literature. At the age of nineteen Mr. Howells received the appointment of Columbus correspondent of the Cincinnati *Gazette*, and at twenty-two he was given the position of news editor of the Columbus, Ohio, *State Journal* under the management of Henry D. Cooke, since prominent in Washington city politics and political preferment. While on the *Journal* he wrote a life of Abraham Lincoln, for a Columbus publishing house and this piece of literary work was doubtless the stepping stone to his promotion, a few years later, to a Consulship at Venice, where was gathered the material for some of his most interesting and popular books, written in after years.

His first appearance in a strictly literary character was also made while residing at Columbus. Mr. A. T. Fullerton of that place sent the first contribution from the West to the *Atlantic Monthly*. It was a poem entitled "By the Dead," and attracted considerable attention. Mr. Howells, who had in a measure, kept up his habit of writing and printing verses, began to cherish the idea of trying his hand on the crank handle of the organ of the muses before the footlights and audience of a critical world. In this he was, as he has been ever since, in his literary efforts, eminently successful. Five of his poems were published in the *Atlantic Monthly* in one year, "The Poet's Friends," "The Pilot's Story," "Pleasure Pain," "Lost Beliefs," and "Andenken." His life of Lincoln netted him $190 and with this money he made a trip to Canada, visiting Montreal and swinging around the circle to Boston, where he first made the personal acquaintance of Mr. James Russell Lowell,[2] then the editor of the *Atlantic Monthly*, and by him was introduced to James T. Fields[3] and Oliver Wendell Holmes.[4]

From Boston he returned to Columbus, where he remained until receiving his appointment as Consul to Venice, where he took up his residence and remained from 1861 to 1865. On his return from abroad he did some writing for the New York *Tribune* and the New York *Times*, and was a salaried contributor to *The Nation* until 1866, when Mr. Fields tendered him the position of assistant editor of the *Atlantic Monthly*. This he accepted and held until 1872 when he was made the responsible editor and remained as such until 1881 when he resigned and was succeeded by Thomas Bailey Aldrich, which position the latter gentleman still holds.

Those who have read Mr. Howells—and who has not? for his books are largely called for abroad as well as at home—upon reading thus much of his history and life, may perhaps ask as to the why of all this great appreciation and success at the hands of the reading world. To this we may safely say that the foundations of this well-earned fame are built of the simple facts of his writing from an American standpoint, and while looking at his characterizations through American spectacles and with eyes that look into his subject matter without any of the blemishes that arise from near-sightedness or moral or mental strabismus of any kind.

He works a field in which he is pre-eminently at home—that of social life—and is content to leave the highways and by-ways of miscellaneous literary labor for others to experiment with as best they may. He handles what he knows he can handle successfully and hence wastes no time in seeking out labyrinthian paths which may

2. James Russell Lowell (1819–91), American poet, literary critic, journalist, and university professor, edited the *Atlantic* from 1857 until 1861. He played a considerable part in fostering Howells' early career. [*Editor.*]
3. James T. Fields (1817–81), a partner in the distinguished Boston publishing firm of Ticknor & Fields, succeeded Lowell as editor of the *Atlantic* in 1861,
and served in that position until 1870. Fields hired Howells as his assistant in 1866 and left the younger man in complete charge upon retiring in 1870. [*Editor.*]
4. Oliver Wendell Holmes (1809–94), Boston aristocrat and distinguished physician, also pursued a successful career as a lecturer, poet, and essayist. [*Editor.*]

lead somewhere and may not. Personally, Mr. Howell scouts the idea of literary inspiration, and in this respect, differs a little from other folks. He even goes so far as to erase the word genius from his vocabulary, as connected with the work-day life of his literary efforts. Upon being asked once, how he reconciled this theory with his own position, he replied, simply that he had a literary bent and that the rest was done by hard work, failing to recognize the simple, but important fact, that that "literary bent" is the very element of genius which with him passes for something else.

He also holds that the "literary life" so much effected, so much quoted, so much over-estimated, is an illusion largely of fancy and imagination. And, furthermore, he holds that the oft-repeated assertion that literary labor is but poorly paid for, is erroneous and unjust. Literary labor, he says, if made a business of, as a lawyer, a physician or a merchant follows his profession or trade, will be found to have equally satisfactory results, the trouble with the pseudo claimants being the false notion of possessing "genius" or of being inspired with a "divine afflatus"—so to speak—of sufficient power to throw off literary gems as a flowing well pours out of its treasures in abundance, without the necessity of industry taking a hand at the pumps to keep the flow full and free. In this we hold Mr. Howells to be about half right and half wrong. Were he not the possessor of a certain degree of literary "genius" he would not to-day be, as he is, the leading writer of American Fiction, albeit his industry, application and perseverance, which are exceptionally thorough, and complete, might be an hundred fold more so than they are.

Mr. Howells writes methodically, systematically and conscientiously. He devotes the morning hours to writing and generally completes at one sitting, what would fill an ordinary page of GOOD HOUSEKEEPING. He erases, re-writes and re-arranges his manuscript with great care and much elaboration, and his proof sheets are a terror to printers, into whose hands his manuscript happens to fall. Of late years he prefers, and does, when circumstances will admit, re-write his work in full. He gives his afternoons and evenings to reading, conversation, driving, walking or any of the ordinary duties of every day life, and is always chatty, sensible, unassuming and delightful in conversation. He says that he has never written a book yet simply for the sake of writing something for somebody to read, but always with the purpose of giving his readers something to think about, that should be useful and profitable to them and to the world as well. He has no hobbies of politics or religion, and no mastering affiliations other than those which his profession as a writer bring him in the world of business, and his pleasant domestic relations hold for him. He is president of one social club and a member of another, enjoys luncheons and small dinner parties where the "feast of reason and the flow of soul" abound, but is not carried away captive by the follies and foibles of what is known as fashionable society life. He has a charming home on Beacon street, Boston, where, with his little family of wife, son and two daughters, in their teens, he lives cosily and comfortably, and the days come and go to him serenely and satisfactorily.

Could anything be more delightful, restful, satisfying, than the daily rounds of such a life? To us who write and read of all this, it certainly looks like the perfection of living. To him of whom we write and read, it may well, as the subject himself says, "seem like a dream," as he turns his eye back over the little more than two-score years, which his memory covers, and recalls the struggles and the trials of his early years, and compares them with the pleasant places into which his lines have now fallen. A dream, indeed, and one which could not have verification in any country under the sun, save that of America!

His has been, is still, and ever will be, an industrious life. He would not be W. D. Howells in idleness, in riotous living or in the *role* of a literary lion and nothing more. He has won his place by his "literary bent" and by constantly narrowing the circle of that "bent" by his habits of industry, his methods of application, and his logical perseverance. The "genius" which he ignores gave him what a writer not long since said of him, a "discernment of a new drift in thought and affairs; a drift which is bringing the well-being of the common people into prominence." This writer calls it "drift," and Mr. Howells, may perhaps, call it "literary bent," but we call it "genius"— a genius of brains and a soul of sense, recognizing the solemn fact that brains without hands are but a poor dependence for subsistence in this work-day world. The same writer just quoted said of Mr. Howells at the time of his leaving the editorial chair of the *Atlantic Monthly*, for the purpose of devoting more time to creative literary work, that in that department "he easily ranks among the best living writers of English." To this we add, as at the beginning of this paper, the title of "the leading writer of American Fiction," and we close the paper with a P. S. assertion that no living writer of Fiction, as pertaining to social life, in America or elsewhere, has ever yet won so prominent a place in the confidence and kind consideration of the world at large, as has William Dean Howells.

# THEODORE DREISER

## How He Climbed Fame's Ladder[†]

WILLIAM DEAN HOWELLS TELLS THE STORY OF HIS LONG STRUGGLE FOR
SUCCESS, AND HIS ULTIMATE TRIUMPH

A MOST UNIQUE AND INSPIRING PHOTOGRAPHIC INTERVIEW.

A POOR OHIO PRINTER BOY WHO BECAME A GREAT NOVELIST.

"I should like, Mr. Howells," said I,[1] by way of opening my interview with the famous novelist, "to learn your opinion concerning what constitutes success in life. You should have the American view?"

"Not necessarily," said the novelist, seating himself.

"Do you share the belief that everything is open to the beginner who has sufficient energy and perseverance?"

"Add brains, and I will agree," said Mr. Howells with a smile. "A young man stands at the 'parting of two ways,' and can take his path this way or that. It is comparatively easy then, with good judgment. Youth is certainly the greatest advantage which life supplies."

"You began to carve out your place in life under conditions very different from those of to-day?"

"Yes. I was born in a little south-eastern Ohio village,—Martin's Ferry,—and, of course, I had but little of what people deem advantages in the way of schools, railroads, population, and so on. I am not sure, however, that compensation was not had in other things."

"Do you consider that you were specially talented in the direction of literary composition?"

"I should not say that. I think that I came of a reading race, which has always loved literature in a way. My inclination was to read."

"Would you say that, with a special leaning toward a special study, and good health, a fair start, and perseverance, anyone can attain to distinction?"

### Early Ideals

"That is a probability, only. You may be sure that distinction will not come without those qualities. The only way to succeed, therefore, is to have them; though having them will not necessarily

---

†From *Success*, 2 (April 1898), 5–6. This bogus interview is made up chiefly of excerpts from Howells' published memoirs. The boastful tone is caused largely by their being taken out of context and framed by Dreiser's words.

1. Theodore Dreiser (1871–1945), American au-thor and journalist, advanced a "naturalistic" view of society in such works as *Sister Carrie* (1900) and *An American Tragedy* (1925), but in his life and his career he was devoted to success and the pursuit of wealth. [*Editor.*]

guarantee distinction. I can only say that I began with a lofty ideal, without saying how closely I have held to it. My own youth was not specially marked by advantages. There were none, unless you can call a small bookcase full of books, which my home contained, an advantage. The printing-office was my school from a very early date. My father thoroughly believed in it, and he had his belief as to work, which he illustrated as soon as we were old enough to learn the trade he followed. We could go to school and study, or we could go into the printing-office and work, with perhaps an equal chance of learning; but we could not be idle."

"And you chose the printing-office?"

"Not wholly. As I recall it, I went to and fro between the schoolhouse and the printing-office. When I tired of one, I was promptly given my choice of the other."

"Then you began life in poverty?"

"I suppose that, as the world goes now, we were poor. My father's income was never above twelve hundred a year, and his family was large; but nobody was rich then. We lived in the simple fashion of that time and place."

"You found time to read?"

"My reading, somehow, went on pretty constantly. No doubt my love for it won me a chance to devote time to it."

"Might I ask how much time you devoted each day to your literary object?"

"The length varied with varying times. Sometimes I read but little. There were years of the work, of the over-work, indeed,—which falls to the lot of many, that I should be ashamed to speak of except in accounting for the fact. My father had sold his paper in Hamilton, and had bought an interest in another at Dayton, and at that time we were all straining our utmost to help pay for it."

"And that left you little time?"

"In that period very few hours were given to literature. My daily tasks began so early, and ended so late, that I had little time, even if I had the spirit for reading. Sometimes I had to sit up until midnight, waiting for telegraphic news, and be up again at dawn to deliver the papers, working afterwards at the case; but that was only for a few years."

"When did you find time to seriously apply yourself to literature?"

### Acquiring a Literary Style

"I think I did so before I really had the time. Literary aspirations were stirred in me by the great authors whom I successively discovered, and I was perpetually imitating the writings of these,—

modeling some composition of my own after theirs, but never willing to own it."

"Do you attribute your style to the composite influence of these various models?"

"No doubt they had their effect, as a whole, but individually I was freed from the last by each succeeding author, until at length I came to understand that I must be like myself, and no other."

"Had you any conveniences for literary research, beyond the bookcase in your home?"

"If you mean a place to work, I had a narrow, little space, under the stairs at home. There was a desk pushed back against the wall, which the irregular ceiling sloped down to meet, behind it, and at my left was a window, which gave a good light on the writing leaf of my desk. This was my workshop for six or seven years,—and it was not at all a bad one. It seemed, for a while, so very simple and easy to come home in the middle of the afternoon, when my task at the printing-office was done, and sit down to my books in my little study, which I did not finally leave until the family were all in bed. My father had a decided bent in the direction of literature; and, when I began to show a liking for literature, he was eager to direct my choice. This finally changed to merely recommending books, and eventually I was left to my own judgment,—a perplexed and sorrowfully mistaken judgment, at times."

"In what manner did you manage to read the works of all your favorite authors?"

"Well, my hours in the printing-office began at seven and ended at six, with an hour at noon for dinner, which I used for putting down such verses as had come to me in the morning. As soon as supper was over, I got out my manuscripts, and sawed, and filed, and hammered away at my blessed poems, which were little less than imitations, until nine, when I went regularly to bed, to rise again at five. Sometimes the foreman gave me an afternoon off on Saturday, which I devoted to literature."

"Might I ask concerning your next advance in your chosen work?"

"Certainly. As I recall it, my father had got one of those legislative clerkships, in 1858, which used to fall sometimes to deserving country editors, and together we managed and carried out a scheme for corresponding with some city papers. Going to Columbus, the State Capital, we furnished a daily letter giving an account of the legislative proceedings, which I mainly wrote from the material he helped me to gather. The letters found favor, and my father withdrew from the work wholly."

"How long were you a correspondent?"

"Two years. At the end of the first winter, a Cincinnati paper offered me the city editorship, but one night's round with the reporters at the police station satisfied me that I was not meant for that kind of work. I then returned home for the summer, and spent my time in reading, and in sending off poems, which regularly came back. I worked in my father's printing-office, of course; but, as soon as my task was done, went home to my books, and worked away at them until supper. Then a German book-binder, with whom I was endeavoring to read Heine[2] in the original, met me in my father's editorial room, and with a couple of candles on the table between us, and our Heine and the dictionary before us, we read until we were both tired out."

\* \* \*

"Then it might be said that you worked at separate and equally difficult tasks, constantly?"

"Perhaps not equally difficult, but, certainly, constantly."

\* \* \*

"Do you believe that success comes to those who have a special bent or taste, which they cultivate by hard work?"

"I can only answer that out of my literary experience. For my own part, I believe I have never got any good from a book that I did not read merely because I wanted to read it. I think this may be applied to anything a person does. The book, I know, which you read from a sense of duty, or because for any reason you must, is apt to yield you little. This, I think, is also true of everything, and the endeavor that does one good,—and lasting good,—is the endeavor one makes with pleasure. Labor done in another spirit will serve in a way, but pleasurable labor brings, on the whole, I think, the greatest reward."

### The Rewards of Literature

"You were probably strongly fascinated by the supposed rewards of a literary career?"

"Yes. A definite literary ambition grew up in me, and in the long reveries of the afternoon, when I was distributing my case in the printing-office, I fashioned a future of overpowering magnificence and undying celebrity. I should be ashamed to say what literary triumphs I achieved in those preposterous deliriums. But I realize now that such dreams are nerving, and sustain one in an otherwise barren struggle."

"Were you ever tempted and willing to abandon your object of a literary life for something else?"

"I was, once. My first and only essay, aside from literature, was in the realm of law. It was arranged with a United States senator that I should study law in his office. I tried it a month, but almost from the

2. Heinrich Heine (1797–1856), German lyric poet and essayist. Howells' early poems were imitations of Heine, so successful that they were occasionally mistaken for plagiarism of Heine's work. [*Editor.*]

first day, I yearned to return to my books. I had not only to go back to literature, but to the printing-office, and I gladly chose to do it,—a step I never regretted."

"You started out to attain personal distinction and happiness, did you not?"

"I did."

### What True Happiness Is

"You have attained the first,—but I should like to know if your view of what constitutes happiness is the same as when you began?"

"It is quite different. I have come to see life, not as the chase of a forever-impossible personal happiness, but as a field for endeavor toward the happiness of the whole human family. There is no other success.

"I know, indeed, of nothing more subtly satisfying and cheering than a knowledge of the real good will and appreciation of others. Such happiness does not come with money, nor does it flow from a fine physical state. It cannot be bought. But it is the keenest joy, after all, and the toiler's truest and best reward."

# ROSWELL SMITH

## Letters to W. D. Howells[†]

Hotel Vendome Boston

Sunday Evig
March 7th. 85

My Dear Howells.

I did not answer your question to day, as to how I like Silas Lapham—I only got ready to answer it—by telling you the critical mood, in which I must necessarily have read it— I have only read to the end of the dinner party—but already I see that your plan was wiser than mine— To lift the average business man it was necessary to go as low down as Silas Lapham—no doubt— You have made him interesting—everybody likes him—as I began to tell you one person going so far as to say he is the only admirable character in the story— I am content—satisfied—more than satisfied— I could not have wished anything better or different—for your sake & in the magazines interest—than this story to hold & charm our new readers— which must number 500.000—I suspect— I hope each of the new 500.000—will buy and read all your other books— I shall tell Osgood to make a point of advertising your books in the May Century—

[†]Unpublished letters in the Harvard College Library. (Errors in the originals have been retained.)

Now let me mention what no doubt you have already thought of—"*The Business Career of Tom Corey*"—why I think he can be made my ideal business man— Pray pardon the suggestion,— I will look up English Copyright Law penalties for you— It is specially penal even on private parties, who sing at a public entertainment—a copyright song—

Yours Faithfully
ROSWELL SMITH

THE CENTURY CO.
33 East 17th Street,
New-York.

March 17, 85

My dear Mr Howells:

I wrote to Mr Warner[1] yester-day with Mr Gilder's approval, suggesting a lay sermon to our British cousins on the London Times' text.

I have read the May installment of "Silas Lapham" with very great pleasure. I do not see how it could be better. It teaches in many ways a much needed lesson—(common sense, which, as has been aptly said is the most uncommon sense in the world). Many a time have I as a lawyer, interposed to prevent a wife from giving up all her property to her husband's creditors with the idea of helping him when he was on the verge of ruin, when the truest kindness to him was that she should keep what she had to enable him to start again.

The great theme I suppose for the coming novel will be the relations of labor and capital. There is room enough for a half dozen authors to write on this subject, and if you ever think of taking it up I should like to talk to you about it. Perhaps there is no country in the world where the abuses of capital are so great as in this country, and where the strife for wealth is so eager, because the opportunities are great, and it is the one god that American society worships. On the other hand, there is no country where what we call Social-ism is likely to take so deep a root and flourish and grow strong as here. It has much [text cut off] and under our form of government, almost no repression. Just as surely as the relations between labor and capital were all wrong in our Southern states under the system of slavery just so surely are they wrong today throughout the entire country. We have tried to treat these great questions through narrations of facts. But when we have got at the facts we have found that the articles bristle all over with libel suits, and seem mere personal

<hr>

1. Charles Dudley Warner (1829–1900), American journalist, essayist, and novelist; he is perhaps best remembered for *The Gilded Age* (1873), which he co-authored with Samuel Clemens (Mark Twain). [*Editor.*]

attacks upon individuals, and, what is worse, were ineffective and uninteresting. Now we are waiting for the coming man to treat them through the medium of fiction. As Dickens[2] reformed the abuses in school life in England, and the Jewish quarter in London so some writer of fiction may yet do a great service in this country, and help to postpone if not prevent the great impending struggle between labor and capital.

Very truly yours<br>
ROSWELL SMITH

W. D. Howells Esq.

THE CENTURY CO.
33 East 17th Street,
New-York.

Mch. 21. 85

My dear Mr Howells:

Last night Mrs Roswell Smith and I had the great pleasure of reading aloud the June installment of Silas Lapham, and our enthusiasm over it is almost boundless. I think the toning down which you have given the proofs is an improvement. One minor criticism I would make. It seems to me I would not have the mother and daughter go to the druggist's to get the bromide—I notice you strike out the laudanum—for there is danger of that sort of suggestion being abused. Is there not a good opportunity to teach the lesson that in cases of such mental trouble, people had better go to the family doctor[3] who would prescribe a simple tonic and sedative, no more important than valerian, for example, though I do not suppose it is necessary to give the doctor's prescription. There is a chance even to let the old doctor give a needed word of warning against resorting to such things inadvisedly. I think this story of Silas Lapham is going to be recognized as the "coming novel" we hear so much about. You have him very much in the condition of the of the man who said he was on the frontier with a party, and when they encountered the Indians, they all separated like a flock of quails, knowing that was the only chance for any of them to escape. It happened however, that the entire party of Indians pursued his trail. They followed him up a ravine, until he came to an impassable wall—There his story ended. One of the excited listeners said—

---

2. Charles Dickens (1812–70), one of the most famous Victorian novelists, gave considerable impetus to social reforms through works like *Oliver Twist* (1837–38), which dealt with Poor Law abuses, and *Nicholas Nickleby* (1838–39), which drew attention to the maltreatment of children in the schools. [*Editor.*]

3. Both lessons—The spiritual adviser has been consulted—the cure of souls—but both are needed to "minister to a mind diseased—"[*Macbeth* V. iv. 40—*Editor.*]

"What did you do?" "Do! Why I died right there,—there was nothing else to do—there was no possible escape."

Now I do not know what you propose to do with Silas Lapham, but in the whole course of my business experience I never knew but one man who took to speculative gambling in business, and especially when he was in business trouble who did not at the same time begin to drink. I used to know the very beginnings of that sort of thing when I lived at the West, by the hot trembling hand. The only man I ever knew who recovered from the passion was a man of past sixty, and he had only given himself up to it for about two weeks. If you go on to the logical conclusion of Silas Lapham he will drink and go to the devil generally, and he will never give up his passion for gambling in business, pursuing the ignus fatuous[4] hope of recovering property. It seems to me that if he does retrieve his character the story will fail in the truth of daily experience, and that the opportunity for a splendid lesson will be lost if, the story ends too precipitately. It may be that you will have to write the business experience of Tom Corey, by way of showing the long miserable record of Silas Lapham's career as a business gambler. When that passion once gets hold of a man it never lets go. I have seen the best and brightest and truest, most honest, upright and conscientious Christian men, who have gone to their death in a few years as the simple result of beginning the career of a business gambler. The demoralization of conscience that comes from drink is bad enough, but the demoralization from the two—gambling and drink, is something frightful.

Of course I do not know your plans, but I should say that Silas Lapham was getting ready to sell the mill property to the British capitalists, concealing the fact of the railroad, and he might get enough to put him on his feet again, then, having got the passion for gambling, it would be impossible for him to resist trying just once more to make enough money to save the house—the result of course would be that he would lose everything, and then—destruction.[5] The story is full of moral lessons and so far, has not a false note in it.

One of the best things in this June installment is the splendid way in which you show up the demoralization of conscience as to divorce. Zerilla and her mother talk about the former getting a divorce and marrying another man as a servant girl and her mother might talk about getting another situation, & in the presence of husband No 1—! That is a good hit—

For a minor criticism, my wife suggests that when Silas comes home from Dubuque there should be a sentence indicating that he had left Irene at the West. I hope Irene is to marry the fellow who owns the Southern Plantation—

There is an old saw which says advice should not be given unless it

4. A false or misleading light. [*Editor*.]    5. Then he is ready to ruin Tom Corey—

be asked. You only asked me to read the installment, and I have volunteered to tell you what I think the situation requires. But now that I have forced myself to write this letter, I am tempted to put it in the fire, which probably you will do when you get it.

Very truly yours
ROSWELL SMITH

W. D. Howells Esq.

THE CENTURY CO.
33 East 17th Street,
New-York.

Mch. 24. 85

My dear Mr Howells:

I have your note of March 22d. Yes, there is a divine power which can reach down to us and which we can grasp, that can lift us out of ourselves. Here and there there is a man like Mr Gough[6] who escapes when the disease of drink has fast hold of him. I did not suppose that you proposed to teach that. I rejoice that you do. But this passion for gambling when once it takes hold of a man is more insidious than the passion for drink. It is so difficult to make a man see the wretchedness and the wickedness of it, and the line seems to him so vague and uncertain between legitimate business with all its risks, and that which is pure speculation and is condoned to everybody who is "successful" in it. Lest the way of escape should be deemed too easy, I suppose you will take care to make the reader and Lapham realize that in his escape he is one of a thousand—and well nigh a miracle.

Very truly yours
ROSWELL SMITH

THE CENTURY CO.
33 East 17th Street,
New-York.

April 6, 85

My dear Mr Howells:

Somebody said to me the other day that there must be a million of men in this country reading Silas Lapham. I queried the opinion, and he went on to say that of one thing he was sure, namely, that a larger number of persons in this country were reading that serial story than ever read a serial story before.

6. John Bartholomew Gough (1817–86), an English-born bookbinder who lived in New York, was saved from alcoholism by taking a temper-ance pledge. Beginning in 1842, he spent the rest of his life lecturing on behalf of temperance. [*Editor.*]

I send you an item cut from the Tribune of Saturday, which is only another illustration of the sad end of the men who get snared in stock gambling. Probably about the ending of your man Rogers. I did not know this Mr Lawrence, but I knew the firm, and also his brother and his guardian. In this connection it occurs to me to say to you that I knew a man who died of delirium tremens who, it was said, had never been drunk in his life, and whose own wife did not know that he was in the habit of drinking. Dr Holland also once told me of a similar case.

Very truly yours<br>Roswell Smith

W. D. Howells Esq.

# ROBIE MACAULEY

# Let Me Tell You About the Rich[†]

To start with there must have been, of course, Grandfather. His story has gone through perhaps as many versions as any American tale, from the glorification by Horatio Alger to damnation by the muckrakers. The 1860s through the 1880s were the years of his rise, the great golden tide of American fortunes. To cite just a few examples: in 1870 William Collins Whitney had been in New York but six years; by 1874 he was to make some $40 millions in the street railway business. In 1870 John D. Rockefeller's small brokerage business in Cleveland was just beginning to prosper. In 1882 Andrew Mellon became the proprietor of his father's Pittsburgh bank—forty years later he was worth between $1 and $2 billion. In 1887 Marshall Field bought out his partner in a Chicago department store and began to accumulate his eventual $130 million. Two of the most contrasting and most interesting Grandfather novels are William Dean Howells' *The Rise of Silas Lapham* and Dreiser's two-part book called *The Financier* and *The Titan*.

*Silas Lapham* is a curious case. In the textbooks of American literature Howells is always tagged as one of the "realists" who were just beginning to dominate fiction in the '70s and '80s—and indeed he had that look and tone. Yet in this story of a ruthless businessman who builds up a fortune and then, because of the most delicate moral compunctions, lets it be taken away, there is something very strange. Looking back on the age of the robber baron, one can only take it as a fantastically atypical piece of "realism."

[†]From *Kenyon Review*, 27 (Autumn 1965), 645–71.

I am not, of course, objecting to the novelists' old habit of taking exceptions. There may just have been that Phoenician who hated the sea, that French aristocrat who admired Robespierre, or that kind-hearted concentration camp commander. But in such cases the fiction writer must make absolutely plain that his subject is anomaly, that his hero is swimming against the current of his times. Howells, for what seems to me a fairly complicated reason, never does.

In 1875 Silas Lapham is one of the new rich men of Boston. His story began on a run-down New England farm where his father one day made the unlikely discovery of a paint mine. The father died poor, but the son, through sharp exploitation and good marketing methods, has risen remarkably fast. As the book begins, he is building a $100,000 house (a great sum in those days—a clerk in his office would make from $400 to $500 a year) in Back Bay, and is even beginning to have a few vague notions about mixing in Boston Society.

The question of Society gets its main exposition in the subplot about Tom Corey's courtship of one of Lapham's daughters—there is at first a small Victorian kind of confusion as to which one he has fallen in love with. The Coreys are an old Boston family, now somewhat on the downgrade, but Howells treats the matter of the acceptance of *nouveaux riches* very gently. Corey's father says:

> "But the suddenly rich are on a level with any of us nowadays. Money buys position at once. I don't say that it isn't all right. The world generally knows what it's about, and knows how to drive a bargain. I dare say it makes the new rich pay too much. But there's no doubt money is to the fore now. It is the romance, the poetry of our age."

There may be some parallel in the fact that Howells, the poor boy from Martin's Ferry, Ohio, found no great resistance in getting to know Hawthorne, Emerson, and Henry James, in being accepted by Boston Society, and in becoming editor of *The Atlantic Monthly*. He does include one comic scene of great embarrassment, a dinner at which Lapham drinks heavily and boasts loudly—but the Coreys remain tolerant even after that.

It is, however, in the main plot where Howells faces the more important issues of money and morality. Lapham's specter of guilt is a former partner, a certain Milton K. Rogers, whose capital Lapham used to found the paint company and whom he then forced out; it is a fairly typical chapter in the history of American business in that era. The woeful Rogers keeps turning up and Lapham keeps giving him a kind of conscience-money in the form of loans for new speculations. Finally these, combined with a number of business reverses, result in a very precarious financial position for Lapham.

There are, however, a number of solutions to the problem: he can accept some of Corey's money for new capital; he can hoodwink his chief competitors; he can sell off certain Western property at great profit to a pair of swindlers who plan in turn to defraud some English investors with it. With the most delicate ethical considerations in mind, Lapham rejects one after another of these escapes; in the end he crashes—with the sympathy and admiration of all around.

The same public that read *The Rise of Silas Lapham* could witness the wholesale business-political thievery of the Grant administration; it is no wonder that they wished to be reassured.[1] Silas Lapham's "rise" was not the financial one but the moral rise over temptation to dishonesty. Already beginning to have some doubts about the ethics of great fortune-building, Americans wanted an example of the businessman who let conscience triumph over greed—and Howells gave them a gentle portrait of one. The accumulation of money, he said, does not necessarily destroy a man's best motives. It need not corrupt. There is no inherent evil in it.

The lesson, of course, has its other side. Silas Lapham *did* go broke, didn't he? It proves again that nice guys finish last, doesn't it? But here is the strangest omission in Howells' fable; Lapham goes broke in a vacuum of moral choice, not in the competitive world of men. He is not—as so many were in those days—driven to make his desperate decision by more ruthless men who want to swallow him up and who care nothing about moral distinctions. It is as if Jay Gould and Commodore Vanderbilt had lived in vain.

Thus from silken rags to moral riches. Howells' "realism" in *Silas Lapham* is not much more respectable than Horatio Alger's; as Frank Norris[2] said, it is the "realism of the broken tea-cup." Its interest comes less from the fictional portrayal of the rich than from what it shows about a wishful popular conception of them. It suggests the forever-ambivalent attitude of Americans, who are charmed by the (public-relations inspired) vision of John D. Rockefeller passing out dimes to children and yet bitter against the malefactors of great wealth. Ours is a country that, in order to protect the chances of the poor and the workingman, puts its trust in millionaire presidents.

If I were to amuse myself by rewriting *Silas Lapham*, I should make it frankly into the typical Grandfather story it ought to be. All Americans of at least three generations are divided into two classes:

1. The administration of President Ulysses S. Grant (1869–77), was marred by corruption and dishonesty at the highest levels, although the chief fault directly attributable to Grant appears to have been his inability to choose trustworthy subordinates. [*Editor.*]

2: Frank (Benjamin Franklin) Norris (1870–1902), was an American "naturalistic" novelist whose major works include *McTeague* (1899) and *The Octopus* (1901). Macauley is referring to an article in *The Wave*, 15 (June 27, 1896) 3, in which Norris contrasts Howells with Zola, who deals in unleashed passions, blood, and sudden death in his romances. "The world of M. Zola is a world of big things; the enormous, the formidable, the terrible is what counts; no teacup tragedies here." [*Editor.*]

the huge grandfather-failed class and the small grandfather-struck-it-rich class. Members of the former are always telling each other how low General Motors shares were just at the time Grandfather went into United Buggywhip so heavily or how Grandfather just shook his head when Mr. McCormick asked him to put a little money into his funny-looking reaping machine. (My own great-grandfather once owned a 100-acre farm where the Chicago Loop is today. But, when the population of the town increased to several thousands, he complained of overcrowding and sold out.) So in my *Silas Lapham* I should continue on a few more chapters to show that, although Grandfather Lapham got great acclaim for going bust while guided by the highest moral principles (especially after that *Atlantic Monthly* fellow wrote a book about him), the actual dismal truth is that he failed because he was a bad businessman.

# Contemporary Responses

*The Rise of Silas Lapham* was serialized in the *Nation* during the winter of 1884 and the spring and summer of 1885. As the novel unfolded in the pages of the magazine, Roswell Smith assured Howells that his story was being read by more people than had ever read a serial story before. In addition to questionable advice from Smith about how he ought to conclude his story, Howells received many letters from other readers, most of them praising the novel and testifying to their pleasure in it. A letter from any pleased reader was always a great satisfaction to Howells, but he particularly enjoyed the responses of other writers whose judgments he respected. As the leading crusader in America for realism in literature, he championed the work of Henry James when it was far from popular and supported the aspirations of younger writers like Hamlin Garland, Stephen Crane, Owen Wister, and Harold Frederic. Their respect for his skill and artistic integrity were important to him.

As soon as the novel was published in book form it was reviewed in most of the literary magazines. The wide popular notice the serial had attracted was reflected in the widely, and sometimes violently, differing critical reactions it aroused. In one of the most sensible initial reviews, Horace Scudder wrote, in the *Atlantic*, that *The Rise of Silas Lapham* "offers a capital example of the difference between the permanent and the transient in art." Scudder saw that Howells was attempting to deal with serious social issues and, despite his graceful humor, to tell the truth. Other critics found the book not merely unamusing and unedifying, but positively vicious and depraved. The reviewer for the *Catholic World* complained that Howells "studies men and women as a naturalist does insects" and described his work as "the progress from man to the apes, from the apes to the worms, from the worms to bacteria, from bacteria to—mud. It is the descent to dirt."

To account for so passionate a denunciation of so genteel a novel one has to remember that as chief defender of realism in American fiction Howells was a kind of lightning rod; he attracted the anger of anyone who saw, or feared that he might soon see, the unpleasant realities of American manners, American capitalism, American "culture," American social diversity pictured in fiction. In its extreme form such criticism implied that literature, like all the arts, was a form of decoration, intended to make life more pleasant for those who could afford it, to comfort readers and help them to forget any unpleasant realities they might be aware of. The goal of such art was taken to be inspiration, and inspiration was best achieved by looking upward toward the ideal rather than downward toward the actual. Realists were accused of being mere photographers, incapable of communicating to their readers the beauty, the pathos, and the inspiration of life. Critics who held such views were influenced by the fact that in late nineteent-century America, taste and "culture" were largely the concern of women. The function of men was to run the affairs of the nation, to carry on trade, to make money. Women were in charge of truth, beauty, morals, culture, and refinement in general. (That attitude is clearly reflected in the Lapham family.)

But even writers, critics and professors who rejected the view that art was a woman's world and took art and literature seriously, sometimes felt that realistic literature was simply too narrow. It neglected the imagination, they claimed, and restricted itself too much to the ordinary, the average of experience. It neglected the heroic, the tragic, and the ideal. Hamilton Wright Mabie's article in the *Andover Review* is a classic statement of this view. It is a calm and reasoned exposition of a position that Mabie would have called "neo-humanist" and Howells would have called "romanticistic."

Howells continued to write and publish until his death in 1920. But whenever a critic reviewed his latest book or reassessed his career, *The Rise of Silas Lapham* was likely to be the standard against which his other works were measured. Howells' reputation as an innovator, a fighter for realism, even a threat to civilized literature, gradually faded, and by the second decade of the twentieth century he was widely regarded as a rather harmless old pussycat, at best charming, at worst dull. A failure to read his novels carefully (or even to remember the titles accurately) resulted in such articles as that in the *Westminster Review* in which the "smart young people" dismissed Howells' achievement because the realism for which he had done battle was now theirs to use free of charge and because they hadn't the wit to realize that Howells' irony was conscious and intentional. Even the affection and respect Forrest Reid shows for Howells serves to denigrate his work because the praise is directed to the most superficial qualities. He liked Howells' purr rather than his bite.

# Friends and Readers

## JOHN HAY

## Letter to W. D. Howells[†]

Cleveland

April 2. [1885]

My dear Howells

I can hardly believe it is I that have so long left a letter of yours unanswered; but I have so many cares of late days that I postpone my pleasures to them. . . .

But Lord love you, the man that wrote Silas Lapham is the man for my money. Mrs. Hay read me the last instalment a few evenings ago, and what with my admiration of the art of it, and my profound sympathy with Silas, I was so wrought up that I felt as if *I* had gone into company too fine for me and got drunk myself. It is awfully good—I am only seized with a terror as to how you are going to keep it up on this level. But of course you know what you are about & it will be a tremendous success.

The Boy thrives and Mrs. Hay sends her love to Mrs. Howells and you. . . .

Yours faithfully

JOHN HAY

†Unpublished letter in the Harvard College Library. As Lincoln's private secretary, John Hay (1838–1905) had been instrumental in securing for Howells the post of American Consul in Venice (1861–65). In addition to his distinguished political career (Secretary of State under McKinley and Theodore Roosevelt) Hay was a poet and novelist whose work Howells had admired in print.

## HENRY NORMAN

## Letter to W. D. Howells[†]

. . . University Club
Madison Square.

New York, April 14, 1885.

Dear Mr. Howells,

\* \* \*

Will you let me allow me to say to you, *sans phrases*,[1] how extremely good your April instalment[2] of "Silas Lapham" seems to me. I have seen nothing equal to it in modern realistic fiction—which is the only kind of modern fiction we care anything about. You have indeed caught "that intangible essence, the commonplace" (if I quote correctly), which is life. Heaven knows that instalment is pathetic enough, yet I made myself a nuisance to my fellow-travelers in a parlor car by laughing over it, too. And I have heard half a dozen people—literary people & judges of such things—express my own opinion about it.

\* \* \*

Yours faithfully,
HENRY NORMAN.

## WILLIAM JAMES

## Letter to W. D. Howells[†]

15 Appian Way
Cambridge, Mar 5. 85

My dear Howells,

Harry will no doubt be rather impatient to learn whether he is likely to lose much by Osgood's failure. If you know in your own case how matters are to stand, can't you tip him a line of information? Or can you tell me how to find out?

Which is most diabolical in a publisher, to pay an author a small percentage, or to promise him a large one & fail? They seem to be a fiendish crew anyhow.

†Unpublished letter in the Harvard College Library. Sir Henry Norman (1858–1939) was an English traveler and writer whose interest in American scenery and customs resulted in several books of memoirs and commentary.
1. *Sans phrases: (French)*, without commonplaces, directly. [*Editor.*]
2. Chapters XIII and XIV. [*Editor.*]
†Unpublished letter in the Harvard College Lib-

rary. William James (1842–1910) was the elder brother of the novelist Henry James and a distinguished philosopher-psychologist. His book *Pragmatism* (1907) did much to turn American thinking out of idealistic and into realistic channels. The first paragraph refers to the publisher James R. Osgood who was going through one of his periodic business reorganizations; both Howells and Henry James published with him.

Your are missed like the d———l at our club dinners. *Pray* come more often! I hope you're all well. I've only read the 1st 3 nos. of Silas Lapham so far, but have squealed with pleasure over every word of it. There isn't a dead line in it—and the endless geniality really nourishes one. I hope you're all well.

Affectly
WM JAMES

# HAROLD FREDERIC

## Letter to W. D. Howells[†]

LONDON OFFICE
NEW YORK TIMES.
203, STRAND, W.C.
May 5, 1885:

My dear sir:

At a private dinner here last evening, confined to some dozen professional men of whom I was the only American, the talk turned upon "The Rise of Silas Lapham", and the expressions of delight in it, and of admiration for it, were so cordial and warm that I yield to the temptation to write to you about them. The guests were mainly men of distinction—artists, writers, scientists and so on—and were certainly all men of fine discernment in literature. They talked a long time, upon many subjects, but upon nothing else was there nearly so much unanimity expressed, or feeling shown, as upon the proposition that in choice shading of character, in deftness of analysis of motives and feelings, and in the quality of life in dialogue, the work marked a distinct advance step in fiction.

They were not able to understand as well as I do, I think, how much more there is in the story—to realize that it means the scrutiny of a master turned for almost the first time upon what is the most distinctive phase of American folk life, but their praise was good to hear, all the same.

I hope you will like my having said this to you. If it impresses you as being a trifle gratuitous, pray explain it on the theory that I haven't borne transplanting very well, and that each one of the eleven months I have spent here has left me more tenaciously fond of all things American, and more intolerant of most things European, than it found me, so that when I *do* hear justice done by

†Unpublished letter in the Harvard College Library. Harold Frederic (1856–98) was a newspaper editor and novelist. His best-known work is *The Damnation of Theron Ware* (1896), a realistic portrayal of the moral confusion of a Methodist preacher. Howells spoke of the book as a major serious novel of which Americans could be proud.

Englishmen to the chief of American novelists I am too proud and glad to keep it to myself.

Faithfully Yours
HAROLD FREDERIC

W. D. Howells, esq.

## CLARENCE E. BUEL

### Letter to W. D. Howells[†]

Editorial Department
The Century Magazine
Union Square, New York

May 9, 1885

Dear Mr. Howells:

A friend of my youth, Mr. Frank B. Felt who is an officer of the Pullman Iron & Steel Co, writes me that he is also interested in a paint company and that you have sunk an imaginary shaft into their mine. He wishes to get even with you by jumping your claim to the name of "Silas Lapham" which he would like to adopt as the trade-mark of "a very superior quality of mineral paint" that they have just begun to manufacture. Hence he has chosen me as a buffer between him and your consent or refusal. My first impulse was to tell him that I thought you would not like to have the title of your book diverted to a commercial use; and then I thought it might interest you to know that Silas has not squelched competition by buying up the Virginia mine, and that a booming Illinois company would like to take *him* into partnership. Treat me as Silas treated Rogers if you like; but what shall I do with my client? He is a good fellow but I don't sympathize with his aspirations.

Yours sincerely
CLARENCE E. BUEL

## W. D. HOWELLS

### Letter to Clarence E. Buel[†]

302 Beacon st.,
Boston, May 11, 1885.

Dear Mr. Buel:

I am sorry that I can't consent to your friend's request, much as I should like to oblige him; but if he wishes to use the name, he can do

†Unpublished letter in the Harvard College Library

†Unpublished letter in the Robert Sinclair Collection, Miami University Library, Oxford, Ohio.

so without my consent. A mineral paint firm in N. Y. objected to my letting Lapham's paint be driven out because it had been identified with theirs from the first, and they didn't want it superseded by "some *cheap mud*"!

Please communicate my desire to your friend with my kindest thanks and regrets. But I really wish he wouldn't.

Yours cordially
W. D. HOWELLS.

# OWEN WISTER

## Letter to W. D. Howells[†]

402 Walnut st.
Thursday, May 21st.

My dear Mr. Howells:

If you are still at leisure to be so kindly disposed as you were last January, my cousin Mitchell will bring you the last fragment of MS., which I forward him to-day, & which finishes the thing. The first draft was finished more than a month ago—but I've been tinkering at it & condensing the whole book wherever I could—\* \* \* I am more grateful to you than I can say. Your remarks have had more influence on my really doubting estimation of what I've done, than anyone's would have had that I can think of. Perhaps this is because they took me by surprise with their favourableness. If you had been severer & less encouraging, I suppose I might have not believed you so easily!!

\* \* \*

We sit in our drawing room and read Silas Lapham aloud whenever it comes. If you like to hear lay readers give vent to their enthusiasm I wish you could hear my father & mother & all of us— And that clergyman the last time! The direct manner in which his impersonal common sense lays bare the obvious fact to those two poor people who are so involved & bedevilled that they can't see straight! Really, I can not tell you how we enjoy it, & how interested we are. One thing I'm going to ask you— Does young Corry see—or did he in earlier—say Nantasket days—see girls of his own class? Was he in the habit of dropping in to various houses in Beacon St—for 5 o'clock tea &c—or do you mean him so far to have been a man indifferent to female society? I ask this—for you never indicate or

†Unpublished letter in the Harvard College Library. Owen Wister (1860–1938) wrote many volumes of fiction, biography, and poetry. His best-known work is *The Virginian* (1902).

allude to any females of Corry's order. That is, I cannot remember any such allusion. I hope this question is not impertinent—

Yours very truly
OWEN WISTER

# HENRY JAMES

## Letter to W. D. Howells[†]

St Alban's Cliff
Bournemouth
May 23*d*

My dear Howells—

* * * I find in your note to my brother that I owe you two letters. Here is one without delay—if you will honour it by such a name. I am down here—& have been for weeks—looking after my sister who, I grieve to say, is in a wretched condition. * * * My only social resource—except that it is a social resource to be out of London in May & June—is Robert Louis Stevenson, who is more or less dying here & who (in case that event should take place) gave me the other day a message of a friendly—very friendly—character to give to you when I should next see you. I shall wait till then—it is too long for a short letter. He is an interesting, charming creature, but I fear at the end of his tether: though indeed less apparently near death than he has been at other times.

I congratulate you heartily on "Silas Lapham"—it has an immense reality & ranks among your highest flights. It is most remarkable. You do catch hold of life & give its impression. —I am sickened by the idiotic, impudent outcry against my tale[1] in the Century—a thing made up of the thinnest, airiest, rashest *guesswork*, & fains, fullest induction from glimpses of New England females in horse-cars 10 & 15 years ago—attacked on the ground of "personality" & invasion of privacy! The fault of my tale is its beastly ignorance & vagueness, as you will easily have perceived. Boston. I hope things are domestically well with you & am, with love to your wife, very faithfully yours

HENRY JAMES

---

. †Unpublished letter in the Harvard College Lib  1. *The Bostonians.* [*Editor.*]
rary.

# The Critics

## WILLIAM MORTON PAYNE

## Recent Fiction[†]

\* \* \*

Those who have been waiting impatiently for the completion of "The Rise of Silas Lapham" may now obtain it in book form, and renew an acquaintance which they have doubtless made to some extent already. If there are any who have resisted the temptation offered by the separate chapters of the story as they have appeared in the Century magazine, their reward is now at hand. We are inclined to think that Mr. Howells has never done anything better than this picture of the self-made American. The material offered him was unpromising enough, but he has bestowed upon it the genial touch of the artist, and made of his homely hero something which comes very near to being a veritable creation. It is almost a new species of work—one which might perhaps be styled the business man's novel—that Mr. Howells has done in this story, and the instant recognition which was accorded it even in its early stages indicates the truth and force of the presentation. People who do not care for novels ordinarily can hardly fail to like this one, and may say, with some sort of not unjust reflection upon novel-writing in general, that here at last are such people as one meets in every day life, and who talk in a natural and familiar way. The interest of such a story is not probably very lasting, but it is very great for the time being, or as long as people continue to talk and act in just the way which it describes.

\* \* \*

## [A Characteristically American Book][††]

\* \* \*

In defiance of his own dictum, Mr. Howells has contrived to tell a very good story in 'The Rise of Silas Lapham.' Obviously he has found some difficulty in making the most of it. He seems to have a

[†]From *The Dial*, 5 (September 1885), 122.
[††]Anonymous review in the *Athenaeum* [London], 12, September 1885, p. 334.

want of perception as to climax, and consequently he is rather wrong (to use a favourite expression of his) as to the point where he should conclude. The reader shuts the book with a sense of diluted interest, but he cannot say that the character of Silas Lapham is not fully developed. The book is characteristically American. English readers have been made sufficiently familiar with Boston life to appreciate Mr. Howells's picture; but they cannot fail to be amused by the *naïveté* of his hit at what he calls Daisy-Millerism while he is drawing a type which one might imagine to be no less irritating to Americans than the famous Daisy herself. It is, however, impossible to differentiate American sensibilities, and English people must be content to be amused. Irene Lapham is delicious. Going over her father's half-finished house, she consults a young man about the library. "I presume with nice bindings it will look very well. . . . I presume we shall have to have Gibbon. . . . We had a great deal about him at school. I believe we had one of his books. . . . Is it Gibbon or Gibbons? . . . I presume we shall have to have Scott's works. . . . He isn't American, though?. . . I always get him mixed up with Cooper." At another place the father points out the advantages of a certain bay window, and tells the young man that the room is to be his girl's room. "It seemed terribly intimate. Irene blushed deeply and turned her head away." Beside such delicacy as this 'Paul et Virginie'[1] itself would seem coarse. But Mr. Howells may be trusted not to exaggerate. The book opens admirably with a quite original device for getting over the standing difficulty of giving the necessary preliminary account of the chief character. Silas Lapham is interviewed by a lively reporter, who effectually prevents his victim from being dull. Mr. Howells's careful attention to details and to the machinery of his story is observable throughout. Every character is perfect in its way, and only on a few occasions does the writer slip into the American habit of overdoing the study of a person's state of mind. Once or twice, however, he has seemed to forget the clever little bit of criticism on George Eliot put into the mouth of one of his girls: "I wish she would let you find out a little about the people for yourself."

\* \* \*

# HORACE SCUDDER

## Recent American Fiction[†]

While a novelist is living and at work, his growth in power is more interesting to critics than the expression of that power in any one

---

1. *Paul et Virginie* (1787), a romance by Bernardin de St. Pierre (1737–1814) in which the heroine loses her life in a shipwreck because she would rather drown than disrobe in public and swim to safety. [*Editor.*] From the *Atlantic Monthly*, 56 (October 1885). 554–56.

piece of work. The Rise of Silas Lapham would probably affect a reader who should make Mr. Howells's acquaintance through it, in a different manner from what it does one who has followed Mr. Howells, as so many have, step by step, ever since he put forth his tentative sketches in fiction. We do not think that Mr. Howells has kept back the exercise of certain functions until he should have perfected his faculty of art by means of lighter essays, but that, in the process of his art, he has partly discovered, at any rate has convinced himself of the higher value to be found in a creation which discloses morals as well as manners. An art which busies itself with the trivial or the spectacular may be ever so charming and attractive, but it falls short of the art which builds upon foundations of a more enduring sort. A pasteboard triumphal-arch that serves the end of a merry masque is scarcely more ephemeral than the masque itself in literature.

The novel before us offers a capital example of the difference between the permanent and the transient in art. Had Mr. Howells amused himself and us with a light study of the rise of Silas Lapham in Boston society, what a clever book he might have made of it! We should have chuckled to ourselves over the dismay of the hero at the failure of the etiquette man to solve his problems, and have enjoyed a series of such interior views as we get in the glimpse of Irene "trailing up and down before the long mirror in *her* new dress [Mr. Howells never seems quite sure that we shall put the emphasis where it belongs without his gentle assistance], followed by the seamstress on her knees; the woman had her mouth full of pins, and from time to time she made Irene stop till she could put one of the pins into her train;" we should have followed the fluctuations of pride and affection and fastidiousness in the Corey family, and have sent a final shuddering thought down the vista of endless dinner parties which should await the union of the two houses. All this and much more offered materials for the handling of which we could have trusted Mr. Howells's sense of humor without fear that he would disappoint us.

But all this is in the story; only it occupies the subordinate, not the primary place, and by and by the reader, who has followed the story with delight in the playful art, discovers that Mr. Howells never intended to waste his art on so shallow a scheme, that he was using all this realism of Boston society as a relief to the heavier mass contained in the war which was waged within the conscience of the hero. When in the final sentence he reads: "I don't know as I should always say it paid; but if I done it, and the thing was to do over again, right in the same way, I guess I should have to do it," he recognizes, in this verdict of the faithfully illiterate Colonel, the triumphant because unconscious attainment of a victory which justifies the title of the story. No mere vulgar rise in society through the marriage of a daughter to a son of a social prince, or the possession of a house on the water side of Beacon Street, would serve as a real conclusion to the history of a character like that of Silas Lapham; as if to flout such an idea, the marriage when it comes is stripped of all possible social consequences, and the house is burned to the ground. In place of so trivial an end there is a fine subjection of the mean and ignoble, and as in Balzac's César Birotteau,[1] a man of accidental vulgarity discloses his essential nobility; with this added virtue in the case of Mr. Howells's hero, that we see the achievement of moral solvency unglorified by any material prosperity, and the whole history of the rise unadorned by any decoration of sentiment.

We have intimated that this bottoming of art on ethical foundations is a late development in Mr. Howells's work. In truth, this is but the second important example. An Undiscovered Country hinted at the possibility of there being other things than were dreamt of in the philosophy of light-minded young women, but it has always seemed to us that the book suffered from its use of an essentially ignoble parody of human far-sightedness. The real break which Mr. Howells made in his continuity of fiction was in A Modern Instance. That book suffered from too violent an effort at change of base. With all our respect for the underlying thought, a respect which we tried to make clear when we reviewed the book, we think that the author's habit of fine discrimination misled him into giving too much value in his art to the moral intention and too little to the overt act. The casual reader of A Modern Instance failed to be sufficiently impressed by the enormity of Bartley Hubbard's guilt.[2] Mr. Howells was carrying over into the region of ethical art the same delicate methods which he had used so effectively in social art. But in affairs which touch the surface of life, such as etiquette, dress, the conventions of society in general, the difference between tweedledum and tweedledee is enormous, while the moment one pushes off into the deeper currents of impassioned human life, mere casuistry ceases to interest one who is struggling with vital problems. A close observer might accept at its real valuation Mr. Howells's reading of those penetrating words of the interpreter of the moral law which made sin to consist in the unacted thoughts of the heart, and found a man who was angry with his brother without a cause to be no better than a murderer; but the rough and ready critic would be impatient at an

<hr/>

1. César Birotteau, protagonist of *Historie de la grandeur et la décadence de César Birotteau* (1838), by Honoré Balzac (1799–1850); Birotteau, aided by his wife, gains some success in the world, then loses everthing because of unsuccessful business dealings; he spends the remainder of his life paying off the debts incurred by his bankruptcy. [*Editor.*]

2. Bartley Hubbard marries a woman whom he does not really love, entangles himself in a series of unethical business transactions, and then abandons wife and child and absconds with borrowed money. He tries surreptitiously to obtain a divorce and is finally shot by a victim of his scandalous journalism. [*Editor.*]

art which seemed to make no distinction between the little and the great in misdemeanor. Nor do we think such a critic unreasonable. If we are to have a portraiture of moral baseness, we have a right to ask for some shadows so deep as to leave no doubt of their meaning, instead of a multitude of little spots of darkness, any one of which may be indicative of turpitude, but all of which taken together do not accumulate into anything more than a character which repels one by its generally ignoble quality.

Was Mr. Howells faintly asserting his continued belief in the artistic justification of Bartley Hubbard, when he introduced him anew in this last story? If he was, we are much obliged to him for not pressing his acquaintance farther upon us. Still, we are so far obliged to him that we must thank him for supplying by means of the juxtaposition a possible comparison between Hubbard and Lapham. They are both self-made men, but Hubbard is essentially vulgar, while Lapham is only accidentally so; the former thrusts his vulgarity through the thin covering of education and aptitude for the world, the latter thrusts his essential manliness through the equally thin covering of an uneducated manner and a hopeless condition of social outlawry.

Nevertheless, though there can be no mistaking Mr. Howells's intention in this novel, and though he uses his material with a firmer hand, we confess, now that we are out of the immediate circle of its charm, that The Rise of Silas Lapham suffers from the same defect as A Modern Instance. The defect is not so obvious, but it arises from the same super-refinement of art. In brief, Silas Lapham, a man of coarse grain and excessive egotism, is, in the crucial scenes, treated as a man of subtlety of thought and feeling. We do not say that the turnings and windings of his conscience, and his sudden encounters with that delicious Mephistopheles, Milton K. Rogers, are not possible and even reasonable; but we complain that the author of his being, instead of preserving him as a rustic piece of Vermont limestone with the soil clinging to it, has insisted upon our seeing into the possibilities of a fine marble statue which reside in the bulk. Moreover, when one comes to think of it, how little the rise of this hero is really connected with the circumstances which make up the main incidents of the story. The relations with Rogers, out of which the moral struggle springs, are scarcely complicated at all by the personal relations with the Corey family arising from the love of young Corey for Penelope Lapham. The Colonel goes through the valley of tribulation almost independently of the fact that he and his are sojourning meanwhile in another half grotesque vale of tears.

This same over-refinement of motive, as supposed in natures which are not presumably subtle, impresses us in the whole history of Penelope's love affair. We feel, rather than are able to say why we feel it, that there is something abnormal in the desolation which falls upon the entire Lapham family in consequence of Irene's blindness and Penelope's over-acuteness. We frankly confess that when reading the scenes, it seemed all right, and we gave ourselves up to the luxury of woe without a doubt as to its reality. But when *thinking* about them (forgive the italics), it seems an exaggeration, a pressing of the relations between these interesting people beyond the bounds of a charitable nature.

But when all is said, we come back with satisfaction to the recollection that Mr. Howells has distinctly set before himself in this book a problem worth solving, and if his statement and solution are presented with an art which has heretofore been so cunning as quite to reconcile one to the fragility of the object under the artist's hand, and this art still seems sometimes to imply the former baselessness, we can at least thank our stars that when we criticise such a book as The Rise of Silas Lapham, we are dealing with a real piece of literature, which surely will not lose its charm when the distinctions of Nankeen Square and Beacon Street have become merely antiquarian nonsense.

# [A Literal, Merciless Representation]†

In 'The Rise of Silas Lapham' Mr. Howells depicts one character distinctively of his time, aggressively of his nation, with a vividness and completeness unapproached in contemporary English fiction, apparently unapproachable by any contemporary writer in the English tongue. Silas Lapham, standing beside Bartley Hubbard, will at least postpone that oblivion which, as a graceful talker in the story says, overwhelms all authors, poor fellows, at last. And perhaps Lapham and Hubbard will get their full meed of praise from remote posterity only. Just now, with so many of them about, it is difficult to find a large public able to appreciate them unreservedly without doing violence to domestic affections. For Lapham is no more a creature of the imagination than Hubbard. He is a literal, merciless representation. With the representation is blended a searching and comprehensive interpretation. Directing and perfecting both is the quick, subtle, mocking spirit of the author, flashing in a phrase or comparison, gleaming in a jest at the sober unconsciousness of the subject who provides the opportunity. From the cleverness of Lapham as literary work it is as impossible to detract as it is to dispute the antipathy his personality excites in people of good taste, or to deny his practical virtues. His almost unmitigated offensiveness is a large part of his truth. His vulgarity is neither exaggerated nor

†Anonymous review in *The Nation*, 45 (22 October 1885), 347–48.

underestimated. To impress his conviction that there is no finer thing in God's universe than Lapham's Mineral Paint, is not to belittle either the quality or quantity of his sentiment. Even to have endowed him with more moral courage than an inherited New England conscience entails and the alert eye of the Puritan wife enforces, would have been to diminish the force of the portrait and to negative its sincerity. Except in literary form, it has, of course, no beauty. And it is in this studied ignoring of beauty, this expenditure of power on the essentially unbeautiful, that the Realist of the passionless every-day falls short of high or good art. There is no inspiration for any one in the character of Silas Lapham. It rouses no tender or elevating emotion, stirs no thrill of sympathy, suggests no ideal of conduct, no notion that the world at large is or can be any less ugly than Lapham and his paint. If it is to be conceded that Mr. Howells and his school are great artists in the highest reaches of their art, then the language is in sore need of words to define Sir Walter Scott and Thackeray.

What has been said of the perfection of Lapham's delineation cannot be applied to all the characters of the novel. Bromfield Corey is a charming contrasting figure, but touched very lightly. Tom Corey, too, commands respect for his persistence in an unpromising love-affair, if not for his taste in the choice of a sweetheart. But the women, especially the young women, are deplorably unattractive, and, moreover, if they represent any truth, it is only half a truth, and the worst half at that. If the young women introduced by Mr. Howells in the novels wherein he stands committed to Realism are representative, the "Woman Movement" in New England should be towards reform of temper and restriction of the freedom of the tongue. But we are disposed to imagine that Boston girls are neither dolts nor vixens, that the passion of jealousy does not rage in their breasts to the exclusion of any other, and that all, whether well-bred Coreys or Laphams of no breeding at all, are not habitually impertinent to their elders, more especially to their helpless, hapless mothers. Here the most unpleasant and the most unnatural girl is Penelope Lapham. Mrs. Corey said she was a "thoroughly disagreeable young woman," and Mrs. Corey did not know that what is called her "drolling" was most brilliant when she was ironically snubbing her relations, or urging her sister to inextinguishable laughter by mimicking their father. Irene Lapham, the beauty, is probably the most extraordinary girl ever graduated from a Boston grammar-school. She mentally connected Sir Walter Scott with a school-fellow who, she said, had a habit of apostrophizing him, prefixing "great" to his name, and she but vaguely conjectured that he was not an American. In a recent speech before a woman's college, Mr. Lowell[1]

---

1. James Russell Lowell (1819–91), American poet, essayist, and critic. [*Editor.*]

said, encouragingly, that he believed they could educate women there who would know the difference between literature and books. If Irene Lapham is not a gross caricature, that college must beware of girls from the Boston grammar-schools, else fulfilment of Mr. Lowell's rosy vision is far off indeed.

The slightest review of this novel would be incomplete without a reference to the illustration of those class barriers in America which excite hostility in the mass of citizens in a republic, and derision or affected incredulity in the subjects of a monarchy. These social distinctions, which are natural and not artificial, have, of course, been harped on by many novelists—grotesquely exaggerated by one or two. Mr. Howells makes their existence and their reason of existence perfectly clear by the simple method of illustrative contrast. Even in a republic—indeed, most of all in a republic—the Laphams are compelled to realize that there are social privileges which money cannot buy. Mr. Howells would have done well to let his effective argument go without comment. But in a paragraph summing up the whole matter he says: "It is certain that our manners and customs go for more in life than our qualities." As an aphorism on society this would be a truism; by extending it to life, the author is narrowing life down to availability as a diner-out.

# [Novel-Writing as a Science][†]

Mr. Howells, the *The Rise of Silas Lapham*, takes several occasions to give vent to his theory of novel-writing. He does well. What he and his kind are really driving at when they write novels is something that many people have been puzzling to find out. It is a good thing that at last he should formulate his purpose in more or less plain black and white. In the following conversation about novels Mr. Howells gives us many hints of his belief:

> 'It's astonishing,' said Charles Bellingham, 'how we do like the books that go for our heart-strings. And I really suppose that you can't put a more popular thing than self-sacrifice into a novel. We do like to see people suffering sublimely.'
> 'There was talk, some years ago,' said James Bellingham, 'about novels just going out.'
> 'They're just coming in!' cried Miss Kingsbury.
> 'Yes,' said Mr. Sewell, the minister, ' and I don't think there ever was a time when they formed the whole intellectual experience of more people. They do greater mischief than ever.'
> 'Don't be envious, parson,' said the host.
> 'No,' answered Sewell, 'I should be glad of their help. But these

† Anonymous review in the *Athenaeum* [London] 12 September 1885, p. 334.

novels with old-fashioned heroes and heroines in them—excuse me, Miss Kingsbury—are ruinous! . . . The novelists might be the greatest possible help to us if they painted life as it is, and human feelings in their true proportion and relation; but for the most part they have been, and are, altogether noxious.'

This seemed sense to Lapham; but Bromfield Corey asked: 'But what if life as it is isn't amusing? Aren't we to be amused?'

'Not to our hurt,' sturdily answered the minister.

We cannot help fancying—the similarity of the names Sewell and Howells seems to favor the notion—that in the character of this minister Mr. Howells himself aspires to enact the part of Greek chorus to his story. At any rate, it is plain from the above passage that Mr. Howells regards the profession of the novelist as quite missionary; and his minister confirms this conclusion by several other dogmatisms. In fact, he uses a crisis of the story to point the moral of his theory, and one of the most vivid impressions taken from *The Rise of Silas Lapham* is that of the Rev. Mr. Sewell, with the air of a Boston Chadband,[1] delivering a severe homily to a pair of old people on the part played by the novels of the old fashion in creating the love-tangle between their children that they have come to consult him about.

It is really very commendable of Mr. Howells to take this high and severe view of his mission in life. And there are many reasons why it is important that we should watch with interest how he proceeds when he sets out to teach the world the way novels ought to be written. There is no use denying it, light literature forms an enormous share—perhaps, with the newspapers, the entire amount—of the reading done by a large mass of our people; and it is useless to pretend that such constant dropping does not wear an impress on the minds and consciences on which it falls. The fact may be deplored, but it is a fact nevertheless and should be recognized. And since it is ever the aim of the church to seize the weapons of the enemy and turn them against himself, there is no reason why light literature should form an exception. The novelist who can handle his art so as at the same time to delight and to better his readers performs a mighty and a good work. Mr. Howells' minister is almost right in placing his influence as next to that of the clergyman.

Mr. Howells has never hesitated to roundly express his contempt for the methods of all the novelists that preceded him. It is not very long ago since he wrote that he and Mr. Henry James, Jr., were the only novelists who understood their business; all others, even Thackeray and Dickens, were only tinkers at the art as compared with these accomplished craftsmen. He goes still further now, and declares in effect that what the others wrote were not novels at all.

1. Chadband is a character in Dickens' *Bleak House*, a pious and eloquent humbug. [*Editor.*]

"Novels are only just coming in," says one of his characters, meaning the novels of Mr. Howells and Mr. James.

This is a great deal to undertake; but Mr. Howells means what he says. His method of writing novels is certainly revolutionary, and we have seen that he writes them with the hope of serving a praiseworthy end. Let us take a glance at Mr. Howells' method, and see whether it is calculated to serve the end he has in view.

The revolution attempted by Mr. Howells is as simple as it is great. He regards novel-writing as science and not as art.

This is, perhaps, a natural outcome of what Mr. Spencer[2] would call heredity and environment. The Puritan mind is scientific, analytical. It is too severe and cold and suspicious to fuse into the constructive enthusiasm of art. And the last thing it would dream of would be to pursue art for art's sake, or even science for the sake of science alone. It must have an object in view, some useful end to serve. Thus it is curious to note how the Puritan mind in Mr. Howells, finding itself, by a freak of circumstance, working at an art, takes it strongly in its hands and transforms it into a science, and a science intended to have a useful application.

Two men study some object in nature, say a plant. One of them will drink in with his eye all its visible beauty, its form, its color, the stirring of the wind and the delicate play of light and shade among its leaves. He seizes a brush and with a few bold strokes reproduces all these traits upon a canvas. That is Art. The other observer plucks up the plant by the roots and brings it home to his herbarium. There he makes minute and careful diagrams of it, probably with the aid of a camera. He measures it and weighs it. He cuts it up into sections and makes drawings of the sections. He analyzes the clay at its roots, he counts its juices and tests for acids in them. That is Science; and therein lies the difference between the novel-writing of, say, Nathaniel Hawthorne and novel-writing as Mr. Howells pursues it.

In this way Mr. Howells has produced the most scientifically realistic novel that has yet been written. M. Zola's[3] books are as the awkward gropings of an amateur compared with this finished treatise. The field that Mr. Howells takes for his investigation is, he tells us, "the commonplace." By studying "the common feelings of common people" he believes he "solves the riddle of the painful earth."

2. Herbert Spencer (1820–1903), English essayist and social philosopher, whose book *First Principles* (1862) did much to popularize the ideas of evolution and of the influence of heredity and environment on individual and social behavior. [*Editor*.]
3. Émile Zola (1840–1902), chief proponent of the French "naturalistic" school of fiction. In his principal group of works, "Les Rougon-Macquart," Zola traced the histories of two French families as their lives were shaped by environment and heredity. Zola's novels were frequently criticized and condemned for their stark realism and joylessly deterministic view of life. [*Editor*.]

Silas Lapham is a type of the self-made American. He has grown rich through the instrumentality of a mineral paint of which he is the proprietor. He lives in Boston and entertains social ambitions for his wife and two daughters. Bromfield Corey is a Boston aristocrat with a wife, two daughters, and a son. The Laphams and the Coreys are thrown together in consequence of a contemplated misalliance between young Corey and one of the Lapham daughters; and in the contrasts and developments that appear among all these "types" is supposed to consist the main interest of the story. There are no incidents that are not sternly commonplace, but everything connected with these incidents and their psychological effect on the actors is analyzed and detailed with microscopic accuracy.

The realism of Mr. Howells has been compared to photography, it is so exact and so minute. We do not think this is a fair criticism. Exactitude and minuteness are not to be quarrelled with on the score of art. They are admissible, and have been admitted, into the finest art. No photograph can be more exact and minute than the little canvases of Meissonier,[4] and the undue rendering of detail does not offend critics in the works of pre-Raphaelite artists.[5] If Mr. Howells adhered to the principles of art, placing the details in their proper perspective, and so forth, we think he should be welcome to as many of them as he pleased. Tourguénieff,[6] in some of his scenes, manages not to omit a single detail, but he manages it with such artistic feeling and skill that the effect is like that of a picture by Meissonier.

Photography is too near akin to art—even though it be a relationship by the left hand—to be used as a comparison for any work of Mr. Howells'. Photography, as generally understood and practised, aims first of all at the picturesque. Art is the sun that warms its horizon; to be as close an imitation of art as possible is its highest aspiration. Now, Mr. Howells, though a mechanic—an anatomist, shall we say?—of exquisite skill, despises art. Therefore his work should be compared rather to a series of scientific diagrams than to photographs. It is not Mr. Howells' details that offend the artistic eye; it is the plans, the sections, the front elevations, the isometric projections he gives of his subjects.

He studies men and women as a naturalist does insects. We read his book on the manners, habits, sensations, nerves of a certain set of

---

4. Jean Louis Ernest Meissonier (1815–91), highly successful French painter whose works typically dealt with domestic or anecdotal subjects. [*Editor.*]
5. The Pre-Raphaelites were a group of mid-Victorian artists and critics, including William Holman Hunt, John Everett Millais, and Dante Gabriel Rossetti, who sought to restore art to its former high role by scrupulous study of natural objects and the portrayal of morally uplifting subjects. [*Editor.*]
6. Ivan Sergeyevich Turgenev (1818–83), a Russian novelist whose "realistic" technique involved a minimum of authorial intrusion, had considerable influence on such writers as Henry James and Howells. [*Editor.*]

people as we might a treatise on the coleoptera.[7] And he investigates and expounds his theme with the same soullessness and absence of all emotion. Even Mr. Henry James, beside this chilly *savant*, appears quite a child of sentiment. He is capable of receiving "impressions"—which, in Mr. Howells' eyes, would be a most unscientific weakness—and he manages to retain some smack of art about the work he does.

Is this kind of novel-writing an elevating pursuit? and is the reading of it beneficial? To these two queries the answer must be emphatically, No.

Novels like *Silas Lapham* mark a descent, a degradation. Of course art is debased when it has fallen so low into realism. Art is ever pointing upward, and the influence of true art upon man is to make him look upward, too, to that vast where his Ideal sits,

—pinnacled in the lofty ether dim,

where all is beautiful, but where all is immmeasurable by him until he beholds it with his glorified intelligence. Science points downward, and when science is unguided by religion it leads its followers lower and lower into the mud beneath their feet. And even as we see some scientists making a distinct "progress" downward from the study of the higher to that of the lower forms of animal life, so in the novel-writing of Mr. Howells we can already mark this scientific decadence. He began with people who were not quite commonplace, whose motives and acts and ideas were a little bit above the common. He now declares that nothing is worthy to be studied but the common feelings of common people; and having begun *Silas Lapham* with people who were inoffensively commonplace, he was unable to finish the book without falling a stage lower. Towards the end he introduces a young woman who speaks thus of her husband: "If I could get rid of Hen I could manage well enough with mother. Mr. Wemmel would marry me if I could get the divorce. He said so over and over again." He introduces a scene in which this young woman, her tipsy sailor-husband, her drunken mother, and Silas Lapham as the family benefactor, figure—a scene that, for hopeless depravity both in the author and subject, out-Zolas Zola. The old woman, who has a bottle in her hand, complains of her son-in-law not giving the daughter an opportunity to obtain a divorce. " 'Why don't you go off on some them long v'y'ges?' s'd I. It's pretty hard when Mr. Wemmel stands ready to marry Z'rilla and provide a comfortable home for us both—I han't got a great many years more to live, and I *should* like to get more satisfaction out of 'em and not be beholden and dependent all my days—to have Hen, here, blockin' the way. I tell him there'd be more money for him in the end; but he can't seem to make up his

---

7. Coleoptera, scientific designation for the    belong. [*Editor.*]
order of class Insecta to which all true beetles

mind to it." Again says this old harridan: "Say, Colonel, what should you advise Z'rilla do about Mr. Wemmel? I tell her there an't any use goin' to the trouble to git a divorce without she's sure about him. Don't you think we'd ought to git him to sign a paper, or something, that he'll marry her if she gits it? I don't like to have things goin' at loose ends the way they are. It an't sense. It an't right." Before Mr. Howells reaches the end of the book he makes even the worthy Mrs. Lapham suspect her husband of infidelity and make a scene, accusing him, in the hearing of her children. It has seldom been our duty to read a book whose moral tone was so unpleasantly, so hopelessly bad; it is a book without heart or soul, neither illumined by religion nor warmed by human sympathy. This is all the more astonishing that Mr. Howells seems convinced that he is fulfilling a high moral purpose in writing it. It might be explicable on the theory that it was the legitimate outcome of the doctrine of total depravity; but it is more probably the logic of the downward progress of godless science. We shall not be surprised if the next book of Mr. Howells deal with characters and feelings that shall be so far below the commonplace from which he has already fallen that even M. de Goncourt[8] will not enjoy reading about them. It is the progress from man to the apes, from the apes to the worms, from the worms to bacteria, from bacteria to—mud. It is the descent to dirt.

But the consolation in regarding Mr. Howells' work is that it is bound to sicken of its own poison. It cannot do any appreciable damage to the novel-reading public, for the very good reason that the novel-reading public, when the present access of curiosity has subsided, are not likely to read it. The force of the novel consists in its popularity, and the popularity of the novel depends on certain well-defined elements, all of which Mr. Howells discards from his work. Dramatic action, surprising plot, thrilling and unusual incidents, interesting and uncommonplace characters, breadth of scene—all of these, among many other things, people look for in their novels, for they look to their novels to take them out of themselves, out of their everyday lives, and to lead them into other worlds for the time being. In these and similar things lies the novel's mighty and subtle spell; and the only way the reformer can succeed in this field is by snatching this spell from the hands of the evil-worker and using it himself as a beneficent power. Mr. Howells seems to have as great a horror of such sorcery as his Puritan forbears had of the arts of the witches of Salem. Therefore he can never hope to reach the class he expects to benefit by his new style of literature. People read novels to be amused, and he hotly repudiates the intention of amusing them. People read novels because they are

8. Edmond de Goncourt (1822–96), in collaboration with his brother Jules (1830–70), wrote novels and criticism that led eventually to the "naturalism" of Émile Zola. [*Editor.*]

"light literature." Mr. Howells offers them heavy literature. Instead of reforming the novel he has transformed it, so that what he produces is not a novel at all. Consequently the people who want novels will not want Mr. Howells'; and this is surely a relief to know. Mr. Howells will be read only by a species of scientific and hard-minded people, which we are led to understand flourishes best in Boston; and this species is past harming. But such a class of readers would be just as well, if not better, satisfied if Mr. Howells called his work by its right name—a treatise—and not by its pseudonym; and it would simplify matters if the scientific school generally were to label their books "Treatise on Commonplace People," "Treatise on Drabs," "Treatise on Drunkards," and so on, as they went through the catalogue.

# HAMILTON WRIGHT MABIE

## A Typical Novel[†]

In "The Rise of Silas Lapham" Mr. Howells has given us his best and his most characteristic work; none of his earlier stories discloses so clearly the quality and resources of his gift or his conception of the novelist's art. As an expression of personal power and as a type of the dominant school of contemporary fiction in this country and in France, whence the special impulse of recent realism has come, this latest work of a very accomplished and conscientious writer deserves the most careful and dispassionate study. If Mr. Howells's work possessed no higher claim upon attention, its evident fidelity to a constantly advancing ideal of workmanship would command genuine respect and admiration; whatever else one misses in it, there is no lack of the earnestness which concentrates a man's full power on the thing in hand, nor of the sensitive literary conscience which permits no relaxation of strength on subordinate parts, but exacts in every detail the skill and care which are lavished on the most critical unfoldings of plot or disclosures of character. Mr. Howells evidently leaves nothing to the chance suggestion of an inspired moment, and takes nothing for granted; he verifies every insight by observation, fortifies every general statement by careful study of facts, and puts his whole force into every detail of his work. In spite of its· evident danger in any save the strongest hands, there is a tonic quality in this exacting conscientiousness which writers of a different school often lack, and the absence of which is betrayed by hasty, unbalanced, and incomplete workmanship. It is this quality which discovers itself

[†]From the *Andover Review*, 4 (November 1885), 417–29.

more and more distinctly in Mr. Howells's novels in a constant development of native gifts, a stronger grasp of facts, and a more comprehensive dealing with the problems of character and social life to which he has given attention. In fact, this popular novelist is giving thoughtful readers of his books a kind of inspiration in the quiet but resolute progress of his gift and his art; a progress stimulated, no doubt, by success, but made possible and constant by fidelity to a high and disinterested ideal.

Nor has Mr. Howells spent his whole force on mere workmanship; he has made a no less strenuous endeavor to enlarge his knowledge of life, his grasp of its complicated problems, his insight into the forces and impulses which are the sources of action and character. If he has failed to touch the deepest issues, and to lay bare the more obscure and subtle movements of passion and purpose, it has been through no intellectual willfulness or lassitude; he has patiently and unweariedly followed such clews as he has been able to discover, and he has resolutely held himself open to the claims of new themes and the revelations of fresh contacts with life. The limitations of his work are also the limitations of his insight and his imagination, and this fact, fully understood in all its bearings, makes any effort to point out those limitations ungracious in appearance and distasteful in performance; if personal feeling were to control in such matters, one would content himself with an expression of hearty admiration for work so full of character, and of sincere gratitude for a delicate intellectual pleasure so varied and so sustained. The evidence of a deepened movement of thought is obvious to the most hasty backward glance from "The Rise of Silas Lapham" and "A Modern Instance" to "Their Wedding Journey" and "A Chance Acquaintance." In the early stories there is the lightness of touch, the diffused and delicate humor, which have never yet failed Mr. Howells; but there is little depth of sentiment, and almost no attempt to strike below the surface. These slight but very delightful tales discover the easy and graceful play of a force which deals with trifles as seriously as if it were handling the deepest and most significant problems of life. Seriousness is, indeed, the habitual mood of this novelist, and in his early stories it was the one prophetic element which they contained. There is a progressive evolution of power through "The Lady of the Aroostook," "The Undiscovered Country," "Dr. Breen's Practice," and "A Modern Instance"; each story in turn shows the novelist more intent upon his work, more resolute to hold his gift to its largest uses, more determined to see widely and deeply. His purpose grows steadily more serious, and his work gains correspondingly in substance and solidity. The problems of character which he sets before himself for solution become more complex and difficult, and, while there is nowhere a really decisive closing with life in a determined struggle to wring from it its secret, there is an evident purpose to grapple with realities and to keep in sympathy and touch with vital experiences.

In "The Rise of Silas Lapham" Mr. Howells has made a study of social conditions and contrasts everywhere present in society in this country; not, perhaps, so sharply defined elsewhere as in Boston, but to be discovered with more or less definiteness of outline in all our older communities. His quick instinct has fastened upon a stage of social evolution with which every body is familiar and in which everybody is interested. The aspect of social life presented in this story is well-nigh universal; it is real, it is vital, and it is not without deep significance; in dealing with it Mr. Howells has approached actual life more nearly, touched it more deeply, and expressed it more strongly than in any of his previous stories. The skill of his earliest work loses nothing in his latest; it is less evident because it is more unconscious and, therefore, more genuine and effective. There is the same humor, restrained and held in check by the major interests of the story, but touching here and there an idiosyncrasy, an inconsistency, a weakness, with all the old pungency and charm; a humor which is, in fact, the most real and the most distinctive of all Mr. Howells's gifts. There is, also, stronger grasp of situations, bolder portraiture of character, more rapid and dramatic movement of narrative. Still more important is the fact that in this novel life is presented with more of dramatic dignity and completeness than in any of Mr. Howells's other stories; there is a truer and nobler movement of human nature in it; and the characters are far less superficial, inconsequential, and unimportant than their predecessors; if not the highest types, they have a certain force and dignity which make us respect them, and make it worth while to write about them. Add to these characterizations of "The Rise of Silas Lapham" the statement that Mr. Howells has never shown more complete mastery of his art in dealing with his materials; that his style has never had more simplicity and directness, more solidity and substance, and it will be conceded that the sum total of excellence which even a reader who dissents from its underlying conception and method discovers in this story is by no means inconsiderable; is, indeed, such as to entitle it to very high praise, and to give added permanence and expansion to a literary reputation which, from the standpoint of popularity at least, stood in small need of these things.

And yet, when all this has been said, and said heartily, it must be added that "The Rise of Silas Lapham" is an unsatisfactory story; defective in power, in reality, and in the vitalizing atmosphere of imagination. No one is absorbed by it, nor moved by it; one takes it up with pleasure, reads it with interest, and lays it down without regret. It throws no spell over us; creates no illusion for us, leaves us indifferent spectators of an entertaining drama of social life. The novelist wrote it in a cool, deliberate mood, and it leaves the reader cold when he has finished it. The appearance and action of life are in it, but not the warmth; the frame, the organism, are admirable, but the divine inbreathing which would have given the body a soul has been withheld. Everything that art could do has been done, but the vital spark has not been transmitted. Mr. Howells never identifies himself with his characters; never becomes one with them in the vital fellowship and communion of the imagination; he constructs them with infinite patience and skill, but he never, for a moment, loses consciousness of his own individuality. He is cool and collected in all the emotional crises of his stories; indeed, it is often at such moments that one feels the presence of a diffused satire, as if the weakness of the men and women whom he is describing excited a little scorn in the critical mind of the novelist. The severest penalty of the persistent analytic mood is borne by the writer in the slight paralysis of feeling which comes upon him at the very moment when the pulse should beat a little faster of its own motion; in the subtle skepticism which pervades his work, unconsciously to himself, and like a slight frost takes the bloom off all fine emotions and actions. There are passages in Mr. Howells's stories in reading which one cannot repress a feeling of honest indignation at what is nothing more nor less than a refined parody of genuine feeling, sometimes of the most pathetic experience. Is Mr. Howells ashamed of life in its outcries of pain and regret? Does he shrink from these unpremeditated and unconventional revelations of character as vulgar, provincial, in-artistic; or does he fail to comprehend them? Certainly the cool, skillful hand which lifts the curtain upon Silas Lapham's weakness and sorrows does not tremble for an instant with any contagious emotion; and whenever the reader begins to warm a little, a slight turn of satire, a cool phrase or two of analysis, a faint suggestion that the writer doubts whether it is worth while, clears the air again. Perhaps nothing more decisive on this point could be said of Mr. Howells's stories than that one can read them aloud without faltering at the most pathetic passages; the latent distrust of all strong feeling in them makes one a little shy of his own emotion.

This failure to close with the facts of life, to press one's heart against them as well as to pursue and penetrate them with one's thought; this lack of unforced and triumphant faith in the worth, the dignity, and the significance for art of human experience in its whole range; this failure of the imagination to bridge the chasm between the real and the fictitious reproduction of it, are simply fatal to all great and abiding work. Without faith, which is the very ground upon which the true artist stands; without love, which is both inspiration and revelation to him, a true art is impossible.

\*    \*    \*

Mr. Howells has said, in substance, that realism is the only literary movement of the day which has any vitality in it, and certainly no one represents this tendency on its finer side more perfectly than himself. Its virtues and its defects are very clearly brought out in his work: its clearness of sight, its fixed adherence to fact, its reliance upon honest work; and, on the other hand, its hardness, its lack of vitality, its paralysis of the finer feelings and higher aspirations, its fundamental defect on the side of the imagination. Realism is crowding the world of fiction with commonplace people; people whom one would positively avoid coming in contact with in real life; people without native sweetness or strength, without acquired culture or accomplishment, without that touch of the ideal which makes the commonplace significant and worthy of study. To the large, typical characters of the older novels has succeeded a generation of feeble, irresolute, unimportant men and women whose careers are of no moment to themselves, and wholly destitute of interest to us. The analysis of motives that were never worth an hour's serious study, the grave portraiture of frivolous, superficial, and often vulgar conceptions of life, the careful scrutiny of characters without force, beauty, aspiration, or any of the elements which touch and teach men, has become wearisome, and will sooner or later set in motion a powerful reaction. One cannot but regret such a comparative waste of delicate, and often genuine, art; it is as if Michael Angelo had given us the meaningless faces of the Roman fops of his time instead of the heads of Moses and Hercules.

\*    \*    \*

The issue between the theoretical realism of the day and the older and eternal realism of fidelity to nature as the basis of all art is the more momentous because it is concealed in many cases by so much nice skill, and so much subtlety and refinement of talent. The divergence between the two is in the nature of a great gulf fixed in the very constitution of things; it goes to the very bottom of our conceptions of life and art. To see nature with clear eyes, and to reproduce nature with deep and genuine fidelity, is the common aim of the old and the new realism; the radical character of the difference between them is made clear by the fact that the realists of the new school deny the existence in nature of the things which the older realists have held to be deepest and truest.

\*    \*    \*

The older art of the world is based on the conception that life is at bottom a revelation; that human growth under all conditions has a spiritual law back of it; that human relations of all kinds have spiritual types behind them; and that the discovery of these universal facts, and the clear, noble embodiment of them in various forms, is

A Typical Novel • 413

the office of genius and the end of art. The unique quality of the Greek race lay in its power to make these universal, permanent elements of life controlling. This is the secret of its marvelous and imperishable influence upon the minds of men. This was the work for which it was so lavishly endowed with genius. The art instinct among the Greeks was so universal and so controlling that all individual thought, feeling, and living seemed to be a kind of transparent medium for the revelation of elements and qualities which are common to the race. What was personal, isolated, unrelated to universal life has largely disappeared, and there remains a revelation, not of Greek character, but of human life of unequaled range and perfection. Every great Greek character is a type as truly as every Greek statue; and it is the typical quality which lifts the whole race into the realm of art. But modern realism knows nothing of any revelation in human life; of any spiritual facts of which its facts are significant; of any spiritual laws to which they conform in the unbroken order of the Universe. It does more than ignore these things; it denies them. Under the conditions which it imposes art can see nothing but the isolated physical fact before it; there are no mysterious forces in the soil under it; there is no infinite blue heaven over it. It forms no part of a universal order; it discovers no common law; it can never be a type of a great class. It is, in a word, practical atheism applied to art. It not only empties the world of the Ideal, but, as Zola frankly says, it denies "the good God;" it dismisses the old heaven of aspiration and possible fulfillment as an idle dream; it destroys the significance of life and the interpretative quality of art.

\* \* \*

\* \* \* It is only when one sees clearly this denial of the spiritual side of life, and sees it in all its results, that one understands why Naturalism inevitably portrays the repellant, and a refined realism the superficial, aspects of life. In this pregnant fact lies the secret of its rigidity, its coldness, its inevitable barrenness. A natural method, a true and vital conception, are always capable of further expansion. Is there anything beyond Zola? He has pressed his theory so far that even his hottest adherents see no step left for another to take. The energetic Naturalist—a man of great force and splendid working power—has left his followers not a single fig leaf to be plucked off the shameless nudity of the "bête humaine"—the human animal—in the delineation of which he rivals the skill of Barye.[1] It is equally difficult to imagine any further progress along the lines of a refined realism; it has brought us face to face with the hard, isolated facts of life, and, having discarded the only faculty that can penetrate those facts to their depths and set them in the large order of the higher reason, there remains nothing more to be done by it. Materialism in

1. Antoine Louis Barye was a French sculptor of animals, often in mortal combat. [*Editor.*]

art reaches its limits so soon that it never really gets into the field at all.

This denial of the imagination, this effort to discard it entirely and banish it into the region of moribund superstitions, is at bottom a confession of weakness. It is the refuge of writers who have inherited the skill, but not the impulse, of the great literary creators, and who are driven, unconsciously no doubt, to adopt a theory of art which makes the most of their strength and demands the least of their weakness. It is a new illustration of the old tendency to elevate individual limitations into universal laws, and to make the art bend to the man rather than the man to the art. We need not concern ourselves about the imagination, as if any man, or body of men, could discard it, or, for any long time, even obscure it; the imagination may safely be left to care for itself; what we need to concern ourselves about is the fact that we are on the wrong road, and that men of genius, unconsciously mistaking the way along which the sign-boards have all been carefully misplaced, may lose time and heart in the struggle to free themselves from misleading aims. We are in great danger of coming to accept as work of the first order that which has no claim to any such distinction, and adopt as the standards of the noblest literary art the very delightful but very inadequate creations of some of our contemporary writers. It is always wisest to face the truth; if the poets of the time lack the qualities which go to the making of great singers, let us acknowledge the fact and make the best of it; if our realistic novelists are more skillful than powerful, more adroit and entertaining than original and inspiring, let us admit this fact also. But, in the name and for the sake of art, let us decline to accept these charming story-tellers as the peers of the great masters, and, above all, let us refuse to impose their individual limitations upon the great novelists of the future. "The Rise of Silas Lapham" and the novels of its class are additions to the literature of fiction for which we are grateful; but it is a great injustice to them and to their writers to insist upon placing them side by side with the great novels of the past.

# MAURICE THOMPSON

## The Analysts Analyzed[†]

Realism in fiction is of French origin, and owes its existence in its present form to clever talents kept well in hand. True genius never had been contented with doing a photographer's work, nor has it

[†]From the *Critic*, n.s. 6 (10 July 1886), 19–20. These remarks were first delivered as an address before the Women's Club of Indianapolis in June 1886.

ever taken kindly to mere reporting. It is safe to say that not one instance of genius, pure and simple, stands forth clearly defined among realistic writers. I should like to make this assertion with due regard for the high value of certain performances of the analytical novelists, but without any reservation or qualification. Genius is a power whose exponent is imaginative lift, and there is no imaginative lift in analytical realism. It may be true that the curiosity and selfishness of any age are tempted and charmed from day to day by pictures and caricatures of commonplace contemporaneous life and manners, much more than by any works of lofty imagination; but this merely proves that nothing else is so attractive to human vanity as a looking-glass. Where is the realistic novel that will live two hundred years? or where is the one that has the right to live a hundred years? It is the fashion to twirl the thumb at Scott's stories now, but the stories do not appear to mind it, they hold their own. Some clever realists affect to laugh down the romances of Victor Hugo, and yet every student of literature feels that one of the strongest voices of all time will live eternally in those romances. Realism is essentially of to-day and for to-day, whilst the ideal creations of genius are for all time. To make a transcript from life is the work of a trained hand guided by a correct vision, and is the mechanical work of the copyist, the product of mere talent. To create something that shall charm the soul of every intelligent beholder throughout the ages, is the act of genius. A photograph is very pleasing; but a work by a master-painter takes hold of the soul and lifts it to heaven!

From the first the realists have felt the slightness of their foothold and have sung their own praises in season and out of season; nor have they hesitated to affect to ridicule all the rest of the world. In their eyes the admirers of Scott and Hugo and Goethe, Milton, Dante and Homer are to be classed with the children who read and believe in 'Jack the Giant-Killer!' It must be understood that I here speak of realists as they are; for in the sense of being true to life, realism is the very soul of poetry and of romance, of painting, of music and of sculpture. There is a difference between making a minutely truthful copy of a landscape and creating a landscape picture which shall forever exhale, so to speak, the fragrance of its maker's genius. The landscape must be true to nature, and it must also be true to imagination, for art at its highest is not the result of cleverly finished transcripting. The novel should be true to human life, but it should also possess some element of that higher life for which the human soul forever pants. Homer and Milton and Shakspeare are realists in the sense of being true to nature, from the artistic point of view, in their greatest works, but it is the elevating force of creative genius which in each instance has secured immortality for both creator and creature. It does not serve the realists' turn for them to say in effect that a novel is not a work of art, nor can they avoid the whip of just criticism by claiming that style is everything and subject nothing, for in either case they admit the low order of their calling.

\* \* \*

I mention this striking characteristic of the analysts as proof of their recognition of the fact that realistic fiction, as we now have it, is a mere vogue which requires the constant care of its votaries to keep it alive. Style and humor count for more, with the analysts, than creative force; indeed, they scout the idea of any more exalted literary power than the power of depicting social life in its commonest and most trivial phases. Genius, from their point of view, is nothing more than a natural aptitude supplemented by training. Of course their doctrine forces them to place great stress upon the importance of ringing the changes on foibles and peccadilloes of character, instead of attempting to imagine noble instances of human self-sacrifice, of lofty aspiration and of soul-stirring passion. They prefer the commonplace *beau* to the hero, and nothing so delights them as the business of mildly defaming womankind under the pretence of analyzing unimportant motives and of drawing the frivolous details of feminine character. Another whim of the realists is their aversion to having a fiction end pleasingly. With them it is 'bad form' to aim at anything but merciless dissection. They deem it proof positive of a fibreless intellect for one to care about the outcome of a story. The persons who languish as characters in their works are left at last in the state of cadavers after a clinical lecture, cut, sawed, picked to pieces, disgraced and abandoned. This is all done in obedience to what the analysts call the 'rigid demand of art.'

\* \* \*

\* \* \* Analytical novels are all alike in form, two parts of trivial conversation to one part of explanatory and quasi-humorous remarks by the author, and they are just as much expected to end dolefully as a certain form of old verse was expected to close with *L'envoy*.[1] The after-taste is the true test of wines and fruits, but the realist insists upon giving to his fiction a lingering tang of vulgarity and hopelessness, with the express understanding that this tang is to be accepted as the badge of high art. In a word, the analysts, and notably those of the United States, are connoisseurs of the commonplace and the ephemeral, a sort of *dilettanti* with a *culte* for infinitesimals and for clinical gymnastics.

---

1. L'envoy is the author's postscript or conclud- ing stanza attached to poems written in certain archaic metrical forms. [*Editor.*]

It has been the boast of novelists that their works are becoming day by day the chief vehicles of popular education. If this be true, what shall we expect? Will the soul grow beyond the stature of its model? If our young men and young women are to be developed by reading the analytical novels of to day, can we hope that they ever will reach heroic proportions? If 'transcripts from life' must all begin on a low plane and close disagreeably, then our children must become pessimists for art's sake, or they must not be taught by the realistic novels. Moreover, it is not puerile or indicative of a fibreless moral substance for one to desire a happy ending to a novel. On the contrary, a taste for disappointing conclusions is an artificial one, acquired at the expense of much that is necessary to perfect moral sanity.

* * *

# "DIPLOMATICUS"

## A Portrayer of the Commonplace[†]

Theodore Roosevelt, in one of his amazing excursions into the realm of literary criticism, gave voice to the opinion that "William Dean Howells is the greatest novelist of our age." It is the somewhat absurd remark of an assertive but commonplace personality. But perhaps for that very reason it forms the most apt introduction to a brief study of an author who evinces an almost morbid love for the commonplace.

And, to be blunt, the commonplace in literature, at least in fiction, has its uses.

It may be asked why people read novels. Doubtless speculative press-critics, in search of a stop-gap paragraph, have often enough put the question and answered it. Probably the reasons they gave are in number and in variety infinite; but the sum total of them all resolves itself into this proposition: people read novels for relaxation.

Most people seek a refuge from the stern, ungilded realities of life in the reading of books wherein is weaved a thread of romance. They seek to drown the cares of their own lot in the following of the fates of other men, in a world of dreams, or at least of romanced and embellished truth. It is seldom, indeed, that this refreshing of the mind will be sought and found in a written portrayal of the

†From the *Westminster Review*, 178 (December 1912), 597–608. "Diplomaticus" is the pen name of an unidentified author.

humdrum, trivial life we lead, in the recital of these little everyday nothings, the sum total of which we call our existence. It is precisely from that *terre à terre*[1] that the novel-reading public seeks escape, and it is no recommendation to its favours that in Howells' works the obsession of it is ever present and ever oppressive.

It is only descriptive art of a very high kind that can make such subjects readable. They are then read with that intellectual appreciation which an artistic *tour de force* never fails to inspire.

To all intents and purposes Howells is a descriptive writer; he is seldom narrative because he seldom condescends to write anything worth narrating. His "novels" are a tissue of trivial incidents in family life, told with an inimitable charm and an aptness and truth that invest them with a freshness and interest they by no means intrinsically possess.

They are as a neck-band of little cameos, admirably finished and polished. Of their kind they are unsurpassed. But it is not the highest kind of literature wherein the reader's attention is constantly leaving the subject-matter to wonder at the descriptive skill of the author. The warmest admirer of Howells would, I imagine, hardly suggest that he is a writer of great books, or a dabbler even in high literature. Such an admirer would be within his rights, and would earn the cordial applause of all were he to characterise him as a writer of charming, even brilliant descriptive prose, a weaver of poetry into the dull fabric of his self-enforced commonplace, a man of acute and fine observation, not poorly endowed with humour, and with a certain facile bonhomie that never fails to charm.

His restriction of himself to the treatment of the commonplace raises curious questions of literary ethics. If a man have a message to tell that will better the world, a story to sing or a picture to draw that will beautify and enrich the world, let him step forward and tell it in his own fashion. He will have deserved well of the public. If a man's soul be angered and tormented at the sight of abuse and misery and evil, and he be moved to eloquent denunciation or vitriolic sarcasm, let him follow his impulse to his heart's content. The world may hate him, but it will respect him and be in his debt.

But what is the standard of literary utility we must set up for a man who has nothing to say, even though he say that nothing brilliantly and well?

\* \* \*

"The Rise of Silas Markham"[2] is one of the most remarkable books in Howells' American-life series. In some respects it is his most important work. He has given it a much stronger plot than usually; it is packed full with human interest and passion, brightened up with a

1. *terre à terre;* (French), commonplace, vulgar, or down-to-earth. [*Editor.*]
2. "The Rise of Silas Markham" is obviously the reviewer's mistaken version of *The Rise of Silas Lapham.* [*Editor.*]

vigorous humour, and told in vivid, realistic language. At times the reader might almost imagine he was persuing a singularly brilliant satire. The sketch of Markham almost comes within this category—the sarcastic exposition of one of those ruthless, energetic Napoleons of American finance of which the world hears so much to-day. But he is an honest Napoleon, as Napoleons go. One might quote at length from such a work. Take the passage at arms between the Mineral Paint King and the reporter:—

> "I've read articles about it (spoiling the landscape with advertisements) in the papers, but I don't see where the joke comes in exactly. . . . I never saw anything so very sacred about a big rock along a river or in a pasture that it wouldn't do to put mineral paint on it in three colours. . . . I say the landscape was made for man and not man for the landscape."

For unconscious humour and sheer indifference to the beauties and real aesthetic joys of life, for sheer disgusting materialism, this speech is hard to beat. The casual, ironically assenting answer is admirable:

> "Yes," said Bartley carelessly, "it was made for the Stove Polish man and the Kidney Cure man."

The book is important in another way; it contains a manifesto, a confession of faith on the part of the author. And this passage is important enough to be quoted in full:

> Bromfield Corey: "You can paint a man dying for his country, but you cannot express on canvas a man fulfilling the duties of a good citizen."
> Ch. Bellingham: "Perhaps the novelist will get at him by and by. If I were one of these fellows, I shouldn't propose to myself anything short of that."
> Bromfield Corey: "What? The commonplace?"
> Ch. Bellingham: "Commonplace? The commonplace is just that light, impalpable, aerial essence which they've never got into their confounded books yet. The novelist who could interpret the common feelings of commonplace people would have the answer to 'the riddle of the painful earth' on his tongue."

In Howells we undoubtedly have such a novelist; perhaps he has the answer to the said riddle (whatever the riddle be) on his tongue. He has certainly not given it to the world at large. Indeed, all he has achieved by his literary glorification of the commonplace is to cause his reader to wonder what his work would have been had he afforded himself a wider scope in subjects.

\* \* \*

In short, with Howells it is more keen observance of the ways of the world than deep insight into the workings of the heart; and we are not sure that the fact does not tell in his favour. One becomes rather tired of these so-called psychological novels wherein the author—generally with very little real knowledge—carefully dissects each of his characters, laying bare each spring of action, exposing his every motive, thought by thought, nerve by nerve. And for deliverance from such nauseous introspection one turns gladly to books such as Howells', wherein, whilst actions are well described, and thoughts finely indicated, there is no attempt at scientifically explaining the origin of either. There is another class of modern novels which is always sure of success, if not of popularity—satirical exposition of a man, an abuse or a class. Howells at times nearly comes within this category, never entirely however.

There is not wanting an element of satire in his works. At times this element becomes so strong as to absorb all other interests, and become the leading "motif."

Yet Howells is obviously enough not a satirist pure and simple, a man who uses his brilliant pen to cast ridicule and the outpourings of irony over the foibles and follies of his fellow-men, to fashion out of the plastic clay of society a gallery of little statuettes of exaggerated and incongruous aspect. Neither is he a moralist who uses sarcasm and realistic description to expose the vices and defects of society, to trace out and publish abroad their causes, their agents, their effects, and by making them ridiculous, adopt the shortest way of ending them. Yet, unintentionally, perhaps, his work not unfrequently has that very effect.

It castigates the snobbery of certain strata in Boston society; it utters a note of mock-indignant protest against the all-absorbing and all-eclipsing power of money; it ridicules the social ambitions of the "nouveau riche," and the awkward situation wherein these very ambitions are apt to land him; it casts a light, sometimes a lurid light, on some not too honest and creditable aspects of journalism and finance. But one feels with his satire as with his psychology that it is incidental, not essential, that it is the natural and inevitable result of exact portrayal rather than the fruit of deep research or profound emotion.

Sometimes this satirical element is entirely, or almost entirely, absent. That is the case in far the larger portion of the "Lady of the Aroostook." Sometimes it becomes the all-absorbing interest, as in page after page of "Silas Markham." But it is at worst gentle satire, loving satire, that excites sympathy rather than indignation, understanding rather than opposition. It amuses us rather than stirs us up, and it amuses us at times rather because it is so human and so true, than because of its being inherently funny.

What moves us to pity or to indignation, according to our several temperaments, is not the satire, conscious or unconscious. It is the exact, minute photograph of American life and manners which the author gives us.

It is a materialistic, superficial, unhealthy life he draws. We are moved, indeed, to disbelief or revolt by some of his sketches of American life.

Everything is so trivial, so matter-of-fact, so glaringly divorced from principle, so utterly devoid of soul.

\* \* \*

There is a glaring lack of unselfish, firm-principled men in that society of conventional machines, sprinkled with unpractical visionaries; men to leaven that society, to breathe health and moral strength into it, to unroll new vistas, new possibilities before it, to instil new life and new ideals into its sluggish and stagnant blood.

\* \* \*

Howells' picture of it is that of a thoroughly materialistic structure, honeycombed with dishonesty, sprinkled with cheap emotionalism, and held together by the thin crust of conventional social varnish.

A man whom Howells wants us to look upon as an unselfish, frank and praiseworthy character is driven to the conclusion that "after all, there is no misery like that of want, and that yonder girl had chosen (in giving up her property to her father's creditors), something harder to bear than her father's shame."[3]

This is offered us presumably as a praiseworthy sentiment; yet it is entirely immoral—setting the dollar-bag above honour.

If American life is indeed founded on that—God help America!

But surely that is not so; and exact and scrupulous and realistic though Howells undoubtedly is, we cannot accept his picture as a correct estimate of American life.

There is too much materialism in all modern life, and there is more of it—a great deal more of it—in American life than in any other.

But there is no society so wholly, so exclusively, one might almost say, so deliberately sordid and materialistic as that which Howells sketches.

It is surely essential that in what purports to be the mirror of a nation's life, all the elements that go to make up that life, that society should be represented.

What should we think of a most beautifully executed photograph of a crowd, from which the pencil of the "retoucheur" had carefully eliminated all the faces, or the hats, or any essential constituent of a crowd? Yet that is precisely what Howells has done. His women are either innocent and beautiful dolls, superficial and intriguing world-

---

3. The quotation comes from Howells' novel *The Quality of Mercy* (1892) and appears on page 243    in the Indiana University edition. [*Editor.*]

lings, or commonplace, though rather erratic machines—his men for the most part fools, rogues, or nobodies.

They act with passion at times, pathos occasionally, humour very often, and selfishness always.

They make up a certain phase of society; not the best, certainly, not the one that gives a nation its ultimate strength and backbone— but the one that is most apparent, that appeals most to a brilliant, superficially acute and slightly cynical observer.

If it had been written as a mordant satire on American society it might be, in part at least, a fine performance. It purports to be the plain mirror of truth, and as such it is a failure. Yet not altogether. William Dean Howells is the portrayer of Italian trivialities and American commonplaces. Some of these realistic and minute descriptions are of their kind probably unrivalled, and certainly unsurpassed.

# FORREST REID

# W. D. Howells[†]

Speaking of modern fiction, Mr. Howells has said: "The moving accident is not its trade; and it prefers to avoid all manner of dire catastrophe. . . . What is unpretentious and what is true is always beautiful and good, and nothing else is so."[1] In his many critical writings he has repeated this, in other words, again and again. His delight in realism, and his intolerance of romanticism, crop up, indeed, at every point. The only excuse for a novel's existence is that it shall give you a faithful picture of life: the mere plot—he has little interest in that, almost a contempt for it. "In one manner or other the stories were all told long ago. . . . Neither arts, nor letters, nor sciences, except as they tend to make the race better and kinder, are to be regarded as serious interests, and they cannot do this except from and through the truth."

The only difficulty here, of course, lies in the precise meaning one happens to attach to the word "truth." For many readers, *Wuthering Heights*, though aiming less at superficial plausibility, will seem, in another and more intimate sense, far truer than Jane Austen's delightful fictions, or than such deliberately unromantic chronicles as *The Lady of the Aroostook* and *April Hopes*. The "truth" of the last two tales (they are both by Mr. Howells) is, in fact, largely a matter of

[†]From *The Irish Statesman*, 1 (27 September and 4 October 1919), 333–34, 359–60.
1. These views are elaborated in Howells' many critical essays. See for instance "Henry James Jr." and "A Call For Realism" in this volume. [*Editor.*]

photographic accuracy; that is to say, it is all on the surface; and, one may add, that in most things he does Mr. Howells' success seems to be largely dependent on his note-books. When he departs from these he is apt to become unconvincing. His realism is seldom the imaginative realism of Tolstoy, of Tourguéneff, of Gorky.[2] He has said that "whatever is true is beautiful"; but he has forgotton Bacon's[3] rather hackneyed words, "There is no Excellent Beauty that hath not some Strangeness in the Proportion." There is too little "strangeness" in Mr. Howells' work: hence, I think, that effect of flatness which so many of his tales produce. Even his style, admirable in its purity, is more remarkable for neatness and cleanness than for beauty. Like the substance of his fictions, it is too seldom touched by imagination; it is essentially prosaic; there is hardly a metaphor, hardly an image, to be found in all his forty or fifty volumes.

\* \* \*

Doubtless, a desire to give a perfectly accurate picture of everyday life is responsible in part for this effect of industrious triviality that so much of Mr. Howells' work produces. The world he sets himself to describe so exhaustively has, one supposes, no particularly high interests. Yet even granting that he gets his picture, that he sees all there is to be seen in it, one cannot help asking, "Was it worth getting?" What exact purpose is served by writing almost exclusively about persons whose acquaintance in real life one would hesitate to make, not on account of any actively disagreeable qualities they might possess (to do them justice, they are entirely blameless and good-natured creatures), but simply from a fear of their proving to be bores? One may be as realistic as one likes, but it is difficult to write a very moving book about absolutely commonplace people in absolutely commonplace circumstances. At the best, one may produce a technical triumph. Mr. Howells might reply that most people are commonplace, and that he "is out" to give a picture of average life; and it is possible, of course (has not Henry James done it for the heroine of *Washington Square?*), to make the dullest person interesting by placing him in a situation calculated to exhibit such spiritual qualities as he may possess. But Mr. Howells, for the most part, is content to leave the situation as humdrum as the people; he has all Flaubert's determination to avoid the exceptional (where it is not a matter of a happy ending), but he has neither Flaubert's matchless style, nor his superb sense of the significant.

\* \* \*

It may be questioned, moreover, if, within its own strongly marked limits, Mr. Howells' work *is* consistently realistic. There seems to be a

2. Maxim Gorky (1868–1936), Russian novelist and playwright, who was an important proponent of "socialist realism." [*Editor.*]
3. Sir Frances Bacon (1561–1626), English statesman, philosopher, and literary man; the quotation here comes from "Of Beauty," number 42 of his *Essays* published in 1612. [*Editor.*]

strain of conventionality running through it, which, from this point of view, must constitute a vitiating element. The happy ending, for example, when it occurs so frequently as it does with him, is not conducive to an appearance of perfect sincerity even in the most optimistic of observers. He says of modern fiction that "the moving accident is not its trade"; yet more than one of his own fables is brought to a pleasant conclusion simply by the introduction of such an accident.* * * It is hard to take perfectly seriously work which is so obviously designed not to offend, and which ignores everything in life that may not be spoken of in the school-room and printed in the popular magazine. One can imagine somebody saying, "After all, if you are going to leave out so much, does it really immensely matter what you put in?"

One might leave it at that were it not for those four admirable novels upon which the reputation of Mr. Howells ultimately must rest. They, however, contain the ripe fruit of so delicate and original a talent that one is inclined to wish their author had written nothing else. Certainly, in comparison, nothing else he has written very much counts.

It was in 1885 that he published the first of these books, *The Rise of Silas Lapham*. It marked an epoch in his work, and far more than fulfilled the promise of the earlier tales. *Silas Lapham* comes so near to being a masterpiece that the hopes of Mr. Howells' admirers must have risen very high indeed. It illustrates all the strength, and very little of the weakness, of his theory of fiction: it illustrates, incidentally, the value of the quality of charm. There is something extremely original, natural, and unassuming about the book. It is full of humour and observation, and of the happiest little touches which throw a kind of glamour of art over a somewhat drab and prosaic subject matter. The opening device, for instance, of having Lapham interviewed for "the *Solid Men of Boston* series," as a means of letting the reader into his confidence, is so remarkably felicitous that one wonders it has never been imitated. No scene of comedy is droller than that describing the flutter aroused in the democratic Lapham household by the arrival of the invitation to the aristocratic Coreys' party. The Lapham family are all magnificently there, and the whole book, with its quiet distinction, has a kind of fine, homely flavour, impossible to describe, but very easy to enjoy. Nothing more "national," more of the soil that produced it, than *Silas Lapham* was, probably, ever written.

As a family chronicle it is in Mr. Howells' work surpassed only by his masterpiece, *The Kentons*, which came seventeen years later. And the two books have much in common. The atmosphere of both is light comedy, with a sprinkling, a summer shower or two, of tears. The interest of both lies in the faithful picture of a family whose tranquility is disturbed by the advent of a suitor for one of the daughters. In both, the parents are simple and unsophisticated people, and the children very loveable. And both show at its highest that rare and most valuable quality of Mr. Howells, his personal charm. In *The Kentons* this charm is indeed so great that it becomes a positive and very rare beauty, a kind of medium through which the whole book is seen. It is hard to imagine anybody *not* liking *The Kentons*. The story is slender in the extreme, but the manner is so light, so good humoured, the portraits are produced so easily, by so natural and graceful an art, the book is so filled with the spirit of youth, with "sweetness and light," is so beautifully balanced and proportioned, that we turn the last page with a sigh of regret. And the execution is as perfect as the conception. As in *Silas Lapham*, the people are more important than the story, and they are exactly the kind of people to make such a story possible, to fit exquisitely into its scheme, which is all grace and lightness and distinction.

\* \* \*

"Neither arts, nor letters, nor sciences, except as they tend to make the race better and kinder, are to be regarded as serious interests, and they cannot do this except from and through the truth." Well, there can be no doubt Mr. Howells' best novels, even some that are not quite his best, admirably fulfil these conditions. They are so kindly themselves, so wise and so humorous, so human and un-affected, that, while reading them, we cannot imagine anything much more delightful than to bask in their sunshine. Their faults are never faults of taste, of slovenliness, of unintelligence, and it is, doubtless, only an ungrateful reader here and there who demands more from them than they offer, and is unsatisfied because a talent, at its best so charming, so delicate and individual, is lacking in one or two qualities which would have raised it to a higher, perhaps to the highest rank.

# Criticism

# Critical Perspectives

Book reviews can be very interesting not only for what they say about the book but for what they tell us about the reviewer as a representative of his time. The reviewer usually reflects the tastes of at least a part of the reading public to which a book is addressed, and his reactions may influence the sales and the immediate reputation of a book. But the chief function of a reviewer is to identify a new book by type, to suggest its special interest or appeal, and to render a quick judgment on its quality. A book review must be current and is often hurried and superficial. If a book continues to be read for seventy years, as *The Rise of Silas Lapham* had by the 1950s, then it deserves, and is likely to attract, more thoughtful and specialized analysis than the initial reviewers were able to provide.

Even during the 1920s and 30s, when Howells' reputation was in near-eclipse, *The Rise of Silas Lapham* continued to be read and assigned in American literature courses. But during the 1940s scholars began to revise their image of Howells. They discovered first that he was a prolific and versatile author whose writing reflected the full spectrum of national life. When they actually read his books they found that he was not the fusty old maid denounced by H. L. Mencken* and that he was not exclusively devoted to describing the smiling aspects of life for the edification of the American girl. And finally they recognized that his reputation as a charming and polished stylist had obscured his penetrating and ironic analysis of American culture and character. By the 1950s a serious reevaluation of Howells was under way, and it led to the current judgment that, along with Mark Twain and Henry James, Howells occupies the mainstream of late nineteenth-century American fiction. In the last two decades, four major biographical studies and more than a dozen book-length critical studies of Howells' work have been published. An edition of all of his plays is now available and a twenty-six volume edition of his fiction, criticism, poetry, and letters is being published. Mere historical interest would not justify or reward the variety of critical viewpoints from which his work is being examined. The seven essays in this section provide a panorama of approaches to the study of fiction, and the fact that each of these approaches reveals something new and admirable about *The Rise of Silas Lapham* is a telling comment on the depth and richness of the novel.

Contemporary critics are no longer much agitated over the threat of realistic fiction to American morals nor over its inattention to ideal conceptions and elevating thoughts. Realism is now generally discussed either as an historical phenomenon that affected all the arts or as a group of techniques by which artists sought to achieve particular effects of verisimilitude. Contemporary critics generally grant Howells the validity of his artistic aims and theories, and they direct their inquiry to the degree of his success. While they

---

*Henry Louis Mencken (1880–1956), American journalist, critic, and essayist, denounced Howells as a Victorian prude whose greatest joy it was to take tea at the vicarage.

do not hesitate to point out his faults, their assumption is that they are dealing with a conscious and accomplished artist, and their aim is to discover and explain how Howells' artistry works.

Donald Pizer's essay focuses on the structure of *The Rise of Silas Lapham*, demonstrating that the mechanics of the book parallel and reinforce its balanced ethical position. William R. Manierre's essay shows us how Howells' narrative technique emphasizes the moral problems of the characters. John Hart sees the novel in terms of the mythic significance of its characters while Harold Kolb presents a symbolic reading. For George N. Bennett, the testing of family relationships is the central concern of the novel. Everett Carter emphasizes the moral aspects of Silas's dilemma, stressing its relation to the larger social morality. Finally G. Thomas Tanselle provides a nearly exhaustive summation of the best that has been thought and said about *The Rise of Silas Lapham* and adds his own revealing observations. The mere existence of the large body of critical opinion, of which these essays are only a representative selection, attests to the fertility and stamina of Howells' novel.

# DONALD PIZER

# The Ethical Unity of *The Rise of Silas Lapham*[†]

Critics of Howells's *The Rise of Silas Lapham* have usually examined its subplot as an excrescence arising from a need to satisfy the popular demand for a romantic entanglement, as a digressive attack on the sentimental self-sacrifice of the "Tears, Idle Tears" variety, or as an overexpansion of the comedy of manners strain in the novel. Each of these points of view has a certain validity. But it is also true that the subplot and main plot have fundamentally similar themes, and that an examination of the thematic function of the subplot will elucidate both the ethical core of the novel and the relationship of that core to a prominent theme in Howells's later economic novels.[1]

I

The main plot of *The Rise of Silas Lapham* concerns Silas's financial fall and moral rise. It revolves around his business affairs and social aspirations, and it concludes with his decision to sacrifice wealth and position rather than engage in business duplicity. The subplot centers on the triangle of Tom Corey and Irene and Penelope

---

[†]From *American Literature*, 32 (November 1960), 322–27. (Footnotes are by Pizer, unless otherwise indicated.)

[1]The most satisfying explications of the novel are by George Arms, *The Rise of Silas Lapham*, Rinehart Editions (New York, 1949), pp. v–xvi; Everett Carter, *Howells and the Age of Realism* (Philadelphia, 1954), pp. 164–169; Edwin H. Cady, *The Road to Realism* (Syracuse, 1956), pp. 230–240; and George N. Bennett, *William Dean*

*Howells: The Development of a Novelist* (Norman, Okla., 1959), pp. 150–161. Cady and Carter have also written excellent introductions to reprints of the novel in the Riverside Editions and Harper's Modern Classics series, respectively. Carter comes closest to discussing the theme of the novel as I do, though he defines it differently and does not analyze the relationship between the main plot and the subplot.

Lapham. Tom is mistakenly believed by all to be in love with Irene. The dilemma caused by his revelation that he loves Penelope is resolved when Irene is informed of the error. Irene then withdraws, leaving Tom and Penelope free to marry.

The dilemma or conflict within the subplot is solved by the use of an "economy of pain" formula. Despite Penelope's willingness to sacrifice herself, Irene must be told of Corey's true sentiments, and Penelope and Corey must be encouraged to fulfil their love. In this way Irene suffers but Penelope and Tom are spared the pain of thwarted love. One rather than three suffers lasting pain. Of the three characters who determine the resolution of the subplot, Lapham realizes instinctively the correct course of action, Mrs. Lapham is helpless and hesitant—this despite her moralizing throughout the novel—and the clergyman Sewell articulates the principle involved and confirms Lapham's choice.

The problem which Silas must solve in the main plot parallels that in the subplot. The three groups who will be affected by his decision are he and his family (Lapham is a participant now as well as an arbiter), Rogers and his family, and the English agents who wish to purchase Lapham's depreciated mill.[2] The crucial point is that the Englishmen are more than mere scoundrels and more than the agents for an "association of rich and charitable people"; they also represent society at large. This fact is somewhat obscured in the context of the financial trickery involved in the sale, since the agents are willing to be cheated. But Howells indicated the social implications of the sale when he immediately compared it to the defrauding of municipal governments. In both instances wealth and anonymity encourage dishonesty, and in both instances dishonesty undermines that which is necessary for the maintenance of the common good— effective city governments on the one hand, fair play and honest dealings in business affairs on the other. Lapham's refusal to sell therefore ultimately contributes to the well-being of society as a whole.

The thematic similarity in the two plots is that both involve a principle of morality which requires that the individual determine correct action by reference to the common good rather than to an individual need. Within the subplot this principle requires Lapham to choose on the basis of an "economy of pain" formula in which the fewest suffer. Within the main plot it requires him to weigh his own and Rogers's personal needs against the greater need of all men for decency and honesty. His "rise" is posited exactly in these terms, for at one point in the events leading up to his rejection of the Englishmen's offer he reflects quizzically that "It was certainly

2. Although Howells hints that the agents are counterfeit rather than real Englishmen, I have followed him in designating them as English.

ridiculous for a man who had once so selfishly consulted his own interests to be stickling now about the rights of others."

The method used to achieve moral insight is also similar in both plots. What is required is the ability to project oneself out of the immediate problem in which the personal, emotionally compelling need or desire is seen out of proportion to the need of the larger unit. In the subplot Mrs. Lapham finds this difficult, and Sewell asks her, " 'What do you think some one else ought to do in your place?' " In the main plot it is no doubt Silas's realization of the honesty that he would ask of other men in a similar situation which aids him in making the same demand of himself. Lastly, as in the subplot, Silas is capable of moral insight, Mrs. Lapham again falters, and Sewell (at the end of the novel) attempts explanations.

One of the functions of the subplot is therefore to "double" the moral theme of the novel, to intensify and clarify it by introducing it within a narrower, more transparent dilemma. The subplot also plays other important roles. Dominating the center of the novel, it is solved before the full exposition of Lapham's business crisis.[3] It occurs, in other words, between Howells's early remark that Lapham "could not rise" to unselfishness in his dealings with Rogers and Lapham's own words at the close which indicate a concern for the "rights of others." The subplot thus contributes to the "education" of Lapham in the correct solution of moral problems. His moral rise is the product of more than a conscience troubled by his earlier treatment of Rogers. It is also the result of his ready absorption of the "economy of pain" formula as a moral guide in the subplot, a formula which he later translates into its exact corollary, the greatest happiness for the greatest number, when he is faced in the main plot with the more difficult problem of the ethical relationship of the individual to society. To sum up, the subplot of *The Rise of Silas Lapham* serves the functions of doubling the statement of the novel's theme, of foreshadowing the moral principle governing the main plot, and introducing Lapham to the correct solution of moral problems.[4]

II

It is possible, at this point, to suggest that the ethical core of the novel can be described as utilitarianism (as interpreted by John Stuart Mill), since both plots dramatize a moral principle in which the correct action is that which results in the greatest happiness for

3. By the close of Chapter XIX Irene has been told of Tom's preference, Lapham has given Tom permission to continue courting Penelope, and Penelope has indicated (in the final words of Chapter XIX) that it will only be a matter of time before she will accept Tom. The problem of the depreciated mill is introduced in the next chapter.

4. Mrs. Lapham's ethical values are a foil to those which Lapham ultimately practices. Her moral beliefs are strongly held but are fragmented; she is helpless and uncertain when a conflict of interests is present and a universal moral criterion is needed.

the greatest number. I do not wish to intimate that Howells consciously employed the ethical ideas of Mill.[5] Rather, I believe that the similarity between Mill's utilitarianism and the ethical principles of *The Rise of Silas Lapham* is probably the result of parallel attempts to introduce the ethical teachings of Christ within social contexts and yet avoid supernatural sanctions. Howells's emerging Christian socialism in the late 1880's is well known,[6] and Mill wrote:

> I must again repeat . . . that the happiness which forms the utilitarian standard of what is right in conduct, is not the agent's own happiness, but that of all concerned. . . . In the golden rule of Jesus of Nazareth, we read the complete spirit of the ethics of utility. To do as you would be done by, and to love your neighbour as yourself, constitute the ideal perfection of utilitarian morality.[7]

That Howells was conscious of the applicability of the Golden Rule to the theme of *The Rise of Silas Lapham* is clear, I believe, from his ironic use of it in connection with Rogers. When Rogers senses that Lapham may reject the Englishmen's offer, his appeal to Lapham is based on the premise that

> "In our dealings with each other we should be guided by the Golden Rule, as I was saying to Mrs. Lapham before you came in. I told her that if I knew myself, I should in your place consider the circumstances of a man in mine, who had honourably endeavoured to discharge his obligations to me, and had patiently borne my underserved suspicions. I should consider that man's family, I told Mrs. Lapham."

But Lapham's answer is the response of a man who is aware of the sophistry of a narrow use of the Golden Rule and who recognizes the necessity for the consideration of a wider range of obligation than individual need. " 'Did you tell her,' " he asks Rogers, " 'that if I went in with you and those fellows, I should be robbing the people who trusted them?' "

### III

There is a twofold advantage in viewing the main and subplots of *The Rise of Silas Lapham* as controlled by a similar conception of moral behavior. First, the novel takes on a thematic unity and structural symmetry. It is within a single moral system, for example, that the apparent conflict between the attack on self-sacrifice in the subplot and Lapham's self-sacrifice in the main plot is reconciled. Penelope's self-sacrifice would diminish the sum total of happiness of those affected by her action, and therefore is wrong; Silas's self-sacrifice

5. John Stuart Mill (1806–73) was the leading Victorian proponent of Utilitarianism, a philosophical system based upon faith in man's innate self-interest as the surest force to provide the greatest happiness to the greatest number. [*Editor.*]

6. See particularly Clara and Radolph Kirk. "Howells and the Church of the Carpenter," *New England Quarterly* (June, 1959), 185–206.
7. *Utilitarianism, Liberty, and Representative Government*, Everyman's Library, p. 16.

increases the happiness of mankind collectively, and therefore is right.[8] Secondly, the theme of the novel anticipates Howells's acceptance of Tolstoy's[9] ethical ideals within the next few years and helps explain his response to those ideals once he encountered them. For in the two plots of *The Rise of Silas Lapham* Howells had already begun working out a belief that man must rise above himself and view life, as, he later explained, Tolstoy had taught him to view life, "not as a chase of a forever impossible personal happiness, but as a field for endeavor toward the happiness of the whole human family."[1] The conviction that man's primary commitment is to mankind was to be one of the themes which Howells emphasized in the series of novels from *Annie Kilburn* (1888) to *A Traveler from Altruria* (1894). In *The Rise of Silas Lapham* that theme appears in a less obvious social context (Howells had to strain for the connection between the English agents and society) and—more importantly—as an obligation which the average individual can grasp and fulfil. His novels during the years following the Haymarket crisis[2] were to examine the theme of man's duty to his fellow men more intensively but less hopefully.

# WILLIAM R. MANIERRE II

## *The Rise of Silas Lapham:*
## Retrospective Discussion as Dramatic Technique[†]

Howells' awareness of the benefits deriving from properly managed narrative perspective and of the dangers of inappropriate authorial intrusion is evidenced not only by his critical writings but by the dramatic rendering of incident in his fiction. If, as is generally granted, *The Rise of Silas Lapham* is his masterpiece, the fact is owing, at least in part, to Howells' discovery of and reliance on a dramatic formula perfectly suited to this particular novel. It is the threefold purpose of this paper to define the formula, demonstrate the extent

8. Cf. Mill, *Utilitarianism*, pp. 15–16: "The utilitarian morality does recognize in human beings the power of sacrificing their greatest good for the good of others. It only refuses to admit that the sacrifice is itself a good. A sacrifice which does not increase, or tend to increase, the sum total of happiness, it considers as wasted. The only self-renunciation which it applauds, is devotion to the happiness, or to some of the means of happiness, of others; either of mankind collectively, or of individuals within the limits imposed by the collective interests of mankind."

9. See note 5 p. 363, above. [*Editor.*]

1. Howells, *My Literary Passions* (New York, 1895), p. 251.

2. A disturbance occurred in Haymarket Square, Chicago, May 4, 1886, after a labor rally. A bomb was thrown, police gunfire ensued, and several people were injured or killed. Ultimately four anarchists were executed for their part in the riot, although they were not even accused of the bombing and only the flimsiest of circumstantial cases could be built to connect them with the bombing or the violation of any specific law. Howells drew a good deal of public criticism because of his efforts to prevent the execution of the condemned men. [*Editor.*]

†From *College English*, 23 (February 1962), 357–61.

of its use in *Lapham*, and suggest its relationship to the novel's structure of ideas.

The device, though open to an almost infinite variety of application, is basically simple, consisting of the discussion in retrospect by various interested characters of specific incidents which have already been presented in staged, set scenes. These incidents, in turn, will usually have been foreshadowed by the generous use of anticipatory detail. Following the occurrence of the antcipated action, whether it be an interview, for instance, or a dinner, or a proposal of marriage, everybody involved, both those actually present and those who, though absent, are in any way interested, are shown discussing what happened—in short, separate scenes linked rather by dramatic relevance and contrast than by authorial commentary or transition. This sequence of foreshadowing followed by incident and retrospective discussion occurs so often in *Lapham* as to create a kind of double anticipation in the reader who, caught up by the specific patterning, looks forward not only to the foreshadowed scene but with equal interest to the ironic counterpoint of the subsequent discussions.

The first three chapters, in their dependence on veiled or explicit reference to previous occurrences, adumbrate the importance to Howells' methodology of retrospective allusion. The interview between Silas and Bartley Hubbard (Ch. I) provides a convenient means of giving the reader an account of Silas' past and of characterizing him by contrast with the flippant reporter. Chapter Two furthers the exposition, introduces other members of the Lapham family directly and, by reference to a meeting between "the Lapham ladies" and "a mother and two daughters" at a "Canadian watering place," introduces indirectly certain members of the Corey group. Another important part of the action gets under way in Chapter Three with the appearance of Rogers. At this point Howells begins to develop his theme of business morality by stressing the conflict between Persis and her husband on the subject of Silas' treatment of his former partner. Exposition accomplished, Howells at once resorts to the formula with which this paper is concerned.

In Chapter Four Tom Corey meets Silas and family at the Beacon Street site; an amusing scene develops in which Irene is alternately embarrassed by the terrible intimacy of references to the "girls' room" and by her father's bragging in Tom's presence. Following this fully developed episode is a series of five separate scenes in which the encounter is variously discussed from contrasting points of view. Silas, driving his family home, airs his views on young men who do not work for a living—a subject to which he "recurred seriously . . . that night" when alone with Persis. This is at once followed by the more extended discussion of Irene and Penelope who, in the privacy of their bedroom, shudder at their father's gaucherie, parody his talk, and gigglingly evaluate Corey's appearance and behavior.

The next two chapters view the meeting from the Corey perspective. Tom's mention of the encounter to his father Bromfield leads to various comments on Boston standards ("there can *be* no standard but ours"), the nouveaux riches generally, the Lapham syntax, the vulgarity of Silas' advertising campaign ("rivalling the hues of nature in her wildest haunts with the tints of his mineral paint"), aristocratic and plebeian mores, and the recurrent theme of Silas' bragging which differs from that of the Corey circle in being "personal" and "about money." When, in Chapter Six, Tom tells his mother that he has met the Laphams at their new house, her only comment is—"It is getting very common down there."

Later in the same chapter, a less extended instance of the technique may be noted. Tom goes to Silas' office and asks to be taken into the business. This occurrence is then discussed alternately by Silas and Persis, by Tom, his mother and father.

Chapter Nine contains a more fully developed example. Once again Tom has met Irene at the new house. This encounter, delightfully presented, proves largely responsible for the misunderstanding of his amatory motives and, as well, portrays Irene's literary ignorance. Tom's later discussion with Bromfield leads to comments on "the average literature of non-cultivated people . . . the bestial darkness . . . [of whom those] . . . who have the habit of reading . . . can [scarcely] imagine." At least the young ladies "in certain ways—to a certain degree . . . had knowledge enough to be ashamed of their ignorance." But Tom's defense of the Laphams as "not unintelligent, . . . as very quick, . . . shrewd and sensible" calls forth the paternal remark, "I have no doubt that some of the Sioux are so. But that is not saying that they are civilized."

Having viewed this second meeting between Tom and Irene from the lofty perspective of Bromfield's social and literary preoccupations, Howells now subjects it to Lapham scrutiny. First, Silas and his wife hold the floor. In contrasting Persis's dawning perception of the essential differences between Laphams and Coreys with Silas' blunt refusal to recognize their significance ("Does that make him any better? . . . My note of hand would be worth ten times what Bromfield Corey's is on the street today"), Howells begins the explicit development of his theme of social education during the course of which Silas comes to realize, albeit dimly, what Persis already suspects—that not quite everything is automatically available to the man with a large bank account.

Next, Penelope and Irene sentimentalize over Tom's offer of a wood shaving ("O Pen, what do you suppose he meant by it?"). Finally, on the next morning, Penelope ("with the quaint modern

American fatalism") and her mother ("with the grim antique Yankee submission") estimate with greater coolness the difficulties of the relationship. Not until the conclusion of this scene can the dramatic presentation of Tom's encounter with Irene really be said to be over.

The sequential patterning recurs again and again in *Lapham*. Howells devotes three separate scenes to retrospective discussions of Bromfield's visit to Silas' office; four to Mrs. Corey's visit to the Lapham residence; five to Tom's declaration of love to Penelope; and three to Tom's offer to put money into Silas' business.

Surprisingly, the technique, so fundamental to this book, almost never appears in Howells' other fiction. (I find but one really striking instance; the sequence beginning with Mrs. Horn's musicale in *A Hazard of New Fortunes*.) Moreover, although the first pages of *Lapham* contain at least seven clear-cut instances, the final pages (Chapters XX ff.) contain but one—the sequence beginning with Tom's offer of financial aid. In his introduction to the Rinehart edition, George Arms maintains that it is precisely this latter portion that "lags" partly because "Howells became too preoccupied with his characters as potentially tragic figures." And Donald Pizer maintains that it is precisely from this point that Howells, having "solved . . . the subplot, . . . [turns his attention to the] . . . full exposition of Lapham's business crisis."[1] In short, one might argue that Howells becomes more involved, less objective and impartial; that, in so doing, he rejects the dramatic device which not only had helped him to maintain a rather strict impartiality in presenting his comedy of manners but had also been at least partly responsible for giving that comedy some of its life and vigor. Clearly, the appropriateness and serviceability of a method better suited to the presentation of a number of ironically juxtaposed viewpoints than to that of a single center of perception decline proportionately as the social panorama recedes into the background, as Silas' moral problem comes to dominate the action, and as, consequently, his perspective becomes central.

I believe that these changes are neither arbitrary nor reflective of altered focus. Accepting the world depicted in Chapters One through Nineteen as given, the narrowed world of the concluding chapters is both logical and inevitable. Undoubtedly there is a "slowing up" in the conclusion, a decrease in tempo that is partly owing to the relative absence of what might be called Howells' dramatic kaleidoscope. In the first nineteen chapters, the succession and multiplicity of brief, ironically contrasting scenes—momentary glimpses from altered perspectives—create an impression of speed, hurried movement, sudden change. This impression is precisely

---

1. "The Ethical Unity of *The Rise of Silas Lapham*," *American Literature*, Vol. 32, No. 3 (1960), p. 324.

right. Laphams and Coreys both are acutely conscious of the rush of events. Silas and family in their social rise unexpectedly confront a world of new and unfamiliar standards, tastes, and taboos with all of which they must conjure. But from the Corey perspective—that of established Boston society—it is the Laphams themselves who represent change and difference. The very haste of their rise constitutes a charge against them.

A sense of hurry is, then, entirely appropriate to the first two-thirds of the book, and the dramatic method under discussion helps provide it. The reverse, however, is true of the last third. Quite properly, Howells stresses the slowness of Lapham's financial decline. Its gradual and grinding nature, its painful sequence of renewed hope followed by new loss of hope, helps to define the full meaning of Silas' temptation and of his victory over it. Explicit statement underscores the decrease in tempo as well as its significance. Pen refers to the slowness with which "the Colonel has gone to ruin," and elsewhere we learn that "the days were going by in a monotony of adversity to him, from which he could no longer escape, even at home." Here, as elsewhere in the novel, tempo reinforces theme.

In still another way, the method under discussion helps to suggest and reinforce meaning. Superficially considered, Howells' treatment of American society appears, in this book, basically complacent, his satire of a stratified Boston, gentle and good humored. On closer inspection, however, one notes that the repeated sequence of dramatically rendered incident followed by series of brief scenes of retrospective discussion, usually critical in nature, implies lack of cohesion, stability, solidarity. The initial episode has been fractured—atomized as it were—by being broken into a number of isolated, more or less fragmentary worlds from the perspective of each of which it is subsequently revaluated. Dramatic fragmentation reveals social fragmentation: a world at odds with itself, characterized by isolation, cross purposes, and misunderstandings.

Opposed reactions to Silas' generosity suggest discord in the Hubbard family even "before [Bartley's] troubles with Marcia had seriously begun." "The old fool's sent it to you as a present." But Marcia "sighed . . . from the bottom of her soul, . . . 'Oh, what a good man!'" Marital and family discord—the keynote to discord elsewhere in the social structure—is a dominant theme from the very first chapter. Mrs. Corey spends her summers in Bar Harbor while her husband remains in Boston. For selfish reasons, Penelope is delighted when she first hears of her father's troubles. Tom, too, is pleased. Persis thanks the "merciful Lord" that the demolished mansion is not covered by insurance. Nanny Corey is pleased that Pen is "going to Mexico. At that distance we can—correspond." And

Pen, after spending a week with her new husband's family, knows that now she won't "feel strange among the Mexicans." Persis is quite incapable of helping her husband when he most needs help. Zerrilla Dewey is anxious to have Mr. Wemmel support her—but first she must get a divorce. In one form or another, and in various degrees of seriousness, separation or antagonism of interest undercuts almost every human relationship in the book.

What Howells has done in the first nineteen chapters is to create a world of fragments which hold together only by adherence to arbitrary, external, and relative standards. Absolute principles are largely irrelevant to its functioning. What happens in the last third of the book is that a man comes face to face with a moral problem requiring a choice based squarely on absolute principles. Society has already abdicated, and the man—this particular fragment—is thrown entirely on his own resources. The meaningful Christianity of an earlier New England might have helped, but America has "outgrown" that. It lives on in Persis as a degraded Puritanism, which, though it enables Silas to recognize the nature of the moral problem involved, lacks the spiritual strength and vitality necessary to give him effective help in making his decision.

And, according to the novel's entire structural and thematic patterning, the social and business worlds of nineteenth-century America have no guidance to offer him. Clearly the world of big business would consider Silas' scruples ridiculous. Is there ever any question in anybody's mind as to precisely what the Great Lacustrine & Polar railroad will do if it should want Silas' mill? It will simply steal it from him. Everybody expects this, but nobody even suggests that there is anything remotely unethical about such behavior. The larger the corporation the less the conscience. And as the individual's relationship with the organization becomes more abstracted, his sense of moral responsibility dissipates. A similar abstraction from the potential victims of Rogers' plot constitutes part of Silas' temptation. That, legally, he would be perfectly safe underscores the lack of society's moral commitment. Silas' remark that "The day of small things was past, and I don't suppose it will ever come again in this country," is not without its significance.

At no point does Howells depict Lapham as a saint. Certain things, however—such as caring for Jim Millon's daughter—or rejecting the Rogers deal—or telling the man from New York all the facts about the business—he has simply "*got*" to do." And by stressing Silas' isolation in each of these instances, Howells rams home the point that the only source of morally responsible action in a fragmented society is the individual human being. Silas "stood in the isolation to which adversity so often seems to bring men." "It was for him alone to commit this rascality—if it was a rascality—or not." Persis "was

helpless now in the crucial moment, when he had the utmost need
for her insight." He keeps from Persis for "dread" of her "blame" his
kindness to Zerrilla. He conceals from Bellingham his behavior with
regard to Rogers and the Englishmen. "He believed that he had
acted right in that matter, and he was satisfied; but he did not care to
have Bellingham, or anybody, perhaps think he had been a fool."

Silas' fear of being considered a fool carries right back to the
method of dramatic fragmentation, in accordance with which each
action receives judgment from multiple points of view, the totality of
which constitutes social sanction. But the sanction of a society such as
that depicted in *The Rise of Silas Lapham* is morally irrelevant, and will
remain so until its members become aware of the principle that each
is ultimately responsible for all. In his sermon on complicity in *The
Minister's Charge*, Mr. Sewell asserts, "you can have a righteous public
only by the slow process of having righteous men and women. . . . If
a community was corrupt, if an age was immoral, it was not because
of the vicious, but the virtuous who fancied themselves indifferent
spectators."

# JOHN E. HART

## The Commonplace as Heroic in
## *The Rise of Silas Lapham*[†]

What gives *The Rise of Silas Lapham* significance in the history of
the American novel is not Howells' "faithful treatment of material"—
all writers strive for an accuracy of statement. His originality of
vision lies, rather, in his ability to recognize and convey the heroic in
"poor Real life." Although Howells made much of the doctrine of
writing what "his fleshy eyes have seen," he insisted that an artist's
duty was to interpret human nature: the novelist, he wrote, should
"seek the universal in the individual rather than the social
interests."[1] Clearly he draws his material from common, ordinary
life, but his interpretation in *The Rise of Silas Lapham* follows the form
and pattern long used for the hero of myth and romance: heroism is
a discovery of self that involves the hero in an unmistakable ordeal
that amounts to a symbolic dying and rebirth. Howells makes the
intent of his method clear in the question Silas puts to Bartley
Hubbard. Silas asks, ". . . so you want my life, death, and Christian
sufferings . . .?" In depicting the motives and passions, the moral and
spiritual sufferings of his hero, Howells shows how the inner vision

[†]*From Modern Fiction Studies.* 8 (Winter 1963).
375–83.

1. These views are expressed by Howells in chapter 21 of *Criticism and Fiction* (1891), and in many of
his reviews and essays. [*Editor*].

of truth that is the discovery of self is recreated out of ordinary events and commonplace happenings. It is this vision of the heroic in the commonplace and Howells' particular portrayal of it that bear critical exploration.

Silas' life is actually the story of self-deception and self-discovery that begins in innocence and ends in wisdom. In one sense the pattern of his life is circular. Silas comes from a Vermont farm and returns to it. But within the circle of wandering, there are two lines of development, one of conquest and one of quest. If conquest is a matter of will, a matter of conscious planning made manifest through overt action, quest is more the inward shaping of character through circumstance and growing awareness. Both the overt action and the inward shaping take place simultaneously. As Silas' conquest takes him from bucolic innocence into the intricate world of Boston, so his success in business shows his awkward failure in the world of personal and social prestige. Yet the very events that bring destruction serve as the series of tests and trials that enable him to recognize the nature of pride and greed, and to understand that real values come, not from external possession, but from moral and spiritual resources that lie within man's nature. Howells did not, of course, discover the pattern of regeneration, but his use of it in portraying the common average business man of his day was both new and startling.

As a way of making the symbolic fall and rise integral to the structure of the novel, Howells uses two major symbols: paint and houses. Both carry a burden of aesthetic, moral, and social meaning, and while they are inextricably linked with the lives of the characters, paint is, in its various stages of manufacture, most closely related to Silas, Mrs. Lapham, and Bromfield Corey. To Silas paint is a matter of commodity. As he says, "the landscape was made for man, and not man for the landscape." Paint is material, money. It has become his passion, his "heart's blood," the driving force behind his way to wealth and power. As symbolic agent, paint is both energy and matter; it can both destroy and create. It makes his financial rise possible, but as Silas grows greedy and ambitious, his greed and pride entangle him in both moral and economic destruction. Yet the paint-mine, like the landscape, remains as a gift freely given, an endless source of moral and creative life to which he can return with renewed understanding after his ordeal in Boston. It is a credit to Silas' moral insight, however, that he names his best grade of paint—the Persis brand—after his wife, whose values and actions, though warped by Puritanical righteousness, are more refined and honest than his own. And in the end, it is the Persis brand that is salvaged from the financial collapse as worthy to compete in a highly competitive market. To Bromfield Corey, paint is hardly a commodity at all, but the medium by which he has once expressed artistic sensibilities as a painter of portraits. If his dilettante interests suggest a loss of vital energy, his indifference to material values accentuates an aesthetic appreciation of life, a cultivated objectivity, a devotion to form and manners. Like the artist or the poet, he is refined, fragile, durable, but he has hardly become involved in the actuality of life. Once he painted it. Now he merely observes it.

The second major symbol is that of houses, and there are four of them. They function not as agent, but as agency. The old farm house in Vermont contains both beginning and end, both source and sanctuary: "I hung on to the old farm, not because the paint-mine was on it, but because the old house was—and the graves." And just as the farm house implies a native innocence, an honesty and uprightness, so the house on Nankeen Square reflects the wealth and greed, the vulgarity and artificiality, the social, moral, and aesthetic poverty which conquest brings. Even the statues of Faith and Prayer become decorative bric-a-brac rather than visual guides of moral attitudes. But the half-built house on Beacon Street perhaps best symbolizes Silas' partially realized aims and aspirations in the social world. It is to be the monument to success and personal aggrandizement. But the classical simplicity of its form and decoration reflects not so much Silas' acquired good taste as his illusory belief that extravagance and hired experts can endow him with taste and position. Similarly, the Corey mansion, inherited from Mrs. Corey's family, not only reflects the air of "aristocratic seclusion," the inherited taste of the new sterile and enervated Corey family, but as scene of Lapham's initiatory ordeal into a world of grace and refinement, it also illustrates the social and aesthetic distance which Silas must travel in order to achieve his goal. Of the four houses the farm house and the Corey mansion suggest real and abiding values in a post Civil War America that found many a rising middle-class hero trying to pass through the Nankeen Squares to the rarefied atmosphere of a Beacon Street. The four houses contain the symbolic movement of the novel: the departure and return, the rise and fall, the destruction and renewal. In a sense, the life, death, and suffering of Silas is a story of paint and houses, a story of energy and matter shaping the destiny of modern man.

In the conquest that moves him from Vermont to Boston, Silas has worked with boundless energy to turn paint into money and property. Two essential ingredients in his success have not come from him at all. He inherited the paint-mine from his father; his wife's "zeal and courage formed the spring of his enterprise." In these early days, the "blunt, outspoken" Laphams have worked toward success together. As Silas says, he mixed paint "with *Faith*" and "the best quality of boiled linseed oil that money will buy." But as success comes, Silas relies less and less on faith, less and less on the old resources. Although Mrs. Lapham warns that he has made paint his god and cannot "bear to let anybody else share in its blessings," she has gradually "abandoned herself to a blind confidence in her husband's judgment, which she had hitherto felt needed her revision." Silas bows easily to his false material gods. He forces his business partner out of the firm, rationalizes his guilt as smart business tactics, and retreats, however uneasily, into his greed for more. Having cut himself off from the familiar moral sources, the strength of his inheritance, the moral wisdom of his guides, he is motivated, not by self-sacrifice, but self-gain, not by inner resourcefulness, but external display. The decaying Nankeen Square district is visual index to the Laphams' social poverty: in spite of the clothes and fine horses, the summers at expensive resorts, the gifts "with both hands" to church and charity, they have acquired neither gesture nor form that insures acceptance in a cultured society. They remain isolated and alone, gaining whatever strength they can from "mutual affection."

Silas' attempt at social conquest demonstrates his inability to realize that acceptance into the world of the Bromfield Coreys demands "something more besides money." Inspired by the apparent interest of Tom Corey in one of the Lapham daughters, Silas envisions himself as the social success that a fine house on Beacon Street may bring. And as he relies on a house to create position for him, so he relies on someone else to conceive it, to bridge, as it were, the aesthetic and intellectual differences between Laphams and the Coreys. His own knowledge is limited. He basks in the architect's tendency towards extravagance and experimentation. Of the architect's talk of permanent art forms, the classical simplicity of design, he understands nothing. He finds greatest pleasure in seeing the piles driven for the foundation, as if he comprehended only the crude, if essential beginnings. He is appalled to think a builder would prefer painted woodwork to the more expensive and fashionable black walnut. While Mrs. Lapham inspects the decoration, he sits ill at ease in what will be the reception room and whittles, dreaming, like a man bewitched, of his new social role and of his daughter's marriage into an aristocratic family. As Mrs. Lapham warns: "You've lost your head, Silas Lapham, and if you don't look out you'll lose your money too."

As Silas' guide and conscience, Mrs. Lapham, for all her righteous warning, hardly understands the nature of Silas' guilt. She senses danger in the sudden appearance of Rogers, the old business partner: "he always manages to appear just at the moment when he seems to have gone fairly out of our lives, and blight everything." Yet she believes that Silas, in lending money to him, has now atoned for the initial fraud: "You've taken the one spot—the one *speck*—off you that was ever there, and I'm satisfied." She does not see that in trying to buy redemption, Silas has only piled sin on sin; unwittingly she has helped to plot his social and financial downfall.

Thus, for all his success in business, Silas knows little of the true nature of self. He has told Bartley Hubbard that man should keep his conscience "as free from paint as you can, if you want much use of it," but has done just the reverse: his passion has made paint his god and increased his greed for personal gain. Holding fast to those values which gratify his pride and inflate his ego, Silas has not yet learned that man's real strength derives from the inner self, from a moral and spiritual concept of life that is in harmony with the inexhaustible and unseen sources in man and nature. Acting as if such strength were his own, he has broken the vitalizing connectives and made his quest merely parody, the pursuit of a delusion. In the language of Emerson, he has become but partial man, a fragment of the total image, a man disunited within himself.[2] Although, finally, Silas must realize these truths for himself, he now needs someone to guide him on the way. As much as anyone else, that guide turns out to be Bromfield Corey.

Although the Corey family is a name that Silas has long hated "as a symbol of splendor which . . . he could not hope to realize in his own," he is awed and elated to have young Tom Corey as an employee in the paint factory, as a guest in his house, as a suitor to his daughter. Actually Tom is the connecting link in the social struggle of which the Laphams and Coreys are only symbols, for Tom is of a new generation, and can combine old idealism with new energy. He has inherited the nose and energy of his forefathers, and he is attracted to paint as an opportunity that honestly interests him for the first time in his life. Since he honors neither social prestige nor family prejudice, he can look on Silas, not as vulgar rich, but as "simple-hearted and rather wholesome." But the backgrounds of the Lapham and Corey families reflect great differences that a mutual interest in paint and houses can hardly unite.

Bromfield Corey, a man who never whittles, is a study in "sterile elegance." He has dabbled in oil painting, in culture, and in life; his judgment has more objectivity than passion. For all his social position, he has long ago discovered that he is not "some sort of porcelain," but "common clay, after all." With values firmly built on moral, aesthetic, and intellectual standards, he has gained the social knowledge and self-insight that prevent a violent sympathy for old certainty or new fashion. Although he acknowledges that money is

2. Ralph Waldo Emerson (1803–82), American essayist, poet, and lecturer, who advocated that man can be guided by an inner voice whose truth transcended the dictates of custom and worldly wisdom. [*Editor.*]

now "the romance, the poetry of our age," the thing "that chiefly strikes the imagination," he clings to the decayed splendor of a "faded tradition," to the belief in "good sense and right ideas," in the mentality and manners that make up the "airy, graceful, winning superstructure" of a society. He sees the Laphams as "rude, native flavours," but without the "sauce piquante." As his reading of the *Revue des Deux Mondes* suggests, he is a man of two worlds; indeed, he is a man of many attitudes and sympathies and understandings.

It is through Bromfield Corey, then, that Silas comes to understand something of the nature of society and self. On a visit to the paint office, Corey acts with courtesy and kindness; he is neither arrogant nor condescending. He is, Silas thinks, "about the pleasantest man I ever did see." Howells spells out the interpretation: where once Silas "could not have imagined any worldly splendour which his dollars could not buy," he now has a "cloudy vision of something unpurchasable," a vision that comes to him "in spite of the burly resistance of his pride." In this moment Silas has caught a glimpse of that impalpable world of being that lies beyond the visible world of matter. But one glimpse is not a gleam of truth, and before Silas can overcome his egotism, his attachment to self, he must be shown the way again and again.

The dinner party at the Coreys, which begins as a tribal masquerade and ends as an unmasked confessional, is an unmistakable ordeal of discovery. Actually, the whole dinner scene is an ironic comedy of manners that exposes both Laphams and Coreys. The invitation is a calculated move: by exposing the Laphams, the Coreys hope to save themselves from an alliance with a family that neither speaks grammatically nor has the habit of wine at the table. For Silas it is the realization of social ambition. There are losses and gains on both sides. A family alliance is achieved; Silas fails miserably to achieve social sanction. But as a result of undergoing what amounts to an initiatory ritual, Silas realizes something of self. Except for Bromfield Corey, the members of the Corey clan, despite the timeless qualities of good taste and form which the house suggests, have much to learn also. Mrs. Corey addresses Silas as General instead of Colonel. At the table Bellingham tucks his napkin in his collar. There are jokes about money and charities. They are, in reality, clannish and vulgar and given to improprieties. They try to dazzle their unsuspecting guests; they lure Silas into a shameful exhibition of bravado. Under the influence of too much wine, Silas monopolizes the conversation, brags of his war experiences, tells how Jim Millon's "hard" death saved his own. The listeners are stunned. They see Silas as a man of "gross appetites, . . . blunt sense, . . . purblind ambition, stupid arrogance." Although Silas feels successful at the time, he realizes next morning that he has disgraced both himself and his family. But in catching this long glimpse of self, he has acquired, as Howells says, a "sense of wrong."

Humility is not easily acquired. Before Silas is able to relinquish the deluding dreams which have fed his ego, he must pass three major crises in his life: the mix-up in the love affair between Irene, Tom Corey, and Penelope; the burning of his new house; and the series of financial disasters. His final rise and reformation are not, as with heroes of romance, a matter of sudden consequence. As Howells says, in real life "the theory of disaster" is not "incessant." Although the direction of Silas' life spells inevitable failure, his reverses are punctuated with hope. The difficult quest of the inner vision is tedious and awesome.

The discovery that Tom Corey loves Penelope, not Irene, forces Silas into the moral sphere for his answers. As he says to Mrs. Lapham, "We don't either of us want anything but the children's good. What's . . . [money] . . . for, if it ain't for that?" It is Silas who senses their inadequacy: "Suppose we don't want Pen to have him; will that help Irene any, if he don't want her?" And it is Silas, not Mrs. Lapham, who sees that they need help in making a decision: Mr. Sewell advises that better one should suffer than all three. It is Silas, too, who understands that in her suffering Irene will be strong as iron and that Penelope will accept her responsibility to Tom without faltering. In this family crisis, Silas proves himself to be gentle, kind, understanding.

As the financial disasters mount, Silas must reckon with the loss of that very foundation on which his idea of success has been based. Money and paint have been his life, and now with the mishandling of funds, the loans to Rogers, the purchase of bad stock, a rising competitive market which can undersell him, he loses the very means on which conquest has been built. Beset by destruction from without and from within—Mrs. Lapham hears of Zerilla and suspects him of supporting another woman—Silas, in silence and alone, must examine the position to which his corrupted conscience and enfeebled sensibilities have brought him. In his agony he sees that he has been a fool. He tells Mrs. Lapham: "I haven't hurt anybody but myself— and you and the children."

Silas' full shock of recognition comes, however, with the destruction of the new house. As symbol of financial success and hope for social privileges, it is his "pride and glory," "his triumphant life's work." Yet just as his grandiose social schemes remain unrealized, so the house is but partly completed. Having resolved to sell it, Silas journeys to it in despair. Alone with his sorrow in the silence, he recalls his long talks with the architect: now he seems to have a feeling for the "simplicity of the whole design and the delicacy of its detail," As Howells interprets, using sound imagery: "It appealed to him as an exquisite bit of harmony appeals to the unlearned ear, and he recognised the difference between this fine work and the obstreperous pretentiousness of the many overloaded house-fronts . . . on the Back Bay." He even detects the "peculiar odour of his own paint," and following a whim, decides to test the chimney. The success of having made the fire inspires him: he feels that he, too, can rise above his adversity. Then as the fire turns into destruction, he knows that with the burning of the house, his last hope for economic and social success has been destroyed. It is ironic that people cannot gossip, as Mrs. Lapham fears, that he has set it on fire himself in order to collect the insurance, for there is no insurance. Completely broken, Silas falls "into the deep sleep which sometimes follows a great moral shock." It is the symbolic sleep of death. When he awakes, he knows that he can neither sell his paint business, nor raise enough money to buy out his competitors. If he sells the worthless mill and stocks, he will be dishonest; if he does not, he will fail. Emerging from the "isolation to which adversity so often seems to bring men," from the trials and tests that have brought material defeat but moral strength, Silas knows that he can and must stand "firm for right and justice."

If, then, Silas' adventure in Boston began as a conquest for financial and social aggrandizement, it has come to serve as a series of ordeals through which he recognizes the need for moral rectitude. Recognition has come, however, not as a matter of triumph over society, but as a by-product of the battle against it. His return to Vermont is a return to the "necessaries" of life, "to the day of small things," to country ways and plain living, to the paint-mine and the old house, to the source of inspiration, which has both led him astray and brought new faith and understanding. Silas' return was, as Howells writes, "as much the end of his proud, prosperous life as death itself could have been. He was returning to begin life anew, but he knew as well as he knew that he should not find his vanished youth in his native hills, that it could never again be the triumph that it has been." Yet, out of his greed and pride, out of the evil generated by social ambition has sprung an understanding of moral self. As Howells says: "Adversity had so far been his friend that it had taken from him all hope of the social success for which people crawl and truckle, and restored him, through failure and doubt and heartache, the manhood which his prosperity had so nearly stolen from him." To be restored to manhood is to discover the nature of self, the native and primal stuff of inner being. Just as a passion for paint and money has nearly destroyed Silas' sense of values, so the return to the paint-mine has aided the redemption.

*The Rise of Silas Lapham* begins and ends with an interview. The interview with Bartley Hubbard, which forms the opening chapter reveals Silas at his boasting best and makes Hubbard a kind of malign helper to our hero's fortunate fall. At the end, the interview with Mr. Sewell, whose role of chance acquaintance and willing guide has helped Lapham atone for his mistakes, reveals the scope of Silas' moral and spiritual growth. Without actually admitting that he ever wronged his partner, Silas owns "that he had made mistakes." Yet, he can also say that "he had been no man's enemy but his own; every dollar, every cent had gone to pay his debts; he had come out with clean hands." Silas has achieved more than clean hands. He has undergone a rebirth that points the way to symbolic ascension. As he says: "Seems sometimes as if it was a hole opened for me, and I crept out of it." The hole is, of course, the still center of creative realization that constitutes self-scrutiny. Having achieved an awareness and conception of self that enables him to overcome the attachment to his pride and greed, having become a man of integrity, Silas can look at himself and his relation to others with the confidence of humility that is truly heroic. Ennobled by the ordeal of experience and "Christian suffering," he can speak freely of his failure with an understanding that bespeaks wisdom.

Howells is not the first to portray the heroic in the commonplace. Such writers as Stendhal, Dickens, Balzac, Irving, Emerson, and Melville had already worked "understandably [at] bestowing form upon reality as given," at depicting a true reflection of the common, the familiar, the low in human life. In a sense, then, Howells is only continuing a literary tradition that had come to focus on real conditions and events. For all his middle-class morality, he is able to attach conditions and events to their roots, to inform them with an inner essence, to illumine and interpret them, to shape them through archetypal pattern and allegorical movement that avoids the stock-types of the romantic novel or morality play.[3] The reality of his vision shows an informed and accurate knowledge of the social, economic, and moral thought of his time; his representation of events, colored as they are in *The Rise of Silas Lapham* by Christian ethics and Greek moderation, is based on rationalistic and empirical points of view, rather than philosophical and historical dogma. It is Howells' major strength that his program of artistic purpose helped him to see the heroic in the "smiling aspects" of "poor Real life."

3. See Erich Auerbach, *Mimesis*, trans. Willard Trask (Garden City: Doubleday Anchor, n.d.), pp. 406–13. [Hart's note—*Editor.*]

# HAROLD H. KOLB

# [The Realist's Symbols]†

\* \* \*

The realistic fiction of the mid-1880's is not symbolic in the traditional sense, but it does employ symbols. The realists deny the transcendental symbolic imagination which ascends from natural facts to spiritual facts, but they do use tightly reined internal symbols, which—like realistic morals—are built into the fabric of the narrative and do not depend on external values for their meaning.[1] Natural facts, for the realists, are symbols of other natural facts.

The symbols of the realists, like their similes and metaphors, are largely devoted to the revelation of character. In *Indian Summer*, Mrs. Bowen's jealousy is caught in the firelight which "flickered upon her face, and threw upon the ceiling a writhing, fantastic shadow, the odious caricature of her gentle beauty." Miss Birdseye, an ineffective, incoherent reformer in *The Bostonians*, is symbolized by her displaced spectacles, a literal natural fact that James borrowed from Elizabeth Peabody.[2] Olive's futile attempt to possess Verena, Basil's eventual victory in separating them, and the ironic fact that Olive first invited Basil to Boston and introduced him to Verena are all captured in James' symbolic stage directions: "Olive put out her hands to hold her, and at this moment one of the *portières* of the room was pushed aside, while a gentleman was ushered in by Miss Chancellor's little parlour-maid." Silas Lapham is fascinated by the symbolic pile driver (a magnification of Silas' great, hairy, pounding fist) which slams home the foundation of his new house: "By gracious! . . . there ain't anything like that in *this* world for *business*."

Lapham's house is in many ways the symbolic center of the novel. Built on the "New Land" on the water side of Boston's Beacon Street, the hundred-thousand-dollar triumph represents the apex of Lapham's financial trajectory.[3] The house is tangible proof that Silas is indeed a "Solid Man of Boston," but the foundation is unsound.

†From *The Illusion of Life: American Realism as a Literary Form* (Charlottesville: The University Press of Virginia, 1969), pp. 122–27. (Footnotes are by Kolb.)

1. In a discussion of *A Modern Instance* Edwin H. Cady notes that Howells' symbols "have no referents outside the immediate field of the novel. They do not point to abstractions of general validity or significance. They function only to give heightened imaginative power to the particular work" (*The Road to Realism* [Syracuse: Syracuse University Press, 1956], p. 214).

2. James argued with his brother William concerning his use of Miss Peabody (who lived until 1894), and he admitted having a "scruple" about the spectacles. See *The Notebooks of Henry James*,

ed. F. O. Matthiessen and Kenneth B. Murdock (New York: Oxford University Press, 1947), pp. 67–68. James also uses the spectacles to symbolize the incoherence of the entire reform movement: "The whole moral history of Boston was reflected in her displaced spectacles."

3. Howells at the time was engaged in a move to Beacon Street. "Drolly enough," he wrote to James in August, 1884, "I am writing a story in which the chief personage builds a house 'on the water side of Beacon,' and I shall be able to use all my experience, down to the quick. Perhaps the novel may pay for the house" (*Life in Letters of William Dean Howells*, ed. Mildred Howells [Garden City, N. Y.: Doubleday, Doran & Co., 1928], I, 366).

The house is a symbol of Lapham's social pretensions and his ruthless extermination of his partner. "There's blood on it," Mrs. Lapham protests; "I shan't live in it." Even the architectural rise which the house represents is superficial: the architect has to maneuver skillfully to circumvent the gauche tastes of the family from Lumberville and Nankeen Square. It is appropriate—even inevitable—that Lapham himself should be responsible for the destruction of the new house; his expired insurance policy provides the final ironic twist.

The Beacon Street fire which warms a curious crowd ("Isn't it perfectly magnificent! . . . I wouldn't have missed it on any account") not only destroys Lapham's multifarious aspirations. It also consumes the money which could have rescued the faltering paint business and puts Silas in the hands of his creditors. The destruction of the house is an integral, functional symbol. It represents Lapham's collapse and, in turn, is a partial cause of that collapse. Appropriately, the smoke-stained shell has the last figurative word: "The windows looked like the eye-sockets of a skull down upon the blackened and trampled snow of the street."

The architectural symbolism in *The Rise of Silas Lapham* is a logical corollary of realistic subject matter. In his concern for ordinary people in their everyday lives Howells puts a strong emphasis on their houses. Ordinary people spend more than half of their everyday lives in their houses, and much of their energy is invested in building, repairing, furnishing, and feathering their nests. The symbolic qualities are irresistible—the house becomes the man. Lapham's Vermont farmhouse represents both his rural origins and his subsequent graceless prosperity. The original ugliness has been "smartened up with a coat of Lapham's own paint, and heightened with an incongruous piazza." The house in Nankeen Square is a monument to expensively indulged bad taste—a medley of green and salmon paint surrounding gray and red velvet wallpaper and gilt modling, topped by a chandelier of "massive imitation bronze." For decoration the Laphams selected allegorical statues of faith and prayer and "a white marble group of several figures, expressing an Italian conception of Lincoln Freeing the Slaves—a Latin Negro and his wife—with our Eagle flapping his wings in approval, at Lincoln's feet."

The rural equivalent of the Lapham drawing room is the Granger-ford parlor in *Adventures of Huckleberry Finn*, full of gaudy plaster parrots, crockery cats and dogs, wild-turkey-wing fans, and "a lovely crockery basket that had apples and oranges and peaches and grapes piled up in it which was much redder and yellower and prettier than real ones is, but they warn't real because you could see where pieces had got chipped off and showed the white chalk or whatever it was, underneath." James also relies on the symbolism of architecture and interior decoration. Olive's narrow parlor, Miss Birdseye's bleak, empty meeting room, and the Tarrants' cottage in Cambridge all express the character of their owners in *The Bostonians.*

\* \* \*

\* \* \* All of Boston is momentarily brought into focus by Miss Kingsbury in *The Rise of Silas Lapham:* "I have often thought of our great, cool houses standing useless here, and the thousands of poor creatures stifling in their holes and dens, and the little children dying for wholesome shelter."

Even the pine shavings from Lapham's new house have a symbolic value in the scene in which Irene Lapham sits on a sawhorse with Tom Corey and pokes at a shaving with her parasol. Ever since George Arms suggested that the scene had an "undertone of sexual symbolism"[4] it has been difficult to read it any other way:

> "You seem to have a great passion for playing with shavings," he said. "Is it a new one?
> "New what?"
> "Passion."
> "I don't know," she said, dropping her eyelids, and keeping on with her effort. She looked shyly aslant at him. "Perhaps you don't approve of playing with shavings?"
> "Oh yes, I do. I admire it very much. But it seems rather difficult. I've a great ambition to put my foot on the shaving's tail and hold it for you."
> "Well," said the girl.
> "Thank you," said the young man. He did so, and now she ran her parasol point easily through it. They looked at each other and laughed. "That was wonderful. Would you like to try another?" he asked.
> "No, I thank you," she replied. "I think one will do."

"What do you suppose he meant by it," Irene asks her sister—a question now shared by the reader. Given Howells' taste, if not his reticence, and given the nature of the *Century Magazine* audience in 1885, the scene cannot be overt sexual symbolism. When Silas merely pointed out to Corey the place in the unfinished house where the girls' room was to be, "it seemed terribly intimate. Irene blushed deeply and turned her head away." There are other problems. Irene, not Tom, is the parasol provocateur and, at that, Irene is the wrong sister: Tom is in love with Penelope. The Freudian response is predictable—a question of role reversal, sublimation, and Howellsian repressions unconsciously bubbling up to the surface. Perhaps, but Howells himself explains the scene in a later passage. Sensible Penelope tells her sister that she was playing with shavings "to hide

4. Introduction, *The Rise of Silas Lapham* (New York: Holt, Rinehart & Winston, 1949), p. xiii.

your embarrassment." It is an adroit symbol of the adolescent social unease which finds a variety of expressions in toe scuffing, tie straightening, button twisting and cigarette puffing.

The nature of Tom's participation should not be overlooked in the scramble for sexual interpretations. Tom has little interest in Irene, yet he endures her ignorance (giving her a reading list as they share the sawhorse) and joins in her embarrassed trifling because he is a gentleman. The Laphams cannot understand a man who is polite to ladies simply for the sake of politeness. This misunderstanding is an important reflection of the Laphams' naïveté, and it establishes the narrative subplot—the Laphams' mistaken notion that Tom is courting beautiful Irene rather than witty Penelope. The triviality of the pine shaving on which Irene builds her romantic castle (she ties it elaborately with a ribbon and cherishes it as a keepsake) underscores the fatuity of her affection. The shaving thus carries a good deal of internal symbolic meaning. Its sexual significance depends, ultimately, on the reader. Like many would-be Freudian symbols, the shaving remains a Rorschach blot.

\* \* \*

# GEORGE N. BENNETT

## [Family Unity in *The Rise of Silas Lapham*]†

The initial episode of the novel succeeds in sounding a positive note. It begins to play on the recurring theme of the simple and unself-conscious dignity of Lapham's own family tradition, which will be of vital importance to the preservation of his integrity. It is a tradition that is easily mocked, as Bartley glibly proves by his questioning: " 'Worked in the fields summers and went to school winters: regulation thing? . . . Parents poor, of course. . . . Any barefoot business? Early deprivations of any kind, that would encourage the youthful reader to go and do likewise?' " In his conventional reverence for motherhood, his pride in his paint, his philistine justification of landscape advertising, and his willingness to talk about himself, Lapham is easy prey for Bartley's clever cynicism. It is Bartley, though, who finally suffers from a comparison, particularly when Lapham momentarily touches on one of the deepest forces of his life—touches only momentarily because, significantly, this is one point at least on which he will not allow himself to brag: " 'All my brothers went West and took up land; but I hung on to the old farm, not because the paint-mine was on it, but because the old house was—and the graves.' " This firm sense of continuity and

---

† From *William Dean Howells: The Development of a Novelist* (Norman: University of Oklahoma Press, 1959), 153–59. (Footnotes are by Bennett.)

of the values of love and devotion to be found in the family unit has been for Lapham and his wife a link with past and a justification of the future. For their children it has created an atmosphere which not only protects them from the outside world but makes any other world largely superfluous. It is, in fact, the very strength of the mutual affection uniting the family in self-sufficiency which contributes to their social ignorance, and one of the complications of theme is the disruption of this solidarity.

The intrusion of Tom Corey is a disturbing element not merely because he represents a different tradition, but because, innocently, he causes the members of the Lapham family to act toward him from motives which are no longer wholly frank and open. It is Lapham, of course, who is particularly devious,[1] and it is his refusal to admit his real motives which provides a measure of his surrender of values. In taking Tom Corey into his business, he insists that he is acting purely from business motives; he is obviously delighted at the invitation to dinner with the Coreys but claims he is acting only in Irene's interest. Neither evasion really deceives Mrs. Lapham, who knows that "in his simple, brutal way, he had long hated their name as a symbol of splendour which, unless he should live to see at least three generations of his descendants gilded with mineral paint, he could not hope to realize in his own."

Howells functions at the peak of his powers in treating the Coreys. Bromfield Corey in particular, charmingly aristocratic and useless, is a labor of love from Howells' pen. Yet it is chiefly by his treatment of Bromfield Corey that Howells introduces the comic aspects of his theme. Having established Corey as the aristocratic dilettante who has deliberately withdrawn from the active commitments of life, Howells permits him to be gracefully witty at the expense of those who take life seriously.[2] The note of indulgence is important:

1. Other members of the family are also affected. The bland assumption that Tom's interest could only be in Irene is not without its bitterness for Penelope, though she at first keeps her resentment from the surface. Penelope becomes guilty of a "potential complicity" and finally, in an excess of conscience, insists on her actual guilt in trying to make Tom like her. Mrs. Lapham, too, is singed by the fires of social ambition, her warnings to her husband notwithstanding. Her conduct during Mrs. Corey's first visit is a sure sign of her loss of dignity and of her nervous desire to please. On that occasion, "In spite of as brave a spirit and as good a conscience as woman need have, Mrs. Lapham cringed inwardly."

2. It is worth noting that Bromfield's objectivity enables Howells to indicate that the displays of vulgarity produced by the impingement of the Laphams on the Coreys' social life are not entirely confined to the Lapham side. When Mrs. Corey reports on her visit to the Laphams, Bromfield is easily able to imagine why Mrs. Lapham appeared "extremely embarrassed and excited": " 'You made her feel so, I dare say, Anna. I can imagine how terrible you must have been, in the character of an accusing spirit.' " He greets her proposal of a dinner with " 'Ah, you overdid the accusing-spirit business, and this is reparation.' " When Mrs. Corey suggests, after it is apparent that Penelope and Tom will marry, that the Laphams are "glad of him on any terms," Bromfield replies in mockery, " 'That is what I have been taught to believe.' " Howells' controlled penetration of character does not waver, however: neither the detachment nor the conduct of Bromfield is affected by his understanding. He continues to regard the forthcoming marriage as "a very disagreeable affair," and it remains an open question whether his resolution to behave as well as he knows how springs from a spirit "safe in the humility he sometimes boasted" or from a spirit "triply armed in pride."

Howells can gain comic relief without abandoning the seriousness of his position. It is for this reason that he resists the patent temptations to farce offered by the famous dinner party at which Lapham makes a drunken fool of himself. Similarly he refuses to enlarge on the ludicrous aspects of the general mistake concerning Tom Corey's intentions toward the Lapham girls, but maintains a firm artistic control over his characterizations by showing Penelope's initial resentment over her secondary role and by indicating that there is no real doubt about how the situation will be resolved.[3]

The spectacle of a man making a fool of himself is, after all, essentially painful rather than comic. It is comic only as it is enclosed in some larger view of human nature—a view which derides the folly of all human action, for example, or, as in Howells' case, a view which includes an awareness of the essential soundness of the victim which will eventually redeem him from his foolishness. A certain amount of comedy arises from Lapham's social ineptitudes, but it is finally the gentlemanliness of Tom and Bromfield Corey that suffers by comparison. They suffer diminution because Lapham's social failure promotes an action from him which is more than social, an act of character possible only to a person who has the moral courage to see himself honestly and to accept the consequences of the knowledge. His apology to Tom Corey is in one sense as excessive as the conduct that necessitated it, but it has its roots in a renewed sense of humility, a renewed sense of distinction between himself and his money.

Lapham's conduct at the dinner party serves to confirm the opinion of Bromfield Corey and his wife that social intercourse with the Laphams is impossible, and the most that Lapham's subsequent apology can produce is a letter of praise from Bromfield. Tom Corey is not unaffected, however, and the experience has more than social meaning for him. Having realized that he was guilty of adding to Lapham's humiliation by remaining aloof from motives of mere gentility, Tom is forced to a revaluation of his whole position in relation to the Laphams. He owns up to the fact that social conduct—at least such relations as his to the Laphams—involves ethical responsibilities and that the possibility of injury is not entirely confined to his family and himself. His proposal to Penelope follows, and the family crisis within the Lapham household results.

It is at this point that the bankruptcy theme (which quantitatively has been in abeyance for seven chapters of about 80 pages) begins to reassert itself. It is typical of Howells' quiet irony, moreover, that the minor theme should continue for a time to overshadow the major, for it is Mrs. Lapham's insistence on revealing this latest complication between the Coreys and the Laphams which prevents Silas from

---

3. When Corey tries to demonstrate his love, Penelope says, "'No! no! I can't let you—yet.'"

telling her of his increasing difficulties with Rogers. But the two themes merge in even more subtle fashion. With a sincerity which has been lacking for some time, Lapham can now state the only terms on which it is possible to resolve the situation: they must act from the motive on which their life together had been predicated—for the good of the children. It is on this basis that he decides that the marriage between Penelope and Tom must be allowed, and his reaction to Mrs. Lapham's suspicion that he may still be acting from unworthy motives—that he is allowing his judgment to be controlled by his desire to have Tom Corey for a son-in-law—dispels any doubt of his sincerity.

Lapham's renewed sense of the values and purposes which had been his before material success clouded his vision is part of the process which enables him to rise to the highest and best that is in him in deciding the business situation from which a legal escape is possible. The standard of "economy of pain" which he had used to decide what would be best for his children cannot be applied to himself. That standard applies to special conditions: when it is to be determined who must suffer when no one is at fault. Penelope's greatest fault remained merely "potential," and in contrast to her father's active guilt even her potential blame is largely forced upon her. Lapham's guilt in his original relation to Rogers is clear from the start and is finally acknowledged by him. Although the whole family must pay for Lapham's original fault, the payment is the loss of their material wealth. Only strict honor can finally redeem Lapham's sin, and redemption brings spiritual compensations not only to him but to the whole family.

\* \* \*

The nature of Lapham's rise and the effects of it on the Lapham family are unmistakable. Irene returns from voluntary exile in Vermont, where she had gone when Tom revealed his true feelings, and in "the shadow of . . . [Lapham's] disaster they returned to something like the old, united life." Lapham is restored to "the manhood which his prosperity had so nearly stolen from him." Ironically, the eventual marriage of Penelope and Tom now produces no social rise because Lapham has returned to the home where he began and because the young couple leave almost immediately for three years in Mexico. Lapham and his wife are now concerned only that Penelope has married the man she loves, and even that satisfaction is tempered by Irene's less fortunate fate.

The novel is brought to a close in a scene which, as George Arms has pointed out, "stands in pleasing symmetry with the Hubbard interview of the first pages."[4] Sewell, the minister who had been

4. George Arms, "Introduction" to W. D. Howells, *The Rise of Silas Lapham* (Rinehart Editions, New York, 1949), xv.

consulted by the Laphams in solving the dilemma caused by Tom Corey and who had confirmed Lapham's solution, visits their Vermont homestead. Sewell's interest in the moral lesson of Lapham's story enables Howells to give final emphasis to his theme and allows Lapham to state in his own words his reflections upon the meaning of the experience which brought him back where he started. Gone is the bragging Lapham of the opening interview; gone is the Lapham who could ease his conscience with a loan whose loss he never expected to matter; gone even is the Lapham who somehow expected that his virtue in refusing Tom Corey's offer of a loan would be recognized by further insistence that it be accepted. The morality which Mrs. Lapham has been preaching throughout the novel, but which she has in a sense been denying by tacitly accepting the benefits of its rejection, is now really Lapham's. And because it has become his through struggle and temptation, it is free from any exaggerated sense of righteousness and heroics. To Sewell's question about regrets, he replies: " 'Seems sometimes as if it was a hole opened for me, and I crept out of it. . . . I don't know as I should always say it paid; but if I done it, and the thing was to do over again, right in the same way, I guess I should have to do it.' "

The mention of Mrs. Lapham suggests another way in which Howells binds his theme of Lapham's moral rise to the family unit. Howells plays on the word *rise* from the start. He describes Lapham's marriage as a "rise in life for him" and continues the same discussion with an account of the relationship with Rogers in which his wife had assumed the role of his conscience. But in this affair Lapham could not "choose the ideal, the unselfish part," he "could not rise to it." Yet it is finally he who achieves moral stature and his wife who fails. She is taught a moral lesson by her husband, and it is because he has risen beyond her that he can administer the lesson without rancor or triumph. During the course of Lapham's business troubles, Mrs. Lapham is led by Rogers to suspect her husband of keeping a mistress. When she discovers her mistake, she draws the same kind of moral application for herself which she has been preaching to her husband: " 'If we're brought back to the day of small things, I guess it's a lesson for me, Silas.' " But the real lesson is in Lapham's explanation of Rogers' motives: " 'Mebbe he believed it,' said Lapham, with patience that cut her more keenly than any reproach. '*You* did.' " This is what Howells had in mind when he opened the whole discussion of the rise in Lapham's life through marriage by commenting that the "silken texture of the marriage tie bears a daily strain of wrong and insult to which no other human relation can be subjected without lesion." It is not irrelevant to remark that Lapham exhibits precisely the kind of character which was beyond the young reporter who introduces his story and whose own story was told in *A Modern Instance.*

\*　　\*　　\*

# EVERETT CARTER

# [Silas Lapham and the Public Morality]†

\* \* \*

Twain was never called upon to formulate his moral code explicitly; but Howells was, and often; and he finally summarized his beliefs concerning the moral function of fiction. There were three levels of immorality in novels, he felt, and we note that nowhere does he speak of immorality as simply the violation of the conventional sexual code. The least pernicious, the most venial sins of the novel are the tickling of our prejudices, the lulling of our judgments, or the pampering of "our gross appetite for the marvellous." These are "not so fatal, but they are innutritious and clog the soul with unwholesome vapors." More immoral is the novel which flatters our passions, and "exalts them above the principles." This kind of novel, he said, is "poisonous," and while it "may not kill" it will "certainly injure." But the mortal crime is committed by the novelist who imagines "a world where the sins of sense are unvisited by the penalties following, swift or slow, but inexorably sure, in the real world. . . ." He produces novels which are "deadly poison: these do kill."

The cataloguing of fictional immorality was based upon the conviction that in the real world, in Howells' world of nineteenth-century America, there was a relation between wrong action and the results of that action; between deed and penalty or reward; the whole structure of his belief depended upon a real world which was fundamentally moral. We may translate "sins of the senses" to mean any usurpation of human reason by human unreason or passion—by the passion of pride as well as love, the passion of possessiveness and acquisition as well as the passions of an unreasoned devotion to an abstract "duty." Any one of these passions, Howells firmly believed, prevented the leading of the good life, individually and socially; and if a novel was to tell the truth about life, it would have to mimic a world in which the supremacy of such passions was penalized by human unhappiness. Sometimes he showed these penalties in operation: the lifelong unhappiness of a professor who, in *A Fearful Responsibility*, acted under false and outdated senses of chivalry and duty, the miserable death of Don Ippolito[1] after the usurpation of his rational faculties by a dreamworld of sentimental unreality, the misery of a Marcia Hubbard[2] who allowed reason to be overcome by physical attraction, the greater degradation of Bartley Hubbard,

†From *Howells and the Age of Realism* (Philadelphia: Lippincott, 1954), pp. 162–69.
1. An Italian priest in Howells' *A Foregone Conclusion* (1875) who allows his infatuation with an American girl to overcome his sense of probabilities. [*Editor.*]
2. The wife of Bartley Hubbard. The story of their ill-fated marriage is told in Howells' *A Modern Instance* (1882). [*Editor.*]

who placed selfish ambition above the emotional health of the society for which he provided news. More often, with typical optimism, his comedies showed the triumph of reason over temporary aberration: the partial satisfaction of Grace Breen[3] in marriage after she had come to terms with her puritanic obsession with duty, the good life Colville[4] found after rejecting the falsities of sentimentalism which had engendered his attachment to Imogene. And finally in 1885, Howells gave this optimism its final expression in *The Rise of Silas Lapham*.

The moral scheme envisioned in this work was ill-served by the simplicity of the book's structure; for in keeping with his earlier dedication to the small, the well made, the unified, Howells wrote the book about a house, the building of which becomes, in almost every respect, neatly symbolic of the moral rise and material fall of its builder, Silas Lapham, the man of industry and commerce. Lapham had turned his native force and energies into the production and marketing of "the best paint in the world," and had devoted his life to its success and his. He told its merits to Bartley Hubbard, the young reporter who came to interview him, with "the intonation of a prayer." And when Bartley asked him for "your life or your money," it was not in jest that Lapham replied that he guessed no one would want his life without his money. He pursued his success, not selfishly, but simply as "someone who had lived to himself" without the knowledge of social good and evil. He defended his advertising which had spread "Lapham's Mineral Paint—Specimen" on every board-fence, bridge-girder, dead wall, barn, and rock in the region; as long as there was no objection from the people that owned the barns and fences, he didn't see "what the public" had got to do with it. He drove his fine trotter down the Boston streets, feeling his sense of triumph as the mare left everything behind her on the road. "And as he grazed a hundred encountered and rival sledges" in his passage, he made his first announcement to his wife that he was going to build a house on the water side of Beacon.

As the first timbers went up, Lapham and his wife stood enjoying it until they sensed someone at their elbow, and it turned out to be Rogers, the man over whom Lapham had rolled on his way to the top, appearing at the moment when the house, the symbol of Lapham's worldly success, was going up. Mrs. Lapham immediately made the identification, and said she would never live in the building, for it represented Lapham's violation of moral law. At this point, the theme of the novel was explicitly stated: "Happy is the man for ever after who can choose the ideal, the unselfish part in such an exigency" (as Lapham's choice in buying out Rogers); and

3. A female doctor, the chief character in Howells' *Doctor Breen's Practice* (1881). [*Editor.*]
4. Theodore Colville's engagement to Imogene Graham, a girl much younger than he, is the central concern of Howells' *Indian Summer* (1886). [*Editor.*]

then Howells bluntly told us "Lapham could not rise to it." The remainder of the tale is concerned largely with Lapham's moral education, his achieving the moral ability to "rise."

To what? To a sense of the morality which binds the social world together, making it imperative that we live for others and not for ourselves. In this moral world, happiness follows when we have pursued the course that will make for the most well-being for the most people. For the world of purely personal relationships, Howells had already explored this morality, which David Sewell, the minister, called "economy of pain," in *Indian Summer*. And for the subplot of *Silas Lapham*, Howells chose the same triadic misunderstanding between lovers, one of whom wants to sacrifice herself, and make three people miserable, instead of just one. The building of the house became a symbol for this relationship, too, for Irene, the young and empty-headed daughter, deceived herself into believing herself beloved while sitting upon a trestle of the house with Tom Corey, and playing her unconscious but nonetheless pointed sexually symbolic game with the wood shavings left behind by the carpenters. The shaving from the house, a sliver of the major symbol, became the symbol for the sliver of personal morality which is part of the large morality of social living.

For as the shaving is to the whole house, so is the complexity of the personal ethic to the social. And it is the social ethic which Howells tried to understand through writing *Silas Lapham*. The "rise," if it is a rise (and there were many, including one English reviewer, who were puzzled by the title, since the story apparently told of a financial disaster), was a rise from barbaric isolation to civilized social conduct, the only means of achieving, if not happiness, at least inner peace. The ability to rise above self-interest to the interest of another, the ability to rise above the interest of another, no matter how close, to the interest of a group, the strength to rise above even the interests of a group to which you have ties of proximity and affection to the interests of the larger society of which you are impersonally a part—these were the successive stages of the salvation of modern man, Howells told us in *The Rise of Silas Lapham*. The first stage was easy—for Lapham. The first stage is personal, with deeply personal emotional rewards granted the simple altruist; and both deed and reward are exceedingly simple to render in the emotional and reward are exceedingly simple to render in the emotional and personalized method of fiction. There was Rogers, a man with a wife (like his own) with hopes (like his), and the act of empathy demanded only the little imagination of which he was capable. But it is not in this easy, first act that social salvation lay, Howells knew, but in an act of the imagination so great that it has yet to be captured in American literature, perhaps cannot be captured in our literature until there are enough of us capable of performing it ourselves. No wonder that poor rough Silas Lapham and the essentially frail structure of well-formed narrative in which he was embedded were not quite capable of giving it full expression.

What is this act of the imagination? It is really the logical demands of the basic faith, the religious faith we may even call it, of Howells and his age in the value of their material world of social appearances. In this world, the acts of devotion of man to man are, by definition, acts of devotion to the only way in which they could conceive of God. Tom Corey, at one point, the crucial point in the story, alluded to the moral act which Howells believed the most significant of his century—the war for the preservation of the Union and the freeing of the slaves, and asked of the action of the common soldier in it: "What has ever been conceived of omnipotence, of omniscience, so sublime, so divine as that?" And the minister, David Sewell, replied quietly: "Nothing." And then he said: "God has never been imagined at all. But if you suppose such a man as that was Authorized, I think it will help you to imagine what God must be." At this point Lapham took his cigar out of his mouth, placed his forearms on the table and said simply: "There's sense in that." This moment, at the Coreys' dinner party, was the hub around which the structure of the novel turned. It was the end of Lapham's dreams of success in Society and the beginning of his realization of the demands of society. As he worked out his salvation, he remembered the minister's words and Sewell became, for him, the preacher of the true religion. When his daughters become involved in a sentimental tangle of meaningless self-sacrifice over Tom Corey, he suggested that his wife visit Sewell whose looks, Lapham said, he liked "about as well as any man he ever saw." And when she did, Sewell threw the light of common sense upon the "traditions which are the figment of the shallowest sentimentality."

Just before the visit to Sewell, Lapham and his wife had been driving the trotter, the same mare in which he had taken so much individualistic pride at the beginning of the story, and this time, preoccupied by their discussion of their children's problems, he ran into another carriage, and the "voice in front of him" shouted, "Where the devil you goin' to?" And Lapham began, from this point on, to understand that the world is a scene of an ethical struggle between a tempting devil and a redeeming God. When an opportunity arose for Lapham to recoup his losses by letting some property buyers beware, his wife said: "It does seem too hard . . . that you have to give up this chance when Providence had fairly raised it up for you." And Lapham replied grimly: "I guess it wan't *Providence* raised it up." It was as near as modern man can come to the devil, for the series of temptations placed in his progress were subtly worthy of the archfiend. At first, it was made possible for Lapham to sin by omission—simply *not* to say something; then the buyers of his worthless property showed themselves willing and eager to be duped since the funds involved were not their own; and finally, Rogers wanted to permit himself to be used as the instrument of evil; sell me the property, he said; what I do with it afterwards is no ethical concern of yours. But Lapham rose to this final temptation saying: "If you think I'm going to help you whip the devil round the stump, you're mistaken. . . ." And that night, he paced up and down while in the next room his wife listened to him and thought of the scriptural words: " 'And there wrestled a man with him until the breaking of the day. . . . And he said, Let me go, for the day breaketh. And he said I will not let thee go, except thou bless me.' " Lapham, at the end, a ruined man, could tell the minister solemnly that he had been blessed and had come out of the hell of selfishness; in his homelier words: "Seems sometimes as if it was a hole opened for me, and I crept out of it."

The nature of the successive temptations of Lapham illustrates the complexities of the problem of social ethics as they spiral out of the simplicity of individual right and wrong conduct, and this complexity when seen against the essentially oversimplified fictional structure is the reason why the novel is so oddly dissatisfying despite its many merits. After unselfishness involving single personalities, an altruism easily visualized, its rewards immediately, intensely, personally warming, comes the welfare of groups, human groups, but with individual faces blurred, individual reactions diluted by immersal in the mass, and the strain on the imagination becomes greater. But then, after the group to which one is tied by bonds of proximity, comes the social body as a whole, something without name, without wife or child, without eyes to cry and heart to suffer, and yet, Howells believed, the most important concept constructed by man in his climb from barbarism to civilized life. It was the well-being of this impersonal personification that Lapham was called upon to place above the well-being of a man's invalid wife ("You want to sacrifice her to a mere idea!" shouted Rogers), and his factory workers ("I don't know what's going to become of the hands in the middle of winter," said Mrs. Lapham). For the Englishmen who wished to buy the land were agents of a community ". . . of an association of rich and charitable people," as they suavely put it, and by insisting that the transaction would hurt no one but those that could afford it, appealed to "that easy-going, not evilly intentioned, potential immorality which regards common property as common prey, and gives us the most corrupt municipal governments under the sun—which makes the poorest voter, when he has tricked into place, as unscrupulous in regard to other's money as an hereditary prince."

This then was the nature of the ethical truth about his society which Howells held in 1885, and which he tried to propound through his novel—a truth difficult of dramatic and imaginative realization because of the almost complete absence of personality in the social organism; it takes an enormous feat of the imagination to envisage this entity and be concerned for its welfare; one must feel the organic complexities and inter-relationships which throb in a modern society; and yet, in order to make concrete such complexity, Howells had chosen, as we have seen, a small, tight, almost allegorical construction where scene reflects character, and symbol reflects moral purpose with almost mechanical consistency, and makes us feel smallness and constriction, instead of greatness and expansion and complexity. The vehicle was simply not up to the burden it had to carry; it was a vehicle suitable to the moral load of the individual social problem of *A Woman's Reason*, or the problems in personal love of *Indian Summer*, or the individual moral dilemmas of *A Modern Instance*. But it could not involve the reader imaginatively in a whole society.

# G. THOMAS TANSELLE

## The Architecture of *The Rise of Silas Lapham*[†]

When the architect Seymour, in Chapter 3 of *The Rise of Silas Lapham*, is discussing with the Laphams their plans for a new house, he suggests a dining room behind the hall because such an arrangement "gets you rid of one of those long, straight, ugly staircases . . . and gives you an effect of amplitude and space." He also hopes that Silas will not insist on a flamboyant material like black walnut, for which there has recently been "a great craze." After all, as a paint manufacturer ought to know, a more everyday material will be just as effective in the end; indeed, "there is really nothing like white paint" for simple dignity. So Howells knew, and he constructed, on a small foundation and with common materials, scrupulously following his blueprint, a house of "amplitude and space" which contains, not a "long, straight, ugly" staircase, but rather two staircases that intersect in many ingenious ways before they finally come together at the upper level.

It is, in fact, this double "staircase," or plot, that has caused more disagreement than anything else about the relative merits of *Lapham*. Any reader sees immediately that the book is made up of two strands

[†]From *American Literature*, 37 (January 1966), 430– cated.)
57. (Footnotes are by Tanselle, unless otherwise indi-

which can be referred to roughly as the "bankruptcy" plot and the "love" plot and that certain characters are involved in both. But the love story is sometimes thought of as not integrally related to the main story of Silas's financial downfall and ethical rise; it has been considered Howells's concession to the public demand for romance. Oscar Firkins once went so far as to say that the two plots "do not concern each other" (though he admitted, "Structurally perhaps [*Lapham*] is the shapeliest of the novels");[1] Howard Mumford Jones has suggested that "possibly [Howells's] two plots interfere with each other";[2] and Harry Hartwick believes that the book "is weakened by Howells's inevitable intrusion of a love affair."[3] The fact that a manuscript summary of the original idea for *Lapham* contains only two sentences referring to the "subplot" has been used by both the detractors of the novel and its defenders.[4] The former consider this document proof that the Penelope-Tom plot, as it finally turned out, is an excrescence which Howells allowed to develop during the composition of the novel but which was not in his mind originally as an important part of the book; the latter, on the contrary, assert that the very development of the second plot beyond the proportions suggested by the synopsis reveals how essential and integral it is—Howells saw that he could not get along without it. Whichever way one argues, it is clear that any final evaluation of *Lapham* as a work of art must meet this question of its basic unity and that any meaningful answer must come from an examination of the work itself as we have it.

1. *William Dean Howells: A Study* (Cambridge, Mass., 1924), pp. 71, 112. In fairness to Firkins, one should have quote his statement that "the story of the business difficulties of the father is united to this love-tale by ties which a logician might blame as inadequate, but which, in an age in which art measures its prosperity by its indifference to logic, criticism must not hasten to condemn" (p. 112).

2. Introduction to the World's Classics edition of *Lapham* (London, 1948), pp. x–xi. Jones explains that "once Howells has got Tom down to Nahant, the conditions of the plot compel him to lose interest in the hero [Tom] as a person; he becomes merely the occasion of tension in the Lapham family and quite fades out at the end. The management of the plot is, I think, the real weakness here." But even as "the occasion of tension" he is serving his function and helping make the two plots work together. A more serious objection to the Corey plot consists of the "good many loose ends" Jones notices in the handling of the Coreys: that Bromfield is too "passive to be effective except as a commentator"; that, although the Corey fortunes shrink, nothing "follows from what would appear to be a plot datum of significance"; and that the two Corey daughters remain shadowy (pp. vii–viii). One may concede, however, that these are undeveloped possibilities for parrellelism without detracting from the impressiveness of the plot integration that is actually achieved.

3. *The Foreground of American Fiction* (New York, 1934), pp. 324–325; at the same time, he alludes to Howells's "able construction of plot," which he considers a "delight." That the romantic element is an "intrusion" is also suggested by Marcus Cunliffe, who talks of what led Howells "to contrive a subplot that seems a little implausible" (*The Literature of the United States*, London, 1954, p. 198).

4. Clara and Rudolf Kirk were the first to describe and comment on this manuscript synopsis of "The Rise of Silas Needham" in their introduction to the American Writers Series, *Howells: Representative Selections* (New York, 1950), pp. cix–cx. Everett Carter, in the introduction to the Harper's Modern Classics edition (New York, 1958), reprints this synopsis (pp. xiv–xv). Recently Kermit Vanderbilt, in "Howells Among the Brahmins: Why 'The Bottom Dropped Out' During *The Rise of Silas Lapham*," *New England Quarterly*, 35, 291–317 (Sept., 1962), has analyzed some of the changes made in the novel from the Needham synopsis to the *Century* serialization to the published book; see especially Part IV (pp. 308–313), where he discusses the enlargement of the "subplot" to such an extent that the book becomes a "general inquiry into the social structure of a new era in America."

The presence of the word "rise" in the title naturally draws attention to the rise-and-fall pattern, and critics have most frequently looked at the structure of the novel in these terms—a social and materialistic rise accompanied by a moral descent in the first part of the book, which reverses itself to become a worldly failure and an ethical success in the last part.[5] But this approach is not entirely successful in showing the relevance of the secondary plot: in fact, although most commentators do feel the need to say something about the construction of the book and usually praise it in general terms, one is surprised to observe how rarely they actually analyze the precise degree of integration of the two plots.[6] There should be some value, therefore, in examining the structure of *Lapham* in detail, for only then shall we have a factual basis for evaluating the two contradictory traditions: that of commending the book's finely wrought structure and of criticizing its superfluous plot. Only then shall we know whether the edifice can support the burden it has to bear or whether it will collapse as a result of inexpert draftsmanship.

I

We may begin, in order to see each part of the book in its proper perspective, by making a quick survey of the over-all plan of the novel before going in more detail into the various parts. *Lapham* falls, quite naturally, into five large movements. One notices, first of all, that the dinner party comes in Chapter 14 and that, since the book contains twenty-seven chapters, this is the exact center, with thirteen chapters on each side. That everything radiates from this central chapter is not a new idea—almost all commentators have observed it. But there is no general agreement from there on as to how the book is divided. George Arms says that the "second part," Chapters 11 to 19, "consists of one highly concentrated sequence, the dinner party and the events anticipating and following it." But it is not clear why one should consider the discussion about what Penelope is to do (in Chaps. 16–19) or Corey's visit to Lapham's office (Chap. 11) as more closely associated with the dinner party than other events earlier or

---

5. Besides Howells's famous comment to Francis Parkman (who had misunderstood the title) that he supposed Lapham's rise to be a moral one, see his remark in a letter to Professor William Strunk that Lapham "was finding out, against his selfish ambition and temptations, what a true rise was"—a letter published by Paul Carter in "A Howells Letter," *New England Quarterly*, 28, 93–96 (March, 1955).

6. The major discussions of *Lapham* will be referred to in later parts of this article, but many briefer comments on the book allude to its structure: Carl Van Doren in *Cambridge History of American Literature* (New York, 1917–1921), III, 80; Alexander Harvey, *William Dean Howells* (New York, 1917), pp. 54, 147; D. G. Cooke,

*William Dean Howells* (New York, 1922), p. 248; Ludwig Lewisohn, *Expression in America* (New York, 1932), p. 253; Booth Tarkington in the Centenary edition of *Lapham* (Boston, 1937), p. xi; Carl Van Doren, *The American Novel* (rev. ed.; New York, 1940), p. 127; Gordon S. Haight in *Literary History of the United States* (New York, 1948), p. 892; Alexander Cowie, *The Rise of the American Novel* (New York, 1948), p. 670; Van Wyck Brooks, *Howells: His Life and World* (New York, 1959), p. 162; Edwin T. Bowden, *The Dungeon of the Heart* (New York, 1961), pp. 108–109; Rudolf and Clara Kirk in the Collier edition of *Lapham* (New York, 1962), p. 9, and in *William Dean Howells* (New York, 1962), p. 106.

later. It seems best, therefore, to limit the dinner party sequence to three chapters—Chapter 14, the one preceding it, and the one following. In Chapter 13 the invitations are sent, the Laphams receive them, and they prepare to go; in Chapter 15 Lapham the next day apologizes to Tom for the way he behaved at the party. These three chapters bear a direct relation to the party, then, and together may be taken as the central pivot.

We are now left with twelve chapters before, and twelve after, this central section. Each of these groups of twelve falls symmetrically into two parts, one of four chapters and the other of eight. In the first half, Chapters 1–4 concern the Lapham family and portray Silas's materialistic "rise"—the interview, plans for the house, and a visit to the house. Beginning with Chapter 5, there are eight chapters devoted mainly to the Corey family, introduced by the conversation between Tom and his father about what work Tom is going to do (Chap. 5). The question of Tom's job, in fact, is the unifying force of this section and brings the Coreys into contact with the Laphams, as their relationship is explored in terms of Tom's romantic interest in one of the Lapham daughters. It is worth observing that, up to this halfway point in the book, one has no basis for referring to the love story as the "subplot" since more than half of the chapters, quantitatively, have been given over to it.

The second half of the novel breaks into the same kind of grouping, though with the opposite emphasis—a four-chapter section (Chaps. 16–19) dealing with the love plot and an eight-chapter portion (Chaps. 20–27) dealing with the bankruptcy plot. This half of the book shows, in both plots, an ethical choice being faced and made. In Chapter 16 Tom declares his love, and in the succeeding three chapters Penelope tries to decide what to do. After she refuses Tom in Chapter 19 (in the vein of romantic self-sacrifice discussed at the dinner party), attention turns to the business plot with Silas's revelation of Rogers's treachery (Chap. 20). The Laphams now discuss the Rogers matter, just as they had wrestled with Penelope's choice earlier, until events reach a crisis, and Lapham, deciding to sacrifice personal financial gain, finds himself in bankruptcy (Chap. 27). The visit of the Reverend Mr. Sewell in the last chapter is not only to be contrasted to the Hubbard interview of the first chapter but is also to be compared with the earlier visit in Chapter 18. That Sewell should be consulted in both the Penelope-Tom affair and in the Lapham-Rogers matter is indicative of the parallelism with which the climactic events of each plot are handled.

Such a way of schematizing the novel brings out the care Howells has taken to keep the two plots in balance. Twelve chapters are dominated by each plot, and they are arranged around the dinner-party chapters with regard for both symmetry and emphasis. It does make sense to speak of the romance as a subplot to the extent that it is placed in the middle of the book, leaving the emphatic positions at beginning and end for the other plot. After we witness Silas as a boasting self-made businessman at the opening, we shift our attention to Tom Corey, so that we are fully prepared for the climax of the theme of "social rise" at the dinner party; then we watch Penelope making her decision (and thus get most of the love plot out of the way in the middle of the book) before turning to Silas's parallel problem in the last block of chapters.[7] The two plots support each other, but the decision in the love plot does seem to be serving as a preparation for Silas's final decision. It may perhaps be convenient to summarize this approach diagrammatically:[8]

| *Chapters* | | | | |
|---|---|---|---|---|
| I. | 1–4 (4) | Business | Materialistic rise | Discussions about house |
| II. | 5–12 (8) | Love | Social rise | Discussions about marriage |
| III. | 13–15 (3) | Dinner | Equilibrium of elements | |
| IV. | 16–19 (4) | Love | Social fall | Ethical choice: Penelope |
| V. | 20–27 (8) | Business | Materialistic fall | Ethical choice: Silas |

The centrality of social relationships and conventions to both plots is evidenced not only by the central position of the dinner party (with its emphasis on etiquette and the relationship between social classes) but also by the general progression of the seasons, against which all the events of the novel are set. As we move into the summer of 1875

7. Similarly, Donald Pizer, in "The Ethical Unity of *The Rise of Silas Lapham*," *American Literature*, 32, 322–327 (Nov., 1960), says that the love plot contributes to Lapham's education because, "Dominating the center of the novel, it is solved before the full exposition of Lapham's business career" (p. 324). Vanderbilt, too, recognizes that "subplot" is not quite the right term (pp. 310–312).

8. It should be noted that the divisions of the novel for serial publication in the *Century* do not coincide, except in one instance (Chapter 12 is the end of the fifth instalment), with the outline suggested in this paper. Though it seems undeniable that serial publication affects structure (when a work is specifically written with such publication in mind), the serial divisions of *Lapham* do not appear to correspond to plot movement so much as to achieve an apportioning into ten fairly equal segments. The ten monthly instalments (from November, 1884, through August, 1885) divide the chapters in the following manner (with the number of pages covered given in parentheses, those in the *Century* before the oblique line, those in the first edition afterward): (1) Chapters 1–2 (14/52); (2) Chapters 3–5

(13/47); (3) Chapters 6–8 (15/52); (4) Chapters 9–10 (12/41); (5) Chapters 11–12 (14/50); (6) Chapters 13–14 (15/52); (7) Chapters 15–18 (13/47); (8) Chapters 19–21 (15/54); (9) Chapters 22–25 (21/74); (10) Chapters 26–27 (13/46). The only division which is out of proportion is the ninth, but if Chapter 25 had been held over, the tenth instalment would have been equally out of proportion. The slight pattern created by the fact that the first and last instalments, as well as the three middle ones (4, 5, 6), each consist of two chapters, is coincidental and of little significance when one considers some of the breaking points these divisions produce: for example, Penelope's refusal of Tom (Chap. 19), surely a climax to be compared with Silas's later decision, is the *first* chapter of an instalment, followed by two others which shift the subject to Rogers and to Silas's financial problems. The division is more understandable, then, as the strategy of a magazine editor (who not only would hope for equal instalments but would try to end an instalment *before* a climactic incident in order to build up interest in the forthcoming issue) than as a guide to the structure of the novel.

in the early part of the book and then through fall into winter and back around to summer at the end, we watch the fashionable classes leaving Boston for their summer homes and gradually returning again. This is the large rhythmic pattern that informs every individual incident and plays a crucial role in determining the date for the dinner party.

The outline of *Lapham* set forth here has the merit of dealing with both plots and of giving each an equal place in the structure: in short, of finding that a symmetrical arrangement of chapters coincides with the pattern of movement between the plots. This is not to deny the value of such a plan as George Arms's three-part division (after Chaps. 10 and 19); what he describes as the "essential movement" of the book—a rising toward material success, followed by two failures, first in "social ambitions" and then in business—is certainly there and is a helpful way of seeing the over-all pattern, but it is most applicable to the bankruptcy plot.[9] One must agree with Arms that there is "a sense of form in *The Rise of Silas Lapham* that is notably fine and in last analysis renders the novel a work of art"; but one must realize that any attempt to examine what creates that sense of form has to show, in addition to the movement of the whole, the inextricability and interrelationship of the parts—in this case, the two plots. One can then discern—to use Mark Twain's phrase about Howells's style—the "architectural felicities of construction" in *Lapham*.

## II

"I never saw anything so very sacred about a big rock, along a river or in a pasture that it wouldn't do to put mineral paint on it in three colours. . . . I say the landscape was made for man, and not man for the landscape." This statement strikes the keynote, not only of the opening chapter, but of the opening section of four chapters. The insensitive pride of the self-made man and the dominance of the business ethic ("The day of small things was past, and I don't suppose it will ever come again in this country,")—illustrated in the figure of Silas—are the motifs of these chapters and are clearly expressed in the interview. But the first chapter introduces certain other matters that are to be important in the structure of the novel as

9. Arms, in his introduction to the Rinehart edition (New York, 1951), pp. xiv–xv, defines his division further (p. xv) by saying that the first part contains "four main sequences" (not specified), the second "one highly concentrated sequence" (the dinner), and the third "a series of hopes and disappointments"; the final moral rise he finds occurring in "two steps": resistance to temptations, then the "testing of [Lapham's] sensibility by Sewell." He also talks of the "pleasing symmetry" of the Hubbard interview at the be-ginning and the Sewell visit at the end, but he believes finally that Howells "does not achieve a richly satisfying relationship between the daughter's conduct in love and the father's in business." John E. Hart, in "The Commonplace as Heroic in *The Rise of Silas Lapham*," *Modern Fiction Studies*, 8, 375–383 (1962–1963), also points out that an interview opens and closes the book (in addition to commenting on the symbols of houses and paint).

a whole. For one thing, we know that it is summer in 1875. Then we have references to Silas's new house and an implied contrast with Bartley's rented apartment and his future house ("There are places in that Clover Street house that need touching up so dreadfully").

We have the allusion to something unpleasant in Silas's short trial of a partnership system, foreshadowing the Rogers affair; we have Bartley's observations on the beauty of Silas's secretary, foreshadowing the Zerrilla episode. That almost everything in the book can be traced back to this interview is a commonplace of Howells criticism;[1] that the foreshadowing is extremely subtle at times (while admittedly mechanical at others) is much less frequently pointed out. Particularly here the theme of social contrasts is introduced, not merely in Bartley's sarcastic replies, but in a number of small touches: Silas keeps his old Vermont house "in good shape" so that he can "spend a month or so there every summer"—just as the best Boston families leave town at that time; he has in his office a "ground-glass door" which he can shut "between his little den and the book-keepers, in their larger den outside"—for he has risen to a class above; he ostentatiously says, "*I* didn't know what the Back Bay was then," when he remembers the scientist alluding to it years before—since he has now obviously "arrived"; he is even referred to in Bartley's article as "one of nature's noblemen." All these details (along with a glimpse of married life on one social level—the Hubbards') work to suggest the social values and aspirations that are an inseparable part of the commercial "rise."

The other three chapters in the first movement develop the story of Lapham's growing domination by materialistic standards in terms of one of its social manifestations established in the first chapter— the new house. Chapter 2 is a flashback to the preceding summer (1874), when the idea of moving to a new house had first come into the Laphams' thoughts, and it traces through the winter the growth of their plans for building; Chapter 3 moves into the spring, when the architect is consulted, and the early summer, when the pile-driving begins; and Chapter 4 describes a family inspection tour of what had been finished by July. The house as a symbol of materialism is evident in many remarks of Lapham's which show that he is taking money as the basis of everything—speaking of his daughters and the improvement in their social position that the new house

1. Arms sums the matter up in speaking of "cross reference" (p. xiv): "Every critic has had something to say about the introduction of anticipatory detail in the first episode, and perhaps in those beginning chapters cross reference is a little too much done." When William Manierre, in "*The Rise of Silas Lapham*: Retrospective Discussion as Dramatic Technique," *College English*, 23, 357–361 (Feb., 1962), uses the terms "retrospective discussion" and "anticipatory detail," he has the same sort of technique in mind: he points out, for example, that the meeting of Tom and Silas in Chapter 4 is discussed from various points of view in five later scenes, or that the "shavings" episode forms the basis of conversation between different persons at four later points (pp. 358–359).

would bring, he asks his wife, "Why don't you get them into society? There's money enough!"; of the architecture, he comments, "And if you come to style, I don't know as anybody has got more of a right to put it on than what we have." The entrance of Rogers in Chapter 3, when Silas and his wife visit the new house, furthers the association of the house with the "business rise"—a rise, it is now clear, accomplished at the cost of some human feeling. Mrs. Lapham sees the structural significance of Rogers's appearance at this time when she says that he "always manages to appear just at the moment when he seems to have gone fairly out of our lives, and blight everything"—his intrusions will punctuate the book with reminders of the price of business success.[2] But the house, a natural symbol of social status, does more than introduce us to the business plot, for the beginnings of the Corey element occur here, too. We first meet the Coreys as early as Chapter 2 (when the Laphams run into them at Baie St. Joan), and it is the Coreys who first make the Laphams dissatisfied with the house in Nankeen Square that had served them for twelve years: Mrs. Corey says, "Nearly all our friends are on the New Land or on the Hill."

It is fair to say, therefore, that the opening movement is centered on the Lapham—business plot (as opposed to the Corey-love plot), but that the construction of the house is an ingenious way to bring in the matter of social awareness, important to both plots, and to make comments about the Laphams' taste relevant—"rich and rather ugly clothes," "abominable frescoes," "a crude taste in architecture," admiring "the worst," lack of "a sufficiently cultivated palate for Souchong," and so on. The romantic interest is also introduced (with a number of clues that Penelope is the more interesting of the girls, even to Tom;[3] and Tom's visit in Chapter 4 prepares us for the next movement, beginning in Chapter 5, when Tom becomes the center of attention. But the focus is not blurred, and we are not allowed to forget that behind the Laphams' rise lies the manufacture of paint, which cannot be used "on the human conscience," that we are witnessing "the effect of the poison of ambition," that only the man who can "rise" to "choose the ideal, the unselfish part" is happy—in short, we are prepared to read, as in Bartley's interview, of Silas's "life, death, and Christian sufferings."

2. George N. Bennett, in *William Dean Howells: The Development of a Novelist* (Norman, Okla., 1959), points out that Rogers appears at "decisive moments" (p. 159). And Richard Coanda discusses Rogers as a devil-figure, playing his role in the Christian drama of Lapham's fortunate fall (*Explicator*, 22, 1963, item 16).
3. Jones, in his World's Classics introduction, points out that most readers do not see these hints about Penelope and suggests, "Keeping this secret down, so to speak, means that Howells is unable to show any clear reason why Penelope rather than Irene should attract Corey" (p. x). But one could argue, rather, that the multiplicity of references to Penelope's attractiveness makes the affair "secret" only to the Coreys and the Laphams and not to the reader.

III

Just after Silas speaks to Penelope at the end of Chapter 4, the scene shifts to another parental relationship. Chapter 5, a discussion between Tom and his father in the Corey library about the possibility of Tom's getting a job, is the first time we have been taken into the Corey home and opens up a group of eight chapters (twice as long as the first part, both in number of chapters and of pages) concerned primarily with Tom—and thus with the love plot. As the romance was subordinate in the first part, so the business plot is secondary here; yet the two are integrated through the elder Corey's concern about his finances and Tom's entrance into Lapham's firm. There are occasional episodes in this part where Tom is not present, but in those cases he is the topic of conversation. Even when the scene is the Laphams' bedroom, as in the brief passage at the end of Chapter 5 which continues from the point where Chapter 4 ended, Silas is talking about Tom and how the paint business would make a man of him. The only intrusion—the Laphams' discussion of Rogers's request for a loan—is inserted, in Chapter 10, between a description of Tom and his father and an account of one of Tom's visits to the Laphams' Nantasket cottage; the Rogers affair is, in this way, placed within the framework of the Corey plot[4] and takes the direction it does so that the only possible tarnish on Lapham's success has, from the Lapham point of view, been removed before the turning point of the book. Lapham's pride and complacency, rising as a result of Tom's attentions to his daughter, now suffer no check from the business plot; rather, with the feeling that reparation has been made, comes a release and an attitude of even greater confidence— symbolized by Silas's decision "to take advantage" of his wife's high spirits (resulting from his loan to Rogers) by "bringing Corey down to supper."

It is this concentration on Tom's affairs which is the most striking aspect of the second movement. The pattern is set in Chapter 5, where the remarks of Tom and his father have to do both with Tom's prospects of a job and with the social distinction between people like the Coreys ("Essex County people . . . just a little beyond the salt of the earth") and the *nouveaux riches* ("the suddenly rich are on a level with any of us nowadays"). The social and the business elements continue to be mixed, though here the business side enters through the Corey heritage (Bromfield's father, "the old India merchant") and through Tom's aspirations in the Lapham firm

4. The degree of integration of the two plots is illustrated by a conversation in this chapter, reminiscent of a number of similar conversations throughout the book. When Mrs. Lapham asks Silas, "How came he to come down with you?," Silas returns, "Who? Rogers?"; when she then explains that she meant "Mr. Corey," Silas appears surprised, "affecting not to have thought she could mean Corey." Harry Hayden Clark, in his Modern Library introduction (New York, 1951), p. xii, calls attention to a similar unifying device.

(equivalent to Silas's ambitions in the social realm). Chapter 6 begins with Tom's visit to his family's summer place, moves into his application to Lapham for a position, and ends with his arrival at the Laphams' summer cottage; Chapter 7 is devoted to this first visit at the Laphams', with business again occupying the middle of the chapter, but it is worth noting that we are not taken into the room where Silas and Tom are talking—the emphasis is on the social and romantic implications of that business interview. In the following chapter, after the Coreys' discussion of their son's relations with the Laphams, Tom begins working at Silas's office. In Chapter 9 there is a similar conversation between Silas and his wife, followed by the visit to the new house with the famous episode of the shavings,[5] after which there is more talk about the Laphams between Tom and his father, and finally we have the Laphams again speculating on Tom's intentions. The next two chapters end with further visits of Tom's to the Nantasket cottage, the second of these describing Bromfield Corey's call at Lapham's office (a business setting with social over-tones) parallel to Tom's first visit to the cottage in Chapter 7 (a social setting with business overtones). The whole movement of eight chapters is divided into two subsidiary parts by the two appearances of Mrs. Corey, in Chapter 8 and in Chapter 12. The Coreys, in Chapter 8, are discussing Tom during Mrs. Corey's brief return to town in July; in Chapter 12, they again talk about Tom and sum up the situation after Mrs. Corey and the daughters have come back in the early fall—and it is then that the Coreys decide they must go through with a dinner.

The building of the house is brought into each of the last four chapters, and the technique of "cross reference" in general is used with as much effectiveness here as in the more celebrated instance of the Hubbard interview. The Zerrilla matter is foreshadowed in references to the "pretty girl" that Tom notices in Silas's office, in Tom's overhearing Silas's advice to her about divorce, and in the "sordidness" of the vignette of the drunken sailor at the end of Chapter 8; the Rogers affair is of course talked about in Chapter 10 (and referred to in Chap. 11); Hubbard's interview is used to make social distinctions between those who read the *Events* and those who read the *Daily*; literary discussions are placed to prepare us for the one at the dinner and to continue the attack on sentimental self-sacrifice. Further, there are suggestions that Penelope is more attractive than Irene, with so direct a remark as Mrs. Lapham's "I

5. Everett Carter, in *Howells and the Age of Realism* (Philadelphia, 1954), discusses (pp. 151, 165) the sexual implications of the scene and the significance of the shaving, "a sliver of the major symbol," as a "symbol for the sliver of personal morality which is part of the large morality of social living." One wonders, however, why it is the female who manipulates the umbrella and why a sliver from the "major symbol" of materialism and selfishness should represent a fragmentation of the "large," presumably altruistic and unselfish, morality necessary for society as a whole.

hope you'll be just as well satisfied, Si, if it turns out he doesn't want Irene after all"; comments about a "temptation" of Silas; and passages reinforcing the whole parallelism of the Coreys' dwindling capital, the Laphams' increasing fortune, and the sentiments of both that dishonest money is to be abhorred. The comparison of Lapham and Corey is not simply a matter of their mutual, if different, interests in business and society, nor of similar situations, like the parents' discussions of their sons and daughters; it extends even to particular remarks: we have Bromfield Corey, late in Chapter 9, saying that "this thing we call civilisation" is "really an affair of individuals," a statement which recalls Lapham's earlier in the chapter, when he says that "a thing has got to be born in a man; and if it ain't born in him, all the privations in the world won't put it there." Finally, one should not overlook remarks which point forward to the dinner, since this entire movement leads up to the decision to have it. As early as Chapter 9, Bromfield says to his son, "One can't do anything in the summer. . . . Still, I can't rid myself of the idea of a dinner."

IV

The center of the novel, in every respect, occurs in the three chapters dealing with the dinner, and it is not surprising that the dinner party has been the most frequently discussed scene in the book and the one that remains in the memory as somehow symbolizing the whole work.[6] Chapter 13 begins with a metaphor that expresses the Coreys' feelings about the dinner in business terms: "Not only the principal of their debt of gratitude remained, but the accruing interest." The tying together of elements, suggested by this sort of metaphor, reaches its highest point in these chapters. The first takes up the Coreys' selection of guests and the Laphams' preparations for attending. Chapter 14 is the dinner itself, memorable largely because of Howells's skill in selecting exactly the right details (Lapham's trouble with his gloves, his leg falling asleep, his cigar ashes on the plate, and the like)—but hardly less so because of Howells's courage in tackling the difficult task of presenting such a climactic scene directly and of giving us the actual conversation. For the structure of the book, this scene is a necessity; Howells's great accomplishment can be measured by the fact that the scene does not strike most readers as a disappointment but rather as an admirable fulfilment of its role as keystone. And Chapter 15 (the shortest and perhaps the most intense in the book), in which Lapham the

6. Carter (pp. 166–167) and Bennett (p. 160), for example, point out the centrality of the dinner party; Booth Tarkington, in his introduction to the Centenary edition, comments on the impression which that scene made on him when he first read it (p. xv); and a dinner scene is used as the jacket decoration for the Modern Library edition.

following day apologizes to Tom for his drunkenness and lack of refinement, does not come as an anticlimax but instead reveals how well the dinner has served as a means of turning the direction of the story.

The dinner is a point of equilibrium with the Coreys and the Laphams meeting ostensibly as equals, and the conversation there draws together all the threads of the book. Since Seymour is present, Silas's new house comes up for discussion, and the talk moves on to the Coreys place, which is in "perfect taste," as the description of its classic simplicity at the beginning of the chapter suggests;[7] and from there the conversation takes a natural turn into architecture in general, which leads to matters of taste in the other arts as well. Before the subject of architecture is passed, however, it is skilfully connected with social distinctions based on wealth and on summers in the country: Bromfield suggests, half seriously, that the "deserving poor of neat habits" might be able to make use of "all the beautiful, airy, wholesome houses that stand empty the whole summer long, while their owners are away in their lowly cots beside the sea," mansions that appear at that season as "long rows of close-shuttered, handsome, brutally insensible houses"—and he can put forward this idea, like Swift's modest proposer,[8] because, as he says, "I spend my summers in town, and I occupy my own house, so that I can speak impartially and intelligently."

The main topic is literature, particularly popular novels like *Tears, Idle Tears,* in which the hero and heroine make "the most wildly satisfactory and unnecessary sacrifices for each other"—"you can't put a more popular thing than self-sacrifice into a novel." It is here that Howells inserts, in the words of the Reverend Mr. Sewell, his

7. The Coreys' house in "Bellingham Place" is based, according to Howells's daughter, on one built by Thomas Buckminster Curtis at 45 Mount Vernon Street, "where my father often dined in his earlier Boston days" (Centenary edition, p. v). In her foreword, Mildred Howells also refers to the autobiographical basis of the novel—extending even to the seasonal pattern. Howells had bought in 1884 "a small house on the water side of Beacon Street"; and, "as there were various alterations to be made in it, he spent most of the summer there overseeing them, while he sent the rest of the family to the country" (p. v). Clara and Rudolf Kirk quote Howells's letter to his father in the summer of 1884 (from *Life in Letters,* Garden City, N.Y., 1928, I, 363–364), commenting on the "miles of empty houses all round me" and on the fact that "nobody else I know sleeps in town"—a letter which the dinner-party conversation in *Lapham* echoes almost verbatim. The Kirks also discuss the connection between Howells's move to Beacon Street from Louisburg Square and Lapham's similar move (*William Dean Howells,* pp. 104–106)—though Lapham's "Nankeen Square" cannot be identified with Louisburg Square, because it is in the South End just off Washington Street (see the opening of Chap. 2). It seems most reasonable to equate "Nankeen Square" with Chester Square, as Clark does in his introduction (p. vii) and James M. Spinning in his notes (p. 518) to the Riverside Literature Series edition (Boston, 1928), or with Canton Square, as Mildred Howells does (p. v). According to Walter Muir Whitehill, in *Boston: A Topographical History* (Cambridge, Mass., 1959), Chester Square was established in 1850 (p. 127), and the wider land in the Neck south of Dover Street rapidly grew in population in the 1850's (p. 122); but by the mid-1860's the flight to the Back Bay was already occurring with such precipitance that people like the Laphams could find many good buys in the area (p. 120). The Laphams bought their Nankeen house in 1863, since, in 1875, they had lived there twelve years (p. 31).

8. In *A Modest Proposal* (1729) by Jonathan Swift (1667–1745) the proposer satirically recommends that the poor Irish relieve their poverty by breeding children for sale as food for the wealthy. To prove his philanthropic disinterest the proposer points out that his wife is too old to bear children, so he will reap no profit. [*Editor.*]

first explicit comments on self-sacrifice and on the relation of fiction to life; to Sewell the unrealistic self-sacrifice in sentimental novels is "psychical suicide," and the effect of the novels is "ruinous." After the ladies leave the room, the conversation turns to reminiscences of the Civil War and the subject of heroism—and sacrifice. Sewell again sums up the general feeling when he says that until a new occasion for heroism arises, "we must content ourselves with the every-day generosities and sacrifices." This brings the group back to the lack of realism in literature, and then Silas, who is always a step behind in the conversation, tells of a war experience that illustrates sacrifice. His story about Jim Millon not only furnishes us with the background information for the Zerrilla episode (and we learn at the end of this chapter that Zerrilla is the Miss Dewey of Silas's office) but shows that Silas himself is indebted to someone else for saving his life (just as Mrs. Corey feels an obligation to Mrs. Lapham for saving hers). Silas's drunken rambling also includes references to Rogers, to the Lapham paint, to Mrs. Corey's charity drive, to the library in his new house, and so on—all of which brings to mind important earlier episodes.

The short chapter which follows is a necessary coda to the dinner scene. In it we witness the beginnings of humility and compassion, not merely in Silas, but in Tom as well. Silas's apology, almost groveling, is perhaps rather extreme, but at least no one can fail to see the difference between this Silas and the boastful man of the first half of the book. The earlier Silas had been saying to his family just the opposite of what he now says to Tom: "you're a gentleman, and I'm not, and it ain't right I should be over you." Silas recognizes that money alone does not make him a gentleman, and Tom is struck by "the tragic humility of his appeal." But Tom, too, has some misgivings, and the last part of the chapter focuses on Tom's reactions to Silas's apology, as a preparation for the ensuing group of chapters which deal (even more intensely than the eight preceding the dinner) with Tom's courtship of Penelope. While Silas is humbling himself, Tom's special interest in the Laphams is revealed by his interruptions ("I have my reasons for refusing to hear you") and by his thoughts ("It had become a vital necessity with him to think the best of Lapham"). He sees Silas as an "offensive boor"; yet he remembers "that which must control him at last," speaking to him "almost with the girl's voice." It is then, in thinking the matter over, that Tom understands how he, too, needs to be humbler, for he had met Lapham's apology "on the gentlemanly ground," selfishly sparing his own feelings, "asserting the superiority of his sort," and "superfinely standing aloof." He also recognizes his family's legitimate concern: "Often he could not make it appear right that he should merely please himself in what chiefly concerned himself";

there was even the possibility of an "injury he might be doing to some one besides his family and himself." All these thoughts border on self-sacrifice; certainly Tom is beginning to be more considerate of others. Just as the two plots involve a similar kind of decision about self-sacrifice, so here, in this one chapter, we observe both Tom and Silas going through a similar change of attitude. The chapter ends with Tom, like Silas, "far as might be from vain confidence" (a surprising position for both of them); and Tom decides to go to Silas to offer "reparation" for the "want of sympathy—of humanity—which he had shown." Tom is now ready to apologize, as Silas was at the beginning of the chapter.

To have accomplished so much in three chapters should be regarded as an astonishing technical performance. It would be difficult to find reasons for concurring in O. W. Firkins's complaint about the "leisurely pace" of the book in which "thirty-one pages are allotted to a dinner at which nothing decisive occurs, to say nothing of the assignment of from twenty to twenty-five pages to the elaboration of pre-prandial arrangements." That "nothing decisive occurs" may be partly true in terms of physical actions, but one cannot deny that a great deal happens here in terms of feelings and attitudes. When Tom thinks of the "chaos" of experience, which at times seems "ruin" and at other times appears to be "the materials out of which fine actions and a happy life might be shaped," he is also describing, one may imagine, the process of the novel itself, by which the disorganized impressions and incidents of life are structured. Once the "form" and "content" are seen as inseparable, the indispensability of these chapters is also recognized; and, conversely, the success of these chapters is that they prove the artificiality of any such division as "form" and "content."

It is not surprising, then, that architecture is a prominent subject in the dinner chapter. One would expect matters related to the major symbol to enter the central chapter; but, beyond that, if *Lapham* is a demonstration of the theory of fiction set forth within it (as it manifestly is), the comments on architecture may be applied to the art of fiction as well. In the literary discussion of Chapter 14 the emphasis (as in *Criticism and Fiction*) is on proportion; Howells realizes that even "realistic" art involves selection—arrangement of details so as to suggest "true proportion and relation" and not "monstrous disproportion." Therefore, despite Corey's belief that novelists (who "try to imitate") are very different from architects (who "create form"), the words Howells puts into Seymour's mouth, comparing present architects with those of the past, may be applied to the artistry of *Lapham* itself: "I think we may claim a better feeling for structure. We use better material, and more wisely; and by and by we shall work out something more characteristic and original."

The center of the book well illustrates how the "material" of everyday life, arranged in "characteristic" proportion, can be "original" through the illuminating metamorphosis that "structure" and form provide.

V

What we may call the fourth movement of the book, Chapters 16 through 19, is parallel in length to the opening movement but carries on the love plot of the second section, bringing to a close the twelve chapters devoted to that plot. This group of chapters, which has an interesting structure of its own, effectively serves to anticipate the final section, which concerns Silas's decision to sacrifice material gain. Not only is the matter of self-sacrifice discussed here as a preparation for Silas's business dilemma, but the way in which the Rogers affair is deliberately postponed because of the urgency of Penelope's problem underlines the quality of anticipation associated with these chapters. When Silas returns home from the office, at the end of Chapter 16, he glares at Tom (who has just declared his love to Penelope) "out of his blue eyes with a fire that something else must have kindled there": he has been talking with Rogers. Then when Silas and his wife go riding, he starts to bring up Rogers (who has been "getting in deeper and deeper" with him), but his wife refuses to listen and says, "There's something a good deal more important than Rogers in the world, and more important than your business." This statement makes clear the structural importance of these chapters in two ways: first, it calls attention to the fact that the Rogers matter is being temporarily pushed aside (Howells wants to emphasize that he is consciously *inserting* the decisive action of the love plot here for a reason); second, it reveals a sense of perspective in its ordering of values, which is to be Silas's chief gain in this section—and one that will aid him in his coming decision. He may once in a while slip back to the purely monetary standard of the "new rich," as when he says that he has a right to consult his minister because he has "contributed enough *money*" to the church; but generally now he can say, "We don't either of us want anything but the children's good. What's it all of it for, if it ain't for that?" So this matter which is "a good deal more important than Rogers" takes priority; and, since it is, after all, the "rise" of Silas that we are interested in, this prior experience provides a frame of reference that makes Silas's final decision all the more meaningful.

These chapters are highly concentrated in time as well as in their attention to the Tom-Penelope relationship. They cover only three days, beginning on the evening of the day after the dinner party and ending about seventy-two hours later, when Tom calls on Penelope after Irene and her mother have left for the town of Lapham; there is then a break of a week before the next section begins in Chapter 20. References to time are correspondingly made more precise: allusions are not to the seasons but to days and hours. We know that the conversation between Penelope and Tom (Chap. 16)[9] occurs three hours after Tom leaves Silas's office. Chapter 17 opens at breakfast the next morning, with Silas making detailed comments about his usual rising schedule; after he leaves, Mrs. Lapham talks with Penelope, who reveals Tom's disclosure of the night before. When Mrs. Lapham sends a message to Silas at the office, he replies that he can meet her at "half-past two," and their ride and discussion of what Penelope should do are the subject of Chapter 18. At suppertime, scarcely forty-eight hours after the Corey dinner, Mrs. Lapham informs Irene that Tom is not in love with her (Chap. 19); this is on Saturday, because Silas tells Irene that "to-morrow's Sunday," and Irene decides she can wait until Monday to go to Lapham. The chapter ends on Monday night: one chapter is thus devoted to Friday night, two and a half to Saturday, and the last half of Chapter 19 to Sunday and Monday. The pace has been slowed in order to concentrate on Saturday, the day when the Laphams are torturing themselves trying to decide what Penelope should do.

Meanwhile, Irene, who tries to make her "sacrifice complete" by performing such services as delivering Penelope's breakfast to her with "an heroic pretense" that she is doing nothing unusual, is not, obviously, the only one overplaying her role. The important "sacrifice" here is Penelope's, and the chief unifying device of these chapters is the repeated comparison of this "sacrifice" with the self-sacrifice in sentimental fiction. During the love scene between Tom and Penelope (Chap. 16), it is Penelope who criticizes the "self-sacrifice" in such novels, says that it is not true sacrifice, calls it "wicked," and pleads for "reasonable" behavior; she concludes that, while "reasonable behavior" would be unusual in fiction, "so it would in real life." She has been reading *Tears, Idle Tears*, the novel discussed at the dinner, and Sewell, who struck out against the book then, returns to the subject of fiction when the Laphams call on him for advice. He enunciates his famous doctrine of economy of pain, asserting that the "false ideal of self-sacrifice" comes from "the novels that befool and debauch almost every intelligence in some degree." Then when Tom calls again—the scene in which Penelope refuses him at the end of Chapter 19—he reminds her of what she had said three nights before about the foolishness of the heroine's actions in the book, and he asks how her own situation is in any way different.

9. This chapter opens with a description of the horrors of the Lapham drawing room, just as Chapter 14, when the Laphams enter the Coreys' house, begins with comments on its "perfect taste."

Penelope reaches her crucial decision at this point in the novel not merely to provide an instance of false sacrifice to be contrasted with Silas's businesss sacrifice but to demonstrate the essential soundness of Silas's judgment, when not encumbered with complicating factors of ambition, money, and prestige. He presents his problem to Sewell with "simple dignity" and finds his own first thoughts corroborated. Both he and his wife had instinctively seen the sense of the "economy-of-pain" solution,[1] but they thought that it must be wrong because their social "rise" had very nearly destroyed their sense of values. Mrs. Lapham had told Penelope, almost immediately, "I couldn't say you had done wrong, if you was to marry him to-day"; when the shocked Penelope describes the course of self-sacrifice that seems attractive to her, Mrs. Lapham says, "Your father would think you were a fool"—and Howells refers to "her strong disgust for the pseudo heroism." [2]

That the whole matter involves, at bottom, the very salvation of one's soul becomes increasingly evident through the diction. It is not simply a question of going to a minister, who points out that the false ideal of self-sacrifice "certainly doesn't come from Christianity"; it is a process of discovery that one is part of "a great community of wretchedness which has been pitilessly repeating itself from the foundation of the world." Silas wrestles with the problem "like a man who meditates a struggle with superior force," and his wife, accustomed "to seek the light by striving," recognizes "the curse of prosperity" and fears the results of Silas's "pride and ambition." When Mrs. Lapham later hears Silas pacing the floor and compares him to Jacob wrestling with an angel, the reader thinks back to this episode, when the family can hear Irene "stirring about in her own room, as if she were busy about many things." The struggle is one of the life or death of the soul, and both Penelope and Silas say that the dilemma is worse than death. We have moved in this section from Tom's declaration of love (Chap. 16) to Penelope's refusal (the last scene of Chap. 19); what has happened in between has prepared Silas for his next trial and has shown that he will now be able to meet it. If the daughters' behavior seems rather exaggerated here, Howells has himself provided the comment on it (and on the internal consistency of art) in Penelope's statement about *Tears, Idle Tears:* "the naturalness of all the rest makes that seem natural too."

## VI

This principle, enunciated by Penelope, may be helpful in analyzing several troublesome aspects of the last part of the novel. It may

1. The term is Sewell's. Howells also explored this idea, as Carter points out (p. 165), in *Indian Summer* (1886).
2. This is not to say that one should not think of others. Lapham tells Penelope that the affair concerns other people, just as the Coreys had brought Tom to see, by the end of Chapter 15, that their whole family was involved. Silas says, "Recollect that it's my business, and your mother's business, as well as yours, and we're going to have our say."

first be said, however, that the last eight chapters complete the symmetry of the book. With their emphasis on Silas's business decision, they round out the twelve chapters devoted to the bankruptcy plot and bring to a conclusion matters introduced in the first four chapters. Further than that, they make a final integration of the two plots and show each member of the Lapham family going through a similar process of inward struggle and hard-won relief. Chapter 20 provides the transition by bringing the treachery of Rogers into the open and following that revelation with a scene between Tom and his mother (in which Mrs. Corey is just as dismayed to learn that Penelope is the object of Tom's attentions as Penelope herself was in the opening chapter of the preceding movement). The next two chapters take us deeper into the Rogers affair and the temptation offered by "those English parties"; they also make further connections between the plots, as when Mrs. Lapham feels that her husband's troubles may help bring Penelope out of her depression. The fourth chapter of this part (Chap. 23) shows Tom in a positive action (not just in being talked about); parallel to the fourth chapter of the earlier eight-chapter section (Chap. 8), in which Tom begins work at the Lapham office, he now offers to put his own money into the firm (thus constituting another in a series of temptations for Silas, a series which mounts in intensity). This chapter defines the organization of the last part of the novel in a conversation between Penelope and her father: "I presume you know I'm in trouble," he says, to which her reply is, "We all seem to be there."[3] Her remark suggests not only the way in which each member of the family faces a problem of his own (or will face one soon) and the way in which all Lapham's problems seem to be reaching a crisis at once and piling up on each other, but also (and more important) the manner in which each individual decision affects the well-being of others.

From here on, the interrelated problems do seem to fall, in accelerating pace, on Lapham's shoulders. The last half of Chapter 23 brings the Zerrilla plot to a crisis (with the first direct presentation of Zerrilla's family—Lapham goes to her flat "in the extremity in which a man finds relief in combating one care with another.") In the next chapter (besides Penelope's reaction to Tom's offer of money) comes Silas's resolution to sell his house, followed by its destruction (just after the expiration of the insurance) in the fire that Silas has himself started. One by one, the ways out of his financial crisis are eliminated. In Chapter 25 Lapham makes his last frantic efforts to extricate himself from his difficulties—by seeing Bellingham, then

---

3. This conversation, in which both Silas and Penelope are speaking of their own affairs, is similar to the one in the next chapter between Silas and his wife, when they realize "that they had each been talking of a different offer."

"those West Virginia people," then the English agents at the hotel. His last temptation, to sell to Rogers who has full knowledge of the value of the property, is successfully passed by the end of the chapter. All that remains is to bring everything full circle. Chapter 26 concerns the failure of Mrs. Lapham's strict but shallow morality ("her instant and steadfast perception of right and wrong, and the ability to choose the right to her own hurt") in yielding to the temptation of suspecting her husband of infidelity; the chapter shows "how she had forsaken him in his hour of trial" and, on top of that, had added another problem to his load. After Mrs. Lapham hears Zerrilla's story in Silas's office and after Irene has returned (during Tom's visit with Penelope at the end of Chapter 26), the way is open for a "rise" in each of them in the final chapter. Mrs. Lapham realizes how foolishly she has behaved and how much she has let her husband down; Silas has shown strength, in contrast to his wife, and is ready to accept financial ruin rather than submit to temptation; Penelope reverses her earlier decision not to marry Tom because she now sees the falsity of self-sacrifice in her case, in contrast to the necessity of it in her father's; and Irene can now place her disappointment in proper perspective, for she has "toughened and hardened," has "lost all her babyish dependence and pliability," and is "like iron." This process of transformation in Irene is one that all four have passed through: "It had been a life and death struggle with her; she had conquered, but she had also necessarily lost much. Perhaps what she had lost was not worth keeping; but at any rate she had lost it."

Silas had lost his fortune but had gained the knowledge that the integrity he began with was worth more. Although people had said that Mrs. Lapham "was marrying beneath her when she took him," Silas's basic good sense and refusal to compromise (reaffirmed for him both in Penelope's case and in his own by Sewell, who visits the Laphams in the last scene of the book) show that his wife is the one who must rise to meet his standard, not the reverse. Social distinctions, like monetary ones, have little relevance to true value—by the end the Laphams did not think "that their daughter was marrying a Corey; they thought only that she was giving herself to the man who loved her." In this world the adherence to principle will result in loss, if not in self-destruction, but peace of mind can be purchased in no other way; Silas's temptation, suffering, and loss are the price he pays for the privilege of returning to the hills of Vermont, where he began. With this paradox (implied by the ambiguity of "rise") at the heart of the book, it is not surprising that the Christian overtones, noticed earlier, are developed in this last part of the book, for most of Jesus's parables are based on the same paradox. The metaphor of struggle spreads out through the book from the important passage at the end of Chapter 25, when Mrs. Lapham, hearing Silas pace the floor all night, thinks of Jacob wrestling with the angel (Gen. 32: 24, 26, 27, is quoted). Before that, Walker had spoken of Lapham as having "a drownin' man's grip round [Rogers's] neck"; Silas later finds "every pulse throbbing with the strong temptation," the decision making him "groan in spirit." The struggle is one against temptations raised up by the devil ("it wan't *Providence*," says Silas), and Lapham in Chapter 25 faces his "tempter," Rogers, refusing to help him "whip the devil round the stump," despite Rogers's invocation of the "Golden Rule" and his reminder that the Englishmen are "Christian gentlemen." Rather, Silas upholds a "mere idea"; he realizes that Rogers's offer to buy the mill property would release him legally of whatever guilt might be involved in the resale to the English agents, but he "was standing out alone for nothing" as "any one else would say." This "nothing," however, has come to mean everything to him. He tells Rogers, "You know that what you've said now hasn't changed the thing a bit." And he ends by moving into the old Vermont farmhouse instead of into a new mansion "on the water side of Beacon."

The house in Vermont that the Laphams return to is "plain," with "no luxuries" and "no furnace in the winter." The family's fortunes have throughout been spoken of in terms of houses, the social symbols of success. Mrs. Lapham expresses the alternatives that sum up the book when she says she will be happy whether they "go on to the Back Bay, or go back to the old house at Lapham." When Penelope learns of her father's difficulties, her first question is, "Shall we have to stay in this house?"; and when the Coreys come to visit their future daughter-in-law, she decides "that they should know the worst at once" and "let[s] them have the full brunt of the drawing-room." If the Nankeen Square house is in contrast to the Coreys', it is no less so to the Vermont farmhouse. And, despite the social pretentiousness of the Back Bay, Lapham's Vermont house and his Back Bay house are not so far apart; his natural dignity had met a responsive note in Seymour, and he had come to understand what the architect was guiding him toward. The design of the Back Bay house "appealed to him as an exquisite bit of harmony appeals to the unlearned ear"; he could see "the satisfying simplicity of the whole design and the delicacy of its detail." The window in James's house of fiction[4] through which Howells looked presents a view organized on these same architectural principles.

VII

This much said, there still remain some vaguely dissatisfying elements in the structure of the last part of the book. The question of

4. In his Preface to the New York edition of *The Portrait of a Lady*, Henry James speaks metaphorically of the "house of fiction," which has "not one window, but a million." Each novelist stands before a different window and represents what he sees from that vantage point. [*Editor.*]

the relationship of the two plots, however, is surely no longer one of these. They are so thoroughly intertwined and so carefully arranged to support each other that their management should rather be regarded as one of the triumphs of the novel. The subtlety of Howells's design is overlooked when one agrees with Firkins that "the bankruptcy story is . . . so much of a laggard that it has almost the look of a trespasser," or with Scudder's similar remark, in his review of the book, about "how little the rise of this hero is really connected with the circumstances which make up the main incidents of the story."[5] There can be no doubt that the two plots support each other, as Donald Pizer has demonstrated, in affirming a utilitarian ethic, with its subordination of individual good to the good of the whole and with its emphasis (as Harry Hayden Clark has noted) on individual responsibility and free will.[6] Rather, one's legitimate feeling of dissatisfaction here may be traced to four elements: (1) the occurrence of the fire, and particularly when it melodramatically comes just after the insurance has expired; (2) the presence of the Zerrilla plot; (3) the telescoping of events in the last chapter; and (4) the suggestions, in the last part, of tragic overtones in what had been, up to then, a comedy of manners—the "lapse in tone" which George Arms discusses (p. xvi). The first two are related, as are the last two, and all will remain, in varying degrees, blemishes on an otherwise imposing edifice.[7]

In terms of the structure as we have been viewing it here, the Zerrilla story is a much more serious problem than the fire. It may be true that when Silas tries out his fireplace the reader feels sure the house is going to burn down; and when, on top of that, the insurance has just run out, the reader may decide that the hackneyed devices of the soap opera are overtaking the book. This is probably part of what Everett Carter had in mind when he called the handling of the house symbol "mechanical."[8] But objections to the fire and its circumstances are based on criteria of probability—that is, of "real-

5. Firkins, pp. 71–72; Horace E. Scudder, *Atlantic Monthly*, 61, 554–556 (Oct., 1885).

6. Pizer, in the article cited earlier, says, "I do not wish to intimate that Howells consciously employed the ethical ideas of Mill. Rather, I believe that the similarity between Mill's utilitarianism and the ethical principles of *The Rise of Silas Lapham* is probably the result of parallel attempts to introduce the ethical teachings of Christ within social contexts and yet avoid supernatural sanctions" (p. 325). Clark's discussion of the "traditional Christian ethics" of the novel is on p. x of his Modern Library introduction.

7. This does not mean that there are no other minor flaws. For example, the point of view is perhaps not thoroughly consistent, with such phrases as the following: "but Mrs. Lapham could not know this, and did not deserve to know it"; "a certain generosity of instinct, which I should not be ready to say was always infallible"; "Mrs. Corey, whose thoughts cannot always be reported"; "Whether Penelope . . . found it more

difficult to harmonise, I cannot say."

8. In both *Howells and the Age of Realism* (pp. 164–169) and his introduction to the Harper Modern Classics edition (New York, 1958), Carter emphasizes the significance of the house as a symbol and as a comment on Howells's art. It is his contention that the "small, tight, almost allegorical construction" of the book "makes us feel smallness and constriction, instead of greatness and expansion and complexity" (p. 169) and is therefore inadequate in a work which involves a feeling for the welfare of society as a whole. The present analysis has attempted to show, on the contrary, that the organic unity of the plots, architectural symbolism, and seasonal metaphors invests the events with universal significance and enhances rather than restricts the commission of the "enormous feat of the imagination" necessary to perceive a truth about the social organism (with its "almost complete absence of personality") in "dramatic and imaginative" terms.

ism"—and it is here that the contrast with the Zerrilla story becomes meaningful. Whatever connections may be found between the Zerrilla affair and the main plots (there have, of course, been foreshadowings of it and allusions to it throughout the book; and it furnishes another example of marital relationships to be contrasted with the Laphams, the Coreys, the Hubbards, and Penelope and Tom), it nevertheless remains an element not smoothly blended into the larger structure. Presumably it is there because in Howells's theory of realism various aspects of life are to be represented in due proportion; Zerrilla is Howells's concession to the more sordid side of "realism," but the matter occupies no larger place in the book, he would say, because it is no more important than that in life.

The same theory of realism, however, cannot account for both the Zerrilla episode and the fire. Despite Howells's reiteration of the fidelity of fiction to real life (and his professed dislike of the "fettering control" of plot as unnatural), he did understand that art necessarily involves selection, and that selection, a conscious process, automatically produces a structure which is artificial in the sense that it does not exist in nature. The test is not, then, whether the Zerrilla story is true to life in its proportions, but whether it is true to the proportions of the work, whether it is "probable" in the Aristotelian sense of harmonizing with internal consistency rather than being "possible" in terms of the world outside the work. This is what Penelope meant when she spoke of the naturalness of one incident in a book being determined by the naturalness of the whole. One cannot ultimately judge a novel except as a work of art, and on these grounds the fire is "probable" in a way the Zerrilla story is not. Edwin Cady's likening of the book to a morality play[9] is a useful way of seeing that it is more than "realistic": the destruction of the house through Silas's own actions is a prerequisite to his rise, both metaphorically and because it pushes him to the last extremity, setting up the proper conditions, as in a laboratory, for the final test. If the device represented by the fire-and-insurance business ordinarily seems trite through its unskilful use in inferior works, its universal validity and its effectiveness should nevertheless be recognized when the episode is set in the framework of such a "satisfying simplicity" of design, observable by even the "unlearned" eye, that it may be considered a classic example of the pattern.

9. In *The Road to Realism: The Early Years, 1837–1885, of William Dean Howells* (Syracuse, 1956), p. 236, and in his introduction to the Riverside edition (Boston, 1956), pp. vi, viii, Cady describes Lapham moving "through a series of morality plays"; he finds the book made up of Silas's growth plus "two other large movements," one focusing on Mrs. Lapham, the other on the Coreys; he pronounces the Zerrilla episode the "least well-digested part of *Lapham*"; he labels the paradox of the rise and fall "an antidote against the falsity of the Horatio Alger tradition"; and he sees in the novel "a concept of form" derived from Turgenev, an "objective" and "dramatic" method. Despite the "dramatic" and "scenic" quality of the novel's structure, Howells had difficulty in dramatizing it, and James A. Herne disliked Howells's adaptation of it for the stage—see Herbert Edwards, "Dramatization of *The Rise of Silas Lapham*," *New England Quarterly*, 30, 235–243 (June, 1957).

The other two matters, relating to pace and tone, require less discussion, though they are greater defects. The last chapter refers to events taking place during a period of five years and is saved only by the concluding conversation between the Sewells and the Laphams from becoming a typical nineteenth-century final-chapter summing up of the fortunes of the characters. George Arms's belief that "the amount of summary narrative [near the end] is relatively too great for the book to hold" (p. xiv) is really applicable only to the last chapter, for it is only there that the shift in narrative method is perceptible enough to be a jarring element in the internal "natural-ness." But the occasional thrusts in that chapter beyond the limits of the main structure do constitue violations of the architectural symmetry. This flaw, however, is a far less serious one (quantitatively and qualitatively) than the "lapse in tone" of which it is a function (since, as the tone grows in solemnity, the tendency increases to state directly rather than to reveal through dramatic scenes). The ques-tion of tone is perhaps not strictly part of a discussion of structure, but it can at least be said (as partial qualification of Arms's excellent point) that Howells takes advantage of opportunities for social comedy to the end (as in the Coreys' reactions to the Lapham drawing room in the last chapter) and that the serious implications of comedy of manners are present from the start (as in the insight with which the Hubbard interview is handled or in the reference to "Christian sufferings"). A much better defense of Howells's ending is provided by William Manierre, who argues that the last third of the book rightly moves more slowly to emphasize the "gradual and grinding nature" of Lapham's financial decline and the isolation of the individual at a time of moral decision.[1] But these observations still do not explain away the undeniable presence of a fundamental shift, one that may be described as from understatement to over-statement, and one which is the most serious weakness of the novel.

That there is no major weakness, however, in the construction of *Lapham* has been the contention of this analysis. It is impossible, of course, to consider structure apart from other elements; if *Lapham* seems impressive in organization, it is only because the basic concep-tion of the whole is sound. A different structure would mean a different novel with different significance. Some readers may be inclined to feel that Howells built better than he knew: but any such assumption about intent, ungenerous or not, becomes irrelevant in the face of a sturdy framework resting squarely on its

---

1. Manierre, pp. 360–361. His point is that the technique of "retrospective discussion" stresses the relativity of various viewpoints and therefore suggests a fragmented society, one which offers Silas no absolute principles and leaves him only with his own individual judgment: thus Howells's shift from dramatic impartiality to an "involved" concern with "a single center of perception" is both "logical" and "inevitable" (p. 359). William McMurray, in "The Concept of Complicity in Howells' Fiction," *New England Quarterly*, 35, 489–496 (1962), also finds the "pattern of move-ment" in Lapham's social involvement.

foundation, giving form to the rooms within and yet shaped by them. As Silas says, "Everybody builds, at least once in a lifetime."

# Howells and the
# Dilemmas of Realism

*The Rise of Silas Lapham* is not only a fine novel but an important document in the development of American literery realism. It is easy to call a work realistic or to talk of an "Age of Realism," but what do the terms mean? Why did certain authors proclaim themselves "realists" and speak contemptously of other writers as "romanticists?" While Howells enjoyed "banging the babes of romance about," as he referred to his attack on sentimental fiction, he was engaged in more than a mere literary squabble. The literary realism that Howells practiced and defended was part of a major intellectual movement in the late part of the nineteenth century. In its wider ramifications it was to result in important changes in jurisprudence, economics, history, applied theology, social legislation and education and in an explosion of interest in new fields such as psychology, sociology, and anthropology. These changes were based on an insistence that life can be lived successfully only on the basis of accurate, objective awareness of actual conditions. When the observed behavior of human beings runs counter to accepted notions of human nature (or divine law) it is the *a priori* standards that are at fault, not the objective observations. The aim of the observer, whether literary or scientific, should be to understand human beings so that institutions, standards, and conventions of behavior and belief might be altered to promote happiness and to fulfill rather than to frustrate and warp normal needs and desires.

Howells did not go to the extreme of Émile Zola, who proclaimed that by means of the "experimental novel" the literary artist could hope "to be master of good and evil, to regulate life, to regulate society. . . ." (*The Experimental Novel & Other Essays,* 1893). But he was committed to the serious social responsibility of literature. He thought it a moral dereliction and a social disservice for an author to ignore or falsify facts or to suggest that foolish, thoughtless, or selfish behavior does not have harmful consequences. He did not advocate stories in which retribution is visited upon the guilty with a terrible swift sword; such a system did not accord with what he saw occurring around him. But he insisted that fiction should deal honestly with the largely unheroic but nonetheless painful problems that plagued the citizens of a new industrial world, citizens who often relied for guidance upon outworn romantic cliches of heroic self-reliance, angelic purity, undying love and noble self-sacrifice.

For Howells then, realism was both a literary allegiance and a moral imperative. But once he had accepted them, as a practicing novelist he had to translate his values and allegiances into artistic productions. For Howells, the first step was negative: the rejection of black and white characters, of effects without causes, of actions without consequences, of authorial interference to rescue or punish characters. C. Hugh Holman sketches more fully the nature of realism in his article and suggests that a failure to read realistic fiction on its own terms may lead to some odd distortions of the literature. In their comments on the work of one another, Howells and Henry James (writing in 1882 and 1886 respectively) announced their mutual admiration and, more important, pointed out the high seriousness each recognized in the work of the other. By 1891 Howells was recognized as *a* dean of American letters, if not *the* dean, and he gathered and edited his "Editor's Study" columns from *Harper's Monthly* in a volume called *Criticism and Fiction*. Chapter Eighteen of that volume, reprinted here, sums up in memorable phrases the defects of romanticistic fiction and defends honest novels against the bad reputation sentimental romances had given them. Larzer Ziff's article on Howells' "literary hospitality" inquires into the novelist's refusal to read life in terms of abstract ideals and suggests that Howells used the surface details of experience as a notation of the deeper experience that Americans were going through, an experience less glamorous but no less heroic than that of medieval knights and Venetian lovers.

A selection from Edwin H. Cady's two-volume biography of Howells sketches for us the way this realistic mind worked. Howells ordered his working schedule in a business-like routine and projected for the world an affable, urbane personality. But his fiction derived not merely from close and shrewd observation of the surface of life but from depths of private experience that often lay maturing for years before he drew on it. This duality in Howells' personality is explored by Robert M. Figg III who points out that as Howells' social concerns deepened he moved from a surface realism to a more penetrating critical realism that would challenge the "conventional acceptances" of his readers and invite them to evaluate realistically the civilization they were helping to create. Finally Charles Campbell shows that Howells' novels may be read not merely as examples of realistic fiction but as arguments for a realistic attitude toward the readers' experience. The novels not only tell stories of characters who find happiness or not according to whether they grasp reality or cling to illusions; the novels also urge their readers to see the same distinction in the world they inhabit.

# C. HUGH HOLMAN

# Of Everything the Unexplained and Irresponsible Specimen: Notes on How to Read American Realism[†]

The realists who dominated the literary scene in America between 1870 and 1900 and whose chief proponents were William Dean Howells and Henry James were self-conscious users of the actual, committed to the doctrine of presenting truthful types of common humanity, and presenting them without the intrusion of the author and with as nearly complete objectivity as they could achieve. Many

†From the *Georgia Review*, 18 (Fall 1964), 316–24.

aspects of the self-conscious theory of realism which these men expounded could be examined. What I should like to do in this brief essay is to summarize a definition of the underlying concept which motivated this period in literary history on the continent, in England, and in America, and then to examine briefly the characteristics which Howells and James each emphasized in the literary figure whom each insisted to have been his chief artistic model, the Russian novelist Ivan Turgenev.

René Wellek, in "Realism in Literary Scholarship," has defined the realism of the Nineteenth Century as "the objective representation of contemporary social reality." He also asserts, "It rejects the fantastic, the fairy-tale-like, the allegorical and the symbollic, the highly stylized, the purely abstract, and decorative. It means that we want no myth, no *Maerchen*,[1] no world of dreams. It implies also a rejection of the improbable, of pure chance, and of extraordinary events, since reality is obviously conceived at that time, in spite of all local and personal differences, as the orderly world of nineteenth century science, the world of cause and effect, a world without miracle, without transcendence, even if the individual may have preserved a personal religious faith." Professor Wellek adds that emphasis on *type* as the "all important association with objective social observation," as almost universal in realist theory. He says, ". . . in fiction the main technical demand of realist theory came to be impersonality, the complete absence of the author from his work, a suppression of any interference by the author. The theory had its main spokesman in Flaubert, but it was also a preoccupation of Henry James." This quality, which Joseph Warren Beach called "the self-effaced author," which Percy Lubbock made the central dogma of *The Craft of Fiction,* and which Wayne Booth, in *The Rhetoric of Fiction,* has brilliantly but not always sympathetically analyzed as "impersonal narration," is not only a technical strategy whose developing importance created the critical concept of point of view; it is also a basic philosophical position about the significance of the actual and the role of art.

Both James and Howells, despite their widely differing backgrounds and intellectual histories and the great differences in their subject matter, shared a common literary master whose work and method each emulated through a large portion of his career, and whose artistic methods both carefully analyzed and briefly praised in critical essays. This literary master was Ivan Turgenev. Howells said of the formative years of his literary career, "My most notable experience without doubt was the knowledge of Tourguénief's novels . . . Tourguénief's method is as far as art can go." In the latter part of his career, the example of Tolstoi's deep moral involvement

1.Märchen: (German), fairy-tale or fable. [*Editor.*]

in social problems led Howells to shift his ultimate allegiance to that Russian novelist; however, even then he believed that Tolstoi, "as an artistic worker," shared the qualities which he had earlier found in Turgenev, and his final greater appreciation of Tolstoi than of Turgenev was a judgment of what James might have called "the quality of their minds" and not of their arts.

\* \* \*

The primary quality which both Howells and James saw in Turgenev was the direct presentation of life with clarity, without interference, and through characters fully realized as people existing in their own right and for no other reason than that they were people. These characters were comprehended with such clarity and completeness that their common qualities were shared by all mankind and their special qualities were shared with their class; thus they became both types of man in general and types of their special social status, without their ever becoming symbols or allegorical figures. James expressed this idea very clearly when he wrote approvingly of Turgenev: "He has no recognition of unembodied ideas; an idea, with him, is such and such an individual, with such and such a nose and chin, such and such a hat and waistcoat, bearing the same relation to it as the look of a printed word does to its meaning." This must have been the quality in James himself which T. S. Eliot was referring to when he said that James had a mind so fine that "no idea could violate it."

Howells declared of Turgenev, "Here was a master who was apparently not trying to work out a plot, who was not even trying to work out a character, but was standing aside from the whole affair and letting the characters work the plot out." And he added, "It was not only that Tourguénief had painted life truly, but that he had painted it conscientiously." James was even more emphatic; he said: "Character, character expressed and exposed, is in all [Turgenev's works] what we inveterately find . . . the simplest account of him is to say that the mere play of it constitutes in every case his sufficient drama. No one has a closer vision, or a hand at once more ironic and more tender, for the individual figure. He sees it with its minutest signs and tricks—all its heredity of idiosyncrasies, all its particulars of weakness and strength, of ugliness and beauty, oddity and charm; yet it is of his essence that he sees it in the general flood of life, steeped in its relations and contacts, struggling or submerged, a hurried particle in the stream. . . . He understands so much that we almost wonder he can express anything; and his expression is, indeed, wholly in absolute projection, in illustration, in giving of everything the unexplained and irresponsible specimen."

These statements of Howells and James about Turgenev remind us of the many similar remarks which other novelists have made about the relationship of their materials to experience. For example, F. Scott Fitzgerald in a letter to Maxwell Perkins[2] on July 30, 1934, defined his art as "the attempt . . . to recapture the exact feel of a moment in time and space, exemplified by people rather than by things . . . an attempt at a mature memory of a deep experience." John P. Marquand,[3] who worked—I think—with some distinction in the realistic novel, in making one of his few critical judgments about fiction, said, "A novel is great and good in direct proportion to the illusion it gives of life and a sense of life. . . . [The reader] should feel that he has been through an experience that may be as real . . . [as] experiences in his own living . . . that he has walked with living people." John O'Hara declared his intention as a novelist to be "to record the way people talked and thought and felt, and to do it with complete honesty and variety." James T. Farrell once defined his method as the attempt to give "the precise content of life in environments described in [a particular] book." And Henry James, in a letter to Robert Louis Stevenson, wrote: "I want to leave a multitude of pictures of my time—so that the number may constitute a total having a certain value as observation and testimony." Clearly this is a tradition of the novel which places a high premium— perhaps the highest—on accurate portrayal of precisely observed people in social situations.

These writers have embraced a mimetic theory of art, one in which the fidelity of the art object to its subject is its highest criterion. James declared, "The only reason for the existence of a novel is that it does attempt to represent life. When it relinquishes this attempt . . . it will have arrived at a strange pass." Howells asserted, "Realism is nothing more and nothing less than the truthful treatment of material." And he defined this truthful treatment of material as the attempt "to report the phrase and carriage of every-day life, . . . to tell just how [the author] has heard men talk and seen them look." Throughout his long career as field-general and spokesman for American realism Howells insisted upon the presentation of the commonplace, in his own phraseology, "the simple, the natural, and the honest." And he believed that the best method by which this honestly-viewed and directly-expressed picture of the actual could be presented to the reader was that which Turgenev had practiced with great distinction. Howells said that Turgenev's "fiction is to the last degree dramatic. The persons are sparsely described, and briefly accounted for, and then they are left to transact their affair, whatever it is, with the least possible comment or explanation from the author. The

2. Maxwell Perkins (1884–1947), who was for many years an editor at Scribner's, played a major role in fostering and shaping the careers of such writers as Ernest Hemingway, F. Scott Fitzgerald, and Thomas Wolfe. [*Editor.*]

3. John Phillips Marquand (1893–1960), John Henry O'Hara (1905–1970), and James Thomas Farrell (1904–1979) are all American writers who have carried on, in one way or another, the "realist" tradition in fiction. [*Editor.*]

effect flows naturally from their characters, and when they have done or said a thing you conjecture why as unerringly as you would if they were people whom you knew outside a book." Howells, who praised Tolstoi beyond measure, could still condemn him for his "didactic" stories which, he declared, "dwindled into allegories. . . . Where Tolstoi becomes impatient of his office of artist, and prefers to be directly a teacher, he robs himself of more than his strength." To show what he means, Howells adds in the same essay that Tolstoi's great quality is his "transparency of style, unclouded by any mist of the personality which we mistakenly value in style, and which ought no more to be there than the artist's personality should be in a portrait." And he condemns the *Kreutzer Sonata*[4] as "terrible" because its author "descended to exegesis." It is also worthy of note that both James and Howells thought Hawthorne's most socially oriented novel, *The Blithedale Romance*, to be his best work; and both considered *The Scarlet Letter* to be flawed by its symbolism and its tendency toward allegory.

The point that I am trying to make—a very simple one, indeed—is that there has been, and still is, a significant movement in American fiction which values very highly the artist's ability to reproduce actuality as a sufficient and admirable end in itself. For some, like Howells, this actuality is largely social and direct. For some, like James, profound epistemological questions raise their heads, and the ability of the artist to know the actual comes under serious question. Yet even James, who virtually invented the psychological novel in his explorations of the accuracy of our reports of the real, in moving into psychological issues enriched but did not abandon the mimetic obligation of the novelist. In his best known critical essay, "The Art of Fiction," he defines the imagination in mimetic—almost classical—terms, calling it "The power to guess the unseen from the seen, to trace the implications of things, to judge the whole piece by the pattern, the condition of feeling life in general so completely that you are well on your way to knowing any particular corner of it." And he gave in the same essay a magnificent definition of psychological experience as "an immense sensibility, a kind of huge spider-web of the finest silken threads suspended in the chamber of consciousness, and catching every air-borne particle in its tissue. It is the very atmosphere of the mind; and when the mind is imaginative . . . it takes to itself the faintest hints of life, it converts the very pulses of the air into revelations."

When the realist concentrates not on symbols or allegories but on

4. *The Kreutzer Sonata* (1889), a novel by Leo Tolstoy, is highly philosophical and places more emphasis on analysis of ideas than on the development of character. [*Editor.*]

> "The beauty and the wonder and the power,
> The shapes of things, their colours, lights and shades,
> Changes surprises—,"[5]

when the realist succeeds in achieving this mimetic goal, he presents us with a picture of complex experience which we are to see and respond to as a segment of life. We may demand of art other things than this—indeed, many of us do—we may feel that such lowly aims are too earthbound for our admiration. But when we read writers themselves committed to such aims, we should be willing to take them on their terms, and not rewrite them into ours in our critical essays. As Northrop Frye[6] lamented in the 1962 Inglis Lecture at Harvard, . . . "we tend to make naïve judgments on literature which assume that literary works form a kind of continuous allegorical commentary. . . ." Leon Edel[7] has commented on what he calls "the bizarre critical image of Henry James," saying that critics have called him a "tragic visionary," a "melodramatist," a "religious visionary," an "allegorist," a "realist," and a "naturalist." And at least one critic has found in sedate William Dean Howells significant phallic symbols. Clearly it is time to do something, and I suggest that that something is again to start looking at realistic novelists in their own terms.

James expressed those terms well when in writing of his master Ivan Turgenev's handling of character, he praised his superiority "to the strange and second-rate policy of explaining or presenting them by reprobation or apology—of taking the short cuts and anticipating the emotions and judgments about them that should be left, at best, to the perhaps not most intelligent reader." He saw Turgenev's value as I would have you see the values of James and the other realists as "absolute projection," as "giving of everything the unexplained and irresponsible specimen."

# W. D. HOWELLS

# Henry James, Jr.[†]

\* \* \*

The art of fiction has, in fact, become a finer art in our day than it was with Dickens and Thackeray. We could not suffer the confidential attitude of the latter now, nor the mannerism of the former, any more than we could endure the prolixity of Richardson or the

---

5. Quoted from "Fra Lippo Lippi" (lines 283–285), by Robert Browning. [*Editor.*]
6. Northrop Frye is a contemporary literary critic, whose most influential work is probably his *Anatomy of Criticism* (1957). [*Editor.*]
7. Leon Edel, American literary scholar, is best known for his five-volume biography of Henry

James and his edition of the novelist's letters. [*Editor.*]
†From the *Century*, 45 (November 1882), 28–29. Until the death, in 1882, of his father, who was also a writer of some reputation, Henry James signed all of his work Henry James, Jr., and was known to the public by that name.

coarseness of Fielding. These great men are of the past—they and their methods and interest; even Trollope and Reade are not of the present. The new school derives from Hawthorne and George Eliot[1] rather than any others; but it studies human nature much more in its wonted aspects, and finds its ethical and dramatic examples in the operation of lighter but not really less vital motives. The moving accident is certainly not its trade; and it prefers to avoid all manner of dire catastrophes. It is largely influenced by French fiction in form; but it is the realism of Daudet rather than the realism of Zola that prevails with it, and it has a soul of its own which is above the business of recording the rather brutish pursuit of a woman by a man, which seems to be the chief end of the French novelist. This school, which is so largely of the future as well as the present, finds its chief exemplar in Mr. James; it is he who is shaping and directing American fiction, at least. It is the ambition of the younger contributors to write like him; he has his following more distinctly recognizable than that of any other English-writing novelist. Whether he will so far control this following as to decide the nature of the novel with us remains to be seen. Will the reader be content to accept a novel which is an analytic study rather than a story, which is apt to leave him arbiter of the destiny of the author's creations? Will he find his account in the unflagging interest of their development? Mr. James's growing popularity seems to suggest that this may be the case; but the work of Mr. James's imitators will have much to do with the final result.

# HENRY JAMES

## William Dean Howells[†]

Mr. Howells has gone from one success to another, has taken possession of the field, and has become copious without detriment to his freshness. I need not enumerate his works in their order, for, both in America and in England (where it is a marked feature of the growing curiosity felt about American life that they are constantly referred to for information and verification), they have long been in everybody's hands. Quietly and steadily they have become better and better; one may like some of them more than others, but it is noticeable that from effort to effort the author has constantly enlarged his scope. His work is of a kind of which it is good that there should be much to-day—work of observation, of patient and

1. Charles Dickens (1812–70), William Makepeace Thackeray (1811–63), Samuel Richardson (1689–1781), Henry Fielding (1707–54), Anthony Trollope (1815–82), George Eliot (1819–80), and Charles Reade (1814–84) were all English novelists; Alphonse Daudet (1840–87), a French novelist. [*Editor.*]

†From *Harper's Weekly*, 30 (19 June 1886), 394.

definite notation. Neither in theory nor in practice is Mr. Howells a romancer; but the romancers can spare him; there will always be plenty of people to do their work. He has definite and downright convictions on the subject of the work that calls out to be done in opposition to theirs, and this fact is a source of much of the interest that he excites.

It is a singular circumstance that to know what one wishes to do should be, in the field of art, a rare distinction; but it is incontestable that, as one looks about in our English and American fiction, one does not perceive any very striking examples of a vivifying faith. There is no discussion of the great question of how best to write, no exchange of ideas, no vivacity nor variety of experiment. A vivifying faith Mr. Howells may distinctly be said to possess, and he conceals it so little as to afford every facility to those people who are anxious to prove that it is the wrong one. He is animated by a love of the common, the immediate, the familiar and vulgar elements of life, and holds that in proportion as we move into the rare and strange we become vague and arbitrary; that truth of representation, in a word, can be achieved only so long as it is in our power to test and measure it. He thinks scarcely anything too paltry to be interesting, that the small and the vulgar have been terribly neglected, and would rather see an exact account of a sentiment or a character he stumbles against every day than a brilliant evocation of a passion or a type he has never seen and does not even particularly believe in. He adores the real, the natural, the colloquial, the moderate, the optimistic, the domestic, and the democratic; looking askance at exceptions and perversities and superiorities, at surprising and incongruous phenomena in general. One must have seen a great deal before one concludes; the world is very large, and life is a mixture of many things; she by no means eschews the strange, and often risks combinations and effects that make one rub one's eyes. Nevertheless, Mr. Howells's stand-point is an excellent one for seeing a large part of the truth, and even if it were less advantageous, there would be a great deal to admire in the firmness with which he has planted himself. He hates a "story," and (this private feat is not impossible) has probably made up his mind very definitely as to what the pestilent thing consists of. In this respect he is more logical than M. Émile Zola, who partakes of the same aversion, but has greater lapses as well as greater audacities. Mr. Howells hates an artificial fable and a *dénouement* that is pressed into the service; he likes things to occur as they occur in life, where the manner of a great many of them is not to occur at all. He has observed that heroic emotion and brilliant opportunity are not particularly interwoven with our days, and indeed, in the way of omission, he *has* often practised in his pages a very considerable boldness. It has not, however, made what we find there any less interesting and less human.

The picture of American life on Mr. Howells's canvas is not of a dazzling brightness, and many readers have probably wondered why it is that (among a sensitive people) he has so successfully escaped the imputation of a want of patriotism. The manners he describes—the desolation of the whole social prospect in *A Modern Instance* is perhaps the strongest expression of those influences—are eminently of a nature to discourage the intending visitor, and yet the westward pilgrim continues to arrive, in spite of the Bartley Hubbards and the Laphams, and the terrible practices at the country hotel in *Doctor Breen,* and at the Boston boarding-house in *A Woman's Reason.* This tolerance of depressing revelations is explained partly, no doubt, by the fact that Mr. Howells's truthfulness imposes itself—the representation is so vivid that the reader accepts it as he accepts, in his own affairs, the mystery of fate—and partly by a very different consideration, which is simply that if many of his characters are disagreeable, almost all of them are extraordinarily good, and with a goodness which is a ground for national complacency. If American life is on the whole, as I make no doubt whatever, more innocent than that of any other country, nowhere is the fact more patent than in Mr. Howells's novels, which exhibit so constant a study of the actual and so small a perception of evil. His women, in particular, are of the best—except, indeed, in the sense of being the best to live with. Purity of life, fineness of conscience, benevolence of motive, decency of speech, good-nature, kindness, charity, tolerance (though, indeed, there is little but each other's manners for the people to tolerate), govern all the scene; the only immoralities are aberrations of thought, like that of Silas Lapham, or excesses of beer, like that of Bartley Hubbard. In the gallery of Mr. Howells's portraits there are none more living than the admirable, humorous images of those two ineffectual sinners. Lapham, in particular, is magnificent, understood down to the ground, inside and out—a creation which does Mr. Howells the highest honor. I do not say that the figure of his wife is as good as his own, only because I wish to say that it is as good as that of the minister's wife in the history of *Lenuel Barker,* which is unfolding itself from month to month at the moment I write. These two ladies are exhaustive renderings of the type of virtue that worries. But everything in *Silas Lapham* is superior—nothing more so than the whole picture of casual female youth and contemporaneous "engaging" one's self, in the daughters of the proprietor of the mineral paint.

# W. D. HOWELLS

# [A Call For Realism[†]]

In General Grant's confession of novel-reading there is a sort of inference that he had wasted his time, or else the guilty conscience of the novelist in me imagines such an inference. But however this may be, there is certainly no question concerning the intention of a correspondent who once wrote to me after reading some rather bragging claims I had made for fiction as a mental and moral means. "I have very grave doubts," he said, "as to the whole list of magnificent things that you seem to think novels have done for the race, and can witness in myself many evil things which they have done for me. Whatever in my mental make-up is wild and visionary, whatever is untrue, whatever is injurious, I can trace to the perusal of some work of fiction. Worse than that, they beget such high-strung and supersensitive ideas of life that plain industry and plodding perseverance are despised, and matter-of-fact poverty, or every-day, commonplace distress, meets with no sympathy, if indeed noticed at all, by one who has wept over the impossibly accumulated sufferings of some gaudy hero or heroine."

I am not sure that I had the controversy with this correspondent that he seemed to suppose; but novels are now so fully accepted by every one pretending to cultivated taste—and they really form the whole intellectual life of such immense numbers of people, without question of their influence, good or bad, upon the mind—that it is refreshing to have them frankly denounced, and to be invited to revise one's ideas and feelings in regard to them. A little honesty, or a great deal of honesty, in this quest will do the novel, as we hope yet to have it, and as we have already begun to have it, no harm; and for my own part I will confess that I believe fiction in the past to have been largely injurious, as I believe the stage play to be still almost wholly injurious, through its falsehood, its folly, its wantonness, and its aimlessness. It may be safely assumed that most of the novel-reading which people fancy an intellectual pastime is the emptiest dissipation, hardly more related to thought or the wholesome exercise of the mental faculties than opium-eating; in either case the brain is drugged, and left weaker and crazier for the debauch. If this may be called the negative result of the fiction habit, the positive injury that most novels work is by no means so easily to be measured in the case of young men whose character they help so much to form or deform, and the women of all ages whom they keep so much in ignorance of the world they misrepresent. Grown men have little

[†]From *Criticism and Fiction* (New York: Harper, 1891), pp. 92–104.

harm from them, but in the other cases, which are the vast majority, they hurt because they are not true—not because they are malevolent, but because they are idle lies about human nature and the social fabric, which it behooves us to know and to understand, that we may deal justly with ourselves and with one another. One need not go so far as our correspondent, and trace to the fiction habit "whatever is wild and visionary, whatever is untrue, whatever is injurious," in one's life; bad as the fiction habit is it is probably not responsible for the whole sum of evil in its victims, and I believe that if the reader will use care in choosing from this fungus-growth with which the fields of literature teem every day, he may nourish himself as with the true mushroom, at no risk from the poisonous species.

The tests are very plain and simple, and they are perfectly infallible. If a novel flatters the passions, and exalts them above the principles, it is poisonous; it may not kill, but it will certainly injure; and this test will alone exclude an entire class of fiction, of which eminent examples will occur to all. Then the whole spawn of so-called unmoral romances, which imagine a world where the sins of sense are unvisited by the penalties following, swift or slow, but inexorably sure, in the real world, are deadly poison: these do kill. The novels that merely tickle our prejudices and lull our judgment, or that coddle our sensibilities or pamper our gross appetite for the marvellous are not so fatal, but they are innutritious, and clog the soul with unwholesome vapors of all kinds. No doubt they too help to weaken the moral fibre, and make their readers indifferent to "plodding perseverance and plain industry," and to "matter-of-fact poverty and commonplace distress."

Without taking them too seriously, it still must be owned that the "gaudy hero and heroine" are to blame for a great deal of harm in the world. That heroine long taught by example, if not precept, that Love, or the passion or fancy she mistook for it, was the chief interest of a life, which is really concerned with a great many other things; that it was lasting in the way she knew it; that it was worthy of every sacrifice, and was altogether a finer thing than prudence, obedience, reason; that love alone was glorious and beautiful, and these were mean and ugly in comparison with it. More lately she has begun to idolize and illustrate Duty, and she is hardly less mischievous in this new role, opposing duty, as she did love, to prudence, obedience, and reason. The stock hero, whom, if we met him, we could not fail to see was a most deplorable person, has undoubtedly imposed himself upon the victims of the fiction habit as admirable. With him, too, love was and is the great affair, whether in its old romantic phase of chivalrous achievement or manifold suffering for love's sake, or its more recent development of the "virile," the bullying, and the brutal, or its still more recent agonies of self-sacrifice, as idle and useless as the moral experiences of the insane asylums. With his vain posturings and his ridiculous splendor he is really a painted barbarian, the prey of his passions and his delusions, full of obsolete ideals, and the motives and ethics of a savage, which the guilty author of his being does his best—or his worst—in spite of his own light and knowledge, to foist upon the reader as something generous and noble. I am not merely bringing this charge against that sort of fiction which is beneath literature and outside of it, "the shoreless lakes of ditch-water," whose miasms fill the air below the empyrean where the great ones sit; but I am accusing the work of some of the most famous, who have, in this instance or in that, sinned against the truth, which can alone exalt and purify men. I do not say that they have constantly done so, or even commonly done so; but that they have done so at all marks them as of the past, to be read with the due historical allowance for their epoch and their conditions. For I believe that, while inferior writers will and must continue to imitate them in their foibles and their errors, no one hereafter will be able to achieve greatness who is false to humanity, either in its facts or its duties. The light of civilization has already broken even upon the novel, and no conscientious man can now set about painting an image of life without perpetual question of the verity of his work, and without feeling bound to distinguish so clearly that no reader of his may be misled, between what is right and what is wrong, what is noble and what is base, what is health and what is perdition, in the actions and the characters he portrays.

The fiction that aims merely to entertain—the fiction that is to serious fiction as the opera-bouffe, the ballet, and the pantomime are to the true drama—need not feel the burden of this obligation so deeply; but even such fiction will not be gay or trivial to any reader's hurt, and criticism will hold it to account if it passes from painting to teaching folly.

More and more not only the criticism which prints its opinions, but the infinitely vaster and powerfuler criticism which thinks and feels them merely, will make this demand. I confess that I do not care to judge any work of the imagination without first of all applying this test to it. We must ask ourselves before we ask anything else, Is it true?—true to the motives, the impulses, the principles that shape the life of actual men and women? This truth, which necessarily includes the highest morality and the highest artistry—this truth given, the book cannot be wicked and cannot be weak; and without it all graces of style and feats of invention and cunning of construction are so many superfluities of naughtiness. It is well for the truth to have all these, and shine in them, but for falsehood they are merely meretricious, the bedizenment of the wanton; they atone for nothing, they count for nothing. But in fact they come naturally of truth, and grace it without solicitation; they are added unto it. In the whole range of fiction we know of no true picture of life—that is, of human nature—which is not also a masterpiece of literature, full of divine and natural beauty. It may have no touch or tint of this special civilization or of that; it had better have this local color well ascertained; but the truth is deeper and finer than aspects, and if the book is true to what men and women know of one another's souls it will be true enough, and it will be great and beautiful. It is the conception of literature as something apart from life, superfinely aloof, which makes it really unimportant to the great mass of mankind, without a message or a meaning for them; and it is the notion that a novel may be false in its portrayal of causes and effects that makes literary art contemptible even to those whom it amuses, that forbids them to regard the novelist as a serious or right-minded person. If they do not in some moment of indignation cry out against all novels, as my correspondent does, they remain besotted in the fume of the delusions purveyed to them, with no higher feeling for the author than such maudlin affection as the habitué of an opium-joint perhaps knows for the attendant who fills his pipe with the drug.

Or, as in the case of another correspondent who writes that in his youth he "read a great many novels, but always regarded it as an amusement, like horse-racing and card-playing," for which he had no time when he entered upon the serious business of life, it renders them merely contemptuous. His view of the matter may be commended to the brotherhood and sisterhood of novelists as full of wholesome if bitter suggestion; and we urge them not to dismiss it with high literary scorn as that of some Boeotian[1] dull to the beauty of art. Refuse it as we may, it is still the feeling of the vast majority of people for whom life is earnest, and who find only a distorted and misleading likeness of it in our books. We may fold ourselves in our scholars' gowns, and close the doors of our studies, and affect to despise this rude voice; but we cannot shut it out. It comes to us from wherever men are at work, from wherever they are truly living, and accuses us of unfaithfulness, of triviality, of mere stage-play; and none of us can escape conviction except he prove himself worthy of his time—a time in which the great masters have brought literature back to life, and filled its ebbing veins with the red tides of reality. We cannot all equal them; we need not copy them; but we can all go to the sources of their inspiration and their power; and to draw from these no one need go far—no one need really go out of himself.

---

1. Boeotia, a region in central Greece, the inhabitants of which were traditionally noted for their dullness of mind. [*Editor.*]

Fifty years ago, Carlyle,[2] in whom the truth was always alive, but in whom it was then unperverted by suffering, by celebrity, and by despair, wrote in his study of Diderot: "Were it not reasonable to prophesy that this exceeding great multitude of novel-writers and such like must, in a new generation, gradually do one of two things: either retire into the nurseries, and work for children, minors, and semi-fatuous persons of both sexes, or else, what were far better, sweep their novel-fabric into the dust-cart, and betake themselves with such faculty as they have to understand and record what is true, of which surely there is, and will forever be, a whole infinitude unknown to us of infinite importance to us? Poetry, it will more and more come to be understood, is nothing but higher knowledge; and the only genuine Romance (for grown persons), Reality."

If, after half a century, fiction still mainly works for "children, minors, and semi-fatuous persons of both sexes," it is nevertheless one of the hopefulest signs of the world's progress that it has begun to work for "grown persons," and if not exactly in the way that Carlyle might have solely intended in urging its writers to compile memoirs instead of building the "novel-fabric," still it has, in the highest and widest sense, already made Reality its Romance. I cannot judge it, I do not even care for it, except as it has done this; and I can hardly conceive of a literary self-respect in these days compatible with the old trade of make-believe, with the production of the kind of fiction which is too much honored by classification with card-playing and horse-racing. But let fiction cease to lie about life; let it portray men and women as they are, actuated by the motives and the passions in the measure we all know; let it leave off painting dolls and working them by springs and wires; let it show the different interests in their true proportions; let it forbear to preach pride and revenge, folly and insanity, egotism and prejudice, but frankly own these for what they are, in whatever figures and occasions they appear; let it not put on fine literary airs; let it speak the dialect, the language, that most Americans know—the language of unaffected people everywhere—and there can be no doubt of an unlimited future, not only of delightfulness but of usefulness, for it.

2. Thomas Carlyle (1795–1881), Scottish essayist, historian, biographer, and social critic, whose view of Victorian culture grew progressively darker over the years. Carlyle's remarks refer to Denis Diderot (1713–84), founder and director of the French *Encyclopédie* and intellectual father of the French Revolution. [*Editor.*]

## LARZER ZIFF

# [Literary Hospitality: William Dean Howells]†

\* \* \*

A year after he became editor of the *Atlantic*, Howells published his first novel, *Their Wedding Journey* (1872), and books of fiction followed at the rate of almost one a year, along with occasional volumes of travel, criticism, and poetry. In his fiction he most clearly realized the promise detected by his elders in 1860, for here he carried into post-Civil-War America a sense of the sturdy morality which sinewed American life. True to his Western origins, however, he did so by concentrating far more closely on the daily actualities of middle-class American life than did the New Englanders. Emerson saw the American democracy as a splendid ground for the individual's realization of the noble purposes which unified humanity, but he spoke of the possibilities in an essentially unhistorical fashion. As John Jay Chapman was to note:

> The ethical assumption that all men are exactly alike permeates his work. In his mind, Socrates, Marco Polo, and General Jackson stand surrounded by the same atmosphere, or rather stand as mere naked characters surrounded by no atmosphere at all. He is probably the last great writer who will fling about classic anecdotes as if they were club gossip.[1]

Howells, with his incredibly detailed sense of the present historical moment—so much so that he was always vulnerable to attacks that he dealt in the petty—did, nevertheless, take his note from Emerson.

The Concord philosopher, unhistorical as he may have been, had called for other writers to bring his ideals to bear on American realities:

> What would we really know the meaning of? The meal in the firkin; the milk in the pan; the ballad in the street; the news of the boat; the glance of the eye; the form and the gait of the body;—show me the ultimate reason of these matters; show me the sublime presence of the highest spiritual cause lurking, as always it does lurk, in these suburbs and extremities of nature; let me see every trifle bristling with the polarity that ranges it instantly on an eternal law; and the shop, the plough, and the ledger referred to the like cause by which light undulates and poets sing;—and the world lies no longer a dull miscellany and lumber-room, but has form and order; there is no trifle, there is

†From *The American 1890s: Life and Times of a Lost Generation* (New York: Viking, 1966), pp. 27–32. (Footnotes are by Ziff, unless otherwise indi-cated.)
1. John Jay Chapman, *Emerson and Other Essays* (New York, 1909), p. 43.

no puzzle, but one design unites and animates the farthest pinnacle and the lowest trench.[2]

The emphasis here is not on the realities; rather, Emerson asks the writer to take them up in order to reveal their transcendental purpose. His immediate followers responded in different ways: Thoreau, for instance, attempted to peel the triviality away from daily life in order to show a core that was one with the life of the Greek heroes and the Hindu gods; while Whitman attempted to pick up every bead of reality and arrange it on a transcendental string of unity.[3]

Howells' novels, with their bickering newlyweds and middle-aged visitors to summer hotels, appeared at some remove from Emerson. He seemed concerned with the meal and the milk in themselves rather than with their animating design. But he only appeared so. The trivialities with which he concerned himself were polarized also, but the polarizing force had changed, had been enfeebled and yet made more flexible by its contact with its materials.

Howells' greatest fictional success in his Boston days was *The Rise of Silas Lapham* (1885), the story of a newly rich vulgarian's social downfall. At one point in this novel Lapham and his young Brahmin[4] employee, Corey, are on an excursion steamer to Nantasket, crowded with specimens of middle- and lower-class Americans out for a good time. Howells looks at them and says:

> The greater part of the crowd on board—and, of course, the boat was crowded—looked as if they might not only be easily but safely known. There was little style and no distinction among them; they were people who were going down to the beach for the fun or the relief of it. . . . In face they were commonplace, with nothing but the American poetry of vivid purpose to light them up, where they did not wholly lack fire.

"The American poetry of vivid purpose" is Howells' equivalent to Emerson's "animating design," and he details the commonplace in order to reveal its underlying purpose as the great unifier in national life.

At the close of the novel Silas Lapham, his scarcely won social status and his commercial winnings tumbling about him to ruin, meets with an opportunity to stem his losses. It will involve a swindle in which a well-heeled and impersonal corporation will be the loser, but in which Lapham will be legally free of any wrongdoing. He resists the temptation and continues his commercial and social

2. Ralph Waldo Emerson, "The American Scholar," in *Selections*, ed. Stephen Wicher (Boston, 1957), p. 78.
3. Ralph Waldo Emerson (1803–82); Walt Whitman (1819–92); and Henry David Thoreau (1817–62), whose attempt to peel the triviality away from life is recorded in his book *Walden* (1854). [*Editor.*]
4. A name borrowed from the highest priestly caste of Hindu society and used jokingly to refer to members of upper-class New England families, especially Boston families. [*Editor.*]

descent, but in so doing he achieves a moral rise. That this hearty vulgarian could make such a decision is believable, Howells demonstrates, because commercialism and social climbing merely form a patina on American life. Scratch the patina and, as in Lapham's case, you find the sturdy, honest country boy who will give no quarter in a fair fight, but who will not take mean advantage of even those who can afford to lose.

Lapham himself had looked at the crowd on the boat on which the author had commented and had said, "But you take faces now! The astonishing thing to me is not what a face tells, but what it don't tell. When you think of what a man is, or a woman is, and what most of 'em have been through before they get to be thirty, it seems as if their experience would burn right through. But it don't." Because it doesn't burn right through, Howells is attracted to it. For him the novelist's task is to reveal in action what the commonplace face does not reveal when glanced at. Thus he will reveal the spiritual cause which lurks in the "suburbs and extremities of nature."

If editorship of the *Atlantic* and undisputed leadership in the field of fiction, capped by *Silas Lapham* in 1885, were not sufficient evidence that the obvious play on his name was justified, that Howells was indeed the Dean of American letters, more was to come: literary Boston extended its ultimate tribute in 1886 by inviting him to succeed Lowell in the Smith Professorship at Harvard. He declined the offer, but the twenty-six years from his Parker House lunch with Lowell to the Harvard invitation formed a success story whose moral was that the expansion of the United States had been matched in literature by an orderly continuity. The West had been won to the East; the East had been bent in the direction of the West.

Howells' critical theme over the same period paralleled his achievement in fiction. He wrote:

> I am in hopes that the communistic era in taste foreshadowed by Burke[5] is approaching, and that it will occur within the lives of men now overawed by the foolish superstition that literature and art are anything but the expression of life, and are to be judged by any other test than that of their fidelity to it.[6]

The test which he was attacking was that which demanded of fiction an idealization of the human condition, which asked of the writer that he lift his readers out of the commonplace by presenting them with models of love, duty, and heroism. Such models, everybody admitted, did not exist except as ideals, but this was all the more

5. Edmund Burke (1729–97), British politician and aesthetician, whose study, *A Philosophical Enquiry into the Origin of our Ideas of the Sublime and Beautiful* (1756), Howells is referring to here, recommends that art should be measured against nature, not merely against art. [*Editor.*]
6. William Dean Howells, *Criticism and Fiction* (New York, 1891), p. 8.

reason why they must be brought into being in fiction. Literature, according to those Howells attacked, was best when it freed itself from the mire of experience and held aloft the beautiful prize, regardless of the prize's lack of relation to the realities of the contest. Ugliness is too much with us in everyday life; fiction should ennoble us by showing us a purer world. In response to this view, Howells' insistence on the simple, the natural, and the honest was, to a large class of readers, merely an insistence on the plain, the dull, and the unedifying.

Howells too, as has been seen, had his ideals, but they were the starting points, the principles which sinewed American life and were to be discovered in a minute scrutiny of it, not the vaguely impossible ends which were to be pursued regardless of the realities. If daily experience had to be falsified in order for the writer to strike a lofty tone, then he should not attempt that tone. Indeed, so committed was Howells to his sense of the American present that even as he rejected the tinsel optimism of the hundred and one tales of lovers who had loved as none had ever loved before, he rejected as unsuitable for the American novelist the tragic note which was struck in the work of Dostoevski.[7] "Very few American novelists have been led out to be shot, or finally exiled to the rigors of a winter at Duluth,"[8] he pointed out. This meant that, though they should not romanticize the realities, still American novelists could concern themselves with "the more smiling aspects of life, which are the more American, and seek the universal in the individual rather than the social interests."[9]

If his remark that the smiling aspects of life were the typically American ones seemed a tempting of the gods, Howells nevertheless had a twenty-six-year professional career to point to as evidence of the validity of his contention. Reporting on his visit to Florence in a book published in 1886, he carried his provocation of the fates to its farthest point: "Poor, splendid, stupid, glorious past! I stood at the windows of the people's palace and looked out on the space in the rear where those culprits used to disturb the signory at their meals, and thanked Heaven that I was of the nineteenth century."[1] So much for the romance that longed for days of yore and conveniently forgot the bestiality of man to man, the grime that gathered on the collar of lace. Plain, unchivalric America of 1886 was less colorful on the surface, Howells felt, but had far more of worth to express, if only the writer could liberate that expression from the resisting commonplace materials in which it resided.

---

7. Feodor Mikhailovich Dostoevsky (1821-81), Russian novelist, author of *Crime and Punishment* (1866), *The Idiot* (1869), and *The Brothers Karamazov* (1880), was both exiled and condemned to execu- tion at different points in his life. [*Editor*]

8. Howells, *Criticism and Fiction*, p. 128.
9. *Ibid.*
1. Howells, *Tuscan Cities* (Boston, 1886), p. 155.

## EDWIN H. CADY

# The Chief American Realist: 1881–1885[†]

\* \* \*

As a professional man of letters in his early forties he was now ready to establish the habits of life and methods of work which would carry him through the next forty years and sixty-odd books. With essential responsibilities narrowed to his family and writing, he had large vistas of personal freedom in control of his time, his energy, and his place and mode of living. Therefore daily, systematic, hard work became an essential part of his formula. It was one of the family jokes that Elinor Howells said he wrote novels like a man sawing wood. His health had been so good for a decade that he had almost forgotten to be hypochondriac; and his stamina had been proved. And his personal growth, as exemplified for instance in the difference between the mind recorded in the notebook he kept for *Italian Journeys* and *Their Wedding Journey* and the one he kept for *Indian Summer* and later works in the eighties, is really striking. The old self-consciously poetic hypersensitivity and temptation to pose are gone. In their place are a balance of mind and accuracy of perception and response reminiscent of Benjamin Franklin. He was nearing the insight he confided to his father toward the end of the decade—that his enforced self-education had been no disaster: "There are some self-made men in this country who would have done well to spend the time making almost anything else; but on the whole the men made by others are worse."[1]

His work habits became professionally well-grooved, and work became a passion, almost a vice, for a man who loved what he did. Consequently he became contemptuous of the flighty author who must wait on inspiration. Why might the Muse not wait as readily on the man who made a business of wooing her as on the man who mooned about yearning for a miracle? "I sit down at my desk and go to work as regularly as if I were in a mercantile or banking office," Howells said, ". . . you can work it out by patient and methodical application." The trick was to discipline oneself to free his time and energies for his best effort. Howells got in the habit of rising between seven and seven-thirty in the morning, sitting down to a substantial breakfast at eight, and being at work by nine. Then he wrote until

[†]From *The Road to Realism: The Early Years 1837–1885 of William Dean Howells* (Syracuse: Syracuse University Press, 1956), pp. 201–6. This biographical study is continued in Cady's *The Realist at War* (Syracuse: Syracuse University Press, 1958).
1. In this book Mr. Cady does not employ conventional footnotes to indicate the sources of individual quotations and citations. Instead, in the "Bibliographical Notes" at the end of the volume he indicates the sources of the information he is synthesizing. See p. 273 in Cady's book. [*Editor.*]

about twelve, never past one o'clock, and had lunch, averaging a thousand to fifteen hundred words of finished production for the day. In a handwriting which deteriorated with the years, he liked to write in extra-large script on half sheets, leaving wide spaces between lines for revisions and piling up huge stacks of paper. He aimed to work three hours a day and sleep eight, and he came to be able to write in trains or hotels, on shipboard, or anywhere there was room. Afternoons he might read or correct proof, but there was always his long constitutional to be walked. Evenings might be given to the theater, to reading aloud with his wife, or to going out.

As Howells' celebrity increased, his public personality continued to be attractive but developed protections. People were surprised on first meeting him to see how quiet, simple, deliberately undistinguished he seemed. He was short, stout, round-shouldered, and peaceable. His "voice had a gentle softness, as though there were twins asleep in the next room." Everyone felt his true kindliness and "absorbent" quality—he seemed really interested in other people and liked to make them talk and unfold themselves rather than parade his own ego. That and his subtle, quick humor gave him great personal charm. But alert observers also saw that in a sense he was armored behind his wit and gentleness. He could not be taken advantage of or pushed into positions he did not like; he was hard to attack. "It is not the attitude of a man who does not think, but more like that of one who does not care always to think aloud," said one sensitive interviewer. "In general he reserves his deeper meditations for himself, as everyone has a right to do. The plane on which he oftenest meets people is one of sensible, considerate, well-balanced reflection on life and books, enlivened by humor and averse to the tediousness of argument." The "colorless Napoleonic face" was full of vitality, the glance of the blue eye exceptionally penetrating; the full mustache was beginning to frost with gray.

All the rest of his career Howells continued to produce plays, essays, poems, reviews, travel pieces—but there was no question about which form enlisted his strongest love. As a brash young interviewer, Van Wyck Brooks[2] "asked him in which, as a man of letters, he took most delight. . . . 'Oh, fiction, fiction,' he replied with a good deal of warmth." Yet, for all his faith in the conscientious application of the seat of the pants to the chair, Howells was just as dependent on the stirring of the waters, on the mysterious and uncontrollable appearance of the creative impulse from the sublogical levels of his mind, as any other artist. Fortunately, he suffered from no such poverty of impulse as some other writers, and his method for dealing with the creative impulse toward fiction, when it came, was as well-grooved as his working day.

2. Van Wyck Brooks (1886–1963), influential  American biographer and literary critic. [*Editor.*]

"My plan is to choose my topic, select the characters I want for the story, choose my locality and time, and then go to work. . . . I generally content myself with choosing the phase of life or the subject that I wish to illustrate, sketch out in mind the principal characters, and then plunge into the work. Most books write themselves when you are fairly started, and I trust to the plot unfolding itself as there may be need. With the portraiture of character it is quite otherwise, and a good deal of reflection is necessary . . ."—thus Howells himself on his method. His system was designed to control himself, not his materials. He was ready to trust his talent and imaginative processes to work out the substance of a book. Academics imagine too much deliberate design in authors, he once protested to Professor Brander Matthews of Columbia: an artist *feels* his way to success; he doesn't *map* it.

For realist Howells, the great thing about fiction was, of course, character. His people absorbed by far the greatest part of his attention and delight. But he rejected the notion that the author is or should be possessed by his characters and lost in his creations: "Never," he said. "The essence of achievement is to keep outside, to be entirely dispassionate, as a sculptor must be, moulding his clay . . ."—or a good actor. By this he did not mean that passion must be absent, but that it must be under artistic command. When the Boston author Robert Grant[3] asked Howells, an old man revisiting the Saturday Club, "how firm a hold he used to have upon his characters," he got a quick, passionate reply: "The grip of a bull dog!" With the characters thus firmly in hand, he could give them their settings and conjecture their fates and significance. All this he could project as a novel: "describe it in 8 or 10 lines, estimate its length, and give its purpose . . ." But he could go no further except by the process of hard, daily work. He would ordinarily refuse to do that until a magazine editor had agreed to accept the final product; and he would steadfastly refuse to elaborate further. The editor had to take the novel in outline if he took it at all and trust the author's imagination and discipline as the author did.

Of course, Howells was begging part of the question of his creative method when he spoke so easily of "choosing" topic, characters, locale, and all the rest. That leaves untouched the question of how the choices became possible. If anyone in a moment of egomania ever pretended that he could create a work of the literary imagination by simple, arbitrary acts of will and logic, it was Edgar Allan Poe, not Howells. Full understanding of Howells' creative processes will

---

3. Robert Grant (1852–1940), Boston jurist and author, whose works include *Unleavened Bread* (1900) and *The Dark Horse* (1934). The Saturday Club, a distinguished Boston literary and dining club founded in the 1850s, included such men as Emerson, Lowell, Longfellow, Holmes, Howells, and James. Grant was a member and wrote its history, *Later Years of the Saturday Club* (1927). [*Editor.*]

require careful study of his notebooks and manuscripts, not all yet available. But it seems clear that his creative impulses came from an esthetic use of memory. Or that the image of the Well as the source of creativity given in John Livingston Lowes's *The Road to Xanadu* applies to Howells' case. Lowes portrayed Coleridge's creative imagination as a mystic Well into which ideas and images from his wide reading dropped as if they were individual fragments with little hooks attached. In the depths of the Well they somehow, often incongruously, became tangled together. Then, when the mysterious energy of creativity troubled the waters, they rose to the surface in new and unpredictable combinations to make themselves available to the conscious, shaping mind of the skillful artist.

Howells' theory was that "an author is merely one who has had the fortune to remember more . . . than other men. A good many wise critics will tell you that writing is inventing; but I know better than that; it is only remembering . . . the history of your own life." His own memory was, as we have seen, much keener than most people's. But his theory of creativity as memory makes sense (in theory and in conjunction with his own various statements about the creation of literature) only if one takes his "remembering" as roughly equivalent to Lowes's "Well." As Lowes saw Coleridge, he seems to have stocked the Well almost exclusively from reading; Howells stocked his from experience of life as well as books. While memory of specific people and events, or indeed direct observation with literature aforethought, gave him materials for his work, what he remembered or recorded was at least as much the response of his own mind and emotions to places, people, and events as anything "objective"—even supposing a man and artist can really see objects as they are. Urged at the age of forty-nine to write a novel of Washington, D.C., he demurred, "I am too old now. I could not stand the going into society to catch the spirit of things."

Leaving for later discussion the question of how a writer may be imagined actually to have placed a "transcript of life" on his page, one needs to avoid being caught in the trap of supposing that Howells did somehow actually reproduce "real life" as it existed around him. As a realistic theoretician he talked a great deal about doing just that. In practice he found his impulses to creativity just where James or Hawthorne found them—in the "germs," the extraordinarily suggestive moments of experience which could set his imagination in motion and eventually make a work of fiction possible. Some of Howells' effects in his work were importantly different from some of theirs, but that is all. His diaries and notebooks follow an interesting rule of preparation for writing. When there are extensive observations of scenes and people, heavily detailed, these are notes for travel books. The notes for serious fiction are records of inward impulses, stirrings of the creative life shaping the work within. The exception to this rule is the special "study" made to flesh out a structure already given but not complete.

When once Howells had "remembered" the basis for a book, he sometimes had to do research to fill in where memory could not serve. In order not to shatter the illusion of life he was creating by falling into anachronisms, he was often at considerable pains to get things "right." While writing *The Quality of Mercy* he felt he needed to know, for instance, just what the police department of a Canadian city would do about a tip that an American embezzler was living there under cover. So he went to Montreal, walked into police headquarters, and solemnly put a hypothetical question to the chief—who immediately pounded his bell and turned out his detective squad to get a first-hand report on the story and be ready to go right to work.* * * The lesson was that he had, indeed, somehow to "remember" in order to do good work. As the genesis of his first major novel, the first big achievement of his free-lance period, *A Modern Instance*, shows, however, he worked best when something had acted to fire his imagination to a very special kind of remembering.

# ROBERT M. FIGG III

# Naturalism as a Literary Form[†]

Ever since Vernon L. Parrington[1] defined literary naturalism as "pessimistic realism," American critics, among them such figures as Alfred Kazin, Richard Chase, and Philip Rahv, have by and large followed suit. Naturalism has appeared to them as identical in *kind* with realism, though different in *degree*. It has been interpreted as an extension of realism, as realism intensified, as a "harsher realism," or as realism carried to the *ntb* degree. This tendency persists even today, as can be seen in two recent collections of realist documents— *Realism and Romanticism in Fiction: An Approach to the Novel* (1962), whose editors call naturalism "a new type of realism," and *Documents of Modern Literary Realism* (1963), whose editor, George J. Becker, tells us that "in essence and in origin naturalism is no more than an emphatic and explicit philosophical position taken by some realists. . . ."

One readily understands this tendency to classify naturalism under the general heading of realism, for most of these commenta-

†From *Georgia Review*, 18 (Fall, 1964), 308–16.
1. Vernon Louis Parrington (1871–1929), American literary scholar; Alfred Kazin, Richard Chase, and Philip Rahv are all contemporary critics who write chiefly about American literature. [*Editor.*]

tors have been mainly concerned with treating the matter from the point of view of literary history, and from that viewpoint naturalism perhaps does appear to be an extension or intensification of realism. But from a strictly literary point of view, it seems to me, the difference between these modes is more than a matter of degree.

\* \* \*

Let us now look at two specific types of American realism, realism of the commonplace and critical realism. The former, according to its chief proponent, William Dean Howells, takes as its subject matter the common, the familiar, the ordinary in American life, and proposes to treat this matter with something approaching faithfulness to the given actualities of life. Its matter is gleaned through empirical observation; its manner of treatment is inspired by a desire for scientific objectivity. It has, too, a social aim, to knit men together in the spirit of sympathy and brotherhood through a recognition of the commonality of their experience. All this is not to imply that realism of the commonplace is a mere photographic treatment of observed actuality. It has its selective criterion: the belief that a proportioned, "average" representation of actuality is closer to the truth than a representation of extremes. It has, too, its faith in value—in a sort of relativistic, pragmatic truth which cannot be determined in an *a priori* manner but must be sought in the observable consequences of human actions. Everett Carter[2] has given us an admirable survey of this aspect of the realism of the commonplace:

> To expose the 'bad *a priori*' that the savage and the untutored were necessarily noble was the motive behind Eggleston's[3] realistic portraits in *The Hoosier Schoolmaster* and *The Circuit Rider*. The falsity of the assumption that the agrarian life of the West was inevitably the good life was the subject of Hamlin Garland's[4] *Main-Travelled Roads* and *Jason Edwards*. The 'pretended absolutes' of the South's chivalric ideals were the targets for John DeForest's[5] criticism in *Miss Ravenel's Conversion* . . . for Mark Twain in *Huckleberry Finn*. . . . A criticism of unexamined 'fixed principles' and closed systems of morality was the motivation for Howells' fiction.

In exposing the bad *a priori* and turning instead to the world of actuality for their reading of truth, these men anticipated what William James[6] was later to call the pragmatic method, that is, "The

2. Everett Carter. *Howells and the Age of Realism*, (1954), p. 153ff. [*Editor.*]

3. Edward Eggleston (1837–1902), historian and regional novelist, author of *The Hoosier Schoolmaster* (1871), *The Circuit Rider* (1874). [*Editor.*]

4. Hamlin Garland (1860–1940), novelist and short-story writer, was a protégé of Howells; *Main-Travelled Roads* (1891) is a collection of his stories; *Jason Edwards: An Average Man* (1892) is a novel written to support the single-tax theories of Henry George. [*Editor.*]

5. John William DeForest (1826–1906), author of the realistic study of the Civil War, *Miss Ravenel's Conversion from Secession to Loyalty* (1867). [*Editor.*]

6. William James (1842–1910), the American philosopher and psychologist, was the brother of Henry James. The quotation comes from Lecture II, "What Pragmatism Means," in *Pragmatism* (1907), pp. 54–55. [*Editor.*]

attitude of looking away from first things, principles, 'categories,' supposed necessities; and of looking towards last things, fruits, consequences, facts." For the dual purposes of bodying forth its proportioned view of actuality and its pragmatic vision of truth, then, commonplace realism necessarily employs selection and arrangement of observed data and hence does not become mere photography. The manipulation of data is solely in the interest of focusing the truth that the author finds operative within the world of actuality. Finally, there is in commonplace realism a sort of optimistic faith that man, through the application of reason to the world of fact, may improve his existence, a faith which was based on the pragmatic assumption that the world of things was full of meaning. The aforementioned principles constitute, of course, a theoretical statement of what realism of the commonplace is, a sort of ideal model of what such realists sought. We would not expect to find a perfect embodiment of this model, the difference between intention and realization in human life being what it is. The closest approximation to an incarnation of these principles is, perhaps, Howells' *The Rise of Silas Lapham.*

The second type of realism we want to look at is what has come to be known as critical realism. As with commonplace realism, its chief theoretician was William Dean Howells, who defined critical realism as an attempt at "dispersing the conventional acceptances by which men live on easy terms with themselves, and obliging them to examine the grounds of their social and moral opinions." Yet in proclaiming this new concept of realism, Howells did not, as Everett Carter reminds us, "discard any of the elements of his former philosophy of fiction. . . ." Critical realism was essentially realism of the commonplace operating on wider and more inclusive grounds, in keeping with Howells' growing awareness that, in the America of the late 1880's, the "smiling aspects" no longer best represented the truth of the American actuality and that the problems of Americans were not so much individual in nature as social. But in shifting grounds Howells kept to "his previous beliefs, with their good-sense and moderation," as Everett Carter has put it, and thus "saved himself from falling into the trap of propaganda." The basis for the socially critical attitude in *A Hazard of New Fortunes,* for instance, is pragmatic rather than doctrinaire: that *laissez-faire* capitalism is reprehensible because of its ruinous and destructive effects upon individuals and upon society as a whole. In his selection and arrangement of the data he has gleaned from observation, Howells still has as his main aim a focused presentation of the truth of the world of actuality. He operates in the faith that, should he manage to capture the essentials of that world in his fictional image, the sensitive reader will necessarily feel his "conventional acceptances" challenged. Thus he leaves the critical inferences largely up to the reader and does not impose them upon him in a direct form, as do the authors of those novels of social criticism which are oriented around a highly prescriptive socio-economic thesis or formula.

In both realism of the commonplace and critical realism, then, there is manipulation of observed data—a selection and arrangement of fictional materials in the interest of embodying the author's view of reality; but the assumptions governing the selection and disposal of these materials are relatively mild and the image of life presented is relatively close to the actual. No highly prescriptive ideas are imposed on the novel, more or less wrenching its materials into shapes and patterns that strike us as distortions of what has been observed in the world of actuality. The "addition" of an unqualified materialistic determinism to a novel based on either of the aforementioned codes of realism—if we can at all imagine such a thing—would have precisely this effect. The incidents of the work would have to be redisposed so as to present the illusion of man as inescapably the creature of forces beyond his control, and the characters would have to be refashioned into relatively "flat" types, representing various examples of passivity, ineffectuality, and futility. Gone would be all pretense that the work presented something approximating observable and verifiable experience, since the idea of the absolute determination of man is but an unproven, and perhaps unprovable, hypothesis. Gone, too, would be the critical purpose and optimistic faith that lie at the heart of both types of Howellsian realism, the idea that man may amend his condition through the application of reason to individual and social problems. The result would be something essentially different from what was before, in respect to both form and significance.

This distinction in *kind* between realism and naturalism was something that Emile Zola, the fountainhead of naturalistic theory, insisted upon in his manifesto, *Le Roman expérimental*.[7] The naturalistic novelist, he tells us, is not simply an observer, but is rather an observer *and* experimenter:

> The observer in him presents data as he has observed them, determines the point of departure, establishes the solid ground on which his characters will stand and his phenomena take place. Then the experimenter appears and institutes the experiment, that is, sets the characters of a particular story in motion, in order to show that the series of events therein will be those demanded by the determinism of the phenomena under study.

In other words, as an observer, the naturalistic novelist gleans "facts" from the world of actuality, just as does the realist. As an ex-

7. *Le Roman expérimental* (*The Experimental Novel*, 1880), by Émile Zola. [*Editor.*]

perimentalist, however, he rearranges or modifies them in accord with the deterministic hypothese of science. Zola admits that the idea of man being governed by an absolute hereditary and environmental determinism is but an *hypothesis,* that science has not yet proven this to be true, though he tells us that physiology and social science will no doubt someday explain such mechanisms. In the meanwhile, the naturalist is to write of man in the spirit of one "who accepts only facts in conformity with the determinism of phenomena," trusting that what he writes is the truth about man. His product thus involves the imposition upon observed fact of a rigid *assumption* about the nature of reality.

\* \* \*

Like the realist, then, the naturalist draws his fictional materials from the world of observed actuality; but, unlike the realist, he does not regard a well-proportioned representation of what occurs in that world as significant enough in itself. He feels it necessary to give authority and significance to observed events through interpreting them in terms of scientific assumptions about the nature of reality. In his novel he therefore imposes upon these materials a narrow and rigid scientific hypothesis, with the result being a distortion of observed data into certain prescribed patterns and forms. Thus we may say that, though the realist and the naturalist draw their material from a common source—the world of actuality—, they use this material in radically different ways, with radically different consequences for the form that embodies their art.

## CHARLES L. CAMPBELL

## Realism and the Romance of Real Life: Multiple Fictional Worlds in Howells' Novels[†]

\* \* \* In *The Rise of Silas Lapham, Indian Summer* and *April Hopes,* [Howells] deals with the theme of the romance of real life in a manner which reflects the rising vehemence of his pronouncements in "The Editor's Study." Howells' theory continually impinges on his fiction; his novels are not so much a fulfillment of his theory as an extended statement of it within a fictional framework. The battle between the realistic and romanticist principles at the center of Howells' fictional world makes it less a portrayal of life and more a commentary upon life couched in a literary vehicle. In this way, Howells' novels are often not so much realistic as they are about realism; their subject is realism as a principle of life and literature in a world dominated by "the foolish joys of mere fable."

†From *Modern Fiction Studies,* 16 (Autumn 1970), 289–302.

Howells admits in his essay, "Novel-Writing and Novel-Reading: An Impersonal Explanation," that he was never able to capture the "barren details" of real life in his fiction: ". . . the novelist must endeavor to give exactly the effect of life. . . . I can never do it, for I was bred in a false school whose trammels I have never quite been able to burst; but the novelist who begins where I leave off, will yet write the novel which has been my ideal." What we see in Howells' novels is the constant attempt to burst the trammels. Although Howells was settled on his theory, he could not write fiction that conformed to it. Instead, he wrote in a self-conscious attempt to pave the way for the true realist who was to follow him. He wrote controlled, literary, argumentative novels which seek to destroy the romanticist frame of mind and to define the proper relationship between fiction and reality.

The characters in *The Rise of Silas Lapham* echo Howells' beliefs about life and literature in their conversations concerning the influence of novel-writers on behavior. Mr. Bellingham paraphrases Howells when he says of the current novelists. "The commonplacs is just that light, impalpable, aërial essence which they've never got into their confounded books yet. The novelist who could interpret the common feelings of commonplace people would have the answer to the 'riddle of the painful earth' on his tongue." Mr. Sewell, the minister, agrees with Howells that novels are the chief intellectual stimulus of the times and that they could be very useful if they "painted life as it is, and human feelings in their true proportion and relation." Instead they do great "mischief" by distorting the facts of life, especially by overemphasizing the ideals of love and duty.

Although the novel's central plot is the moral rise of Lapham, the realism battle is omnipresent as a sub-plot. The confused love affair involving Lapham's daughters and [Tom] Corey parallels the situation in *Tears, Idle Tears*, the sentimental novel that prompts the discussion among the characters. Howells brings this romanticistic fictional world into juxtaposition with his own in order to make his point. Penelope Lapham, although she can see the flaws in the morality of the sentimental novel, is too much infected with the poison to fully differentiate the two worlds. She decides, as did the heroine of *Tears*, to sacrifice everyone's happiness for a false ideal of duty. But she is in the wrong novel for such impostures, and in the end she comes to her senses and sees the value in Mr. Sewell's theory of the conservation of heartache.

Penelope's final decision is inevitable because she is not acting in a world of romance. As the elder Corey—the ironical artist of this novel—has assured as earlier, ". . . practically the human affections . . . reconcile themselves to any situation that the human sentiments condemn. . . . the right sister will be reconciled; the wrong one will be consoled; and all will go merry as a marriage bell. . . . Why, it's quite like a romance!" What Corey means of course, beneath the irony, is that it is not at all like a romance but according to the normal pattern of human behavior. Howells never tires of reminding us that novelistic assumptions are defeated in his fictional world. Thus Lapham's financial decline is not constant and without relief although "Our theory of disaster . . . borrowed from the poets and novelists, is that it is incessant." In the same way, the Coreys are not reconciled to their son's marriage to Penelope Lapham at the end, although "These things continually happen in novels." Howells is always defining the battle lines between realism and romanticist illusion, and thus changing his fiction into an argument. He is too concerned about life, too much of a realist, to write realistic fiction as he defined it. Moreover, he sees a web of literary illusions that must be dispelled before the reading public can appreciate an art of the commonplace.

Howells' fictional world tends to turn in on itself in its excessive concern with the relationship between fiction and reality. Thus the reader's attention is called to the novel as a construct when Howells, in [a] passage in *Indian Summer*, . . . gives his characters a perspective on their own author:

> "Oh, call us a passage from a modern novel," suggested Colville, "if you're in the romantic mood. One of Mr. James's."
>
> "Don't you think we ought to be rather more of the great world for that? I hardly feel up to Mr. James. I should have said Howells. Only nothing happens in that case!"
>
> "Oh, very well, that's the most comfortable way. If it's only Howells, there's no reason why I shouldn't go with Miss Graham to show her the view of Florence from the cypress grove up yonder."
>
> "No, he's very particular when he's on Italian ground," said Mrs. Amsden, rising.[1]

Within this "real" fictional world where characters can speculate on what they would do if they *were* characters in a novel, the interest centers around an attempt to see life as a fiction. Imogene Graham, fascinated by Colville's tragic past, makes him "the hero of her carnival dream." The metaphor of the dream reveals how she tries to fictionalize life. Colville counsels her against waking dreams because they give "a false view of things." Imogene, however, is unconvinced:

> "Why should dreams be so very misleading? I think there's ever so much in dreams. The most wonderful thing is the way you make people talk in dreams. . . ."
>
> "That's when you're sleeping. But when you're waking, you make people say just what you want. And that's why day dreams

1. Page references to passages from *Indian Summer* are to the CEAA approved text (Blooming-  ton and London: Indiana University Press, 1971). See p. 173.

are so bad. If you make people say what you want, they probably don't mean it."

"Don't you think so?" (pp. 116–117)

Imogene, in effect, tries to write herself and Colville into a sentimental novel of her own making. She will restore his youth, save him from his past, contemning all selfish considerations. The idea at first seemed like something she "had read in a poem or a novel," but it soon becomes her only concern. She manages to draw Colville into her fiction and make him say what she wants to the extent of an engagement.

Colville is the detached realist who speaks Howells' language; yet he is unable to hold the balance between the realistic and romanticist principles. Howells allows the center of the novel to be dominated by the sentimental fiction created by Imogene; the reader, however, is, along with Mrs. Bowen and Mr. Waters, always aware of the absurdity of the affair. In the end, the realistic vision asserts its supremacy, and Colville sensibly marries Mrs. Bowen.

Conversation in *Indian Summer* is continually concerned with novels. Imogene has no understanding of real literature; she dismisses each author with a surface judgment which she mistakes for his essence. At one point she shocks Colville by being enthusiastic over an edition of *The Marble Faun*[2] illustrated with photographs; this gross confusion of reality and romance epitomizes the theme of the novel. * * *

---

2. *The Marble Faun* (1860), a romance by the American author Nathaniel Hawthorne (1804–64). [*Editor.*]

# Selected Bibliography

There is no complete edition of Howells' works. When it is completed, the most inclusive edition will be "A Selected Edition of W. D. Howells" in twenty-six volumes, currently being published by the Indiana University Press with texts bearing the seal of the Modern Language Association's Center for Editions of American Authors. Six volumes of Howells' selected letters are being published by G. K. Hall; volumes One and Two were published in 1979. The only other attempt at a collected edition is the "Library Edition" issued by Harper Brothers in 1911, but only six volumes of this edition were ever published . All of Howells' dramatic works appear in the single-volume *The Complete Plays of W. D. Howells*, edited by Walter J. Meserve (New York University Press, 1960). Two major collections of Howells' correspondence have been published: *Life in Letters of William Dean Howells* (Garden City, N.Y.: Doubleday Doran & Co., 1928) 2 vols., edited by his daughter, Mildred Howells, and *Mark Twain–Howells Letters* (Cambridge, Mass.: Belknap Press of Harvard University Press, 1960), 2 vols., edited by Henry Nash Smith and William M. Gibson.

Until the Indiana edition's bibliographic volume is published, the most complete listing of Howells' writings is likely to remain *A Bibliography of William Dean Howells* (New York Public Library, 1948; reissued by Arno Press, N.Y., 1971) prepared by William M. Gibson and George Arms. A very ambitious bibliography compiled by Vito J. Brenni (Scarecrow Press: Metuchen, N.J., 1973) is useful for its organization of Howells' work according to genre, for its inclusion of writing about Howells, and for its indices, but it is unfortunately marred by many inaccurate and questionable entries. Guidance in finding books and articles about Howells is provided in George Fortenberry's chapter on Howells in *Fifteen American Authors Before 1900* (Madison: University of Wisconsin Press, 1971) edited by Robert A. Rees and Earl N. Herbart. More complete is the listing in *American Literary Realism* (special issue, 1969) with a supplement in the same journal, 5 (Spring 1972). The special Howells issue of *Modern Fiction Studies*, 16 (Autumn 1970) also contains a bibliography.

It would be pointless to list all of Howells' works here, but the following partial list will provide some idea of the variety of his book publications and of the span of years they embrace.

†*Poems of Two Friends* (1860)
　*Lives and Speeches of Abraham Lincoln and Hannibal Hamlin* (1860). A campaign
　　biography.
†*Venetian Life* (1866)
　*Suburban Sketches* (1871)
*\*Their Wedding Journey* (1872). Howells' first novel.
*\*A Chance Acquaintance* (1873)
†*Poems* (1873)
†*A Foregone Conclusion* (1875)
　*Sketch of the Life and Character of Chester A. Arthur* (1876). A campaign biography.
　*The Lady of the Aroostook* (1879)
†*The Undiscovered Country* (1880)
†*A Fearful Responsibility* (1881)
　*Doctor Breen's Practice* (1881)
*\*A Modern Instance* (1882)
　*A Woman's Reason* (1883)
*\*The Rise of Silas Lapham* (1885)
*\*Indian Summer* (1886)
*\*The Minister's Charge* (1887)
†*Modern Italian Poets* (1887). Translations and commentary.
*\*April Hopes* (1888)
　*Annie Kilburn* (1889)
*\*A Hazard of New Fortunes* (1890)
*\*The Shadow of a Dream* (1890)
　*A Boy's Town* (1890). A memoir of Howells' Ohio boyhood.
†*Criticism and Fiction* (1891)
*An Imperative Duty* (1892)
*\*The Quality of Mercy* (1892)
　*The World of Chance* (1893)
　*My Year in a Log Cabin* (1893). A memoir.

*A Traveler From Altruria (1894). A utopian romance.
†Stops of Various Quills (1895). A volume of poems.
†The Day of Their Wedding (1896)
†he Landlord at Lion's Head (1897)
  An Open-Eyed Conspiracy (1897)
  Stories of Ohio (1897). A history for schoolchildren.
  The Story of a Play (1898)
  Their Silver Wedding Journey (1899)
*Literary Friends and Acquaintance (1900). Essays on American authors and literature.
*The Kentons (1902)
  The Flight of Pony Baker (1902). A Boy's Town story.
  Letters Home (1903)
*The Son of Royal Langbrith (1904)
  Miss Bellard's Inspiration (1905)
†Fennell and Rue (1908)
*My Mark Twain (1910). Reminiscences and criticism.
†New Leaf Mills (1913). A narrative based on a Howells family utopian experiment.
*The Leatherwood God (1916)
*The Years of My Youth (1916). An autobiography up to 1860.
†The Vacation of the Kelwyns (1920)

*These titles have been published as part of the Indiana University edition.
†These titles will be included in the completed Indiana University edition. This edition will
also include three volumes of Howells' critical writings, and a single volume containing all
of his poetry.

## BIOGRAPHY AND CRITICISM

This list is intended only to provide an introduction to the large body of Howells criticism by
directing the reader's attention to the leading critics and scholars, to the great diversity of
interpretation, and to the breadth of Howells' interests and relevancies.

### BOOKS

Bennett, George N. William Dean Howells: The Development of a Novelist. Norman, Okla:
    University of Oklahoma Press, 1959.
Bennett, George N. The Realism of William Dean Howells, 18891920. Nashville: Vanderbilt
    University Press, 1973.
Cady, Edwin H. The Road to Realism: The Early Years, 18371885, of William Dean
    Howells. Syracuse: Syracuse University Press, 1956.
Cady, Edwin H. The Realist at War: The Mature Years, 1885–1920, of William Dean
    Howells. Syracuse: Syracuse University Press, 1958.
Cady, Edwin H., and Frazier, David. The War of the Critics Over William Dean Howells.
    Evanston: Row, Peterson, 1962.
Carrington, George C. The Immense Complex Drama: The World and Art of the Howells
    Novel. Columbus: Ohio State University Press, 1966.
Carter, Everett. Howells and the Age of Realism. Philadelphia: Lippincott, 1954.
Ebel, Kenneth. Howells: A Century of Criticism. Dallas: Southern Methodist University
    Press, 1962.
Fryckstedt, Olov W. In Quest of America: A Study In Howells' Early Development as a
    Novelist. Cambridge: Harvard University Press, 1958.
Garlin, Sender. Howells and Haymarket. New York: AIMS Occasional Papers, 1979.
Gibson, William M. William Dean Howells. University of Minnesota Pamphlets on American
    Writers, no. 63. Minneapolis: University of Minnesota Press, 1967.
Hough, Robert L. The Quiet Rebel: William Dean Howells as Social Commentator. Lincoln;
    University of Nebraska Press, 1959.
Kirk, Clara M., and Kirk, Rudolf. William Dean Howells. New York: Twayne Publishers,
    1962.
Kirk, Clara M., and Kirk, Rudolf. William Dean Howells: Representative Selections, Rev.
    Ed. New York: Hill and Wang, 1961.
Lynn, Kenneth S. William Dean Howells: An American Life. New York: Harcourt Brace
    Jovanovich, 1971.
McMurray, William. The Literary Realism of William Dean Howells. Carbondale: Southern
    Illinois University Press, 1967.
Vanderbilt, Kermit. The Achievement of William Dean Howells: A Reinterpretation.
    Princeton: Princeton University Press, 1969.
Wagenknecht, Edward. William Dean Howells: The Friendly Eye. New York: Oxford
    University Press, 1969.
Woodress, James L. Howells and Italy. Durham: Duke University Press, 1952.

### CHAPTERS AND ARTICLES

Arms, George. "The Literary Background of Howells' Social Criticism." American
    Literature, 14 (November 1942), 260–76.

Baxter, Annette K. "Howells' Boston and Wharton's New York." *Midwest Quarterly*, 4 (Summer 1962), 353–61.

Bryan, James E. "The Chronology of Silas Lapham." *American Notes and Queries*, 4 (December 1965), 56.

Budd, Louis J. "William Dean Howells' Defense of Romance." *PMLA*, 67 (March 1952), 32–42.

Carter, Everett. "The Palpitating Divan." *English Journal*, 39 (May 1950), 237–42.

Cawelti, John G. "The Self-Made Man and Industrial America." In *Apostles of the Self-Made Man*. Chicago: University of Chicago Press, 1965.

Clark, Harry H. "The Role of Science in the Thought of W.D. Howells." *Proceedings of the Wisconsin Academy of Science, Arts and Letters*, 42(1953), 263–303.

Eakins, Paul John. "The Howells Heroine." In *The New England Girl*. Athens, Ga.: University of Georgia Press, 1976.

Edwards, Herbert. "The Dramatization of *The Rise Of Silas Lapham*." *New England Quarterly*, 30 (June 1957), 235–43.

Eichelberger, Clayton L. "William Dean Howells: Perception and Ambivalence." In *The Chief Glory of Every People: Essays on Classic American Writers*, ed. Matthew J. Bruccoli. Carbondale: Southern Illinois University Press, 1973.

Foster, Richard. "The Contemporaneity of Howells." *New England Quarterly*, 32 (March 1959), 54–78.

Fox, Arnold B. "Howells' Doctrine of Complicity." *Modern Language Quarterly*, 13 (March 1952), 55–60.

Frazier, David L. "Howells' Symbolic Houses: The Plutocrats and Palaces." *American Literary Realism*, 10 (Summer 1977), 267–79.

Girgus, Sam B. "Howells and Marcuse: A Forecast of the One-Dimensional Age." *American Quarterly*, (March 1973), 108–18.

Habegger, Alfred. "Nineteenth-Century American Humor: Easygoing Males, Anxious Ladies, and Penelope Lapham." *PMLA*, 91 (October 1976), 884–97.

Jenkins, R. B. "Howells' *The Rise of Silas Lapham*." *Explicator*, 36 (Spring 1978), 37–40.

Millgate, Michael. "The Emotional Commitment of William Dean Howells." *Neophilologus*, 44 (January 1960), 48–54.

Pizer, Donald. "The Evolutionary Foundation of Howells' *Criticism and Fiction*." In *Realism and Naturalism in Nineteenth Century American Fiction*. Carbondale: Southern Illinois University Press, 1966.

Salomon, Roger B. "Realism as Disinheritance: Twain, Howells and James." *American Quarterly*, 16 (Winter 1964), 531–44.

Stephens, Gary. "Haunted Americana: The Edurance of American Realism." *Partisan Review*, 44 (January–February 1977), 71–84.

Taylor, Walter F. "William Dean Howells." In *The Economic Novel in America*. Chapel Hill: University of North Carolina Press, 1942.

Trilling, Lionel. "W. D. Howells and the Roots of Modern Taste." *Partisan Review*, 18 (September–October 1951), 516–36.

Tuttleton, James W. "William Dean Howells: Equity as the Basis of Good Society." In *The Novel of Manners in America*. Chapel Hill: University of North Carolina Press, 1972.

Van Westrum, A. Schade. "Mr. Howells and American Aristocracies." *Bookman*, 25(March 1907), 67–73.

Vorse, Mary Heaton. "Certain Overlooked Phases of American Life." *Critic*, 43 (July 1903), 83–84.

Wells, Gerald K. "The Phoenix Symbol in *The Rise of Silas Lapham*." *South Atlantic Bulletin*, 40 (May 1975), 10–14.

# NORTON CRITICAL EDITIONS